THE
FUGITIVE'S
GIBRALTAR

THE FUGITIVE'S GIBRALTAR

*Escaping Slaves and Abolitionism in
New Bedford, Massachusetts*

KATHRYN GROVER

University of Massachusetts Press
AMHERST

Library of Congress Cataloging-in-Publication Data
Grover, Kathryn, 1953–
The fugitive's Gibraltar: escaping slaves and abolitionism in New Bedford, Massachusetts / Kathryn Grover
p. cm
Includes bibliographical references and index.
ISBN 1-55849-271-2 (alk. paper)
1. Fugitive slaves—Massachusetts—New Bedford—History—19th century.
2. Abolitionists—Massachusetts—New Bedford—History—19th century.
3. Antislavery movements—Massachusetts—New Bedford—History—19th century.
4. New Bedford (Mass.)—History—19th century. I. Title
F74.N5 G84 2001
326′.8′0974485—dc21
00-048878

British Library Cataloguing in Publication data are available.

This book is published with the support and cooperation of the
University of Massachusetts Boston.

To the people of New Bedford

CONTENTS

ILLUSTRATIONS

ACKNOWLEDGMENTS

I have lived in New Bedford, Massachusetts, for nine years and during that time have worked independently from my home. So it seems ironic, if only to me, that this book has woven me into a web of connection and support I could not have imagined when I started.

After three years of trying, and another year of trying without hope, I received a National Endowment for the Humanities Fellowship for College Teachers and Independent Scholars to undertake the research for this book. I am indebted to NEH, and to the additional support I received from the Frank C. Munson Institute of Maritime Studies at Mystic Seaport Museum and the New Bedford Cultural Council, for enabling me to put almost all of my freelance work on hold for a little more than a year in order to concentrate on this project. I live uneasily with the knowledge that while I have been able to discover a great deal about New Bedford's community of color, its fugitive slaves, and its abolitionism, this is a place so rich in primary resources that much remains untapped. The New Bedford Free Public Library is a positive treasure in this city, and I am grateful both for its remarkable collections and for the unfailing assistance of Paul Albert Cyr and Tina Furtado in its local history and manuscripts divisions. Paul Cyr even from time to time hastened his project of abstracting the city's nineteenth-century newspapers to help me, and without the abstracts I could not have found the wealth of local detail that fueled this project. The New Bedford Whaling Museum is also an invaluable resource, and I am grateful in particular for the assistance of Judith Downey, Mary Jean Blasdale, and Laura Pereira. I am also more indebted than I can say to Charles Watson of Roger Williams University in Bristol, Rhode Island, who made his research on the protection papers, crew lists, and probate records of New Bedford's people of color available for my use. I could not have done this project at all within the time available to me without his help. John Piltzecker and Michael Caldwell of the New Bedford Whaling National Historical Park, founded in 1996, have taken a strong interest in the project and have worked hard for its support. Ilene Horowitz and Michael Bachstein prepared the maps for this book.

I am grateful to Robert L. Hall of Northeastern University, Shirley Wajda of Kent State University, Charles Backus, then director of Syracuse University Press, David D. Hall of Harvard Divinity School, and Paul Wright of the University of Massachusetts Press, all of whom supported this project from its inception. Other people were of immense help to me by providing leads and information I had trouble tracking down on my own. I thank Ruth Caswell of New Bedford's Spinner Publications; Richard Kugler, then curator at the New Bedford Whaling Museum; Martha S. Putney; Jeffrey Bolster of the University of New Hampshire; Gary Collison of Pennsylvania State University; Rudolph M. Lapp; Cynthia Griffin Wolff; Nancy Osgood; James Driscoll of the Queens, New York, Historical Society; Mae G. Breckenridge-Haywood of Portsmouth, Virginia; John Buescher; Jeremy D'Entremont; Bob Huddleston; Lllewellyn Howland III; Guy Washington of the National Park Service; and Philip J. Schwarz of Virginia Commonwealth University, who shared his research on Leonard Grimes from the Executive Papers of Virginia Governors. My notes, I hope, indicate their many specific contributions. Melissa Morgan Radtke of Midlothian, Virginia, a colleague from our days together in Rochester, New York, researched Portsmouth and Norfolk newspapers for me when I had run out of time for research trips, housed and fed me when I could visit, and even, because she knows my weaknesses so well, made reservations for my overnight stay near Dulles Airport. I thank her and her family for their interest, affection, and support.

I also want to acknowledge many institutions and their staff both for retaining materials related to New Bedford's antebellum history and for their help, in particular the wonderful Department of Rare Books and Manuscripts at Boston Public Library. Roberta Zonghi, curator of rare books, has been impressively efficient, kind, and knowledgeable, as have Susan Glover Godlewski and William Faucon. Elizabeth Bouvier of the Division of Archives of the Supreme Judicial Court of Massachusetts researched and provided copies of many important cases. I thank also Bernard R. Crystal of Columbia University's Rare Book and Manuscript Library, Bill Cretes at the National Archives and Records Administration in Washington, D.C., Thomas Knoles at the American Antiquarian Society, Phil McCray, then of Cornell University Archives, Karl Kabelac at the University of Rochester's Rush Rhees Library, Carolyn Davis at the George Arents Research Library for Special Collections at Syracuse University, Gail Redmann of the District of Columbia Historical Society, Stephen Z. Nonack of the Boston Athenaeum, Paul Mahoney at the Massachusetts Archives, Martha H. Smart at the Connecticut Historical Society, Jamelle Tanous Lyons at the Fall River Historical Society, and Bonnie Hardwick of the Bancroft Collection, University of California at Berkeley. I also relied upon the collections of the Library of Congress; the Historical Society of Pennsylvania; the District of Columbia Public Library; the Massachusetts Historical Society; the Rhode Island Historical Society; the Friends Historical Library at Swarthmore College; Houghton, Widener, and Lamont Libraries at Harvard University; the G. W. Blunt Library at Mystic Seaport Museum; the Portsmouth, Virginia, Public Library; the Sergeant Memorial Room at the Norfolk, Virginia, Public Library; and the Library of Virginia.

I save my deepest thanks for last, and these are all due to New Bedford people and institutions. Lee Heald, director of programs at the New Bedford Whaling Museum, engineered that institution's sponsorship of the writing phase of this project, supported by a generous and indeed indispensable grant from the Henry Howland Crapo Charitable Foundation. Julian E. Youngblood, descendant of the Reverend William Jackson, very graciously spent hours with me talking about Jackson and sharing photographs, documents, and his transcriptions of Jackson's letters, journals, and autobiography. Mr. Youngblood is a kind and generous man who deserves a biography in his own right, and I am deeply gratified that he permitted me to know more about his family. Randall B. Pollard, grand historian of the oldest black Masonic lodge in the nation, the Prince Hall Grand Lodge of Massachusetts, also permitted me to interview him about his great-great-grandparents, William and Lucinda Clark Bush, and their nephew Leonard Grimes. He and Mr. Youngblood are rightly protective of their legacies, and I feel honored to have had access to them.

Finally, I owe an enormous debt—practical, intellectual, and spiritual—to Carl J. Cruz of New Bedford Historical Society, founded in 1997 to study and interpret the lives of people of color in this region. Carl's interest in the region's population of color is constant, deep, and active. Before there was a New Bedford Historical Society there was Carl Cruz, and the city should be thankful for that. I often feel a little sick to think what I would not know if I did not know Carl, if we had not questioned each other and puzzled out so much in scores of telephone conversations, if we did not talk so much about standards of proof in a subject so surrounded by legend, if it were not for the generosity he has always shown me. Because I work alone, to have been able to build this sort of collegial relationship with Carl Cruz has meant more to me, and more to this project, than I can articulate.

K. G.

THE
FUGITIVE'S
GIBRALTAR

FIGURE 1. North side of lower Union Street, New Bedford, daguerreotype by Morris Smith, 1849. Courtesy Old Dartmouth Historical Society / New Bedford Whaling Museum, New Bedford, Mass. One of the earliest known photographic street views of the city, Smith's image shows the Mansion House, with its colonnaded second-story porch, at center. Originally the home of William Rotch Sr., the dwelling was converted to a hotel in 1828. Fugitive William Henry Johnson worked there for a time, probably in the 1830s, and British abolitionist Joseph Sturge talked with a fugitive waiting tables there in 1841.

INTRODUCTION

THIS BOOK is about New Bedford, Massachusetts, that part of its antebellum community formed by fugitive slaves, abolitionists, whaling merchants, and free people of color, and how aid to fugitives fit into an abolitionist's ideas about the movement. I was drawn to write it to answer one large, probably unanswerable, question. Can a place have a soul, as the fugitive George Teamoh put it, that inclines it toward tolerance? In pursuit of that essentially ahistorical query, I found myself almost unwittingly involved in other issues—how a prosperous community, perhaps the most prosperous in the country, spun and fell in love with its own mythology at an early point and how the presence of fugitive slaves wove itself into the legend its people made. Indeed, the willingness of New Bedford people to harbor and help fugitives is arguably at the very basis of the city's spiritual understanding of itself as a place apart from and more open than all others.

By any contemporary measure, the number of fugitive slaves living in New Bedford before the Civil War was high: local white abolitionists put it at anywhere from three to seven hundred at different times between 1845 and 1863. In his 1858 history of the city, the first ever published, New Bedford's Daniel Ricketson even declared, "It is said that at one time in the early part of the present century there was hardly a house in the place which did not give shelter and succor to a fugitive slave."[1] Ricketson almost surely overstated the case, but there is no question that an unusually large number of escaped slaves found a home, however briefly, in the city. In New Bedford this study has identified one hundred fugitives by full name, another ten by first or last name only, and more than seventy whose presence but not names are recorded. Those who have been identified can, I think, safely be judged an indeterminably small part of the total.

Yet almost nothing was known about these persons, locally or more broadly. Local historians and some residents knew that the merchant and abolitionist Rodney French had once rung the bell at Liberty Hall to warn fugitives of the rumored approach of slave catchers. They have been proud to claim that Frederick Douglass made New Bedford his first home after escaping slavery in 1838, that Henry "Box" Brown had been publicly feted on his arrival in 1849. City residents who read the newspaper in 1910 learned that William Ferguson, a longtime city messenger, had escaped slavery aboard a Boston-bound coal schooner in 1847. However, just as popular history has often been reduced to the biographies of its heroes, the contour and content of the universe of people of color in New

Bedford, to say nothing of that segment who were fugitives, were largely unstudied and unknown.

Thus this investigation aimed to be both documentary and analytic. I wished to uncover and record the presence of individual fugitives in the city, even as I recognized that most official records of the community would be mute on this score. Studying fugitives involves a sort of double bind because, first, their movements and presence were supposed to be clandestine and, second, as people of color, they were in large measure invisible in most northern communities. Tracing them in maritime New Bedford is complicated by the fact that the use of aliases was common not only among fugitives but among mariners generally.[2] Yet not all of the traditional sources, fortunately, were unrevealing. Town clerk Henry Howland Crapo's important memorandum of tax delinquents between 1839 and 1842 shows remarkable candor and a penchant for biography. The records of the New Bedford Overseers of the Poor, created when the town was incorporated as a city in 1847, are marvelously detailed accounts of the life histories of many of the community's poor and identify scores of relief applicants as fugitives. This fact runs counter to historical understanding; as historian Leonard Curry argued in 1981, "Blacks were routinely excluded from the ranks of the 'deserving poor' in many cities" and thus were ineligible for "outdoor relief," or the distribution of fuel, food, and sometimes cash to needy city residents. One might expect fugitives in particular to be left to their own devices, for they could not of course claim legal settlement in a community. Applicants who could not establish such a claim were usually asked their previous place of settlement, and poor relief administrators would then wrestle with their counterparts in that place about whose responsibility the applicant was. Yet this was not the case in antebellum New Bedford; people of color regularly received assistance, especially with firewood or coal in the beginning or midst of a winter, and fugitives in particular were given fuel and groceries, it seems, quite readily. Whether New Bedford was unusual in this respect is a question that cannot be answered until the poor relief records of comparable communities are analyzed.[3]

Combing other official records—federal and state censuses, city directories, tax lists, probate records, and, in New Bedford, whaling crew lists and seamen's protection papers—was vital not only to establishing a picture of the settled community of color (and how settled it truly was) but to speculating about possible fugitives. This investigation compiled information on the city's population of African descent in federal and state censuses between 1790 and 1860 and in city directories from their first appearance, in 1836, through 1859. These directories indicated people of color with a "c." after their names from 1836 through 1845 and were surveyed selectively after that date. Because Crapo, compiler of the first directories, was so methodical about how streets in New Bedford were numbered and usually indicated corner residences, it has been possible to use the directories to plot the residential and business distribution of people of color in the city, to analyze change in this distribution over time, and to compare New Bedford to other port cities for which such data have been analyzed.[4]

Protection papers and crew lists add a wealth of detail about New Bedford's mariner population that does not exist for people in inland cities. First required by the federal government in 1796 to protect American sailors against impressment and to authorize assistance should a sailor become somehow marooned in a foreign port, seamen's protection papers identified a seaman by name, listed his age, height, complexion, hair type, and eye color, and recorded either or both his place of birth and place of residence (fig. 2). Each was witnessed, a fact that helped pinpoint the importance of such boardinghouse keepers as William P. Powell and William Vincent in housing, outfitting, and orienting men of color new to whaling and to New Bedford.[5] From 1803 Congress also mandated that vessel captains submit to customs collectors a list of names, birthplaces and residences, and descriptions of the crew on board before the vessel could be cleared for a voyage (fig. 3).[6] Collating people's statements about their place of birth in all of these records hinted at the efforts of many people of color to conceal their true origins and in turn their possible fugitive status; in some instances, such as Ferguson's, such suspicions were confirmed through other sources, such as William Still's invaluable history of the Underground Railroad or Joseph Ricketson Jr.'s letters to the abolitionist Weston sisters. And these records, combined with the returns of whaling vessels in Alexander Starbuck's exhaustive *History of the American Whale Fishery,* permit corroboration of the statements such fugitives as John W. Thompson and John S. Jacobs made in published narratives about their voyages and thus heighten one's confidence in their essential truthfulness at a time when accounts of fugitives' lives and escapes were often doubted.[7]

Compiling official demographic records of the city's population of color also made it possible to identify some of those fugitives who stayed in New Bedford and some who moved on. The city is said to have been on the main eastern travel corridor from the South to the free states and to Canada. In 1893 a Medway man who had assisted in the escape of fugitives to Massachusetts denied that he was ever a "station keeper" because his town was "out of the general course of travel from the South to Canada. . . . The more common routes I think were up the Connecticut Valley—and from New Bedford through the Eastern part of the State." Elizabeth Buffum Chace, an abolitionist and former Quaker, identified another route from or through New Bedford to Fall River, Massachusetts; Valley Falls, Rhode Island (her home); Worcester, Massachusetts; and Vermont and recalled in detail how she helped one fugitive who came to her door in Quaker women's clothing—a useful disguise because of its deep and shadowy bonnet—on his way from New Bedford to Canada.[8]

Because of the kind of place New Bedford was—wealthy, racially diverse virtually from its settlement, still influenced by a once-pervasive Quaker ethic, and, it seemed to some, surprisingly enlightened on matters of social reform—the city

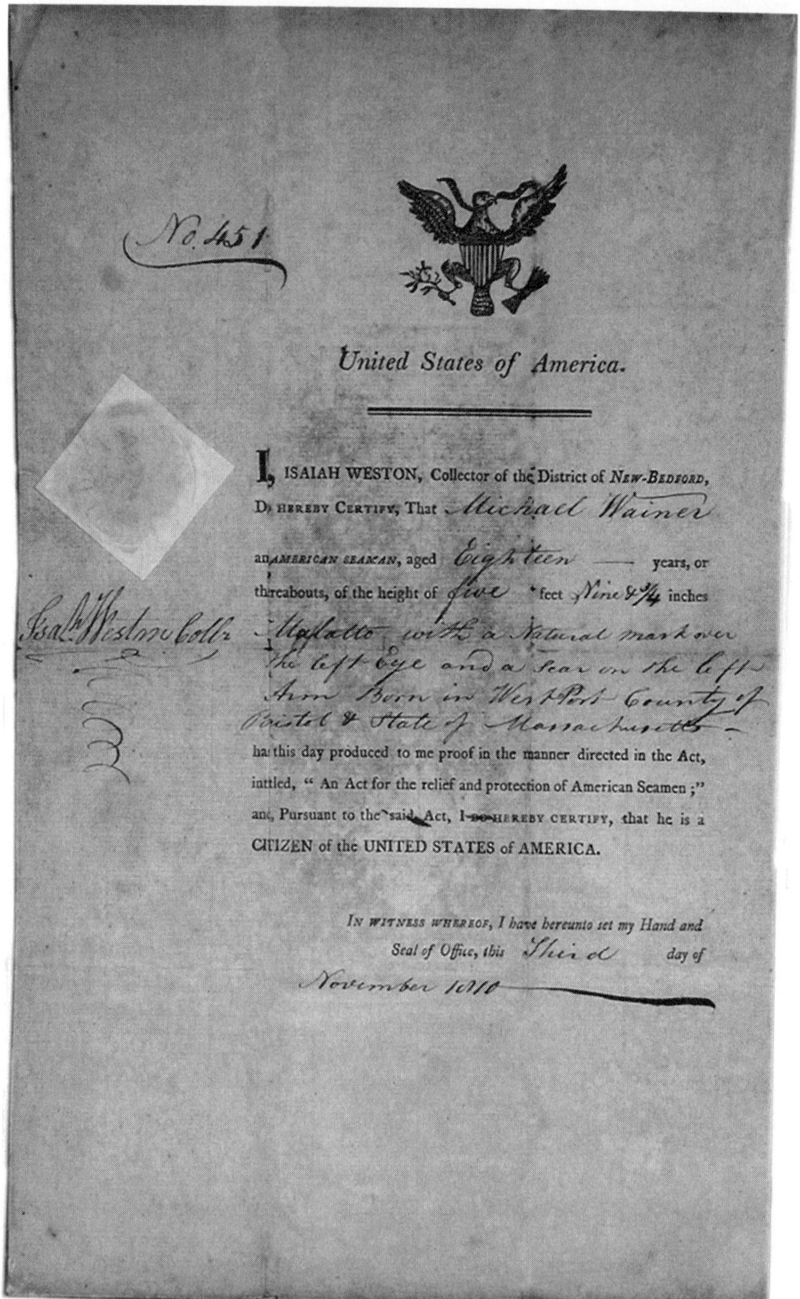

No. 451

United States of America.

I, ISAIAH WESTON, Collector of the District of *NEW-BEDFORD*, DO HEREBY CERTIFY, That Michael Wainer an AMERICAN SEAMAN, aged Eighteen — years, or thereabouts, of the height of five feet Nine & 3/4 inches Mulatto with a Natural mark over the left Eye and a Scar on the left Arm Born in WestPort County of Bristol & State of Massachusetts — has this day produced to me proof in the manner directed in the Act, intitled, "An Act for the relief and protection of American Seamen;" and, Pursuant to the said Act, I DO HEREBY CERTIFY, that he is a CITIZEN of the UNITED STATES of AMERICA.

IN WITNESS WHEREOF, I have hereunto set my Hand and Seal of Office, this Third *day of* November 1810

Isa.h Weston Coll.r

FIGURE 2. Seaman's protection paper for Michael Wainer, 3 November 1810. Courtesy Carl J. Cruz, New Bedford Historical Society. The son of Paul Cuffe's business partner, Michael Wainer was second mate on Cuffe's *Traveller* on its first visit to Sierra Leone. The vessel left nearby Westport on 25 November.

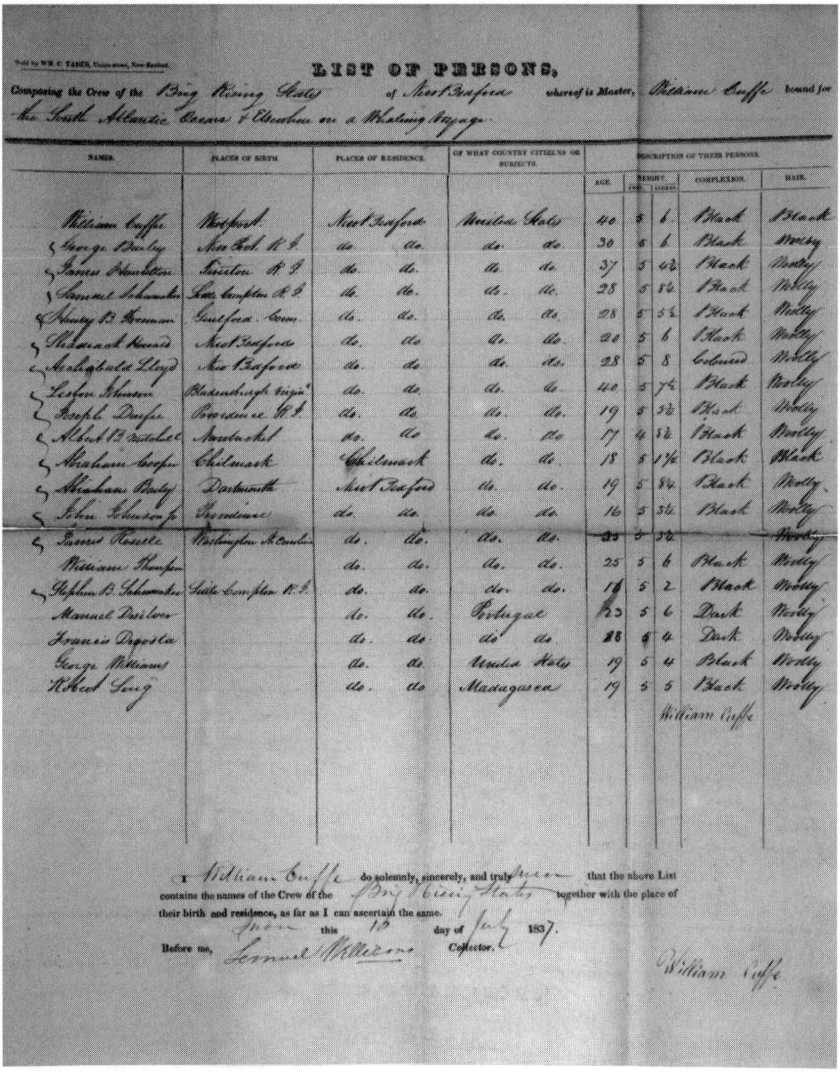

Sold by WM. C. TABER, Union-street, New-Bedford.

LIST OF PERSONS,

Composing the Crew of the Brig Rising States of New Bedford whereof is Master, William Cuffe bound for the South Atlantic Ocean & Elsewhere on a Whaling Voyage.

NAMES.	PLACES OF BIRTH.	PLACES OF RESIDENCE.	OF WHAT COUNTRY CITIZENS OR SUBJECTS.	AGE.	HEIGHT. FEET.	HEIGHT. INCHES.	COMPLEXION.	HAIR.
William Cuffe	Westport	New Bedford	United States	40	5	6	Black	Black
George Bailey	New Port R. I.	do. do.	do. do.	30	5	6	Black	Wolley
James Hamilton	Tiverton R. I.	do. do.	do. do.	37	5	4½	Black	Wolley
Samuel Schumaker	Little Compton R. I.	do. do.	do. do.	28	5	8½	Black	Wolley
Henry B. Freeman	Guilford. Conn.	do. do.	do. do.	28	5	5½	Black	Wolley
Shadrack Howard	New Bedford	do. do	do. do.	20	5	6	Black	Wolley
Archibald Lloyd	New Bedford	do. do	do. do.	28	5	8	Coloured	Wolley
Lisbon Johnson	Bladensburgh Virgin^a^	do. do.	do. do.	40	5	7½	Black	Wolley
Joseph Durfee	Providence R. I.	do. do	do. do.	19	5	5½	Black	Wolley
Albert B. Mitchell	Nantucket	do. do	do. do	17	4	5½	Black	Wolley
Abraham Cooper	Chilmark	Chilmark	do. do.	18	5	1½	Black	Black
Abraham Bailey	Dartmouth	New Bedford	do. do.	19	5	8½	Black	Wolley
John Johnson Jr	Providence	do. do.	do. do.	16	5	3½	Black	Wolley
James Russell	Washington N. Carolina	do. do.	do. do.	[illegible]	5	5½		Wolley
William Thompson		do. do.	do. do.	25	5	6	Black	Wolley
Stephen B. Schumaker	Little Compton R. I.	do. do.	do. do.	16	5	2	Black	Wolley
Manuel Dasilver		do. do.	Portugal	23	5	6	Dark	Wolley
Francis Degosta		do. do	do do	28	5	4	Dark	Wolley
George Williams		do. do	United States	19	5	4	Black	Wolley
Robert Long		do. do	Madagasca	19	5	5	Black	Wolley

William Cuffe

I William Cuffe do solemnly, sincerely, and truly swear that the above List contains the names of the Crew of the Brig Rising States together with the place of their birth and residence, as far as I can ascertain the same.

Sworn this 18 day of July 1837.

Before me, Lemuel Williams Collector.

William Cuffe

FIGURE 3. Crew list for the *Rising States,* William Cuffe, master, 18 July 1837. Courtesy National Archives and Records Administration. The *Rising States* was a black-owned vessel that usually carried a high complement of men of color in its crew. George and Abraham Bailey were the sons of Quaco Bailey, an early landowner in the town's Hard-Dig section and a resident since at least the mid-1790s. This voyage was George Bailey's sixth, and he served as first mate. It was the second and last voyage for the *Rising States;* damaged in a gale that killed four of its crew, including Cuffe, the son of mariner Paul Cuffe, it was condemned at the Cape Verde Islands in December 1837.

attracted others to describe it more narratively in its antebellum years. Twelve fugitive slave narratives—those of Henry "Box" Brown, Leonard Black, William Grimes, Harriet Jacobs, John S. Jacobs, Thomas H. Jones, Edmund Kelley, George Teamoh, John W. Thompson, and the three accounts of Frederick Douglass—are about escaped slaves who lived for some time in New Bedford, and all offer invaluable information about the community. The narratives of the Boston Vigilance Committee's Austin Bearse and of Jonathan Walker and Daniel Drayton, white mariners who attempted unsuccessfully to rescue fugitives from the South, also touch upon New Bedford people and events; Walker and Bearse once lived in New Bedford, and Drayton took his life in the city.[9] James Bunker Congdon, a bank clerk and municipal official descended from Rhode Island Quakers, prepared comprehensive accounts of numerous local incidents that bear on the history of the city's population of color; his elder brother Joseph began collecting materials about them, particularly about the Afro-Indian merchant mariner Paul Cuffe, before 1850. The Quaker whaling merchant Samuel Rodman Jr. kept a diary for more than thirty-seven years; because he was committed to such reforms as temperance and, for some time, antislavery, his diary is deeply informative. Charles Waln Morgan, a former Quaker and Rodman's brother-in-law, kept diaries intermittently that show his own involvement in antislavery and abolition and kept business records that document his relationships with specific New Bedford people of color. William Still, the dedicated secretary of the Philadelphia Vigilance Committee, chronicled the often-harrowing stories that escaping slaves told him in both his journal and his book, which also reprinted letters fugitives sent him. Still's connection to New Bedford as a fugitive "depot" was more than occasional, and the accuracy of his statements is corroborated in other sources over which he had no influence or control. Three of the five older Weston sisters of Boston and Weymouth, abolitionists to a woman, taught school in New Bedford at various times between 1836 and about 1846 and seem to have been assigned to the city to whip up abolitionist fervor. Their many letters, now at the Boston Public Library, are wonderful expositions of the ideas of the abolitionist "Boston Clique," rich in gossip about New Bedford abolitionists, and informative about fugitives when other documents are not. Because of them the importance to the cause of such men as Joseph Ricketson Jr. emerges; without them the fact that Ricketson was probably the most committed white abolitionist the city ever produced would probably have been lost to the record, as it is today in local public memory.

In this book I look at New Bedford from the time it was set off from the township of Dartmouth in 1787 until the first men of color walked to William Street to enlist in the Civil War regiment that Massachusetts governor John A. Andrew had struggled to create.[10] New Bedford was in some respects different from most other New England places. For one thing, its economy remained based almost solely on maritime commerce when other cities in Massachusetts, even port cities, had turned to the production of shoes and textiles (fig. 4). Indeed,

FIGURE 4. "Storing Oil," stereoview by T. E. M. White, 8 August 1870. Used with permission of the Board of Trustees of the New Bedford Free Public Library. Portuguese laborer Joseph Lima shovels seaweed as whaling merchant Joseph Ricketson II (not the abolitionist Joseph Ricketson Jr.) stands to his right. At this time New Bedford still had only one textile mill; despite the profitability of its pioneer Wamsutta Mills, city capitalists did not build another until 1871, when Potomska Mill opened in the South End.

some residents were decidedly opposed to the development of industry in the city. "We deem it a curse to be immersed in manufacturing—a curse particularly heavy upon the poor and suffering operatives," Daniel Ricketson proclaimed on learning of the proposed enlargement of the Wamsutta Mill, the city's first and only textile mill before the Civil War. "Alleviate their condition as we may, by sumptuary and other legislation, which is still to be done, yet so long as avarice is a trait of human character, will the poor become its victims." New Bedford ought to content itself, Ricketson argued, with its "legitimate fields . . . agriculture and commerce." The Nantucket and New Bedford abolitionist Isaiah C. Ray agreed. At the mills of Lowell and Manchester, New Hampshire, he wrote, mill girls were tied to penurious schedules, lived and worked in stifling conditions, and stood helpless in the face of "Abbott Lawrence robbing the poor girls of a large per centage of their labor. . . . Well I ask are not riches to be despised when it is ground out of the vitals of poor country girls who are driven by the devilish 'Fashions' to work in the vile place?" Both Ricketson and Ray seemed oddly oblivious to the ways in which whaling resembled industry—the abysmal conditions of life and work on many whalers, the degree to which agents, crimps, outfitters, and even owners and masters exploited crew.[11] In manufacturing towns the need for unskilled labor was, naturally, in industry, which was almost uniformly closed to people of color. But New Bedford needed unskilled labor on its wharves and its whalers at a time when the industrial economy had begun to offer better wages[12] and when unsavory stories of corporal abuse, mutiny, and desertion had begun to gather around whaling and discourage young, northern, rural white men from signing on. In historical terms whaling, more than any of the relatively tolerant maritime trades, had welcomed the participation of people of color, and as white and immigrant labor entered the factories the decks and forecastles of whalers may have grown especially dependent on whalemen of color at least until the 1850s. Those laborers in turn viewed whaling, despite its disadvantages, as one of the only occupations available through which they might support themselves and their families.

Second, New Bedford had always maintained a dissenting attitude, settled as it was by persons who either wished to be at a considerable remove from colonial Massachusetts governments or had been cast out by them—Baptists and Quakers in particular. Just as white citizens of early Dartmouth had objected to the mandate to settle an orthodox minister among them, before 1800 citizens of color protested their exclusion from the franchise when they in fact paid taxes on their real property. A schism rent the local Society of Friends in the early 1820s, well before the Hicksite schism affected the sect at large. The Unitarian congregation that developed from the separation of "New Light" Quakers was more radical than most; after the Civil War its minister, William J. Potter, disdained membership in the Unitarian-Universalist Association on the grounds that it was too conservative. A certain "live-and-let-live" philosophy seems to have pervaded early Quaker life in this region and, many would argue, has persisted into the current day.

Moreover, the community learned to deal with transience from an early point. Even among its settled population many men were virtually transient because of the amount of time they spent at sea. Occasionally someone like Crapo heard news of these men, or caught up to someone who knew where they were: in 1839 he wrote of John Robbins, a black waiter at the Mansion House, "He left here in debt last spring. Heard he had gone whaling from Newport—since heard he was in a New Orleans packet—He belongs in Dedham," and in 1840 Crapo stated that the tax delinquent Augustus Gerry had "gone to New Orleans & from there to Liverpool—thinks he will be at home in spring to go whaling."[13] Moreover, even though the town's settled population was small in the 1800s, its "floating population" was large. Abolitionist John Bailey once complained to the *Liberator* that fugitive slaves stood out in such a small place, but clearly it was possible for many people to become "lost in the living mass" of transients who found shelter for short terms along the city's waterfront and in its poorer neighborhoods. Some sources indicate as much. Between 1845–52 and 1858–64, when the officially enumerated population of color in New Bedford ranged around 1,250 persons, the overseers of the poor identified more than 260 men, women, and children of color who were never recorded in any other local listing of residents. Even the Reverend William Jackson's records of Second and Salem Baptist churches, which might be expected to reveal the more settled part of the population of color, named one hundred persons whose names appear nowhere else.

For the sake of their main industry townspeople tolerated an entirely distinct maritime culture, one that turned the predominant Quaker-influenced one of New Bedford virtually on its head. At least into the 1820s in New Bedford, most Friends dressed plainly, did not use profanity, drank moderately if at all, and did not play music or attend dances; sailors, by contrast, dressed flashily, swore and drank profusely, and carried on boisterously in the streets, rum shops, and boardinghouses. By the mid-1850s, for every settled, moderate, orthodox Quaker there were thirty-seven footloose, seemingly libidinous sailors.[14] As whaling went further afield and native-born crew grew scarcer, those transients became more exotic, and the city may have grown more cosmopolitan as a result. In 1928 the economist Elmo Hohman noted that New Bedford whaling crews included "Portuguese and mulattoes from the Azores and Cape Verde Islands, Spaniards, Swedes, Norwegians, Danes, Dutchmen, Germans, Frenchmen, Englishmen, Scotchmen, Irishmen, Gay Head Indians, negroes from the United States, Africa, and the West Indies, Maoris from New Zealand, Kanakas from the Sandwich Islands, natives from other South Sea Islands, and half-breeds who represented the crossing of many different stocks." Charles T. Congdon, a New Bedford native and New York City journalist, recalled the universe he confronted in his hometown in the 1830s and 1840s:

> The whale-ships recruiting at the Sandwich or Society Islands brought back, besides oil and bone, not a few tattooed natives, with the sound of whose astonishing language I was familiar, though I did not understand a word of it. These Kanakas, as they were called, were harmless, simple, fond of rum, and, I suspect, often swindled out of the little money which their voyages brought them. Ships, indeed, came to us from all parts of the world. We had often walking about swarthy Portuguese sailors, and mariners of the true broad-bottomed Dutch type, puffing their long pipes mildly. I knew by sight, almost as soon as I knew anything, the flag of every important sea-going European nation,—the Union Jack of England, the different tricolors of France, of Germany, and of Russia, the yellow signal of Spain. All these nations wanted oil and candles, and came to New Bedford in pursuit of those commodities. Sometimes, when the wharves were full of ships, our streets—there were only two or three of much consequence—were really brilliant and bustling.[15]

The diversity that whaling created continued after the industry ceased in the 1920s: today more than 60 percent of New Bedford's population is of Portuguese descent (a figure that includes many Cape Verdeans; the Cape Verde Islands were under Portuguese rule until 1975), about 7 percent is of Hispanic origin, and another 4 percent is black non-Hispanic.[16] Because of that diversity, this book uses the term "of color" whenever possible. People of African descent in New Bedford were from many parts of the world, not just from the American South, and other people who were not of African descent, including Native Americans, Hawaiians, and even some Azorean islanders, were often labeled as black.

Finally, even as Samuel Rodman and others occasionally complained about the low pitch of abolitionist sentiment in New Bedford, the town was never identified as "pro-slavery" and was far more apt to be depicted, especially by Southerners, as overrun with radical abolitionists. New Bedford was not the Newport, Rhode Island, of which British abolitionist Joseph Sturge complained, for example, or the Northampton, Massachusetts, whose abolitionism Lydia Maria Child described as "lifeless." New Bedford was not William Lloyd Garrison's native Newburyport. In a letter responding to the Underground Railroad historian Wilbur Siebert's request for a description of his role in the "organization," Thomas Wentworth Higginson replied petulantly, "There was *no* organization in Mass answering properly to the usual description of the U.G.R.R. . . . I don't understand your map with lines leading to Newburyport for instance. That was a very proslavery place & I don't remember a fugitive slave there while I lived there (1847–52)."[17]

Having always been interested in the dynamics of communities and how great global and national events play out locally, I have hoped that a detailed study of abolitionism and the passage through and presence of fugitives in New Bedford could cast—if not by itself, then in combination with other local studies on these subjects—a brighter light on the issues in these fields generally. This examination has documented that New Bedford residents were actively assisting fugitive slaves before 1793, the year to which Siebert assigned the "first recorded evidence of befriending the runaway in Massachusetts, in a manner often employed later by Underground operators."[18] It will clarify, I hope, the role of both Quakers and free people of color in the movement to assist fugitives in the North and in their passage to other countries. In this connection it will demonstrate how the issue of forcible resistance ultimately created a chasm between most white and virtually all black abolitionists. Among many Quakers it was the violence more than the inequality of the master-slave relation that impelled their opposition to slavery. When New Bedford's William Rotch Jr. wrote to the Providence abolitionist Moses Brown for details about his brother John's mistreatment of slaves aboard his vessels in 1789, it was Rotch's peace testimony, not his antislavery testimony, that was the more inflamed. "I have been endeavouring to find what instances of barbarity could be substantiated that have been exercised by N. England ship masters both to slaves & crew, . . ." Rotch wrote. "One instance I am informed of occurd in a ship of thy brother Johns of the slaves attempting to rise & that many of them were killed in attempting to quell them. . . . I likewise hear that another (or the same) who succeeded to the command of Johns vessel by the death of the Capn & mate & perhaps by the name of Wolf was so inhuman as to take a child an infant by the feet whose crying afflicted him & repeatedly whipd it before its mother & one made an attempt to burn it by thrusting it into the Caboose."[19] But just as the abhorrence of violence had once turned many Quakers to anti-slavery reform, the possibility of violence stood between them and the most decided antislavery advocacy they might have demonstrated, short of becoming a Jonathan Walker or a Daniel Drayton—that of actively assisting fugitive slaves. Anyone might have expected them to do so after the Fugitive Slave Act; Quakers were consistently uninterested in the hegemony of civil law over God's law. But the idea of forcible resistance made them leery and fearful of white abolitionists who defied the act's provisions, mostly because they tended also to advocate the use of force to aid and protect fugitives. These were the very abolitionists whom black abolitionists regarded most highly, for among them the commitment to the use of violence to resist slavery and the Fugitive Slave Act had become virtually unanimous.

Finally, this book may serve as a useful contribution to the debate about the Underground Railroad's level of organization. Historian Larry Gara was certainly correct when he argued in 1963 that "although the underground railroad was a reality, much of the material relating to it belongs in the realm of folklore rather than history," the countless stories about tunnels, caves, hidden and underground rooms: New Bedford has as many of these stories as any place associated with the movement of fugitives from the South. Gara also demonstrated persuasively that the Underground Railroad was orchestrated by people of color in at least as great a measure as by white abolitionists. But his view that "abolitionists had no centralized organization, either for spiriting away slaves or for any other of their activities" seems to have been a reaction to some of the boldest declarations in what has always been a very sparse literature. In a 1933 issue of the *Journal of Negro History,* for example, E. Delorus Preston Jr. argued that the Underground Railroad "was a system, a highly developed and thoroughly organized system, that mysteriously aided fugitive slaves, in their frantic efforts to escape miserable slavery, to freedom." It may be, as Gara asserts, "that many Americans believed in the existence of a widespread and highly organized underground railroad operated by abolitionists to run slaves out of the South," yet Preston never made any claims for its *central* organization, and to my knowledge no one involved in assisting fugitives at the time (except perhaps Henry Bibb) claimed that the infrastructure of their assistance was "highly organized."[20] Unfortunately, however, later Underground Railroad historians have tended to take Gara's argument—which corrected public legend, not the claims of participants—as the basis for an argument that the Underground Railroad was a series of haphazard connections, or simply not organized at all. I believe that this analysis demonstrates the opposite, and perhaps a more sophisticated level of organization than Gara believed existed. Just as Gara conceded "the existence of . . . regionally organized assistance" in the area embracing Wilmington, Delaware, the southeastern counties of Pennsylvania, and Philadelphia, the regular passage of fugitives between Norfolk and Portsmouth, Virginia, and New Bedford, sometimes by way of Philadelphia and sometimes directly, suggests the existence of systematic communication and connections over a far wider region. In the absence of any participant's having stated as much, the sheer number of fugitives from those places in this northern port is perhaps the strongest evidence that is apt to emerge. That Thomas H. Jones sent his wife and children to a white abolitionist in Brooklyn whom he already knew, that slaves seeking escape often knew which vessel captains were likely to be sympathetic, that New Bedford fugitives knew when family and friends had made their escape, that Harriet Jacobs figured out a way to learn her former owners' itineraries and her children's conditions when they made their way North before she did—all of these facts and countless others point to the presence of a system of communication, leading often to assistance, that spread widely along the Atlantic coast. It is doubtful that Wilmington–Philadelphia and New Bedford–Norfolk are the only instances that, as Gara put it, "give the legend a basis in fact." While it is patent that no Underground Railroad "headquarters" existed, with "disciplined conductors, controlling directors, and planned excursions into the South," it does not follow that the system was "of a haphazard nature."[21] I believe that this book demonstrates it to have been something more, and I hope that future works analyzing the presence and travel patterns of fugitives in other places will make connections only hinted at in the most reliable nineteenth-century accounts of this "passage to freedom."

1

"The True Ring of Freedom"

You may recollect the circumstance that took place a few weeks since, the attempt to capture a slave, who escaped to this place in a vessel from Norfolk, Va., they came at that time very near capturing him. We have just now got information that his owner has offered a high reward for him and that they have actually formed all their plans to take him without any delay. We think it imprudent for him to be here after the boat arrives, and I could not think of any better plan than sending him to Fall River, if you can keep him out of sight for a short time.

ON 18 FEBRUARY 1854, during a winter when the *American Beacon* of Norfolk claimed that slaves were escaping "almost daily" from that port, the New Bedford merchant Andrew Robeson asked Nathaniel B. Borden of nearby Fall River to conceal a fugitive from the man who claimed to own him.[1] Robeson did not identify the owner or the fugitive, but by that time slaveholders in more than one southern port city had reached the limit of their endurance with New Bedford. The city's Free Soil newspaper, the *Republican Standard,* noted nine days earlier that "the descendants of John Smith, out in Virginia . . . are lashing themselves into a furry [*sic*] in regard to our quiet little city of New Bedford" because a group of Norfolk-area slaveholders, probably including the one to whom Robeson alluded, had failed in their attempt to seize escaped slaves in New Bedford about a month before.

These slaveholders—one Major Hodsdon, James M. Binford, Mrs. Smiley, and one or two others[2]—had left Portsmouth in early January "in pursuit of their property," the *Beacon* stated, and one of them had visited New Bedford on 7 January, a Saturday, apparently on a scouting mission. The *Standard* reported that the man returned to Boston Saturday evening but came back to New Bedford with "two or three assistants" the following Monday morning. In Boston Hodsdon had retained a lawyer and contacted the U.S. Attorney, who sent a letter directing Deputy Marshall John D. Hathaway in New Bedford "to keep a lookout, to make his plans for securing the fugitives, and to write him by every mail of the progress he made in the prosecution of his duty." But Hathaway, despite the fact that the Fugitive Slave Act of 1850 mandated his cooperation, failed to respond to the attorney's query, and so Hodsdon and his party themselves went to New Bedford—"that den of negro thieves and fugitive protectors," as the *Beacon* acidly put it. Once there, Hodsdon told the *Beacon,* Hathaway told them that he "had recognized the negroes, and told the street he found them upon, but told them they were gone. He would give them no further satisfaction, except to let them know where the black friends of the negroes at present resided. Going there, the negroes were not to be found."[3]

The frustrated Hodsdon told the *Beacon* that he and his fellow slave owners had done everything they could to keep their mission and its purpose secret; they had even, he said, "disguised themselves, went in different directions and used every endeavor in as silent a manner as could be, to discover the whereabouts of the fugitives." Yet their careful procedure was fruitless in New Bedford, he charged, "so generally was the matter bruited [about] and so well posted was every citizen upon the subject." Hodsdon claimed that their reclamation effort "had been made a topic from the pulpits on the day before"; moreover, bells were chiming all over the city when they arrived, "the tolling being a species of telegraph they use in that sink of iniquity and lawlessness, to let the inhabitants know that masters or officers are in search of their slave property." The Valley Falls, Rhode Island, abolitionist Elizabeth Buffum Chace may have recollected the same incident when she wrote her antislavery memoir in 1891. A man who claimed to own the fugitive in one escape she aided had written to a Boston newspaper about his reception in the city. "He said that, when he arrived in New Bedford, the bells were rung to announce his coming, and warn his slave, thus aiding in his escape; and that, every way, he was badly treated. The truth was, as we afterward learned, that he arrived at nine o'clock in the morning, just as the school-bells were ringing; and he understood this as a personal indignity."[4]

The *Beacon* was outraged by the treatment the Virginians had received in the North and fumed at Edmund Anthony, the editor of the *Republican Standard,* for referring to Hodsdon and his associates as "scoundrels" in print. To the *Beacon* and other Virginia newspapers, the *Standard* was "the organ of the Black Guards, black fugitives, and rowdies and Negro stealers of that rank stew of fanatics and outlaws," and Anthony was "the amanuensis and private secretary of the Darkies."[5] New Bedford merchant Rodney French was another who raised their ire. A little more than two years before, merchants in New Bern, North Carolina, had resolved to boycott a vessel owned in part by French, a Free Soiler and later mayor of the city (1853–54), because they believed him to be "foremost in the lead of the opposition" to attempts to enforce the Fugitive Slave Act. French, New Bernians claimed, "did by his arts and public speeches endeavor to influence and excite the abolition part of his town to resist" the law—to the extent, they averted, that "he called on the fugitive slaves and free negroes to arm themselves and prevent the taking away runaway slaves." The merchants of New Bern pledged not to give French any business nor even to lighter the vessel's load "over the Swash" at the mouth of the harbor, to urge other port towns not to send any goods by the vessel, and to keep an eye on French's schooner and assure that it be searched before it left port. They hoped, they said, to send French's vessel away "without a barrel of freight."[6]

French answered that his vessel was in New Bern only because heavy rains had kept its captain from loading lumber at Bay River, that he occupied only a "humble place in the ranks" of antislavery reform, and that, when Southerners spoke of slaves being returned to lawful owners, he believed the Declaration of Independence made clear that there was no "slave upon this continent who had escaped from his 'lawful' owner." To French, beloved by Free Soilers but distrusted by New Bedford's more moderate abolitionists, the Fugitive Slave Act was "the most disgraceful, atrocious, unjust, detestable, heathenish, barbarous, diabolical, tyrannical, man-degrading, woman-murdering, demon-pleasing, heaven-defying act ever perpetrated in any age of the world by persons claiming to have consciences and a belief in a just God."[7] Like many other New Bedford merchants, he had long had commercial relations with the South and owned property there, but he told New Bern merchants he would give it all up rather than accede to the conditions they placed on trade:

> Gentlemen, we hold, or rather most of us [in the North], this way, that there is not a slave in his chains down South, who has not a right to his immediate, unconditional liberty. Who can successfully deny this? . . . God forbid that any panting fugitive from the prison-house of bondage should ever tap at my door and be turned away empty. No matter now close upon his heels are his pursuers. I prefer to have my lot cast with that proscribed and persecuted class, rather than enjoy the "employment," "for a season," of those who can only "extend the hand of friendship" upon condition that I assist them in "carrying out, in good faith, the Fugitive Slave Law."

In 1854, evidently responding to an article its editors had seen in that "greasy sheet," the *Republican Standard,* the Petersburg, Virginia, *Express* urged southerners to more drastic action than simply boycotting one trading vessel:

> The *'little village of Petersburg'* (which, by the way, is as large in population and resources as the great whaleopolis of New Bedford) may not be able by withdrawing its patronage from the New Bedford merchants, to paralyze the entire operations of the whale-fisheries, but let the whole Southern States, whom the authorities of New Bedford have insulted, determine to buy no more of their Winter-strained oil, and we should soon see what would be the effect. The dull glimmer of the *Standard* would no longer be perceived. The whole available fleet of whaling ships would probably be sent to the coasts of Senegambia to bring 'niggers' to Brazil. New Bedford, magnificent as she is now, and shining with the gloss of the spoils with which she has been smeared, would share the fate of Athens and Corinth; she would soon be
>   "Grease, but living grease no more!"[8]

Edmund Anthony seemed to take a perverse pleasure in publishing the withering commentary of the southern press. "The newspapers of negro breeding Virginia have been intensely exercised in regard to our city, the *Standard,* whale oil,

&c, &c, ever since" Hodsdon, whom Anthony called "a dealer in babies, in mothers, and in negro humanity generally," had failed to find the escaped slaves. Like most other city residents in the antebellum heyday of whaling, he assigned a more positive value to New Bedford "grease." The city's motto is *lucem diffundo,* "I pour forth light," a declaration many seem to have taken both literally—sperm whale oil being the best illuminant then available—and figuratively. "It cannot be denied," local poet and author Daniel Ricketson wrote in 1853, "that a highly respectable portion of the citizens of New Bedford have ever been the firm and constant friends of the Temperance, Peace and Anti-Slavery enterprises." And certainly fugitives saw the city similarly. In 1855 William Still of the Philadelphia Vigilance Committee tried to persuade the Norfolk slave Thomas Bayne, alias Sam Nixon, to head for Canada because it was, in his view, "the safest place for all Refugees; but it was in vain to attempt to convince 'Sam' that Canada or any other place on this Continent, was quite equal to New Bedford. His heart was there, and there he was resolved to go." For George Teamoh and other fugitives slaves, New Bedford was "our magnet of attraction," "the fugitive's Gibraltar."[9]

Abolitionists of both races agreed. Samuel J. May reflected that when Frederick Douglass escaped from Baltimore in 1838, New Bedford was "the best place, on the whole, to which he could have gone," and Douglass himself stated in his first autobiography in 1845 that of all the evidence of industry, beauty, and prosperity that impressed him during his first days in the city, "the most astonishing as well as the most interesting thing to me was the condition of the colored people, a great many of whom, like myself, had escaped thither as a refuge from the hunters of men. I found many, who had not been seven years out of their chains, living in finer houses, and evidently enjoying more of the comforts of life, than the average of slaveholders in Maryland." On a visit to New Bedford in late July 1837, Charles B. Ray, a native of Falmouth, Massachusetts, who had been educated in part in New Bedford schools and was then editor of the *Colored American,* wrote that "the people of color here are, perhaps, according to their number, better off than in any other place." When antislavery lecturer and Boston minister A. T. Foss visited New Bedford for the first time in 1860, he confessed to his audience that he had always wanted to speak in the city "because they had the true ring of freedom here."[10]

To the city merchant Charles Waln Morgan, writing just after the passage of the Fugitive Slave Act in September 1850, New Bedford was without question "one of the greatest assylums [*sic*] of the fugitives," and opposition to the law was "the ruling sentiment of this town." Most contemporary writers tended to attribute these facts to the influence of the Society of Friends, who, though much diminished as a sect by 1850, were believed to have set an enduring tone for life in New Bedford. "There is, and there ever has been, in New Bedford since its origin, a strong leaven of the old fashioned Quaker principles," Ricketson wrote in 1853, "and though not so ardently represented by the 'peaceful sect' as it was wont to be in past and more prosperous days of the Society of Friends, still the

FIGURE 5. *South parlour of Ab^m Russell Esq. New Bedford,* watercolor by Joseph Shoe-maker Russell (1795–1860), 1848. Courtesy Old Dartmouth Historical Society / New Bedford Whaling Museum. Russell's retrospective view of his parents' County Street parlor about 1812–15 is a picture of Quaker austerity; the walls have only a narrow wallpaper border, the architecture is plain but dignified, and on the mantle is what appears to be a collection of shells. Both men and women wear their hats in the house. Russell's wife, Sarah Schumaker Russell, sits in the only upholstered armchair.

most casual observer will perceive the influence of their principles upon this community." The journalist Charles T. Congdon recalled of the 1830s city in which he was raised, "The town was antislavery from the start, being full of Quakers,— it was founded, in fact, by one of that denomination—and the people were all Abolitionists before William Lloyd Garrison began his wonderful work." The normally critical Douglass felt less apprehensive in New Bedford when he saw "the broad brim and the plain, quaker dress, which met me at every turn . . . 'I am among the Quakers,' thought I, 'and am safe.'" Even those less favorably disposed to Quakers in general, such as the Weston sisters of Weymouth and Boston, attributed the town's relatively welcoming climate to the presence of Friends (fig. 5). "The descendents [*sic*] of the early Quakers begin to remember that they ought to have a testimony offer in this matter," Caroline Weston wrote to her cousin Wendell Phillips in 1845 from New Bedford, where she was teaching school, "as many among them remember when the *garrets* of Thomas Arnold and Wm Rotch the elder were constantly tenanted by runaway slaves (forwarded to their care by Moses Brown of Providence) which explains how it was that this place became a refuge for slaves—(there are now living here more than four hundred)." [11]

Congdon and Weston both erred slightly: the people of New Bedford were not all abolitionists even after William Lloyd Garrison began to work for the immediate emancipation of American slaves, Joseph Russell did not become a Quaker until 1766, after he founded the town, and evidence suggests that in the post-Revolutionary days of Moses Brown and William Rotch fugitives were as apt to be sent from New Bedford to Providence as the other way around. But the view of New Bedford as a place that Quaker culture had made both hospitable to people of color and prepared to make a stand for the fugitive has clung to the city into the current day. Not only do local sources tout this view continually, but historians have fostered it as well. [12]

Certainly New Bedford's heritage of Quaker-induced dissent is a strong one. The city may be in New England, but it chafed from the beginning at the kinds of towns Separatists and Puritans established. It did not have a central common with a meetinghouse at one end; indeed, it had no meetinghouse at all for the first thirty years of its existence as a village. Those who initially inhabited the vast township of Dartmouth, from which New Bedford was set off in 1787, tended to settle in dispersed fashion, on large farms on or near the township's many tidal rivers and amid Apponagansett, Acoaxet, and Acushnet peoples, small bands of Wampanoag Indians who were later referred to simply as "Dartmouth Indians." Purchased from the Wampanoag sachem, Massasoit, and his eldest son, Wamsutta, by enterprising men of Plymouth Colony in 1652, Dartmouth's seventeenth- and eighteenth-century population was probably much the same as one Mr. Fayerweather described Rhode Island's in 1760: "Quakers, Baptists, Fanatics, Rantters, Deists, and Infidels swarm in that part of the world." [13] Local historian Zephaniah W. Pease simply described early Dartmouth's settlers as "a class not particularly Puritan." From an early point, the towns of southeastern Massachusetts were reluctant to seek out, settle, and pay for ministers of the "Puritan orthodoxy," a tendency that dogged the colonial leaders of first Plymouth and then Massachusetts Bay into the 1700s. According to one Congregational minister, the failure to plant the church successfully in such towns as Tiverton, Freetown, Nantucket, and Dartmouth made their people "ignorant, erroneous and vicious," a dangerous tendency in lands that bordered Rhode Island, "the place where Satan hath his throne." [14]

By 1686 enough Quakers had settled in Dartmouth to establish a meetinghouse, and the Quaker population was greatly supplemented beginning in the 1750s by many former residents of Nantucket, whose ancestors had come to settle that island from dissenting towns in northeastern Massachusetts and southern New Hampshire. [15] These are the Quakers who left Nantucket for a harbor deep enough to float whaling vessels grown more massive and heavy by the need, even in that day, to go further afield for whales. The Acushnet River separating New

FIGURE 6. Bird's-eye view of New Bedford waterfront, stereoview by Stephen F. Adams or Gilbert D. Kingman, 1867. Courtesy Old Dartmouth Historical Society / New Bedford Whaling Museum. This early view of the city's harbor looks over the masts of whaling vessels to the broad Acushnet River, Fairhaven on the opposite shore, and the river's confluence with Buzzards Bay.

Bedford and Fairhaven was one of two main north-south rivers in southeastern Massachusetts, and even Bartholomew Gosnold had noted its virtues during his exploration of the coast in 1602. Rising as a brook, the river grew so deep and broad in its short path to the sea that it offered excellent harbor for deepwater vessels (fig. 6).[16] When the Nantucketers (principally members of the Rotch family, who comprised the preeminent whaling firm on the island) arrived, Joseph Russell of Dartmouth had been running four whaling sloops from the village for about a decade. In 1765 Joseph Rotch, who had worked his way from cordwainer to whaling magnate in forty years on the island, bought land of Russell, financed Russell's candleworks, the first in the village, and by 1769 had established the firm of Joseph Rotch & Son in "Bedford at Dartmouth."

Joseph Rotch had joined the Society of Friends on Nantucket in 1734, and Joseph Russell and his family were accepted into the Dartmouth Monthly Meeting of Friends in 1766. By the Revolution, more than half of all churches in Bristol County were either Baptist or Quaker, compared with 15 percent of churches elsewhere in Massachusetts, and the greatest concentrations of Quakers in the county had settled in Dartmouth and Swansea. By that time the village whaling merchants were largely Quaker—such men as Isaac Howland, Barnabas Taber, Barnabas Wing, and Benjamin Allen. One local account attaches a firm geographic dimension to this phenomenon.

> Bedford Village was located on the River front of two farms, separated by Elm Street. The north farm belonged to the Kempton descendants and they were Pilgrim and not Quakers. By some strange fate, the persons to whom they sold land, belonged to the same religious persuasion as themselves, so North Bedford was Presbyterian and attended the meeting house of Dr. West, at Acushnet. It approved the Revolution.
>
> South of Elm Street, was the farm of Joseph Russell, the leading Quaker. Most of the men to whom he sold land were of the same sect, and so were the merchants and wealthy men of the village. . . . It was practically a fact that the residents north of Elm Street worked for the Quakers, who lived south. Here were the wharves, storehouses, oil-works and most of the wealth . . . the residents south of Elm Street sought to avoid any relation with the war, as they were pleased to interpret that principle.[17]

Indeed, by the Revolution the Dartmouth Monthly Meeting's position on peace was well established. The Revolution had provoked numerous disownments for joining the militia or navy, manufacturing or repairing firearms "for the use of war," helping build and equip forts, and having anything to do with "prize goods," presumably obtained from privateers holed up in New Bedford harbor. In November 1776 Benjamin Howland III castigated himself before the meeting overseers "for going in company with those that took guns in order to be used in the military service"; exactly a year later Joseph Russell apologized formally for carting prize sugar "a small distance." Not all needed the discipline of the meeting to bear their testimony: William Rotch Sr., then living on Nantucket, was asked during the early years of the war about bayonets he had stored since taking them as part of the estate of an insolvent Boston debtor in 1764. Rather than sell them—instruments, he said, "purposely made and used for the destruction of mankind"—he threw the bayonets into the ocean.[18] The Friends' peace testimony, however, did not keep the whaling vessels of Nantucket and New Bedford from constant harassment and obstruction (England was by that time the principal market for the products of both fleets)[19] nor the British from burning Bedford village in early September 1778 on suspicion that its warehouses were filled with stolen goods deposited there by privateers registered, it is said, in other ports.

In 1782 Joseph Rotch, who had fled to Nantucket during the war, returned to rebuild his mainland whaling enterprise but lived only two years longer; after his death his grandson William Rotch Jr. came to the village to take over that branch of the family business. By the 1790s the village was again thriving.[20] William

Rotch Sr., whose efforts to establish a branch of the business in Dunkirk, France, were largely thwarted by the French Revolution, returned to America in 1794 and settled with his son Thomas in New Bedford by 1795. The next year he retired at age sixty-two and turned over his firm to his son-in-law Samuel Rodman, who had been managing company affairs on Nantucket, and by 1798 Rodman and his family had also moved to New Bedford. The Rodman family had an extensive kin network that helped forge close ties between New Bedford and Philadelphia in this early period: the sister and daughter of Samuel Rodman married Philadelphians Samuel Rowland Fisher and his nephew William Logan Fisher, and the younger Fisher came as an apprentice to William Rotch Jr. in New Bedford in 1795.[21] In 1791 Quaker Thomas Hazard Jr., a descendant of the Narragansett planter Robert Hazard and husband of Rodman's sister Anna, had settled in New Bedford. The Rotch clan dominated New Bedford whaling then and for the next quarter century: as Samuel Rodman wrote to Long Island Quaker Isaac Hicks in 1799, "There is not a Ship in this harbor but what belongs to our family."[22]

The Rotch-Rodman family now permanently joined others who had long lived in Dartmouth, having come to the sparsely settled area either from places closer to the center of Plymouth Colony, from Rhode Island, or at an earlier date from Nantucket. The Kempton and Delano families, the latter settling largely across the river in Fairhaven, descended from the original Plymouth grantees. John Russell, from whom Joseph Russell descended, had come from Plymouth to settle in Dartmouth by the early 1660s. By the 1690s part of the large and far-flung Benjamin Howland family had come from Plymouth to Dartmouth, and the families of James, Matthew, and Weston Howland were all in New Bedford village by the 1790s. The Pope family, in Dartmouth by the 1670s, was also from the Plymouth area. The Taber family lived in Dartmouth from the 1720s, the Ricketson family since at least the 1740s, the David Coffin family from the early 1770s. Rhode Island families included the Rodmans and the families of Joseph Anthony, Caleb Greene, Joseph Austin, Caleb Congdon, and Cornelius Grinnell, all living in and around Bedford village by the 1790s.

By 1795, according to Rotch family apprentice Jeremiah Winslow of Maine, Bedford village had no more than eleven hundred inhabitants and portions of only four streets "passable with carriages"—Union, climbing gradually west from the waterfront perpendicular to the Acushnet River; Water Street, then the closest street parallel to the river; part of Second Street, or the second parallel to the waterfront; and part of Bridge Street, running roughly parallel to Union Street to connect with the bridge that spanned the Acushnet River to Fairhaven. "There was no way out of the town, either to the North or South, but through the main street to the top of the hill," William Logan Fisher wrote in the same year. "Then the road diverged either way." This road at the top of the hill was County Street, which ran from Clark's Cove on the south along the high ridge above the village core and north toward Freetown and Taunton. Two other roads soon connected the village to portions of Dartmouth: one, Kempton Street, ran from the village's northern section west to Smith Mills in North Dartmouth, and the other, Russell's Mills Road, ran from Allen and Dartmouth Streets through its south end west to Russell's Mills in what is now South Dartmouth (fig. 7). Water Street ended, Winslow wrote, on the south at the brick home of Cornelius Grinnell, one of only two homes built completely of brick in the village and the only one with end chimneys instead of a single center one. Before 1795 the only meeting-house was that of the Friends, one block south of Union Street. One newspaper, the *Medley*, served the village—though not, in Winslow's or Fisher's opinion, adequately. There were two schoolteachers, one possibly self-trained physician, and, as one might expect in a settlement so preponderantly Quaker, one lawyer and no court; "the inhabitants were more disposed to settle differences by arbitration," Winslow wrote, "than to trust to 'the glorious uncertainty of the law.'"[23]

Of the major commercial powers of antebellum New Bedford, the families of only five were not present by 1800. By 1803 John Avery Parker, originally from Plympton but living in Westport since the 1790s, had moved into the village. By 1808 James Arnold, who married the daughter of William Rotch Jr., had come to Bedford village from Providence. Philadelphian Andrew Robeson, who married Samuel Rodman's granddaughter Anna, was living in Bedford by 1817, and two years later, Charles Waln Morgan, also of Philadelphia, married Rodman's daughter Sarah and moved to the village. Of the families who were instrumental in rebuilding the village and the whaling industry after the British raid, only the Kemptons, Popes, and Parkers were not members of the Society of Friends, and the increasing wealth of the industry was almost wholly in the hands of Friends.[24]

Moreover, the center of the whaling industry had begun to move from Nantucket to New Bedford. At the beginning of the war Nantucket sent out 150 whaling vessels, or 49 percent of the entire colonial fleet; Dartmouth was a distant second with 80 vessels. By 1793 Nantucket initiated 124 voyages to Dartmouth's 90. In the early 1820s, after a slow recovery from the Jeffersonian embargoes and the War of 1812, whaling voyages from New Bedford and Fairhaven surpassed those from Nantucket for the first time, and for all time (fig. 8).[25] From that point until after the Civil War the profitability of the industry, and the prosperity of the city, were virtually unimpeded. Between 1800 and 1830 the population of the town grew 74 percent, from 4,361 to 7,592 people, but the income from whaling spiraled, from about $300,000 to $3.5 million, an increase of more than 1,000 percent. The Boston *Traveller* described the spectacle New Bedford offered in 1830: "Notwithstanding all we had been told of the thriving condition of the town and the wealth of its inhabitants, we were unprepared to witness the forest of masts in the harbor and the crowded state of the wharves. A fleet of whale ships and other fishing vessels had a few days before returned, loaded with the most valuable spoils of the ocean; and rendered the appearance at this time, perhaps, unusually bustling. . . . New-Bedford, next to Boston, has the largest amount of tonnage of any port in Massachusetts."[26] By 1845 New Bedford was the fourth-largest port in the country on this measure, behind only New York

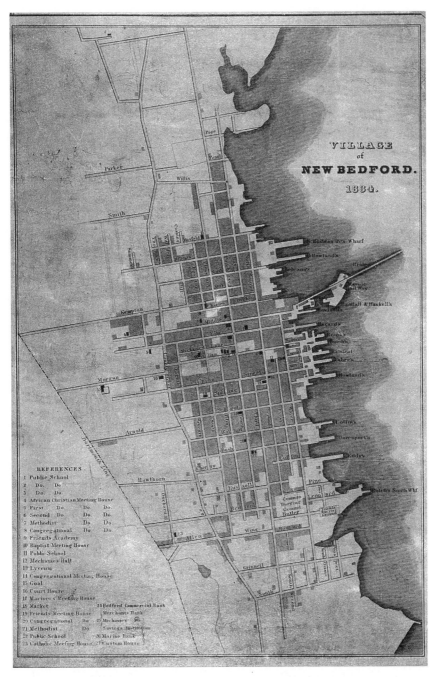

FIGURE 7. "Village of New Bedford, 1834," surveyed and drawn by J. Congdon and published by Pendleton, Boston. Courtesy Old Dartmouth Historical Society / New Bedford Whaling Museum. The shaded areas on this map appear to show developed sections of the village; the range of estates with their grounds along County Street is shown, as are a few estates remaining in the settled core east of County Street.

FIGURE 8. Southeastern Massachusetts and the New Bedford region.

City, Boston, and New Orleans; it handled nearly twice as much tonnage as Philadelphia (fig. 9). By that year more than 250 whalers ran out of New Bedford;
the fleet reached its pinnacle in the early 1850s, with about 310 vessels. In 1846,
far from the local industry's best year, those vessels returned 40,138 barrels of
sperm oil, 89,146 barrels of whale oil, and 580,862 pounds of whalebone, or baleen. The raw goods were together valued at $3.5 million, about 41 percent of the
value of American whaling products as a whole. Ten thousand mariners manned
the city's fleet, and thousands more worked in the shoreside occupations that
supported it and processed its products. Caulkers and shipwrights built and repaired the ships, barks, and whaleboats, stevedores loaded and unloaded them,
blacksmiths made harpoons and lances, coopers made barrels for storing oil and
other products, bakeries made ship's bread and biscuit, tailors made sailors' clothing, other men worked in the long, low ropeworks and cavernous sail lofts; still

others ran the boardinghouses, dining rooms, taverns, and brothels, essential features of maritime culture. The vessels returned with the bright-burning oil of sperm whales, too expensive for household use but the choice of lighthouses and many public buildings and the finest oil for lubricating the works of the country's new industrial economy. From the head of the sperm whale came spermaceti, a pure product that needed no processing and was fashioned into the best candles; from its gut, if a whaling crew were lucky, came ambergris—scarce, highly valued, at the time a chief constituent of perfume, and, according to the whaling historian Elmo Hohman, "an infallible aphrodisiac in various Mohammedan countries." From toothless whales, those that strain their food from seawater through massive plates of fringed cartilage (baleen) in their jaws, the industry

FIGURE 9. *View of New Bedford from the Fort near Fairhaven,* lithograph by Fitz Hugh Lane from a sketch by A. Conant, 1845. Courtesy Old Dartmouth Historical Society / New Bedford Whaling Museum. Lane's harbor view suggests the variety and volume of shipping from New Bedford before midcentury; one whaling vessel heads toward the wharves as another, at far right, makes its way out of the river into the Atlantic; two whalers are moored in the harbor; a schooner is hove to near the Fairhaven shore; sailboats, rowboats, and the steamer *Massachusetts* ply the Acushnet; and a profusion of masts is visible in the background at right.

FIGURE 10. New Bedford harbor from the foot of Middle Street, stereoview by T. E. M. White or Gilbert D. Kingman, probably 1859. Used with permission of the Board of Trustees of the New Bedford Free Public Library. Seaweed-covered casks line the shore between Front Street and the Acushnet River. Local historian Zephaniah Pease recalled in 1918 that casks protected in this way "covered every wharf along the waterfront of New Bedford. The leakage saturated the soil, and the air was redolent with the heavy odor."

took whale oil, put to the same purposes as sperm oil, and the baleen itself for the stays in corsets, the ribs of umbrellas, the handles of whips, fishing and divining rods, bows, pen holders, shoehorns, brushes, painters' graining combs, and other products that needed to be at once strong and flexible. Indeed, even as the development of the petroleum industry after 1859 spelled the end of whale oils in lighting, the international demand for baleen kept the industry alive into the 1920s. Draymen and workers carted or rolled casks of oil from the wharves, where they lay covered in seaweed to keep them from drying out, to the candleworks and oil factories that processed the raw products. For all the beauty and industry that impressed nineteenth-century journalists, it is astonishing that virtually none mentioned how foul the city must have smelled (fig. 10).[27]

By midcentury whaling ranked third among Massachusetts industries in the value of its products and fifth in the country. It was an industry that, at least until about 1845, expected receipts above what most land-based industries could promise, and one in which considerable capital investment coupled with spectacular risk could create awesome profit for owners and agents. For crew, however, returns grew less and less attractive over the first half of the nineteenth century. All crew were paid a "lay," or a proportion of a voyage's profit, that typically ranged from ⅛ to ½₀ for a captain to as little as ½₀₀ for a "green boy" who had no prior experience on a whaling vessel. One recent study of whaling voyages between 1840 and 1858 found that some boys signed onto crews for extraordinarily "long" lays of ¼,₅₀₀; more than twenty others signed on simply for clothes or board.

The lay system in effect transferred part of the risk involved in a voyage from owners to crew; a vessel that came back half-empty yielded poor compensation for everyone aboard. From the lays were subtracted the cost of a sailor's outfit (his clothes, sea chest, soap, and other necessary articles), any advance he might have been given to support his family in his absence, and any purchases he made from the captain's "slop chest," a shipboard store from which he could buy tobacco and anything to supplement his outfit; seamen often complained that the outfits furnished them ashore were so inferior that they could not avoid making purchases from the slop chest. Seamen paid interest on advances, outfits, and these purchases, but owners paid no interest on wages held until the end of the voyage. On the 1839–43 voyage of the *Francis Henrietta,* lays ranged from ¹⁄₁₆ to ¹⁄₃₀₀; Samuel Rodman and Charles W. Morgan, who together owned one-half of the vessel, each earned $8,438.70 on the voyage, while six of the twenty-six members of the crew below the rank of mate earned less than $30.00 each, one as little as $8.40. And over time the wages paid to certain whaling crew began to pale in comparison to those of shoreside work and even of the merchant marine, with which whaling wages had compared favorably earlier in the century. By the 1850s men of color were increasingly constrained to the roles of cook, steward, and unskilled hand on board a whaling vessel, and both cook and steward earned less than one-half of what they might have made ashore if all employment opportunities had been open to them. Cooks' monthly wages in the 1850s ranged from as high as $35.00 to as low as 55¢.²⁸

These rates of compensation, coupled with strict shipboard discipline and the cramped, noxious, and dangerous conditions of life and work aboard a whaling vessel, compelled Hohman to describe the occupation as "at its best . . . hard, and at its worst . . . the lowest condition to which free American labor has ever fallen." While touting the possibilities of advancement in a whaling crew in 1842, one agent in the same breath told J. Ross Browne, an Irish American who had grown up in Kentucky, that a whaling vessel "is a place of refuge for the distressed and persecuted, a school for the dissipated, an asylum for the needy." Browne was shocked that he had to share his forecastle barracks on the *Bruce* with men of color and dark-skinned Portuguese sailors recruited on the way and blamed their presence on poor wages, want, and naïveté:

> Why are the crews composed, for the most part, of foreign outcasts? Because they can be obtained at a lower rate of compensation than Americans, because they have never been accustomed to Republican institutions, and are willing to submit to oppressive and despotic treatment; because, having been all their lives suffering from hunger and want, they are easily satisfied with the poorest fare, because, in short,

they are more easily cheated, more servile, more ignorant, and more depraved than the generality of Americans inveigled into the same service. . . . Abolish all these abuses, and Americans will man our vessels. There are thousands of enterprising young men in this country who would be glad to find employment in the whale fishery, if they could do so without becoming slaves.[29]

Labor turnover was high in the industry and increased over time; on the six voyages of the *George Howland* between 1840 and 1866, turnover was 63 percent of the original crew, thinned by desertion, discharge, and death.[30]

Still, the global demand for whale oils was so insistent that by the 1850s New Bedford was often set forth as the wealthiest city in the country—even, some claimed, in the world—and it was something of a sport among journalists and others to compute the per capita wealth of its residents. "Probably no city in the Union, perhaps no city in the world can show such an amount of property in proportion to the number of inhabitants," the *Whalemen's Shipping List,* which kept track of the industry and the comings and goings of its vessels, reported in 1854. "Taking the last United States census as the basis of population, a division of the wealth of the city would give to every man, woman and child in New Bedford, a fraction over $1615 each." According to statistics of real and personal wealth reported in the *Republican Standard* exactly a year later, per capita wealth was $1,265.83, and the wealth of the average city poll tax payer was of course considerably higher—$5,979.84. In 1860 the New York *Evening Post* calculated it this way: "In case of an equal distribution of property to every male citizen twenty-one years of age, the amount would be above $4,300 apiece, and if divided among all the inhabitants the share of each man, woman and child, would exceed $1000. There is not a city in the Union with such an aggregate of wealth according to the population. A fair proportion of its tax payers are women, and their assessments, it is worthy of note, are by no means less than the average of the valuations set to the other sex. With such an abundance of 'this world's goods,' New Bedford ought to be an urban paradise."[31]

In closing the *Post* seems both to have taken a gibe at Quakers as well as to have expressed its suspicion that New Bedford was something short of an urban paradise. Indeed, one local historian has written that there were "two New Bedfords" in these years, "one a fair and dignified village on the hilltop, where were patrician mansions, with opulent gardens, the homes of the whaling merchants and captains," the other "squalid sections where the sailors and those who preyed upon them, the saloons, where delirium and death were sold, the boarding houses, the dance halls and houses where female harpies reigned and vice and violence were rampant."[32] And New Bedford's wealth was of course not distributed equally. In 1855 property value by ward ranged widely, from $2,704.54 per taxpayer in Ward 6, the extreme south end of town, to $12,953.29 per taxpayer in Ward 5, the County Street district. From the early 1830s, when temperance reform took hold of the town, officials cast a worried eye on the "squalid sections." In 1836 Debora Weston wrote that the village, whose population had just been

FIGURE 11. Bethel Street from Union, photograph by Fred Palmer, about 1900. Courtesy Old Dartmouth Historical Society / New Bedford Whaling Museum. No antebellum views exist of the village's boardinghouse districts, but Palmer's photograph of the boardinghouses lining Bethel Street documents that most had been built before 1850. Palmer's view is one of few that show what much of the housing in the downtown core must have looked like at the height of the whaling era. Nearly all of these frame structures were leveled in 1916 for the city's new whaling museum.

counted as 11,113 persons, had "50 grog shops"; in 1852 another municipal survey uncovered 78 "liquor shops" and 56 "houses of ill repute" in the city, 37 of the former and 21 of the latter in Ward 4, the principal commercial and working-class district, alone. In these districts children "go about begging pig's livers at the expense of their integrity," one reformer wrote in 1840, and "disorderly dances, dog and rooster fights, obstructing the side-walks" were common occurrences in the north part of Ward 4 near the city's railroad depot, an area that came to be known as "Holy Acre" in the early 1900s. One temperance and vice campaign in 1856 swept down on the waterfront Arctic Saloon in Ward 4 and hoped to have made "dancing, fiddling, drinking and high times generally . . . 'institutions' of the past on First street."[33] But in these districts lived most of the workers and crew on whom the city's industry depended (fig. 11), which may explain why municipal efforts to eradicate crime and waywardness were sporadic, if not half-hearted.

Still, New Bedford seemed to have a generous share of individuals who cared about the well-being of the town's laboring people and those less fortunate; among them were what the historian William J. Frost has termed "outward-looking" Quakers. Unlike inward-looking Friends, who tended to be "tribalistic" and to minimize their contact with the attractions and corruptions of the world at large, outward-looking Friends took a more "humanistic" view of their role in society. This philosophical division within the sect extended to the issue of slavery. Although Friends of both types opposed slavery, inward-looking Friends, the historian Jean Soderlund has noted, "were less interested in abolition at first, though they eventually came to view slaveholding as one kind of worldly behavior that must be purged from the meeting." Outward-looking Friends, following the lead of Anthony Benezet, John Woolman, and Nantucket's Elihu Coleman, were more apt to focus centrally on eliminating slavery as adherence to the Quaker testimony that all people are equal in the eyes of God and equally capable of cleansing themselves of sin.[34]

As Soderlund has pointed out, the "handful" of abolitionists in this country before the Revolution were largely Friends or thought of themselves as Friends,[35] even if the sect itself tended to set a "gradualist, segregationist, and paternalistic" tone for the antislavery movement before William Lloyd Garrison and the American Anti-Slavery Society began to call for immediate abolition of slavery in the early 1830s.[36] And Douglass was not the only fugitive who associated Quakers with the same commitment to equal rights and loving assistance that whites did; narratives document that a good number of escaping slaves believed antislavery reform to be vital among people who called themselves Friends. One of the earliest known fugitives in southeastern Massachusetts, Robert Voorhis, "the Hermit of Massachusetts," had heard much "of the hospitality of the Quakers (or Friends,) . . . as a class who were zealous advocates for the emancipation of their fellow beings in bondage" and relied on their assistance in both of his early 1790s efforts to escape Charleston, South Carolina (fig. 12). Quakers figured critically in the escapes of Georgia fugitive John Brown, Kentucky's William Wells Brown (who took his name from an assisting Friend), Leonard Black, Peter Robinson, and Fall River's James Curry, to say nothing of the scores aided by Thomas Garrett in Wilmington, Delaware; by Abigail and Elizabeth Goodwin in New Jersey; by Elisha Tyson in Baltimore; by Passamore Williamson, Isaac T. Hopper, and Lucretia Mott of Philadelphia; and by Friends in other cities. One abolitionist who accused Quakers of negrophobia and proslavery sentiment in 1851 nonetheless conceded in the *Liberator*, "Strange to say, the black people, many, too many of them, will run mad, almost, after a Quaker!"[37]

Yet numerous documents attest the fact that abolitionism among Quakers was a personal decision, as it was among Americans of other creeds, that depended on one's interpretation of the sect's principles. Although individual monthly and

ROBERT THE HERMIT.

FIGURE 12. "Robert the Hermit," wood engraving in *Life and Adventures of Robert, the Hermit of Massachusetts, Who Has Lived 14 Years in a Cave, Secluded from Human Society* . . . (Providence, R. I., 1829). Courtesy John Hay Library, Brown University, Providence.

yearly meetings of the Society of Friends took an early stand against their members' participation in slave trading and slaveholding, historians and contemporar-
ies agreed that the society as an organized religious body seemed more interested
in purging slave owners from its fold than in achieving freedom and equity for
slaves. "Now they have become a sect, and have become conservative, and care
very little about the great principles that brought their fathers forth, and out, in
former times," New Bedford's Isaiah Ray, a birthright Quaker, wrote in 1847,
noting that Friends in his day seemed to adhere only to the sect's discipline and
to lack a creed altogether. "They are scrambling after money with the world, and
their philosophy is left to be taken up by individuals." Samuel Rodman, Daniel
Ricketson, and John Bailey made similar observations about the local and New
England Yearly Meetings at this time.[38]

The Quaker historian Thomas Hamm has pointed out that Friends tended to
oppose slavery on two grounds—the suffering that slaves endured and the fact
that unfree people were kept from understanding and living their lives "according
to the light within them." But these beliefs did not always, or even usually, impel
Quakers to embrace the notion that blacks were whites' "social equals," as Jean
Soderlund has put it. Samuel Ringgold Ward, a fugitive slave and Congregationalist minister, noted as much. "They will give us good advice. They will aid in
giving us a partial education—but never in a Quaker school, beside their own
children. Whatever they do for us savors of pity, and is done at arm's length," he
wrote ruefully.[39]

Increasingly, as Garrisonian immediatism took hold of the antislavery movement, Quakers "were not as a religious sect, much more friendly than others to
the immediate emancipation of the enslaved without expatriation," Unitarian
minister Samuel J. May wrote. "They were disposed to be colonizationists rather
than abolitionists."[40] Elizabeth Buffum Chace noted the presence of this tendency at one New England Yearly Meeting of the Society of Friends at Newport,
where during the meeting's long discussion of slavery "almost everybody was
against us," she wrote. "They denounced the *Liberator,* Garrison was an infidel,
slavery could only be cut off gradually, the colored race must be colonized in
Africa." Quakers at the meetings she attended generally "disapproved of Friends
uniting with other people in public meetings or in philanthropic work, they did
not think the slaves should be set free all at once, and they did not want their
daughters to marry negroes," Chace wrote. "I remember making an appeal to a
Quaker cousin of mine, by asking him if he did not think the slaves should be
freed, and his only reply was, 'I shouldn't want to see a black man sitting on the
sofa beside my daughter.'"[41] Reform-minded Quakers like Chace often met with
more than the disapproval of their monthly meetings: the Smithfield, Rhode Island, meeting disowned her father, Arnold Buffum, because of his antislavery
work, and Isaac T. Hopper and Abby Kelley were disowned by their meetings for
the same reason.[42] Chace herself resigned from her meeting, as did James Munroe
from his in East Greenwich, Rhode Island, because of what he perceived as its

"almost total apathy to the miseries of three millions of the great brotherhood of man, deprived of every right that humanity can claim, and subjected to every outrage that humanity can suffer."[43] In 1835 the perceptive critic and abolitionist Lydia Maria Child identified the issue at hand in an approving letter about Philadelphia Quaker Sidney Ann Lewis's refusal to take down a sign advertising her sale of antislavery writings and cotton goods made with free labor: "I wish this spirit were more universal among the Quakers; but many excuse themselves, by saying they must not mix with the world—that Israel must dwell in his tents. If *our* way does not seem right, why can they not work in their own way? Assuredly, they would, and so could others that make similar objections, if they truly loved the work for Christ's sake. Assuredly, they would, if they remembered 'those who are in bonds as bound with them.' They do not realize the condition of the oppressed, and the spirit of the world is with them in this very fear of acting *with* the world."[44]

Some Quakers discerned this tendency as distressing as well. After attending a quarterly Friends meeting in early April 1843, Samuel Rodman Jr. reported that the meeting's answers to the "queries" it routinely received from various Yearly Meetings "did not indicate any special advance in the temperance reform, but on this subject as well as others, particularly that of slavery, the quiet temperament which in modern times has characterized the Society, if it does not leave them behind others, gives them no claim to the precedence which was formerly accorded with justice to this over other sects." After a Monthly Meeting for Discipline the following January, Rodman noted with some chagrin how far behind New England's Quakers as a sect were in antislavery reform.

> The London Gen'l Epistle was read on which I took occasion to remark on the difference in the practice of Friends in Great Britain and this country in relation to slavery. There they ever show themselves alive and ready to act and do act independently and in union with others for the suppression of the enormous traffic and the abolition of slavery, remote as they are from the scenes of its accumulated wrongs, while here they show to a very great extent, and particularly in New England, a practical dereliction of this great subject though our own government gives it sanction and support and derives a direct income from the horrible system. I thought it worthy of consideration whether this practical abandonment of this great department of Philanthropy in which the Soc'y had formerly been prominent was not the cause of the disaffection which had been this day the occasion of an exercise of discipline in the case of Anna Maria Bailey [daughter of New Bedford abolitionist jeweler John Bailey] and whether the disaffection from the same cause if continued would not spread and be the means of making further inroads within our borders.[45]

Lydia Child put it more succinctly in a letter to the abolitionist Caroline Weston: "Pity that a sect founded on such high and broad principles should be buried in the mere shell of lifeless forms." But, she added, "when a Quaker *has* a soul, what large ones they have!"

New Bedford had its share of inward-looking Friends—after a spate of induced

FIGURE 13 (LEFT). William Rotch Sr. (1734–1828), oil on canvas by unidentified artist after a portrait by Edward D. Marchant (1806–87), about 1850. Courtesy Old
Dartmouth Historical Society / New Bedford Whaling Museum. Marchant probably
painted the original work during an 1825 visit to New Bedford, when Rotch was ninety-
one years old. Daniel Ricketson described his attire to be "of the true William Penn
order—a drab beaver, drab suit, the long coat and waistcoat, knee-breeches with
silver-buckles."

FIGURE 14 (RIGHT). William Rotch Jr. (1759–1850), half-plate daguerreotype by unidentified photographer, about 1845. Courtesy Old Dartmouth Historical Society / New
Bedford Whaling Museum.

manumissions in the late 1780s and 1790s, the New Bedford Friends Meeting
minutes rarely mention antislavery—but it also had an influential group of large-
souled ones.[46] In 1716, the year John Farmer was disowned by the Friends Meeting
in Newport, Rhode Island, for publishing without the meeting's approval a letter
calling for the unconditional manumission of all slaves Quakers owned (Farmer
was later disowned for the same reason by the Philadelphia Meeting), the Nantucket and Dartmouth Meetings had both formally called for all Friends to "to
forbear for time to come, to be in any way concerned in purchasing any slaves."[47]
William Rotch Sr. and his sons William Jr. and Thomas each held important
positions in the New Bedford Meeting hierarchy and were adamant and active
antislavery workers from at least the 1780s (figs. 13 & 14). So were those who
married into this family—Samuel Rodman Sr.; Thomas Hazard Jr., whose father
in 1730 refused a large inheritance of slaves from his own father, Robert, one of
the famed "Narragansett planters" of Rhode Island; and James Arnold, son of the

Providence abolitionist and Quaker Thomas Arnold. In 1790 William Rotch Jr., Thomas Arnold, and Thomas Hazard Sr. were founding members of the Providence Society for Promoting the Abolition of Slavery, for the Relief of Persons Unlawfully Held in Bondage, and for Improving the Condition of the African Race. The society's founders included twenty-six men from Massachusetts, among them Joseph Austin, James Davis, Caleb Greene, Isaac Howland Sr. and Jr., James Howland, Humphrey Howland, Peleg Howland, Ebenezer Perry, Abraham, Barnabas, Caleb, and Seth Russell, and Daniel Ricketson; all were New Bedford residents, and two others, John Howland and Jeremiah Austin, lived in the towns of Dartmouth and Westport. All of the founders living in what was originally Dartmouth were Friends, and they made up two-thirds of the Massachusetts members of the society.[48]

William Rotch Sr. was a member of a committee appointed by the New England Yearly Meeting to visit all Friends' meetings in the region and "investigate their antislavery testimony"; the committee advised in its 1770 report that Quakers set free all slaves they owned unless they were too young or too old to support themselves. In these same years, Rotch was in court for having paid wages directly to Prince, a slave owned by the heirs of Nantucket's William Swain, rather than to the heirs after Prince served on a whaling voyage on Rotch's whaling vessel *Friendship.* The court of common pleas on Nantucket is said to have manumitted Prince in consequence of the voyage, and the decision is supposed to have ended the legal employment of slaves on New England vessels.[49] Rotch frequently purchased the indentures of men of color for his whaling crews; in 1785, trying to arrange the passage of the *Canton* from Nantucket to London, he wrote his son William Jr. and son-in-law Samuel Rodman to secure "the Indentures of the Masters of some of the Blacks, with their full power, not only to retain their present voiges, but to secure those whose apprenticeship may not have expir'd in future vizt. Geo. Lawrence for his Black man, Peter Macy for his Boy—and a full Power from Edward Bourn of Sandwich for his Jo Cunnet. . . . Shubl Lovell respectg his Joe Tobey. . . . I dont recollect the other Blacks nor their situation."[50]

Rotch may have been interested in people of color at least in part because they represented much-needed crew on the labor-scarce island and in early New Bedford, but his interest in antislavery was more than pragmatic. In early November 1787 Rotch wrote Providence abolitionist and Quaker merchant Moses Brown about Quakers and the proposed federal Constitution:

> Thou queries how friends can be active in establishing the new form of government, which so much favours slavery, alas in this point I must refer thee to some advocate for it, as to my own part my heart has been often pained since the publication of the doings of the Convention; and much disappointed I am as I had entertained some hope that so many wise men, would have found some system of Government, founded on equity & justice, that thereby it might have acquir'd some strength and energy, and that it might be on such a basis that we as a Society might lend our aid in establishing it so far as it tended to peace and morality; but we may say in truth

that the wisdom of man (as man) can or shall not work the righteousness of God; and whatever high encomiums are given to it (the Constitution) it is evident to me it is founded on *Slavery* and that is on *Blood,* because I understand, some of the southern members utterly refused doing anything unless this horrid part was admitted.[51]

At the time Rotch and Samuel Rodman were involved in the case of Cato, a black slave whom Rodman had hired of his Newport owner John Slocum two years earlier. Cato had come to look upon Nantucket, and his life in the Rodman family, as his "assylum," and Rodman and Rotch tried to convince Slocum to free the man. Slocum refused, but after much "friendly" persuasion he finally agreed to manumit him in a year's time. "Slocums proposal was to lodge it [the manumission document] in the hands of one of his own children," Rotch wrote to Brown, "but this base intimation was rejected by Cato's friends, & S. Rodman has it in possession; Cato is a very honest orderly man set out yesterday on his new year [of] slavery, he is I believe near forty years old, and altho it is but for a year, yet the darkness of that heart that requires it, gives me so bad an opinion of this man, that I think in this enlightened age, he ought not to lay claim to any great degree of Christianity." Rotch confessed to Brown, "My heart is warm'd toward those poor blacks and I feel sometimes willing to spend and be spent if I could contribute to their encouragment."[52]

By the late 1780s William Rotch Jr. had taken up his father's antislavery testimony and was if anything more willing to "spend and be spent" in the cause. In 1789, on behalf of the Providence Abolition Society but largely with his own funds, he sued the owner and master of the brigantine *Hope* on the charge of having fitted out as a slaver in Boston in June 1788, three months after the Commonwealth of Massachusetts had passed a law banning the slave trade. After selling its cargo of 116 slaves in the West Indies in February and March 1789, the vessel put ashore at Acoaxet (now Westport, the westernmost town in what was originally Dartmouth), its crew fled to Rhode Island to escape the Massachusetts law, and the *Hope's* captain came to New Bedford to clear the vessel's cargo for Newport, where its owner lived. Rotch hired Boston attorneys Thomas Dawes Jr. and Christopher Gore to prosecute the case. In March 1791 the Court of Common Pleas at Taunton found for the Abolition Society, but the *Hope's* owner immediately appealed; in October the Supreme Judicial Court upheld the lower-court ruling, as did the court at Boston in February 1792.[53] Rotch by this time was heavily involved in collecting information on instances of cruelty aboard New England ships to "slaves & crew" and in supporting antislavery in any way he could. To Rotch, the uprising of slaves in Santo Domingo in 1791, in which the recently freed Toussaint L'Ouverture took active part, was an event to be applauded. Among "the thinking people of New England whose minds are unclouded with the dark seeds of slavery," he wrote to his uncle Francis, "it is looked upon that the struggle on the part of the Negroes & Molattoes is as just as was the American struggle for liberty."[54]

2

Origins

In 1853 New Bedford native William Allen Wall (1801–85), a trained artist with a penchant for historical scenes, visualized for a generation far removed how the city's whaling industry might have begun. Wall completed *Birth of the Whaling Industry* five years before Daniel Ricketson published the first history of the city, so he must have come by his impressions largely from stories told him by his father's generation, perhaps among them people who had had a hand in New Bedford whaling's early years. In a place awash in prosperity, it is easy to imagine how colorful, nostalgic, and monumental those stories must have been even in Wall's boyhood. *Birth of the Whaling Industry* was the second in a trio—with *Gosnold at the Smoking Rocks* (1842) and *Old Four Corners, New Bedford* (1855)—which may have been the first truly commemorative historical scenes ever produced of the city.

Unlike *Gosnold at the Smoking Rocks,* which depicted the explorer's 1602 trading overture with Indians at the mouth of the Acushnet River, neither of Wall's other two scenes had by their subject matter to feature people of color. Yet both did, and more or less centrally. In the right foreground of *Old Four Corners* Wall placed a man and two women of color, at least one of them a tradesperson, talking together on lower Union Street. The painter's view of the inception of New Bedford whaling features both a Native American and a man of African descent, both of them working men. *Birth of the Whaling Industry* (fig. 15) shows a sloop hauled up on the Acushnet shore near Center Street, the already legendary site of Joseph Russell's first tryworks. In whaling's first century these one-masted sloops did the lion's share of the industry's work, and by 1765—two years after the date the boy in the painting's right foreground, clearly Wall's stand-in, is carving into the stump behind Russell—Russell and his partners had put four sloops weighing each about fifty tons to the pursuit of whaling from New Bedford. This sloop might have gone after right whales in coastal waters or sperm whales in the warmer waters of the tropics and subtropics; Nantucket whalers had been taking sperm whales for half a century by the date of this view.[1] In either case the vessels would have brought back to shore whale blubber, cut into large strips and packed

FIGURE 15. *Birth of the Whaling Industry*, oil on canvas by William Allen Wall, 1853. Used with permission of the Board of Trustees of the New Bedford Free Public Library.

in casks assembled on board, to be rendered or "tried" into oil on land. *Birth of the Whaling Industry* shows Russell's rude tryworks, with a whale's jawbone slung onto the roof; within six years of this view Russell, under the supervision of Joseph Rotch's Nantucket firm, would begin building the city's first candleworks nearby.[2] As vessels grew larger and spent years at sea rather than months, the facilities for trying out blubber were incorporated on the vessels themselves.[3]

In the right foreground of *Birth of the Whaling Industry*, two men cut blubber and pour oil into casks. Next to them, at center, a cooper pauses in his work on a barrel to talk, Wall wrote in a description accompanying the painting, to "an Indian, who, with his baskets and moccasins for sale or barter, is seated upon a broken mast"; one man kneels to inspect a pair of moccasins. Behind this group men are at work on the hauled-up sloop, and to their left in the foreground Joseph Russell, "in his broad-brimmed hat and Friendly coat, the founder of New Bedford and the father of her whale-fishery," sits with his back to the painter as he talks with a man of color—"evidently one of the old stock of Guinea negroes, some old 'Pero,' 'Quash,' or 'Pompey,' " Wall wrote in an oddly objective way— who is holding the reins of Russell's horse.

By 1763 whaling was a century-old American industry, and Nantucket was at its pinnacle. Vessels from the island had crossed the equator, penetrated the Davis Straits, Baffin Bay, Hudson Bay, and the Gulf of St. Lawrence, and that year they reached the northwestern coast of Africa in the whale hunt. Two years later whalers would stop for the first time at the Azores, the Cape Verde Islands, and the islands of the Caribbean.[4] By the 1760s new markets had opened for whale oil, which impelled swift growth in the industry and a consequent change in its method of recruiting crew. Native Americans living on Long Island, Cape Cod, and Martha's Vineyard had been whaling since the industry's first days in the 1650s and 1660s, and they were more than half of Nantucket whaling crews beneath the rank of mate between 1725 and 1734. In 1730 55 percent of Nantucket whaling crews were Indians, some of them recruited on the mainland, and as vessels grew larger so did crews and the consequent recruiting effort. By the next decade the island was no longer able to meet the industry's labor needs, and one 1746 report states that many of the nine hundred Indians living on Nantucket had come from the Vineyard (which had three distinct bands of Wampanpoags at Gay Head, Chappaquiddick, and Christiantown) in search of "better employment." That Wall's painting shows the Indian and the man of color not in whaling garb but as a trader and a servant is telling, and surprisingly accurate: an epidemic in the summer of 1763 had virtually extirpated Nantucket's Indian population, and in that decade probably only 12 percent of the island's whaling crews were Indian; an even smaller proportion, 8 percent, were black.[5] Much the same proportions must then have prevailed in Dartmouth's far smaller fleet; Dartmouth enumerators reported only thirty-four slaves living in the settlement in 1755, and no census accounted for the number of free people of color at this early date. The greatest numbers were in the already thriving commercial ports of Boston (989 slaves) and Salem (77). By 1765 the number of black and mulatto people in Dartmouth had risen to sixty-one, and they were outnumbered by Indians, enumerated at seventy-five. By that time Boston's black population had declined to 811.[6]

The Nantucket historian Edward Byers has noted that whaling vessel owners began to recruit blacks, either directly or through agents, toward the end of the 1700s; the number of people of color living on Nantucket rose from 44 in 1746 to 274 in 1820.[7] As the whaling industry grew, owners sometimes used New York City and Boston agents to find men in the larger port towns of the Northeast. Between 1769 and 1776, only from 16 to 30 percent of William Rotch Sr.'s crews were Nantucketers. Rotch also hired crew from individuals on the mainland, including Thomas Smith Jr. of Sandwich on Cape Cod, who regularly sent him Indians from the Mashpee settlement, and Oliver Smith, a merchant in Stonington, Connecticut, who in 1770 sent Rotch twenty Indians and men of color for whaling crews. Oliver Smith is known to scholars of slavery as Colonel Oliver Smith, to whom the African Venture Smith was sold in about 1760. One of the first American slave autobiographers, Smith was born about 1729 to a tribal prince in Guinea. He was taken aboard a Rhode Island slaver when he was six years old. Purchased by the vessel's steward, Smith was not killed by the smallpox virus that swept through the ship on its middle passage, nor was he sold with the rest of the captured Africans in Barbados; instead he was brought back to Rhode Island to the Narragansett plantation of his purchaser. After a failed escape attempt when he was twenty-two, Smith was sold repeatedly and then purchased by Oliver Smith, who permitted him to hire his time that he might purchase his freedom. Venture Smith owned a sloop in which he carried on trade in wood between Long Island and Rhode Island, and about 1773 he made at least one whaling voyage under the auspices of Oliver Smith. Whether Smith ever sent him to a Rotch vessel in Nantucket is not known.[8]

Though neither crew lists nor protection papers exist from the years before 1796 to verify the possibility, there is no reason to doubt that similar staffing practices occurred in New Bedford toward the end of the century, even though labor was easier to secure on the mainland. In February 1771 58 of 1,521 males over the age of fifteen were "negro or mulatto," or about 3.8 percent of the population, and even though by 1776 black adult males may have made up a slightly smaller share of the adult male population in the town, still a greater proportion of total local population was black than prevailed in the state as a whole (1.8 percent).[9] The population of people of color was sufficiently congregated by 1778 that their settlement was identified on an early map. After the British raid on 5 September, Major John André annotated a map of Bedford's harbor, from Ricketson's Neck in South Dartmouth on the west to West Island in Fairhaven on the east, with a list of the properties destroyed. It shows the principal concentrations of settlement on both shores with small black squares and landowners' names, and just between homes labeled "Maxfield" and "Kempton" is an area called "New Guinea" (fig. 16). Sandwiched between County Street and the long stretch of marshland that gave rise to Allen's Creek, New Guinea seems to have occupied roughly the same location that the West End, a neighborhood composed largely of persons of color, has occupied to the current day. That this settlement should have borne this name, at least among whites, is not surprising: it was the term almost uniformly ascribed to black settlements in the coastal Northeast. Nantucket's neighborhood of color was so labeled, as was, at least occasionally, Plymouth's Parting Ways, settled near that town's border with Kingston about 1779. Black neighborhoods in Boston and New Haven were also called New Guinea.[10] The geography of such New England settlements seems to have been one of two types depending, probably, on the age of the town in which they arose: either they were in waterfront areas already disheveled and abandoned as middle-class residential areas in such older cities as Boston and New Haven, or they were set off in an initially remote corner of a newer village whose waterfront was still growing and still inhabited by artisans and merchants, as they were in Nantucket and New Bedford. The 1790 census data suggest that no such neighborhood could have been identified in New Bedford: only thirty-eight persons of color were enumerated in the village. All but five of them lived in the households of

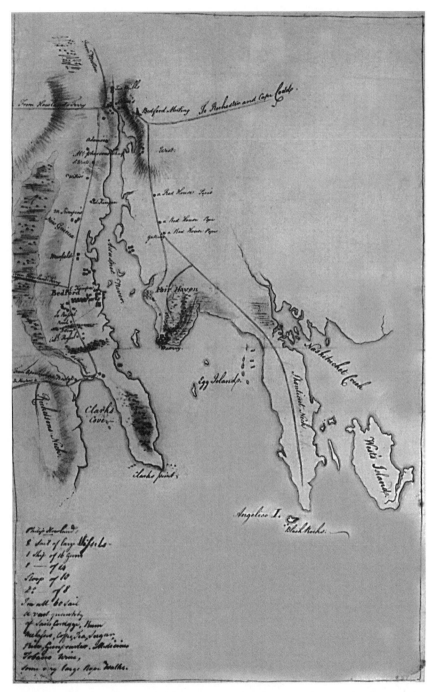

FIGURE 16. Bedford Harbor, finished topographical map with notes by Major John André identifying New Guinea, 1778. Courtesy William L. Clements Library, University of Michigan.

white persons, and those five persons in black households lived in fact in only one, that of Aaron Childs. The discrepancy between André's map and these statistics is the first suggestion of the possibility that the census, as it has been presumed perennially to do, undercounted the population of color, that probably a substantial number of people of color were living in Bedford's west end and in other parts of the village. William Logan Fisher once recalled eating descented skunk at the "restaurant" of "a nice old colored man named Pero," who lived two or three miles west of the village (perhaps in Dartmouth) and noted, too, that the "small Indian wigwam or cottage" of Sarah Obadiah near Clark's Cove was something of a tourist attraction in the village's early years.[11]

By 1790 Bristol County recorded 794 people of color in its population and had moved from ninth among Massachusetts counties in the number of people of color in 1754 to third, again behind only the most commercially developed and maritime-oriented counties of Suffolk and Essex. In that year, 174 nonwhite persons lived in Dartmouth, Westport, and New Bedford. By 1800 the number of people of color in these towns was 405, an increase of 132 percent that brought their share of the population to 4.3 percent.[12] These towns contained good farmland, but the growth in the economy was almost entirely due to maritime trade and whaling. The increase in the population of color is surely related to that maritime economy.

Wall identified the man of color in *Birth of the Whaling Industry* as having, like Venture Smith, come from Guinea, and he suggested a series of names typical among New England slaves and black servants—Pero, Quash, Pompey. Whether Wall knew it or not, Joseph Russell in fact owned slaves named Quash and Pero at the time; they were probably among the thirty-seven males of color living in Dartmouth in 1765. Russell, born in Dartmouth, was accepted into the Dartmouth Monthly Meeting of the Society of Friends in April 1766, though he may have "followed the Meeting"—attended its services and observed its customs of dress and address—before being formally admitted as a member. Six years after his acceptance, however, the meeting disciplined him and Isaac Howland II, also a slave owner, for "running goods," presumably military, intoxicating, or illegally acquired ones. Isaac Howland had run afoul of the meeting often in the past. In 1764 the meeting sent members to visit him both for marrying a non-Quaker and for being "in the practice of the slave trade," and it found the paper he submitted "signifying his sorrow" for both offenses insufficiently apologetic until September 1765. Three months later the meeting permitted Howland to move to Rhode Island, where he learned spermaceti manufacture, and he then returned to New Bedford. Only a month after he and Russell were reported for running goods, the meeting declared both, with Rebecca Slocum, "offenders . . . by their keeping their Negroes in bondage when they are fit for freedom after they have been repeatedly admonished to comply with ye order of friends." By January 1774 Russell still refused to accede to the meeting's wishes, but by September the visiting committee finally persuaded him to free his two "negro men," Quash and

Pero. In April of the same year Isaac Howland freed his slave Pero. Howland has long been reputed to have been the last person in Dartmouth to free a slave when he manumitted Primus in January 1777, but John Akin still owned an Indian named Hazzard, whom he freed the next month.

Both Quash and Pero took Joseph Russell's last name, as Pero did Isaac Howland's. Quash Russell died in 1807 by drowning in a mill pond at the head of the Acushnet River, now the town of Acushnet; Pero Russell was one of seven free men of color in Dartmouth, including John and Paul Cuffe, who in 1780 signed and delivered a petition to the Massachusetts Governor's Council and House of Representatives protesting the fact that they were taxed but not allowed to inherit property or vote. Pero Howland, born about 1746, also signed this petition; he remained in Dartmouth until his death in September 1829. Records make it possible to identify only one other of the approximately thirteen men and women of color whom Dartmouth Quakers held as slaves and freed between 1774 and 1777. Caesar Slocum, freed by Peleg Slocum in November 1774, may have served in the Revolutionary army after his manumission; he and two other people of color were listed in their own household in the Dartmouth census of 1800.

What became of the other slaves Friends freed in these years—Primus, owned by Isaac Howland II; Luce and Vilot, one of them underage when John Russell freed them in September 1774; London, whom Peleg Slocum freed in November 1774; and the unnamed slaves owned by William Sandford (one, a female) and Rebecca Slocum (at least four, three adults and "one or two" underage)—is not known; their names cannot be found in any census or tax listing. Cato Slocum and Martha Slocum, who married in January 1798, may have earlier been members of Rebecca Slocum's household. What became of slaves owned by others—the seven, one of them a boy named Robin, whom merchant Seth Pope mentioned in his will in 1727; Venter, purchased at public auction in Dartmouth in 1769 by blacksmith Elnathan Sampson and spermaceti manufacturer John Chaffee and freed by them the next year; the two for whom Leonard Jarvis received "prize shares" from continental agent Daniel Tillinghast in May 1778; those claimed by Benjamin Hathaway, George Hitch, John Louden, William Shaw, and Truman Taber, each shown with one "servant for life" in the Massachusetts tax valuation list of 1771—is also mysterious, especially because in most cases not even so much as their first names were recorded.[13]

How these early people of color came to Dartmouth, however, can at least be suggested. Many, like Venture Smith, probably reached southeastern Massachusetts by way of a Rhode Island slaver. Beginning in the 1720s until the slave trade was banned in the United States in 1808, Rhode Island nearly monopolized the business, capturing more than one hundred thousand Africans; these statistics made it a small player in the international slave trade but the principal player in the American colonies. Almost two-thirds of Rhode Island's slavers exchanged Africans in the West Indies for cash, sugar, and molasses, the last commodity turned into rum in, usually, Rhode Island; rum itself was used as currency in

Africa. Though Rhode Island slavers sold most Africans in the Caribbean, they annually brought between 3,200 and 4,000 to the American colonies; one historian estimates that about 1,200 people of color were brought into New England each decade between 1700 and 1750. The slaves brought to Rhode Island were usually only those who could not be sold in the Caribbean or the South or those brought only until they could be shipped to a more demanding market.

Isaac Howland, living in Rhode Island in 1758, may have been the focus of complaint in the Dartmouth Monthly Meeting because that year he was captain of the Newport slaver *Dolphin*, bound for Barbados to sell 145 Africans. In the same year, at least two vessels, the sloops *Dove* and *Abigail*, carried 150 Africans directly into Rhode Island. Between December 1754 and June 1763, at least 713 Africans arrived in Rhode Island aboard at least thirteen vessels. The Sephardic Jews Aaron Lopez and his father-in-law, Jacob Rivera, settled in Rhode Island in 1752 and remained active in the slave trade until the Revolution, when they moved to Leicester, Massachusetts; Samuel Rodman, orphaned in Newport at the age of thirteen, apprenticed with Rivera and worked with Lopez in his whaling and mercantile endeavors before moving to Nantucket and then to New Bedford. During the war his mother and sisters also moved to Leicester to escape the British occupation of Newport. The relationship between Rodman and the Riveras was not unusual; commercial, family, and religious ties bound many families with a history of slave trading to New Bedford people.[14]

Before 1765 less than 10 percent of all Rhode Island slave trade vessels sold Africans in Rhode Island, but by 1755 Rhode Island's slave population was almost double that of Massachusetts. Of the former colony's 4,679 slaves, almost half lived in Newport County (in 1766 Abraham Redwood of Newport ranked as New England's largest slaveholder, with 238 persons), and another 1,446 lived and worked on the large, plantation-like estates of Kings (now Washington) County, principally in North and South Kingstown. There, as many as forty slaves on a given plantation raised sheep for wool and cattle for beef, milk, and cheese, grew corn and tobacco; and raised and helped to train pacer racehorses. Many of these animals and commodities were then sold in the West Indies.[15] In 1755 one of every four people in South Kingstown was a slave, and even the tiny towns of Tiverton and Little Compton, bordering Westport, Massachusetts, had more than 160 slaves in their populations in 1748–49. In contrast, only 61 slaves lived in all of Bristol County by 1754, and the entire slave population of Massachusetts was 2,423, just 271 more than lived in Newport County alone.

Many New Bedford people of color born before 1825 had Rhode Island origins; it is most likely that they or their parents had been sold to the large mercantile slave owners of Newport or the larger plantations at North and South Kingstown, at Greenwich, and on Jamestown Island. New Bedford people may have purchased these Africans from such interests or directly from vessel owners through private or public sale. Even after 1750, when the demand among New Englanders for slaves began to decrease, slave sales and auctions took place even in Massachusetts: Jay Coughtry, a historian of the slave trade, has identified the June 1763 auction of twenty-three Africans in Rehoboth, about twenty miles west of New Bedford, as the last notice of a local slave sale. And, largely from the 1770s forward, manumitted Rhode Island slaves or their descendants may have come to New Bedford for work.

At least twenty New Bedford men and women of color were born in either Newport or Jamestown, including the mariners Newport and Pompey Gardner, Experience Fairweather and her sons Edward, James, and Leonard, and the antislavery activist Henry O. Remington, whose mother, named Acoombah, may well have been born in Africa.[16] At least nine persons of color born before 1820 came to New Bedford from North and South Kingstown. Among them were the laborer and mariner Abraham Rodman, who may have descended from slaveowning members of the Rodman family living in South Kingstown and who later worked with Frederick Douglass on the city's wharves, and Weighty Potter and her daughter Experience; judging by their names—especially Weighty, the term Friends used to describe a particularly influential member of the sect—both must have been owned and named by Quaker slaveholders. About twenty persons born before 1820 came from Little Compton and Tiverton, including such leaders in New Bedford's community of color as John Briggs and Samual Gray (the latter of whom also signed the 1780 petition) and the mariners Benjamin and Job Cook, Caezer Green, Fortune Howland, James Hamilton, and Ebenezer Hunter. Whether they were enslaved, manumitted, or born free when they came to New Bedford is not known, though there are documented cases of slaves whose freedom was purchased for them in the eighteenth century. Samuel Rodman not only assisted in purchasing the freedom of John Slocum's Cato on Nantucket in the late 1780s, but he also paid $250 to Christopher Mardenborough of Newport to free his slave Jack and $126 to Abraham Rodriguez Rivera for the remaining two years of servitude his slave Cato was to have completed.[17]

Another African-born man who came to Dartmouth by way of Rhode Island was Kofi, a West African of the Akan or so-called Coromantee people from the Ashanti region, now central Ghana. He was brought to Newport as a boy in 1728 and came into the hands of the Quaker Ebenezer Slocum, who either purchased him or acquired him through his wife's dowry. In February 1742 Slocum sold Kofi, then between fifteen and twenty years old, to his nephew John Slocum, the only Dartmouth resident among the 162 largest slaveholding families in colonial New England.[18] Within a decade John Slocum manumitted him.[19] By this time he spelled his name Cufe, a slight Anglicization; like most Akan people, he was named for the day of the week, Friday, on which he was born. Before 1860 at least six New Bedford people of color claimed, like Cufe Slocum, to have been born in Africa, and one historian has argued that probably more than 75 percent of all slaves brought to New England in the 1700s were African-born. In New Bedford one was Violet Proctor, the oldest person in the New Bedford almshouse when she died there in 1853. Reputed then to be 108 years old, she had earlier told a reporter for the *Republican Standard* that she had been aboard "the ship at the time the tea was thrown overboard in Boston harbor, just prior to the commencement of the Revolutionary War." Thus she may have come to New Bedford initially in the employ of the Rotch family, part owners of the ship *Dartmouth,* whose tea cargo was thrown overboard at the famed Boston Tea Party on 3 September 1773.[20] As late as 1864 men born in Africa still found their way to New Bedford; in October of that year the overseers of the poor recorded the case of Peter Makela, "age 30 Born at Makela, Coast of Africa—to state N.B. about 3 weeks ago, in Bark Mermaid, whaler—is sick and destitute, at the house of Sylvanus Allen c, No. 98 South Water St.—Allen wants him provided for." The overseers spent ninety cents to buy Makela a ticket to the state almshouse.[21]

At about the time that he was freed, Cufe Slocum married Ruth Moses, a Wampanoag from Dartmouth, and began a family there and on Cuttyhunk, the island on which Bartholomew Gosnold had landed in 1602. He supported his family as a carpenter and a cartman, carrying sails, rigging, and other ship's stores back and forth to the mainland, and with this income he bought a farm of more than one hundred acres in Dartmouth in 1766. After he died in 1772, his thirteen-year-old son Paul traveled to Bedford village to sign onto a whaling crew. As many former slaves and their immediate descendants did, Paul took his father's given name as a surname. Known to the world as Paul Cuffe, he went on to build and own six vessels, carried on a successful career in the coastwise trade, and initiated the first black-led effort to populate Sierra Leone with resettled American blacks in 1810 (fig. 17).

Like Cuffe Slocum, Quash Russell was Ashanti; his name, a variant of Quashee, is the name given to boys born on Sunday.[22] Abraham Quash, listed in his own household in the 1790 Dartmouth census, made his or his father's West African day name his surname as well. Others whose names are West African in origin kept them as given names, such as Quaco Bailey (from the male name for Wednesday) and Cugo Canady, whose first name surely derives from the Monday male name, Cudjo.[23] The surname of the African Indian Quanwell family may derive from Kwame, the male day name for Saturday; in the first federal census a free man of color named Joseph Quawm is listed in a household of three in Dartmouth. Variously listed as Quan, Quanawin, or Quonwell, the first of this name in Dartmouth was Peter Quanawin, a "molatte man" from Tiverton who came to Dartmouth to marry Martha Job, an Indian, in 1763. Twenty years later he bought three acres of land in Dartmouth next to "Boggy Meadow Spring," land he continued to own until his death in 1816. A farmer and mariner, he lived in New Bedford on six rods of land he also owned, and at his death he possessed "part of a Dwelling House thereon standing viz. one stove room & one bedroom with the Chamber over & Celler under them with a priviledge to pass & repass in the Entry & a priviledge in the well it being in the West End of said Dwelling House."[24]

Joseph Quawm or Quanwell, identified in one deed as a "mustee man" (part

FIGURE 17. Captain Paul Cuffe (1795–1817), engraving for Abraham L. Pennock by Mason & Maas from a drawing by John Pole, Bristol, England, 1812. Courtesy Old Dartmouth Historical Society / New Bedford Whaling Museum. This engraving shows Cuffe in silhouette, a customary mode of portraiture among Quakers, and below him his *Traveller* between the shore of Sierra Leone on the left and North America on the right.

Indian and part African), acquired about twenty acres in the Clark's Cove section of Dartmouth between 1789 and 1805 and seems to have been operating a boardinghouse by 1800. James Quanawin or Quanwell, also described as mustee, apparently spent most of his life at sea, making at least eight voyages on whalers from New Bedford; his son Joseph Quanwell (called Joseph Quanwell 2 to distinguish him from his older contemporary of the same name) was also a lifelong mariner. He moved into New Bedford when he was eight, about 1807, and went on his first voyage when he was sixteen, on the William Rotch Jr. and Sons' whaler *Barclay*. Quanwell returned with the *Barclay* in November 1817 and shipped out in 1819 on another Rotch family whaler, the *Midas*. On that twenty-one-month voyage to the whaling grounds off Brazil, Quanwell grossed a remarkable $917.22. He then shipped at least three times more through 1840, and by 1849 he owned a house on Ray Street, next door to the property owned by black mariner John Lewey. Buying the property, valued at three hundred dollars in 1849, must have consumed his available savings, for by March 1847 his struggle to make ends meet impelled him to visit the New Bedford Overseers of the Poor for wood and groceries.[25]

Place names are also clues to persons who may have been slaves: parents gave day names, but slave owners bestowed both place and classical names. Lorenzo Greene's survey of the fifty-two fugitive slave notices that mentioned slave names in New England newspapers between 1718 and 1784 found that most were place or Christian names (only four had African day names); Gary Nash's analysis of 258 slaves freed by will in Philadelphia before 1750 or mentioned in church records there before 1775 found that only 5 percent bore such place names as London and York, usually reflecting a master's place of origin or business. In New Bedford, the population of color included Glasgo Corey, a "negro man" living in Dartmouth in 1759 and a New Bedford resident from 1800 to 1820; Lisbon Johnson, a mariner from Bladensburg, Virginia, who probably lived at William P. Powell's boardinghouse for mariners of color when he first came to the city in the mid-1830s; London Richmond, who lived in Westport from 1790 until his death and shipped with Paul Cuffe; and members of the Boston family of Nantucket and New Bedford. Emanuel Goree, who married in Dartmouth in 1802 and owned property in New Bedford through at least 1817, was probably named for Goree Island, off Dakar, West Africa, a major holding station for Africans bound for slavery in the Americas.[26]

In late eighteenth-century Philadelphia Nash found that 16 to 17 percent of slaves bore such classical names as Caesar, Scipio, Cato, Jupiter, and Parthena; Greene found classical names less prevalent in New England than place names. Caesar, Cato, Jupiter, and Scipio are all given names among New Bedford people of color, Caesar in particular. Caesar Treadwell, born between 1740 and 1775, came to southeastern Massachusetts from New Jersey and married a white woman from Barnstable in 1792; he lived in a house in the Clark's Cove section of the city, now known as the South End, until he died in the 1840s. Poor relief records for his daughters Jane and Martha confirm that he was a slave either before or when he came to New Bedford. Scipio Rome, whose name combines both a classical and a place name, was born between 1740 and 1785 and was living in New Bedford by 1810. From 1837 or 1838 he lived at the end of Middle Street, then developing into a black neighborhood, and he may have been the Scipio whom merchant Joseph R. Anthony employed in September 1823 to plant strawberry and raspberry plants on his Seventh Street property.[27]

In Philadelphia biblical names were as prevalent as classical names, but, because they tended to be given to children generations removed from slavery, they are not an indicator of possible slave origin in the way that African and classical names tend to be. Nash found that the names of Philadelphia black adults and children between 1775 and 1790 were far more likely to be English names, less likely to be biblical or classical names, and far less likely to be African or place names. Some African names were Anglicized: Cudjo might become Joe and Quaco Jack in the first American-born generation.[28] Another clue to possible slave origin are Spanish names or Christian names used as last names; John Thornton has noted that after Angola was christianized about 1600, Christian names spread through west central Africa. First names such as Manuel and Domingo (or, shortened, Mingo, sometimes classified as an African name) may have an origin in Angola or Portuguese slavery; Emanuel and Manuel were quite common names among people of color in New Bedford, Domingo less so, and because the city's population included Portuguese and Afro-Portuguese people since whalers first reached the Portuguese islands it is hazardous to presume an Angolan origin based on these names alone. Angolan Africans also tended to have double names. Thornton suggests that Angolan naming patterns "may be the origin of a common pattern in the Caribbean basin today in which people have what normally are given names as surnames, among them Charles, Joseph, Pierre, or Francois. These names are transmitted as surnames in European naming systems, but their origin as last names may well reflect the pattern so widely seen in central Africa." Thus it is at least possible that such New Bedford men as Manuel and Antone Joseph (a name borne by at least three men in the city in 1856), Antone, John, Joseph, and Peter Francis, Manuel James, Antone Domingo, and William Vincent descended from Angolan people.[29]

Early New Bedford was also populated by "mustees," persons who parents were African and Native American. In southeastern Massachusetts, as elsewhere, the sex ratios that prevailed among people of color and Native Americans throughout the eighteenth century tended to promote marriages between blacks and Indians, as did the general proscription against marriages between white and "colored" persons. The 1765 census found thirty-seven black males and twenty-four black females in the town of Dartmouth, which reveals the decided preference among slaveholders everywhere in the Americas for men; in the same year thirty-five Indian men and forty Indian women lived in Dartmouth, a statistic suggesting the loss of Indian men in military service during the French and Indian wars. These ratios favored the marriage of black men and Indian women; so, too, did the fact that the children of Indian women were considered to be free. John M. Earle wrote in 1861 that "by far the larger proportion" of marriages between Native Americans and people of color were "Negro men to Indian women."[30] At least fifty men of color (variously identified as "negro," "black," "mulatto," and "mustee") married women of the Dartmouth, Gay Head, Chappaquiddick, Mashpee, Narragansett, and Middleborough tribes, all Wampanoags of southeastern Massachusetts and the islands. Black women married Indian men, but in far fewer numbers: no more than ten marriages of this sort are known to have occurred in New Bedford and its surrounding towns by 1860, and often Indian women married mustee men.

Racial identities in New Bedford were hardly fluid, but they were certainly ambiguous. Often a man such as Jesse Webquish Jr. was identified as an Indian in his seaman's protection paper and in crew lists but classed as "colored" in the census or city directory. Amos Haskins, a master mariner whom the local newspaper identified as "an Indian of the Narragansett tribe, and . . . a native of Mattapoisett" in 1859, was always classified as either mulatto or black in censuses; his wife, Elizabeth Farmer, was of African descent, and two of his daughters married men of color (fig. 18). About 1850 Amelia Hawes of Fairhaven painted a portrait of "Indian Annis" or "Black Annis" Sharper just a year before she moved to the

FIGURE 18. Amos Haskins, one-sixth plate daguerreotype, about 1850. Courtesy Old Dartmouth Historical Society / New Bedford Whaling Museum.

town's almshouse (fig. 19). She was probably Anna Sharper, identified in Fairhaven censuses between 1820 and 1840 as black.[31] In 1857 Albert Bierstadt, just back from three years of study as a painter in Dusseldorf, painted the portrait of Martha Simon, whom he identified as "the last of the Narragansetts." She was probably Wampanoag, and a year later Daniel Ricketson called her the "one solitary specimen of a full-blooded native . . . to be found within the precinct of the old township of Dartmouth."[32] But men and women with the surname Simon, Simons, Simonds, or Simmons were often classified as black in New Bedford directories and censuses. Deborah Peguin, identified as a Dartmouth Indian, married "Lonnon, a negro," in Dartmouth in 1757, but other women with the same surname (a variant of which may have been Pequit, borne by Indian women who married into the Cuffe family) were identified as mulatto or mustee. James Bunker Congdon, the New Bedford bank clerk whose brother Joseph collected African American historical materials at an early date, was aware of how intermixed people of African descent had become locally. In a long and deeply sarcastic reply to an 1863 inquiry from Samuel Gridley Howe of the American Freeman's Inquiry Commission about the "position, morally, mentally, socially of the African in New Bedford? Not of the mixed races,—of the pure African descent,"

Congdon cited marriage not only with Indians but with men from the islands of the South Seas, Hawaiians (who in those days were referred to as Kanakers or Canackers), as well as others:

> No human being can select from among the "colored people" of New Bedford, those who are of "pure African descent." . . . I have no skill that will enable me to pick out those who are <u>untainted</u> with the blood of other races. . . . With the staple of the African there have been mingled the blood of Massasoit and Uncas. Fayal has sent its contribution, and the feeble Cannacker and the sturdy and warlike Marquese have added to the diversity. But, as in all other communities of coloured people, the great majority is composed of those who are of pure African blood and such as have

FIGURE 19. *Indian Annis and the Thomas Taber House,* oil on canvas attributed to Amelia Hawes, about 1850. Courtesy Old Dartmouth Historical Society / New Bedford Whaling Museum. Called "Black Annis" or "Indian Annis," Anna Sharper was born sometime between 1740 and 1775 and was the widow of Hezekiah Sharper, a New Bedford mariner of color who died before 1 May 1810. His estate, worth $92, included a dwelling house appraised at $30 and household items worth $4.20, including a "Large Bible & Hymn Book." After Sharper's death, his widow moved across the river to Fairhaven.

mingled with it, in a greater or less degree, that of the Caucasian race. If the blood of the two races is not the same, it must be allowed that it mingles easy. And so generally and in such palpable proportions has this mingling process been accomplished, that the pecuniary and social statistics of the North regards them, not as Africans but in a peculiar and more significant sense as Americans, and in treating of them make no more reference to Congo than to Crim Tartary.[33]

Indeed, New Bedford's population of color grew culturally more complex with the ever-widening sphere of whaling from the port. Since 1765 whaling vessels had been mooring off the Cape Verde Islands, a Portuguese colony from the late 1500s whose plantations had been manned by West African slaves virtually since that time, and sending whaleboats to the island of Brava for meat, fruit, vegetables, salt, and other supplies. Captains also recruited Cape Verdeans to fill out crews thinned from desertions, illness, and death. Joseph Antone, a founding member of New Bedford's African Christian Church, the city's first black church, was in New Bedford from at least 1821, when he married Sally Auker, a Dartmouth Indian. He was then about twenty-four years old. Unlike many Cape Verdeans, Antone was not a mariner; he was a laborer who worked at George Howland's candleworks in the late 1830s and early 1840s. Antone was a common surname, sometimes anglicized to Anthony, a common Quaker name in southeastern Massachusetts as well as first name; Joseph Antone lived in New Bedford at the same time as Antone Joseph, also from the Cape Verde Islands. Cape Verdeans similarly might have Domingo as a first name (Domingo Barrows, in New Bedford by 1841) or last (Antone Domingo, a mariner who shipped from New Bedford in 1840); Manuel or Emmanuel was a very common first name. Before 1855 at least twenty Cape Verdeans, only one of them a woman, had settled in New Bedford. Despite the fact that they often thought of themselves as Portuguese, enumerators routinely listed them as black.[34]

The same tendency applied to Sandwich Islanders, who were present in small numbers in New Bedford from the late 1820s. As early as 1823 between forty and sixty whaling vessels cruising in the Pacific stopped at Honolulu for provisions, shore leave, outfitting, and crew recruitment, and by 1840, eight years before the first whaling vessel passed through the Bering Strait to the Arctic Circle, some four hundred whalers stopped in Hawaiian ports annually. In later years, as the length of voyages stretched to between four and five years, they both outfitted and recruited in the islands and used them as a transshipping point, sending home part of their oil and bone cargo in other vessels and returning to the Arctic hunt.[35] In 1844 an estimated five hundred to six hundred "Kanakas" were crew on American whalers. New Bedford whaling crew lists that year show twenty among the 217 whaling crew of color, men with such colorful names as John Sunday, Tom Marquise, William Canacker, and one simply identified as Friday; Samuel Fortune (aboard the bark *Fortune*) and Robert Tahita were from "Otahita" or Tahiti, one of the Society Islands. In 1834 a group of Sandwich Islanders who had come down with cholera in New Bedford were identified as John Bull,

Tar Bucket, Jose, Milo (named for the ship on which he had come to the port), Tom, Jack, Harry, Charley, and Rope Yarn.[36] Sandwich Islanders were also commonly named for a vessel's captain or a great man of American history, very often John Adams or John Quincy Adams; Sandwich Islanders with both names lived in New Bedford in the mid-1850s.[37]

Some fourteen of these whalemen remained in New Bedford long enough to be listed in a census or a directory, and nine of those fourteen are listed after 1855, by which time New Bedford controlled half of the entire American whaling industry and nearly three of every four of the city's whaling vessels were bound for the Pacific or Western Arctic.[38] They were very largely mariners. John Swain, born between 1802 and 1807 on the Sandwich Islands and listed as a laborer in New Bedford by 1841, applied for assistance from the city's overseers of the poor in 1861, at which time the secretary took down a detailed account of his life at sea:

> John B. Swain, Kanacka, has wife Emma & 1 child Emma A. Went to Nantucket in 1833, brought from Mowee by Capt Obed Swain, in ship Awashonks, went next voyage from Nantucket in ship Clarkson Capt Wm Plasket, gone nearly 4 years next in ship Japan, Capt John Toby, gone about 3 years, next in ship Edward Cary, same captain, gone 4 years, next in Potomack, Capt Oliver C. Swain, gone a little more than 3 years, next in same ship, Capt Charles Grant, 46 months, next in ship Levi Starbuck, Capt Jernegan gone 46, then in Bark Elizabeth of Westport Capt Francis, left here in six months came home sick. Arrived home in Jan 1859, says his wife moved here from Nantucket soon after he sailed in the Elizabeth. He sailed in May & she came here Augt, the family has lived here since says he owns a house & lot at Nantucket on York St bot of Barzilla Burdett, cost about 600.00, says Capt Obed Swain has the paper & he (John B) dont know anything about it says he is not Naturalized, lives 178 Kempton order on SW McFarlin 1.50 1/4 ton coal. When he came home from the Elizabeth (sick) he came in Bark Azor [?] Capt Butts, he brought John, that he calls his child with him at that time, he is no relative of his, was acquainted with John's father at Fayal [in the Azores] & he wished to take John & bring him here & send him to school. Emma never had any child.[39]

Swain died in New Bedford a little more than two months later, leaving his wife, Emily, born in the West Indies, and a nine-year-old boy named John Swain, born in Portugal in 1852.

At least one of the small number of Hawaiians who settled in New Bedford boarded black and Polynesian seamen. Joseph Dunbar, born in Hawaii about 1802 and a New Bedford resident by 1836, married Charlotte, the daughter of Joseph Quanwell, after her first husband died in the New Bedford almshouse that year. With her husband often at sea—he made at least three whaling voyages between 1838 and 1849—Charlotte Dunbar took in men of color on a regular basis at 66 South Second Street, the home she inherited from her first husband. Charles W. Morgan's papers show a $5.50 payment to her for boarding "Chas Canacka" before he shipped out in the *Hector* in 1838. In 1841 she boarded three black mariners, though all at the time were listed as being at sea. Charlotte Dunbar may have done so to offer a better place for her husband's countrymen to board; at that time James and Mary Dyer, whose boardinghouse was in the seamy lower Howland Street section of town closer to the waterfront, took in "destitute" Sandwich Islanders in part because black mariners were said to shun the place. Cholera broke out at this boardinghouse in 1834, but in 1837 and 1838, when Dyer was serving a prison term for assault, Morgan was paying the board to Mary Dyer for Charles Coffin, John Adams, and Charles Canacka. Coffin and Canacka also stayed at Dunbar's, and in April 1839 both Adams and Canacka deserted.[40]

A few New Bedford people of color came from other exotic places. Anthony G. Jourdain came from Suriname, a Dutch colony since the early 1600s. Jourdain was a barber and fashionable hairdresser in New Bedford from at least 1836 until the mid-1850s when he, as did other enterprising men of both races from the city, went to California (fig. 20). Jourdain came first to Martha's Vineyard and married Hepsabeth Johnson, a Gay Head Wampanoag, and he is said to have come to the island at the same time as William Adrian Vanderhoop, also born in Suriname. Probably also a slave or descended from one, Vanderhoop married Beulah Salisbury, either Indian or mustee, on the Vineyard in 1837; Beulah Vanderhoop was instrumental in effecting the escape of the fugitive Edinbur Randall in the fall of 1854.[41] In the 1850 census, the first to list the names of every individual and his or her place of birth, fifty people out of a total population of color of 1,008 were born outside the United States. Three were born in Chile, surely reflecting the habit of New Bedford whalers to stop at the port of Valparaiso. Thirty-three persons listing their birthplaces as Manila, Guam, Santa Cruz (in the Canary Islands), the Azores (or Western Isles), the Cape Verdes, Hawaii, the island of St. Helena, and the islands of the Caribbean probably also made their way to New Bedford on whaling vessels. Seven came from Canada (six of them from Nova Scotia, where people of color had lived since the 1780s), and seven more from either Ireland or England; the latter may have come aboard returning trading vessels that had brought oil, candles, and other goods to Europe.

Over time the number of transient and settled whalers of color was supplemented by the movement of rural people to the cities, particularly to ports. The black population of Dartmouth actually exceeded that of New Bedford until the 1820 census, when the former began to slip sharply and the latter to climb rapidly. In the difficult decade of the War of 1812, the white population of New Bedford dropped by more than 30 percent, but the population of color rose by 12 percent. Between 1820 and 1830, prosperous years despite fluctuations in the price of whale products, the white population nearly doubled (93 percent), rising from 3,734 persons to 7,209; the nonwhite population grew somewhat more slowly, at a rate of nearly 80 percent. Over the next quarter-century, however, black population growth outstripped white in New Bedford, its greatest increase, 87 percent (from 383 to 715 persons), coming in the 1830–40 decade. Thus the share of the city's total population that was black rose steadily, from 5.0 percent in 1830 to 7.5 percent in 1855.

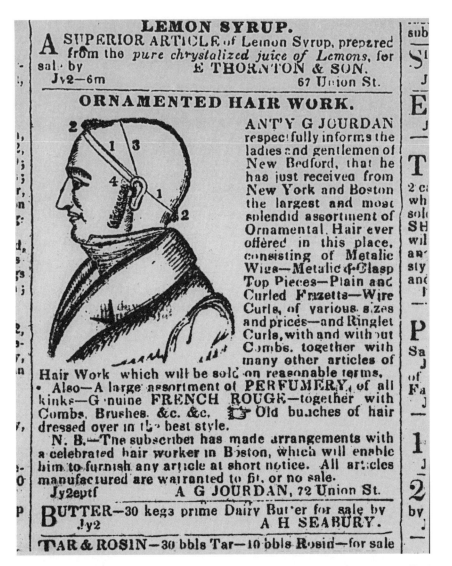

Figure 20. Advertisement for Anthony G. Jourdain's hairdressing shop, New Bedford *Mercury*, 2 July 1841. Used with permission of the Board of Trustees of the New Bedford Free Public Library.

As Massachusetts port cities both active in trans-Atlantic trade, New Bedford and Boston might be expected to have had similar populations of color, the only difference perhaps being in a greater proportion of foreign-born blacks in New Bedford owing to the wide reach of the city's whalers. But in 1850, and probably for many decades before that date, the demographic profile of New Bedford's population of color was quite different from Boston's, and its proportion of foreign-born blacks was smaller. Slightly less than 5 percent of New Bedford blacks were born outside the United States, compared with 16 percent of Boston's (half of them from Canada). Yet in a sense, New Bedford's population of color could be called more cosmopolitan than Boston's, and probably than that of almost every other city in the Northeast. Less than 40 percent of all Massachusetts blacks in 1850 were born outside Massachusetts; in Boston more than 55 percent were born out of state. Philadelphia veered closer to homogeneity than Boston: in 1850 only 45 percent of all persons of color were born outside Pennsylvania.[42] But in New Bedford, fully 63 percent of all people of color in the 1850 census were born outside Massachusetts. Among whalers, of course, the proportion was far higher: 121, or 78 percent, of the 154 black whalemen shipping out of New Bedford in 1850 listed a birthplace other than Massachusetts.

And New Bedford's population of color was proportionately far larger than that of Boston. At the end of 1853, 1,600 people of color lived in New Bedford, whose total population was 18,000; only 900 more lived in Boston, a city of 140,000. The smaller city was 8.8 percent black at that time; Boston was 1.8 percent black. No city in the Northeast at the time, including Philadelphia, had a higher proportion of people of color in its population.[43] By mid-1857, 16.7 percent of all people of color in Massachusetts lived in New Bedford.[44] Moreover, while the black populations of most of the Northeast's cities tended to decline between 1850 and 1860, a fact many historians attribute in part to the passage and enforcement of the Fugitive Slave Act of 1850, the black population of New Bedford increased from 1,047 persons in 1850 to 1,518 persons in 1860, or from 6.3 to 6.8 percent of the population.[45]

New Bedford also had a smaller proportion of northern-born blacks among its population. Roughly 52 percent of Boston's black population was born in New England, Massachusetts included; only 43 percent of New Bedford's people of color claimed to be native New Englanders. The proportion of black Bostonians from all the northern free states (adding New York, Pennsylvania, New Jersey, Ohio, and Michigan to New England) was about 62 percent of the total population of color. New Bedford's black population born in the North was 53 percent. In short, Boston was more apt to have foreign- and northern-born people of color than New Bedford was. What remains is the South, and it is here that the most remarkable differences between New Bedford and most other northern cities become clear. Of 1,999 persons of color in Boston in 1850, 332, or 16.6 percent, listed a birthplace in the slave states. In New York City, 15 percent of 14,000 people of color had been born in the South. In New Bedford, 302 of 1,008 persons of color in the 1850 census listed a southern birthplace, or 29.9 percent. Predictably, only Philadelphia, sitting virtually on the Mason-Dixon line, had more southern-born people of color—about 7,200 of 19,422 persons, or 37.2 percent.

Two aspects of New Bedford's 1850 population may signify that the southern-born population was greater than statistics suggest. First, seventy-five men and women of color in New Bedford told census takers that year that they did not know where they were born. For another forty-four the enumerators left place of birth blank, which may mean the persons in question were not home when the enumerators visited and that someone else claimed not to know the resident's birthplace. If this is what the difference between "unknown" and a line left blank was meant to indicate, to state that one does not know where one was born suggests one of two possibilities—either genuine or feigned ignorance. The fugitive Samuel Ringgold Ward once wrote that his parents deliberately kept him and his siblings "quite ignorant of their birthplace, and of their condition, whether free or slave, when born; because children might, by the dropping of a single word, lead to the betrayal of their parents."[46] That ignorance was occasionally a pretense is suggested by the very high numbers of persons who gave different birthplaces to census takers (and ship masters) in different years. In the 1850 and 1860 censuses, for example, the laborer William Ferguson told enumerators that he did not know his birthplace. But for some reason, he told the state census taker in 1855 that he had been born in Virginia, and in 1848 the overseers of the poor stated outright that he and his wife Nancy were "Runaway Slaves." When Ferguson died in New Bedford in 1910, the reporter for the New Bedford *Standard-Times* related his escape from slavery to New Bedford in 1847 in great detail. The laborer Caleb Handy listed his birthplace as unknown in 1850, as Virginia in 1855, and as Massachusetts in 1860; an entry in the city's poor records states that his four children were born in Maryland between 1838 and 1847 and that the family came to Massachusetts in 1849.[47]

Similarly, a large number of men, particularly men of color and foreigners, were entered onto New Bedford crew lists with their name, race, and the statement "no proof," which meant they had no protection paper to verify their citizenship when they signed on. In an examination of crew lists between 1803 and 1840, Martha Putney found 2,028 men of color on the crews of 79 whaling vessels shipping from New Bedford as well as a "large numbers of 'no proofs,' " many of whom, she has argued, were probably men of color.[48] In a sample of 65 men of color who were among the crews on 32 voyages from New Bedford in 1841, Putney found another 93 men whose description was unclear or who had "no proof." She also found the number of "no proofs" to have increased "substantially" after 1822. In 1850 117 whaling vessels sailed from New Bedford with 2,814 men on board; New Bedford Port Society records have data on 114 of those 117 voyages, involving 2,787 men, or an average of 24.4 men per crew. Of this total, 109 men were identified as mulatto or black in complexion and with "wooly" hair, or .956 man per crew; those with no proofs totaled 526, or 4.61 per crew. From 20 September (two days after the Fugitive Slave Law passed) until the end of 1850, all of these measures increased. The average crew size rose to 27.79, the number of men of color rose to 1.02 per voyage, and the number of men with no proofs rose to 6.13, which lends slight support to the possibility that no proofs were often fugitive slaves.[49] Why a fugitive would want to undertake such a venture is patent: as John Thompson put it, "I thought I would go on a whaling voyage, as being the place where I stood least chance of being arrested by slave hunters." He and others in the early 1840s were likely to be at sea for almost three years; by 1858 the length of the average whaling voyage had increased to forty-three months.

Yet establishing anything more than suggestive about the presence of fugitives on whaling vessels may never be possible; to date, only six cases are known, five of them by name. The ability to document the presence of others is fatally clouded by several factors. The logs kept on whaling voyages were official documents and thus were unlikely to record the presence of fugitives, both white and black mariners frequently used aliases, and most men escaping masters were surely not inclined to be candid about their backgrounds. Philip Piper listed his birthplace as New York City in the protection paper he received in June 1836 before he shipped out on the whaling vessel *America* in July. But in the 1850 census, he and the rest of his family, except for his father, listed their birthplaces as Virginia (probably Alexandria) or Washington, D.C. Henry Steward told census takers in 1855 and 1860 that he had been born in Pennsylvania. However, his protection papers, a crew list, and his New Bedford tombstone show his birthplace as Queen Anne's County, Maryland. Steward shipped on the Fairhaven whaler *Favorite* in August 1846 and returned with the ship in November 1849. He seems then to have quit the sea, and by 1860 he was listed in the census as a fruit dealer. Nine years later he died, and his will, signed with a mark, clearly states his origin. He left one dollar to each of his two children, "both of Maryland," and added, "said children are really named Elizabeth and Cordelia Steward but have sometime been named or styled Brooks—These two daughters are the only children I have & were born in Slavery and have been so long separated from me that the above identification is made." Whether Steward was a fugitive when he came to New Bedford is not known; he may have been freed or purchased his freedom after his children were separated, or sold away, from him. Moreover, how many mariners lied about their places of birth is impossible to determine. The fact that Piper, Steward, John Thompson, and others are known to have done so, however, suggests strongly that the actual number of southern-born mariners in the whaling workforce may have been much higher than protection papers and crew lists indicate and that fugitives in whaling crews may have been more abundant than more direct evidence has so far suggested.

Comparing protection papers to population figures in 1850 is also mildly suggestive of fugitive origin. According to the birthplaces they had recorded on crew lists, the men of color who left the city on whaling vessels in 1850 were more likely to have been born abroad than the city's population of color as a whole, about 9 percent compared to just under 5 percent. In addition, black whalemen were more likely to claim northern birthplaces, more than 67 percent of the total compared to 53 percent of New Bedford black residents. But the distribution within northern states is striking: only 10 percent of New Bedford's population of color listed northern birthplaces outside New England, while fully 35 percent of black whalemen did. The difference between these two last statistics is almost matched by the difference between southern-born black residents of the city (29.9 percent) and southern-born black whalemen (17.5 percent). In 1851, when the number of black whalemen almost doubled to 290 persons, a slightly smaller percentage (16.2) claimed a southern birthplace and a greater percentage (70.3) claimed a northern one, with fully 41 percent of the free-state total claiming a birthplace outside New England. That a greater proportion of black whalemen said they came from northern free states than was part of the city's black population as a whole suggests several possibilities. One is that opportunity awaited blacks on whalers but not in New Bedford generally. Another is that black men born in the South who wanted to secure a berth on a whaling crew concealed that fact so as not to raise the suspicion of agents, captains, and owners that they were fugitives. Some may have been free and did not wish to be turned away on the strength of that suspicion; others certainly may have been fugitives. Instead, they stated their last place of residence, however fleeting their stay may have been. Indeed, although early crew lists included both place of birth and place of residence, later ones tended to list only birthplace or residence and frequently were mute about which question was asked. That more New Bedford black residents than black whalemen listed southern birthplaces may reflect the fact that most of the 1850 census was compiled before the Fugitive Slave Act was signed into law.

The birthplace profile of the 1855 state census tends to support the view that persons of color claiming to have been born in the Middle Atlantic states of New York, New Jersey, and in particular Pennsylvania may actually have been born in the South. The proportion of persons claiming to have been born in the North is remarkably similar in 1850 and 1855—53.3 percent in the earlier year and 53.1 percent in the later. A state-by-state analysis, however, shows a marked decline, from 18.4 to 9.5 percent, of those claiming a Middle Atlantic birthplace. By contrast, the proportion of the population claiming to have been born in the South is considerably higher in 1855 New Bedford than it had been just five years earlier, rising from 29.9 percent of the population of color to 42.9 percent. The number of persons claiming a Virginia birthplace in 1855 more than doubled, from 102 to 341 persons, and the number of persons born in every other slave state also rose. But the actual numbers are misleading because the population of color overall also grew, from 1,007 in 1850 to 1,540 in 1855, a 52.9 percent increase. The proportion of Maryland-born people of color declined by 0.6 percent, of persons from the District of Columbia by 1.0 percent, and of persons from Georgia by 0.3 percent. By contrast, the proportion of Virginians increased from 10.1 percent of the 1850 city population to 22.1 percent, which accounts virtually entirely for the difference between the proportions of southern-born persons as a whole between 1850 and 1855. Moreover, another 16 persons claimed simply to have been born in the "South," while 20 others claimed birthplaces in southern states rarely seen in previous New Bedford censuses—Tennessee, Missouri, Mississippi, and Kentucky. Another revealing difference is the almost entire disappearance of persons claiming not to know their birthplace. In 1850, "unknown" appeared in the birthplace column of 75 people of color, or 7.4 percent of the city's population of color. In 1855, it appeared in only one. The number of blank birthplaces also declined, from 44 persons (4.4 percent) in 1850 to 14 (0.91 percent) in 1855.

To what degree the 1855 census reflects true population growth or a more thorough enumeration, the latter coupled with a lessened reluctance to reveal one's birthplace, is impossible to determine. Either way, raw census data, combined with the many people of color who supplied different birthplaces to different enumerators, supports the possibility that a considerable number of fugitives lived in New Bedford, before and especially after the Fugitive Slave Act. But not all southern-born people of color were former slaves, and just as the number of fugitives is indeterminate, so is the number of free southern-born blacks who made New Bedford home for some time. Other sources reveal their status and cumulatively suggest that free blacks from the South were also present in the city in appreciable numbers.

One was Lewis Fleetwood, who claimed Washington, D.C., as his birthplace and came to New Bedford with his wife, Maria, and their daughter, Maria, on 29 May 1839, according to his testimony in November 1848 before the overseers of the poor. That he should have recalled the date of his arrival so precisely seems on its surface surprising. However, the District of Columbia register of free negroes, which included manumission records as well as certificates of freeborn status, indicates that Fleetwood had been freed only four days earlier. A record for 25 May 1839 states, "Dr. Robert E. Kerr, in consideration of $300, manumits Louis Fleetwood, who is twenty-six years old, has a dark black complexion and is five feet five inches tall. He has a scar above his left eyebrow, a wart on his left little finger, and a scar on his right arm above the elbow." Fleetwood's date of birth as recorded in his manumission and in the 1850 New Bedford census are within three years of each other. District marriage registers also contain a record of the union of Louis Fleetwood and Maria Wise on 26 December 1838. Once having settled in New Bedford, Lewis and Maria Fleetwood had three other children, Lewis A., Charles, and Benjamin, between 1841 and 1845. By 1845 Fleetwood was a porter at the city's Mansion House, but by 1847, out of work with a wife and four children to support, he twice applied for and received coal to get through the winter of 1848–49. Later in 1849 he got a job as a waiter on the steamboat *Massachusetts*. In October 1853, perhaps hoping to make enough money at sea to support his family more comfortably, he took out a seaman's protection paper and eventually signed on as steward on the *William Penn*, probably a coastwise

FIGURE 21. Mrs. Lewis Fleetwood and her children, daguerreotype, about 1850. Courtesy Old Dartmouth Historical Society / New Bedford Whaling Museum. Lewis Fleetwood might have had a photograph made of his wife and his two youngest children, Anne and probably Benjamin, before he went to sea on the *William Penn* in 1853. Maria Wise Fleetwood always claimed Washington, D.C., as her birthplace, but whether she was free at the time of her marriage is not known.

trading vessel (fig. 21). There he lost his life, swept from the top-gallant foremast as the vessel wrecked off Cape Hatteras in late September 1855.[50]

Enoch G. Bell also came from Washington to New Bedford a free man. He first appeared in the 1849 city directory as a waiter at the City Hotel; according to the 1850 census, he had been born in Washington, D.C., about 1814–16, and was then a waiter in the home of John Avery Parker, the wealthiest man in the city. By 1855 Bell was a ropemaker living on Kempton Street with his wife, Ann E., aged thirty-six, and his children, Lewis A., born in Washington between 1840 and 1845, Catharine S., also born in the District in the same years, and Anna P., who had been born after Bell came to Massachusetts. By 1855 as well, a mariner named Lloyd Bell, born in Washington between 1805 and 1807, was living in New

Bedford. The District's register of free blacks includes what are surely the records of both Bells. The register states that on 31 December 1829, "George Bell, in consideration of one dollar, manumits his children, Lloyd, aged about nineteen, Rachael Ann, aged about seventeen, and Enoch [George] Bell, aged about fifteen." About six years later, for some unknown reason, George Bell again manumitted Enoch: "George Bell, a colored man of Washington, in consideration of the natural love & affection which I have and bear to my son Enoch George Bell a slave to me, and in further consideration of one dollar, manumits Enoch George, who is about twenty-one years old." After 1860 neither Lloyd nor Enoch and his family were living in New Bedford, and the 1870 District census lists Enoch Bell, age fifty-five, a laborer who owned five thousand dollars' worth of real estate, his wife Ann Eliza, age fifty-seven, his children Lewis D., a twenty-eight-year-old clerk, Celestine, age twenty-three, and Annie P., a nineteen-year-old teacher. The coincidence of names and birthdates in every instance, except in the name "Celestine" (perhaps Catherine S. was Catherine Selestine), makes it almost certain that the New Bedford and District of Columbia records refer to the same men.[51]

The Washington free negro register also contains records of the freeborn status of William Bush and his sister Louisa in July 1847, just a year or two before a man of color by that name appeared as a laborer in the New Bedford city directory. His 1850 census listing indicates a District birthplace and lists as well his wife Lucy, born in Maryland (fig. 22), and their children, ranging in age from twenty-five to twelve—Susan, James, Mary, Louisa, Martha, Josephine, Anna, and Andrew. In 1855, James was no longer living with his parents and had apparently left New Bedford, and Eliza Bush, aged 50 and born in Virginia, had been added to the household. Louisa was then living nearby with William and Julia Bush Castle. In 1852 Bush operated a grocery store on South Water Street, amid the boardinghouses and outfitters, but by 1855 he was running one of those boardinghouses himself, around the corner on Coffin and First Streets. From other accounts, including a family Bible, it is known that Bush's wife Lucy's maiden name was Clark and that she was the sister of Archibald Clark, whose father, also named Archibald, had lived in New Bedford since 1836. The District register has a marriage record dated 14 September 1820 for William Bush and Lucy Clark as well as certificates of the freeborn status of Julia Ann Bush, about twenty years old in 1842, and Susan Bush, identified as William's daughter. A marriage record also exists in the same register for Julia Ann Bush and William Cassell dated 11 November 1845. That these accounts describe the same family seems clear; the Louisa identified as William Bush's sister is probably the Eliza Bush shown living in his household in 1855, the year Bush's daughter Louisa was living with the Castles, her sister and brother-in-law.

Manumission records exist for Lucy Clark Bush, born in 1805, and three of her children, all listed in the family's 1850 New Bedford household. On 12 October 1827, a woman named Sarah Kyle swore in the register "that Lucy Bush, a mulatto

FIGURE 22. Deacon William and Lucinda Clark Bush, photograph, 1860–65. Courtesy the descendants of Deacon William and Lucinda (Clark) Bush.

woman aged about twenty-three, was manumitted by James Pumphry. Lucy has three children: Julia Ann, aged six, Susan Ann, aged four, and James William, aged two, who were born long after Lucy's manumission." Four years earlier, Pumphry had sold an Eleanor Clarke, born about 1800, to James Warren, who then freed her. On the same day that she testified to the manumission of Lucy Clark and the free status of her three children, Sarah Kyle also swore "that Eleanor Clarke was born free, as were her three children. Archy, aged ten, Cornelius aged eight, and John, aged six years." Despite the contradiction about Eleanor Clarke's status, Archibald and John Clark both became New Bedford residents. Archibald first showed up in New Bedford as a single mariner in 1827 using the name Archibald C. Lloyd; he married Sarah Coquet, probably at least part Indian, in New Bedford in February 1828. He remained a mariner all his life, shipping aboard the famed black-owned whaler *Rising States* in 1837 and probably cooking on whaling and trading vessels in the 1840s. In 1849 or 1850 Clark went to California, where he died in the latter year. John C. Clark was also a mariner; his father witnessed his protection paper in 1831, when he was twenty.

From these data a probable scenario emerges. Archibald Clark Jr. came to New Bedford to go whaling in 1827, married a local woman in 1828, and encouraged his father to settle there by 1836. The next to come might have been James Bush, William's eldest son and Archibald Clark Jr.'s cousin; he was listed as a laborer living at the corner of Kempton and Cedar Streets in the 1849 directory. In 1864 Bush's daughter Josephine, then married and seeking coal from the city, told the overseers of the poor that she had come to New Bedford with her father and his family on 1 December 1849. By that time William Bush, his wife, his daughters Julia Ann and Susan, and his son James had certificates of freedom on file in Washington. So did Eleanor Clark, but whether she died before Archibald Clark Sr. moved to New Bedford or afterward is unknown. Then, sometime between 1850 and 1855, William Bush's daughter Julia and her husband, William Castle, also moved to New Bedford.[52]

Unlike Enoch G. Bell and his family, the Bushes and Fleetwoods stayed in New Bedford. The widowed Maria Fleetwood became a washerwoman to support her young family. When he was nineteen, her son Lewis became one of the first men of color to enlist in the Fifty-fourth Massachusetts Volunteer Infantry and was wounded at Fort Wagner. The daughter of her son Charles was Juan F. Drummond, the first female physician of color in Massachusetts. William Bush's daughter Martha married William H. W. Gray, a sergeant in the Fifty-fourth, and was permitted to serve as a nurse to the Fifty-fourth and Fifty-fifth Regiments, filled with men of color she had grown up among in New Bedford (fig. 23). And William himself played a profound and central role in the city's community of color and in antislavery work. Some of New Bedford's white abolitionists actively aided fugitive slaves, and some made a point of celebrating that fact either at the time or later, after the Thirteenth Amendment extinguished slavery altogether. Such men of color as William Bush left no records at all of the roles they played.

FIGURE 23. Martha Bush Gray and her husband, First Sergeant William H. W. Gray, photograph by H. C. Foster, Charleston, S. C., 1863. Courtesy Carl J. Cruz, New Bedford Historical Society. During the war, claiming "what I want is to be useful," Gray sought permission from her congressman to go South to nurse "the sick and wounded" of the Fifty-fourth Regiment. "I have in the 54th Regt. my Husband, two cousins, and no less than seven young men that I have taught in the Sabbath School, these with the three young men that boarded with my Father, (Wm. Bush) is all very near to me, and it makes my heart bleed when I think of them with so many others, suffering for what I could do for them, if I was only permitted to do so. . . . I am anxious to do all that I can for them, and my country also." Both she and her husband died without ever having received pension benefits.

But from what evidence remains it seems clear that before he came to New Bedford and afterward, he probably knew more about, and did more for, the fugitive
slaves living in and passing through the city than anyone else then alive. After
most white abolitionists had finished exclaiming over them, the fugitives who
came to New Bedford were for the most part left to their own devices, and it was
then, it seems, that the abolitionists of color took up the fugitives' long-term
cause and interests as their own.

3

Fugitives, the Sea,
and the Coasting Trade

WHEN HE WAS A BOY, living in Fairhaven on the east side of the Acushnet River just after 1800, Joseph Bates itched to go to sea. "In my school-boy days," he wrote in a narrative of his "long life on shipboard," in 1868, "my most ardent desire was to become a sailor. I used to think how gratified I should be if I could only get on board a ship that was going on a voyage of discovery round the world. I wanted to see how it looked on the opposite side."[1]

For slaves, however, getting on board a ship had a different meaning. When Frederick Douglass was sent from his owner's Talbot County, Maryland, plantation, to service in Baltimore, the sight of a vessel running down the Chesapeake Bay from the city gnawed at him. "You are loosed from your moorings, and are free," he wrote, remembering how he felt, "I am fast in my chains, and am a slave! . . . You are freedom's swift-winged angels, that fly round the world; I am confined in bands of iron! O that I were free! O, that I were on one of your gallant decks, and under your protecting wing." Going to sea was not a romance for Douglass and other slaves, as it was for such free white men as Joseph Bates. "To a fleeing apprentice, dissatisfied with the 'bondage' of work ashore, to a runaway slave, the sea might appear the only real shelter," the historian Jesse Lemisch has argued. "The presence of such men, fugitives and floaters, powerless in a tough environment, makes *wanderlust* appear an ironic parody of the motives which made at least some young men go to sea."[2]

Although many of the early residents of color in New Bedford were probably former New England slaves or their children, some may well have reached New Bedford aboard coastal trading vessels. For alongside the city's whaling industry grew a very active trade with ports from Nova Scotia to the West Indies. In whaling's early decades some vessels cruised the southern Atlantic for whales only in summer and returned to Nantucket and New Bedford to refit for trading voyages to southern ports in the winter. The city's *Medley* and *Columbian Courier* regularly reported vessel clearances for North Carolina, Virginia, and Georgia ports from late October through December and returns generally from mid-February through late April. But as the hunt for whales took the industry farther afield after about 1800, whaling vessels did not typically moor in southern harbors. It then became far more likely that Caribbean- and southern-born people of color reached such coastal cities as New Bedford aboard the schooners and sloops that traded New England manufactured products for the raw goods that made northern enterprise possible.

New Bedford merchants such as Joseph Rotch had been trading sperm and whale oil for tobacco, pork, and naval stores—tar, turpentine, oakum, pitch, and lumber—with merchants in North Carolina ports since the 1760s. In late November 1791, William Rotch Jr. sent two men "to such parts of Georgia as may be thought best or other parts of the Southern States" to harvest "the best Live Oak & red ceder" for framing two ships. Any surplus they acquired was to be sold, Rotch directed, on the "Savannah or Charlestown [sic] Market." A year later, Rotch's letterbook listed his widely dispersed connections with merchants in Alexandria, Petersburg, Winchester, and Lynchburg, Virginia, and in New Garden, North Carolina (where many Nantucket Quakers had settled at the beginning of the Revolution), as well as in England, France, and Ireland. That same year, the first issue of the village's first newspaper, the *Medley*, reported vessels clearing for New Bern, North Carolina; Savannah, Georgia; the Chesapeake; and the West Indies. Two years later Rotch placed a notice in the *Medley* advertising the sale of Baltimore flour as well as pitch and turpentine.[3] In these years, before the Erie Canal made western New York the nation's breadbasket, the best commercial grain crops were grown in New Jersey, Pennsylvania, and Maryland, and New Bedford merchants purchased flour principally in the ports of Alexandria, Philadelphia, and Baltimore. Shipbuilders bought lumber, already scarce in southern New England by the 1790s, from the forests of the lower coastal South. Commerce through New Bedford in southern flour, barreled beef and pork, rice, lumber, naval stores, tobacco, and, somewhat later, cotton remained strong through the Civil War, in part because the village was never especially well connected by road to western forests and farms; waterborne trade was vastly more efficient and economical. As the historian Gary Collison has pointed out, New Bedford was only five hundred miles from Norfolk, Virginia, at the mouth of the Chesapeake Bay; a coasting vessel could make that trip in four or five days. The ports of Wilmington, Washington, and New Bern in North Carolina were only between a half-day and a day farther south.[4]

The first documented fugitives in New Bedford had probably reached the village in a coastwise vessel about eight years after the case of Worcester's Quock Walker had banned slavery in Massachusetts—thus creating a feasible free place to which to escape—and about two years before the passage of the first Fugitive Slave Law in 1793.[5] Thomas Rotch, brother of William Rotch Jr. and soon to become a public Friend, had just arrived in New Bedford from Nantucket in June 1791 to run the family's candleworks and ropewalk. A man of color referred to only as John had come to New Bedford at about the same time, presumably with his wife and family, and Rotch wrote Providence abolitionist Moses Brown that "motives of humanity" induced him to take the man into his home. Somehow, by early summer 1792 Rotch and Thomas Hazard Jr. had discovered that John's reputed owner intended to visit New Bedford in order to take him and his family back, and Hazard quickly went to Providence to consult with Brown about the case. On 24 June he sent John to Providence with a letter for Brown.

> This will be handed thee by the black man in whose case I consulted counsil when last at Providence, we think considering all circumstances, it will be best for them to leave this place in the most private manner, that no person here may know where they have gone, so that when the person who is in pursuit of them arrives, he may not be able to follow them   in order for greater security, they have changed their names, we shall find places of security for three of his children here, there will be himself, his wife with a young child, and one large girl about sixteen years old to find places with you, this girl can be put out where she can earn her living immediately, his wife perhaps with thy friendly assistance can get into some sober family where her industry may support herself & child.

Both Hazard and Rotch assured Brown that John had been a good and faithful worker in the family enterprise for about a year; Hazard called him "very industrious, honest & sober" and suggested that Brown may be able to find work for him at some Providence workshop "till some more convenient place can be found for them." Hazard explained that John's eldest daughter accompanied him "in order to get her placed out first," presumably in domestic work, after which John would return to New Bedford "for his wife & young child." In a postscript Hazard again stressed "the necessity of using great secrecy & caution his family will be seen no more in this town they being removed from the place where they have lived." By 1 July, it seems, John had returned to retrieve his wife and two of his children; Thomas Rotch wrote Brown on that date that "parental tenderness added to the danger of his knowing the persuer" made it unsafe to leave behind his son, whom Hazard and Rotch had hoped to secrete in New Bedford with two of the other children.[6]

The case of John and his family was surely fresh in the mind of William Rotch Jr. (Hazard had told Brown he acted only in the absence of Rotch, on Nantucket when the reclamation was threatened) when he wrote on 10 July 1792 to his uncle Francis, then at Dunkirk, France. "I have pledged myself a faithful friend to the abolition of the slave trade & slave holding," Rotch wrote, "and am almost daily concerned in protecting the injured Africans and promising their liberation where any pretence can be found to avoid the law & Massachusetts being the only state in the Union where slavery dare not rear her head we have abundance of them seek refuge here."[7] Rotch was not entirely correct: Vermont had abolished slavery in its constitution of 1777, five years before Massachusetts declared it void by judicial decision, but it was certainly true that Massachusetts was a more accessible and promising haven after 1783 for escaping slaves than Vermont would ever be.

The three other documented fugitive arrivals to New Bedford in the 1790s probably represent an indefinitely small portion of those who actually came to the city on vessels running back and forth to southern ports in that decade. On 26 August 1794, Noah Stoddard, master of the schooner *Betsey,* placed a notice that he had discovered a stowaway negro on board after four days out from Richmond, Virginia. Stoddard claimed that the young man "had concealed himself unbeknownst to me" and that "it appearing inconsistent for me to return, the wind being ahead, I proceeded on my voyage, and landed him in this Port— He calls his name BOB, is 19 years old, and says he belongs to MOLLY BIRD, a Widow, in *Charles City.*" Stoddard published the notice in New Bedford and, probably, in Richmond newspapers to avert kidnapping charges and possible liability; by placing it, he noted, he had taken "every legal method . . . to prevent the Owner losing the property, in my power." In late April 1797 William Taber of the sloop *Union* used almost identical language about "the wind being ahead" when he advertised that a twenty-seven-year-old fugitive named James had stowed away at York River (fig. 24). Yet James had been found on the day after sailing, not after four days at sea. Whether Bob or James were ever claimed and taken back to Virginia is unknown. A year earlier, ship master Allen Shepherd advertised the desertion of "a black Sailor, by name JESSE CARPENTER," described his manner and his sailor's clothing, and offered a ten-dollar reward for his return; Carpenter could have been a fugitive who escaped once the ship *Eliza* reached free soil. Certainly Harry and his wife Lucy, living with two different owners on Maryland's Eastern Shore and brought to New Bedford almost exactly two years later, were fugitives. Harry's owner, not the vessel's captain, placed the notice of their escape; this fact, and the language of the notice, strongly suggest that Harry's owner believed the captain who brought them away had conspired to take them:

> Ran Away, on the night of the 28th ultimo, from the subscriber, living in Somerset county, Maryland, on Pocomoke river, a Negro man named HARRY, about 23 years old—thick and well set—of a dark complexion, with thick lips and full eyes.— HARRY has a notable scar on or near the outside of one of his ancles, occasioned by a burn, also is marked on or near the calf of one of his legs by the bite of a dog— and may, perhaps, bear on the back of his neck some marks of a blister plaister, applied to it while he was sick.
>
> HARRY is supposed to be carried off by a certain THOMAS WAINER, of Westport, in Massachusetts, a Mulatto, who traded here, and cleared out as Capt. of a small vessel from Westport—came to the port of Snowhill, Maryland, where he got a load of corn and staves, and cleared for Norfolk, Virginia, whence, he said, he intended for Westport, whither I suppose him to have gone.
>
> Negro LUCY, wife of said HARRY, and the property of Wm. TINCLE, Hatter, at Snowhill, aforesaid, is supposed to be with him, and in a state of pregnancy.

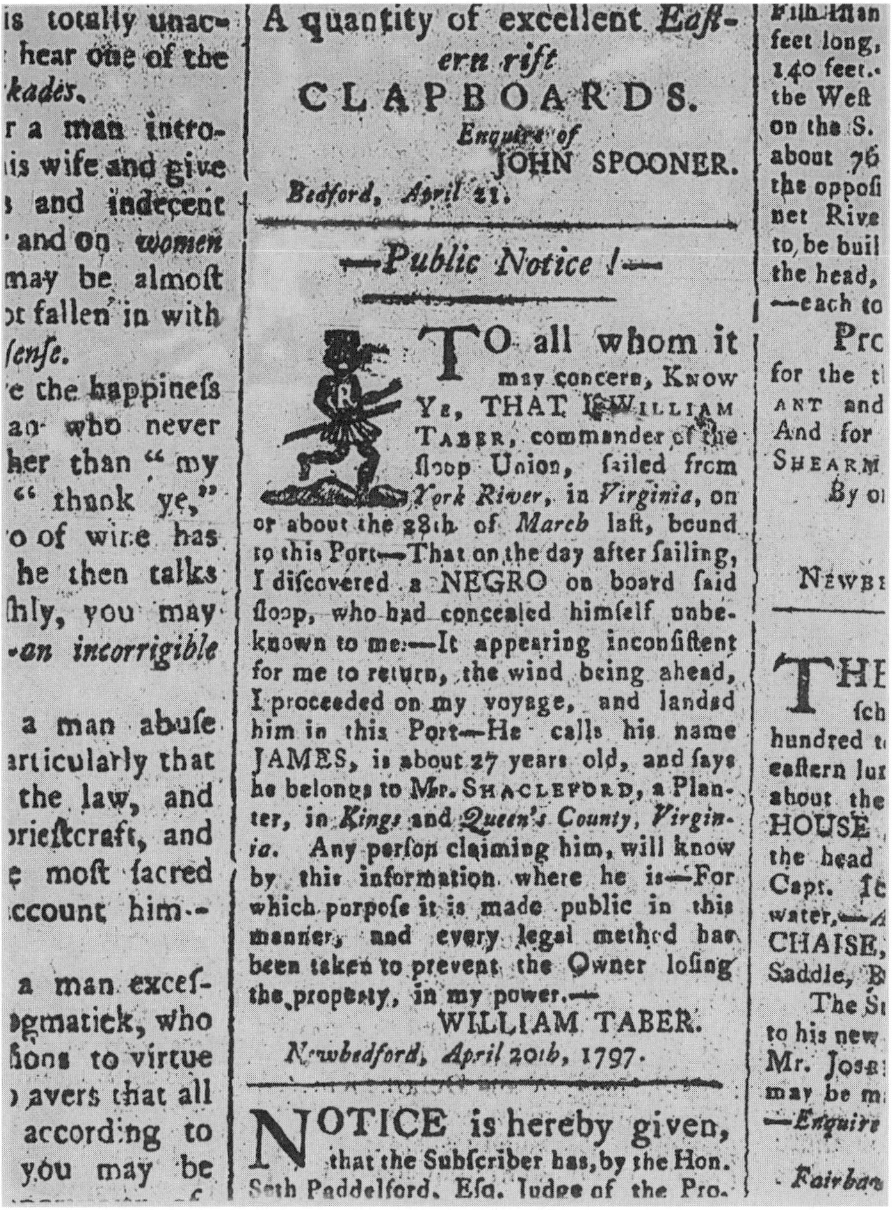

A quantity of excellent *Eaft-
ern rift*
CLAPBOARDS.
Enquire of
JOHN SPOONER.
Bedford, April 21.

—*Public Notice !*—

TO all whom it
may concern, KNOW
YE, THAT ISWILLIAM
TABER, commander of the
floop Union, failed from
York River, in *Virginia*, on
or about the 28th of *March* laft, bound
to this Port—That on the day after failing,
I difcovered a NEGRO on board faid
floop, who had concealed himfelf unbe-
known to me:—It appearing inconfiftent
for me to return, the wind being ahead,
I proceeded on my voyage, and landed
him in this Port—He calls his name
JAMES, is about 27 years old, and fays
he belongs to MR. SHACLEFORD, a Planter, in *Kings* and *Queen's County, Virginia.* Any perfon claiming him, will know
by this information where he is—For
which purpofe it is made public in this
manner, and every legal method han
been taken to prevent the Owner lofing
the property, in my power.—
WILLIAM TABER.
Newbedford, April 20th, 1797.

NOTICE is hereby given,
that the Subfcriber has, by the Hon.
Seth Paddelford, Efq. Judge of the Pro-

FIGURE 24. "Public Notice!" *New-Bedford Medley,* 28 April 1797. Used with permission of the Board of Trustees of the New Bedford Free Public Library.

Whoever delivers the said HARRY to me, at my house, shall receive FORTY DOL-
LARS—and in proportion is secured in any gaol of the United States, so that I get
him.

SAMUEL SLOANE
near King's Ferry, Somerset county, Mary'd.
April 8th, 1799[8]

Thomas Wainer, then twenty-six, was the son of Michael Wainer, a man of
African and Native American descent who was the business partner of Westport
mariner and merchant Paul Cuffe. At the time, Thomas Wainer was master of
Cuffe's *Ranger,* a seventy-ton schooner that Cuffe ran between the New Bedford
customs district (which included Westport), the Down East ports of Maine and
New Brunswick, and such cities as Philadelphia, Wilmington, Delaware, Norfolk, and Savannah. With his share of oil and bone from his first whaling voyage,
Cuffe had purchased iron for the *Ranger,* his third vessel, in 1793 and finished
building it in 1795. Cuffe and Michael Wainer sent cargo to Norfolk that year
and tried to load Indian corn on the Nanticoke River at Vienna, but unidentified
whites, alarmed at the *Ranger's* all-black crew, at first attempted to prevent the
vessel from landing. Cuffe eventually succeeded in purchasing three thousand
bushels of corn and returned with it to Westport. Thomas Wainer's trip in the
vessel to the Eastern Shore may have been the vessel's next voyage, which seems
to have involved a return by way of Philadelphia; just two days after Samuel
Sloane placed his runaway notice, that city's *Daily Advertiser* noted the entry of
the schooner *Ranger,* having made a ten-day passage from New Bedford.[9]

Although the antislavery sentiments of Michael and Thomas Wainer are not
recorded, Paul Cuffe's are well documented. Cuffe is best known for having conceived and organized the first black-sponsored effort to resettle American people
of color in Sierra Leone, where in 1792 the British abolitionist Thomas Clarkson
resettled some eleven hundred former slaves who had either supported the British
during the Revolution or were confiscated from Loyalist owners and had initially
been settled in Nova Scotia. William Thornton, an English-born Quaker who
hoped to resettle the seventy manumitted slaves he had inherited from his father,
a sugar planter on the British West Indies island of Tortola, traveled along the
eastern seaboard to advance the idea, talking to William Rotch Sr. and to the Free
African Society in Newport in 1787. By 1811 the colony had been populated by
black Nova Scotians, maroons from the British West Indies, Africans native to
the region, Kru tribespeople, and more than one thousand Africans the British
had retaken from slave ships. But making the colony viable required more than
settlement, especially insofar as sympathetic Friends on both sides of the Atlantic,
at once philanthropic and business-minded, wished to encourage it. In March
1797, after talking with the captain of a vessel just returned from Sierra Leone
about the colony's progress, William Rotch Sr. reported what he had learned to
the Quaker merchant Samuel Rowland Fisher of Philadelphia:

They have recently found spontanious growth of a most excellent kind of coffee equal to the Moco which promise great advantage but I find very little prospect of trade except in the article of rum which wholly prohibits us—Benson says great attention is paid to the education of the Black Children and that they make a great progress in their learning—He further informed me that Danes had established a similar Colony further down upon the Coast and have so far discountenanced Slavery, that the trade with men are looked upon with disgrace and are only allowed a few years to collect their debts and settle accounts—Thus we see the progress of that desiarable [*sic*] work which I hope will one day change the fertile country of Africa into a land of plenty & happiness.[10]

Cuffe probably learned of Sierra Leone through Rotch, which whom he had a commercial and personal relationship since at least 1800, through his extensive network of Quaker trading partners, and through the Free African Society of Newport, a port he often used. Clearly his aim was to erase this trading deficit between the African settlement and both England and the United States. Indeed, his interest in the project stemmed much less from the belief that free people of color could not coexist in a land that condoned black slavery—as Thornton himself had put it in 1786, speaking for many white colonizationists, "There can be no sincere union between the whites and the Negroes"[11]—than from an interest in developing a free labor economy that might compete with slavery. During his first visit to Sierra Leone, Cuffe revealed this interest in a letter to William Allen, an English Quaker who had helped organize the African Institute of London, or "the Friends of Civilization in Africa." "This countery is a Country of fertility," he observed, "and is I believe from information is Suitabel for Shugar. Cane could be Raised Equal to the Westindies and instead of Paying ½ of a Dollar per pound for Shugar might have Plenty for Exportation. Coffee is found to grow Naturaly Wild in the Desart Cotton indgeo and rice is Natural to this countery." Five years later Cuffe wrote to Simeon Jackson, a free black merchant in Savannah, about how to raise rice and asked Jackson if he might recommend someone knowledgeable in rice cultivation who would be willing to establish and operate a rice mill in Sierra Leone. He had earlier explained to Allen that his aim was "to Replace to the Africans a trade in Lawfull and Leaguall terms in Lue of the Slave trade," an objective he reiterated in an August 1816 letter to the black cleric Peter Williams Jr. in New York City. "In consequence of what Thee mentioned (viz) That We The people of Coular might Establish A mercantile Line of business from The United States to Africa &c. Should this Still be your mind and your purpose To carry it into Effect This fawl We have no Time to Loose." About two weeks earlier in a letter from his Westport home to Thomas McTroy, an aspiring emigrant from nearby Providence, he had laid out his essential stipulation for the trip. "If thee goes to that Part of the world," Cuffe cautioned, "thee must Set thy face against all Slave trade for that trade is ruinous to that Country and is Conterary to All Christian Institutions."[12]

In mid-March 1811, during his first voyage to Sierra Leone aboard his brig

Traveller, Cuffe wrote in his logbook, "my time implyd in prusing Clarksons Records on abolishing Slavery which often Ba[p]tized my mind in the Line of his proceeding," and in October 1816 he lent the second volume of this title along with other works on the subject to Sarah Howard, who two years earlier had married Cuffe's son-in-law, the widower Peter Howard of New Bedford (fig. 25). Howard wrote Cuffe that she had just completed six months of schooling at Randolph Academy, south of Boston, and hoped to teach a three-month term in Westport, presumably at the school Cuffe had set up for the children of his large extended family perhaps as early as 1797. On a trading voyage to Baltimore in 1812 Cuffe had visited Daniel Coker and George Collins, free men of color who had established an "African School" there, surely to apply whatever he learned to the operation of his own institution.[13] In addition to Clarkson's history, Cuffe lent Howard "an essay on the slavery and commerce of the human species," "an essay on the impolicy of the African slave trade," "an abstract of the evidences delivered before a select committee of the house of commons," and "elias hicks observations on slavery." In 1811 he lent one James Reed "8 books . . . on the abolishing of the Slave trade," which suggests his library of such works was not only lent freely to anyone who wished to educate themselves on the subject but was also probably quite comprehensive for its time.[14]

Cuffe's trading brought him into contact, probably not incidentally, with Quakers and others along the coast who were opposed to slavery. He corresponded with and was a houseguest of Elisha Tyson of Baltimore, member of the Maryland Society for the Relief of Free Negroes and an active abolitionist who is claimed to have helped "countless slaves" escape to the free states and Canada.[15] In 1814 John F. Mercer, former governor of Maryland, wrote Cuffe for advice about where to educate two "slave offspring" recently freed by his daughter Margaret; "from prejudice of Coulor," Cuffe explained to Samuel J. Mills, head of Andover (Massachusetts) Theological Seminary, "he [Mercer] could wish to have them removed into the northern Stats, where they Could be placed under Some pious Charactor and educated Sutible to enjoy the improvements of thair fortens."[16] Cuffe wrote also to the educator and geographer Jedidiah Morse, to Joseph Clark, who ran a school for black children in Philadelphia, and to Plainfield Academy in Connecticut, to inquire about educating the boys, and at Mercer's request he offered up his own "Common Countery School House," where he had schooled three boys from Sierra Leone a year or so earlier.[17] But in the end, with the assistance of William Rotch Jr., the boys were sent to schoolmaster Benjamin Tucker in Philadelphia. Cuffe also secured the commitment of Tyson in Baltimore, James Bryan at Wilmington, Delaware, Samuel R. Fisher in Philadelphia, New Bedford's Abraham Barker, then in business in New York, and Moses Brown in Providence should the boys' passage north need assistance in any way. Then, in 1817, Cuffe was approached by the executors of the estate of Virginian Samuel Gist, whose will had manumitted his several hundred slaves. Only months before his own death that year, Cuffe went to William Rotch Jr. for advice about how

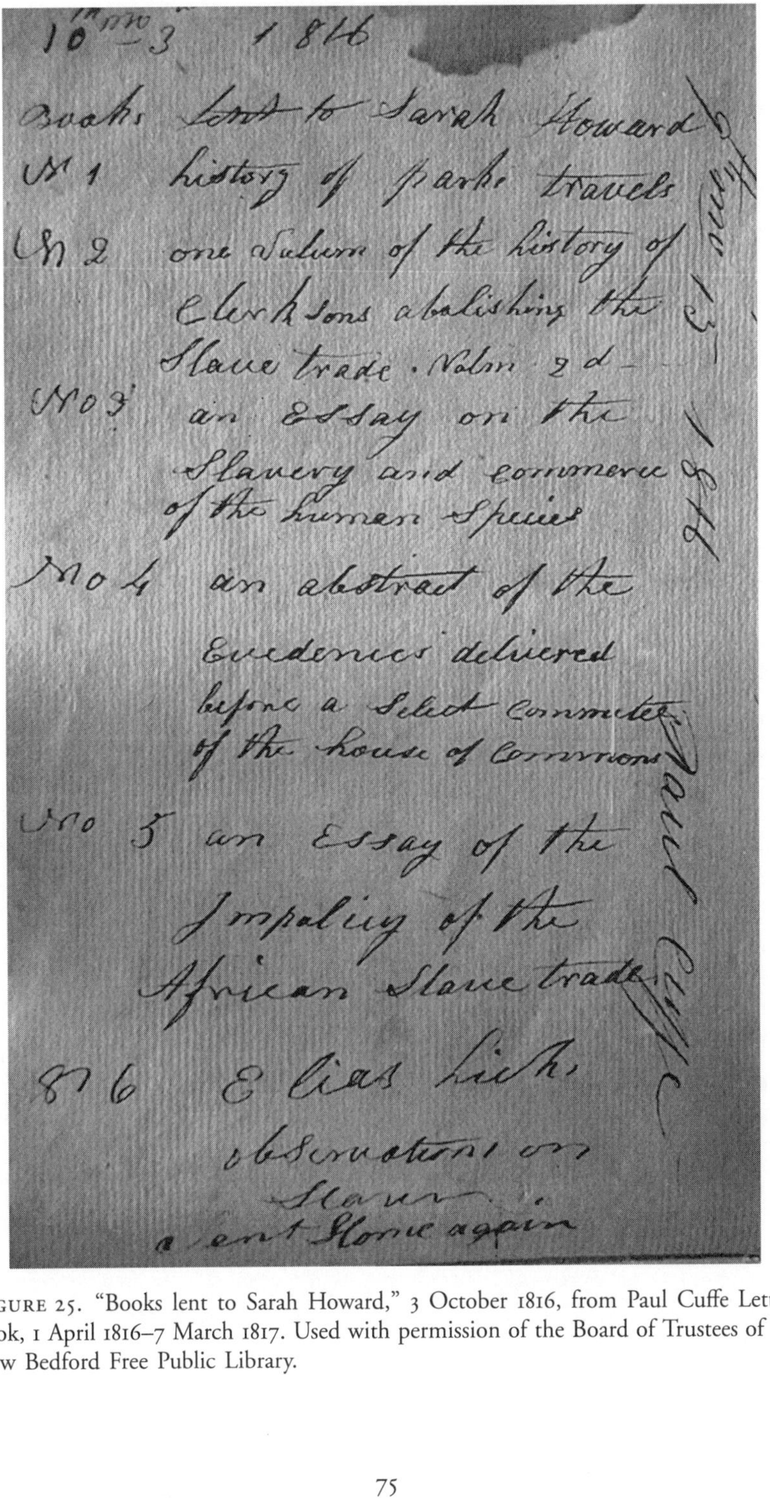

FIGURE 25. "Books lent to Sarah Howard," 3 October 1816, from Paul Cuffe Letter-book, 1 April 1816–7 March 1817. Used with permission of the Board of Trustees of the New Bedford Free Public Library.

to proceed. Rotch in turn wrote to his brother Thomas, by then resettled in Kendal, Ohio, with his wife, Charity.

> Paul Cuffee is concerned for the right colonization of between three & 400 Slaves near Richmond whose owner having recently died in England has left them free and ordered his lands sold for their use, by the laws of Virginia, if freed they must leave that state and Paul has been applied to by the Executor for advise where to place them, he has suggested their being settled in Ohio or Indiana; & he has just recd a letter from Thos Dean. Agent to the Brother Town Indians informing he was soon to go to Indiana to provide Land for those Indians to remove to and suggested that their settlement might offer a convenient place for the immigration of those few Blacks.[18]

Thomas Rotch thereupon wrote to several persons to ascertain the legal proscriptions about settling free blacks in the midwestern states. He asked Benjamin Ladd among others whether "this may not be a favourable moment to enforce the necessity of an alteration in the present Law of our State with respect to the admission of the black people to equal privilege with ourself"; he reasoned that living as he and Ladd did in "a widely extended Country of fertile land a great part of which remains in an uncultivated state . . . thousands or even millions of those unhappy sufferers might be admitted to settle and become by degrees (as they emerge from the state of degradation to which they have been subjected) useful members of Civil Society." Initially with Rotch's aid, and after litigation that extended past his death in 1823, Gist's freed people were resettled near Hillsboro, Ohio, in the 1830s.[19]

A self-taught man and a devout Quaker, Cuffe could not square slavery or racial inequality with his worldview. On a trip to New York City in May 1812 he was moved to put a query before the United Society of Methodists conference in that city after an encounter he described in his journal: "As I Was traveling in the Street With my guide he kindely introduced me to two Methodist preachers Who accosted me thus, 'Do you understand English?' I answered them, 'There Was a Part I did not understand (Viz) that of one Brother professor makeing merchandize of and holding in Bondage their Brother professor this parte I Should be glad they Would Clear up to me.' We bid Each other farewell With [out] any further Conversation." To Cuffe it was "very trying" that "many persons, who profess being enlightened with the true light" seemed yet to condone slavery, and he asked the Methodist conference "to clear this stumbleing block, and lighten the load that lays heavy on one who wishes well to all mankind."[20]

Such attitudes inspire the question whether Cuffe may have carried numbers of escaping slaves north on his trading voyages; after all, his crews were often entirely composed of men of color, and his repute among leading Quaker merchants in the East may have kept his vessels above suspicion. Moreover, he lived at a time when fugitive slave traffic was probably small, not widespread enough to generate the clamor among slaveowners so often voiced in the 1840s and especially the 1850s. No known records document that Cuffe himself carried fugitives, though the Wainer notice does indicate that at least two made their way north on a vessel his family owned. The Wainer family itself dispersed throughout the Northeast in the early 1800s, with one branch settling on Oneida Lake in western New York and another for a time in London, Ontario; Gardner Wainer, the son of Cuffe's partner and himself a Quaker, evinced his early support of the free produce movement in a letter to John Cuffe, Paul's brother, in 1832 from London: "There is a good deal said and a doing for our oppressed Breathern the affrican Raice, they are coming in by Vessel loads from the Slave States the free ones and now let us all be willing to Clap Shoulder to the Work the avice is Given not to make use of none of the cottons shugar & molases   here is a store keep for that use to Keep nothing but what is free and they are about to imploy a coullard man To Cart it about the Streets it claims the attention of allmost every Class of people it is thought by some that this Store will be a very Graite one   the Quakers or friends are working hard for them in all their yearly meetings."[21]

As free men of extraordinary prosperity for their time, Paul Cuffe and Michael Wainer were surely unfavorably impressed with the condition of the enslaved people of color they encountered along the coast and waterways of North America. There is little doubt that they encountered them often, and they were more apt to find them than whites along the wharves in port cities and at plantation landings. In a region with few cities, with their pools of tradespeople and services, and few white male laborers, men of color did the lion's share of both unskilled and artisanal work in the South.[22] They were so critical to the economy of southern ports, the historian Ira Berlin has argued, that "probably nothing arrived or left these cities without some black handling it." Black workers not only cultivated and harvested plantation and forest products, but they also transported them down the South's tidal rivers to coastal cities; both free and enslaved men of color in those ports loaded, unloaded, worked on, and provided equipment and services to the vessels that carried those products to markets. Throughout the 1700s, more than half of the population of Charleston, South Carolina, was of African descent, and in colonial South Carolina more men of color were working on ships and in maritime trades than in any other occupation except agriculture and woodworking. In the 1700s and 1800s, North Carolina black women peddled fish and shellfish, sold meals to sailors, and did their laundry; some black men worked on the docks as stevedores and draymen; and others worked on board, as ferry operators, stewards, cooks, mechanics, or engine room help, or as pilots guiding vessels down the coastal rivers and between southern cities.[23] Thomas H. Jones, born in Hanover County, North Carolina, in 1806 and brought to the coastal city of Wilmington at the age of nine, worked for a time as a stevedore loading and unloading vessels coming in and out of Wilmington before he escaped slavery (fig. 26); between 1796 and 1802 Henry Jackson Jr., whose free son William made his way to New Bedford by the late 1840s, apprenticed as a pilot with his father, a slave and the master of the pilot boat *Nancy* on

Virginia's Rappahannock River (fig. 27). People of color were so prevalent on the vessels and wharves of the South that some writers considered it strange to find white people among them at all. In his escape effort the fugitive William Singleton assumed the fisherman he saw at dusk on Adams Creek in Craven County, North Carolina, was black and hailed him for assistance. He "must be a colored man," Singleton wrote in his slavery narrative, "because the white people as a rule do not fish." The tendency of men of color to work on vessels or in maritime trades tended generally to increase throughout the South during the first half of the nineteenth century. By 1850, fully two-thirds of all employed men of color in Baltimore's second ward, which embraced the Fell's Point shipyards, were working on vessels, on the docks, and in ropewalks and other maritime industries.[24]

The historian Jeffrey Bolster has amply documented the roles of men of color on northern vessels, and the works of Ira Berlin, Gary Nash, Marcus Rediker, and others have shown the extensive participation of black men and women in the northern shoreside trades that supported maritime commerce.[25] Their presence was so thoroughly taken for granted that the Boston Vigilance Committee was able to use them as a subterfuge in its fugitive rescue efforts, as Thomas Wentworth Higginson once explained: "I belonged to several secret societies in Boston aiming to impede the capture of fugitive slaves; it was also afterwards planned to distress slave claimants. One of these societies owned a boat, in which men used to go down in the harbor to meet Southern vessels. The practice was, to take along a colored woman with fresh fruit, pies, &c—she easily got on board & when there, usually found out if there was any fugitive on board; then he was sometimes taken away by night."[26]

That people of color were central to the success of the North American maritime economy as a whole can be judged by several accounts. In 1828 the Senate Foreign Relations Committee voiced its objection to the American Colonization Society's plan to resettle American blacks in Africa because of the effect it would have on labor supply and costs in seaport cities. In February 1843 155 Boston vessel owners and masters, and a sprinkling of abolitionists, sent a petition to the U.S. Senate and House claiming that the southern states' various Negro Seamen's Acts, which called for the imprisonment of free sailors of color until northern vessels left their ports, greatly harmed not only the interest of these mariners but "the commerce of these States." These global issues were echoed in countless local incidents: one slave trader in pursuit of two fugitives working a packet running between Charleston and a Florida port was warned that the vessel's captain would probably be unwilling to let them leave his service because they had become "quite valuable to him."[27]

Southern slave society was disintegrated in many ways, among them a vast divide between the world of the plantation and the world of the port. Plantation slaves lived generally far separated from other plantations, had their numbers supplemented regularly by newly enslaved Africans, and tended to have far less contact with the world outside. Gerald Mullin has found that plantation slaves

FIGURE 26. Thomas H. Jones, frontispiece engraving from *The Experience of Thomas H. Jones, Who Was a Slave for Forty-Three Years* (Worcester, Mass., 1857). Courtesy Carl J. Cruz, New Bedford Historical Society.

FIGURE 27. Bible belonging to Henry Jackson, grandfather of the Reverend William Jackson, private collection, photograph by John Robson. This small volume is inscribed on the inside front cover, "Henry Jackson. His book the year of our Lord 1791 Henry Jackson his book Febuary [*sic*] the 4 1792/ the schooner nancy of rappahonock [*sic*] pilot boat." Henry Jackson's son and namesake also worked in the maritime trades before leaving Norfolk for Philadelphia after Nat Turner's rebellion in the early 1830s.

in colonial Virginia were far less apt to be able to speak English well enough "to pass as free men in town" should they decide to escape. By contrast, slaves living in southern ports and other towns tended increasingly to be "American-born creoles" who were skilled and often permitted to travel. Many had been permitted to hire their time, knew the ways of white society, knew what they needed to do to attempt to pass as free or to escape. Henry "Box" Brown, born in 1815 outside Richmond, wrote that his trips to the mill several times a year with his brother were "the means of furnishing us with some information respecting other slaves, otherwise we would have known nothing whatever of what was going on anywhere in the world, excepting on our master's plantation." Frederick Douglass recalled how the Lloyd plantation slaves who worked on the sloop *Sally Lloyd* "were esteemed very highly by the other slaves, and looked upon as the privileged ones of the plantation; for it was no small affair, in the eyes of the slaves, to be allowed to see Baltimore."[28]

Based on his work in eighteenth-century Virginia, Mullin has suggested that slaves' origins (whether African- or American-born) and their fluency with English established their location in the hierarchy of work available to them. This milieu—whether they worked in the field, in the household, or in a workshop, for example—in turn governed how thoroughly and quickly they assimilated to "colonial values." The nature of this assimilation and the type of job they held determined the type of resistance men and women of color offered toward slavery. Plantation slaves with poor English skills who attempted to escape were more apt to do so in groups and more often suspected to be "lurking"—to use the standard term of contemporary runaway slave advertisements—either in the surrounding area, around plantations from which they had been sold (and where family members and friends remained), or around places to which spouses, parents, and children had been sold. In March 1812, when slaveowner James K. Goodloe advertised the escape of a slave carpenter named Robin in the *Raleigh Register and North Carolina State Gazette,* he postulated that the fugitive was "supposed to be lurking after the family of Mr. Robt. Harwell, who owns said negro's wife, and who is on his rout to the Mississippi Territory, for the purpose of selling her."[29] Indeed, in response to northern concerns that fugitives from the South would ultimately mount a serious challenge to free labor in the North, fugitives countered that ties to family held many slaves whose condition might otherwise prompt the desire to escape in the South. "The northern people think that if slavery were abolished, we would all come north," Douglass stated in an early public appearance in Lynn, Massachusetts, in 1841. "They may be more afraid of the free colored people and the runaway slaves going South. We would all seek our home and friends, but, more than all, to escape from northern prejudice, would we go to the south." The fugitive Leonard Black argued that if people of color were treated equitably, they would probably prefer to remain in the South rather than make a "rush for the north, overwhelming the workingmen in this region with misery and despair. . . . Give us pay for our toil, and we will work at the South."[30]

Slaves working in cities, in towns, and along rivers and the coast were more likely to escape by themselves either to a colony's most densely populated places, to attempt to pass there as free, or out of the South altogether. As Mullin has put it, their resistance was not directed inwardly, toward the plantation, but outwardly "in the sense of setting and goals: they were determined to get as far as possible from their masters and the plantation. Their flight from and repulsion of the plantation, moreover, were a fitting corollary to the psychological consequences of their training and work routines." In his work on colonial South Carolina runaways, Philip Morgan has also found that runaways generally tended to be "acculturated, highly valued, and therefore probably atypical slaves." Although historians have often noted that, as Morgan put it, "these advertised runaways represent only the most visible tip of an otherwise indeterminate iceberg," one-fifth of the male and female runaways identified in South Carolina newspaper notices were described as skilled. "A skilled, native-born, male runaway who was able to speak English well," he has argued, "was more likely to pass as free or attempt to leave the colony than a runaway who was his exact opposite."[31]

In Virginia, North Carolina, and South Carolina, enslaved men who worked in maritime occupations were among the most likely to run away. In South Carolina skilled slaves were 11.3 percent of all slaves listed in inventories between 1730 and 1779. Slave "watermen," generally men who fished or worked as crew or operators on vessels, were 8.6 percent of all skilled slaves in the colony, yet nearly one-quarter (24.9 percent) of all skilled slave runaways in South Carolina between 1732 and 1782 were watermen. "The independent, self-reliant existence of watermen, with their obvious access to a means of escape, no doubt accounts for their prominence among skilled runaways," Morgan has stated. Mullin's findings in Virginia are almost identical: between 1736 and 1801 almost 25 percent of Virginia's skilled runaways were mariners. "So important was the correlation between acculturation and the mobility factor, that two types of semi-skilled slaves—watermen and waitingmen—whose tasks required them to travel frequently, reacted outwardly to slavery. More fugitives capable of passing as free men, in fact, came from these occupations than from any others."[32] Although some historians have questioned Mullin's findings about the relation between assimilation and the propensity to escape slavery, most agree that watermen escaped in "disproportionately high numbers" relative to their presence in the slave population.[33]

As these studies indicate, the number of notices placed in southern newspapers that allude to the maritime skills of fugitives is large. In March 1793 one New Bern, North Carolina, slaveowner advertised a forty-shilling reward if his "Negro Boy named Jack, about nineteen years old," was apprehended in Craven County and four pounds if taken outside the county. "He was late the property of Captain

Hosmer," the advertisement explained, "and as he was brought up to the sea, I expect he will try to get on board of some vessel, with an intention of going to New-England, where he was born. . . . If he has left this town I suppose he will try to get to Washington to take shipping there. All masters of vessels, and others, are hereby forewarned from harbouring, employing, or carrying him away, as the subscriber is determined to prosecute with the utmost rigor of the law, any person so offending." The admonition to masters of vessels was standard in fugitive notices surely because, as David Cecelski has pointed out, "runaway slaves regularly headed to the coast instead of attempting overland paths out of bondage." In June 1820 another New Bern slaveowner sought the capture of Sam, "by trade a Carpenter;—he is also something of a Seaman. I have been informed that he has procured a Seaman's Protection and obtained forged Free Papers. He has, no doubt, already gone or will attempt to go to some of the Northern sea-ports." Frederick Douglass relied on a similar subterfuge—foregoing forgery and using instead another man's protection paper—to effect his escape eighteen years later. Because the descriptions on protection papers were so general, as James Fenimore Cooper pointed out, "they not unfrequently fitted one man as well as another."[34]

Simple knowledge of the people and ways of a waterfront could make escape possible. Harriet Jacobs, whose *Incidents in the Life of a Slave Girl, Written by Herself* was a sensation when it was published in 1861, came from a family of seafaring men in the coastal city of Edenton, North Carolina. Her uncle Mark worked as a steward aboard a vessel, an in-law named Stephen was a sailor who escaped to the North, and her brother Joseph escaped by vessel in 1828 and, after his capture, a second time by vessel from New Orleans. When Jacobs escaped slavery in 1835 and felt she must leave her first Edenton hiding place, a slave woman friend brought her "a suit of sailor's clothes,—jacket, trowsers, and tarpaulin hat" so that she might disguise herself. "Put your hands in your pockets," her friend advised, "and walk ricketty, like de sailors." Together they walked to an Edenton wharf, from which a black "seafaring man" (probably Stephen) rowed Jacobs to a vessel to hide for the night. Her friends then hid her in a swamp until her uncle Mark could find another place to secrete her. But Edenton officials, sensitive to the possibility that northern vessels were carrying slaves to freedom, had begun intensive shipboard inspections at this time, so Jacobs put her sailor's clothes back on, used charcoal to darken her face, and walked with a black friend to her own grandmother's house, where she hid in a tiny crawl space for a month short of seven years without the knowledge of her children, living in the same house, or her owner, living a few blocks away. She then got a message to her friend Peter, another "trustworthy seafaring person," so that he might post letters she wrote home when he arrived in New York City; thus she hoped to fool her owner into thinking she had already made her way north. In 1842 Jacobs finally escaped. Her friend Peter arranged with one vessel's captain to take her to the North, she walked to the wharf at night, her uncle Mark rowed her out to the anchored ship, and the captain "showed her to a little box of a cabin." He advised her to stay below whenever a sail came in view, but otherwise she might be on deck; by the third week of June she stepped ashore in Philadelphia.[35]

Jacobs never named the captain or the vessel on which she made her escape, but the exposure of northern mariners to southern slavery inclined some to aid such escapes as hers. Austin Bearse, a native of Barnstable on Cape Cod who worked on a coastwise schooner trading in South Carolina ports from about 1818 to 1830, saw enough of it to provoke his systematic participation in the Boston Vigilance Committee; his first fugitive rescue took place in 1847 at the behest of the Quaker Mott sisters, then living in Albany, New York. In his *Reminiscences of Fugitive-Slave Law Days in Boston* (1880), Bearse described scenes that must have been familiar to many northerners on trading voyages:

> It is well known that many New England vessels are in the habit of spending their winters on the Southern coast, in pursuit of this business—for vessels used to run up the rivers for the rough rice and cotton of the plantations, which we took to Charleston. We often carried gangs of slaves to the plantations as they had been ordered. These slaves were generally collected by slave-traders in Charleston, brought there by various causes, such as the death of owners and the division of estates, which threw them into the market. Some were sent as punishment for insubordination, or because the domestic establishment was too large; or because persons moving to the North and West preferred selling their slaves to the trouble of carrying them. We had on board our vessels, from time to time, numbers of these slaves—sometimes two or three, and sometimes as high as seventy or eighty. They were separated from their families and connections with as little concern as calves or pigs are selected out of a lot of domestic animals. Our vessel used to lie at a place called Poor Man's Hole, not far from the city. We used to allow the relatives and friends of the slaves to come on board and stay all night with their friends, before the vessel sailed. In the morning it used to be my business to pull off the hatches and warn them that it was time to separate, and the shrieks and cries at these times were enough to make anybody's heart ache. . . . In my past days, the system of slavery was not much discussed. I saw these things as others did, without interference. Because I no longer think it right to see these things in silence, I trade no more south of Mason and Dixon's line.[36]

By that time in his life, Bearse claimed, he had seen slavery in ports all over the world, but what he witnessed on southern rice and sugar plantations and in New Orleans was *"full as bad* as any slavery in the world—heathen or Christian. People who go for visits or pleasure through the Southern States, cannot possibly know those things which can be seen of slavery by shipmasters who run up into the back plantations of countries, and who transport the slaves and produce of plantations."

At this time many shipmasters were engaged in such trade. Bearse himself was probably living in New Bedford when he became a subscriber to the *Liberator* in 1837,[37] and across the Acushnet River in Fairhaven Joseph Bates had turned toward abolition after experiences similar to Bearse's. Bates shipped as a cabin boy on a European voyage in 1807, when he was fourteen, and in 1815 he made his first coastwise voyage from New Bedford to Alexandria, Virginia. He sailed, often among black crew, on trading vessels to Alexandria, Baltimore, and European ports through the 1830s, and as he rose through the ranks his reform spirit quickened. He turned against alcohol, swearing, and in any way profaning the Sabbath, and as master he began to enforce such proscriptions on his own vessels. Then Bates began to propagate the gospel aboard his ships, but because the American Tract Society refused to sponsor the distribution of antislavery documents, he rejected its form of evangelism. With other Fairhaven residents, he organized the town's first antislavery society about 1835. Antislavery was not the last of Bates's enthusiasms: he became a Millerite in 1839 and remained an Adventist for the rest of his life.[38]

New Bedford vessels were quite commonly found in southern ports through the years Bearse and Bates described. Merchant manifests for New Bedford trading vessels exist from 1808. Though quite incomplete when compared against the shipping and maritime columns of local newspapers—many records of the New Bedford custom house have not survived—they nonetheless document an active trade with southern ports. In 1808 Joseph Howland, William Rotch Jr., and Stephen Mosher were regularly sending apples, sperm oil, spermaceti candles, and plaster to Alexandria and Charleston; Isaac Cory, a Westport merchant who was for a time partners with Paul Cuffe, sent whale oil, apples, potatoes, and cheese to Richmond in that year as well. Vessels returned to New Bedford with ship stores, flour, corn, bacon, barreled pork, and lumber. By early 1812 almost every vessel registering a cargo in New Bedford was bound south, usually to Norfolk, Alexandria, and Richmond in Virginia, Wilmington, Washington, and New Bern in North Carolina, and Savannah. Of twenty-three manifests surviving from the month of January 1815, eleven were of vessels embarking for or returning from the South, often from Elizabeth City, North Carolina; George Howland's *Emily*, built in New Bedford, was registered in Elizabeth City in 1815. By the midteens, shoes, harness, ceramics, and wool and felt, often in the form of hats, were common cargoes; the shoes and hats could have been destined for plantation slaves.[39] Between January and May of 1815 nearly half (67 of 138) of all existing manifests were for vessels trading with the South, and this count may actually underestimate the number. Cuffe's *Traveller,* which left New Bedford for Wilmington, Delaware, in May 1808, was listed as returning from the port it had most recently visited—Bristol, Rhode Island. The tendency to list a vessel's most recent port of call might have been common. When the *Rising States* of nearby Rochester left in June 1808 it headed for Savannah, but when it returned later that year it was listed as having come from New York City.

Not only did New Bedford merchants trade frequently in southern ports, but several key members of this elite had family connections there; as Cecelski has noted, a "sizable contingent of sea captains and shipping merchants" had resettled in North Carolina from New England and New York "during the cotton and naval stores boom." Because Quaker merchants preferred to trade whenever possible with other Quakers, New Bedford commercial men probably relied more heavily than other merchants on networks of kin and Friends along the eastern seaboard. Some of these southerners were relocated Nantucket Quakers, who left the island and its crippled whaling industry behind just before the American Revolution. In the early 1790s William Rotch Jr. traded extensively with William Coffin Jr. of New Garden in Guilford County, where most Nantucket Quakers resettled. Rotch also traded with Joseph Anthony at Lynchburg, Virginia, who may have been related to the Anthonys in southeastern Massachusetts. The antebellum New Bedford merchant Abraham Barker had sent his younger brother Jacob to apprentice with Isaac Hicks in New York in the late 1790s, and by the 1830s Jacob's son Abraham was partners in a New Orleans brokerage business. New Bedford's Whitridge family had commercial and family ties to Whitridge and Company in New Orleans and Thomas Whitridge and Company in Baltimore, William C. Whitridge confessed in an 1838 letter to Benjamin Rotch, then attending Harvard College, that he had left New Bedford for New Orleans "in pursuit of wealth" in 1837, when the nation was in the throes of the financial panic.[40] Merchant William Tallman Russell also traded candles and whale oil with Thomas Whitridge of Baltimore through the 1820s, as well as with Richard G. Howland of the same city and merchants in New Orleans, Charleston, and Norfolk.[41] Branches of the Rodman and Hathaway families lived in and around Norfolk and Portsmouth, Virginia, and New Bedford merchants shipped oil and candles to Howland and Sons (sometimes Howland and Brothers) in Norfolk in the 1850s.[42] Earlier Thomas H. Howland, son of New Bedford merchant Weston Howland, was a member of a commission house in Alexandria, no doubt buying flour and other agricultural goods to be shipped north on family vessels.

One such vessel was the sloop *Regulator,* owned by Weston Howland and John Avery Parker. The *Regulator* is referred to as a "flour packet" because it principally carried flour on a regular schedule between Alexandria and New Bedford. The trip from Alexandria to New Bedford could be a swift one—on 8 November 1816 the New Bedford *Mercury* reported the arrival the day before of "sloop Regulator, Chadwick, 4 days from Alexandria, with 600 bbls flour, to the Captain, J. A. Parker, Weston Howland and others"—but more commonly voyages lasted about three weeks as the vessel loaded and unloaded goods at other ports, including Norfolk to the south and St. Andrews (probably New Brunswick) to the north. Only two manifests exist for the vessel between 1815 and 1818, but the *Mercury* recorded at least ten clearances and corresponding arrivals of the vessel in these years. Usually the sloop was in the command of Samuel Chadwick. On one of these voyages between 1815 and 1818, Chadwick carried three or four people of color to New Bedford. One of them was William, or William Mason; two others were married—the man named George, the woman's slave name not indicated—and there was probably also a free man named William Butler. By some accounts, Butler told Chadwick that the other three were also free people; by others, Chadwick knowingly took the slaves north.

Cecelski has suggested that among New England mariners and merchants who resettled in the South were some who "no doubt . . . held abolitionist sympathies"; one was the son of a slaveowner in New Bern, North Carolina, whom Robert Purvis, a Philadelphia African American leader and merchant, identified in a letter to the Underground Railroad historian R. C. Smedley in the early 1880s. "Through his agency," wrote Purvis, "the slaves were forwarded, by placing them on vessels engaged in the lumber trade, which plied between Newberne and Philadelphia, and the captains of which had hearts." This slaveholder's son has never since been identified, though the records of the first Boston Committee of Vigilance document that Captain Samuel Howland, whose father owned the slave Joseph Johnson, carried Johnson north from New Bern in December 1846 aboard the schooner *Erma & Julia*. Johnson, the records note, was a seaman, "has been before the mast five years." It seems at least possible that Howland was the New Bern merchant whom Purvis described.[43] Both Vestal Coffin and his cousin Levi, born in Guilford County, North Carolina, of Nantucket Quaker parents, were active in assisting fugitive slaves from the mid-1810s. They descended from the same ancestors as New Bedford's David, Timothy G., and William C. Coffin, the last a committed abolitionist.[44]

Cecelski has argued that "the presence of an escape route along the East Coast was indeed widely known both locally and among northern abolitionists," and the contemporary account of Daniel Drayton certainly suggests as much. Like Fairhaven's Joseph Bates, Drayton was drawn to a life at sea after his family moved near the Delaware River in New Jersey just before the War of 1812, and probably by the mid-1810s, when he was a teenager, he signed on for his first trading voyage as a cook on a sloop carrying wood down the Maurice River in south New Jersey to Philadelphia. According to his 1853 memoir, Drayton spent "the best years of my life" in the coasting business between St. John, New Brunswick, and Savannah, and visited most of the ports and coastal rivers between these points, including New Bedford. "My trading up and down the bay, in the way which I have described, of course brought me a good deal into contact with the slave population," Drayton recalled, "No sooner, indeed, does a vessel, known to be from the north, anchor in any of these waters—and the slaves are pretty adroit in ascertaining from what state a vessel comes—than she is boarded, if she remains any length of time, and especially over night, by more or less of them, in hopes of obtaining a passage in her to a land of freedom."[45]

William Grimes, a fugitive who made his way to New Bedford by June 1816, was the sort of man Drayton must have encountered, and his escape relied on the sympathies of northern mariners. Born in 1784 in King George County, Virginia, Grimes was sold eight times, had unsuccessfully attempted to escape slavery at least four times and been jailed as a consequence, and had worked as a plantation house servant, a field hand, a barber, a stableman, and a hackman before he was thirty years old. Sold to an agent for the U.S. Navy near the end of the War of 1812, Grimes worked as a hackman in Savannah and then, despite his troublesome reputation, was permitted to hire his time; he worked on board the captured British vessel *Epervier* and then as a cook and steward on the federal vessel *James Monroe*. As his 1824 narrative recounts, Grimes was in Savannah when the Boston-registered brig *Casket* arrived:

> I went with a number more to assist in loading her. I soon got acquainted with some of these Yankee sailors, and they appeared to be quite pleased with me. Her cargo chiefly consisted of cotton in bales. After filling her hold, they were obliged to lash a great number of bales on deck. The sailors, growing more and more attached to me, they proposed to me to leave, in the centre of the cotton bales on deck, a hole or place sufficiently large for me to stow away in, with my necessary provisions. Whether they then had any idea of my coming away with them or not, I cannot say, but this I can say safely, a place was left, and I occupied it during the passage, and by that means made my escape. The evening before the brig was to sail I went with a colored man (a sailor on board) up into town and procured some bread, water, dried beef, and such other necessaries that I should naturally want. It was late in the evening, and he being a Yankee sailor, I directed him to walk behind me in the capacity of a servant, (as they would consider me his master, the watch or guard being all on their posts;) he did so, and we procured every thing necessary for me, took them on board, and I stowed away in the hole left for me, where I myself went and remained until we arrived at the Quarantine Ground, New York. I will here mention that during my passage I lay concealed as much as possible; some evenings I would crawl out and go and lie down with the sailors on deck; the night being dark, the captain could not distinguish me from the hands, having a number on board of different complexions.[46]

The irony of escaping amid the commodity that Southerners argued necessitated slavery cannot have been lost on Grimes or any of the numerous other fugitives who concealed themselves in that way. After the *Casket*'s master discovered Grimes aboard off New York, he had the fugitive put ashore on Staten Island. From there Grimes walked to New Haven, Connecticut, but on seeing a relative of one of his former owners there Grimes moved on to Southington, then back to New Haven, then to Newport, and then on foot to New Bedford, where he got work as a servant in the home of John Howland in June 1816.

That fall Grimes opened his own barber shop, and "kept a few groceries" while he continued to work for Howland. In his autobiography Grimes said he was then the only black barber in New Bedford, but he was not the only person of color operating a business in the village. By 1817 William Mingo, born in Westport, had a dry goods partnership with white merchant Philip Allen II, possibly at a store in bordering Dartmouth.[47] Paul Cuffe, in the last year of his life by the time Grimes came to the village, had been trading sheep and African camwood, hides, and ivory in New Bedford for at least a decade and in July 1809 had formed a partnership with his sons-in-law, Peter and Alexander Howard. The Howards, former slaves, twin brothers, and carpenters, had come to Westport about 1806, perhaps with Cuffe, and were working on his schooner *Alpha* when they met

Cuffe's daughters Naomi, then twenty-three years old, and Ruth, then seventeen. In an early August 1807 letter to Philadelphian John Parrish, an unidentified correspondent termed the brothers "exceptions" to the general state of people of color, many of them apparently fugitives, in the southern New England states:

> Massachusetts . . . has been overrun [?] with a set of poor lawless creaters, claiming protection, from their own masters, and too frequently returning kindness with ingratitude. There are however exceptions which I note with pleasure—in the next township lives Paul Cuff, the owner & Master of a fine ship in Philadelphia a few months since. He is a man whom I suppose to be worth 20,000 Dollars, of more extensive credit & reputation than any other in the township—and his family settled about him with equal reputation who are also much respected. His daughters married twin Brothers who were formerly Slaves. They are carpenters, & are now finishing for themselves in this town, a most commodious and comfortable house.[48]

At first with their father-in-law and by 1811 on their own, Peter and Alexander Howard traded in West Indian goods and groceries as well as in foodstuffs, cloth, earthenware, flax, leather, cotton, tobacco, snuff, and sugar from every mid-Atlantic and southern port (fig. 28). From 1811 until 1820 their tax assessments were the highest of any people of color in the town. Peter Howard had died before William Grimes arrived in New Bedford, but his brother continued in business and briefly became partners with the black trader Richard Johnson, whose origins are as obscure as the Howards'.[49] Johnson appears to have come to New Bedford about the same time the Howards did. Since April 1806, when he bought land in the town's commercial core from the white mariner Nathaniel Hathaway, he had also been a trader on Water Street in the village. The black activist and historian William C. Nell, who knew Johnson, stated in his *Colored Patriots of the American Revolution* that Johnson was a mariner in early life "and filled every capacity from a cabin boy to a captain." Nell stated that Johnson was taken prisoner in the War of 1812 and confined for six months, though shipping manifests and newspaper advertisements make clear that he was in town and actively engaged in coastwise trading in late April 1812, mid-November 1813, from February to mid-April 1814, and in mid-January 1815. Johnson was partners with Alexander Howard from 1815 until June 1817, when he again went into business for himself, and after Alexander Howard's death about 1825 Johnson married his widow, Ruth Cuffe Howard.

When Grimes came to New Bedford in 1816, the village in general remained depressed from the effect of the War of 1812 on American shipping of all kinds; the gross value of all whaling industry exports had dropped from a high of $606,000 in 1807, before the first Jeffersonian embargo was enacted, to as little as $10,000 in 1814 and stood at $175,000 for the year between 30 September 1815, nine months after peace had been declared, to 1 October 1816.[50] During the war, as William Rotch Sr. wrote to his son Thomas, "our town has felt much by Captures amt $200,000 already & much more exposed, & the laboring poor would

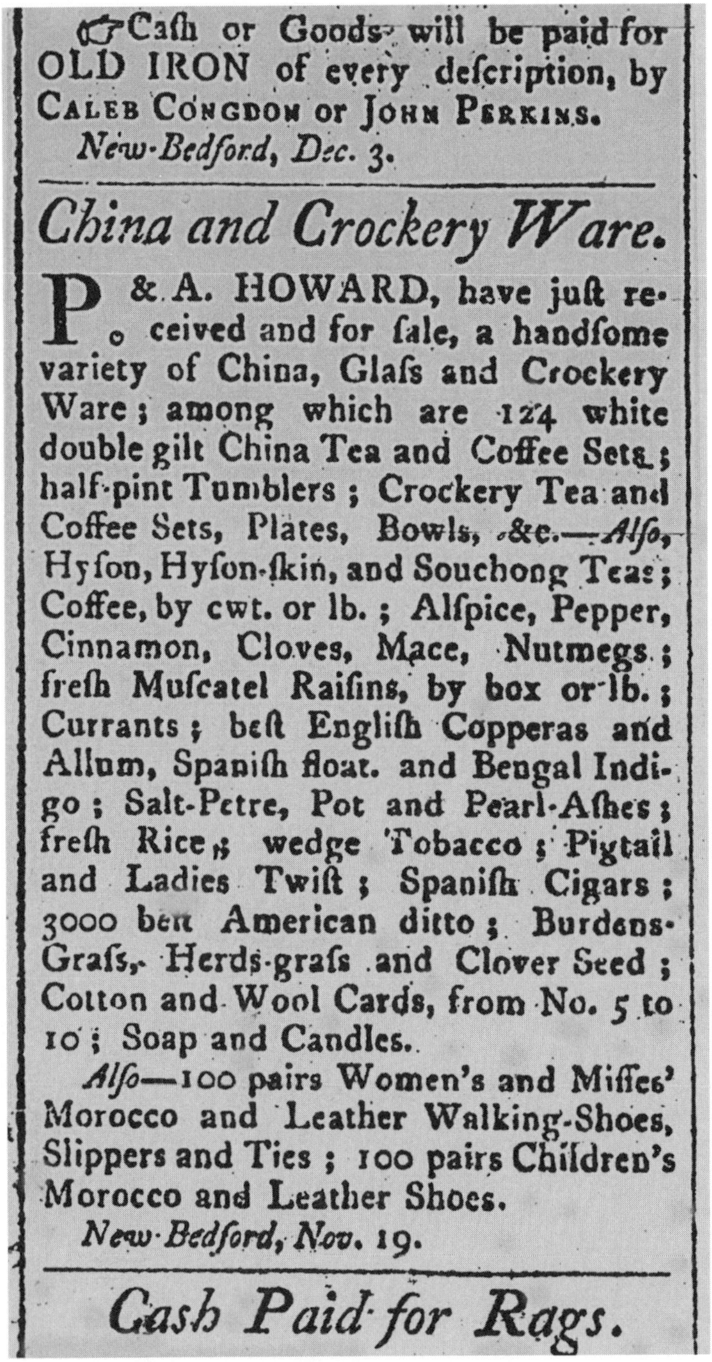

> ☞Cash or Goods will be paid for
> OLD IRON of every description, by
> CALEB CONGDON or JOHN PERKINS.
> *New-Bedford, Dec.* 3.

China and Crockery Ware.

P & A. HOWARD, have just received and for sale, a handsome variety of China, Glass and Crockery Ware; among which are 124 white double gilt China Tea and Coffee Sets; half-pint Tumblers; Crockery Tea and Coffee Sets, Plates, Bowls, &c.—*Also,* Hyson, Hyson-skin, and Souchong Teas; Coffee, by cwt. or lb.; Allspice, Pepper, Cinnamon, Cloves, Mace, Nutmegs; fresh Muscatel Raisins, by box or lb.; Currants; best English Copperas and Allum, Spanish float. and Bengal Indigo; Salt-Petre, Pot and Pearl-Ashes; fresh Rice; wedge Tobacco; Pigtail and Ladies Twist; Spanish Cigars; 3000 ben American ditto; Burdens-Grass, Herds-grass and Clover Seed; Cotton and Wool Cards, from No. 5 to 10; Soap and Candles.

Also—100 pairs Women's and Misses' Morocco and Leather Walking-Shoes, Slippers and Ties; 100 pairs Children's Morocco and Leather Shoes.

New-Bedford, Nov. 19.

Cash Paid for Rags.

FIGURE 28. Advertisement for P. & A. Howard, New Bedford *Mercury*, 14 January 1814. Used with permission of the Board of Trustees of the New Bedford Free Public Library.

have felt much more of the pressure had not they Brother Wm. & Sam'l [Rod-
man] employed many men in repairing vessells & removing the Rock before
Wm's house, Sam'l not less than 30 or 40 men, & Wm perhaps near 20."[51] The
town's population does not appear to have declined, but the rate of growth in
its white and black populations slowed considerably during the decade.[52] And
though there may not have been a significant influx of people of color from outside the region, it does appear that the movement from rural to more urban places
had begun among people of color. Of the four coastal towns of old Dartmouth,
rural Dartmouth and Westport were home to nearly 63 percent of all persons of
color in 1800 and about 61 percent in 1810; by 1820, however, the proportion of
people of color living in these rural towns had dropped to 48.5 percent. For the
first time more than half of the area's black population lived in the commercial
towns of New Bedford and Fairhaven. Statistics on the number of people of color
in white and black households respectively also suggest, if only tentatively, declining opportunity for people of color in rural areas. The proportion of people of
color living in black households climbed from 88.6 percent to 96.3 percent between 1800 and 1810 but dropped back to 93.7 percent in 1820 in Dartmouth and
Westport combined. In New Bedford and Fairhaven, 59.7 percent of all people
of color lived in black households in 1800 and only 49.7 percent did so in 1810,
but by 1820 69.5 percent of people of color lived in black households in these
commercial places. That the portion of the population of color living in black-
run households is consistently lower in New Bedford and Fairhaven suggests the
greater demand for domestic help in these more populated and prosperous towns
as well as, possibly, the greater presence of transient and single people, as opposed
to families, there.

In Westport were such large families as the Cuffes and Wainers, together comprising eight of seventeen black households in the town in 1810 and fifty-one of
its seventy-five persons of color.[53] In Dartmouth was the eleven-person household
of the late Benjamin Cook, a black mariner originally from Tiverton, Rhode Island, who had lived in Dartmouth since 1791. Identified in deeds as a "mustee
man," he had died in the summer of 1815 from a fall into the lower hold of a
vessel then in Virginia. His wife, Catherine, remained with her large family in
Dartmouth until the mid-1830s, when she moved into New Bedford to live with
her daughter and son-in-law. The couple's sons Edward and Pardon both became
mariners. Pardon, who married Paul Cuffe's daughter Alice, was one of very few
black whaling captains.[54] Isaac Simons, who was probably Native American or
mustee, also had an eleven-person household, but probably some of them were
boarders; the town frequently paid him to shelter, feed, and care for indigent
Indians, blacks, and "foreigners."

Cook and some parts of the Cuffe and Wainer families may well have been
boarding single mariners at the time as well. Pero Howland, a free man since Isaac
Howland's manumission of 1774, was seventy years old in 1816 and was still living
in Dartmouth with his wife of fifteen years, Jane Almy, and two others in his

household. Quash Anthony also lived in Dartmouth and had been a "free negro" since at least 1771, when he purchased four acres of land on the west side of Clark's Cove. By 1795 Anthony owned more than thirty acres in the town. Peter Quanwell (or Quanawin) was another early landowner who in 1783 bought three acres in Dartmouth for "25 silver dollars." He and his wife, Martha Job, a Dartmouth Indian, had by then been married twenty years. She seems to have left Quanwell in 1795, when her husband announced in the *New Bedford Medley* that he would not be responsible for her debts, and by 1800 she was listed in her own Dartmouth household. By 1810 Peter Quanwell appears to have moved into New Bedford and taken as a second wife a Hannah White of Westport. About two months before William Grimes came to town, Quanwell died and left six rods of land in the village and the east half of a house.[55]

In New Bedford, along with Richard Johnson and the Howards, were such men as Jeremiah Easton, who was apparently a truckman; in 1814 and 1815 Alexander Howard paid him for carting fish. Caleb Johnson, born 1784 in New York State, had married Mercy Terry of New Bedford in 1806 and was probably a laborer and a farmer; he owned land on Kempton Street in what was later called the Cannonville section, possibly in the section earlier called "Hard-Dig." His two sons became mariners. The clothes cleaner Thomas A. Williams, whose grandson's 1931 obituary claimed he had come to the city in 1781, was about to marry a Mary Mahoney in New Bedford in November 1816. If not at that time, he appears to have been outfitting sailors by the late 1820s.[56] Cesar Tredwell had been living in New Bedford village since 1810 with his wife, Deborah, a white woman from Barnstable whom he had married in 1792, and his five children, Deborah, Jane, Martha, Thomas, and William. His daughter Jane's 1849 poor relief record states, "Cesar was a slave who came from N. Jersey owned a house, the easternmost in the road east fm orphan's home lived there many years." Parts of the Quanwell family had moved into the village by 1816 as well, including Joseph Quanwell, who had twelve persons in his New Bedford household in 1810 and may have been boarding mariners; he owned almost five acres in the Clark's Cove section of the village. Another Joseph Quanwell, son of James Quanwell of Dartmouth, had come to New Bedford at the age of eight in 1807–8 and first went whaling in 1815–16.

Grimes himself did not last long in New Bedford, a fact he attributed to the collective indiscretion of the town's people of color and to the false accusation of a white woman. People of color had somehow fallen into the routine, he stated in his narrative, of coming to his place in the evenings to socialize and dance late into the night. These visitors "had finally got so much habituated to take to their own heads in rioting and carousing," Grimes wrote in his rather self-serving account, that his landlord asked him to close the shop, "to which I replied, yes, sir, I will very gladly, for I see the colored people have imposed upon me." He returned to work for Howland but two months later was implicated, apparently falsely, in the attempted rape of a woman who lived below his shop. Arrested twice on the same charge, Grimes was ultimately acquitted, and he left the city. Much of the rest of his life he spent in New Haven as "old Grimes," running a restaurant, barber shop, and clothes cleaning shop near Yale College.

Northern vessels were not only a means of escape but also a source of work for southern black mariners; for Grimes they were both. Seamen of color who claimed slave-state birthplaces were well represented in northern crews before the Civil War. Between 1803 and 1821 the proportion of Philadelphia's black mariners born in bordering Delaware and Maryland ranged from 26.2 to 34.8 percent of the total and was consistently the highest proportion of all black mariners shipping from this city in these years; when those black sailors claiming to have been born in other slave states are included, the proportion of southern-born Philadelphia black mariners was 39.7 percent of total black crew in 1803, 47.6 percent in 1811, and 45.8 percent in 1821. At least one of every three Philadelphia black seamen listed Delaware, Maryland, and Virginia birthplaces in 1830 and 1850. Farther north the proportion was smaller but still significant: though three of every four black crew members in Newport, Rhode Island, between 1803 and 1820 claimed to have been born in New England, 13 percent identified a southern birthplace; of 1,065 black men sailing from Newport between 1820 and 1857, 133, or 12.4 percent, were born in a slave state. Of 1,516 men of color sailing from New Bedford between 1803 and 1841, 13 percent listed a slave-state birthplace; protection papers for the 3,000 black men sailing on foreign voyages between 1809 and 1865 show that 500, or 17 percent, were born in the South.[57]

According to Bolster, southern plantation owners believed that maritime work made slaves "insolent" and "independent," an assertion that seemed proven by the fact that black boatmen had been key figures in Gabriel Prosser's rebellion in 1801 Virginia; a boatman named Sancho, implicated in Prosser's rebellion, used men of color who operated ferries, rafts, and vessels along the Roanoke River to spread news of another revolt planned for Easter 1802. These boatmen in turn relied heavily on slave artisans, who traveled relatively freely in the area, to help spread these plans to plantation slaves. In 1823 Charleston slaveholders bemoaned the fact that vessels arriving from the North almost always had at least two men of color employed on board, "Abolition Societies in the North," they charged, would no doubt "intrigue, through this class of persons, with our slave population," who would surely be "seduced from the service of their masters in greater numbers."[58]

In the North boatmen had in fact been active in early revolts and antislavery work. Crispus Attucks, the son of an African and a Nantucket Indian who ran away from his Framingham, Massachusetts, owner in 1750, worked on whaling crews and as a ropemaker in Boston before his attempt to persuade Massachusetts governor Thomas Hutchinson to keep British soldiers from taking colonists' jobs and his subsequent, fateful role in the Boston Massacre. In 1807 Paul Cuffe's first biography related how planters on Maryland's Nanticoke River had interpreted the presence of his sloop *Ranger* and its all-black crew in 1796. "The white inhabitants were struck with apprehension of the injurious effects which such circumstances would have on the minds of their slaves," the *Monthly Repository* of London noted, "but perhaps they were more fearful that, under the veil of commerce, he had arrived among them with hostile intentions," to spirit slaves away or incite them to rise up against their owners.[59] Despite northern abolitionists' claims to the contrary, Southerners grew only more certain that such intrigue conspired systematically against their interests as time passed.

4

The 1820s:
Beginnings of Activism

IN NOVEMBER 1822 Nathan Johnson, then about twenty-seven years old, stood in a large room inside Nelson's Tavern in New Bedford listening to the agent of a Virginia slaveholder attempt to convince two local magistrates that he ought to be permitted to take a man of color back to slavery. This man, then called John Randolph, had been living in the village for at least four years, and perhaps longer; he had a wife and probably a child by the time of the hearing. Nathan Johnson had lived in New Bedford probably a little more than three years; he had married the black woman Mary J. Mingo Durfee in the village on 24 October 1819. Where Johnson came from is obscure; he was either born into slavery in Virginia, as some accounts allege, or as either a slave or free man in Philadelphia, about 1795. His wife, always called Polly, had been born in nearby Fall River and had been married once before; she was ten years older than Nathan. By late January 1820 Polly Johnson was doing domestic work in the home of Charles Waln Morgan, who had moved from Philadelphia to marry Samuel Rodman's daughter Sarah in June 1819 and to begin his career as a whaling capitalist. The Johnsons were probably living in the Morgan home, then on Union Street at the western edge of the village's commercial core, when census takers visited the home in 1820. By March 1822 Nathan had himself probably been working for the Morgans for some time; the man Morgan referred to in a letter at that time as "my black man Nathan" was almost certainly he.[1]

Johnson's attendance at the hearing about John Randolph may have been his initiation into fugitive slave activism; no earlier record of his long abolitionist career is known. More than fifty years later, when he was quite an old man, Johnson told a reporter for the New Bedford *Republican Standard* that while he stood in attendance at the hearing "a person stood behind him with a heavy pair of tongs in his hand ready to brain him if there was any attempt made for Randolph's liberation." The level of feeling at the hearing was patently intense. It had been called because Camillus Griffith, an agent for "parties living in the vicinity of Alexandria," had just failed in his effort to seize two alleged fugitives on Nantucket and, frustrated, had come to New Bedford after a third. The people

Griffith sought to apprehend were three of the four who had come to New Bedford on the *Regulator* between 1815 and 1818—a William Mason, a man of color named George and his wife, whose name in slavery was not known, and a free black named William Butler. Mason had taken the name John Randolph and settled in New Bedford; George was then known as Arthur Cooper and lived with his wife Lucy on Nantucket. Where the Coopers and Randolph had come from is not entirely clear. In one account Butler is said to have helped the three escape the plantation of Hancock Lee of Fairfax County, Virginia, but Griffith claimed that the Coopers were owned by David Ricketts and Randolph by the estate of Edgar McCarty. Lucy Cooper may have been free.

In late October 1822 Griffith went to Boston at the behest of Ricketts and McCarty's estate to obtain a "process" from the federal district court by which he might apprehend the Coopers and Randolph. The presiding judge refused his request on the grounds that the Fugitive Slave Law of 1793 did not necessitate such a warrant. Under the law, however, the state marshal whom Griffith then prevailed upon clearly felt bound to provide him a deputy, and, with this unnamed man and a power of attorney Ricketts had given him, he proceeded to Nantucket on 25 October. Griffith later testified that he and the deputy "were in the act of removing" the Coopers from their home in Nantucket's New Guinea neighborhood "when a large assemblage of persons collected round the house and seemed to set us at defiance." Griffith sent the deputy to the back of the house to keep the Coopers from escaping by a rear door, but, Griffith stated, "the threats of the mob alarmed him," and the deputy retreated. Griffith was meanwhile arguing with Francis G. Macy, a cousin of William Rotch Jr., about his legal right to apprehend the couple and their children. Sylvanus Macy then charged that the power of attorney Griffith produced was a forgery. "We are not in Virginia now but in Yankee town," Griffith claimed Sylvanus Macy said to him, "and we want those colored people to man our whale ships and will not suffer them to be carried back to bondage."[2]

Called to the scene while this discussion ensued on Nantucket, a local magistrate told Griffith that the laws of Massachusetts did not recognize slavery and that he would arrest Griffith if he attempted to carry the Coopers off. Griffith replied, predictably, that federal law authorized him to apprehend fugitives from service and asked the magistrate, identified only as "Esq. Folger," "if he did not consider the State laws of Massachusetts subordinate to the laws of the United States." "No," Folger is claimed to have answered, and by this time, Griffith was informed, Thomas M. Macy, Francis's son, had "put his Quaker coat and hat on George [Arthur] and assisted him and his wife and children out of the window and carried them off to a place of greater safety"—in fact, to Folger's house. "I had the mortification to be entirely defeated," Griffith wrote, and so decided to attempt to fulfill his responsibility to the other slaveholder he represented.

Armed with a power of attorney from Thomson T. Mason, administrator of the estate of Edgar McCarty, Griffith went to New Bedford on 5 November in pursuit of Randolph, who, he said, "was well known to me." Griffith claimed that he simply went to Randolph's house and brought him before the local magistrates; he did not provide details. Records of the state's case against Griffith, however, charge that he and one Charles Drew "did make a violent & cruel assault & harm the said John Randolph[,] did then & there beat, wound & evil intreat out with a certain dangerous weapon made of iron, & called a handcuff, did unlawfully & injuriously strike & wound him, the said John Randolph in & upon the face & mouth." The writ also claimed that Griffith, while trying to arrange the local hearing at Nelson's Tavern, had in effect held Randolph for an hour against his will and "without any lawful warrant, or any legal authority whatever." In a separate trial, Randolph himself charged that Griffith had not only hit him but had thrown him to the ground and beaten him about the head with the handcuff; he also said Griffith had visited him four days earlier and, wielding two pistols, threatened to kill him.[3] Whatever occurred, somehow Griffith managed to bring Randolph before the local magistrates. They, he said, "refused to take cognizance of the case," and Griffith then told the deputy sheriff that he should accompany Griffith and Randolph to Taunton, "where justice can be found." On hearing this plan, Griffith charged, Randolph tried to escape through a window, "and when I attempted to stop him I received some blows." Nathan Johnson's recollection differed. "Randolph was perfectly passive," the *Republican Standard* reported him to have said, "and he, (Johnson) was never more ashamed of a man in his life, after the boasts he had made that he would fight it out."

Griffith struggled to get Randolph into a carriage, but before he could leave Thomas Rotch, the son of William Rotch Jr., and William W. Swain served Randolph with ten writs of debt they claimed Randolph owed them. Griffith immediately assumed they were "fictitious claims . . . brought for the avowed purpose of getting him out of my possession." He contended that Randolph was a slave and therefore unable to contract debts, but Rotch and Swain prevailed upon the sheriff to serve the writs. So powerful were these Quakers in the region's politics, Griffith swore, that "they would have him removed from his office" if the sheriff had refused their demand. So Randolph was taken to jail in Taunton, and an infuriated Griffith went back to Boston to get a writ of habeas corpus.

As soon as Griffith left, according to his testimony, Swain and Rotch dropped the charges against Randolph, who "made for New Bedford" the same day and boarded a vessel for New York the next; his friends in the city later reported that he had stayed in New York only a few days before shipping out to Barbados. In the meantime, Griffith charged, Swain and Rotch "pursued" him "60 miles to Boston" and less than an hour later had him arrested for assault. He was taken to Taunton, put in jail, and was there served with a second writ for damage against Randolph. Griffith said he was kept in a "dungeon" for thirteen days at $1,600 bail. The case was postponed to the April 1823 term, which allowed Griffith to gather witnesses, "although every artifice was practiced by these men in New Bed-ford (calling themselves Friends,) to keep back the evidence."

Griffith claimed his witnesses proved that Randolph had first assaulted him, but in order to clear himself of the assault charge, he had to prove, he felt, that Randolph was a slave. Indeed, the entire case hinged on Randolph's questionable status. Griffith asked Butler, who "knew Randolph as well as I did," to testify. In court Butler said he had known Randolph "five or six years since in Virginia; that he was then a slave and that his name was William; but when I asked him the question to whom did he belong, the magistrate, Mr. Cobb, stopped him short and observed, the witness need not answer the question, and if I wanted to prove the identity of the negro I must bring proof from Virginia." The court declared in the interim that Randolph did not owe service to anyone, questioned Griffith's authority to seize him "while resident within the limits of Massachusetts," and held that "an administrator in another State cannot take possession of property belonging to his intestate here without having first obtained letters of administra-tion in this State," which Griffith had tried but failed to do. The court then found Griffith guilty but continued the case to the next term "for the opinion of the whole court," which appears to have overturned the earlier ruling. Randolph's suit against Griffith was tried in October 1823 and continued to April 1824, when it was dismissed and Randolph was ordered to pay Griffith court costs. Randolph, however, was not to be found.[4]

William Butler, according to Thomson Mason, returned to Fairfax County in December 1822, but when news of the case became general he "absconded and we have since received information that he is again in New Bedford." Several men of color with the surname Butler, at least one of them probably born in the South, lived in New Bedford in the early 1820s, but no William Butler was ever recorded in the city. Arthur and Lucy Cooper remained on Nantucket, where Arthur be-came a vocal opponent of colonization.[5] Whether Samuel Chadwick, the master of the *Regulator,* was complicit in the escape of the Coopers and Randolph is unclear. When he returned to Alexandria in the vessel he was arrested; an account in the Alexandria *Herald* labeled him one of those "kidnappers who command their [the North's] coasters." The acting governor of Virginia at the time stated in an application for the extradition of Butler that Chadwick assisted Butler in the plan to carry the fugitives north. Chadwick claimed in a deposition that But-ler had told him the three were free people. Certainly Benjamin Lindsey, the Quaker editor of the *Mercury,* would have applauded Chadwick if he had helped them escape. Though in later years he was far less inclined to take such a decided stand on the issue, Lindsey's account of the incident three days after Randolph's attempted rendition shows the typical Quaker disdain for legal solutions:

When the worst features of a system so abhorrent are exhibited to us, we do not stop to investigate a plea of legal power; we are strongly impelled by a higher impulse—

that of NATURAL RIGHT and COMMON HUMANITY. To see a man who for years has deported himself creditably in his humble sphere, dragged from his family, manacled, and forced towards perpetual bondage, and all for no other crime than the exercise of that freedom to which, by the law of nature every man is entitled, and to remain unmoved by the spectacle, would argue, to say the least, a most unenviable coolness of temperament. We are happy to state, that through the zealous exertions of several of our citizens, the attempt to which we allude has been frustrated. Similar attempts have been recently made at Nantucket, and have been equally unsuccessful.[6]

Why these Virginia slaveholders permitted more than four years to pass before attempting to reclaim the Coopers and Randolph was never explained in the records that have survived. Perhaps they had been emboldened by the successful efforts of Southerners to abort the slave insurrection planned by Denmark Vesey. When news of Vesey's project to take Charleston, South Carolina, with a force of slaves erupted in June 1822, the city's slaveholders alleged that it "was advised, set on foot, and arranged by the agency of free Negro sailors on board Northern vessels." Vesey had worked as a mariner earlier in his life, and several principals in the Vesey plot admitted that black seamen had spread news of the proposed rebellion. No evidence pointed to the complicity of northern "free Negro sailors," but state legislators nonetheless promptly enacted the first of the southern states' Negro Seamen's Acts. The South Carolina law was actually a more general effort to control the actions of people of color in the state—its title was "an act for the better regulation and government of free negroes and persons of color, and for other purposes"—but its third section applied specifically to "any free negroes or persons of color" working as "cooks, stewards, mariners, or in any other employment" on board vessels from any port other than those of South Carolina. The law's third section mandated that any person of color aboard any vessel would be put in jail until the vessel left port and that vessel masters were obligated both to take the prisoner away and to pay the expenses of this detention. Any captain who did not comply was liable to pay a fine of one thousand dollars and to spend at least two months in jail himself, and any black sailor who had somehow averted imprisonment was to be sold as an "absolute slave." The fourth and fifth sections of the act passed a share of these slave sales on to any sheriff who enacted the law and compelled the Charleston harbormaster to report the arrival of all persons of color entering the port. The United States Supreme Court a year later deemed the South Carolina act unconstitutional, a ruling the state largely ignored except insofar as it amended the law slightly so that black mariners would be whipped and warned out of the state rather than sold straightaway.[7] Laws with slightly differing provisions but identical intent passed in Georgia, North Carolina, and Louisiana in 1829 and 1830 and in Florida and Alabama by 1842.

Other slave revolts had been planned and attempted in the eighteenth and early nineteenth centuries, but Vesey's was clearly the most alarming to that date.

The higher proportion of southern-born black seamen on New Bedford vessels bound for foreign as opposed to domestic ports may well reflect the fact that the Negro Seamen's Acts discouraged black men from taking too active a role in the coastwise trade. As late as 1846 the black activist William P. Powell complained that "the Charleston, Mobile, and New-Orleans ports are closed against" black mariners because of "unconstitutional Southern laws" banning their free entry.[8] Yet that some black men continued to work as crew on trading vessels is undeniable, as later events amply testify.

Thus by the early 1820s the South had grown tense over the relation of the coastwise trade, much of it originating in the North, to the institution of slavery. The 1820s was also a difficult decade for New Bedford in economic, spatial, social, and racial terms. Whaling had rebounded after the close of the War of 1812, though somewhat slowly at first; while no vessels were recorded to have left on whaling voyages from New Bedford in 1812, 1813, or 1814, ten cleared for the Pacific and south Atlantic grounds in 1815, twenty-five in 1818, and thirty-six in 1820. The village's whaling fleet was beginning to eclipse that sailing from Nantucket; by 1823 New Bedford's was larger, and it would remain so throughout the whaling era. Yet the industry had daunting supply-and-demand problems in the early 1820s especially, surely complicated by the Panic of 1819. The price of a gallon of sperm oil had fallen at the end of the war and then increased to eighty-eight cents a gallon in 1820, the highest it had been since 1811. But then the price per gallon dropped sharply to sixty-six cents in 1821 and to forty-two cents in 1823. The price of a gallon of whale oil more than doubled in the last year of the war, when it reached seventy-seven cents, and then plummeted to twenty-eight cents a gallon in 1819; the price then hovered unsteadily around thirty cents a gallon through 1829. Only whalebone, not as yet the valuable product it would be after the Civil War, rose more or less steadily, from eight cents a pound in 1816 to eighteen cents a pound in 1827.[9] And while the nation's whaling fleet as a whole tended to land progressively more barrels of both whale and sperm oil between 1818 and 1824, the New Bedford fleet experienced more uneven progress. In 1820 the city's whalers returned 12,330 barrels of sperm oil and 21,130 barrels of whale oil, an extremely good year. But in 1821, while sperm oil production rose to 14,201 barrels, whale oil production fell by two-thirds, to 7,724 barrels; then in 1822 sperm oil dropped more than 71 percent while whale oil output doubled. Sperm oil output in 1823—28,038 barrels—was double what it had been in 1821, but then it plunged again to 5,839 barrels in 1826.[10] Whaling was an expensive industry, requiring large capital outlays for constructing or refitting vessels and outfitting them; moreover, its returns were slow to accrue and highly uncertain. Vessels, if they were not wrecked, sometimes did not acquire a full load for two to four years, and some returned to port with oil and bone insufficient to pay the expense of the voyage. In the early 1820s returns clearly did not permit further capitalization of the fleet, and until 1827 merchants were not able to send more vessels to sea than the thirty-six that had left port in 1820.[11] "Our business in both kinds of oil is miserably depressed," Charles W. Morgan noted in a letter to William Logan Fisher in March 1824:

> We thought it had last winter reached its lowest ebb, but the abundance of the supplies of late will pour such immense quantities into market next fall—and so many depend upon sales to pay their debts—that it may yet go lower—Father [Morgan's father-in-law, Samuel Rodman Sr.] does not seem anxious to sell and will I think be found at the end of two years with a pretty large stock—we are sadly puzzled what to do with our ships—as freights will not pay their expenses—and some people send them to the fisherys seemingly to get them out of their sight for the longest time with the least loss.[12]

"Money is lost on every voyage," Morgan wrote Fisher one month later, and about a year earlier, in January 1823, Joseph R. Anthony had recorded in his diary "a great scarcity of money among the greater part of the inhabitants of the town." Still, whaling had returned enough to the village's vessel owners and agents by the late 1810s and early 1820s that they were able to improve their lives in profound, and profoundly material, ways. Between 1818 and 1820 new families formed; William Rotch Rodman, Samuel Rodman Jr., Benjamin Rodman, Charles W. Morgan, William W. Swain, Francis Rotch, William Rodman Rotch, William C. Taber, and Joseph R. Anthony married. And by 1822 a significant segment of the village's most affluent families had begun to claim land at the top of the rise from the waterfront, from County Street west, as their new domain. Up to 1821, almost all home building among the most prosperous residents had occurred in an area hard by the waterfront, between Water Street, from which several wharves jutted into the river on the east, Second Street on the west, and Union and Middle Streets on the south and north, respectively. It was here that both Andrew Robeson and his brother-in-law Benjamin Rodman built their estates in 1821. But by that time Robeson and Rodman were the only ones to choose to build in the district. Nearly everyone else of means planning to build chose sites on the still-rural reaches of the County Street bluff for their large, often colonnaded, mansions in Greek Revival style and expansive, landscaped grounds surrounding them. In 1821 and 1822 James Arnold, the brothers Joseph and Thomas Rotch, and Charles W. Morgan were all having mansions built for them on or just below (east of) County Street; in 1820 William Rodman Rotch purchased the house Gilbert Russell had built on County Street in 1805.[13]

Building that year was not confined to dwellings. Also in 1822 the village's congregation of Quakers erected a new and larger meetinghouse, a building that might well have been visible testimony against what New Bedford's leading Friends viewed as a distressing drift from plainness among younger members of the congregation, the "outward ease and prosperity, and wordly possessions and honors, begetting pride and highmindedness, and dwarfishness in religion" that seemed to mark the attitude and actions of these congregants.[14] Much more severe and plain than any of the mansions being built at the time and even than the sect's first meetinghouse of 1785, moved diagonally across Spring Street, the new brick-faced meetinghouse arose at a time when the meeting's response to the evident prosperity of many Friends was beginning to diminish its influence. And even though the controversy had nothing to do with the cause of the slave, the escaping slave, and the free people of color living in the village, it opened a seam in abolitionism as local whites understood and practiced it.

The 1820s schism among Friends was not the first time the sect's elders had called to task those who seemed to take lightly their testimony about plainness and dealings with the world. Virtually since it was constituted, the Dartmouth Monthly Meeting had, like other Quaker meetings, brought before it Friends who had strayed from the sect's various testimonies; in 1772 one David Allen was condemned for "being in company with the rabble at the time called Crismas and shot a Goos," which he repented in writing and in person. During the Revolution the meeting had been preoccupied with violations of the peace testimony, chiefly in the form of enlisting in the armed forces or dealing in prize goods, but afterward it grew more intent on eradicating the "defects among our youths and others respecting plainness and other defects . . . amoung us as a meeting which hinder the groth and spreading of the pure seed of life." The meeting brought before it seven men who confessed to having "some time past joined a consider-able large company in an entertainment, with roasting and eating quawhoks, whereat were also provided victuals and spiritous liquor, and after pertaking of the same, with mirth and merriment we (with said company) repaired to a house where was musick and dancing, and so far joined with them, as to remain at the house till the company dispersed." Like Allen, the seven men condemned themselves and begged the meeting to "pass it by as to let us remain under their care." Through the 1780s and into the 1790s the meeting had also condemned members for marrying non-Quakers or "nigh in kind," for swearing or being otherwise "unbecoming in conversation," for sleeping during the meeting, for gambling, for dealing in liquor, even for tying back one's hair with a "riband," a clear departure from "that simple Plainness that we profess."[15]

In the late 1810s and early 1820s the same sorts of infractions presented themselves to the meeting's elders, but those who were cited seemed far less inclined to come before the meeting to renounce their waywardness. When a committee of Friends visited merchant William Rodman Rotch in 1821 to reason with him about having married non-Quaker Caroline Stockton of Princeton, New Jersey, committee members found him "in a pleasant disposition towards Friends, but not at all disposed to make that satisfaction that we think this Meeting could consistently accept of"; when his brother Thomas was reported for having "con-tribute[d] on a late occasion of public rejoicing, to the expense of a band of mu-sic, and otherwise to aid and countenance some of the proceedings of the day," the committee that visited him reported that "he justified his deviations, and had no desire to be continued a Member of our Society." The tendencies among

younger Quakers were distressing on a personal level as well. In 1819 Samuel Rodman lamented the fact that his son William Rotch Rodman had "never been
satisfied with reasonable and moderate things. . . . In his determination to be rich
he has embraced schemes that common judgement and foresight would have
turned from with disgust." The younger Rodman went on to build County
Street's fanciest mansion in 1833 and, according to Charles Morgan, left his accounts "in great confusion" at his unexpected death in 1855. Joseph Anthony
noted that the Quaker hallmarks of thrift, simplicity, and moderation would have
stood many in good stead during the late winter of 1823, when sperm oil prices
were falling. "Retrenchment of expenses of living is the cry on all sides," he wrote,
"but few are ready to commence."[16]

But more troubling to the meeting was a series of requests for dismission from
its most prominent members. In February 1822 James Arnold, a wealthy merchant and son-in-law of William Rotch Sr., asked to withdraw from the sect "on
the ground of want of unity with Society in the administration of the Discipline."
Charles W. Morgan reported in a letter to William Logan Fisher in Philadelphia
that the reasons Arnold gave at the meeting "were excellent & clear indeed & I
united with all except 'giving up the ship.'" Morgan added that in the midst of
this upsetting event—Morgan predicted, "I guess the meeting will take no notice
of the request," and in fact the meeting did not accede to Arnold's request until
July[17]—Nathan Johnson asked to be admitted to membership in the New Bedford Friends Meeting.

> At that meeting my black man Nathan sat during business and towards the close,
> rose & informed the meeting that he had no wish to intrude, but believed it to be
> his duty to request to become a member of that Society . . . speaking very well &
> properly, the request received due notice, and is under care of overseers. I was entirely
> ignorant of his views or intentions—though he is quite plain & has been very exem-
> plary in every respect for a long time—I fancy they will have to receive him and thus
> make up for James's loss—Frank says they will have a new light in a dark lantern—
> So, I have no doubt others suspect, from his location in my family—but I know
> nothing of his sentiments.[18]

Morgan's use of the term "new light" was highly specific, for New Bedford
Quakers were soon split by a controversy between Old Lights and New Lights
that had already affected the Quaker congregation in Lynn. The controversy was
not in its essence a new issue for Friends: the tension between the authority of
the Inner Light and that of the Bible or of the Discipline as interpreted and
enforced by a meeting's elders shook the sect at regular, if unpredictable, intervals.
Beyond this fundamental doctrinal dispute, however, lay a grave concern over
waning deference to the meeting's authority. In the context of the general religious enthusiasm of the time, these dissenting New Lights were more emotional,
less apt to acquiesce to ecclesiastical authority, and less concerned (and some of
them clearly not concerned at all) with what deviations from plainness and ortho-

doxy might signify. Clearly they had come to believe that the "Old Lights" in control of the New Bedford Meeting had made, as William Lloyd Garrison once said of churches in general, "strict outward observance a test of Christian character."

New Lights interpreted Quakerism differently. Energized by the radical "public Friends" (essentially traveling minsters) Mary Newhall (or Newell) of Lynn and Hull Barton of the Hudson Valley, they saw themselves as closer to the sect's tendency to concentrate on the "inner light" within each person, the "still, small voice" that, once heard, establishes a direct communication with God. Old Lights were alarmed, at base, by an individuating process Newhall had begun in Lynn: attending more fully to the inner light made the hierarchy of Quaker meeting seem a "dead formality," Newhall charged, and naturally diminished the authority of the meeting over the actions of its members. Even the circumspect Charles Morgan was affected by New Light thinking, as he explained in one 1822 letter to William Logan Fisher written after the Lynn meeting disowned Newhall in March 1822. "The more I have arrived at and cultivated self examination the less I have found to do with Society or individuals. I feel clear entirely clear from all, and have no connexion with or rather preference to any body of people on earth though I have not at all felt it my place to denounce that nominal membership with the Quaker society, that my birth accidentally gave me, and I do not look or wish to look forward to a separation from them, though as far as I have yet seen my habits and practice are likely to differ from them in things deemed essential."[19]

Repeated instances of individuals attending meetings other than Orthodox Quaker ones, particularly those run by disowned Quakers such as Newhall, were the most unsettling signs of disaffection. Newhall's sermons in New Bedford drew numbers of Quakers; as Joseph Anthony observed of one of her appearances in February 1823, "So many members of the Friends Society attending the meeting gives much umbrage to the Old Lights." On 19 March 1823 the meeting's elders examined Mary Rotch and her sister Elizabeth Rodman, the wife of William Rotch Jr., "for their unity with M. Newell, &c." In April, one Old Light stood up in meeting and called both Newhall and Mary Rotch "contentious and disorderly," which prompted immediate rebuke from merchant Andrew Robeson. In July 1824 the meeting received two complaints against Joseph Rotch, the son of William Rotch Jr. and the brother of William Rodman and Thomas Rotch, first for "being present at places where music and dancing were performed" and second for having "manifested a want of unity with Friends, by countenancing Individuals disowned by our society, so far as to promote and in various instances to attend Meeting appointed by them, or on their account."[20] James Arnold's wife, Sarah, had even been converted by an itinerant Methodist minister and, with her daughter Elizabeth, was denied membership in the meeting in October 1825; at the same meeting Andrew Robeson resigned and Elizabeth Rotch was denied. Disownments and voluntary dismissions mounted: Mary

Rotch was denied in August 1824, Samuel Rodman Sr. resigned in October that year, William Coffin resigned in May 1826, and, probably signifying the worst for the meeting, William Rotch Jr. first asked to be released as an elder and then was denied membership in September 1829. To Benjamin Rodman, disowned in September 1824 and an early supporter of Newhall, the elders of the New Bedford meeting were "a corrupt branch of a corrupt tree."[21]

Friends had been numerically at their strongest between 1815 and 1820, but with the disownments and withdrawals beginning in the early 1820s, their ranks thinned markedly; between 1845 and 1855 the number of Friends in the city fell from 571 to 267.[22] In the 1820s alone the New Bedford Friends Meeting lost most of the more prosperous and reform-minded members of its congregation.[23] There were important exceptions to the general rule of defection: George Howland Sr. and Jr., among the wealthiest of the city's whaling merchants, never left the Society of Friends (fig. 29), nor did Samuel Rodman Jr. or William C. Taber, among the most active of local abolitionists. On the whole, however, those who remained tended to be a more inward-looking group. In the 1820s one New Bedford Old Light Quaker, Job Otis, deplored the tendency of some Quakers to promote free schools for people of color and to join tract societies, for while "these things might be well in themselves, . . . yet . . . in their several relations, bearings and tendencies there was a snare in them, tending to sap the strength of the Society in various ways."[24] New Bedford Friends did not do as Morgan predicted and admit Nathan Johnson to membership, and discussion of antislavery and concern for people of color had long since disappeared from meeting minutes.

The declining power of the Friends Meeting in the village may have created a vacuum of leadership that spread beyond the sect to the village at large, much as historian Edward Byers has suggested occurred somewhat earlier on Nantucket.[25] A lack of political and moral authority seemed to affect various aspects of life in New Bedford. Joseph R. Anthony, disowned for marrying his cousin Catherine Russell in 1820, noted in March 1823 that the whaler *Persia* had returned to New Bedford and begun unloading her cargo on a Sunday, a "wicked" practice in the minds of many local people. At town meeting less than a month later, a divide emerged over whether all of the village's children were to be educated with public funds.[26] James Arnold and Quaker Joseph Shoemaker Russell argued against increased expenditure for public schools, a proposal offered by Timothy G. Coffin, one of the few birthright Quaker lawyers in the village and the son-in-law of merchant John Avery Parker, who was not a Friend. Anthony noted of the issue, "It was the wish of the lower with some of the middling class of the inhabitants of the town & most of Holmes' society [local Congregationalists] with J. A. Parker & Tim. G. Coffin at their head, to have all the children of the Town to be educated together at the public expense in town schools, but they found the town too aristocratic to carry a thing of this kind into operation." The move for universal public education in New Bedford failed by a vote of 189 to 142, a fact that

FIGURE 29. George Howland Sr. and his sons George Jr. and Robert Browne, oil on canvas by William Allen Wall, about 1840. Courtesy Old Dartmouth Historical Society / New Bedford Whaling Museum. Wall symbolized the family's virtue and prosperity in the backdrop, a column and the house flags bearing the family firms' private symbols waving from the topmasts of whaling vessels.

suggested considerable contention over who should determine how the village would develop.[27]

Certainly how the village had developed by the 1820s suggested the absence of any overarching public control over what whaling had wrought. Because no maps or directories exist of New Bedford in this decade, it is difficult to picture the town's particular geography at that time. Other accounts suggest, however, that local historian Zephaniah Pease's contention that there were "two New Bedfords" by the mid-1820s was a valid one. Whaling had created the imposing homes on County Street as well as the "squalid sections" of boardinghouses, taverns, brothels, and dance halls. And these sections were not geographically distinct from the most active commercial areas; Thomas A. Williams's clothes-cleaning shop, Richard Johnson's store, and the mansions of Benjamin Rodman and Samuel Robeson were within two or three blocks of one another, and all of them were within a block or two of the wharves. Samuel Rodman Jr., Benjamin's brother, lived at the northwest corner of Middle and Water Streets, scarcely a block from the site of New Bedford's first mob action—another indication of the absence at the time of clear political authority.

This action was actually two incidents separated by three years and known as the "Ark riots." Both riots, in 1826 and 1829, began in one of the three areas Pease identified as derelict—Hard-Dig, extending from an undetermined point on the north side of Kempton Street west toward and over the border with Dartmouth. But they both concluded in an area Pease did not mention, a cove at the base of High Street, just north of the bridge to Fairhaven. On the shore of this cove was a jerry-built structure called the Ark, which was actually a house built on top of the hull of the abandoned whaler *Camillus* with the sternboard of the dismantled Nantucket whaler *Ark* affixed to its upper deck (fig. 30). The *Ark* had left Nantucket on its maiden whaling voyage in February 1819 and returned with a respectable cargo but apparently in distress; the vessel was broken up in 1822.[28] The *Camillus* had been bought in Boston and sailed from New Bedford in June 1821; it returned a year later only to be condemned. Thus New Bedford's Ark did not appear on the waterfront until the latter year. The strange edifice had a promenade deck of sorts about four feet wide running around the entire hull and accessible by a flight of stairs from the shore. One newspaper account of the Ark affair, published almost thirty years later, enlarged the promenade's width to twenty feet and added that the space inside was divided into thirty apartments that rented for a dollar or a dollar fifty a month; each of these tenements had a bar, this report noted, "making some thirty places in this 'marine' block where liquors were dispensed for purposes other than medicinal and mechanical." According to the local historian Leonard Bolles Ellis, "respectable families in moderate circumstances" were the Ark's first tenants, but it rapidly became "a brothel of the worst character" and a "moral offense to the community." Ellis termed Hard-Dig "a notorious neighborhood . . . occupied by the dangerous and vicious classes" and "a constant menace to good order"; in the 1850s one editor called it "the *Five*

FIGURE 30. *The Ark,* watercolor by William Swift (1834–1911). Courtesy Old Dartmouth Historical Society / New Bedford Whaling Museum. The date of this painting is unknown, but it is retrospective; Swift was active in the area between 1865 and 1911.

Points of this region."[29] Pease had identified two other unkempt sections—Chepachet, in the area of what was then called Cannonville (which may have bordered Hard-Dig and is now the city's Buttonwood Park), and the Marsh, south of the most densely settled part of the city at the foot of Howland Street, between Water Street and the river. Thus the waterfront north and south, and the city's main artery to the west, were hemmed in by these unsavory districts.

Areas like these existed in every port, and they tended, as in New Bedford, to be heavily populated by persons of color. The northeast slope of Boston's Beacon Hill was known as "Nigger Hill," which in 1817 one white minister labeled a "sink of sin." In 1821 the Massachusetts legislature appointed a commission to determine whether to limit the admission of free blacks—"a species of population," its mandate stated, "which threatened to become both injurious and burdensome"—to the commonwealth and publicly complained about "violent riots in that part of the town, where persons of colour are collected in great numbers" over the past several years. In 1823 Boston mayor Josiah Quincy initiated a campaign against illegal bars and taverns and himself led raids into the black sections of Beacon Hill. In October 1824 an argument over yielding right-of-way on Providence sidewalks appears to have triggered a riot in that city's Hardscrabble section, home to poor people of color at the city's northern edge, which destroyed every house in the district. The next year a crowd in blackface carrying noisemakers and pitchforks mobbed the black section of Boston's North End to force an end to its disorderly activity; another Boston mob rioted in the "Nigger Hill" section on 14 July 1826.[30]

Similar trouble seems to have begun in New Bedford at the same time, although it did not erupt as a crowd action until the end of August. On 18 July 1826, four days after the Boston riot, Samuel Rodman Jr. wrote in his diary that a woman had hung herself at the Ark two weeks earlier; that night, he wrote, he heard "the cry of murder" that seemed to him to be "coming up from the Ark and going up Water street." When he looked out his window toward the Ark, he saw lights and heard "much talking," but he was unable to make out what was said. "I have not heard any particular cause for the disturbance," he wrote, "but such is the character of the families inhabiting that disgraceful building and that of those who frequent it that it would not be at all strange if murder should be committed in their drunken and libidinous orgies." The Ark was a graphic affront to order, as Rodman noted, "by reason of the conspicuous position, plan, and height of the building and the little restraint which governed the conduct of the tenants &c"; the "carousing which frequently took place there, the profane and libidinous conversation and language which those most contiguous were obliged to hear and the dissolute manners of the men towards the women" were all "forced upon the observation of the neighborhood for a considerable distance in a westerly and easterly direction."[31]

Yet the demise of the Ark occurred as a result of an incident that took place in Hard-Dig. On 4 August, a little more than two weeks after Rodman first heard the rumors of murder emanating from the structure, boys picking blueberries in Hard-Dig happened upon the body of a white man partly concealed by dead leaves. Though his identity was never established, many assumed it must have been the corpse of a local ship carpenter who had recently disappeared and that he must have been murdered, Rodman reported, "at some small house of bad character kept by people of color about a mile from this village." Indeed, the only things uniting the Ark and Hard-Dig was the suspicion of murder and, by inference from contemporary accounts, the existence of people of color in both places. Local law officers stayed away from these districts, one retrospective account noted, and so an undefined group of citizens decided to take matters into their own hands. Rodman reported that this "part of our population" wished first to destroy the Ark but did not because a child had died in the building and had not yet been buried. Instead they assembled on Kempton Street and vented their excitement on Hard-Dig, where they destroyed "three small houses and a barn which was also inhabited by persons of bad character." Ellis identified one of these houses as belonging to Jake Peterson, "a leader of the place," a man of color who kept a "resort" in the neighborhood; Pease called Peterson "a disreputable character." The only local record of his presence in New Bedford is his marriage to a black (or Indian) woman named Patty Simonds two years earlier. One County Street resident who witnessed the riot told Ellis "he distinctly heard the shouts of the mob and the blows of the axes." The damage was done in two hours, and the group deemed it so effective that its members planned, rumor had it, to destroy the Ark the next night. The Ark was owned by one Asa Smith, who apparently was white.

The following evening, Rodman reported, "the throng in the streets in our neighborhood" made it clear that "something was meditated and expected." The rumors of the raid were sufficiently convincing that five families who lived in the Ark packed their belongings and left the place, but some remained and armed themselves with stones and bottles of hot water to defend the building. Rodman reported that after sundown some in the crowd that had assembled by the bridge began to throw rocks and then hauled a "Quaker" gun—a cannon loaded with sand or mud—to the spot to frighten the fractious tenants. Ellis noted that someone in the crowd even "rammed home an imaginary cartridge and stood ready to apply the match" when, at about ten in the evening, the remaining occupants abandoned the structure to the aggressive crowd. Then men with axes and crowbars went to work dismantling the Ark, but, as Rodman noted, the building "was unexpectedly strong" and "cost them much and severe labor." About 2:30 in the morning, by which time, Rodman stated, "they had got most of the sideboarding knocked down, all of the partitions, & some of the rafters of the roof down," flames appeared near the dismantled chimney. The fire seemed to surprise those wrecking the structure as well as those watching the demolition, Rodman noted, though a later account stated that tar barrels had been brought down in order to set fire to the vessel. The attackers called for water, but no fire apparatus was present; the crowd rapidly dispersed. The flames spread to an adjacent barn, a nearby house, William W. Swain's candleworks, and the tryworks and cooper's shop adjoined to that candleworks. Cinders fell on Rodman's house, but the night was so calm that the firemen who soon appeared were able to save it, the house near the barn, and the candleworks.

The equivocal Lindsey at the *Mercury*, while he acknowledged that the Ark was "a most offensive and indecent brothel," nonetheless deprecated the crowd action. Though he had disputed the authority of human law in the case of John Randolph, Lindsey now argued that civil law must this time hold sway. "If nuisances exist," he argued, "it is not for individuals to assume to themselves the right and to exercise the power of rectifying them by violent measures. The authority of the law is the only proper means for the remedy of public grievances." Rodman's interpretation was different. Like Lindsey, he pointed out that "the civil laws had not been tried, the impression of its inadequacy had not been proved, & it might be incorrect"; perhaps "regular measures" might have put an end to the scandalous proceedings at the Ark. Yet the riot, he noted, appeared "justified in the view of the actors by the infamous character of the house, and the alleged insufficiency of the existing laws to afford a thorough remedy." The crowd, in other words, perceived that the police power in the city feared, was unable, or simply refused to exert control over these seemingly lawless sections.

The town, as represented in the voice of the *Mercury*, did seem to wish to disown the event. In response to a report of the Ark incident in the *Taunton Reporter*, Lindsey made no reference at all to that neighborhood and stated only that the three or four "houses (or huts) alluded to were in the town of Dartmouth, and were occupied by coloured persons, of abandoned character." The crowd's action aimed to settle the question of who would act to put down "the profligacy which has characterized a large part of the coloured inhabitants or residents of our town," as Rodman put it. He could not himself condone the "harshness and illegal character" of the rioters' actions, but he hoped they would "be of permanent usefulness in restraining in some degree the licentiousness of their conduct, and more particularly in deterring any citizen of a different class from outraging decency and the obligations of the social relation, as in the case of the owner of the Ark, by concentrating in the heart of a respectable neighborhood such prolific seeds of moral pestilence."[32]

Yet they were not. Three years later, amid regular reports in the *Mercury* of disclosed slave insurrection plots in the summer of 1829, trouble arose again. Using the hull of another old whaling brig, the *Indian Chief*, whose three voyages since 1821 had brought disappointing results, Asa Smith had rebuilt the Ark some five hundred feet west of the old horror. The *Mercury* noted that this second Ark "transcend[ed], as a den of abominations, any thing that tradition has to relate of Ark the first." The business seems then to have been run by Titus Peck, a man of color who had been born in Bristol, Rhode Island, sometime during the Revolutionary War and had moved to New Bedford at least as early as 1820. Later in life, when he was in his eighties and about to be sent to the state almshouse, a local poor relief official described Peck as "a miserable drunkard" who "has been drifting around, all his life." Pease called him "a bully and desperado . . . his power was so great that it was said that the Selectmen dared not interfere."

But the crowd that set upon the Ark this time was not so tentative. Again the attack on the structure seemed to have nothing directly to do with incidents there; it was provoked, Samuel Rodman wrote, by "the barbarous outrage committed on a white man a mile or two from this place on the road to Dartmouth village by colored men as the maimed man asserts." Again, Hard-Dig was apparently the site of the incident. Ellis connected another event to the attack: Mrs. Josiah Richmond, who apparently witnessed it, told him that some citizens believed Ark residents had that spring set the fire that destroyed the Elm Street Methodist Episcopal Church. Had the fire not been contained, it might well have set the town ablaze, as the church's lower story stored full casks of oil. Ellis said a "reign of terror" then ensued until the second Ark riot erupted. Rodman noted that "for almost every night last week there had been some threatenings of an intention to destroy that building" despite the fact that officials had called a town meeting "to abate by legal proceedings the nuisance occasioned by the turbulent and unmoral practices of the occupants of the 'Ark.'" About town were heard ominous and inscrutable warnings—"Jerry, keep dark north end," "Keep dark south end," and "Jerry is in town." Town officials hoped that citizens would let the law take its course, but Rodman observed ruefully that "the perpetrators of the outrage had no such intention." This time, a smaller crowd—Ellis put it at about twenty-five people—appeared in masks, "dressed in coats turned inside out, trousers covered with white canvas at the knees, and slouch hats," and with a hook and ladder truck began at about ten in the evening of 23 August to batter the Ark and burn it down. Two other buildings Asa Smith owned, another two dwellings, and the barn that belonged to Rodman's father "which I formerly occupied," Rodman noted, were also destroyed. One of the burned dwellings was known as the Howard house, on North Second Street, which Ellis noted "bore a reputation similar to that of the Ark"; upon learning the mob's intention, Benjamin Rodman met them at the house, which cannot have been far from his own, and told the assembled crowd that the residents had left. "There are eleven of us," the masked men said, and cheered, leaving Rodman baffled; the group set fire to the house despite his effort to stop them, and they passed attorney Timothy G. Coffin over their heads and "out of harm's way" after he attempted to "read the Riot Act" to them. Most accounts imply that the crowd was rather good-natured.[33]

Rodman wrote, "So complete was organization of the actors that very little disturbance was made by their proceedings," and this time the *Mercury* almost applauded the attack. "There certainly is a great difference between the riotous outbreakings of a turbulent spirit, impelling to promiscuous outrage and violence," the newspaper pointed out, "and operations, although unsanctioned by law, which tend to a specific purpose of at least, imagined good; and are characterized in the process by as much order and regard for decorum as marked those of Saturday evening." Still it would be better to let the law handle such matters, the *Mercury* suggested, as it attempted an objective evaluation of the growing town's predicament. "As with other maritime places, there is a degraded class of population brought within our borders, which can only be kept within the bounds of decency by vigorous police regulations. As the navigation of the port increases, the necessity for such regulations becomes the more apparent, and we have not the least doubt but that, perceiving the need, there will be found both the disposition and the ability in those unto whom it legally appertains to second the general wish, by adopting adequate measures of prevention in a matter of such growing importance to the community."[34]

After the second Ark riot and a fire a month later that ravaged three "tenements" built and owned by Thomas Rotch on Bridge Street, just south of the Ark site, the town seemed at last willing to act by appointing a 110-man Committee of Vigilance to keep an eye out for more trouble. And by June 1830 private citizens, among them Samuel Rodman Jr., created a new society for the "moral improvement of seamen," which became the long-lived New Bedford Port Society. The founders hoped that boardinghouse keepers would ban liquor from their premises, keep better order within, and "have them closed for the night at 10 o'clock."

In a letter to the editor endorsing the new organization, one "Philonautes" im-
parted "a word to the Sailors": "the benevolent individuals who are acting for you
in this place, are acting for your good," he assured any who might be reading.
"The[y] wish to promote your temporal good. They wish you may have more
property, more self-respect, more independence, a better lot in every respect—a
better hope on the ocean, and better homes on the land."[35] But "the effectual
defiance of the law" that the Ark riots represented continued despite the town's
effort to extend its paternal—perhaps better termed patronizing—hand; arson
grew more frequent, and another "lawless mob" set fire to the homes of people
of color in Dartmouth, probably in Hard-Dig.[36]

Sandwiched between the two Ark riots was a riotous event of quite a different
character, instigated by several of the village's most prominent men of color. One
of them was Nathan Johnson, who had been working for Charles W. Morgan
since at least 1821.[37] By 1829 Johnson was working as the superintendent of a
bathing house on William Street in downtown New Bedford, and by 1836 the
city directory referred to him as a trader. His wife, however, was a confectioner
of wide repute by 1835, and he had entered the catering and confectionary business himself by May 1830. An advertisement he placed in the *Mercury* at that time
stated that he had for sale "Fresh Bordeaux Almonds; superior (French) Olives,
Olive Oil, Prunes, Cocoa Nuts, Oranges, Lemons, Lemon Syrup, shelled Almonds, Spices, &c. &c. Confects, Jellies, Ice Cream, Cake, Candies, &c. as usual
Refreshments served up in the best manner, and charges moderate."[38] By that
time, Johnson owned a shop and a house on Seventh Street, the former Quaker
meetinghouse (held until 1831 by a group of New Lights), and land enough west
of the meetinghouse for another structure. Johnson had also grown interested in
abolition by this time, as his attendance at the John Randolph hearing of 1822 at-
tests.

On 28 March 1827 Johnson, Thomas Williams, William Vincent, Norris Anderson, George Allen, Thomas A. Green, and about twenty other people whose
identity was never revealed went with clubs and stones to a house inhabited by a
man named John Howard. They broke down the doors, smashed the windows,
threw rocks at Howard, and then beat him. Court records are mute on the provo-
cation, but Samuel Rodman Jr. revealed it in his diary. As an eyewitness to much
of the Ark riot the preceding August, Rodman, along with about fifty other persons, was called to testify about the event in Taunton at the Superior Court's
April 1827 session. "There were know nothings then as now," one 1856 account
of the Ark riot observed, and no evidence was presented that permitted any one
of the rioters to be charged. Rodman left Taunton early the next morning, but
his father stayed for the pending trial "of Nathan Johnson Norris Anderson &
others for an alleged riot occasioned by a visit of a coloured man from New York
or farther south whose object it was to get information of run-away slaves."[39] A
jury declared Johnson and his codefendants not guilty, and they were immediately released.

Like Johnson and Thomas A. Williams, most of the identified rioters were men of color of some standing. Anderson owned and operated a soapworks on Ray Street in the city's north end; William Vincent ran a boardinghouse for black sailors and became the city's first agent for the *Liberator*. Howard, whom they attacked, may have been the black mariner John E. Howard, possibly from Baltimore, who lived in New Bedford from about 1820 until his death in 1848. But whether Howard was an informer about fugitive slaves or the man who sought information is not known.[40] The account does establish, however, the beginnings of organized action as well as a growing militancy among New Bedford people of color. During these years the first organized signs of black antislavery activism emerged generally: the Massachusetts General Colored Association, an all-black antislavery society, was founded in 1826, and the black newspaper *Freedom's Journal* issued a call for the nation's first convention for people of color in 1827. Yet the Ark and the Howard riots predate the development in New Bedford of organized abolitionism, which many historians of antebellum crowd actions have identified as one of the main causes of racial rioting. The first documented New Bedford lecture calling for the emancipation of American slaves—by Benjamin Lundy at the old Quaker meetinghouse—did not take place until late June 1828; the New-Bedford Union Society, an auxiliary to the annual colored people's conventions that began in 1830, was apparently not formed until October 1833.[41] The fear that organized abolitionism would destabilize and topple the prevailing political order thus cannot explain the racial rioting in New Bedford, Providence, and Boston in the 1820s. Nor is it likely that the pressure for jobs exerted by a growing number of European immigrants can be held to account. New Bedford's economy expanded rapidly as the 1820s progressed, but it remained largely mercantile when most other cities in Massachusetts, even coastal cities, had turned to the manufacture of shoes and textiles, the major employers of new immigrant labor. As late as 1855 the city was the seventh largest in the commonwealth but ranked near the bottom in its percentage of foreign-born.[42]

It seems far more likely that the city's changing social geography, an emerging differentiation in the occupation and use of its spaces, instigated the Ark riots. The historian David Scobey has argued that urban dwellers construe spaces, particularly such public spaces as the street and the sidewalk, into social "cartographies" that delineate territories and boundaries, "itineraries" that define how spaces are to be used, and "choreographies" that guide how one travels through space. The street, Scobey has asserted, plays a major role in "the spatial script of class formation."[43] Through the War of 1812, most New Bedford merchants, affluent and middling, lived in waterfront sections, and during the trying 1810s population growth had slowed considerably. But between 1820 and 1830 New Bedford was growing more than twice as fast as Boston, which was more than ten times larger in 1820 (3,947 persons in New Bedford to Boston's 43,298) but only eight times larger in 1830 (7,592 to about 61,400).

As prosperity returned to whaling, the town was filling with people, which must in itself have been a remarkable sight. In part, New Bedford's population grew by dint of population losses in the rural places around it. Dartmouth was almost as populous as New Bedford in 1820 (3,636 persons, compared with New Bedford's 3,947), but by 1830 New Bedford's population had nearly doubled, while Dartmouth's grew by only 6.3 percent. The same held for the population of color. Together, Dartmouth and Westport had nearly as many people of color (222) in 1820 as New Bedford and Fairhaven (236), but by 1830 the urban black population (417 in New Bedford and Fairhaven) far outstripped the rural (204). The permanent nonwhite population in New Bedford grew from 160 persons in 1800 to 213 persons in 1820 to 383 persons in 1830; in Dartmouth it declined from a high of 223 in 1820 to 132 in 1830.

And population growth in urbanizing New Bedford at this time introduced the first substantial group of transient people, among them, as the historian Paul Boyer has put it, "young men from the country" who came to be viewed as a "rootless, unstable element particularly vulnerable to the city's temptations." Transient white and black people, certainly many more than census enumerators captured, lived on the margins of society and drifted into town in hopes of getting work on whaling crews, on the wharves, or in the oil, candle, or ship's bread factories; especially the seamen among them populated the waterfront boarding-houses, basements, rum shops, and brothels between voyages. In a milieu where many still abided by Quaker customs of dress and decorum, this new, quite literally floating population must have been startling to behold. And their inherent transience was amplified by the nature of life and work in the whaling industry.

Perhaps they were the citizens "of a different class" whom Rodman identified, the people like Asa Smith who flouted "the obligations of the social relation." Joseph Anthony made an equally obscure reference in his diary in early April 1823 when he noted the "considerable opposition to the old town officers" mounted by "the needy Shaylers that have come into the town the year or two past" in addition to the Congregationalists in Sylvester Holmes's church. Whomever they meant to designate, there is no doubt that the size and nature of the population were changing dramatically and that the prevailing mode of social control—the benevolent paternalism of affluent, mostly Quaker, men—was not adequate in this altered universe. As the *Mercury*'s Lindsey pointed out after a fall 1830 riot in Hard-Dig, "Our town along with its commercial growth has acquired and is acquiring a class of population, for the due subordination of which the ordinary restraints of a country village are altogether insufficient." In 1838 Jeremiah Winslow noted woefully the change in the town to which he had moved as an apprentice to William Rotch in 1795: "The once quiet Village has become the residence of many strangers of doubtful character; the wise and the prudent no longer possess that salutary influence which induced others to act for the public good, the scum of society for a time has had control, and the post of honour is a private station. Unbounded extravagance has succeeded a well ordered economy, and the productions of the four Quarters of the Globe are put in requisition to gratify the appetites of modern Epicureans."[44] Just as Massachusetts legislators worried about the influx of free people of color, New Bedford in the 1820s may have grown alarmed at the presence of many unknown persons in the village who did not come from Quaker families and who neither understood nor respected the quiet force of respectability and affluence that had theretofore preserved the town's "good order."

Boyer has argued that the compact coastal cities of British North America before 1790 were composed of "stable, socially diverse neighborhoods" in which people of all classes and occupations huddled in the principal commercial areas where churches and other such community centers were also located. As new people flooded these cities, these areas changed markedly, especially after the Panic of 1819; tight-knit neighborhoods began "the long decline into slums" at the same time that "an older political order based on deference to elite figures gave way to a system based on the manipulation of a mass electorate."[45] As New Bedford's affluent merchants abandoned the waterfront for the higher, quieter, more pastoral reaches of County Street, the question of who controlled waterfront spaces became a dangerously open one. Though no documents suggest it, one imagines that the women and children especially of wealthy families came to know less and less of these places, and to avoid, if not fear, them more and more. "Those whose walks are limited to the fairer parts of our city," the New York Society for the Prevention of Pauperism warned in 1823, "know nothing of the habits, the propensities and criminal courses, of a large population in its remote and obscure parts," sections that had grown so unapproachable in Boston by 1861 that the compiler of the city's first atlas simply described them as "full of sheds and shanties" rather than attempting to map them.[46] And the fact that, as Pease noted of Hard-Dig and the Marsh, "the constabulary seldom entered these precincts" suggested that police power had also left them up for grabs.[47] That Providence's Hardscrabble riot of October 1824 grew out of a dispute over who had right-of-way on sidewalks is not surprising in this regard. In Providence as in New Bedford it may have been a struggle between permanent residents who traversed these districts regularly going to and from work or to and from town who objected to the visible ways of the impermanent population, and perhaps equally to the cultural differences of new residents who represented the "different class" to which Rodman referred. Moreover, as Leonard Curry has shown, all documented antebellum urban riots occurred between April and October and were often in July and August; the Ark riots both took place in August, when people spend far more time on the streets and sidewalks, which "were, with few exceptions, the only unsegregated places in the city."[48]

The Ark riots indicate undeniably that this contest over space had a racial dimension. The presence of many more people of color in the city in the 1820s, largely single men who intermingled with white men and women in such places as the Ark and who exhibited the rootless and robust ways of seamen, must have been unsettling to New Bedford. It was probably more unnerving to people who were not in control of the city's whaling fleet and who did not comprehend or need to accept how far-flung the search for crew had to be.[49] Assuming that men of color from the South were among those walking the streets of New Bedford, they represented the first of many culturally strange or exotic people in the city, there well before the Hawaiians and other South Sea Islanders whose presence Melville and other chroniclers of the antebellum city so vividly described. If transient seamen were unnerving, so too must the greater presence of southern-born people of color—more expressive, more "aesthetically inclined"—have been both alluring and nettling.[50] Joseph Anthony's description of the visit of a black theatrical troupe to the village in January 1824 suggests as much. "Much sport is anticipated," Anthony wrote, and added that he had attended the group's performance of "Pizarro" the next evening at Cole's Tavern. He termed it "quite a burlesque of the stage" and noted, "One of the fair damsels gave us two good songs." But after a week of performances, the selectmen had had enough of this "sport," banned the performances, and threatened to bring the "African Corps" to court if it did not desist.[51] Even though no accounts of the Ark riots mention promiscuous relations between the races in their descriptions of "licentious" behavior, fear of miscegenation, or racial "amalgamation" as it was often termed in the antebellum years, may have been planted in these crowd actions; as David Roediger has noted, "the crowds singled out places in which Blacks and whites took common sensual pleasures: brothels, taverns and the homes of interracial couples." Still, that unknown and different people, including black people, came to congregate in waterfront neighborhoods probably represented the greater grievance: their presence, to some white residents, constituted an invalid claim on districts that these whites had never relinquished, even if the elite had.[52]

The Howard riot of 1827 was also an extralegal action, an effort to create order in a place on which town officials, including the police, had turned their backs. And the fact that it took place in the frenetic times between the two Ark riots cannot be insignificant. Rodman's passing reference to the trial and the brief court record are the only surviving accounts of this 1827 incident, and it is tempting on their basis to suggest that the action of Johnson, Anderson, Williams, Vincent, and others may have been an effort on the part of the community of color not only to protect escaped slaves but also to police itself at a time when the perceived profligacy of some of their race was broadcast in the press and surely on the street—or perhaps to impress upon the minds of local whites that the same class and cultural divisions that prevailed among them held also within the black population. There were respectable men like Johnson, and there were disreputable men like Peck and like Howard (who, if he was John E. Howard, had married a white woman). Indeed, census data suggest a highly stable population of color at this time. Even though there were more black men than women (212 to 171, according to the 1830 census), about one in five males and one in four females were under the age of ten, which suggests strongly that families had formed in the 1820s. Of the 145 people of color listed by name in the federal census or municipal tax rolls in 1830 New Bedford—that is, heads of household—109 were listed in later or earlier censuses, later city directories (by 1836), or later or earlier seaman's protection papers; only 32, or 22 percent, could be found in no other listing. Even though the census is obviously biased toward the settled population, this degree of permanence seems remarkable.[53]

How many of these people of color were fugitives is impossible to discern from existing records, though the assault on John Howard's house by Johnson and other men of color at least hints that there were more than a few. One January 1824 crew list for the New Bedford whaler *Abigail* stated overtly that one member was a "runaway slave," although the man had claimed on his protection paper to be free and a Massachusetts native. In July 1830 the *Mercury* reported matter-of-factly that "*Mingo Elsey,* a slave belonging to a gentleman in Baltimore, is now in this town for the purpose of soliciting donations to assist him in the purchase of his freedom. Persons disposed to aid the cause of suffering humanity by contributions for this object may learn the circumstances of the cause by calling on Mr. T. I. DYRE, of this town." At about the same time Joseph M. Smith, who escaped North Carolina as a stowaway on a lumber ship, arrived in New Bedford, as he told a reporter on his hundredth birthday in 1911: "I waited until the captain went down below to dress for going ashore, and then I made a dash for liberty . . . when the ship tied up at the wharf at the foot of Union Street. . . . I was over the edge and in the midst of an excited crowd. 'A fugitive, a fugitive,' was the cry as I sprung ashore. . . . Had never heard the word 'fugitive' before and was pretty well scared out of my wits. But a slave had little to fear in a New Bedford crowd in slavery days . . . they stood aside and let me pass."[54]

The fact that the Taunton jury acquitted Nathan Johnson and his cohorts of assault in 1827 also seems to indicate general sympathy for the plight of escaped slaves. And this, coupled with the presence of enterprising black businessmen in the waterfront commercial district, must have seemed encouraging to such fugitives as Grimes, Randolph, and Smith, however long they remained in town.

5

The 1830s:
Organizing Antislavery

BY THE EARLY 1830s the packet sloop *Rodman,* owned by New Bedford merchants Franklin Tobey and Benjamin T. Ricketson, ran regularly between New York City and New Bedford. It carried both passengers and freight, and in good weather its captain, Charles L. Wood, could make the trip between the two cities in less than a day's time. City people often took passage on the *Rodman,* merchants for business trips, families for visits to friends and relatives in New York and, after an overland trip by coach, in Philadelphia. Charles W. Morgan traveled this route often, for he had not only family in the Philadelphia area but numerous business interests that drew him there.

Sometime between 1831 and 1834, the wealthy New York merchant John Jacob Astor put a man of color named William Henry Johnson (fig. 31) on the *Rodman* to New Bedford. Born on a Richmond, Virginia, plantation in 1811, Johnson, along with his mother, had escaped on the schooner *Tantovy,* loading at Richmond with flour bound for New York. An unidentified member or members of the crew found the two a place to hide in the forecastle.[1] As the *Tantovy* approached Sandy Hook it was disabled in a gale, and as its captain cut away the mast on deck, Johnson and his mother emerged from below. At that moment, as Johnson told the story, a fortuitous wave came up and washed Johnson and his mother overboard. Somehow they managed to find a rock in the harbor large enough to cling to until a British vessel rescued the two and deposited them on shore at Long Island. Johnson worked at a Jamaica farm and then moved to New York City, where he got work as a dishwasher at the fashionable Astor House. There he remained until, while at home one night, he heard his former Richmond overseer's voice asking if he were there on the other side of the door. Aping a woman's voice as best he could, he sent the man to a house farther up the street and then fled to Astor at the Astor House. The next day he stepped off the *Rodman* onto New Bedford's Centre Wharf.

During the 1830s Johnson was one of an undetermined number of fugitive slaves who came to New Bedford; later in the decade Frederick Douglass reported that a "great many" of the people of color then living in the village, himself in-

FIGURE 31. William Henry Johnson, photograph by unidentified photographer, date unknown. Courtesy Carl J. Cruz, New Bedford Historical Society.

cluded, "had escaped thither as a refuge from the hunters of men." By the time Johnson arrived, the community of color had already organized its own church and was in the midst of organizing the town's first antislavery society. And by the time the fugitive John S. Jacobs arrived in 1839, the community had created a debating society named for British abolitionist William Wilberforce, had set up a separate antislavery society for women which regularly participated in the annual antislavery fairs, and had begun to organize those who could vote into what the *Mercury* called "the colored Abolitionists." In the same decade white abolitionists organized as well, and the city's seemingly favorable attitude toward antislavery reform had drawn attention to it in other quarters. For the most part, though, except when a peculiar set of circumstances seemed to demand biracial effort, white and black antislavery reformers tended to act independently of each other in the 1830s. Their issues were not always the same. And while William Lloyd Garrison's call for immediate abolition began to tug at the seams of white antislavery reform almost as soon as it was organized, New Bedford's black abolitionists seemed only steeled by Garrison's campaign.

Johnson is variously said to have arrived in New Bedford in 1833 or 1834, though he may have been in the city by August 1831. On the sixteenth of that month in New Bedford, a short (five feet three-and-one-half inches) black man named Henry W. Johnson claiming to have been a native and resident of Boston and born in 1810 took out a seaman's protection paper.[2] The document was witnessed by James C. Carter, who ran a boardinghouse for seamen on Ark Lane, near the site of the infamous boardinghouse-brothel that was demolished in 1829. Boardinghouse proprietors were the most frequent witnesses to such certificates, a fact that indicates their larger role in helping seamen find and secure a berth and a suitable outfit. On 30 September 1833, a black man of the same description calling himself William Johnson took out another protection paper in New Bedford, this time claiming to have been born in Newark, New Jersey, and using as a witness William P. Powell, who had been in the village since about 1829, had himself shipped out on one whaling voyage, and by late 1832 was probably running a boardinghouse of his own for black sailors. This short man could well have been the fugitive; as a boy on the plantation of one Andrew Johnson, he had been trained to ride race horses, a role he filled until he was in his early twenties. He would therefore have been kept slight. Johnson once recalled having been buried in a heap of stable hay, manure, and other waste, with a straw extended more than a foot through this pile to supply him with air, in order to reduce his weight before one apparently crucial race—evidently his last, as he escaped soon afterward.[3] Exhumed from the pile, Johnson came within the weight limit and won Andrew Johnson a $50,000 purse. Johnson gave William Henry Johnson $250 of that prize. He never described how his live burial affected him, but soon after the race he made arrangements, with the help of and a little extra money from his master's daughter, to escape.

Why Astor sent Johnson (who called himself Henry until about the Civil War) to New Bedford is unclear. Perhaps Johnson himself suggested the village; he might have known other Richmond people of color who had settled there. The blacksmith Lewis Temple was living in New Bedford by June 1829; Henry Wheaton was listed as a householder in the village in 1830 and witnessed the protection paper of his son Thomas that year; Peter Nelson, a house carpenter, came from Richmond to New Bedford between about 1828 and 1839. It also seems at least possible that Astor, knowing Johnson's former overseer was in the neighborhood, sent the fugitive to New Bedford with the thought that he might find a berth as a greenhand and escape aboard a whaler. Johnson may have taken out a protection paper with the same idea in mind, but, with no evidence of being pursued and with other work available, he may have decided to stay ashore.

The choice to settle exposed him to an emerging infrastructure of antislavery activity. The Massachusetts General Colored Association, the first antislavery organization in the state when it was organized in 1826, gave physical and financial support to Garrison when in 1831 he founded the *Liberator* to argue against the American Colonization Society and to espouse immediate rather than gradual emancipation of American slaves. By its fifth issue, in May 1831, black boardinghouse keeper William Vincent had become the newspaper's New Bedford agent. Judging by the 1830 New Bedford census, Vincent was one of three men of color operating boardinghouses for black mariners; he had twenty-three people of color in his household, eighteen of them men between the ages of ten and fifty-five. Vincent had lived in New Bedford since about 1826, when he began to witness protection papers for men of color; of the thirteen he signed between that year and 1834, eight were for men who claimed Philadelphia or nearby birthplaces in Pennsylvania, including his own son William Jr. His son Edward, who took out a protection paper just after his father died in December 1836 (witnessed by the white merchant John Coggeshall, whom William Vincent named executor in his will), claimed to have been born in New Bedford, so Vincent may have been living in town by 1820 or 1821.

That Vincent wrote his will in 1832 suggests that he may have been quite old and perhaps unwell, which may also account for the fact that aside from his role as *Liberator* agent, his name does not appear in the records of early 1830s antislavery efforts. By the 1 November 1831 issue of Garrison's paper Vincent had been joined as New Bedford agent by Richard Johnson, by then a prosperous merchant. Johnson, according to Garrison himself, had subscribed to the *Liberator* since its first issue, and by 1831 he had certainly had the experiences at sea that tended to incline many sailors to a serious consideration of human rights. William Nell had chronicled Johnson's early maritime career, including his incarceration during the War of 1812, and in 1824 he was threatened with arrest under the invalidated but still enforced Negro Seamen's Act of South Carolina. In that year Johnson was supercargo (the officer in charge of the vessel's commercial concerns) of the trading vessel *Rodman,* whose venture he and the white merchant Peleg Crowell had jointly financed. Stopping at Charleston during its return voyage from the West Indies, the *Rodman's* black cook and one black sailor were jailed, but Johnson's commercial connections in the city intervened on his behalf, arguing that he could not be jailed because he was "neither cook, sailor, nor stevedore," the occupations specified as liable to imprisonment under the act. According to abolitionist Samuel J. May, Charleston's mayor "demurred some time, because as he said, such a man might do more harm among the slaves, than if he had not risen from the menial situation, to which the free blacks are usually condemned." Johnson ultimately "gave bonds for his good behavior" and was permitted to leave.[4]

In 1829 Johnson transferred land he owned on Middle Street to the first church of color in New Bedford, the African Christian Society, of which his second wife, Ruth Cuffe Howard, had been a founding member three years earlier. In 1832 he chaired a meeting of the town's people of color to pass resolutions opposing colonization. "In whatever light we view the Colonization Society," the meeting resolved, "we discover nothing in it but terror, prejudice and oppression"; its effect on public opinion the meeting deemed "more prejudicial to the interest and welfare of the people of color in the United States, than slavery itself" and its proposal to repatriate American blacks nothing more than an excuse for the public at large "to withhold from us knowledge and the means of acquiring

subsistence, and to look upon us as unnatural and illegal residents in this country." Johnson seems to have opposed colonization for many years, certainly long
before Garrison did. In March 1814 Paul Cuffe reported him to be "Some what
Cool on the Subject" of supporting organizations of African Americans "for the
good Caus of Africa" and with an eye toward encouraging settlement in Sierra
Leone, but Johnson nonetheless appears to have donated one hundred dollars
"and no furthe[r]" to Richard Allen's effort to organize such a group in Philadelphia. Cuffe's letter to Allen suggests not only that Johnson had ties in Philadelphia but that he knew Allen, a leader in that city's black community since 1787.[5]
Johnson was a delegate to the third annual convention of free people of color
in Philadelphia in 1833, appointed to the committee to prepare its address, and
appointed a vice president representing Massachusetts. On 19 October 1833 he
and others organized the New-Bedford Union Society, an antislavery society designed as an auxiliary of the colored convention, and in May 1834 the membership appointed him its representative to the convention's fourth annual meeting.
He was chosen treasurer of the local group at its annual meeting, held at his
Water Street home, in late October that year.[6]

No records are known to exist of the New-Bedford Union Society, but occasional *Liberator* articles indicate others active with Johnson in the group. In its
first year the corresponding secretary was William P. Powell, the New York–born
boardinghouse keeper who was also a founding member of the American Anti-
Slavery Society. The Reverend Jacob Perry, elected president of the Union Society
in late October 1834, had come to New Bedford from Providence to become
pastor of the African Christian Church. Lewis Temple, the Richmond blacksmith
who went on to invent the Temple toggle iron, the most significant technological
improvement in the whaling industry before the 1850s, was elected vice president
at that time. Johnson's son Richard Cummings Johnson was named corresponding secretary; he and his brother Ezra Rothschild Johnson would assume their
father's agency of the newspaper *Colored American* by the early 1840s. John C.
Briggs, a laborer born in Tiverton, Rhode Island, who spent his boyhood years
in the New Bedford home of George Howland Sr. and worked for him as an
adult, was named assistant secretary. On the group's investigating committee were
the laborers David S. Fletcher and Augustus Munroe and the barber William
Berry. The origins of most of these men are mysterious. The brothers Richard C.
and Ezra R. Johnson were born in New Bedford in 1808 and 1814, respectively,
but their father's place of birth is not known. Nor is Berry's or Fletcher's. Munroe
told census takers in 1850 that he had been born in Massachusetts and told the
state enumerators in 1855 that his birthplace was Virginia. Berry told 1850 enumerators that he did not know his birthplace but told census takers in 1855 and
1860 that he had been born in Ohio. Probably only three—the Johnson brothers
and Briggs—were native to the region.

The preference of New Bedford's people of color to organize their own antislavery society seemed to follow, deliberately or coincidentally, the lead of Boston's black activists. There the Massachusetts General Colored Association had made a room in Boston's African Meeting House available to Garrison and his cohorts when they met to organize the New-England Anti-Slavery Society on 6 January 1832. The association's members were avid supporters of the *Liberator* and were present at the January meeting, but they elected to remain within their own society at that time.[7] So, too, did the members of the New-Bedford Union Society after the formation of the Anti-Slavery Society of New Bedford on 4 July 1834—if, indeed, they had been offered the opportunity to join.

Within the white community, William Rotch Jr. and his nephew Samuel Rodman Jr. were the first to enunciate formal antislavery principles in the 1830s. In October 1831 Rodman hosted Benjamin Lundy's second visit to New Bedford, and in mid-January 1832, probably at the behest of the newly organized regional antislavery society, he canvassed the town for signatures to a petition he intended to lay before Congress to abolish slavery in the District of Columbia. Rodman also distributed printed circulars seeking signatures throughout Bristol County and sought the aid of others to do so on Nantucket and in Barnstable and Dukes Counties.[8] In early July that year he escorted Rhode Islander Arnold Buffum, one of the New-England Anti-Slavery Society's first agents and the father of a family of abolition-minded children including Elizabeth Buffum Chace, as he presented antislavery lectures in Fairhaven and at the Congregational and African churches in New Bedford.[9]

Just as the cleric Perry had been prominent in early black antislavery activism in New Bedford, a minister was at the fore of the fledgling local movement among whites in the town. John Overton Choules, who assumed the pastorate of the First Baptist Church of New Bedford in August 1833, had been born and brought up in England and could remember when his grandfather had taken him to visit the great abolitionist William Wilberforce. At the second annual convention of the New-England Anti-Slavery Society, in 1834, Choules told the audience how Wilberforce had taken the boy upon his knee and had shown him the symbol of the Society for the Abolition of Slavery in England—a kneeling African in chains, his face and clasped hands reaching toward heaven, above the caption, "Am I Not a Man and a Brother?" Choules, like other abolitionists able to date his conversion to the cause to a precise moment, said he became devoted to antislavery after meeting Wilberforce and declared to the assembled delegates that a recent trip to the South had proved to him that "perpetuation was the determination of slaveholders." Fortunately, public sentiment about antislavery seemed to him, as well as to Lundy and Garrison, to be changing. "Five years ago," the convention proceedings reported, "he was told that no anti-slavery minister would be able to get a pulpit; now those same persons were ready to say, God be with you."[10]

Choules was elected one of four vice presidents of the Anti-Slavery Society of New Bedford at its founding in July 1834, and he gave its first address. William Rotch Jr. was elected president of the new group. The oil manufacturer Joseph

Ricketson, Choules, whaling and textile merchant Andrew Robeson, and the banker Joseph Congdon were elected vice presidents, and Congdon's younger brother James Bunker Congdon was named recording secretary. Attorney John Burrage was elected corresponding secretary, and John F. Emerson, a teacher and later principal of New Bedford High School, was made treasurer. All professionals or leading merchants, none of these men was then a member of the Society of Friends. Robeson had been denied membership in October 1825, Ricketson in November 1828, Rotch in September 1829; Choules, Burrage, and Emerson were never Friends, and the Congdons were children of a Providence Quaker disowned by the New Bedford Monthly Meeting in March 1790, though James Bunker Congdon joined the local Friends after the Civil War.[11]

Still, the group enunciated nonviolent principles much as Garrison and his cohorts had for the New-England Anti-Slavery Society. "While we seek to elevate the character of our coloured population, and to do all in our power to put an end to slavery," its constitution averred, "we wish to have it distinctly understood, that we look with abhorrence upon every attempt to resort to physical force for the attainment of these ends, and that we shall not, directly or indirectly, countenance the use of any means for the accomplishment of the objects we have in view, but such as are in accordance with obedience to the laws of our country, and the benign principles of the Christian religion." The document's third article elaborated on its first stated aim; the society proposed "to elevate the character and condition of the people of colour, by encouraging their moral, intellectual and religious improvement, by correcting the prejudices of public opinion, and by endeavoring to obtain for our colored citizens, an equality with the whites in civil and religious privileges."[12] By this time, the Massachusetts General Colored Association had become an auxiliary of New-England Anti-Slavery Society and had subsumed its activities within it, but New Bedford's people of color seem generally to have remained aloof from the Anti-Slavery Society of New Bedford throughout the 1830s. The patronizing tone of its constitution, its primary emphasis on the need for improved "character" among people of color, probably did not sit well with them.

At the time that the two antislavery societies were formed in New Bedford, the *Mercury*'s Lindsey (who reported the formation of the Anti-Slavery Society of New Bedford but not of the New-Bedford Union Society) began to take a wary tone about abolitionists, if not abolitionism. He had perhaps grown nervous over the alleged connection between North and South in the Nat Turner rebellion: people in both regions had charged that the surreptitious distribution of the 1829 tract *Appeal to the Colored Citizens of the World*, written by the black Boston clothes dealer, David Walker, to encourage slaves to protest their condition actively, had helped foment Turner's attempted slave insurrection of August 1831.[13] The growing number of antislavery societies, and of mob actions related to stifling them, seems also to have touched off a hostile response among the more moderate.[14]

On 11 July 1834, a week after the Anti-Slavery Society of New Bedford was formed, Lindsay published without comment the New York *Commercial*'s account of the "row" at the city's Chatham Street Chapel "occasioned by the studied mixture of the blacks and whites" at an antislavery gathering. "The rows of seats back of the orchestra were filled *alternately* with blacks and whites—an earnest of the projected amalgamation—and a white man in a clerical dress, introduced two 'dingy Desdemona's' into a pew and took his seat between them! These proceedings, so clearly intended to outrage public taste and feeling, produced the results which the projectors of the excitement probably intended." The New York paper pronounced the meeting "a failure" and attributed the "negro riot" that was alleged to have occurred during it to the "misguided efforts of Arthur Tappan and others in the cause of immediate emancipation." In early August the *Mercury* decried the effort of a minority of "fanatics" to create an antislavery society in Fall River despite the opposition of most of those who had assembled to consider it at the town's Baptist church. A majority of the committee appointed to address the issue reported in favor of creating such an organization, but when the meeting opposed the proposal "a slight disturbance occurred, and fears of a riot were entertained, but by a timely adjournment it was prevented. Thus it is with fanatics in all cases," Lindsey surmised. "After having submitted to the voice of an assembled multitude and finding themselves defeated, they indiscretely attempt to force their doctrines down until an over excited community visit them with a punishment created by their own foolhardiness. They afterward formed a society."[15]

Almost a year later, Lindsey failed to cover the late April visit of the Reverend Samuel J. May to New Bedford but did report the controversy May's lectures provoked in Taunton later that month. Converted to immediatism after hearing Garrison speak in Boston in October 1830, May, a Unitarian, had in 1835 become the general agent and corresponding secretary for the Massachusetts Anti-Slavery Society (the new name of the New-England Anti-Slavery Society after it became an auxiliary of the American Anti-Slavery Society in February that year) and promptly embarked on a lecture tour promoting the cause of immediate abolition. Samuel Rodman Jr., who went with his son Edmund to hear May speak at the North Baptist Church in New Bedford on 19 April, felt that he spoke about slavery "with much force of reason and eloquence"; two days later, May himself noted in a report to the *Liberator*, "a large addition was made to the number of abolitionists" when he spoke at Sylvester Holmes's "Orthodox Society" (Congregational). Jonathan Walker, a master mariner living in New Bedford at the time, may have been one of these converts—in 1848, after his imprisonment for attempting to help fugitives escape, he wrote that the first slavery lecture he had ever heard was May's "some fourteen years ago"—but Holmes himself was not. May told Garrison that Holmes, though "zealous for moral reform . . . has not yet escaped from the delusion of colonization"; he left with him "Judge Jay's Inquiry, which I think will dispel the confidence he may still have in that Impracticable and ungenerous enterprise." After the meeting with New Bedford Congregation-alists, Andrew Robeson's son took May to speak before about two hundred people of color at the African Christian Church. William Rotch Jr., Joseph Ricketson, and "one or two other abolitionists" attended the lecture as well. "I was very much pleased with the appearance of a great portion of them," May reported to Garrison, as though he were more familiar with stereotypes of people of color than with the people themselves. "They looked intelligent and kind. They were well dressed—few of them gaudily."[16]

May then went on to lecture at Fairhaven, Sandwich, and Plymouth, and by the end of April he presented several lectures in Taunton. Afterward, citizens of the town called a series of meetings, the *Mercury* reported, "for the discussion of the question whether it was constitutional, legal or expedient to form a society in Taunton auxiliary to the New England Anti Slavery Society and whether the religious, moral and social condition of the blacks could not be accomplished by other and better means than by immediate abolition, &c." As in Fall River, the majority of the five to seven hundred persons who attended the meeting opposed creating such an auxiliary and instead adopted, in an "almost unanimous" deci-sion, a resolution that it was inexpedient to form an antislavery society in the town. "During the whole of the discussion, it is added, there was but one opinion expressed of the evils, moral, political and social, of the legalized traffic in human blood," Lindsey reported. "The *modus operandi* by which the evils could be re-moved seemed to be the only difficulty in getting at the question."[17]

Clearly Lindsey was not inclined to downplay instances of opposition to orga-nized antislavery work, and that he reported none about the New Bedford society at the time of its creation suggests that none was immediately expressed. Despite the fact that the town had racially separate antislavery societies, New Bedford was already beginning to earn a reputation as a place with unusual racial relations. Lindsay reported that a New Bedford man of color named George Tillman, stay-ing at Boston's Lafayette Hotel, refused to give up his seat at the breakfast table at the insistence of a southerner, who "pushed him away" for his seeming impu-dence, and that Shadrach Howard, the teenage son of Ruth Cuffe and Alexander Howard, had knocked over a pedestrian in a New Bedford street and was sum-moned before the local police court. Then in June 1835 the black boardinghouse keeper James Dyer, who had lived in the area since about 1820, beat James Bunker Congdon with a cowhide strap on Water Street because Congdon, in September 1834, had traced a local cholera outbreak to Dyer's boardinghouse and had pub-licized the conditions he confronted there. Congdon, then a town selectman, variously described Dyer's South Water Street house—four rooms, a two-room cellar, and a garret—as a "little building" and a "hovel" that could house five or six people comfortably but sheltered Dyer's family of "five or six persons" and eighteen or nineteen boarders, all "Canackers" from the Sandwich Islands. The boarders had no bedding, and one who could speak English told Congdon that Dyer had flogged them and "gave them rum every day." He fed them, Congdon claimed, raw vegetables and spoiled pork. The men who recovered at the town's makeshift hospital (among them, it was later discovered, three Native Americans from the Pacific Northwest) were sent to the boardinghouse of Moses Shepherd, a man of color who lived on upper Elm Street. The disease spread to others living in what was clearly a marshy section near Dyer's house and killed thirteen people, including Jacob Johnson, an aged and devout man of color who had "been employed in cleaning out a hole at the foot of Union Street where the washings of the street had accumulated" when he was taken ill. For assaulting Congdon Dyer was fined thirty dollars and court costs (another twenty dollars) in the Court of Common Pleas, a sentence that, Lindsey noted with some embarrassment, invited scorn from at least one New York editor. "'Our colored brethren' seem to be in clover in New Bedford," Lindsay quoted him to have written. "One of them, doing a good business, can afford to flog a white man once a week, or nearly so, for the sake of amusement." Dyer also assaulted Edward W. Greene, a physician and member of the local board of health who had visited the boarding-house with Congdon, and ultimately was sentenced to four years in prison. Yet the damage done to New Bedford's reputation by the earlier fine had already, in Lindsey's view, been done.[18]

That New Bedford seemed rather more favorable toward abolition than other Massachusetts cities and that some of those most sympathetic were leaders of its prosperous whaling industry must have attracted the Weston sisters, whose noses, proverbially, were always near to the ground to flush out energy and money in support of the cause. Caroline, Anne, and Debora Weston (born in 1808, 1812, and 1814, respectively) were among the era's most active and radical abolitionists, and their eldest sister, Maria, born in 1806, edited the antislavery annual *Liberty Bell,* orchestrated (with Anne) the annual antislavery fairs in Boston and else-where, and for a time edited the *National Anti-Slavery Standard* (figs. 32 and 33). In 1830 Maria married Henry Grafton Chapman, whose father and namesake was an affluent Boston merchant who, like the Quaker James Mott in Philadelpha, refused to deal in slave-grown cotton. The Chapman family were abolitionists from an early date and, like the Westons, were Unitarians. The Weston sisters were considered to be central to the so-called Boston Clique of abolitionists. Caroline, Ann, and Debora remained single and supported themselves as teachers, but a major part of their lives was devoted to organizing abolitionists wherever they might be found. All four were founding members of the Boston Female Anti-Slavery Society, created in 1833 as an auxiliary to the New England Anti-Slavery Society.[19] By August 1835 Anne and Debora Weston were both in New Bedford and had probably been dispatched there to begin a massive petition drive. On 1 August Anne wrote Maria that "petitioning for the District" (that is, for the abolition of slavery in the nation's capital) would be easier in New Bedford because Burdett Washington, probably an escaped slave, had "told his story" at Holmes's church the day before. "He came to the Abolitionists a few days previous and was kindly received. Brother Choules behaved like a man & a brother,"

FIGURE 32. Debora Weston, undated photograph in William Lloyd Garrison Collection. Courtesy Massachusetts Historical Society.

FIGURE 33. Maria Weston Chapman, daguerreotype by unidentified photographer, about 1846. Courtesy Trustees of the Boston Public Library.

Anne wrote, using the abolitionist motto with her tongue at least slightly in her cheek. "He told the preliminaries in a manner that was good in the extreme . . . the man then told his story, many tears were shed, & then a collection taken up of 102 dollars & 2 rings. Was'nt that pretty well."[20] The need to identify sources of funds for the always struggling cause was often foremost in Maria's mind, as she indicated in a letter to Debora about a woman who was probably also a fugitive:

> How is Lucilla Tucker? We (the Boston Female Anti-Slavery Society) have paid 14 dollars on her account to Jas Easton of N. Bridgewater who carried her from Boston to Bridg^{er} kept her there for some time I forget how long gave her medical attendance & finally carried her to N. Bedford. We owe him $13 more. How to get it I know not. We have just paid $400 to the cause—paid [illeg] to a a [*sic*] man from Kentucky whose humanity has brought him into trouble—25 for printing sundry tracts—and where to look for a cent I know not—I wish to get this 13 from N. Bedford. I wish Andrew Robson would come to our rescue. Try.[21]

Anne Weston may have been in New Bedford to size up the town and to prepare her younger sister Debora for petition work; according to historian Deborah Gold Hansen, the Boston Female Anti-Slavery Society began a petition campaign "conducted with antislavery societies throughout the North" early in 1836, and Anne Weston "oversaw the distribution and collection of these petitions for the society, assigning different individuals the responsibility for their dispersal in each of Boston's wards as well as in every town in the state."[22] By January 1836 Debora Weston was teaching school and working as an assistant to New Bedford High School principal John F. Emerson. In her first years in the city she clearly viewed New Bedford as a backwater; she was homesick for her sisters and the abolitionists' circle of Boston. That she had more or less been assigned to New Bedford is clear in a letter she wrote Anne at the time:

> I have no pleasure in any of these brethren. Br Emerson is the stoutest of any of them & he longs to have a lecturer come & stir them up, or rather should I say stir him up, for he knows what he wants. Br Choules I think exerts a very bad influence here. Did I tell you that the society bought 500 copies of Dr Channings letter to give away, but poor creatures I believe they did it through ignorance, for when I expostulated with some of them, they said that perhaps it was done inconsiderately & br Emerson said that he was thinking of something else or he should have opposed it. . . . I want to come home so much that I can hardly stay. Though every thing is so pleasant here, the truth is I dont like the thought of coming back. I dont fellowship anything here. However what must be must be.[23]

That the Anti-Slavery Society of New Bedford had invested in William Ellery Channing's "letter"—probably his book *Slavery,* published in 1835—signified to Weston that local abolitionists assumed that because Channing was Unitarian he must be a true abolitionist. Channing, however, did not support immediate emancipation and was critical of the tactics of abolitionists, which he believed so

extreme as to hurt their cause. Weston seems to have suspected that Choules was
more a Channingite than a Garrisonian, as she and her sisters most emphatically
were. Patently, Weston felt, she had a great deal of work to do in constructing
abolitionism of the right sort in New Bedford, and her letters make clear how
truly *organized* the organization of antislavery was in the 1830s. Abolitionism in
this decade cannot be characterized as the mere agglomeration of private sentiments, as it might have been when local people in Nantucket and New Bedford
thwarted the efforts of slave agent Camillus Griffith in 1822; it was, whenever it
could be, a series of carefully orchestrated events that were not only staged but
widely publicized. Debora Weston helped assemble New Bedford women into
their own antislavery society, worked clandestinely in the 1840s with local black
and white activists to test the segregated practices of such institutions as the New
Bedford Lyceum and the New Bedford and Taunton Railroad, and then engineered the public outcry that ensued upon the failure of both to respond grace-
fully to the challenge of integration. She ceaselessly sponsored petition drives,
pricked at local churches for refusing to read notices of antislavery meetings, and
badgered Garrison to make sure speakers arrived in New Bedford when local
racial controversies would give them the greatest impact. When men like Lindsey
and others expressed concern about what they perceived as "the rashness of enthusiasts" in abolitionists, it was such people as Maria Weston Chapman and her
sisters that they must have had foremost in mind. The Westons, like Garrison,
did intend to incite abolitionist outrage and in the process to bring down such
venerable customs as public segregation; they believed as Garrison did, that "new
truths" are, and should be, "disorganizing in their operation."[24]

What Garrison perceived to be the ineluctable action of truth others, like Lindsey, viewed as the onset of chaos. From early December 1829 to December 1830,
both whites and blacks were arrested in Savannah, Atlanta, Richmond, New Orleans, Charleston, and Wilmington and New Bern in North Carolina with copies
of Walker's *Appeal,* and several mariners, both white and black, were incarcerated
for distributing multiple copies. New and stiffer Negro Seamen's Acts were put
in place. And the South's alarm about the spread of "seditious" literature allegedly
designed to encourage slave revolt culminated in a riot at the Charlestown, South
Carolina, post office, an action aimed to stop the flow of pamphlets such as Walker's and those distributed by the American Anti-Slavery Society.[25] But, just as
blacks and whites set up separate antislavery reform organizations, Walker had
meant for literate blacks to read his address to illiterate slaves, while the AAS had
not intended to reach a black audience. Through Samuel J. May the AAS publicly
admitted that it had sent antislavery pamphlets into the South but made clear
that its object was to convince slaveholders and other white Southerners "of the
exceeding wickedness of the system" of slavery. "In no case," May stated, "did we
send our publications to slaves" because they were not addressed to them, and
the AAS knew that few could read them even if they had been.

In a speech before the Massachusetts Anti-Slavery Society, May also disavowed "the foolish tale that we would encourage amalgamation by intermarriage, between the whites and blacks" and stated that, on the contrary, "one of our objects is to *prevent* the amalgamation now going on, so far as can be done, by placing one million of the females of this country under the protection of the law." For its part, the Massachusetts Anti-Slavery Society denied having circulated "any tracts of an inflammatory nature in the Southern states" and having had any wish to "incite discord." Lindsey at the *Mercury* chided northern abolitionists for their foolhardy mail campaign and proposed in its stead a program of far more modest intention. "Instead of liberating the southern Slave they are firmly rivetting the chains upon him," he wrote. "Would it not be pure patriotism in them, instead of throwing themselves at such a time upon their *constitutional rights,* to set themselves about devising means to remedy, or at least not to increase the evil which they have already brought upon the people in whose cause they profess to engage—to restore if possible to the blacks the same liberty which they held before the present commotion commenced."[26]

The charge that the abolitionists' campaign aimed to uproot American institutions was amplified at the same time by the suspicion that "foreign," specifically British, abolitionists were trying to agitate United States citizens to the same end. On the same day that English abolitionist George Thompson's lecture at Lynn was met with hostility and riot, the Anti-Slavery Society of New Bedford met a strange obstacle to their meeting at the town's North Christian Church. In a public letter meant to set the record straight about what happened, society president William Rotch Jr. pointed out that three of the five trustees of the church had granted the society permission to use its facility for its meeting, another was out of town, and the fifth had opposed the request. As the group met, suddenly they were interrupted by singing from the church's gallery.

> It appears that that was the regular evening for rehearsal with the choir. But an instance cannot be mentioned, in the history of that house or any other in town, in which a meeting of the choir has taken precedence of another meeting allowed to be held by the proper authority.... We therefore say, that the singing, by which the disturbance was commenced, was unauthorised, and a device premeditated by a portion of the choir, to interrupt the proceedings of the Anti-Slavery Society. The course adopted by the choir was hailed with applause by those who were disposed to disturb the public peace and all further efforts on our part to be heard, were entirely useless. Not wishing to create disturbance, we then quietly left the house.

Rotch argued that the obstreperous choir violated the society's constitutional right to discussion and that the group had "kept within [the] sacred enclosures" of the Constitution's mandate to exercise that right responsibly. "We claim the right to be heard in vindication of our opinions and our measures, since they are so boldly and so frequently denounced as subversive of the peace and safety of the union," Rotch declared, making a slightly sarcastic nod to the prevailing hostility toward antislavery reform. "We rely on sound reasoning, arguments and incontrovertible facts to sustain our principles."[27] But Rotch's assurances were not

sufficient to prevent the organization of antiabolitionist sentiment in New Bedford. In late August, what Lindsey termed a "very large and respectable" group
of citizens assembled to express formally its views on the "course pursued by
the Anti Slavery Associations of New England." Of the twenty-one members of
the committee that called the meeting, eight were whaling or trading merchants
(though generally not the town's most prosperous), four were attorneys or law
enforcement officials (including John H. Clifford, attorney general of the commonwealth in the 1850s, and Thomas Dawes Eliot, by the 1850s an abolitionist
himself), two were dry goods merchants, two worked in insurance and banking,
and two were artisans.[28]

The committee declared its belief that the Union could withstand anything
except "a deep sectional misunderstanding" like the one abolitionists were then,
they believed, trying to foment. As "good friends of order and of the continuance
of our Union," the group decried the "puerile and . . . inflammatory" character
of some abolitionist literature and, like Lindsey, argued that "we cannot but believe that the great mass of Anti Slavery publications recently scattered over our
country, are calculated to seal the ears and close the eyes of the South, and indeed
combine in one body the slave holding states against the rest, rather than en-
lighten them upon a subject which they better understand." In its resolutions the
New Bedford committee managed to touch upon almost every worry (except
miscegenation) abolitionists ignited—the alarming possibility that abolitionists
wished to encourage a massive slave revolt; the fear that immediate emancipation
would flood the North with low-cost black labor and force widespread unem-
ployment upon laboring whites; the concern that foreign insurgents were making
a play to topple American institutions and leave behind a chaotic rubble; and the
fact that women were being permitted to play a role in public antislavery meetings. The "alarming excitements" abolitionists instigated "have recently threatened the subversion of the laws and . . . portend the rule of anarchy in different
portions of our land," the committee wrote, and members wished to quiet the
concern of the South about what the North really thought. In their view, the
antislavery societies of New England and the Middle States had embarked upon
"a course marked by a headlong and reckless philanthropy, in which neither present danger, nor the safety and tranquillity of all are judiciously considered—a
course which if adopted by the North unanimously, would instantly dissolve the
Union—a course in which children and foreigners are invited to participate;
whereas so serious and momentous a question should be left only to the consideration of grown men and citizens." Because only the South could eradicate slavery,
it was the duty of the North "to leave the subject to the calm consideration of the
benevolent and thinking among them," the group concluded. The committee, as
its resolutions finally pointed out, was against slavery, but only if slavery could be
ended "without sacrificing the rights and endangering the domestic safety, and
impoverishing the white population."

Aside from a fundamental antipathy for slavery, New Bedford's abolitionists and antiabolitionists had another feature in common: both were primarily interested, as was the American Anti-Slavery Society, in speaking to white people in the belief that only whites convinced of the moral error of slavery could end the institution. Even the aggressive Weston sisters were not interested in mobilizing the community of free people of color, which was an internal effort rarely helped along by the visits of abolitionists of either race. Whites and nonwhites did occasionally work in concert in the 1830s—in 1835 Anne Weston reported that three of the fifteen New Bedford delegates attending an upcoming antislavery convention in Fall River were black,[29] and black and white women sometimes worked together to produce goods and set up tables at the annual antislavery fairs. Later, the Westons may have instigated the efforts of men of color to join New Bedford's Lyceum. But generally the New-Bedford Union Society seems to have set and followed its own course.

Whether the Westons' petition drives embraced the black community is not known, but it seems unlikely that the 1837 petitions presented to Massachusetts lawmakers by the New Bedford community of color had been sponsored by the Boston Clique. In April of that year, Ezra R. Johnson and "122 other Coloured Citizens of Massachusetts," all male, petitioned the Massachusetts House "on the subject of slavery and the slave laws"; this document was accompanied by another signed first by Johnson's stepmother, Ruth, and "106 other colored ladies" of the state, the great majority of them New Bedford women.[30] These petitions were not about the favorite subjects of the Boston Female Anti-Slavery Society—banning slavery in the District of Columbia and the new state of Texas, protesting the admittance of Arkansas as a slave state—but rather objected to policies that directly and specifically impinged upon the rights of people of color. They protested, first, the Negro Seamen's Acts, by then in place in nearly every southern state, and, second, the laws that banned or severely regulated the admission of free persons of color into southern states. The petitioners claimed that they "do know and can prove, that several worthy citizens of this Common wealth have been seized in southern ports and for no other reason than the color of their skins" and that "many" Massachusetts citizens had been "presumed to be some runaway slave," jailed, and, if no testimony of their freedom was proffered, sold into slavery to pay the costs of their imprisonment. "Some of them have been redeamed [*sic*] from bondage," the petitions noted, "but others have been hurried off beyond the reach or knowledg [*sic*] of their relations or friends."

Most of the events for which New Bedford's people of color organized in the 1830s similarly revolved around an organic sense of their own rights. In this decade they seem to have settled on Richard Johnson, Nathan Johnson, and William P. Powell to lead and represent them. Nathan Johnson attended the second annual free colored people's convention in 1832 and the third, with Richard Johnson, in 1833; he attended the fourth with Jacob Perry, minister of the African Christian Church. Both Johnsons visited Samuel J. May when he came to speak in New Bedford in 1835; May commented that Richard Johnson "somewhat resembles our friend James Forten of Philadelphia," a prosperous sailmaker and leader in that city's black community. Nathan Johnson was elected one of the two vice presidents of the Fifth Annual Convention for the Improvement of Free People of Colour, a meeting Powell also attended. In the *Liberator* Powell and others thanked both "Capt. Vanderbelt" of the steamer *Lexington* and the "select boarding house" of Serena Gardner in Philadelphia for the quality of the accommodations and treatment extended them, notices that foreshadowed the 1840s interest in segregation issues. By the mid-1830s Powell ran his boardinghouse for mariners of color on temperance principles, and he once recalled with pride "that free black sailors had distributed David Walker's Appeal to slaves in the South." An active abolitionist all his life, Powell may have helped Walker in his efforts to circulate the *Appeal* in this way while he was living in New Bedford.[31] Richard Johnson, in addition to serving as subscription agent for the *Liberator* and helping to organize the New-Bedford Union Society, had also tried to sell subscriptions to the New York newspaper *Colored American,* despite the "pressure in money affairs" that weighed upon the country after the Panic of 1837.

By this time William Henry Johnson had probably taught himself to read by struggling through the law books in the office of Timothy G. Coffin. When he came to New Bedford, one of his first jobs had been to sell soap on commission— two cents per cake—possibly for the black manufacturer Norris Anderson or for Zenas Whittemore. Whittemore, who was white, was an early subscriber to the *Liberator* and for decades employed Henry O. Remington, a central figure in New Bedford's community of color. Benjamin Lindsey then appears to have hired Johnson to carry the *Mercury* to subscribers, and Johnson added to his income by working as a stevedore on the docks, a sawyer, a lamplighter, and a domestic for the families of Seth Russell (at six dollars a month) and John Henry Clifford (at thirty dollars a month and board). In 1836 he married the widow of the Hawaiian mariner Peter Perry at Clifford's house, where he was then working. For a time he also worked at the city's Mansion House, its earliest hotel and the former home of William Rotch Sr., where he earned twelve dollars a month. On learning that Johnson had taught himself to read, Coffin gave him "copies to imitate" to help him learn to write. Johnson then began to read law in the New Bedford office of Francis L. Porter, and by 1842 had qualified for the bar. But by the late 1830s he had also turned his mind to antislavery reform. He joined the Wilberforce Debating Society, organized by 1839, and by the early 1840s he had joined the antislavery lecture circuit. Johnson's trajectory, though established earlier than most, was not unusual for a fugitive in New Bedford. Both John S. Jacobs and Frederick Douglass, who also came to the city in the 1830s, set upon markedly similar paths. Each had been illiterate: Douglass taught himself to read and write before escaping slavery; Jacobs developed these skills on a New Bedford whaling vessel and Johnson in a New Bedford law office. As they strove to support themselves through whatever work they could find, all three men came to the antislavery podium conscious of their lack of erudition and polish. Yet they each made a forcible impression because they showed slavery, to use Johnson's words, "just as it is."

That the village was attractive to people of color in the 1830s is unquestionable. It was a highly active port by that decade, and whaling and maritime trade, its principal industries, were historically the most welcoming of all occupations to men of African descent.[32] For the first time, the rate of growth among the population of color outpaced that of the white population; the white population of New Bedford grew by 57.2 percent in the 1830s, but the black population increased by 86.6 percent. The earlier rural-to-town migration became more pronounced. The ratio of urban to rural population among blacks—that is, that part of the population living in New Bedford and Fairhaven, the commercially oriented parts of what had been Dartmouth—was almost the inverse of what it had been in 1800. Then, 37.8 percent of the black population lived in New Bedford and Fairhaven; in 1830 67.5 percent did. The differential grew more extreme during the 1830s: by 1840, 93.4 percent of all people of color in this region were living in New Bedford and Fairhaven, 87.2 percent in New Bedford alone. And where nearly a third of the village's black population lived in the households of whites in 1820, only 12 percent did by 1830, which indicates the growing possibility that a family of color could live a relatively independent life. No white household in Westport, Dartmouth, or Fairhaven was home to more than a single person of color, but in 1830 New Bedford some whites had two or three black men, women, and children living in their households, probably working as domestics and as coachmen and porters in their businesses. The proportion of the black population living in white households fell only slightly, to 10.9 percent, by 1840, which suggests a fairly constant demand for domestic help in the town's affluent households.[33]

Still, it was clearly possible for people of color to establish themselves in New Bedford by the 1830s. Paul Cuffe and Peter and Alexander Howard had all died long before, but Richard Johnson had grown prosperous enough to own a share of the whaleship *Francis* in 1835 and to become sole owner of the *Rising States* in August 1836. By 1842 Johnson doubled his share of the *Francis* from one-sixteenth to one-eighth and also owned part of the whaler *Washington*.[34] New Bedford assessors valued his property in 1837 at $13,800. When he died in 1853, Johnson's estate was appraised at $31,637, including several buildings and land. By 1835 Nathan Johnson, apparently not related to Richard, owned what Samuel J. May termed a "very pretty estate" including a large lot, at least two houses, and residential and commercial property in other parts of town; in 1849 he was taxed for $15,500 of real estate and $3,200 in personal estate. He and his wife ran a fancy confectionary patronized by the city's wealthiest residents, and at one point Johnson ran a bath house and a dry goods store and owned a share of the whaleship *Draper*.[35] William Mingo, earlier in a Dartmouth dry goods partnership, had moved into New Bedford by 1830 and worked as a cabinetmaker. When he died in 1837, Norris Anderson owned a house, lot, and soap factory valued at $3,700 on Ray Street, in a neighborhood north of downtown that abutted the wharves above the bridge to Fairhaven. Next door, just to the south, was the two-story boardinghouse of James W. Harris, also black, who had come to New Bedford to go to sea about 1830 and worked and lived at first in the home of whaling merchant David R. Greene. When Harris died in 1846, his 113 Ray Street house, barn, and outbuildings were valued at $2,500.

By the late 1830s Richard Johnson's sons, Richard C. and Ezra R. (who had trained as a sailmaker but is said to have been unable to earn a living as one in New Bedford), seem to have assumed much of the responsibility for their father's trading business. It seems clear, too, that the firm also outfitted sailors; the brothers advertised in the *Colored American* for "five or six first-rate tailoresses" to work in New Bedford, probably sewing clothes for seamen.[36] Near their Water Street business was the clothes cleaner Thomas A. Williams, whose shop was "a few doors South of the 'Cheap store' near the Four Corners." Lewis Temple, the blacksmith, was farther south still, in a shop on Coffin's wharf at the foot of Walnut Street. On North Water Street was the boardinghouse of William P. Powell. Black stevedores such as Abraham Rodman and John Briggs, boardinghouse keepers such as William Vincent and James Carter, ropemakers and riggers, caulkers and coopers all worked and sometimes lived in the waterfront area.

Commentators of both races, including Samuel J. May, noted with surprise the prosperity of such local people of color as Nathan and Richard Johnson, which indicates how unusual it must have been generally. In 1837, when the black activist Charles B. Ray visited New Bedford for the *Colored American,* he noted that men of color wholly owned the whaleship *Rising States* and that "nearly all" of the black "resident citizens" owned their own village homes and lots, "and many a number of houses, and are quite rich." Property ownership was not as wholesale as Ray suggested—in the same article he estimated that only fifty of New Bedford's twelve hundred people of color owned real estate—but what New Bedford people of color had been able to achieve relative to black populations in other American cities seemed generally impressive. Ray stated that the real property owned by people of color in the village was collectively worth seventy thousand dollars; six years later Ezra R. Johnson put the total at one hundred thousand dollars, "and gradually increasing."[37] "We have few in affluent circumstances," Johnson averred, but he and his brother Richard C. Johnson were among those few, thus presenting the real possibility of acquiring, if not wealth, at least some financial stability.

It was chiefly this possibility and its occasional realization that impressed African American leaders about New Bedford. They cared little, if at all, whether these features arose from the need of black labor on whaling and other vessels or from that need combined with a certain civic predisposition, shaped by Quaker ideology, to the idea of equal treatment. People of color were not treated as equals in New Bedford, but that they could achieve at all was the fact that resonated with people of color elsewhere, North and South. Ray declared that New Bedford's black population was "better off than in any other place."[38]

Ray's visit was not made at the request of white abolitionists, and it is equally improbable that whites initiated the efforts of New Bedford's citizens of color to mobilize for the 1837 elections. The legal basis of black suffrage in Massachusetts is murky; nonetheless, while some free states, including Rhode Island, Connecticut, and New York, had attempted to restrict the franchise to white males, black men seem to have been eligible to vote since the state's constitution was ratified in June 1780.[39] New Bedford's black voters met at the African Christian Church in early November 1837 to propose their own list of candidates to serve as representatives to the Massachusetts General Court (meaning the Senate and House) and resolved as well "to interrogate all candidates in this county for legislative offices" on four issues—whether liberty was "the birthright of all men"; whether the United States Congress had the power, and should immediately employ it, to abolish slavery in the District of Columbia and in the territories; whether Congress had the authority and responsibility to abolish the "internal or domestic slave trade"; and whether they would vote to instruct all federal representatives to preserve "to the people" the freedoms of speech and the press and the right to petition "or remonstrance." These citizens, among them Richard C. and Ezra R. Johnson, John Briggs, William P. Powell, and Nathan Johnson, also expressed an early lack of faith in the two-party system. "We have not as yet discovered any sincerity in either party," they declared, and viewed it to be their duty as abolitionists to "stand aloof from all political parties" and vote only for men who responded favorably to the group's four queries.[40]

The black community in New Bedford managed to organize in spite of and probably partly because of the hostility they faced throughout the 1830s. The response to the second Ark riot did seem to stifle activities citizens found objectionable around the Ark, which continued to be a small enclave of largely black settlement, but racially motivated attacks continued at Hard-Dig; to Lindsey the neighborhood remained a "haunt of infamy and vice," and even the 1845 city directory called it a "neighborhood of bad repute."[41] Rodman recorded that "a lawless mob" had burned down two houses occupied by people of color in this district in October 1830, an event that occurred after a drunken militia muster and prompted a counterattack on the part of several men of color. In late November the Supreme Judicial Court found three men, Consider Andrews, William Young, and David Healy, guilty of rioting "at the house of Joshua Drew, in New-Bedford" and sentenced them to six and seven months of hard labor at the town's house of correction; a man of color named Leonard M. Gibson was also found guilty of assault and battery on one Elihu Mosher and sentenced to two months' hard labor at the same place.[42]

Four years later a fire of unstated origin, in a town where arson was not uncommon,[43] struck a range of commercial and residential buildings on South Water and First Streets, including two small tenements on First Street that Richard Johnson owned and rented to families. Rodman noted in his diary, "Ten or twelve buildings including two torn down on the ast [*sic*] side of First Street to stay its ravages were destroyed, most of them large and all on the west of Water Street dwelling houses, one of them occupied by a large number of poor families who could do but little more than escape from the fury of the flames with their lives." One year after that, a group of fifteen to twenty sailors, who had come to New Bedford from New York City "to get on whaling voyages," set upon Hard-Dig and with "bullet and buckshot" killed a man called Henry Mariner. The surname of the murdered man suggests strongly that he was a seaman and that he may have been a South Sea Islander, who were often given either straightforward or jocular names by the masters who registered them in foreign ports. The *Mercury's* account of this riot did not describe any racial dimension, but in a letter to his boyhood friend Benjamin S. Rotch, a young Joseph Ricketson Jr. stated, "There was a row up to 'Hard dig' last night; some sailors undertook to tear down a niggers house and the 'nig' shot two of them, one slightly & the other very dangerously." On the same day Rodman noted that "an affray at a house of ill fame in Dartmouth about 1 mile on the Smith Mill's Road" had left one man dead and another badly wounded. Mariner, the *Mercury* noted, was put immediately into a wagon and taken down to his boardinghouse in New Bedford, where he died of his wounds at four o'clock in the morning.[44]

In later years Joseph Ricketson, probably the most steadfast and active of the city's white abolitionists through the 1840s and 1850s, stopped using the term "nigger." But Debora Weston used it on occasion in letters to her sisters, a tendency that suggests how far at bay even some of the most sympathetic white abolitionists kept people of color from their lives and activities, particularly in the organizing 1830s. More conservative members of the community, such as the Episcopalian minister Nathaniel T. Bent, with whom Weston boarded in her first terms of teaching in New Bedford, were of course more apt to express negative ideas about people of color. In early 1837 Debora Weston wrote of having gone "up to Nathan's [Johnson] to get some free labour candy" (that is, produced by free, not slave, workers) and to ask about the antislavery meeting he and "Old Andrew Robeson" had attended at the request of the local antislavery society. (It may have been a meeting of the Bristol County Anti-Slavery Society, organized on 1 August 1836 at the region's first celebration of "the anniversary of the great deliverance of the oppressed in the British West Indies.")[45] "I had a real powwow with him," she wrote to her sister Anne, "& he said that both & [*sic*] he & Mr. Robeson thought it was the best meeting they ever attended. Mr. Bent thinks Nathan takes great airs upon himself, for he & his wife went in a carriage."[46]

Nathan Johnson was not alone in selling goods produced by free labor in the 1830s; in 1838 Ezra and Richard C. Johnson advertised "free labor produce" at their grocery at 25 South Water Street. They offered both white and brown sugar, molasses, rice, and coffee, perhaps produced by free black West Indian labor.[47] Debora Weston made a point of wearing silk stockings and gowns in preference to ones made of cotton. Within the next year the black community had organized its Wilberforce Debating Society and the New Bedford Female Union Society.

Society officers Sarah Ann Rosier, Amelia J. Piper, Cynthia Potts, Mary Ann Kendall, and Christina F. Newell announced in the late summer of 1839 that they would sponsor their own fair on New Year's Day of 1840 to raise funds for the *Liberator* and the Massachusetts Anti-Slavery Society and reported that the group met twice weekly to knit and "talk over the wrongs of our countrymen and women in chains, and pray that the time will soon come when every yoke shall be broken—when all oppression, (whether it be southern slavery or northern prejudice,) shall cease in our land and the world." In August 1839 the Wilberforce Debating Society held a public meeting to celebrate the birthday of British abolitionist William Wilberforce with an address by the tailor Paul C. Howard, Paul Cuffe's grandson and Shadrach Howard's brother, who held the audience "in breathless silence for near three quarters of an hour," the *Liberator* reported.

Two months earlier New Bedford's citizens of color had convened to voice their disapproval of the new Massachusetts Abolition Society, formed by antislavery advocates who had begun to mirror the fears of the population at large— that Garrison and his supporters were insurrectionists because they disdained the political process, repudiated the authority and castigated the timidity of pastors and church organizations, and welcomed the participation of such women as the Grimké sisters and Abby Kelly in antislavery meetings.[48] Chaired by boarding-house keeper William P. Powell, the meeting termed "distinct and palpable false-hoods" the new organization's charges that the "old" Massachusetts Anti-Slavery Society "lent its sanction to the peculiar sentiments of the Non-Resistance Society" and required its members not to vote. The meeting charged that the new organization had been founded by "certain *clerical, political jugglers*" and was a "dangerous institution, and unworthy of our confidence and support"; if these dissidents "through their *desperate recklessness,* succeed in removing the old landmark (the Mass. Anti Slavery Society,) the *tried* friends of the slave will soon become an easy prey to the violence of popular fury, and Slavery, the curse of this great nation, fatten on the spoils of victory!" The meeting endorsed the participation of women in the movement both because it was their "chartered right" and because without them "the bleeding slave" would lose "their invaluable services." It threw its entire support behind Garrison, "the bold and uncompromising opponent of American slavery."[49]

The most significant evidence of the political sophistication of New Bedford's citizens of color, though, was their perceived influence in elections, particularly in 1839, when they offered Nathaniel A. Borden as a candidate for the Massachusetts House of Representatives from Bristol County. Borden, a Nantucket native then about thirty years old, had been a mariner in the late 1820s but became partners with the former slave Thomas T. Robeson in a restaurant and grocery in New Bedford by the late 1830s; he was very often an officer of meetings of people of color and went on to play a central role in the desegregation struggles of the 1840s. Throughout 1839 the candidates for key state office had issued responses, often rather less than direct, to abolitionists' queries about their antislavery platforms, and by late November the citizens of color had resolved, as Borden put it, "that in union there is strength, and united we will be." The meeting resolved not to vote for any candidate for governor, lieutenant governor, or the legislature who did not openly support immediate abolition and that any abolitionists "who let predilections for party predominate over their acknowledged sense of duty are hypocritical in their professions and false to the principles of true republicanism." At the meeting, New Bedford people of color endorsed the senatorial candidacies of Whigs Seth Whitmarsh and Nathaniel B. Borden, Fall River's most prominent white abolitionist, and Van Burenite Foster Hooper.[50] "The 'Bristol County Abolition Sc,' have *run* or rather got out their nominations for office," Debora Weston reported to Maria Weston Chapman in early November. "Wendell Phillips for Gov—Rodney French, Borden, & two others all I believe supports of the old soc. . . . The whole town is up in arms about the Elections, which are very closely contested, & as the col'd people hold the balance of power   all the politicians are violent abolitionists."[51] She presented a more serious analysis in a letter later that month, when a second election had been called to fill other seats:

> The col'd people here, who by the way, control it is said the election, held a meeting last week & passed excellent resolutions. I will send you the paper. Saturday afternoon I saw John F Emerson, whom the whig party put up to get abolition votes. . . . I expect in the course of these elections to come out bright non-resistance I could see John's mind, which when I went to Boston was in an excellent state, beginning to be warped by party notions. He was complaining of the col'd people, who he said passed very good resolutions, but yet were not going to act up to them—They were going to vote a democratic ticket.[52]

That Weston and apparently others believed the votes of New Bedford's colored citizens could determine the election seems on its face absurd; according to the 1839 voters' list published by the city, registered voters (that is, men) of color numbered, at a minimum, seventy-three and were only 3.3 percent of the 2,215 voters in New Bedford. But the election returns show how those seventy-three and indeed even fewer votes might have acted as a powerful swing. Edward Everett (whose letter to Edmund Quincy endorsed immediate emancipation based on the success of the plan on several of the British West Indies islands) won in New Bedford and in the state at large against Marcus Morton, whose antislavery sympathies were widely doubted. Wendell Phillips, a candidate for lieutenant governor, received fifty-one votes in New Bedford but lost overwhelmingly. In addition to supporting Whitmarsh, Nathaniel B. Borden, and Hooper, the "colored abolitionists" also supported Whigs George Howland Jr. and John F. Emerson; Van Burenites Rodney French, John Bailey, and Isaac Taber; and independents Joseph Ricketson, Nathaniel A. Borden, and John Burbank for representatives. Like Phillips, Borden and Burbank each received fifty-one votes, which strongly suggests the existence of a bloc of voters of the sort Borden himself had wished for in the late October meeting of black citizens. It seems likely that those fifty-one were men of color, whose votes Weston believed critical in the election. And indeed, while fifty-one votes could win a seat for no one, they may well have swung the election to particular candidates. In New Bedford 1,643 voters were recorded in the election, and representatives needed half of those votes, or 822, to win a seat in the House. In its report on the local election results, the *Mercury* rather brashly affixed a typographic dagger to the names of Howland, Emerson, French, Taber, Bailey, Ricketson, Burbank, and Borden and stated in the key, "The names to which this mark is prefixed were voted for by the colored Abolitionists." John F. Emerson, a man of little renown locally except among abolitionists, received the most votes of any candidate—865—but only fifty-eight votes separated him from his least successful Whig challenger, and only forty-three votes clinched his victory. George Howland Jr. was the second most popular candidate, with 844 votes, and Isaac Taber the third, with 824 votes. Morgan, the only candidate whom the abolitionists of color had not endorsed, squeaked into the house with 823 votes, only one more than he needed for election; though he had friends and business relations with more people of color than probably any other white merchant in New Bedford at the time, voters of color might have perceived in him the same quality Debora Weston had—that he "is swayed about by every wind of doctrine." All three of the candidates black abolitionists supported for state senator won in New Bedford, though only Hooper and Whitmarsh carried the county.[53]

Into this gathering atmosphere of political potential came not only free blacks but fugitives. When Charles B. Ray came to New Bedford in 1837, William Rotch Jr. spent one morning telling stories of the "cases of fugitives, in which he had participated," none of which Ray described specifically. In November 1837 black and white abolitionists worked together to place five-year-old Elizabeth Bright secretly in New Bedford, unbeknownst to her reputed owners and Massachusetts courts. Elizabeth Bright was a slave whose mother had died shortly after giving birth in Mobile, Alabama, and who in 1837 lived in the family of Henry Bright in Alabama before they moved to Cambridge, Massachusetts. On 17 November, apparently while Bright and his wife were not at home, John and Sophia Robinson, a black couple who claimed no affiliation with any antislavery group, went to the Brights' Cambridge home and took the girl away to their own home in Boston. The Brights accused the Robinsons of kidnapping the girl, while for their part the Robinsons claimed to have been motivated by the fear that Bright would return to the South and plunge the child back into slavery. According to the *Mercury,* Bright "promised emancipation," told the "Anti-slavery Society" that he would give the group five hundred dollars if he should ever take Elizabeth back to a slave state, and then took out letters of guardianship from the probate court (which, the newspaper added, "effectually was emancipating the child"). Henry Bright then brought writ of habeas corpus against the Robinsons.

Yet according to a decision of the Massachusetts Supreme Judicial Court in August 1836, Elizabeth Bright could not be emancipated because she was free from the moment she stepped onto the soil of Massachusetts. Chief Justice Lemuel Shaw's ruling applied originally to the case of Med, a six-year-old enslaved girl brought north by a Mrs. Samuel Slater of New Orleans and freed through the efforts of the Boston Female Anti-Slavery Society. When society members failed to persuade Slater to free the girl, they brought a writ of habeas corpus against her. As the *Mercury* pointed out, seemingly as a warning to others who might attempt such action, Shaw ruled that "an owner of a slave in another State, where slavery is warranted by law voluntarily bringing such slave into this state, has no authority to detain him against his will, or to carry him out of the State against his consent for the purpose of being held in Slavery." Thus a slave brought even temporarily into Massachusetts was thereupon free permanently.[54]

The decision scandalized many and immediately became an important precedent among abolitionists. Lydia Child, a member of the Boston Female Anti-Slavery Society, cited the opinion of the editor of the Boston *Commercial Gazette* that the ruling "is much to be regretted; for such cases cannot but injure the custom of our hotels, now so liberally patronized by gentlemen from the South." "Verily, Sir Editor, thou art an honest devil, and I thank thee for not being at the pains to conceal thy cloven foot," Child wrote witheringly to the New York Quaker Esther Carpenter.[55] In the Med case, attorneys were able to prove that Mrs. Slater meant to return to the South—one witness indeed claimed that she planned to sell the girl in New Orleans to pay for the expenses of her northern trip—but the assurances of Henry Bright that he had no intention of moving from Cambridge worked to the detriment of the Robinsons. The *Mercury* reported that the court advised the couple that "it would materially operate in their favor" to bring Elizabeth when they appeared for sentencing, yet in court in mid-December 1837 they failed to do so.[56] The sentencing was postponed until January 1838 to offer them another opportunity.

The court charged the Robinsons with having concealed the girl "for nearly four months," but a letter from Debora Weston to her sister Maria makes clear that Mrs. Robinson had brought the girl to New Bedford a day or two after she was taken from the Brights' home. "Tell Maria that the little child of Henry Bright's which Mrs. Robinson brought here is doing very well & is nearly recovered from a *very* bad cold which it had," she wrote on 19 November, two days after the alleged kidnapping. "The N. B. ladies are going to do every thing they can for her. The child is contented & happy. Tell this to Mrs. Robinson."[57] By early January, the *Mercury* had learned "from the testimony of a colored man named Ames . . . that the child had been brought to New Bedford by some persons unknown, and was found among the colored people here in good health." The Robinsons did at last bring her to court in January, whereupon they were ordered to restore Elizabeth to the Brights and were each sentenced to four months in "common jail" and a two-hundred-dollar fine. Two black Boston property owners posted bail in the amount of one thousand dollars when the Robinsons announced their intention to appeal.[58]

FIGURE 34. Frederick Douglass, by unidentified photographer, 1842–43. Courtesy Gregory French. The earliest known photographic view of Douglass, this daguerreotype shows him in his early twenties at the end of his years in New Bedford.

Clearly, even if New Bedford's black and white abolitionists pursued their own paths in antislavery reform, in instances where immediate action was called for—often involving fugitive slaves or slaves brought north by southern owners—the level of organization and cooperation between them was high. Like the escape of William Henry Johnson and the rescue of Elizabeth Bright, Frederick Douglass's escape was a biracial effort in its later stages (fig. 34). Johnson's escape had capitalized on the maritime connections between South and North and the likelihood of finding seamen sympathetic to antislavery, but Douglass's used the maritime connection in a different way; it banked on the ubiquitous presence of mariners of color along the eastern seaboard.

In his first and unsuccessful attempt in 1835, Douglass had forged protection papers for himself and four other slaves, who together took a canoe into the Chesapeake Bay and hoped to use the North Star to guide them out of Maryland. "Our reason for taking the water route was, that we were less liable to be suspected as runaways," he wrote; "we hoped to be regarded as fishermen; whereas, if we should take the land route, we should be subjected to interruptions of almost every kind." In his second attempt, in September 1838, he used another man's protection paper, dressed himself in sailor's clothes, came north on the railroad to Wilmington, Delaware, took a steamer to Philadelphia, and finally took a train to New York. Lonely and bewildered, Douglass spent his first night "among the barrels on one of the wharves" and in the morning was approached by a sailor who took him to David Ruggles of the city's Vigilance Committee.

Ruggles hid Douglass at the corner of Lispenard and Church Streets for several days while Douglass waited for his fiancée, the free woman Anna Murray, to arrive from Baltimore. After they were married, Ruggles decided to send Douglass, trained in caulking, to New Bedford on the supposition that he could get work on whaling vessels fitting out for sea.

Though there is no known evidence of it, Ruggles may have written to white abolitionists in New Bedford to arrange for them to meet Douglass in Newport, where the steamer *John W. Richmond* would deposit the couple. However it occurred, after the *Richmond*'s overnight run the Douglasses found themselves standing on the wharves of Newport in front of a stagecoach headed for New Bedford. There "two Quaker gentlemen who were about to take passage on the stage,—Friends William C. Taber and Joseph Ricketson,—who at once discerned our true situation, and in a peculiarly quiet way, addressing me, Mr. Taber said: 'Thee get in.' I never obeyed an order with more alacrity," Douglass wrote in *Life and Times of Frederick Douglass,* his final and most revealing autobiography. Taber and Ricketson had the stage driver take the couple to the Seventh Street home of Nathan and Mary Johnson (figs. 35 & 36), a fact that at least hints at the possibility that Johnson had housed other fugitives before that time; so, too, does the fact that Douglass carried with him a letter from Ruggles to Johnson.[59]

Johnson told Douglass, who had changed his name from Frederick Bailey to Frederick Johnson in New York, that he should probably drop his new surname on the grounds that "nearly every slave who had arrived in New Bedford from Maryland" had taken the name Johnson, "much to the annoyance of the original 'Johnsons' (of whom there were many) in that place." That the surname was assumed certainly suggests that they were fugitives, not freed people. Of 1,008 people of color in the 1850 New Bedford census, the first to indicate birthplaces, none with the surname Johnson claimed to have been born in Maryland; most stated a Massachusetts, Pennsylvania, New York, Connecticut, or New Jersey birthplace, and two claimed to be native to Virginia. Because Douglass's statements about New Bedford can usually be verified in other sources, the incongruity between his report on Johnsons and the census may signify two possibilities, not mutually exclusive: first, those Maryland fugitives named Johnson were no longer living in New Bedford by 1850, and, second, Johnsons in the 1850 census lied to enumerators when they cited northern birthplaces. The "original" Johnsons to whom Douglass referred were probably the family of Richard Johnson, the widow and sons of Jacob Johnson, and the family of Caleb and Mercy Johnson, who lived in Cannonville near Hard-Dig. Richard, Jacob, and Caleb Johnson had lived in New Bedford since at least 1806. In town at about the time Douglass came were Lisbon Johnson, a mariner who never claimed any birthplace other than Bladensburg, Virginia; James H. Johnson, who declared an unknown and a New York birthplace in different censuses; and William Henry Johnson, the Virginia fugitive who had arrived earlier in the same decade. One other Johnson,

FIGURE 35 (LEFT). The rear, older section of Nathan and Mary Johnson's home, 21 Seventh Street, New Bedford; photograph by John Robson. Now facing south, the house, built anywhere between 1800 and 1825, may originally have faced east toward Seventh Street. This view shows the back of the Federal-style house with what appear to be the original splayed lintels over the windows. The higher, more stylish front added about 1857 is visible at far left; a narrow rear addition enclosing a staircase was added in the twentieth century. The Johnsons had occupied this early dwelling since 1826; it had earlier been used as a school. It is the only extant structure in New Bedford associated with Frederick Douglass.

FIGURE 36 (RIGHT). View of 21 Seventh Street, about 1895. Used with permission of the Board of Trustees of the New Bedford Free Public Library. Probably photographed to record snowstorm damage, this view of Seventh Street shows the Nathan and Polly Johnson house at far right. In April 1857 Polly Johnson received the city's permission to move the older dwelling at 21 Seventh Street to the rear of the lot and to add onto it; this shallow structure with Greek and Gothic Revival details was the result.

Philip, was a mariner whose protection paper states his birthplace as Talbot County, Maryland, where Frederick Douglass was born, but after he left New Bedford on the whaling vessel *Rodman* in 1839, no record exists of him in the village.

Because of the number of Johnsons in the village, Nathan Johnson suggested that the fugitive take the name Douglas, for the heroic Scottish lord from Walter Scott's *Lady of the Lake,* which Nathan Johnson was then reading.[60] If Nathan Johnson was from Philadelphia, he may have added the final "s" to honor the family of Robert and Grace Douglass, prominent in that city's black community at the time Johnson probably came to New Bedford. In his first days in the village, Douglass, like Ray and others, was impressed by the standard of living among its people of color; many who had very recently been slaves lived in better homes and more comfortably than the typical Maryland slaveowner, he wrote in his first narrative of 1845.[61] Within days of his arrival, Douglass wrote in *My Bondage and My Freedom*, "I put on the habiliments of a common laborer, and went on the wharf in search of work." He found day's work loading oil onto a New York-bound sloop moored at Gideon Howland's wharf at the foot of North Street (fig. 37), just north of the Fairhaven bridge; by 1841 he lived in a boardinghouse on Ray Street in this neighborhood. He borrowed Nathan Johnson's "wood-horse and saw" and cut cord wood. Then Douglass sought a job in his field, caulking. He went to see Rodney French, a trader whose reputation among fugitive and free blacks would later grow large, and asked for work caulking or coppering a ship French was then fitting out. As skilled work, Douglass recalled, caulking paid two dollars a day in New Bedford at the time, double what common laborers earned. French hired him, but, at the report that all the white caulkers would walk off the job if he began to work among them, Douglass chose instead to return to the unskilled labor pool and worked for French presumably at shoreside tasks. Douglass also "dug cellars—shoveled coal—swept chimneys with Uncle Lucas Debuty—rolled oil casks on the wharves—helped to load and unload vessels—worked in Ricketson's candle works—in Richmond's brass foundery" on the bellows. To this list in his 1855 account he later added moving "rubbish from back-yards," cleaning the cabins of vessels, and working as a waiter for John Henry Clifford, an attorney who had married into the John Avery Parker–William H. Allen families and had served as a state representative; Clifford had also hired William Henry Johnson in the 1830s.

Douglass found day's work "an uncertain and unsatisfactory mode of life, for it kept me too much of the time in search of work." But soon he obtained his first steady employment, at the candleworks of Joseph Ricketson, one of the two men who had invited him aboard the stagecoach at Newport. There, among an all-white workforce, he rolled and lifted oil casks until the winter slack season. Then he went back to the wharves to work for George Howland ("a hard driver," Douglass called him, "but a good paymaster") fitting out two whaling vessels—first the *Java*, which sailed at the end of May 1839, and then the *Golconda*, which left New Bedford in early December of the same year. At Howland's wharf, just south of Union Street, he worked with John Briggs, Solomon Peneton, and Abraham Rodman, all men of color. Briggs had been brought up in George Howland's household, Peneton was a Maryland-born mariner and laborer who worked as a waiter for Howland's son George Jr. in the 1840s, and Rodman was a mariner who had probably descended from slaves in South Kingston, Rhode Island. Lucas Debuty or Debety, with whom Douglass did chimney sweeping, was of unknown origin but was probably a Virginian by birth. By his death in 1844 Debety owned two houses in the emerging black neighborhood on Middle Street.[62]

FIGURE 37. Stevedores roll casks along a New Bedford wharf in this undated photograph by Martin & Terrill, New Bedford. Used with permission of the Board of Trustees of the New Bedford Free Public Library. The whaling vessels *Henry Smith* and *Josephine* are shown docked, the *Josephine* behind. The stones in the foreground may be from wharf construction, or they could be ballast; coasting vessels sometimes shipped out with ballast to pick up freight in southern ports.

Debety does not appear to have been politically active, but Peneton, Briggs, and Rodman were. Rodman was part-owner of the vessel *Rising States;* Briggs was an officer of the New-Bedford Union Society, a member of the African Christian Church, and one of the men of color who laid out the abolition strategy the community of color articulated in November 1837. Peneton, who had come to New Bedford probably from Baltimore by April 1832, played a major role in many of the black community's antislavery activities from 1840 until he moved to California in the early years of the Civil War.[63] Douglass described these three men as "sober, thoughtful and upright, thoroughly imbued with the spirit of liberty," and he was drawn irresistibly into their political sphere. "I was now living in a new world," he wrote, "and was wide awake to its advantages." The people of color in New Bedford seemed to him "much more spirited than I had supposed they would be. I found among them a determination to protect each other from the blood-thirsty kidnapper, at all hazards"; they were, he wrote, "educated up to the point of fighting for their freedom, as well as speaking for it." He heard stories of how the community of color had banded together to threaten publicly a man of color who had himself planned to inform on a fugitive slave,[64] and he found its active members so articulate at the first antislavery meetings he attended that he sat silently, feeling unable to add anything to what was put, it seemed to him, so well by others.

Though Douglass was nearly penniless in his first winter, an unidentified agent advanced him a subscription to the *Liberator*, whose message set his soul "all on fire" (Garrison's own phrase) and made the paper "next to the bible" in Douglass's estimation. It was probably the newspaper he tacked up near the bellows at Richmond's foundry to read while he worked. Soon after beginning to receive the *Liberator* in January or February 1839, Douglass recalled, he went to a lecture Garrison gave in New Bedford's Liberty Hall. This lecture was probably the one Garrison presented on 13 April 1839 and may have been the first he ever gave in New Bedford. It appears to have been the meeting that impelled Samuel Rodman Jr. to a more active role in antislavery reform as well. After Garrison's lecture—"interesting and impressive, liberal in the application of denunciatory passages of Scripture to the sin of slavery but generally in a very calm and serious manner," Rodman wrote approvingly—Rodman met for the first time "this man of whom I have [heard] so much." His reaction to Garrison was a common one. Rodman expected a formidable and fiery personality but instead encountered "not that striking appearance of a great man that I had fancied, but more meek and serious in his aspect, consistent with the sentiment of religious trust and self devotion to the great cause in which he is engaged."[65] At a party the next evening at his brother Benjamin's home, Debora Weston noted, "All that clique were there & all talking abolition—Sam Rodman seemed in a very good way. He is very anxious to see Elisabeth Hayward's pamphlet, Garrison having mentioned it in his lecture. If you can get it I wish you would send it to me for he is worth converting people say." On 16 April Rodman attended his first antislavery meeting, that of the county antislavery society. "I had never attended similar m'gs and had a curiosity to see the proceedings," he wrote, and added that the meeting, "not large," was made up in the morning mostly of "the delegates and colored people." That night, at the home of Andrew Robeson, Rodman dined with Garrison and found himself somewhat less impressed with the editor, "on the score of humility not being disposed to so charitable an opinion of the intention and efforts of some others in the same cause or of those who have the unhappiness to be born in the district where slavery has from time immemorial or since the early settlement of the country been prevalent as I think justice would warrant."[66]

About a month before Frederick Douglass first heard Garrison speak in New Bedford, he had given his first known public address, against colonization, at the African Christian Church on 12 March 1839. By that time he had joined the Wilberforce Debating Society—William Henry Johnson recalled having argued

against him in that forum, that intemperance was a greater evil than slavery—
and had become a class leader and preacher in the African Methodist Episcopal
Zion church, not yet formally organized and meeting then in a school building
on Second Street. Douglass also registered to vote in 1839.[67] Yet he seems to have
been uninvolved in the circumstances surrounding the suspected return of three
women to slavery in Georgia, despite the fact that he shared living space with
them in Nathan Johnson's house. Just as Johnson's home was Douglass's first refuge in 1838, it had played the same role for the women of the Gibson family
since 1834.

In June that year, a plantation owner named Patrick Gibson from Creighton
Island, Georgia, off the coast at Darien, came to New Bedford aboard a lumber
sloop named, ironically, *Northern Liberty,* with the three women and one boy
of color. According to the later testimony of Thomas Cole, who operated at
inn on South Water Street near the Four Corners, "Gibson arrived in May or
June   was introduced to me by the Capt of the Sloop Said he had some children
with him which he 'wish to have educated'   Inquired for a suitable person to
have the care of them—I recommended Nathan Johnson   sent for him—and
an agreement was made with him." "In the summer of 1834 John Williams came
into the office a good deal excited," Richard C. Johnson testified, "said there were
some persons in the street below who had been brot from the south and wanted
me to go down and see them. Went down and found a woman and two or three
children sitting near the corner. (Four corners) some one said that they were brot
to the north to be set at liberty and educated and that a certain person who stood
by had brot them I supposed it was Gibson I did not interfere any further." Later,
Johnson stated, Patrick Gibson "introduced himself to me said he has some children at N. Johnson which he had brot here to educate. There was a boy with
him."[68]

The women were Betsey Gibson and two daughters, Helen and Jane, whom
she had conceived with Gibson. Another woman of color Gibson called Margaret
had also come to New Bedford; she may have been Patrick Gibson's daughter,
conceived with an enslaved woman named Mary, or his granddaughter. By 1855
she had taken the surname Molyneux, the name of Gibson's business partner who
was also the British consul to Savannah in these years. The boy was named Toby.
At the time, Betsey was thirty-four years old, Helen eleven, Jane seven, and Margaret no older than nine; Toby's age and genealogical place within the large number of Gibson slaves are not known. Gibson had probably come to know about
New Bedford through Joseph Howland, a master mariner who had worked in
the coasting trade between Savannah and New Bedford between 1818 and 1831,
and Gibson was one of many Southerners who regularly came north for his
health. He vacationed often at Newport, and on this occasion he left New Bedford first for a "vapor bath" and medicines in New York City and then for the
warm springs at Saratoga, New York. He wrote Nathan Johnson from Schenec-
tady that August that if Johnson could not find work for Toby, Gibson would

pay his board; he had already arranged to pay two hundred dollars each quarter for the support of the Gibson women. Johnson placed the children in school, and Gibson wrote him often to ask after his family; to report on their enslaved kin and friends on the Creighton Island plantation; and to send them peaches, potatoes, and cloth for dresses. His letters show him to have been a solicitous father. "I don't let them want for any thing that is necessary for their comfort & good," he wrote Johnson, and he often asked how they did at school and how they responded to the cold weather of the North. "Be sure & give the children plenty of blankets in the colder winter nights & any thing that they want you can get for them," he wrote Johnson one October. "Write me now and then how they are & how they come on."[69]

Gibson's correspondence indicates that he or his associate Edmund Molyneux brought members of the Creighton Island slave community to Newport during the summer; in June 1835 he wrote Johnson to say that "Betsey's sister Nan" would be in South Newport with the Molyneuxs that summer to serve as nurse to their new child. Betsey might visit, "but," he cautioned, "don't let any of the children go with her—when I come they may perhaps go there." The year before he had promised that "Grand Ma Cloey," the mother of Betsey and Nan, would visit them the following summer and that Margaret's mother "will be able come & see her." In February 1836 Gibson wrote that "Grandma Cloey . . . wishes to go & see them all next May or June   Capt. Boles of the Sloop America from your quarter has promised to carry them on when he goes."[70] Gibson himself came to New Bedford at least once to visit the women.

Then, in February 1837, Gibson died unexpectedly. Whether he had promised the women their freedom has never been determined, though Georgia law prevented him from doing so without express permission of the legislature. Joseph Howland later testified that Gibson "said he wished to free his slaves   He had at one time an idea of setting at New Providence   also of going to Van Diemans land   He had a great regard for his slaves   was a very kind master. I understood from him that he brot his children to the north to free them and educate" them. But if Gibson meant to manumit them, he had not altered his will to reflect the intention, whether it was legally permissible or not. This fact, however, was unknown to New Bedford people at the time of Gibson's death. After Johnson was notified of the event and was assured by Gibson's nephew that Molyneux "will manage the affairs" of the estate, he heard nothing until mid-August of 1837, when Molyneux sent him the board payment and informed him, "I think it probable that Betsey & the children will return to Georgia this fall." But the Gibsons remained in New Bedford, and the tone of Molyneux's letters grew increasingly inquisitive about Johnson's accounts of the costs associated with housing them. Then in mid-April 1839 Molyneux informed Johnson, "I am making arrangements with my friend Robert Johnston of New Port R. I. to send Betsey & the children with him to Jamaica & I request you will send them to Newport or wherever Mr. Johnston fixes to sail from."[71]

Molyneux told Johnson and others that he intended to resettle the women, along with members of their family then still on Creighton Island, in Jamaica, where slavery had become illegal on 1 August 1838. In mid-May 1839 Molyneux wrote again to say the arrangements were in place and to direct Johnson "to take them to Newport & see them safe on board." Johnson, however, was suspicious. He did not bring the women to Newport for the June sailing, which prompted an angry letter from Molyneux. "You must not expect any more money from me either for board or education or clothing," he wrote, "as you have thought proper to prevent the People going to Jamaica I suppose it is your intention to pay for their support in New Bedford."[72] Molyneux continued to quibble over Johnson's accounting of the women's expenses and declared, snippishly, "Betsey must now support herself by her own labours. Any orders for Betseys going to Jamaica ought to have been obeyed & you should have turned her out of Doors."

Molyneux then began to make arrangements to retrieve the women again, and in October 1839 he wrote Johnson to say that Captain Howland would arrange to have them transported in a sloop to Savannah. Johnson remained leery of the whole scheme, as David W. Ruggles later testified.

> I heard that Mrs. Gibson & family were about to leave tomorrow & called to see them. Nathan Johnson was present at that time. We had some conversation about their going to the South. The Woman said that she had made up her mind to go & trust in God. N. J. remarked that it seemed almost like going into the lions den & that there was great danger that they would be again enslaved & at the same time said that he should feel almost unwilling to go and if it was for himself he would not; but that he felt confident from his last letter from Mr. Mollyneux that they would be sent to Jamaica. Mrs. Gibson said that Mr. Gibson had frequently told her that it was his intention to settle the family somewhere under the British Government. This is the substance of a conversation I heard a day or two before the family left town.[73]

Johnson set off with the four women in early November 1839, a decision that this time aroused the interest and intervention of whites in New Bedford. Benjamin Rodman traveled to Newport to talk Johnson out of letting the women go, and they all returned to New Bedford on Rodman's promise that he would write Molyneux to learn his intentions. Rodman asked to know the terms of Gibson's will and any other information that "shall enable the friends of the persons in question to judge whether the change will be for their real benefit and the promotion of their happiness." Molyneux's response was brief and curt. "If you [?] to write to me again you will be pleased to pay the postage. . . . With the exception of the fact of the Slaves alluded to having been sent to New Bedford for education every circumstance stated in your letter is untrue." Rodman had the letter and his response printed in the *Mercury*. "By Mr. Molyneux's answer you will learn that there was no foundation for the expectation entertained that they were either going to Jamaica or to enjoy the freedom which they are now legally entitled to," he wrote.[74] In the meantime Henry Jackson, the white pastor at New Bedford's

First Baptist Church for the past year, wrote to a friend in Savannah to secure a copy of Gibson's will, which was published in the *Mercury* on 29 January 1840. It made clear that Gibson had given thirty-four of his slaves to Molyneux, including "Toby, my driver, and his wife Chloe, with their issue, to wit, Betsey and her two children Helen and Jane, now in New Bedford, Massachusetts. . . . Mary (daughter of Lydia) and her children to wit, Margaret, now in New Bedford, Catherine and Adeline and her future issue, Lydia (Mary's mother) and her grandsons."

Johnson and others had not known that Georgia law banned Patrick Gibson from freeing his slaves, and as a consequence of having taken the women to Newport in November he was accused of kidnapping them in order to return them to slavery. In a letter to her Aunt Mary, Debora Weston reported that Gibson had "bequeathed to Edward Molyneux . . . 'my slave Betsey & her three children now residing in N. Bedford'. Gibsons own children remember, to him & to his heirs, forever, I believe was the expression. After church to-night Mrs Ricketson is going to call with me at Mr Jacksons to see the correspondence," she wrote. "The coloured people are much excited against Nathan & at the ball the waiters refused to serve under him—& they were obliged to get Tom Robison," or Roberson, another man of color who was a grocer and caterer in town at the time.[75] Yet the enusing investigation by the Young Men's Anti-Slavery Society of New Bedford, founded in March 1836, concluded that Johnson "cannot be charged with having violated his duty as a faithful guardian of their rights, or as a member of the society."[76] The Gibson women remained in New Bedford, and by 1855 other former slaves named in Gibson's will as Molyneux's property were living in town as well. Helen Gibson married the black activist Shadrach Howard, Jane married the black mariner Robert Piper, and Margaret married a man whose surname, Cook, alone is known. Before 1850 Margaret's sister Catherine had settled in New Bedford and married black leader Jeremiah B. Sanderson; her mother Mary and her grandmother Lydia were also members of the Sanderson household. By 1855 Adeline, the sister of Catherine and Margaret, was also living with the Sandersons, and other members of the family were with other relations in town— Robert, Lydia's grandson, and Charles, another child of Mary.

Samuel Rodman Jr. was probably correct when he observed in late December 1839 that "the abolition zeal of our community is not warm enough to resist a low point in the scale of Farenheit [*sic*]," but the fact remains that such fugitives as Douglass and William Henry Johnson found themselves in a community that wielded some political force. They chose to stay to become part of it. In the early 1840s both joined the antislavery lecture circuit, an activity for which life in New Bedford had effectively apprenticed them. But not all fugitives felt so safe in the town, so apparently secure in the thought that they would not be pursued northward by former owners or owners' agents like Camillus Griffith. In July 1839 a man with no protection paper named William Henry signed on to the crew of the bark *Hope*. On the *Hope's* crew list Henry's age is listed as twenty-three and his birthplace as Petersburg, Virginia, but his race is not designated. The *Hope* set sail for the Indian Ocean on 11 July and returned about two years later, in late May 1841; shortly afterward Henry was listed in the city directory as a laborer working at 36 High Street. This address was the home of Gideon Richmond, a white shipwright doing business as Wilcox and Richmond at Robeson's wharf, on the river just north of High Street. In 1839 Wilcox and Richmond owned the *Hope,* and Henry was listed as a man of color living at 36 High Street in 1839 and 1840. Henry Howland Crapo, New Bedford's meticulous town clerk and recorder, also noted that Henry was "a runaway slave," the only man so designated in the clerk's 1839–41 memorandum of local tax delinquents.

Another fugitive who chose a rather immediate trip to sea was John S. Jacobs, who later joined Douglass and Johnson on the antislavery circuit.[77] Jacobs was the younger brother of Harriet Jacobs, who in 1861 achieved considerable attention with the publication of her *Incidents in the Life of a Slave Girl.* He escaped slavery in 1838, three years after she went into hiding and four years before she was able to leave the crawl space of her grandmother's home and flee to New York City. His fourth owner, Samuel Treadwell Sawyer, was elected to the U.S. Congress from Edenton, North Carolina, in August 1838 and took Jacobs with him to Washington, D.C. Jacobs had learned by that time to conceal his true antipathy to slavery: "I grew sick of myself in acting the deceitful part of a slave," he wrote in his 1861 autobiographical narrative, "and pretending love and friendship where I had none. Unpleasant as it was thus to act, yet, under the circumstances in which I was placed, I feel that I have done no wrong in so doing." He presented such a convincingly faithful aspect that Sawyer, preparing for his marriage in Chicago, brought Jacobs with him. Together they passed through Niagara Falls, Buffalo, and Chicago and then went into Canada, where the only obstacle to Jacobs's escape then was his reluctance to tell a lie about himself in order to obtain a seaman's protection paper. So he returned to New York City with Sawyer and concocted a strategy to escape. Day by day he brought out a few clothes, "as if to be washed," from the Astor House, where he and Sawyer stayed, and then took his trunk out on the pretense that it needed repair. One of his "old friends from home" then living in New York picked up the trunk and packed it with Jacobs's clothes. After assuring that all of the errands he was to do at Sawyer's behest were done, he wrote a note to Sawyer (signed, "No longer yours"), boarded a boat for Providence, and then somehow "went through to New Bedford," where he stayed several months.

When he reached New Bedford, probably in May or June of 1839, someone whom Jacobs did not identify introduced him to "Mr. William P———, a very fatherly old man, who had been a slave in Alexandria." Most likely Jacobs had met William Piper, a hostler in his early fifties who had been born in Alexandria and had come to New Bedford sometime between 1825 and 1830. Whether he and his family were fugitives or free is not known. Piper lived on the south end of South Sixth Street, near the neighborhood that was soon to be referred to as

Dog Corner; though it gained an unsavory reputation like Hard-Dig's, it was also home to some of the longest-lived families of color in the city, Lewis Temple's and Cuffe Lawton's among them. Piper's oldest children, Robert, Philip, Sarah Ann, Amelia, and Augustus, were all born in Alexandria; his daughter Rebecca was born after his move to Massachusetts. When Jacobs arrived in town, Piper was working as a hostler for William Rotch Rodman, whose six-year-old mansion was the finest on County Street.

Jacobs had written that the sons of his first owner had been instructed not to teach him to read or write, and so the first thing he did in New Bedford was to attempt to "raise myself above the level of the beast, where slavery had left me, and fit myself for the society of man." He tried to work during the day and attend night school in the town but found his work schedule often kept him from school. Thus he determined that "the better plan would be to get such books as I should want, and go a voyage to sea." Apparently without a protection paper, he signed as crew on the *Francis Henrietta*, a whaling vessel half owned by Charles W. Morgan and his brother-in-law Samuel Rodman Jr., William Rotch Rodman's brother; it thus seems likely that Piper was instrumental in getting Jacobs aboard the vessel. He was one of three men of color in the crew, two of whom had no protection papers. The other was John Williams, a native of the region who clearly joined the crew to escape for another reason: he was suspected of having murdered a Gay Head Wampanoag woman named Prudence Hennet or Cooper the night before, at the Hard-Dig "hut" of a man of color named Samuel Gale, alias Samuel Spenser.[78] Morgan was not above taking men out of jail to fill berths on his whaling vessels—he paid the jail fees of four men so that they could ship out on the *Rodman* in August 1840—and it should not be surprising if he or his agent asked few questions of men who wished to ship. Jacobs shipped at a 1/130 lay, and he was not the most poorly compensated man on board; many others shipped at 1/145, 1/185, and 1/200 lays, while one man even signed on at 1/300 lay. Williams, who had apparently been to sea at least twice before, signed on at 1/65 lay, which suggests that he was a boatsteerer or possibly the ship's steward or cook. But Morgan figured he was due only slightly more than sixteen dollars, because— predictable in view of his alleged crime—he deserted in "Juan Hernandes," the island Juan Fernandes off the coast of Chile.

But Jacobs stayed with the *Francis Henrietta* throughout its long voyage of three years, six months, and sixteen days and made, he said, "the best possible use of my leisure time on board" by keeping in view his aim—to earn enough money to buy his sister's freedom—and by learning to read. Others had availed them- selves of the long stretches of idle time a whaling voyage often included: the rec- ords of the whaler *Rebecca*, which sailed from New Bedford in September 1791, include the purchase from the ship's slop chest of a spelling book by James Smith, one of its "Negroe oarsmen," and Paul Cuffe often read antislavery publications on his voyages south and to England and Sierra Leone.[79] William Powell, whom Jacobs may have known—Jacobs shipped out on 1 September 1839, and Powell left New Bedford to open another temperance boardinghouse for seamen of color in New York City sometime after 26 September that year—certainly advocated that black mariners use their time to that end and suggested that the practice was somewhat common:

> On board of whale-ships the crews are generally unlettered men, or rather, a large proportion are ignorant of the rudiments of a good common school education. No one can imagine, but those who have performed a whaling voyage, the thirst the men have for mental cultivation. The forecastles are turned into schoolrooms. There you will see the *cook,* the *steward,* and two or three of the crew, under the tuition of their several teachers, busily engaged in their primary lessons; and others studying *navigation,* and taking *Lunars,* under the instruction of the captain or mates. By close application during the voyage, an unlettered man may acquire the art of reading, writing and arithmetic. Now this is the case with a large majority of coloured men in the whaling service, that when having acquired a thorough knowledge of the art and skill of capturing whales, together with navigation and seamanship, it qualifies them to fill the offices of boatsteerers, third, second, and first mates, and sometimes captains of whaling vessels.[80]

Powell's views on the prospect for advancement among black mariners did not represent the reality of the situation at any time in the history of whaling, just as his estimates of the number of men of color in the whaling service were far higher than their real representation on crews.[81] Still, his *National Anti-Slavery Standard* series on seamen of color is the only contemporary account of their presence and participation in the American maritime industry, and it did ring true for a few men like Jacobs. Time in the black boardinghouses and on vessels also honed the antislavery conscience of men such as Powell and Jacobs. Powell kept an engraving of Crispus Attucks in his boardinghouse dining room, persisted after the time of David Walker's *Appeal* in using stewards and other black mariners to distribute antislavery tracts, and claimed that his sailors' homes, even as they formed his income, were created "for the purpose of promoting the moral and social welfare of colored seamen. That not only shipwrecked destitute sailors, but, also the flying fugitive slave, always found shelter, food and raiment without money and without price." In New Bedford, and later in New York City, Powell was fluent in "travel craft," or "the ability to seek out the keepers of information vital to the survival of a black traveler in strange and probably hostile places," including fugitive slaves, and helped numerous men of color find berths on New Bedford whalers.[82] His New York boardinghouse offered a reading room, a library, and regular discussions on issues confronting black mariners; Frederick Douglass called the place "an *Oasis* in the desert, when compared with the many houses where seamen usually congregate."

How many men of color escaped slavery by joining a New Bedford whaling crew as Jacobs did cannot be determined, and documented instances are few. Including Jacobs, only six such cases have been identified. Based on her analysis of crew lists, however, Martha Putney has pointed out that the number of persons on crews listed as "no proofs" (having no seaman's protection paper) increased markedly after 1822—her sample of 1841 and 1842 whaling voyages from New Bedford found the "no proofs" in fact outnumbered known men of color—and has argued that these men were "mainly blacks and foreigners." In New Bedford the number of seamen of color on whaling vessels increased rather dramatically in 1837, climbing from twelve the year before to fifty-nine in 1837, to sixty-two in 1838 and 1839, and to 107 in 1840.[83] The percentage of those men claiming slave-state birthplaces also rose, from 8.3 percent of all black crew in 1836 to 24.2 percent in 1839, while the proportion of black crew claiming free-state birthplaces fell from 83.3 percent in 1836 to 61.2 percent in 1839.[84] If these voyages had been coastwise trading trips, such statistics would seem to document the effect of the Negro Seamen's Acts from 1823 forward, which were claimed to have discouraged most (though clearly not all) northern-born men of color from seeking berths on such trips. But whalers, nearly all of them bound for the South Atlantic, Indian, or Pacific Oceans, almost never made stops in southern ports, which makes the decline in men of color claiming northern birthplaces and corresponding rise in southern-born black crew harder to understand. It may indicate the flight of both free and enslaved mariners of color to the North as the South grew increasingly suspicious and controlling of its black watermen, and with the almost virtual exclusion of men of color from the North's new factories, whaling—an occupation that by then articulate whaling men often compared to slavery—may have been the only occupation truly open to them. An analysis of the real levels of participation of black men in such other maritime lines as the merchant marine and the navy would help pinpoint the specific appeal of whaling among them, but the fact remains that whaling vessels offered fugitives advantages that no other branch of maritime or shoreside work could. Fugitives who managed to secure a berth on a whaler with a false, forged, or borrowed protection paper or with none at all, like John S. Jacobs, found themselves in a place from which retrieval was so unfeasible as to be almost impossible. They might leave their own country forever by deserting and settling in a part of the world more to their liking; Putney has argued that the increasing rates of desertion and discharge among no proofs and others from the 1820s onward suggests strongly "that slaves used this road to freedom and that it was probably much more frequently travelled than the overland route of the historic 'underground railroad.'"[85] Or they might, like Jacobs, return after a long and successful voyage, with money in their pockets to buy the freedom of family still enslaved in the South and with ideas about the kind of power they might wield.

6

The 1840s:
Caste and "the Liberal Spirit"

IN 1841, three years after Great Britain had emancipated the slaves laboring on its West Indian possessions, Joseph Sturge, a prosperous wheat merchant from Birmingham, England, toured the United States. Sturge stopped at some of the sites other European visitors included on their American tours, such as the seaside resort of Newport, Rhode Island, but his trip had a different aim. Sturge was an abolitionist, and he wished to determine for himself the "actual state of feeling and opinion" on universal emancipation among professing American Christians, particularly Quakers. He also wanted, he wrote, to bolster and aid those working toward emancipation and to "introduce the English anti-slavery reader to a better acquaintance with his fellow labourers in the United States." In New York, Washington, Philadelphia, and smaller Quaker enclaves in Pennsylvania and New Jersey, Sturge discerned a great measure of "passive anti-slavery feeling" but a distressing avoidance of the issue as well; by the time he left Philadelphia, he was sad and depressed "that so many of the very class of christian professors, who once took the lead in efforts for the abolition of slavery . . . should now be so discouraging, and holding back their members, from taking part in so righteous a cause."

With the Quaker poet and abolitionist John Greenleaf Whittier, a close friend of Garrison in his early years, Sturge attended the New England Yearly Meeting of the Society of Friends in Newport in June. While other tourists marveled at the stylish estates of affluent summer residents, the regular visits of many "southern families of wealth" to Newport had the opposite effect on him. The presence of these southerners had, he wrote, "the effect of materially adding to the vast amount of complicated pro-slavery interests which exist in the free States, as well as of diffusing pro-slavery opinions, and feelings, throughout the entire community."[1] Sturge's disappointment in the actions of his fellow Quakers intensified during the yearly meeting. Presented with a request from a quarterly meeting that it "encourage more action" with respect to the abolition of slavery, the yearly meeting, quietly and without debate, referred the petition to committee. The meeting took the same action on the London Yearly Meeting's epistle on slavery

FIGURE 38. Andrew Robeson (1787–1862), *carte de visite* by Bierstadt Brothers, New Bedford, 1862. Courtesy Old Dartmouth Historical Society / New Bedford Whaling Museum. Among the most enigmatic of New Bedford abolitionists, Robeson was born in Philadelphia and married Anna Rodman, daughter of Samuel Rodman Sr., in 1810; the couple moved to New Bedford in 1817. Garrison, the Westons, and other Boston-based abolitionists viewed Robeson as one of the most stalwart and generous supporters of the cause in the state, and he presided often over antislavery meetings in New Bedford.

and then turned the entire subject over to its meeting of sufferings. The perfunctory manner in which abolition was addressed troubled Sturge, as did the "plain intimation" of its letters to other meetings that it would not condone "Friends uniting with any of the anti-slavery associations of the day."

Still, Sturge was convinced that, "especially where the deadening commercial intercourse with the South does not operate," some New England Quakers and others showed "genuine anti-slavery feeling." One such place was New Bedford, which he visited shortly after the Newport meeting. At worship services on 20 June at the Friends meetinghouse, he wrote, "I had the pleasure of witnessing the coloured part of the audience, placed on a level, and sitting promiscuously with the white, the only opportunity I had of making such an observation in the United States; as, on ordinary occasions, the coloured people rarely attend Friends' meetings." Before the meeting Sturge and Whittier "called on a number of persons friendly to abolition," including Andrew Robeson (fig. 38), who accompanied Sturge on a visit to Eliza Rodman's home; the next day Robeson returned to show her the portrait of Thomas Clarkson that Sturge had given him. That night Sturge attended a party at the home of William Congdon Taber, a local bookseller and still a member of the Society of Friends.[2]

In New Bedford Sturge encountered not only positive sentiment on abolition but a fugitive as well. At the Mansion House he was waited on by a man who had escaped slavery "some years before" (see fig. 1). The waiter might have been William Henry Johnson, whose twelve-dollar monthly wage suggests that he was a waiter there. But the slave Sturge met had encountered severity on the part of his master that Johnson never mentioned. "The idea of running away had been first suggested to his mind, by reflecting on his hard lot, being overworked, and kept without a sufficiency of food, and cruelly beaten, while his owner was living in luxury and idleness, on the fruits of his labour," Sturge wrote. "He had been flogged for merely speaking to one of his master's visitors, in reply to a question, because it was suspected he had divulged matter that his master did not wish the stranger to know."[3]

The fugitive Sturge encountered may have been one of a number of far more anonymous men of color living in New Bedford by the 1840s. Robert Goldsborough, who worked at the Mansion House in 1841, may have come to New Bedford the same year, and he stayed in relative obscurity until he left for California about 1856. George and Fanny Thomas had been living in the town since 3 March 1840. He was a laborer, and the Thomases rented a house in back of the African Christian Church on Middle Street. Both were illiterate. In 1850 they each claimed to have been born in New Jersey, in 1855 they simply told enumerators they were born in the South, and in 1860 they stated that they had been born in Georgia. Eight months before he died in September 1861, George Thomas applied for poor relief, at which time he told city officials that both he and his wife had been slaves and gave the exact date of their arrival in Massachusetts.[4] Nothing more is known about them, but the Thomases at least made it into the public record; another fugitive who came to New Bedford at almost exactly the same time did not. Letters, and one scarcely fictionalized account, refer to him only as Abraham. The day after the Thomases came to town, Debora Weston sent a letter about him to her sister Maria by way of Isaac C. Taber:

> Today at noon Abraham came with your letter. I did not know him though I thought I had seen him before, which was a mistake. He kept talking about his family, & removing his family. Pinda I suppose he meant. I liked him very much. He wanted me when I wrote to tell you that he got here safe. He was put he said in the Jim Crow car, but rode in the inside of the stage I understood him. He wants you to tell Pinda that at the place where he is staying are two old acquaintances of his, who came from the very place he did, Savannah I suppose & that he has not the least trouble in getting along—I told his story to Mr. Howland, who was much interested & thinks he can give him some work immediately. There is great feeling for runaway slaves here, & it is rather a recommendation than otherwise. I dont doubt he will prosper. I should not think it at all safe though to publish his story, which is a great pity, for there never was a prettier one—Why did he not go to Guiana?"[5]

Six months later, William C. Coffin, who is said to have brought Frederick Douglass to public notice the next year, wrote Maria Chapman to report on Abraham's situation:

I received your letter requesting me to inform Abraham of the arrival in Boston of the amiable Mr. Hogan by this mornings mail. I immediately went in search of him and informed him of the fact, he did not seem to be at all alarmed—feeling perfectly safe surrounded as he is by kind friends who are willing to do all in their power to prevent his falling into the hands of his christian slave-holder.

He thinks it would be better for Pendas to remain where she is for the present as Hogan might discover his whereabouts if she should attempt to come to him, which I think is good advice. He wished me to say that he was well, and that he should have paid Penda a visit in a week or two had he not received this information. He wishes to know if Hogan's wife is with him and whether he intends to remain in Boston during the winter.[6]

Ever alert to the potential publicity value of gripping slavery tales, and despite her sister's concern about its effect on their safety in hiding, Chapman wrote her only anti-slavery novel based on Abraham and Pinda. *Pinda: A True Tale,* published by the American Anti-Slavery Society the same year, tells the story of this Savannah slave whose husband, initially left behind in Georgia, was named Abraham; Chapman, however, mentioned neither New Bedford nor anything about their situation after they were reunited in the North. Pinda had been brought north by her owner's wife, a Mrs. Logan, and had escaped during a trip to New Hampshire. Some nineteen months later, Abraham managed to escape to Boston. "How I got here you must not tell," Chapman, in the novel, had him caution his wife upon their meeting in Boston, "for it may bring kind people into difficulty, and close up the way to those who are left behind." Chapman stated that the fugitive Abraham planned either to go to Canada or Guiana. Instead, as she had done with Lucilla Tucker and perhaps also Elizabeth Bright, she helped arranged his move to New Bedford. What became of him and Pinda after 1840 is not known.[7]

One of the issues in Pinda's case came to the fore in New Bedford almost immediately after Sturge's visit, and the case illustrates well how the idea of forcible resistance split white abolitionists as it strengthened both the resolve and the organization of black abolitionists in the village. In early July 1841 the well-known sea captain Joseph Dunbar lay gravely ill at his South Sixth Street home in New Bedford. His condition was so serious that his daughter, married to the Richmond, Virginia, commission merchant Henry Ludlam, left immediately for New Bedford with her husband and an eighteen-year-old enslaved girl, all at the time vacationing at Virginia's Old Point Comfort. The Ludlams had hired the service of the girl, Lucy Faggins (or Louisa Fearing, as the newspaper accounts sometimes referred to her), for one year.[8]

Accounts of the incident, none of them directly from Lucy Faggins, differ markedly, but the bare facts are these: upon learning that a slave had been brought into New Bedford, several white and black abolitionists tried to make her aware that, as of the 1836 Med decision, she was free once she entered Massachusetts. They secured a writ for her removal from Dunbar's house and presented her at a hearing before Judge Samuel Sumner Wilde in Boston, who pronounced her free.

Boston abolitionists accompanied her away from the courthouse, where her story, by most accounts, ends. The case, at least to those involved, hinged on whether Lucy had been told beforehand that she was technically free in Massachusetts and whether she wished to remain in the state after the Ludlams had gone.

Henry Ludlam told the *Mercury* that he had made Lucy aware of the plan to visit New Bedford "and after distinctly stating to her, that if she accompanied us she would be a free girl as soon as she reached Philadelphia, asked her whether she would avail herself of the privilege or return with us to Richmond. She chose the latter, and said she never wished to be separated from her brothers and sisters."[9] The New Bedford *Register,* a short-lived competitor to the *Mercury,* stated that Faggins "had been told that the Abolitionists and Colored people of New Bedford were very bad people, and she must not go out, or have any thing to say to them, as it would be their object to entice her away for the purpose of selling her, and that it was an every day occurrence for cart loads of Colored people to be sold in our market and sent away in chains."[10]

Faggins's presence in New Bedford was already known to the Reverend Thomas James, pastor of the local African Methodist Episcopal (AME) Zion Church and a former New York slave who had escaped in 1822, five years before the state's gradual manumission law made all slaves held there free. James had just moved to New Bedford in 1840 and had met Faggins in the Jim Crow railroad car on his return from a visit to New York. He invited her to visit his church while she was in town, and when she failed to appear he asked two women of color (one of them a teacher, he said) to accompany him to Dunbar's house. Still another account claims that the fugitive William Henry Johnson, from Richmond himself, also visited the Dunbar home with James. According to Ludlam, Faggins had been free to travel about New Bedford visiting family friends with the couple's children, and, he told the *Mercury,* "I have in passing through the kitchen frequently observed that she had negro visitors, but never by word or look have I expressed to her or to them any disapproval." But James and his party, he said, made the mistake of calling at the front door. "If they had applied at the kitchen as the other negroes did," Ludlam wrote, "they would not have met with any interference."

James described the encounter differently to a member of the board of the New Bedford Anti-Slavery Society. When he and the two women met Ludlam at the front door and asked to see Lucy, the *Register* reported, Ludlam refused to allow them in. "She is a Slave and my Servant," the newspaper quoted him to have said; "you shall have no conversation with her, and I wish you to go away." James reported that Ludlam said, "Lucy is my slave, and slaves don't receive calls." Yet somehow William Henry Johnson had managed to elude Ludlam, as "S. T." (probably the Quaker Susan Taber) stated in a letter to Debora Weston:

They were met at the door by Mr. L, who desired to know their business. We have come to make a friendly call upon your sevt.—was the reply, whereupon the gentleman became very angry—told them his servant had not and *should* not have any associates among the col'd people—and desired them immediately to leave the house. While they were in the midst of this altercation Henry Johnson a shrewd col'd fellow (whom I forgot to mention as one of their number) slipped round the house into the kitchen and found greatly to his surprise that she was a person whom he had known in VA. He lost no time in acquainting her with her right to freedom. She told him she should like to be free—but it was evident she was afraid to say so before the other servants for fear it would get to her master's ears.[11]

When the New Bedford Anti-Slavery Society learned about the incident, either James himself or the Reverend John M. Spear, then pastor of the First Universalist Church of New Bedford and a member of the town's antislavery society, sought to secure a writ of habeas corpus claiming that the girl was unlawfully restrained and aiming to gain her release from the Ludlams. "It was evident they intended to keep her from the influence of abolitionists and as no such case had before occurred here we did not know how far we could lawfully proceed," Taber wrote. She added that the society felt it best to have Spear consult the abolitionist attorney Ellis Gray Loring in Boston about the best course, "so secret were all these movements that very few were aware of any action in the case." According to his account, James went to Boston with unidentified others after Henry Howland Crapo, the local justice, refused them to grant the writ. The supplicants returned with "an officer of Boston" whom Taber and James identified only as "sheriff Pratt,"[12] who went immediately to the local antislavery meeting and asked Spear and the Methodist minister Joel Knight to accompany him to serve the writ at Dunbar's house; according to Taber, "Knight was not known to them [the Ludlams] as an abolitionist."

Taber and the *Register* claimed that the officer of the court also asked Henry Johnson, as Taber put it, "to be within hailing distance if his evidence was needed and others were told to perambulate the streets in that vicinity for fear they should try to convey her away privately." The *Mercury* reported that "the family were alarmed by finding the street gradually filling up with a crowd of colored people—and soon afterwards by the entrance of an officer with a writ of habeas corpus, from Boston, directing him forthwith to carry the body of the servant before Judge Wilde in Boston." As the Ludlams talked to the officer, the *Mercury* account stated, "a crowd of negroes in the street had increased to a pretty large number, and it is known that some of them were armed with bludgeons." Faggins was reportedly so scared that she hid under the ailing Dunbar's bed, but the *Register*'s account, and the public testimony of both Spear and Knight, painted a different picture of the event. The number of people of color in South Sixth Street "did not, at any time during the evening exceed fifteen or sixteen, they were not armed with bludgeons, as stated in the *Mercury;* they stationed themselves several rods distant from the house, and remained perfectly quiet. Their object was to prevent the inmates of the house from smuggling the slave away."

The *Mercury* claimed that Faggins had hidden "in order to escape from these officious friends, and could only be persuaded to yield herself upon the promise that she should go back to Virginia and see her brothers and sisters and cousins, if she wished. She was taken to the house of a respectable clergyman by the sheriff, with a full escort of her pretended friends . . . the girl, who was as free as air to come and go when and where she pleased, has been imprisoned for two days and three nights, under the name of *liberty.*" The *Register* countered that Dunbar himself wished the girl to be set free and in fact that his health improved after Faggins was taken to Boston—though he did die within the month. Taber told Weston that the conversation between Pratt and Ludlam lasted almost two hours, during which "the Ls to be sure made every possible effort [to] secure their prey." Ultimately, however, Pratt prevailed. The Ludlams "were very unwilling that she should be taken to the house of an abolitionist fearing that she would be influenced and desired that Mr. Knight would take her home with him," she wrote, so Helen Gibson, a woman exactly Faggins's age whose freedom hinged on the same 1836 state law established in the Med case, was asked to stay the night with her in an upper-floor bedroom of Knight's home. James related that he and others "prepared to lie down before the door" to prevent her abduction. However, Ludlam had apparently told Faggins that the people of color meant her harm and told her to hang a handkerchief in her window should she wish rescue; she did so, and when she explained to James why, he summoned twenty men "from the colored district of the place, they took seats in the church close at hand, ready for an emergency." Ludlam and some twelve other men came with a ladder to Knight's home, but they fled when the men James had called together walked out of the church toward them. "The entire town was now agog over the affair," James wrote.[13]

In the morning Pratt took Faggins to Boston for a hearing before Massachusetts Supreme Court Justice Samuel Sumner Wilde. Samuel Sewell and Loring represented Spear and the antislavery society, while Boston attorney Charles P. Curtis and New Bedford attorney Harrison Gray Otis Colby represented the Ludlams. Colby, who two years earlier had arranged the purchase of the wife and three children of New Bedford restaurateur Thomas T. Robeson, "knew that he had the wrong side of the question," Taber wrote. "Slavery is a terrible curse, as blighting as a pestilence," Colby wrote in his diary at the time of the Robeson incident, but he took the Ludlams' case anyway.[14] James claimed that Wilde postponed the hearing and asked him and others to bring Faggins to his home so that he might speak with her and inform her of her rights.

Ludlam testified in court that the dark stories Faggins related about New Bedford's abolitionists were Faggins's own imagining and that, once he left her at the New Bedford rail depot, "I never saw her again until I past her in the Court room in Boston, surrounded by a crowd of white and black abolitionists, who were in constant conversation with her—even then I did not exchange a word with her, she went fresh from their hands into the Judge's room." Wilde reportedly took Faggins into his chambers and simply asked her whether she wished to stay with

Ludlam or in Boston. "Intoxicated with all the glowing accounts that had been given to her of a life in Boston," Ludlam observed in the *Mercury*, "it is not strange that she at the moment forgot her former ties, and concluded to remain with her new friends." In a letter to the *Liberator*, Boston black activist William C. Nell reported that "a large concourse of friends" took Faggins to the AME Bethel Church of Noah C. W. Cannon in West Centre Street, where she was congratulated and a collection taken up for her benefit. In a report on the case reprinted in the *Mercury*, the New York *Courier and Enquirer* declared that Wilde had "left her to the tender mercy of the Abolitionists, under which blessed patronage she will undoubtedly become very soon the inmate of the Almshouse, for such poor creatures thrown helpless upon society hardly ever fail to become dissolute and abandoned." Despite the newspaper's prognosis, by 1850 Faggins married Isaac Henson, a former slave and probably a fugitive from Maryland, in New Bedford and lived most of her life in the city (fig. 39); by 1848 her sister Martha and Martha's husband-to-be, Henry Onley, had moved to the town from Richmond as well (figs. 40 and 41). An article in the *Boston Morning Post* offered another reason why Lucy Faggins chose to remain in Massachusetts, and why her sister may shortly have joined her. "She did not wish to go back to Virginia," the *Post* reported, "because she had reason to believe that the estate on which she was brought up would soon be sold, and herself with it, as her former master was dead."[15]

Faggins remained in Boston for some time after her hearing because of the controversy her case triggered locally. In a letter to Nell, Jeremiah Burke Sanderson, a New Bedford native and barber who became a central figure in the community of color in California in the 1850s, noted a rumor that Ludlam had received a letter stating that Faggins was "very anxious to return" to him and that the writer would "deliver her into his (Mr. L's) hands" for two hundred dollars. Sanderson believed the letter to be a forgery and added, "I hope that young Lady will not come to New Bedford for the present at least, it would n't be safe just now." The event, he said, "had raised a storm of anti abolition excitement amongst us. Abolitionists are perfectly calm, possessed, while it is raging around them; I am now, if I was not before, (if the inhabitants of New Bedford exhibit a fair specimen of northern feeling in relation to slavery,—and I presume they do, rather a favorable one—) convinced, that abolitionists have much, very much to do, if they would see slavery abolished peacably."[16] For Weston's benefit, Susan Taber presented an extremely revealing account of the local reaction to the Faggins case:

> And now what does the world say? Why the whole community is in an uproar Capt. Robert Gibbs thinks the d----d abolitionists deserve to have their necks stretched— and I suppose many others are of his opinion. . . . Doubtless we shall have your commiseration when I tell you that we are so unfortunate as to offend by our measures a scion of the illustrious house of Ricketson. The redoubtable Daniel told J. B. [John Bailey] a few days since that the abolitionists in this place had become so

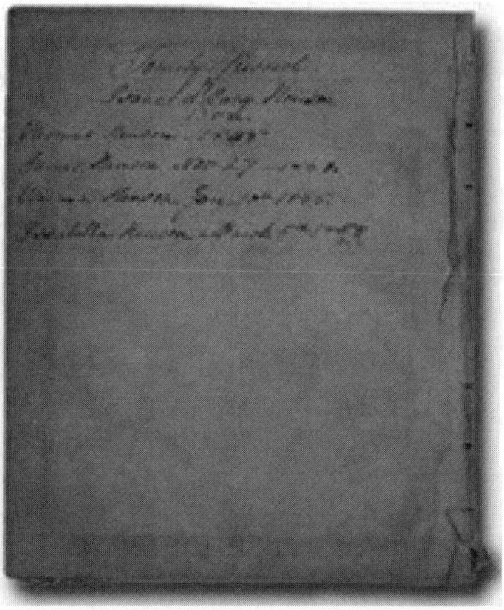

FIGURE 39. Family record of Isaac and Lucy Henson in the Onley family Bible, 1850s. Courtesy Carl J. Cruz, New Bedford Historical Society. The Onley Bible is one of the only records that document the kinship of Louisa Faggins Henson and Martha Faggins Onley.

FIGURES 40 AND 41. Henry Joseph Onley and his wife, Martha Faggins Onley, oil on canvas by unidentified artist, 1855–59; private collection; courtesy Carl J. Cruz, New Bedford Historical Society. In New Bedford by 1850, both Henry and Martha Onley never stated the same birthplace twice in state and federal censuses between 1850 and 1860; they may well have been fugitives. Martha Onley, like her sister Lucy, was actually from Richmond; Henry Onley was born in Charles City, Va. The couple had five children and lived in New Bedford for the rest of their lives.

mean—no respectable person would act with them—every man who could be called
respectable was leaving our ranks &c. When urged to mention some instances he
named Whittier and Sturge and concluded by saying—my father and I cant act with
you. Oh terrible!! . . . Sunk so low that even Daniel R. cant have fellowship with us.

But to be serious Deborah—we have had to encounter much reproach and oblo-
quy. Nothing but a firm conviction of the righteousness of our cause could sustain
us under such a weight of falsehood and contumely as is heaped upon us—we know
now how to appreciate in some small degree the trials through which you have
passed. We have been told that our conduct was inhuman in the highest degree.
Even Samuel Rodman thinks our measures quite too precipitate: 'we ought to have
waited until there was some change in Capt. D——'. No one appeared to be aware
of the possibility of her being taken out of the state while we were patiently waiting
for Capt. D—— to die. I do not mean to speak lightly of the affliction of this family—the sick man has been a great sufferer in body and mind, and I know that those
who were active in the matter would most gladly have been released from the necessity of entering his house on such an errand . . . as it was they took every precaution
to prevent disturbance and if the invalid was in any way a sufferer by this affair on
his family must be the responsibility. Brother James says Mr. Colby admitted while
in conversation with him that the abolitionists who came for the girl behaved in a
perfectly gentlemanly manner   he had no fault to find with them on that score.

Now that this chattel person is beyond their reach they have become desperate.
They are determined if possible to ruin Spear. He went to the gaol a day or two since
on one of his missions of love intending to obtain the release of a man confined there
for drunkenness. Baylies put a writ on his hand, saying 'I shall serve it in a few days:
you had better look round for bail.' I have seen a copy of it. S. is therein accused
of enticing away Ludlams property therby [sic] putting him to great expense and
inconvenience—and also of falsely and maliciously swearing that the girl's liberty
was restrained. The trial is to come on in November. Do you think it probable that
L.—— will be so foolish as to persevere in this lawsuit? His property! I suspect he
will find some difference between our laws and those of Virginia in respect to what
he is pleased to call his property.

. . . You ask what the Parker faction say—They are boiling over with wrath.
John A. Parker met John Bailey in the market and charged him with guilty and inhuman conduct in going to the house of a dying man and dragging the poor frightened
girl from under his bed where she had secreted herself through fear of such as he.
After he had pretty much exhausted his vituperation, father John told him with the
greatest nonchalance that he was not out of his own house all that evening.

The Faggins case took place before Daniel Ricketson's professed conversion to
abolitionism, which he himself dated about 1844–45.[17] It probably offended the
non-Quaker Parker because Dunbar was his son-in-law, and he maintained a
business relationship with Ludlam. But Parker himself was not sympathetic to
slavery. His abolitionism is legendary but entirely undocumented, though it is
known that before the war he often allowed the city's citizens of color to use his
grove for West India emancipation celebrations. Still, until the emergence of the
Republican Standard in 1850, the *Mercury* was probably the newspaper most New

Bedford residents read, and Parker probably took its interpretation of the affair—which it termed "one of the most inhuman acts of brutality, committed under the color of law, that was ever perpetrated in a civilized community"—to be credible.[18] Rodman's objection was probably based too on the unseemly rumor that Faggins had had to be dragged from under Dunbar's bed, the sort of confrontation that he, still a Quaker, could not condone. To Nell this and the allegation that Dunbar's house was surrounded by a noisy throng were nothing but "proslavery facts."

The Faggins incident showed how the issue of nonresistance, probably the most tenacious of all Quaker principles, could splinter abolitionist sentiment even in a supposed bastion of the movement, and how easily even active opponents of slavery could be convinced that abolitionist extremism foreshadowed some sort of doom. As the New Bedford and Nantucket abolitionist Isaiah C. Ray noted in one 1842 letter, "I am an Abolitionist, and that in Nantucket, is very unpopular, if a person is a plain outspoken Abolitionist. He may be an antislavery man, and pass along very well, but if he is an Abolitionist, he will be traduced, slandered, ... and every thing that malice can inflict."[19] James noted that "the respectable and wealthy classes, as well as the lower orders, at that time regarded abolitionists with equal aversion and contempt." Quakers and former Quakers of New Bedford, who composed a large portion of the town's active antislavery reformers, seemed both dismayed and affronted by the violence that abolitionist activities seemed to invite, the stories of black men and women carrying clubs, of Lucy Faggins being dragged from beneath the dying man's bed. Some, like John Spear, were members of the New England Non-Resistance Society, formed in 1838, and were unalterably opposed to the use of physical coercion to fortify the cause. Some, perhaps the same men, were alarmed at the rise of a younger generation of abolitionists whose positions and language seemed to embody an aggressiveness that confirmed the worst fears of the moderate wing of antislavery reform, to say nothing of the public at large.

In New Bedford that new generation was represented by Rodney French (fig. 42), a trader who had helped form the Young Men's Antislavery Society in 1836 and whose political sympathies and motives nettled the town's Whig establishment. In later years Charles Morgan called French "verbose & violent," and Samuel Rodman reported the disruptive effect of his participation at local temperance and town meetings in 1841. Rodman suspected that French's commitment to temperance was secondary "to the ascendency of his political friends in town, County, or State, and to the personal consequence which he thence hopes to attain." For his part the *Mercury's* Lindsey was scandalized by the resolution French offered, in concert with radical abolitionists Nathaniel P. Rogers and Stephen Foster, at the 1841 meeting of the New England Anti-Slavery Society. On the question of clerical support for abolitionism, French and his cohorts asked the convention to declare "that the church and clergy of the United States, as a whole, constitute a great brotherhood of thieves, inasmuch, as they countenance

FIGURE 42. Rodney French (1802–82), by Phineas G. Headley and James E. Reed, about 1870. Used with permission of the Board of Trustees of the New Bedford Free Public Library. Headley and Reed must have inherited this image from another photographer, for French had died by the 1890s, when they became partners.

and support the highest kind of theft—manstealing, and duty to God and the oppressed, demands of abolitionists that they should denounce them as the worst foes to liberty and pure religion, and forthwith to renounce them as a Christian church and clergy." Even Garrison, never kind to the clergy, was more moderate. He suggested that of the "responsible classes" in the free states they "stand wickedly pre-eminent, and ought to be unsparingly exposed and reproved before all the people." The opposition of Garrison and Charles C. Burleigh to French's resolution helped assure its failure—despite the fact that, the *Mercury* noted, "a majority of the *ladies* invariably went in favor of the harshest epithets."[20] Even such firebrands as Wendell Phillips seemed leery of French: in May 1844 Caroline Weston, then teaching in New Bedford, wrote Phillips that should he decide to come lecture in the town, "Polly Johnson shall freeze her best ice & ice her best cakes," but "Rodney French shall not provide his dinner to Wendell."[21]

Yet while the community of white abolitionists seemed to be unraveling from such "unhappy dissencions" as the Faggins case and the widening rifts between Garrisonians and more moderate and more radical branches of the movement, these events did not trouble the village's black activists. Its members, including James and the fugitive William Henry Johnson, had initiated the effort to free

Faggins and had played a central and well-orchestrated role throughout the proceedings. Almost to a person, the abolitionists of color remained staunch Garrisonians, even refusing to support the proposed creation of a newspaper specifically for people of color on the grounds that it would merely be an organ of the "clique" that formed the "new" American and Foreign Anti-Slavery Society.[22] One May 1840 meeting of citizens of color praised the "old" American Anti-Slavery Society for "its determination to adhere to original and pure Anti-Slavery principles" and charged that only "the foul spirit of prejudice" could have inspired the "new organization" to emerge largely because women had been permitted to take part in old organization activities and governance. "As its tendency is to exclude a large portion of the well-tried friends of the Slave, on account of their sex," the meeting reasoned, "we should not be surprised if its next step is to exclude another portion on account of *colour.*" The principles underlying the American and Foreign Anti-Slavery Society "are as *foreign* to freedom and equality," the meeting concluded, "as the Slave code of Georgia is to the Declaration of American Independence."[23] In 1843 the community chose not to send delegates to the Buffalo National Convention of Colored People both because it had not invited women and because it seemed to devote too much attention to the nation's free people of color. "Bound as we are, by indissoluble ties to our downtrodden, enslaved brethren, our condition can never be materially altered while 3,000,000 of them remain in the condition of goods and chattel," the New Bedford meeting declared.[24]

The community was also beginning to produce its own spokesmen. By 1841 Frederick Douglass had spoken twice publicly against the colonization movement. The day after his third speech, before the Bristol County Anti-Slavery Society in New Bedford on 9 August that year, Douglass traveled to an antislavery meeting on Nantucket and there met New Bedford bookseller William C. Coffin.[25] Coffin, who had heard Douglass preach at an AME Zion service on Second Street, invited him to address the Nantucket convention. The second of his two Nantucket speeches was so impressive that John Collins, general agent of the Massachusetts Anti-Slavery Society, asked him to be a lecturer for the society on a three-month trial basis. So began the career of Douglass, the first lecturer of color who was actually both a slave and a fugitive, and he immediately sensed the power of the story he could tell. "Fugitive slaves, at that time, were not so plentiful as now," Douglass wrote in 1855 of his earliest lecturing, "and as a fugitive slave lecturer, I had the advantage of being a *'brand new fact'*—the first one out. Up to that time, a colored man was deemed a fool who confessed himself a runaway slave, not only because of the danger to which he exposed himself for being retaken, but because it was a confession of a very *low* origin! Some of my colored friends in New Bedford thought very badly of my wisdom for exposing and degrading myself." "We are told *Douglass* is a feigned name," the Hingham *Patriot* reported after several speeches Douglass made there in November 1841, "and that there are but two or three individuals to whom he has confided his story, as he well knows that if his old master learns his 'whereabouts,' he must return to captivity." Douglass's testimony, guarded as it was, was nonetheless revolutionary in antislavery rhetoric, and his eloquence impressed nearly everyone who heard him. The New Bedford–born journalist Charles T. Congdon recalled of Douglass's speeches in support of the fugitive George Latimer in 1842, "His was pure natural oratory, requiring no allowances, and as free from turgidity and bad taste as if he had been trained in the severe school of Webster, or had studied to good purpose the classical orations of Edward Everett. . . . Antislavery speeches were then frequently interrupted, but the sharpest of such intruders never meddled with Mr. Douglass without being sorry for the temerity."[26]

By the time John S. Jacobs returned to New Bedford on the *Francis Henrietta* in mid-February 1843, Douglass was surely the most popular lecture on the antislavery circuit (fig. 43), and the fugitive William Henry Johnson was about to follow Douglass's lead. In late May 1840 Johnson went to New York City to attend the annual meeting of the American Anti-Slavery Society, and he was a delegate from New Bedford at its 1843 annual meeting. In mid-August that year he and David W. Ruggles, whose origins and connection to New York's David Ruggles are mysterious, left to give a series of antislavery lectures in Maine. At a small town near Augusta, where, he noted, "to my great surprise, they had never heard an antislavery lecture . . . before," word had got out that "a slave"—that is, Johnson—"would address them in the evening on the subject of slavery." The two "New-Bedford boys" were able thereupon to secure the largest church in town for their address. Johnson began with hymns and readings from scripture and then took as his text the thirteenth chapter of Hebrews—"Remember them that are in bonds as bound with thee." In a letter to William Lloyd Garrison later published in the *Liberator,* Johnson described the effect he had on Maine audiences:

> I had not been speaking more than 20 minutes, before more than one half of the congregation were weeping; and I never saw more interest in a meeting, since I have made myself acquainted with the anti-slavery enterprise. . . . Having been under the influence of slavery ourself so long, we do not appear before the people with excellency of speech or of wisdom; but in the language of the apostle Paul, declaring unto them the testimony of God. We told the congregation on Sabbath last, that we appeared before them as the representatives of two and a half million of slaves in this boasted land of liberty; and only wish to relate the conclusion of those whom we left behind us just as it is. And we did so, while we were engaged in promulgating those truths, I glanced my eyes across the house—and such weeping eyes I never beheld in an anti-slavery meeting.[27]

By the time Jacobs returned, the community of color had lost one of its most active figures and was about to lose, for a few years, another. William P. Powell had moved to New York City late in 1839 to create a temperance-based boardinghouse for mariners of color like the one he had started in New Bedford, and by June 1841 he had taken on Nathaniel A. Borden as his new partner in the enterprise. New Bedford native Jeremiah Burke Sanderson, then about twenty years

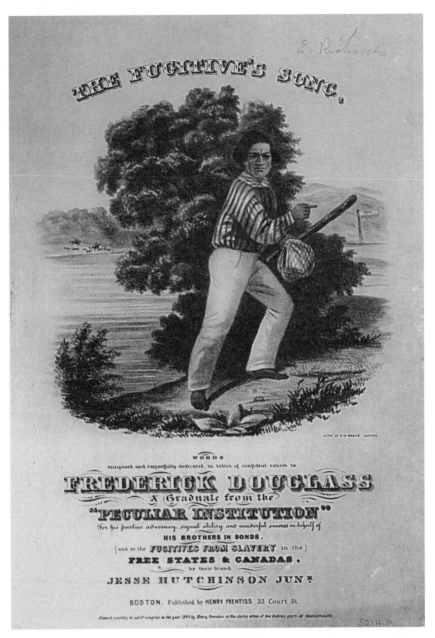

FIGURE 43. "The Fugitive's Song," composed by Jesse Hutchinson Jr., Lynn, Mass., and published by Henry Prentiss, Boston, 1845. Probably issued shortly after Douglass wrote and published his first autobiography, the cover of this sheet music commemorates his escape. By 1845 Douglass was living in Lynn, also home to the reform-minded Hutchinson Family Singers. Douglass and the Hutchinsons frequently shared the anti-slavery stage until his removal to England in 1846. Courtesy Library Company of Philadelphia.

old, took over the *Liberator* agency from Borden (fig. 44). Sanderson had met William C. Nell in New Bedford in 1840 and began a lifelong correspondence with him that June. While working as a barber in New Bedford, he became active in antislavery meetings, serving as secretary of the 1840 meeting of citizens of color in support of Garrison's "old" American Anti-Slavery Society. He was one of a group of local black activists who attended the Nantucket antislavery meeting that launched Douglass's career; abolitionist Parker Pillsbury declared Sanderson's own address on that occasion the best he had ever heard on slavery. By January 1842 the Massachusetts Anti-Slavery Society asked him to join the antislavery lecture circuit.[28]

Other men whom Douglass knew well, including Solomon Peneton and John Briggs, were also growing more involved. And the community had begun to mobilize itself to end segregation in public facilities, an effort precipitated by the David Ruggles affair of July 1841. Racial discrimination had been a fact of life in New Bedford as elsewhere for decades; Paul Cuffe had complained of it in the first two decades of the century, and Samuel Rodman noted in May 1839 that Nathan Johnson had been badly treated en route to the American Anti-Slavery Society convention in Newport. He had come from New Bedford in a carriage with Andrew Robeson but was "rudely forced from the Bar Room" at Hazard's Tavern. Robeson "rebuked" the innkeeper, and somehow Rodman heard of it, for he chose to stay at another inn when he reached Newport himself.[29] On New Year's Day 1841 Coffin wrote Debora Weston about local abolitionists' first successful protest of railroad company segregation policies, which took place probably as New Bedford residents were returning from the Boston Female Anti-Slavery Society's annual fair:

> We had taken our seats in the cars when on looking round our friend Borden was missing. Suspecting the cause and not being willing to lose so good a companion I immediately went in search of him, and found him colonized without his consent in the "Jim-Crow." I persuaded him to leave it and take a seat with us. He had hardly got himself comfortable seated, before the Conductor appeared, full of wrath, and ordered him out. This of course we could not consent to without first telling the gentleman what we thought of such an unrighteous proceeding, and immediately opened our fire upon him. Arnold, Ann, Mary and myself,—all joined, the girls (forgetting they were out of their "appropriate sphere," in their eagerness to protect an insulted brother) did their part and our poor conductor not expecting such opposition, retreated, leaving us in possession of the field.[30]

The first such case to receive public notice, however, was Ruggles's effort to gain equal treatment aboard the steamer *Telegraph* between New Bedford and Nantucket in early July of the same year. Ruggles apparently had come to New Bedford on 12 June aboard the New Bedford and Taunton Railroad, a branch line that had opened slightly less than a year before. En route, he said, he had taken a seat in the "long car"—as opposed to what the railroad company termed the "small car, divided into two parts and having no communication with each

FIGURE 44. Jeremiah Burke Sanderson (1821–75), undated photograph taken after his migration to California in 1854. Courtesy Oakland Public Library, Oakland, Calif. In New Bedford Sanderson married Catherine Gibson or Molyneux, one of the former slaves of Patrick Gibson; in California he pioneered public education for black children in both Sacramento and San Francisco.

other except by a window." Conductors directed "persons intoxicated and otherwise offensive" to one part of this small car, "attached to every train," and people of color to the other part. Because Ruggles did not seat himself in this car, he said, he was "assaulted and indeed nearly suffocated." Then, en route a week later to Nantucket on the *Telegraph,* he attempted to purchase a first-class passage (for two dollars) so that he might have "all the privileges of the Boat" rather than be allowed only forward-deck privilege. The *Telegraph*'s captain, Lot Phinney, refused to sell Ruggles a first-class ticket and then, Ruggles claimed, assaulted him, took his "private papers," and left him on Nantucket (on the return trip to New Bedford, however, Phinney unaccountably accepted Ruggles's proffered two-dollar fare). Then, on 6 July, Ruggles again attempted to sit in the railroad's long car en route to Boston "when he was visited by one of the Conductors and ordered to leave the car," a local antislavery society report stated. "This he refused to do, on the ground of his right to hold and enjoy what he had purchased, and the conductor left the car. Soon after, the superintendant employed by the company with two or three other persons entered the car and violently assaulted the person of Mr. Ruggles, tearing his clothes and dragging him from his seat, and out of the car. He demanded his trunk, which had been placed in the baggage car, but the train was allowed to proceed with it to Boston, and he has not yet recovered it." The society, along with a meeting of citizens of color that Douglass chaired at the end of June, publicly deplored Ruggles's treatment, but his case against the railroad was unsuccessful.[31]

The New Bedford and Taunton Railroad earned itself regular and scathing notice in the *Liberator* thereafter. According to Garrison, the Boston and Worcester Railroad showed "no exclusiveness," the Norwich and Worcester Railroad "no unwarrantable distinctions," and the Nashua and Lowell Railroad was "equally free to all," but aboard the New Bedford and Taunton Railroad, human rights were "shamefully outraged still." The Eastern Railroad, running from Boston northward, also maintained "an odious distinction on account of color, and a bullying propensity to carry it out," the *Liberator* stated, and in October 1841 the *Colored American* printed as corroboration an account of the "colorphobia" Frederick Douglass encountered on the Eastern between Garrison's hometown of Newburyport and Portsmouth, New Hampshire.[32] New Bedford natives Shadrach Howard and Jeremiah Sanderson tested the New Bedford and Taunton Railroad again in February 1842 and received worse treatment than Ruggles had. Because New Bedford abolitionists returning from the county antislavery meeting at Taunton had filled the small car by the time they arrived, Howard and Sanderson claimed they took the only seats available—in the front, "long" car. Confronting them, conductor George Bird told them to move and then assaulted Howard because, apparently, he was not moving fast enough to exit. Rail company employees and Howard then fought each other, Howard drawing a "common three-bladed" knife at one point, and despite Bird's efforts to eject him from the train the conductor reluctantly permitted him to travel to Taunton. Howard and Sanderson were soon afterward arrested and tried before the county court of common pleas the next month.[33] Abolitionists like Rodman and Elizabeth Buffum Chace found these practices unacceptable and often seated themselves with people of color on their way to and from antislavery meetings; even New Bedford attorney John Henry Clifford, whom Frederick Douglass characterized as "pro-slavery" and "about the most aristocratic gentleman in Bristol county," unwittingly protested the practices of the railroad company by acknowledging Douglass's presence on the train between Boston and New Bedford. Nantucket abolitionist and whaling merchant Nathaniel Barney took a much bolder step: as a stockholder, he publicly urged the directors of the New Bedford and Taunton Railroad to reconsider "the proscriptive character" of their actions, and eighteen months later he sold his stock. Barney ordered the corporation's treasurer to turn his dividends over to Francis Jackson of Boston for the benefit of Garrison, "in view of his faithful and undeviating advocacy of the rights of humanity."[34]

Abolitionists also called unfavorable attention to the exclusionary practices of churches, a controversy stimulated locally by Debora Weston's effort to have New Bedford ministers read an announcement, probably about the upcoming anti-slavery fair in Boston, from their pulpits in late December 1839. In a letter to her sister Caroline, she noted that Thomas M. Smith, the Congregationalist minister, and Theodore W. Snow, pastor of Grace Episcopal Church, refused to read the notice, and in February Smith, Snow, Henry Jackson of First Baptist Church on William Street, and Isaac Bonney of the Elm Street Methodist Church an-nounced in the *Mercury* that they expected to be consulted about announcements they were asked to read and should not be accused of a "breach of christian cour-tesy" if they refused to read them otherwise. "I have made such a fight here in town about the ministers who refuse to read notices & by publicly proclaiming that I wont go to church where such things are perpetrated I am getting things into a very good way," Debora wrote confidently to her sister Anne in March 1840.

Douglass ridiculed both Bonney and Jackson in his last two autobiographies and in several of his early speeches. At Bonney's Methodist church he was directed to sit not on the main floor but in the gallery with "about a half dozen colored members"; he at first assumed the reason was that they were "unconverted" as he was. But when Bonney served the sacrament of the Lord's Supper to the entire white congregation and then asked the black members to take communion after-ward, Douglass noted, "the colored members—poor, slavish souls—went for-ward, as invited. I went *out,* and have never been in that church since." A deacon at Jackson's church told Douglass people of color were not allowed in the church at all during one revival meeting. And in a November 1841 speech in Hingham, Douglass described the indignation one white woman displayed when passed a cup at communion from a woman of color at the unidentified church of a pro-fessed abolitionist minister; the white woman left the church. "Such was the reli-gion *she* had experienced," Douglass commented. He added another tale from the same revival. "Another young lady fell into a trance—when she awoke, she declared she had been to Heaven; her friends were all anxious to know what and whom she had seen there; so she told the whole story. But there was one good lady whose curiosity went beyond that of all the others—and she inquired of the girl that had the vision, if she saw any black folks in Heaven? After some hesitation, the reply was 'Oh! I didn't go into the *kitchen!* "[35]

The Elm Street Methodist Church was not the only church in New Bedford to offer a "negro pew." Charles Congdon recalled that even the liberal Unitarian Church, at least during the ministry of Orville Dewey in the 1820s, had "a pew for black people, though I never saw any blacks in it. Under the circumstances they declined very properly to pray with us, but set up a tabernacle for themselves in the outskirts of the village [the African Christian Church on Middle Street, organized in 1826], where they could make as much noise as they pleased; and sometimes they pleased to make a great deal." Segregated churches were thus often a matter of choice. In 1832 John Cuffe, a Quaker in practice but apparently never one formally, wrote to his sister Freelove Slocum, "Why do the collored run after the Whites and joins their churches—and are called brothers and sisters and partake of the same bread and wine and yet are held as slaves and are treated worse than the Dumb Beast of the field . . . I do not think that the collored people have no right to joine no society Except Such as do not hold them in slavery and fight not . . . if they do join them helps to keep Negroes in slavery and whip and kills us and yet call us Breathern   Christ was a collored man so worship him."[36] After his treatment at Bonney's church, Douglass came to the same conclusion.

After their faceoff over the issue of reading antislavery notices, the Weston sisters planned another confrontation over segregated seating in churches, first persuading one congregant to bring up the "negro pew" question in his church and then asking their cousin Wendell Phillips whether the purchase of a meeting-house pew by a man of color, accomplished through a third party, could be successfully contested. "Is not the black man's right to sit in his pew good against the world?" she asked. "The friends here think some of fighting this battle but wish to know how the matter stands at first."[37] Weston may have been referring to the battle forming over the New Bedford Lyceum, a lecture association that had been organized by the town's elite for the public's edification. Aired extensively in local, state, and antislavery newspapers, the Lyceum issue crowned the controversy over segregation in New Bedford and sullied the town's reputation as a haven of racial tolerance. How the issue arose is somewhat unclear, but it appears that white abolitionists deliberately staged the confrontation after people of color had asked for tickets to a certain lecture and had been refused, as Debora Weston explained in an October 1845 letter: "I met Thomas A Greene & walked round the square with him talking about the Lyceum difficulty . . . he wanted to extinguish the matter quietly by putting every thing back to where it was[,] selling tickets to all, but if he could not do that, he was going to try to make the objectors bring it up, but he rather thought the best way was to propose a black man for a member. . . . Mr Emerson has found a nigger who will apply for admission to the Lyceum, Borden, an excellent man. So here we are."[38]

Emerson's minutes of this meeting and the Westons' letters indicate that Andrew Robeson nominated Borden for membership, a motion that failed by a vote of fifty-five to twenty-one. Samuel Rodman Jr., merchant Abraham Barker, and Greene protested the action, Greene publicly criticizing the Lyceum for "rejecting a man who bore as fair & irreproachable character as any one in the community. He believed he was as little stained & defiled with the leprosy of the world as any man & on every consideration & principle was entitled to be received as a member of the Lyceum." Rodman's brother Benjamin, who once had given Weston a pair of free labor silk stockings and had questioned the authority of the Quaker elders in the early 1820s, was among those who opposed the admission of people of color—principally, it seems, on the grounds that no one "should attempt to question them in regard to the manner in which they voted (which no one had done)," Emerson wrote; "they assured us they should answer no such impertinent questioning." Samuel Rodman then allowed the protest to be set aside and offered in its place two resolutions—to rescind the Lyceum's vote to sell no more tickets and to sell tickets to anyone "without distinction of sect party or color." Lyceum members passed the first resolution but rejected the second, and then a proposal that people of color be admitted free to the house's north gallery passed, "a ruse by which the proscription was sought to be concealed by a semblance of liberality and thus make it the more secure, thereby in effect adding to injury," Samuel Rodman observed. "So inveterate is the prejudice against the unfortunate race in this com'y."[39]

Caroline Weston, in Boston when the Lyceum vote took place, wrote Phillips that the Lyceum was "doomed" and that its proceedings, in the eyes of abolitionists who relished controversy because of what it might do for the cause, "have been rich beyond my warmest expectations." The town "rocked with excitement," she said, between Lyceum meetings during the controversy, and she recounted what occurred when David W. Ruggles's name was offered for membership:

> after much discussion of a somewhat vulgar character, David was "debarred" from the privileges of the Lyceum—by a vote of 13 to 10 or some such number—a multitude of motions followed—the abolitionists fought their battle as well as troops so untrained could be expected to do—they are without eloquence, without habits of business (of this sort) without experience or knowledge of the use of Parliamentary rules—they could only testify & fight—& this they did valiantly . . . The abolitionists certainly were entrenched on martyrs ground—Joseph Ricketson rushed forward & as his father's son should contending with numerous disadvantages spoke long & distinctly & *well*—amid the hisses & laughter of the meeting which he finally succeeded in bringing to order—Sammy Rodman came to the rescue & made a noble speech & was supported by Thomas A. Greene, Andrew [Robeson]—dear Andrew—cant speak but his silence is more eloquent than words.[40]

With Joseph Ricketson at her shoulder urging her to make it "sufficiently pious," Caroline Weston wrote the protest that Samuel Rodman had offered and then withdrawn at the earlier Lyceum meeting. Rodman, Joseph and Daniel Ricketson, Andrew Robeson, John Emerson, William Coffin, and others had signed the protest, and after the decision to admit people of color to the gallery Emerson resigned his Lyceum office and Daniel Ricketson returned his tickets. The Westons then set to work to organize a wider protest against the Lyceum's actions. They made sure that Garrison knew about the controversy, and, when she learned that the Lyceum had invited Charles Sumner and Ralph Waldo Emerson (no stranger to New Bedford, as he had occupied the Unitarian pulpit on a temporary basis in the late 1820s) to speak that fall, Caroline worked to engineer their refusal. She wrote to M. M. Brooks, a friend of Emerson in Concord, to ask that he be apprised of the facts. Brooks responded that William J. Rotch, the Lyceum's president, had described the incident similarly to Emerson in a letter but differed only in the view "that the affair originated from dissatisfaction on the part of some, at the contiguity of the coloured people to the whites in the Lyceum, and that they did not probably forsee the result." Brooks assured Weston that Emerson would not lecture on the grounds "that the most ignorant they being most in need of the instruction" the Lyceum offered were being excluded. Brooks wrote, "I am sometimes selfish enough to regret ever having been an Abolitionist, it has opened before me such a knowledge of injustice and wrong that my soul is at times crushed, and my reason reels, my faith in God is lost and I am for a while thus most wretched of all beings an Atheist—I am sorry that the people of New Bedford should have done what they could to increase the wretchedness. . . . Mr. Emerson says his friend Benj Rodman should have signed that protest. Why has he not?"[41]

Caroline Weston then asked Phillips to tell Sumner about the "proscription" and to ask him to write a letter stating why he declined to speak in New Bedford. "If he [Emerson] will give his reasons in a letter to Mr. Green to be laid before the audience that he is expected to address he will do great good," Weston told Phillips, and noted that Sumner's letter should "be written as soon as these proceedings are made public—which will probably be in the course of the next week. Meanwhile," she added, "the quarrel is one of the prettiest that I was ever engaged in—& the richness of incident is indescribable."[42] Clearly embarrassed by the whole affair, Joseph Ricketson wrote Phillips to make sure he knew "for the credit of my native town that the very first men and the descendants of the first inhabitants are opposed to such proceedings." He wrote Phillips, "Almost every one of the signers of the Protest are and have been Officers of the Lyceum," and of those who did not, including Benjamin Rotch, William J. Rotch, Edmund Rodman, J. H. W. Page, Abraham Barker, John Howland, and George Hussey, "they are among our wealthiest, and first men, against whose moral character there cannot be found a blemish, & although they have not all signed the protest they notwithstanding conceded with us in everything else, and boldly declare their opinions. . . . Barker & Howland & Mr. Hussey are Quakers, men of wealth and high standing—but there were some Quaker on the other side."[43] About a week later, Caroline Weston asked Phillips to write an article for the *Liberator* about the Lyceum. "I would write it myself or send to beg Garrison to do it knowing how overburdened with cares & perplexed you must be—but that would break Joe's [Ricketson] heart which is *quite* set upon you doing this—in vain will have been his sleepless nights & his testimonies by day his battles in insurance offices & his separation from friends if *you* who are to him the Cause incarnated will not do this for him."[44]

In January 1846 the incident unfolded much as Weston had planned it. Emerson and Sumner both made public the letters of refusal they had sent to Rotch, and the *Liberator* and *National Anti-Slavery Standard* (by then edited in part by Maria Weston Chapman) printed them in full. Emerson wrote to Rotch, "Now, as I think the Lyceum exists for popular education, as I work in it for that, and think that it should bribe and importune the humblest and most ignorant to come in, and exclude nobody, or, if anybody, certainly the most cultivated,—this vote quite embarrasses me, and I should not know how to speak to the company . . . the vote appears so unkind, and so unlooked for, that I could not come with any pleasure before the Society." Sumner's letter made direct reference to New Bedford's reputation for "refined hospitality and liberal spirit" and added that, because "the New Bedford Lyceum has recently undertaken to establish, within its jurisdiction, a distinction of *caste* which had not been there recognized before," he could not lecture in the town, which he had never visited, for to do so "might seem to lend my sanction to what is most alien to my soul."[45]

By the time the Lyceum controversy erupted, the Westons and Phillips had won Joseph Ricketson over thoroughly to their sort of abolitionism and had converted his brother Daniel, who only four years earlier had labeled local abolitionists as "mean." Though he claimed that antislavery sympathies had been planted within him as a boy by his parents, friends to both Lundy and Garrison, Daniel Ricketson dated his abolitionism to 1844, when from a speech Phillips made "I learnt the true and consistent doctrine of disunion—an uncompromising disunion with Slave-Holders; and from that day without one moments wavering, that is since the gubernatorial election of 1844, I have not cast a vote under the constitution of the united States, believing as I do that it is cemented with the blood of the Slave." Ricketson introduced a resolution at the January 1846 Massachusetts Anti-Slavery Society meeting applauding the refusals of Emerson and Sumner, and in the local *People's Press* he described the "spirit" of the Lyceum's action as one "which would better become a body of Southern Slave holders, than an intelligent assembly of New England people. . . . This is the spirit that binds more firmly the fetter to the slave—this is the spirit that makes the Southern autocrat feel secure in his nefarious traffic—this is the spirit of allegiance to the bloody Moloch of the South!"[46]

By the fall lecture season of 1846 the Ricketson brothers had helped formed an alternative, the New Bedford Lecture Association, as "a standing protest against *caste*," Jeremiah Sanderson stated; Andrew Robeson was president and Joseph Ricketson secretary. In a letter inviting Horace Mann to speak before the new group, Joseph Ricketson assured him that the lecture association was formed "not with any disrespect to the Old Lyceum, but that every one may have a chance to hear the lectures," and he noted in addition that the Lyceum had simply not been able to secure sufficiently interesting speakers. Indeed, in 1847 the Lyceum invited Herman Melville but no antislavery lecturers, while the Lecture Association offered Sumner, Theodore Parker, Mann, and the Unitarian ministers James Freeman Clarke and John Weiss. Ricketson wrote Debora Weston about the Lyceum's response:

> You cannot tell what a mess the Lyceum are in—They had hoped and so far deceived themselves to think that by the recinding [*sic*] of their "odious vote," we should have no lectures this winter & were all taken by surprise, when our course was announced . . . they announced their lectures on the same day we did and by the advertisement enclosed you can judge for yourself—they say we are obstinate. . . . They had a meeting last evening & reduced their tickets from two dollars to fifty cents & yesterday they were trying to sell their tickets to colored people at that price, when only two years ago, they have got two dollars—verily what a fall was theirs.

Ricketson added that "one large colored man has purchased a ticket & says it may happen that he may set side of 'Capt Merrill,'" one of the Lyceum members who had proposed setting off the gallery for people of color. "Theres fun a head," Ricketson concluded. But he himself did not find it immediately: on the day the lecture association's series was announced in the *Mercury* in 1847, people he thought were friends refused to vote for him as a director of the town's Commercial Bank. The move disturbed him so much that he refused to run for reelection as secretary of the New Bedford Port Society, run by essentially the same individuals, and told Weston that "others may take care of the Port Society—I shall concentrate my little strength in behalf of the cause of Humanity, cheerfully & willingly."[47]

The Lyceum matter was so explosive partly because of the divide it revealed within New Bedford's elite and because of the town's already vaunted reputation for tolerance. Although individuals had organized private schools for children and adults of color, by the late 1830s black and white children attended public schools together. "The public schools are all open," Debora Weston wrote to Maria in April 1837, "and black children admitted on terms of the most perfect equality." Douglass noted similarly of the town's schools at his arrival in 1838: "in New Bedford, the black man's children—although anti-slavery was far from popular—went to school side by side with the white children, and apparently without objection from any quarter." Ten years later J. B. Sanderson wrote to Douglass that the same conditions prevailed. Yet other testimony suggests that discrimination existed within the classroom. Charles Congdon recalled of his public school that "the black boys were seated by themselves, and the white offenders were punished by being obliged to sit with them," while William Wells Brown's daughter Josephine stated that children of color "had to occupy a seat set apart for us" in New Bedford schools of the late 1840s. But that the public schools of the town were open to children of color at all was viewed as a true novelty.[48] Contemporary observers also found it remarkable that public meetings, usually antislavery meetings, were not segregated. Charles W. Morgan had noted that "the coloured & white people [were] seated promiscuously" at Garrison's antislavery lecture in April 1841, Sturge had used the same term when he attended the Friends meeting in June that year, and Frederick Douglass noted the same tendency when he spoke in New Bedford on behalf of the imperiled fugitive George Latimer in November 1842. "From the eminence which I occupied, I could see the entire audience," he wrote to Garrison for the *Liberator,* "and from its appearance, I should conclude that prejudice against color was not there—at any rate, it was not to be seen by me; we were all on a level, every one took a seat just where they chose, there were neither men's side, nor women's side; white pew nor black pew, but all seats were free, and all sides free."[49]

Just as the desegregation controversies frayed the abolitionist fabric, the protection of such fugitives as Latimer seemed to strengthen it. In the fall of 1842 Latimer and his wife had hidden in the hold of a vessel between their native Norfolk, Virginia, and Baltimore and had then fled to Philadelphia and finally to Boston. On 20 October, just days after they arrived in the Massachusetts capital, a white employee of Latimer's master recognized him and arranged for his arrest. When abolitionists failed to secure Latimer's release by writ of habeas corpus, they called for mass meetings and a petition drive through the length and breadth of the commonwealth. After a New Bedford antislavery meeting on 31 October, Andrew Robeson "fell into my arms," Anne Weston wrote to her aunt Mary and sister Debora. "He was full of Boston & the Slave." The next evening she went with the free black abolitionist Charles Lenox Remond and William Coffin to a crowded meeting at the town hall about Latimer. There Remond and Frederick Douglass protested Latimer's rendition and urged support of his legal defense fund. "I have the best evidence that a great good has been done," Douglass wrote to Garrison. "It is said by many residents, that New Bedford has never been so favorably aroused to her anti-slavery responsibilities as at present." James B. Gray, Latimer's Norfolk owner, ultimately decided to sell the man for four hundred dollars, much less than he had originally requested, and Latimer himself appeared before a packed house at the Bristol County "Latimer Convention" in New Bedford on 18 January 1843. "At the close of that ev'g there was an attempt at a disturbance by the boys to break up the m'g," Samuel Rodman noted in his diary, "but they did not succeed either in the house or by the false alarm of fire which they endeavored to raise in the streets."[50] Ultimately the huge Latimer petitions, signed by more than one hundred thousand people, bore fruit in the so-called "Latimer statute," or Massachusetts personal liberty law, of 1843, which forbade state officials from assisting in the rendition of fugitive slaves within Massachusetts and directly responded to the U.S. Supreme Court decision of the previous year in *Prigg v. Pennsylvania,* which permitted slaveholders to pursue and return slaves in any state without due process but absolved state officials from any responsibility to enforce the 1793 Fugitive Slave Law.[51]

In the midst of this excitement, John S. Jacobs returned to New Bedford on the *Francis Henrietta.* While the vessel lay in the harbor, a man he knew and referred to only as R. P. (probably Robert Piper, a mariner and son of William Piper) took a shore boat to the vessel to tell Jacobs that his sister Harriet had escaped and in fact had been to New Bedford to look for him. Jacobs had earned $356.83 on the voyage and another $10 for helping unload the ship, money he planned to use to buy his sister's freedom. He immediately went to New York and found his much-changed sister at the Astor House, the hotel from which he had accomplished his escape five years earlier. Harriet told John that her brother's former owner claimed that the abolitionists had lured him away in New York; John told her he had needed no such enticement "to stimulate his desire for freedom."[52] The news about John had hastened Harriet's escape. By 1843 she and her brother moved to Boston, and John Jacobs spent the next several years trying to keep his sister's whereabouts a secret from the Norcom family of Edenton, who claimed her. In a letter to Sydney Howard Gay written from Chelsea, a small city just north of Boston, Jacobs described how Dr. Norcom, having heard that Harriet was living in New York, had written a letter to "the New York blood hounds" about her and how the doctor's son and son-in-law (Daniel Messmore) had somehow written Harriet directly.

> The old Dr writes his to New York to be put in to the hands of the smartest polease officer in the city, offering $100 reward for her ann after having discribed her as menutely as posable he sais that he dont wish to sell her at any price he wants to get her to make an ensample of her for the good of the institution—the young Dr writes as if he had just come from a camp meeting, his hole head is full of love the purest of the Delilah kind he is afraid that she is not happy an comfortable away from all of her friends and relatives and after assuring her that the family still entertain the most friendly feelings towards her he then begs her to write him where she is that he might restore her to her former happiness (hell).

Jacobs added that the family wanted Harriet "to return home or buy her self but as my sister has not the means of buy her self and finds these cold regons more healthy than the suny South they will have to love each other at a distance the sweetest love that can exist betweene master and slave."[53]

By 1846 John Jacobs had begun to work for "the oppressed the world over," writing to Sydney Howard Gay about a former Edenton slave who was considering a return to slavery and helping guide a fugitive on a New Orleans vessel out of Boston harbor and to safety. Then in late fall 1847 Jacobs embarked on an

FIGURE 45. Jonathan Walker, by unidentified photographer, about 1870. Courtesy Massachusetts Historical Society.

antislavery lecture tour with Jonathan Walker (fig. 45).[54] Born in Harwich, Massachusetts, and a master mariner in New Bedford in 1836, Walker had tried to help seven slaves escape in his own boat from Pensacola, Florida, to the Bahamas in June 1844 but fell ill en route; eventually two sloops overtook Walker's vessel and imprisoned him and the fugitives in Key West. In November Walker was taken to court and placed in a pillory. Onlookers hurled rotten eggs at him, and a local marshal branded his right hand with the initials "S. S.," for "slave stealer." He remained in prison until late May 1845, leaving a wife and eight children without support. New Bedford residents took the case to heart. The *Mercury* reported that those who had known Walker in New Bedford felt him to be "a respectable, kind-hearted New England man." Two weeks before Walker received his infamous "branded hand," Caroline Weston noted in a letter to Wendell Phillips's wife Ann, the local elite had called a meeting to raise funds for his legal expenses.

> You would have laughed to see the meeting which was got up here—The Whigs quite desperate—all on fire with compassion and indignation—the Abolitionists quite in the background & Clifford, Eddy, Charles Morgan & the Ricketsons, Page, Bartlett, Joseph Grinnell & others carrying their hats round for money—every other man was acting as collector—they got about $100 tho' it was a rainy night, so much

so that very few ladies got out. . . . Wm Coffin resigned here as Sec of the meeting as soon as he understood how it all was—& Thomas Hathaway also—they thought it foolish to shew any thing upon a <u>lawyer</u>.[55]

By August 1845 Walker had committed his story to paper and traveled to Boston to show it to Maria Weston Chapman, who urged him to publish it. It may have been at this time, too, that abolitionist Henry Ingersoll Bowditch commissioned the Boston daguerreotypists Albert Sands Southworth and Josiah Johnson Hawes to photograph his branded hand (fig. 46). *The Trial and Imprisonment of Jonathan Walker* was published in Boston the same year that Walker was released, and he began traveling through New England giving antislavery lecturers and selling his narrative soon afterward. Living in poverty in Plymouth in the fall of 1847, and grimly convinced that "among the Cape people and masters of vessels there, . . . with very few exceptions, there is no interest manifested in behalf of the enslaved millions of this country," Walker set off on an extensive lecture tour with Jacobs, through upstate New York, in late November. Jacobs, as his letter to Gay suggests, appears to have been the superior orator; the *National Anti-Slavery Standard* termed him a speaker "scarcely excelled by any of his predecessors."[56]

Walker's exploit was a celebrated rallying point among abolitionists, but it was not the only attempted slave rescue of 1844. That year Calvin Fairbank of western New York was convicted in Kentucky of having assisted in the escape of the Lexington slaves Lewis Hayden and his wife. Hayden managed to make his way to Canada and to Detroit by 1845, but Fairbank was sentenced to fifteen years in a Kentucky prison. Abolitionists immediately recognized Hayden's possible value to the cause and seem to have encouraged him to settle in New Bedford. "Lewis Hayden has won the esteem and friendship of all with whom he has become acquainted, and is a rare young man," Garrison wrote to Gay in late March that year. "Should he conclude to return, and take up his abide in New Bedford, I think he can be made very serviceable to our cause." Hayden and his wife did settle in New Bedford but, it appears, only briefly. By May 1846 they moved to Boston, in time Lewis Hayden raised the money that assured Fairbank's release, and he became a central figure in the Underground Railroad in Boston.[57] The perpetrator of the other 1844 rescue, Charles Turner Torrey, was not so fortunate. A "pealer" whom Garrison found "decidedly objectionable" because of his affiliation with the "new" American and Foreign Anti-Slavery Society, Torrey nonetheless was actively sympathetic to the cause of the fugitive slave. He was arrested on 25 June 1844 in Baltimore on the charge that he had helped the slaves of Bushrod Taylor of Winchester, Virginia, escape, was convicted, and died in jail in May 1846.[58]

Neither Torrey nor Fairbank had a commercial interest in the areas where these slave escapes took place, but Fall River's Gilbert Ricketson had such a stake in the port of Portsmouth, Virginia. Ricketson's return of a fugitive who had stowed away on his schooner *Cornelia* in that port in 1844 drew another line in the sand

FIGURE 46. *The Branded Hand,* daguerreotype by Albert Sands Southworth and Josiah Johnson Hawes, Boston, about 1845. Courtesy Massachusetts Historical Society, gift of Nathaniel Bowditch 1930.

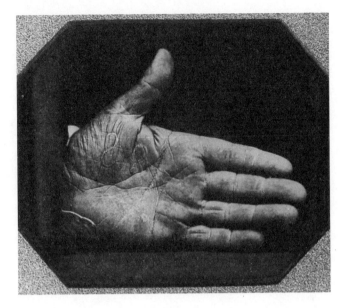

between antislavery people and abolitionists. The *Cornelia,* owned in part by Ricketson's uncle Joseph Ricketson Jr., plied the trading routes between New Bedford and the South regularly in the 1840s. The vessel was loading with corn at Portsmouth's Railroad Wharf on 12 December 1844 when a Norfolk slave named Tom, the property of one John Rutter (or Rudder), hid aboard the *Cornelia.* Gilbert Ricketson, the *Cornelia's* captain, discovered Tom when the vessel ran aground near dusk the same day. Reports state that Ricketson took Tom, the *Cornelia's* black steward, Henry Boyer, and another black crew member identified only as Smith in a small boat back to Portsmouth.[59] Boyer was promptly arrested on the charge of "having advised or persuaded" Tom to escape.

At Boyer's trial, John Rutter claimed that Tom was helping to load the *Cornelia* when Boyer asked him "if he was free the witness replied that he was not, . . . the prisoner then told him if he would do as he told him that he could be benefitted . . . the prisoner told him to go down in the forecastle of the vessel when the witness concealed himself in a [illegible] where some canvass was placed . . . he remained there until the afternoon when he was removed to another place by the prisoner who told him they were going to search the vessel." Boyer was accused additionally of having secured provisions for Tom. When Ricketson discovered Tom, an unidentified New Bedford correspondent wrote to Garrison in late December, he insisted on taking Boyer and Smith with him to Portsmouth, "and I am told that Smith says, the Capt. instructed the slave what to say, and advised him to accuse them both of being privy to his being on board; but for this I will not vouch."[60]

When news of Ricketson's action reached New Bedford, James B. Congdon, then chair of the town's board of selectmen, contacted a Norfolk law firm to secure counsel for Boyer, but it was too late: a week after the incident, Boyer, despite assurances that he had counsel "of the highest standing," was tried, con-victed, and sentenced to four years in a Virginia prison. Congdon's effort not-withstanding, New Bedford seemed far more outraged about Ricketson's action than Boyer's fate. Joseph Ricketson, apparently ill at the time Boyer was seized, published a notice in mid-January 1845 disclaiming any sympathetic association with his nephew's action. "I am desirous as an owner of said vessel, as far as my own interest is concerned, to say, that I had much rather it would all have been jeopardized, or even lost forever, than such an act in which I might in any wise have been connected, should have occurred," he wrote. The notice appeared in local and antislavery papers, and Ricketson may also have written the anonymous letter to the *Liberator* describing Gilbert Ricketson's return to New Bedford.

> Capt. Ricketson called on me, on his return, stating that he had called for the pur-pose of letting me know the difficulty he had got into. 'What difficulty?' said I. 'You have heard, I suppose, that I found a slave on board my vessel.' 'Yes,' said I, 'and you carried him back—did you not?' 'Yes,' said he. 'Well,' I replied, 'You did very wrong in so doing.' 'Why,' he replied, 'I should never have dared to go back there again, if I had brought him away.' 'So,' said I, 'you'll not only return your brother into bond-age, but jeopardize the liberty of your own townsman, for the sake of interest.' . . . He evidently feels guilty, for he had not called on Boyer's wife since his return, or given her any information in relation to her husband! Previous to this, he had always had his washing done by Boyer's wife.[61]

Gilbert Ricketson responded defensively in the same newspapers, claiming that his uncle was the only one who did not approve "the course I took" in re-turning Tom to Portsmouth and that he would have put both his own liberty at risk and exposed the vessel's owners to financial penalty. "Would the other large owners have justified me in putting their property at hazard," the vessel's captain asked, "because Mr. J. Ricketson was willing to risk the loss of his small share? I think not."[62] Gilbert Ricketson saw himself as a clear-headed pragmatist, as self-interested as any man and certainly no more self-interested than most aboli-tionists.

> The way I look at the subject, a man's own freedom is of more consequence to him-self than is the freedom of his neighbor, or any other person. Hence, the reason why I chose to return with the slave Rudder, instead of trying to bring him to New-Bedford. I considered liberty of as much value as Patrick Henry did, whom the New-Bedford abolitionists quote with so much approbation. Rather than run the immi-nent risk of a 10 years' deprivation of that liberty, incarcerated in the Virginia State prison, I preferred doing as I did . . . however much Torrey and a few others may fancy this kind of life, I, for one, choose to keep clear of such service, if I can. I know

that, in coming to this conclusion, I shall offend my *very particularly sensitive* friends of the ultra abolition school in New-Bedford and elsewhere, *which I am very sorry to do*. . . . Doubtless, they would have deemed it quite a Godsend to their cause, if, instead of being here at home with my family, I were at this moment employed at hard labor in the Virginia State prison, for attempting to get a slave free. It would have been rung all through Massachusetts, as Walker's and Torrey's cases have been. The Liberator and Chronicle, John Bailey, Frederick Douglass, Wm. Lloyd Garrison, and other kindred prints and souls would have thundered forth their anathemas against southern tyranny; but their thunders, though very loud here at home, would have died away long before they reached the narrow confines of the Virginia penitentiary.

New Bedford residents who met in January to consider Boyer's case applauded Joseph Ricketson, "a worthy son of a noble sire," for his repudiation of Gilbert Ricketson, but discussion of Boyer himself virtually disappeared from letters and newspapers. Instead, Garrison and the ever-opportunistic Weston sisters saw in the case a golden opportunity to evangelize New Bedford. In early January and early February, Garrison wrote to tell abolitionist John Bailey that he would not be able to attend any meeting about Boyer because of illness in his family and noted too that many other of the movement's best speakers were otherwise engaged. "I am sorry it so turns out, and you will be sorry too," Garrison wrote apologetically. "I see the opportunity is a good one, arising out of Capt. Ricketson's infamous conduct, (rendered still worse by his impudent and profligate defence,) to make a grand anti-slavery stir in New Bedford, and regret the arrangements cannot be made according to the desire of the friends."[63] For her part, Caroline Weston urged the popular Wendell Phillips to capitalize on the *Cornelia* incident by making an appearance with Garrison in New Bedford:

> There is to be no meeting if you cannot both come & as soon as we know when you will come we will proceed to agitate—The public mind here is charmingly disposed for an uproar—the Boyer case furnishing a test by which to try people & abundance of them of fair character enough hitherto have been weighed in the balances & found wanting. The selfishness & meanness of the wharves [?] & the churches shine out visibly. . . . There is great discussion going on & the community is just in the right state to be attacked. . . . You must come—I believe that the feeble Philanthropy of this place can be blown into a blaze & the wealth turned into the right channel—Come & do it—We have converted Daniel & there is every prospect of his staying converted—I think we are sure of Joe too—& there is a hundred thousand dollars to begin with—If you will come, we shall send for Quincy & May—The Hutchinsons &—I have written to Garrison urging him to come as has Mr. Emerson—& I charged him as I now charge you . . . it is very important that the Mass Antislavery Soc. should march in—Drums beating & colours flying & take possession of New-Bedford.[64]

But Phillips and Garrison did not come to make a "grand anti-slavery stir" in the town, and Gilbert Ricketson's criticisms of abolitionists must have stung more deeply as a consequence. Ricketson found the widespread condemnation of his action—including Garrison's comment that he "seems to be so utterly debased in mind as to be incapable of appreciating how good and noble it is to suffer in a righteous cause, rather than to inflict suffering on others"—hypocritical.

> All this talk about freeing the slaves in this way, is very beautiful in theory—it looks well on paper, and sounds well in resolutions; but when you come to put it in practice, then *comes the rub*. I would that every slave in the United States were set at liberty; but I have no idea, at present, if I can avoid it, or becoming a martyr in the anti-slavery cause, especially when I see such men as Garrison, Leavitt, Edmund Quincy, Bailey, Emerson, and others of the same kidney, so careful to keep themselves out of harm's way at the North, when, if there is any truth in the doctrine they preach, they ought to be in the slave States, beautifully engaged in the work they so much approve—that of unriveting the shackles of the bondmen. Do we find them so engaged? Not at all. . . . They can easily meet at Liberty Hall, New Bedford, and pass resolutions, denouncing me for having done acts contrary to the Divine law, as they allege; but all this does but little towards setting the slave free. . . . Why don't they fit out a vessel or two, and go out themselves to Norfolk or Charleston, and attempt to put in practice what they so highly applaud? . . . Do they expect to make a cat's-paw of me in a service they are unwilling to undertake themselves?

The *Cornelia* case received scant notice after Gilbert Ricketson's defense was published at the end of February 1845. One January account noted that Boyer's wife and three children were destitute, and at the June Massachusetts Anti-Slavery Society meeting Phillips presented a resolution condemning the "dastardly act" of Ricketson, which "has virtually locked the prison door upon Henry Boyer, and doomed to a ten-fold worse slavery than before, a poor fugitive slave." But nothing appears to have been done to secure a pardon for Boyer, and no newspaper, antislavery or otherwise, mentioned the fate of the slave Tom. Boyer apparently served his full term and had returned to New Bedford by late April 1849. "Boyer the man who was in my vessel the Cornelia & imprisoned in Virginia was in town last week on his way home," Joseph Ricketson wrote Debora Weston at the time. "I did not see him—I understand his wife is about being married to another man—there is a little notice of this in the Liberator of this week taken from a Sandwich paper." Boyer may have left New Bedford after his disappointing 1849 return.[65]

Henry Boyer was not the only man of color to be incarcerated for assisting fugitives. Indeed, there were just enough cases exposed in newspapers to fan the popular concern that blacks were key figures in what by then was called the Underground Railroad; such suspicions about black mariners had after all given rise to the Negro Seamen's Acts. Leonard Grimes, who had settled in New Bedford at about the time Boyer went to prison, had himself been imprisoned on the charge of having helped the seven slaves belonging to Joseph Mead of Loudon County, Virginia, escape on 26 October 1839 (fig. 47). Born free in Leesburg, the seat of Loudoun County, on the Potomac some two hundred miles northwest of

Washington, D.C., Grimes moved to Washington as a boy, married as a young man, and began to use his hackman's trade as a cover for assisting fugitives out of Virginia. On 10 March 1840, when he was about twenty-five, Grimes was convicted on what even the court admitted was circumstantial evidence of having taken a slave named Patty and her six children in his hack to Washington; the fugitives, the *Alexandria Gazette and Virginia Advertiser* reported, were believed to have reached Canada. Because so many had testified to Grimes's "very high character," he was sentenced to the lightest penalty his crime demanded—a fine of one hundred dollars and two years in the state penitentiary. Just before he entered prison, he signed a deed in trust with his uncle William Bush, to whom he apparently was in debt at the time, for his property at the corner of H and 22d Streets in Washington, Bush was to take care of Grimes's wife and children while he was incarcerated.[66] Several efforts to gain a pardon for Grimes failed. He probably served his full term and within two years left the South for New Bedford, where he set up a grocery and provisioning store with another man of color, Lewis Thomas, on lower Middle Street. Grimes seems to have remained in New Bedford for about three years; in June 1846 the couple's fourth child, Leonard E., was born there. In 1848 Grimes and his family moved to Boston, where he organized the city's Twelfth Baptist Church, known by the 1850s as the "fugitive slave church." After the Fugitive Slave Act passed in 1850, about forty members of Grimes's congregation fled to Canada, and his parishioners raised $1,300 in 1854 and 1855 to purchase the freedom of famed fugitive Anthony Burns. Grimes himself traveled to Baltimore to arrange the exchange of funds for Burns.[67]

That Grimes had actively assisted fugitives in and around Washington is corroborated by the stories passed down by the descendants of William Bush. "Prior to his residence in New Bedford Deacon Bush was actively engaged in assisting the fugitives, helping them across the border from Virginia & Washington," Bush's granddaughter, Anna Jourdain Reed, wrote in an undated memorandum. "It was while thus engaged that a nephew, an able and ardent assistant, was apprehended with a carriage filled with run-away slaves. He was arrested and sent to prison. This nephew in later years became the well-known and beloved pastor of the Twelfth Baptist Church in Boston, the Rev. Leonard Grimes." Grimes might have come to New Bedford because kin had already settled there. Archibald Clark, the brother of William Bush's wife Lucinda, had moved to the town from Washington in 1831, probably with his son John, and that year took as his second wife the Jamaica-born widow Nancy Davis Boyer. His son and namesake by his first wife, probably Eleanor Clarke, may have moved to New Bedford earlier, about 1827; he was then using the alias Archibald C. Lloyd, and contradictory assertions about Eleanor Clarke's slave status suggest that her son may have been a fugitive. However the actual genealogy played out, William Bush and his family moved to New Bedford shortly after Grimes left for Boston—and after his or his wife's reputed involvement in the ill-fated *Pearl* incident may have come to light.[68]

Daniel Drayton's effort to help seventy-seven (some accounts claim seventy-six) slaves escape from Washington on the hired schooner *Pearl* in April 1848 was an interracial collaboration, in both its execution and its undoing (fig. 48).[69] Like Fairhaven's Joseph Bates and the Boston Vigilance Committee's Austin Bearse, Drayton was awakened to the inequities of slavery through years of working on coasting vessels running between Savannah at the South and St. John's, New Brunswick, down East. In his early years he had turned a "deaf ear" to the queries of slaves who approached him at southern landings and ports in an effort to gauge his willingness to help them escape. "At that time, according to an idea still common enough, I had regarded the negroes as only fit to be slaves," he later wrote, "and had not been inclined to pay much attention to the pitiful tales which they told me of ill-treatment by their masters and mistresses." But, partly by dint of a religious awakening, he changed his mind; he came to approach the subject much as Harriet Beecher Stowe later did, as an infamy that involved the forcible shattering of families.

> The idea of having first one child and then another taken from me, as fast as they grew large enough, and handed over to the slave-traders, to be carried I knew not where, and sold, if they were girls, I knew not for what purposes, would have been horrible enough, and, from instances which came to my notice, I perceived that it was not less horrible and distressing to the parties concerned in the case of black people than of white ones. I had never read any abolition books, nor heard any abolition lectures. I had frequented only Methodist meetings, and nothing was heard there about slavery. But, for the life of me, I could not perceive why the golden rule of doing to others as you would wish them to do to you did not apply in this case.

Drayton concluded it "very right and proper" to help slaves escape; indeed, he wrote, "the more dangerous it might have been to render such assistance, the more meritorious I should have thought the act to be." He declared specious the occasional claim among southerners that slaves were happy in their situation and only thought of escaping at the suggestion of northern abolitionists. "There is not a waterman who ever sailed in Chesapeake Bay who will not tell you that, so far from the slaves needing any prompting to run away, the difficulty is, when they ask you to assist them, to make them take no for an answer. I have known instances where men have lain in the woods for a year or two, waiting for an opportunity to escape on board some vessel." Drayton became so moved by the plight of slaves that he made "one or two attempts," unsuccessfully, to help them escape. Then, in the summer of 1847, Drayton and his only assistant, "a small black boy," were unloading a cargo of Delaware Bay oysters at the White House wharf in Washington when a man of color came aboard "and, observing that I seemed to be from the north, he said he supposed we were pretty much all abolitionists there," Drayton wrote. "I don't know where he got this piece of information, but I think it likely from some southern member of Congress."

According to Drayton, the man told Drayton that he brought a message from a free man of color whose wife and five children were slaves. They wished to

FIGURE 47. Leonard Grimes, photograph by G. H. Loomis, Boston, 1860 or 1861. Courtesy Carl J. Cruz, New Bedford Historical Society.

FIGURE 48. Daniel Drayton, engraving in *Personal Memoir of Daniel Drayton, for Four Years and Four Months a Prisoner (for Charity's Sake) in Washington Jail. Including a Narrative of the Voyage and Capture of the Schooner* Pearl (Boston, 1853). Courtesy University of Massachusetts at Dartmouth.

escape because the owner had threatened to sell them all when the wife tried to purchase her freedom. At the time, slaves assuredly took this as no idle warning: the firm of Franklin and Armfield in Alexandria, part of the District of Columbia until 1846, sold as many as one thousand slaves a year to cotton belt owners in the deep South and was one of the largest slave dealers in the union.[70] Drayton took the party to Frenchtown, New Jersey, where the woman's husband was waiting for them, and later heard "that the whole family are comfortably established in a free country, and doing well." To Drayton it was an "exploit," one he wished to repeat: he had not seen much success in his life, and he came to view carrying slaves to freedom as his life's mission.[71]

Accounts differ, but the *Pearl* incident seems to have begun with a letter Drayton received in February 1848, probably from the free Washington carpenter Daniel Bell, the free domestic servant Paul Jennings, or Jennings's brother, asking for a meeting in Baltimore the next month. Bell's family, freed at their owner's death, was suddenly endangered when the owner's heirs contested his will. At a meeting the correspondent said he had heard about Drayton's earlier rescue and begged him to undertake another for "a family or two" whose members expected at any moment to be sold. Drayton—reluctantly or wholeheartedly, depending upon the account—said he would consider it and ultimately agreed to the plan.[72] He chartered the New Jersey–registered *Pearl* from one Edward Sayres and went to Washington, arriving with a load of wood at White House Wharf on 13 April 1848. Jennings stated that Drayton assured him he would take "as many . . . as want to go," a claim Drayton himself made. But Horace Mann, who engineered Drayton's defense after his arrest, claimed the slaves had stowed themselves in the vessel's hold while the captain was away from the wharf; when they came on deck later, Mann said, Drayton "was as much astonished as any body at the number of fishes that had got into his net."[73]

Bell and Jennings, with the assistance of the free black butler Samuel Edmondson, are believed to have passed word of Drayton's plan to slaves in and around Washington. On the night of 13 April, ironically during a massive citywide celebration of the expulsion of Louis-Philippe and the declaration of the French republic, Bell's family, Samuel Edmondson, five of his siblings, and Mary Ellen Steward, claimed by Jennings's former owner, Dolly Madison, and some sixty others made their way to the foot of Seventh Street. Lucinda Clarke Bush, a mulatto free woman married to William Bush and often taken for white, is said to have gone to homes in Washington to retrieve the slaves under some ruse and to have taken them to the *Pearl*. That Drayton and William Bush knew each other seems well established: Bush was termed his "old friend" in a later newspaper account. At this juncture, too, Drayton's betrayal took root: a black hackman named Judson Diggs, who carried other slave passengers to the vessel, informed their masters. The slave owners at once hired a steamer and overtook the schooner, returned in both vessels to Washington, and threw the entire party in jail. Between forty-five and forty-one slaves from the *Pearl* were traded to New Orleans (though a yellow fever epidemic there forced their return to Baltimore within the month). New York abolitionists, organized by Brooklyn Presbyterian cleric Henry Ward Beecher, managed to purchase the freedom of five of the six Edmondson children; Beecher's sister, Harriet Beecher Stowe, interviewed Mary and Emily Edmondson for *Uncle Tom's Cabin* and paid for their private school education. The freedom of some members of Bell's family was also purchased, but the rest were returned to slavery.

For his part, Drayton was confronted with an enormous bail of one thousand dollars for each slave he had taken on board and was charged with 115 counts of larceny and transporting stolen property. Boston abolitionists arranged for Drayton's defense; he was tried numerous times through May 1849, and in the end spent four years and four months in prison. "If a man wishes to realize the agony which our American slave-trade inflicts in the separation of families," Drayton wrote, "let him personally feel that separation, as I did; let him pass four years in the Washington jail." Slave owners believed he had been financed by northern abolitionists. Drayton was paid, but he never revealed by whom, and he said he had taken the mission on as his "protest against the infamous and atrocious doctrine that there can be any such thing as property in man! We can only do according to our power, and the capacity, gifts and talents, that we have. . . . I could not talk, I could not write, but I could act. The humblest, the most uneducated man can do that."[74]

One historian has termed the 1848 *Pearl* incident "the most audacious of all such enterprises down to John Brown's raid on Harper's Ferry eleven years later," and if Lucinda Clarke Bush had been involved the scandalous and ill-fated rescue would certainly have been enough to compel her family's move to New Bedford, some six months after Drayton's various trials had concluded. Lucinda's brother Archibald Clarke and part of his family already lived in the city, and even though Bush and most if not all of his family were free, he may have worried that Lucinda's reputed role in the escape attempt would come to light and cause her arrest and possible return to slavery. In New Bedford Bush and his family probably first lived at 128 Third Street, Clarke's home, and returned to live there in the 1860s. "Many fugitives from slavery found refuge beneath this roof," Bush's granddaughter Anna Jourdain Reed has written, but it was in a "more capacious dwelling that Deacon Bush gave shelter and protection to the many who came to his door, oftimes in groups of five, six or more." The fugitive George Teamoh would attest as much in the mid-1850s. By that time Bush was both a laborer and boardinghouse keeper on South Water Street and later on Coffin Street, also on the south side of the waterfront; Reed probably meant to indicate one of these dwellings.

By the time Bush settled in New Bedford, the town had clearly come to be perceived as a destination, if only a temporary one, for fugitives. In her reminiscences Elizabeth Buffum Chace stated that a fairly systematic connection between the South and Canada had been put in place in the region after 1839.

From the time of the arrival of James Curry at Fall River and his departure for Canada, in 1839, that town became an important station on the so-called underground railroad. Slaves in Virginia would secure passage, either secretly or with consent of the captains, in small trading vessels, at Norfolk or Portsmouth, and thus be brought into some port in New England, where their fate depended on the circumstances into which they happened to fall. A few, landing at some towns on Cape Cod, would reach New Bedford, and thence be sent by an abolitionist there to Fall River, to be sheltered by Nathaniel B. Borden and his wife, who was my sister Sarah, and sent by them to my home at Valley Falls, in the darkness of night, and in a closed carriage, with Robert Adams, a most faithful Friend, as their conductor.[75]

At Valley Falls, Chace recalled, she and her husband prepared fugitives for the rest of their voyage north. The couple took them to the Providence and Worcester Railroad depot and put them under the care of a trusted conductor, who at Worcester secured the fugitives' transfer to a railroad running into Vermont. In that state, a Unitarian minister Chace identified only as Young met them and sent them into Canada. "I used to give them an envelope, directed to us, to be mailed in Toronto," she wrote, "which, when it reached us, was sufficient by its postmark to announce their safe arrival, beyond the baleful influence of the Stars and Stripes, and the anti-protection of the Fugitive Slave Law." Other evidence suggests that fugitives were at some point directed to New Bedford. Mansfield Jackson escaped from his Suffolk, Virginia, owner by stowing away on the brig *Relief* in Norfolk, which he had helped to load, on 14 June 1841. The *Relief* was bound for St. John's, New Brunswick, but when the captain discovered Jackson after a week at sea he put in at Newport to arrange the fugitive's return. Jackson had been tied up but managed to free himself, stole a boat, and landed on Goat Island in Narragansett Bay. The *Mercury* reported, "We learn that the blacks have taken him in charge, and have contributed money and clothes to his relief, and would convey him to New Bedford."[76]

The next year John Thompson was directed to New Bedford. Thompson, then thirty years old, escaped his Maryland plantation on a stolen horse and hoped to board a steamer across the Chesapeake Bay to Baltimore and the North but, advised against trying, walked into Columbia, Pennsylvania, a well-known fugitive stopping point and home to several active white and black abolitionists. He worked on a farm outside the town for six months, but the arrival of slave catchers in the neighborhood suggested, he wrote, that it might be "best for me to go to sea." Thus he went to New York, where his inexperience at sea kept him from getting a berth as an able seaman in the merchant marine. He apparently had met a man who was an agent for New Bedford whaling merchants, for Jackson "was advised to go to New Bedford, where green hands were more wanted, and where, I was told, I could go free of expense." The agent put him on board a vessel bound for the port, and once there "I was told," he wrote, "I could only go before the mast as a raw hand, as a great responsibility rested upon the cook, or steward, of a whaling vessel, bound upon a long voyage, one of which places I preferred and solicited." Thompson then went to a different merchant, Gideon Allen, who was preparing the *Milwood* for a trip to the Indian Ocean and needed "both cook and steward."

> I approached him with much boldness, and asked if he would like to employ a good steward, to which he replied in the affirmative, asking me at the same time if I was one.
>
> I told him I thought I was. So, with much parleying we agreed upon the price, when he took me down to the vessel, gave to my charge the keys of the cabin, and I went to work as well as I knew how.
>
> The following day the Captain, Mr. Aaron C. Luce, came on board with Mr. Allen, who introduced me to him as the captain of the ship, with whom I was going to sea. The captain looked at me very suspiciously, as much as to say, you know nothing of the duties of the office you now fill.[77]

At the New Bedford boardinghouse at which Thompson lodged was a cook who had trouble finding work because his "deformed feet" kept him from climbing the rigging, a job cooks sometimes had to do when whaleboats were in pursuit. The man promised to teach Thompson stewardship if he in turn would recommend his instructor for cook. Allen hired both. On 21 June 1842 Thompson took out a seaman's protection paper, claiming his birthplace as Adams County, Pennsylvania, just west of where he had lived after escaping slavery, and three days later he swore similarly on the crew list of the *Milwood*. Two other men of color signed on as well to the crew of about thirty men. The vessel left New Bedford 25 June, but Thompson soon found himself so seasick that he was unable to perform his steward's duties. The cook did his work and then, with some resentment, told Luce that Thompson had never been a steward before. When Luce confronted him, Thompson confessed:

> "I am a fugitive slave from Maryland, and have a family in Philadelphia; but fearing to remain there any longer, I thought I would go on a whaling voyage, as being the place where I stood least chance of being arrested by slave hunters. I had become somewhat experienced in cooking by working in hotels, inasmuch that I thought I could fill the place of steward."
>
> This narrative seemed to touch his heart, for his countenance at once assumed a pleasing expression. Thus God stood between me and him, and worked in my defence.
>
> He told me that had circumstances been different, he should have flogged me for my imposition, but now bade me go on deck, where I could inhale the fresh air, and I should soon be well. I did so and soon recovered.
>
> The captain became as kind as a father to me, often going with me to the cabin, and when no one was present, teaching me to make pastries and sea messes. He had a cook book, from which I gained much valuable information.
>
> I was soon able to fulfill my duty to the gratification and satisfaction of the captain, though much to the surprise of the whole crew, who, knowing I was a raw hand, wondered how I had so soon learned my business.

Thompson's idyllic time at sea was unusual in the whaling industry, persistently charged with ill treatment and abuse of seamen and beset with desertion and mutiny. By the time he went to sea, whaling was no longer desirable, if it had ever been, and agents throughout the Northeast resorted to low measures to secure crew for the vessels. Just as a murderer had boarded the *Francis Henrietta* with John S. Jacobs, a white Brooklyn firefighter implicated in a crime was on board the *Milwood* with Thompson, and both Charles Morgan and Samuel Rodman recorded having gone to jail to find crew in the 1840s.[78] J. Ross Browne recounted the measures taken to assure that he would board the *Bruce,* which shipped out on a whaling voyage from New Bedford about three weeks after the *Milwood* left. Browne and his friends had signed up after seeing a notice on the New York wharves that six "able-bodied landsmen" were wanted for a New Bedford whaling voyage. They applied to the agent, who wove for them a tale that decades earlier had drawn farm boys from all over the Northeast to New Bedford: "Whaling, gentlemen, is tolerably hard at first, but it's the finest business in the world for enterprising young men. If you are *determined* to take a voyage, I'll put you in the way of shipping in a most elegant vessel, well fitted, that's the great thing, well fitted. Vigilance and activity will insure you rapid promotion. I haven't the least doubt but you'll come home boat-steerers. . . . There's nothing like it. You can see the world; you can see something of life!"[79] Browne began to suspect something was awry when the agent secured an officer to watch him and his friends during their voyage to Providence so that they did not escape and made sure that a debt for the voyage was charged against their wages.

As John Jacobs had, Thompson secured his earnings from Allen upon returning with the *Milwood* in June 1844 and returned to his family in Philadelphia. But other fugitives who came to New Bedford in the 1840s came to stay. Samuel Rodman recorded in his diary in early May 1843 that he was trying to help "an old colored man" named David Norfolk and his wife, both "formerly slaves in Virginia," find a small house in the town where they might live "during their remaining years."[80] No man of color with that surname was ever recorded as living in the town, which suggests that he may have used an alias and thus may not have been free when he came to New Bedford. In 1844 Thomas U. Allen escaped from his Richmond, Virginia, owner, while in the process of trying to purchase his freedom. He came to New Bedford, where he became the first pastor of the Second Baptist Church, the first Baptist congregation of color in the city.[81] New Bedford abolitionist John Bailey wrote to Garrison in August that year, "A schooner arrived here two or three days since from the South, with two 'chattels personal' on board, about eighteen or twenty years of age. They like New-Bedford so well, that they have concluded to make this their residence for the future."[82] And in 1845 Daniel Ricketson, in his annual report as secretary of the New Bedford Benevolent Society, told the pitiable story of "an old and decrepit colored man" about whom the society had learned from a Providence newspaper article.

We soon after reading this sketch encountered the old man in one of our streets, and learned from him, that he was a poor old worn out slave from Virginia, who had been in the service of several masters for over 70 years—during which time he had met with many hardships, and had been more severely treated both by sea & land. After being worn out in the service of slavery, he was sold for $5.00 a short time before our interview with him to the master of a small vessel bound to Providence R. I. On his arrival there, he left the vessel, an opportunity undoubtedly being given for his escape, & came to New Bedford. We found him very poor & destitute of every comfort, sleeping on the counter of a poor clothes dresser in the basement of a small house on 1st Street—and picking up what little he could by sawing wood—a more patient suffering creature we never met with—he made no complaint, and appeared astonished when with the friends of our Society, we procured him a comfortable straw bed, and some blankets and a small quantity of provisions which he cooked at night for himself by the clothes dressers little coal stove. The same poor old man is now here. He is usually seen with a saw horse strapped to his back, and a staff in his hand, limping along humbly touching his hat to almost every one he meets. Let us speak a good word for him—a more worthy object or a more deserving one we have not among us. His name is Daniel Ball. Give him a trifle then when you shall chance to meet him—my word for it you will be heartily repaid.[83]

Ball remained in New Bedford and boarded at 24 First Street, across from and slightly south of the home and shop of Thomas A. Williams, the clothes dresser who probably housed him when he first came to town. He remained poor: in 1846 the newly constituted New Bedford Overseers of the Poor gave him a half ton of heating coal.

At about this time, Caroline Weston put the number of fugitives living in New Bedford at more than four hundred, which, if true and if the city's 1847 census was in any way an accurate count, would have meant that one of every two and a half persons of color officially recorded as residents of the town was an escaped slave. As he wrote to Garrison early in 1846, John Bailey believed that New Bedford's reputation as a haven for fugitives had made abolitionists there susceptible to imposters who proclaimed fugitive status to secure money and other assistance:

We are peculiarly situated—here is one of the fugitives' depots. There is scarcely a week passes but that more or less of that oppressed race arrive here, and are thrown immediately upon our hands for protection and support, all classes turning them over to the abolitionists to be fed, clothed, and provided for. In the large cities it is not so. A few hundred fugitives in the city of New-York would be but a few drops in that ocean of human beings, and would soon mingle and be lost in the living mass. But here, they preserve their identity. They are strangers, and we take them in. In so doing, we are sometimes taken in ourselves.[84]

To avoid being "taken in," poor relief administrators and abolitionists were always careful to secure as many details of a fugitive's story as possible. The record books of the Overseers of the Poor, constituted officially when New Bedford became a city in 1847, often express doubt about certain stories and show that overseers sometimes checked on details when they could before providing coal, wood, and groceries to those who sought their aid. In February and March 1848, the city's poor relief accounts record the extension of aid to five families of "runaway slaves"—Peter and Margaret Ann Stevenson and their eighteen-year-old daughter Mary, born in North Carolina, who arrived in New Bedford in May 1847; William Chase, identified as a fugitive, Emeline Chase, and an eleven-month-old child named Samuel, who had come to New Bedford most recently from New Jersey in November 1847; Thomas and Mary Peaker and William and Nancy Ferguson, whose places of origin were not identified and who received aid in February 1848; and William and Susan Nolan and their two Maryland-born children, three-year-old William P. and seven-month-old Joseph. Of these families, only that of William Ferguson was recorded by the same name in any census, tax, probate, or directory listing. Ferguson, in fact, remained in New Bedford for the rest of his life, but he seems to have tried to keep his origins out of the official federal record at least until the Civil War: he told federal census takers in 1850 and 1860 that he did not know his birthplace, though he told a state enumerator in 1855 the truth—that he had been born in Virginia. In 1910, nine years before he died, Ferguson told his story to the New Bedford *Standard Times.* Born a slave in Gloucester County, Virginia, Ferguson had been sent at the age of eleven to Norfolk to work for a butcher. At about age twenty-five, in April 1847, he stowed away on the coal schooner *Pornony* for Boston and, for a reason he did not identify, came directly to New Bedford. He arrived in the city on the day it was celebrating the election of its first mayor, Abraham Hathaway Howland.[85]

The William and Emeline Chase listed in the poor relief records in November 1847 and a family of the same name whom John Bailey described in a *Liberator* notice in late January 1848 were probably the same. That month, a woman Bailey referred to only as the "wife of Aaron Chase" came to ask him if he could get information about her husband. She and her two children had left Mount Holly, New Jersey, a few days after her husband's brother, "Commodore Chase," escaped slaveholders who had come to capture him. Commodore Chase had come to New Bedford, and Aaron Chase's wife had followed. Aaron Chase was apparently taken at Mount Holly. Mrs. Chase noted also that another family, that of the blacksmith John Taseo, had left Mount Holly at the same time for New Bedford. Bailey stated that Taseo had never been able to pursue the trade he learned in slavery in New Jersey and in New Bedford "came out with his basket the other morning, asking for bread! I gave him some, for which I am liable to a fine of $500, by the laws of our pious Christian rulers—at least, I should be, in some of the States of the Union."[86]

Neither Taseo nor any of the Chases are listed in any formal record of city inhabitants; they may have believed they were still hunted and may have moved on, perhaps to Canada. Other fugitives are known not to have stayed in New Bedford for long. John Armstrong, known in slavery as John Hill, came to New Bedford in early March 1847 aboard a packet from Baltimore. In that city he had taken care of the horses and carriages of two Bostonians, who told him that if he could escape they would hire him in Boston; Armstrong probably told this story to New Bedford abolitionist Isaiah C. Ray, a shoemaker and later an attorney, who sent him on. Ultimately Armstrong was placed with a family in Pembroke, Massachusetts.[87] And Alexander Duval, an escaped slave from Baltimore, settled in New Bedford with his free wife Mary Ann and their four-year-old daughter Martha on 3 October 1848. He worked as a cooper, a trade in which jobs were usually seasonally available in the city, but early in 1851 he saw his former owner on a New Bedford street and immediately made arrangements through the Boston Vigilance Committee to leave for England. Former New Bedford boarding-house keeper William P. Powell met Duval and fellow fugitive Francis S. Anderson in Liverpool, where he then lived, and he wrote Mary Ann Duval in March 1851 to report their safe arrival. Powell also expressed the hope that the family might be reunited in "old England," but it was a hope never realized: Mary Ann Duval was, according to the overseers of the poor, "unwell" and "destitute" and often in need of their support. She did domestic work, sometimes living in the homes of the whites she worked for, but by 1859 she lived in one of the poorest parts of town, the Marsh at the foot of Howland Street. After a brief moment of glory as an antislavery speaker in 1851, Alexander Duvall was one fugitive who did not achieve popular acclaim in England: for most of his first six months there, he was unable to find work and begged on the streets.[88]

The story of Henry "Box" Brown, the most sensational fugitive in New Bedford during the 1840s, may be the most fully documented of all escapes and well illustrates not only how the Underground Railroad operated in specific terms but also how the urgency and drama of fugitive slave cases captivated abolitionists of every stripe. Born in 1815 in Louisa County, Virginia, Brown was one of those plantation slaves who saw a larger world, having been designated to carry grain to a mill in an adjacent county several times a year. When his master died, his family—his parents, his sisters Jane, Robinnet, and Martha, and his brothers Edward, John, and Lewis—was broken up, and Henry became the property of his master's son. About March 1830 William Barrett sent Brown to Richmond, forty-five miles from the plantation, to work in his tobacco factory (manned, Brown said, by 150 people of color, 30 of them free). When his wife and children were sold to a North Carolina slaveholder in August 1848, he began to contemplate escape.[89] Around Christmas that year, he revealed an escape plan with Samuel A. Smith, a white Richmond shopkeeper who agreed to help him for a fee of eighty-six dollars, and James Caesar Anthony Smith, who worked in the shop. J. C. A. Smith, the minister of a black church and, Brown later wrote, "the conductor of the under-ground railway," thought the proposal too risky.[90] And then Brown had an epiphany. As he prayed to God for guidance, "the idea suddenly flashed across my mind of shutting myself *up in a box,* and getting myself conveyed as dry goods to a free state."

Brown's plan was not novel: a New Orleans fugitive nearly suffocated by crating himself up in 1825, and just before Brown's plan came to him, a Charleston slave who had packed himself in a crate with a jug of water and a loaf of bread had been discovered among the freight on a vessel when, having exhausted his supplies, he was forced to reveal his presence. About two weeks after helping Brown crate himself up, Smith tried the same tactic with another fugitive.[91] But the success of Brown's escape and drama surrounding it made him almost instantly famous. The principal players in Brown's escape, in addition to Samuel Smith, J. C. A. Smith, and the fugitive himself, were James Miller McKim, William Still, and Lucretia Mott in Philadelphia, Sydney Howard Gay in New York City, and Joseph Ricketson Jr. in New Bedford. McKim, a former Presbyterian minister who had left the church over theological differences, was the publishing agent and later corresponding secretary for the Pennsylvania Anti-Slavery Society; he worked closely with William Still, the executive secretary of the interracial Philadelphia Vigilance Committee. Still was the youngest child of Levin and Sidney Steel, who had moved from New Jersey to Philadelphia in 1844; his mother was a fugitive, and some of his siblings had long since been sold to owners in the South.[92]

In early March 1849, McKim was visited in Philadelphia by a Richmond merchant, probably Samuel Smith, who, he wrote, "was very desirous as to secure the escape of a man in that city who was held as a slave. He proposed to ship him by overland express in a box to this city." McKim thought the plan too dangerous, but the man "overruled my objections, satisfied me that the plan was feasible, said as a merchant he frequently shipped large boxes in that way &c &c. All he wanted he said was a man in Phil[a] who would engage to receive the box." The merchant told McKim that Brown had "saved a good deal of money by doing over-work" and was willing to give one hundred dollars to anyone who would accept the shipment. McKim said he would accept the box and that Brown might keep his money.

Several delays and misgivings on McKim's part then ensued, but ultimately the merchant wrote to say the box, addressed to a James Johnson at 31 North 8th Street, "a fictitious address," had been put in a railroad freight car bound for Philadelphia (one of the engravings of the unboxing of Brown, printed in Still's 1871 book about the Underground Railroad, shows the address as "Wm. Johnson, Arch St., Philadelphia"). McKim asked an express agent to be on hand to remove and deliver the crate ("this express man suspected I suppose what was going on but had sense enough to <u>know</u> nothing," McKim recalled) as soon as it came in. When McKim arrived at the anti-slavery society office just at daylight, as the merchant had telegraphed him to do, a box marked "this side up" was sitting just inside the door. "The express wagon had left & I entered the office alone dreading lest I should find the man inside dead," McKim wrote. "You can better imagine than I can describe my feelings when tapping on the box & calling out 'all right?' the prompt reply came from within—'all right sir.' I never felt happier in my life hardly." With Still, the printer Lewis Thompson, and C. D. Cleveland (who had helped support Daniel Drayton's family in Philadelphia while he was in prison) on hand, McKim cut the hickory hoops that held the box shut, lifted its cover, "& up rose—with a face radiant with joy & gratitude—one of the finest looking men you ever saw in your life. . . . I wish all the world could have witnessed the scene of opening that box. It was a most thrilling scene" (fig. 49). "He was about as wet," Still wrote of the event, "as if he had come up out of the Delaware." Brown sang a hymn of praise that he had planned to sing if he arrived safely, and McKim took him to his home and then to the home of James and Lucretia Mott, where he recuperated.[93]

The dimensions of Brown's box became almost as legendary as the exploit itself. McKim wrote that it was "3 feet by 2 8 in high & 23 ½ wide," Still recorded it at two feet eight inches deep, two feet wide, and three feet long, and as New Bedford's Charles W. Morgan heard it described in April it was one foot eleven inches deep, two feet six inches wide, and three feet two inches long.[94] According to McKim, the box had "almost imperceptible cracks at the joints." Brown

FIGURE 49. "Resurrection of Henry Box Brown," engraving in William Still, *The Underground Railroad* (1871). Still, secretary of the Philadelphia Vigilance Committee, is shown at center holding the box cover. In later depictions of the event, Still is not represented, and a man of color looking a great deal like Frederick Douglass, who was not present, is shown at right.

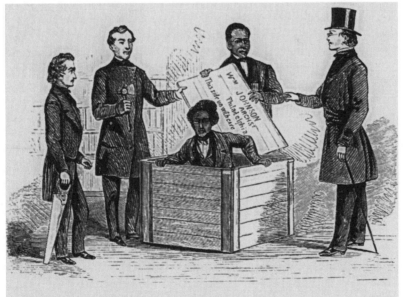

RESURRECTION OF HENRY BOX BROWN.

inserted himself into the box in a sitting position and carried with him, McKim said, "a beefs bladder containing about ½ gallon of water, some biscuit & a large gimlet," the last to bore holes in the box should his air supply diminish.

> He soon became thirsty but found the water was of more use to him to bathe his temples & face than to drink, so he kept wetting his temples & fanning himself with his hat all the way. He was 21 hours boxed up, having been put in at 3 [?] A.M. one day & taken out at 6 A.M. the next. The box was 6 times shifted after leaving Richmond, and at none [?] of these times was any regard paid to the 'this side up'. . . . he was twice set down with his back, shoulders, & head downwards, once was in the railroad, and here he turned himself, right, but the next time was when he was put on the deck on board the steamer that crosses the Chesapeake. Here he was surrounded by a number [of] passengers, some of whom stood by & others sat on the box. All were quiet & if he had attempted to turn he wd have been overheard. He therefore had to continue in that position for 20 miles. His veins in his temples he said were swollen as thick as his finger.

McKim identified Brown as a worker in a tobacco factory and noted that his pregnant wife and three children had been sold to a trader and "carried south"— a Methodist preacher in North Carolina had purchased them—the August before. "He resolved after his family were torn from him that he wd be free or die in the attempt," McKim wrote on 28 March. "The result proves how well he kept his word. I sent him yesterday morning to New York to be forwarded from there to a place of safety further North."

Still wrote that after spending several days at his own home, Brown went on to Boston, but he seems to have abbreviated his account; McKim's and other correspondence make clear that Brown was sent to New York and then immediately to New Bedford, where he arrived the evening of 29 March.[95] "I received your very valuable consignment of 200 pounds of Humanity last evening and as merchants say will dispose of it to the best advantage," wrote Joseph Ricketson Jr., clearly delighting in the language of subterfuge associated with fugitives, to Sydney Howard Gay of New York. "The storage and incidental expenses shall be light, as I have plenty room enough for a short while, and I hope I shall receive more than the ordinary commission in disposing of it as most probably what I do receive will come from Heaven."[96] Ricketson first referred to him as "Henry Smith," but he crossed out "Smith" and wrote "Brown" above the line; in a letter to S. A. Smith, McKim referred to him as "Clark." The "Box" in his name, according to Still, had been added in Philadelphia. Ricketson told Gay that Brown had "staid at my house last night & took breakfast this morning." Brown's finger, which Smith had injured purposely so that Brown would have an excuse not to work, was "very bad," Ricketson wrote, and Brown had been to the doctor that morning. Ricketson also added, "Henry's sister is at service here and is a very nice woman," but because of the uncertainty about his surname and the possibility that his sister was using an alias she cannot be definitely identified. "He has many friends here who former [sic] lived in Richmond," Ricketson told Gay; "he will remain with them for a while—& I think with their assistance & my own he can get along." Ricketson apologized for the haste in which he wrote, laying it to the fact that he had been busy all that morning "in writing & devising a scheme for the colored man who lives with me to get his wife & 3 children from Maryland they being free & he having run away last October."[97]

At the end of April 1849 Ricketson wrote his friend Debora Weston about New Bedford's response to Brown and his fantastic escape:

> The man appears to be a fine fellow, has found considerable employment—he has worked several days for me & if I commence manufacturing oil again I think I can give him constant employment. Noble as was the sentiment uttered by Patrick Henry, "Give [me] liberty or give me Death," how much nobler and more difficult was the carrying out of the spirit of the sentiment in the case of this man. Every one that hears of it or seen him are astonished. They all glorify in it & I think it will have a strong tendency to cement the Anti Slavery feeling here. Only one man, and he an exdivine of the Orthodox School, Pardon G. Seabury, doubted the veracity of the story as Mr. Robeson informed me, but he no longer doubts, for as we were standing at the Post Office last Friday, the man came along and I informed him Mr. Seabury of it; it was 'prima facie' evidence. Orthodoxy stood abashed; God's image in an ebony case confronted it too strongly; what says he? you dont mean 'that nigger', yes, says I, there is the Hero; such I'll give up says he were it not for <u>exposing</u> the <u>express</u> I would call a town meeting and show him up. His name is Henry Brown [Smith crossed out] and he is the greatest Lion [?] of the age—[98]

Whaling merchant Charles Morgan heard Brown's story, perhaps from the fugitive himself, at a party during his first week in New Bedford:

> Sarah & I went to Wm J Rotchs to tea but came home early—I there heard a singular account of the escape of a slave who has just arrived here which I must record—He had himself packed up in a box about 3 ft 2 in long 2 ft 6 in wide & 1 ft 11 in deep and sent on by express from Richmond to Philadelphia—marked "this side up"— He is about 5 ft 6 in high and weighs about 200 lb—In this way he came by cars & steam boat to Philad near 25 hours in the box which was quite close & tight had only a bladder of water with him and kept himself alive by bathing his face and fanning himself with his hat. He was twice turned head downwards & once remained so on board the steam boat while she went 18 miles—which almost killed him and he said the veins on his temples were almost as thick as his finger. Yet he endured it all and was delivered to his antislavery friends safe & well—who trembled when he knocked on the box and asked the question "all right["]—and the answer came promptly "all right sir"—I think I never heard of an instance of greater fortitude & daring and he has well earned the freedom which he will now enjoy—[99]

Morgan never made a better case for his moderate abolitionism than his almost unwitting description of Brown having earned the freedom that more forthright abolitionists, such as Daniel Drayton, claimed to be his natural possession.

The remarkable similarity between McKim's and Morgan's accounts of the escape suggests that Brown had even then told the story so often that its details were virtually scripted in his mind. But it seems clear, too, that he was already fully aware of the publicity value of his story. Still noted that when Brown left Philadelphia, he was "evidently feeling quite conscious of the wonderful feat he had performed" and seemed anxious to share it on the antislavery circuit. He wrote (with Charles Stearns) and had published the first edition of his narrative that year, when he also began work to raise funds to create a grand panorama about slavery that he might unveil during his lectures. Panoramas were the rage at the time, and in New Bedford Benjamin Russell and Caleb Purrington had just completed their *Panorama of a Whaling Voyage*. The work, a vast canvas twelve feet high and nearly thirteen hundred feet long rolled onto two spindles and unwound as the narration demanded, debuted in New Bedford in December 1848 and was on view at Boston's Amory Hall by early April 1849; thus Brown might have seen it in either place and taken it as his model.[100] Through the fall of 1849 Brown traveled through the region to lecture and raise money for the work.[101] His *Mirror of Slavery*, some fifty thousand square feet divided into forty-six scenes that traced the history of the slave trade through the West Indian emancipation and a "Grand Tableau Finale—UNIVERSAL EMANCIPATION," was first exhibited in Boston in mid-April 1850, narrated by Brown and "an all-black company of assistants." Brown took the panorama to other cities in New England and, after two agents of his former owner attempted to capture him on 30 August, went with it and J. C. A. "Boxer" Smith to England. For four years he, initially accompanied by Smith, lectured in England about his escape. Brown sometimes sang a ballad he had written about it, sometimes at the beginning of a lecture jumped from the box, which he had saved and shipped as well, and once even recrated himself in it for the ninety-minute train trip between Bradford and Leeds.[102]

Two months before Brown made his escape, the fugitive William Wells Brown had brought William and Ellen Crafts to New Bedford to speak at Liberty Hall (fig. 50). The Crafts' escape from Georgia was almost as sensational: Ellen, called in the antislavery press "the white slave," cut her hair, dressed as a male planter, and, to mask her lack of beard, covered her face with a muffler and pretended she had a toothache. To complete the effect and ward off any close inspection, she also carried her right arm in a sling, walked with a cane, and aped deafness. William, her husband, acted as her servant. They stayed in hotels in Charleston and Richmond and passed without incident through Baltimore, en route to Philadelphia for, they said, medical treatment. Once they reached the free states, their story was widely publicized; according to Andrew Robeson, who reported their New Bedford visit for the *Liberator*, city residents "were eager to see them," including many not often seen at antislavery meetings. When Brown brought the Crafts on stage, "an expression of astonishment" issued from the assembly, presumably because Ellen was so fair. According to Robeson, a woman in the audience asked her "if they called her a nigger at the South," and she responded, "Oh yes, they didn't call me any thing else; they said it would make me proud."[103]

FIGURE 50. Margaret Virginia Onley, Mary Ann Holmes, and William Craft, tintype, 1865–70. Courtesy Carl J. Cruz, New Bedford Historical Society. The Crafts, who fled to England in the 1850s, returned to the United States after the Civil War and may have been photographed with Onley and Holmes, both New Bedford women, in Boston. Margaret Onley claimed to have been born in Massachusetts in 1847 or 1848, but family tradition holds that her middle name honors her birthplace; she may have come to New Bedford as an infant with fugitive parents. Mary Ann Holmes, born in 1823 in Virginia, may also have been a fugitive; she and her husband, John, appear to have settled in New Bedford between 1853 and 1855.

Frederick Douglass, who resolutely refused to offer the exact details of his escape until his 1893 autobiography, charged that the practice of publicizing these dramatic escapes "has neither wisdom nor necessity to sustain it." He added pointedly, "Had not Henry Box Brown and his friends attracted slaveholding attention to the manner of his escape, we might have had a thousand *Box Browns* per annum. The singularly original plan adopted by William and Ellen Crafts, perished with the first using, because every slaveholder in the land was apprised of it. The *salt water slave* who hung in the guards of a steamer, being washed three days and three nights—like another Jonah—by the waves of the sea, has, by the publicity given to the circumstance, set a spy on the guards of every steamer departing from southern ports."[104]

Douglass was surely correct, but the other side of the equation was the effect these stories had upon the resolve of antislavery people in the North. After the Crafts spoke in New Bedford, the meeting pledged unanimously to "extend to those fugitives from slavery escaping into this State, the same protection of life, liberty, and the means of pursuing happiness, that we claim for ourselves, and, so far as it is in our power, Massachusetts shall never again be made the hunting-ground of slaveholders." Such famed fugitives as Box Brown and the Crafts inspired these declarations, but they applied even to the most obscure fugitives, the ones whose names are never mentioned in the letters of abolitionists who helped them elude the grasp of pursuing agents and slaveholders. For every Box Brown in New Bedford, there were scores of other fugitives who saw no virtue in being candid about their origin and who stayed out of sight as well as they might. They were men like Stethy Swons, whose fugitive status may have been known only to other fugitives until his daughter revealed it in a deposition aimed at securing his Civil War pension benefits. Or they were children like Isabella White, who as a four- or five-year-old in 1849 was shipped to New Bedford in a barrel labeled "sweet potatoes" and kept in the home of merchant Loum Snow until she was old enough to work in domestic service. By 1849 the city seemed to have put itself on the line for escaped slaves, on the edge of the year that turned probably as many antislavery sympathizers into active abolitionists as it turned moderate abolitionists away from the fight.

7

The 1850s:
"Very Poor Hunting Ground"

As 1848 turned to 1849, as Quakers and former Quakers were wont to do, Charles Waln Morgan (fig. 51) took a moment to reflect on the past year and express his hope for the coming one. "And so this eventful year," Morgan wrote on New Year's Eve. "God grant that if I live to record the passage of another, I may feel that I have made some advancement in spiritual things, and have loosened the shackles that now dog me so much—and prevent any actual usefulness or active benevolence." All his life Morgan had fought temptation—first the urge in the 1810s to rush as a volunteer to quench every fire in Philadelphia, then the tendency to invest in too many potentially capital-draining enterprises at once. As prices for sperm oil were climbing higher than ever before, he hoped to extricate himself from the debt he had undertaken in support of less fortunate industries—principally, the blast furnace at Bloomsburg, Pennsylvania, and the nearby Duncannon iron works that he co-owned with William Logan Fisher. He listened to Horace Greeley speak in New Bedford in late November 1848 and felt ashamed of himself. "There is nothing which under my present situation is so galling, as the idea that with my ample means, I am not able to forward so good a work or any great or good work," Morgan wrote in his diary. "Oh! that my warning voice could be heard by all who are about engaging in projects beyond their ability & thereby involving themselves in debt, shew this slavery, which which [sic] will hamper and cripple all your efforts to do good to others or to yourself." His debt he termed a "dreadful thraldom," and he wished to live long enough to free himself of it and "shew to the world, that I have not thus enslaved myself from a sordid love of gold—and endeavour to benefit others from those accumulations it has cost me so much time & sufficiency to accumulate." [1]

The boom in sperm and whale oil prices occurred, Morgan noted, "in the midst of unprecedented dullness for almost every thing else," and New Bedford was not shy about showing its good fortune. A journalist for the New York *American* called the city "a perfect New England town, built up by the industry and peculiar enterprise of its inhabitants, and rendered a place of delightful resort by the taste and beauty displayed in the erection of some of its private edifices, the

FIGURE 51. Charles Waln Morgan, miniature portrait by unidentified artist. Courtesy Old Dartmouth Historical Society / New Bedford Whaling Museum. This small portrait shows Morgan as a young man, perhaps around the time of his 1819 marriage; he was then twenty-two.

exquisite arrangement and rural embellishments of its private grounds, and the hospitality of its citizens." Herman Melville called it "the dearest place to live in, in all New England . . . nowhere in all America will you find more patrician-like houses, parks and gardens more opulent, than in New Bedford."[2] Indeed, as 1849 began, the town seemed almost radiant to Morgan. New Bedford had snow on the ground, and during the day of 5 January he wrote, "The sloping hill sides . . . of the city are covered by a gay & moving throng enjoying the amusement of coasting which is a perfect mania among our people at present, of nearly all classes sexes ages & colours—all mixed together and all orderly & good humoured"; as day turned to night, Morgan returned home and listened with his much-loved family to the city's Unitarian minister, John Weiss, read from "Dickens new Christmas tale."

Amid the rising wealth of the whaling industry came the news of the discovery of gold in California, both fantastic and portentous in Morgan's mind. In early December 1848, a week before one of his whaling vessels returned to port with a fantastically profitable cargo, Morgan noted the stories he had heard about "the wonderful gold region in California" and how thousands were already headed there. "It seems to be pretty well established that one man can gather from $20 to $100 worth a day," Morgan wrote, but he awaited more firsthand news as city-registered whaling vessels returned from the Pacific; "what is to be the end of all this it is hard to say." Ten days later the reports seemed more worrisome to him. "The gold fever is at its height," he wrote, "all previous amounts are confirmed and there can be little doubt of an immense influx of gold—and a vast flocking to the Gold regions—But I fear only evil sooner or later will ensue." Despite his forebodings, Morgan's overriding desire to "pay my debts, and avoid all speculation for ever" impelled him to take what he hoped would be one last risk—sending his bark *Magnolia* to California with freight and passengers.[3]

Morgan was far from the only New Bedford citizen who hoped to realize some profit from California bounty. Away from the County Street eminence, along the "dreary streets" and ramshackle buildings that Melville described near the waterfront and in the sections of town that affluence had not affected, men of color also aimed to rid themselves of debt by trying their luck in the gold fields. From mid-December 1848 through early April 1850, men who had never or rarely been to sea—Lloyd H. Brooks, Daniel Sullivan, George Fletcher, Noah White, Peter Nelson, Nathan Johnson and his stepson George Page, Thomas Buchanan, Ezra R. Johnson, Samuel Woodland—took out seamen's protection papers and bought or earned passage on one of scores of ships that left the city for San Francisco.[4] Nathan Johnson owned a substantial amount of property in New Bedford and ran an apparently successful catering and confectionary business, but by the late 1840s he owed his creditors; Thomas Buchanan's William Street bathhouse was not successful enough that he could pay off his mortgage on it. Both, as it happened, were in debt to Charles W. Morgan. So was Samuel Woodland, who left with his wife to do the washing and chores of a vast number of single miners and others who flooded the gold regions and floated in and out of San Francisco. Men of color from other places came to New Bedford to board the ships. T. E. Randolph, who had escaped Virginia slavery in December 1848 and was living in New Bedford in 1849, left for California by 1851 and stayed there. Men who listed their residences or birthplaces as Charleston, South Carolina; Washington, D.C.; "the state of Virginia" or "the state of North Carolina"; Baltimore; Easton, Maryland; New Orleans; and Suffolk and Richmond in Virginia all took out protection papers in New Bedford in 1849 and probably went west instead of whaling. In the 1850s New Bedford lost to California more of its most prominent men of African descent, including Jeremiah B. Sanderson, Shadrach Howard, and Solomon Peneton.[5] Some, including Ezra Johnson, returned, but a good many did not. Those known to have stayed did in California as they had done in New Bedford: they became founders and leaders of the politically organized black community in that territory.

Morgan stayed in New Bedford trying to extricate himself from his financial problems by selling most of the *Charles W. Morgan* to the up-and-coming whaling merchant Edward Mott Robinson (father of the infamous investor Hetty Green), and holding his sperm and whale oil off the market (while selling to a British vessel the portion the crew of the *Morgan* owned) until the meager supply on hand drove the price still higher. As he waited, the status of the California territory became a sensitive topic, with President Zachary Taylor claiming that the people living in the territory, not Congress, ought to decide whether slavery should be permitted there. As ever, the territorial question brought slavery talk to the fore. In January 1849 Morgan recorded having "an animated discussion on slavery" with the Reverend John Weiss and William J. Rotch, "Mr. Weiss taking the ultra antislavery ground WJ Rotch the opposite—I in the middle as usual." Weiss often made Morgan think about the way he lived his life, at one time criticizing "the worldliness and coldness so prevalent among us—our tongues only professing that we are not ashamed of that gospel [of Christ], while our lives gave the lie to these professions." Morgan wrote sorrowfully, "I felt it like an arrow in my heart." In another sermon Weiss preached charity for Washington Goode, a man of color in Boston who had been convicted of murder on circumstantial evidence and sentenced to die. Morgan wrote that many, Weiss surely included, were trying to persuade Governor George N. Briggs to commute the sentence; Joseph Ricketson wrote that he and others had secured almost 750 signatures on local petitions to that end. "Mine contained 69 names only," he wrote Debora Weston, "but they were the most respectable and influential men in the city." Weiss made a speech and wrote resolutions on Goode's behalf. "Weiss is too good for a Reverend," wrote Ricketson, a decidedly more radical man than Morgan.[6]

In the fall of 1849 Californians created a constitution that banned slavery, an action that helped inspire a series of resolutions related to slavery on the part of Kentucky senator Henry Clay. In late January 1850 Clay proposed that Congress admit California as a free state, ban the slave trade but continue to permit slavery in the District of Columbia, recognize that as a federal legislative body it had no authority to interfere with the trade in slaves between states, and make more stringent the provisions articulated for returning fugitive slaves in the act of 1793. The proposals engrossed Congress. Morgan wrote in early March that federal legislators were "still absorbed in the slavery discussion & little else attended to Mr. Webster is to speak Thursday and I think his speech will decide the action of the North—I think California will be admitted & I fear some concessions to slavery will be made . . . perhaps it is necessary," he averred.[7]

Webster's speech, which in advocating above all else the preservation of the Union essentially endorsed Clay's proposed "compromise," infuriated abolitionists and did not sit well with many moderates, including Morgan. "This evening reading Mr. Websters speech upon slavery," he wrote on 11 March "—it does not seem to suit the North—& I fear I cannot sympathize with him." He was much more impressed, as one might expect a Quaker-bred man to be, with William Henry Seward's spirited characterization of the compromise as "radically wrong and essentially vicious" and his declaration that "a higher law" than the U.S. Constitution forbade slavery. Seward, Morgan wrote, "will make no compromise— and is willing to risk all for preventing the extension of this curse and disgrace of America—I sympathize more with these views than with Websters," he concluded. Clay's proposals about the rendition of fugitives—specifically, that such cases be placed under federal jurisdiction, thus overriding the personal liberty laws that such states as Massachusetts had enacted to guarantee some legal rights to accused fugitives—irritated Morgan. "As to sending back fugitive slaves—they might as well ask us to keep slaves ourselves," he wrote. Even the *Mercury* responded somewhat peevishly to Webster's conciliation:

> With respect to fugitive slaves, we utterly oppose all laws for their capture and surrender. While we have always condemned slave stealing, we have always condemned, and do still condemn slave catching; and we may say in all frankness that we consider the northern man degraded who lends himself to the capture of a fugitive slave. It may be true (though we doubt it) that Congress is bound to pass laws for the capture of slaves—but no one can say that the States are bound to make similar laws, nor that State officers can be compelled to do the bidding of Congress We go further. We hold that the States have a perfect right to compel their officers to attend to their appropriate duties and abstain from the performance of any service in behalf of any other legislative or executive authority. Let Congress compromise as they will and pass slave-catching laws as they will—we trust not one jot or tittle of the law of this State will be modified with respect to slave-catching.[8]

Congress's long debate on the compromise made many, Morgan included, uneasy. By the end of July, Taylor having just died in office to be replaced by pro-compromise Millard Fillmore, he decided he favored the compromise bill—"anything," he declared, "that will settle or quiet this vexed question without abandoning the principle of opposition to the extension of slavery—we must allow it where it is and grant it the rights it now possesses—but do nothing to extend it." When the Senate defeated the compromise in late July, Morgan seemed to waver in his support for the proposal, though he believed Clay's efforts to bolster support for the Union "great & grand." "No one can see what is to be the result," Morgan wrote on 1 August 1850. "This is a dark day for these United States—what a curse this slavery has been to the *whole* country."[9]

As the debate in Congress wore on, tension grew. The day after Morgan declared in his journal that slavery was not a sectional matter, news reached New Bedford that a mob had attacked Frederick Douglass in Columbus, Ohio, where he had gone to speak. Earlier that summer several men had assaulted him on the street in New York, and in Columbus, the *Mercury* noted, Douglass "barely escaped with his life." The day after that, 3 August, Hard-Dig was again beset with rioting. "The peaceable inhabitants in that quarter were disturbed and alarmed," a correspondent signed "Law and Order" wrote in a letter in the ensuing *Mercury,* "to the great interruption of their needed repose after the labors of the week, and two of them were seriously wounded by the ruffian and unprovoked attacks of the devotees of intemperance and licentiousness, who nightly congregate in that locality—wounded too in a manner which shows life and limb were in imminent peril." Late in August, some thirty fugitive slaves, including Douglass and Mary and Emily Edmundson, gathered at Cazenovia, New York, to pass resolutions of advice to their cohorts (fig. 52). "In running away," slaves were told "to take their master's best horses, and provisions, money, and arms, and use the arms, if

FIGURE 52. Abolitionists' meeting of fugitive slaves at Cazenovia, N.Y., daguerreotype by Ezra Greenleaf Weld, August 1850. Courtesy Madison County Historical Society, Oneida, N.Y. Frederick Douglass is shown seated, second from left; Gerrit Smith stands just to the left behind him. Mary (left) and Emily Edmundson, whose escape aboard Daniel Drayton's *Pearl* had been thwarted but whose freedom had been purchased by Henry Ward Beecher and Harriet Beecher Stowe, stand to each side of Smith.

required . . . to keep clear of all sectarian churches that will not preach abolition from the pulpit, to join no political party, and send their children to the schools exclusively for colored children. To aid them they say they can only furnish pocket compasses, and in the dark nights they can run away."[10]

Throughout this unsettling time, slaves continued to escape. "It is almost an every day occurrence for our negro slaves to take passage [aboard a ship] and go North," one correspondent complained to the Wilmington, North Carolina, *Journal* in October 1849, just after the fugitive Thomas H. Jones had made his circuitous way from that city to New Bedford. A slave stevedore in Wilmington, Jones learned late in 1848 that plans were afoot to re-enslave his free wife and children—technically, slaves in that state could not be manumitted without a special legislative act—and so arranged with a schooner captain to carry his family to New York, where they stayed in the Brooklyn home of Robert Cousins Jones's letters and fugitive slave narrative make clear that he had known Cousins previously and was certain that Cousins would assist, which bolsters Cecelski's claim that both slaves and northern abolitionists knew of a coastal escape route, or routes. Sometime after 30 August 1849, Jones persuaded the steward of the turpentine brig *Bell* to stow him in the hold, but the turpentine made Jones so ill that he moved to a different part of the ship. There the captain found him, made for port in New York, and went ashore, Jones believed, to arrange for his rendition. Jones set to work in the interim making a raft of loose lumber on the ship, made his escape on it (fig. 53), and was picked up in the harbor by sympathizers who took him to Brooklyn; then, by way of Hartford, Springfield, and Boston, he came to New Bedford, probably in October 1849.

Probably in May that year the fugitive Joseph Jacobs, the son of Harriet and nephew of John S. Jacobs, returned to New Bedford after almost three years at sea; he had escaped Edenton, North Carolina, in 1843, a year after his mother had. John S. Jacobs had returned on the *Francis Henrietta* that year and at his sister's request took care of Joseph. He probably placed the boy as an apprentice in the office of the Boston weekly newspaper, *The Saturday Rambler,* but according to Harriet, once other employees learned he was black, "insults and abuse" forced him to leave. "Having no one to advise him," Harriet wrote (though certainly her brother John must have), Joseph shipped out on an unidentified whaler. Candid about his Edenton birthplace, he secured a protection paper in late July 1846. After his return he may have followed his uncle to Rochester, New York, where by April 1849 John Jacobs had opened an antislavery office and reading room; the next year, both numbered themselves among the gold rush horde.[11] In late April 1850 Jacob Bigelow, referred to in Underground Railroad literature as the "general manager" of the network between Philadelphia and Washington, D.C., wrote the New Bedford abolitionist Isaiah C. Ray about a woman named Araminta, who was probably of African descent and may well have been a fugitive. Bigelow, who had helped secure the purchase of the Edmundsons after the *Pearl* incident, wrote, "Araminta has just left my office,

FIGURE 53. Thomas H. Jones aboard his makeshift raft in New York harbor, engraving from *The Experience of Thomas H. Jones, Who Was a Slave for Forty-Three Years* (1857; reprint, New Bedford, 1871). Courtesy Carl J. Cruz, New Bedford Historical Society.

prepared to start for New Bedford on Monday morning 29th inst. I have advised her to go to Phil.ᵃ on Monday, leave there Tuesday morning at 6 o'clock by the Camden & Amboy R. R. which will land her near to the Fall River Boats Whf— To be sure to take that Boat on Tuesday evening for New Bedford. If no accident prevents, this will be her course."[12] And, according to historian Gary Collison, the fugitive Shadrach Minkins may have escaped Norfolk in May 1850 in the schooner *Vesper,* bound for New Bedford, and then have gone on to Boston— and his apprehension in February the next year.[13]

Then in August 1850 an incident occurred that showed how thoroughly committed New Bedford's black abolitionists had become to forcible resistance. About the time Minkins may have landed in New Bedford, a slave referred to only as Mary "took advantage of a favorable opportunity" and escaped with her two children from her Baltimore owner, George W. Whim. By mid-July 1850 she was in New Bedford and had secured work at the Franklin House, a hotel across from the city's railroad depot at the foot of Pearl Street. It was not a fashionable part of town. Two years earlier the *Mercury* reported a "great haul" at the Railroad House, "one of the dens of infamy in the outskirts of the city, near the Railroad Depot," in which local law officers rounded up some forty persons, "chiefly half-grown boys, together with nine females, who were enjoying a 'checked-apron ball' "; two years later the city announced its intention to clamp down on the "disorderly dances, dog and rooster fights, [and] obstructing the side-walks" that took place at the "houses of bad repute" around the depot. The Franklin House must have been notorious as well: Mary's New Bedford friends "were unwilling to have her stay in a house with such a reputation," a report later stated, but she intended to work there until they could help her find a better situation.[14]

On the last day of August two white men entered the Franklin House and attempted to seize Mary while she worked. At first report one of the men was identified as a constable from Pawtucket, Rhode Island. The rumor held that he had a warrant to arrest a man believed to be there, and upon entering, the *Republican Standard* reported, "a colored woman ran out of the house and across the fields and took to the woods. We are told that the occupants of the house desired to get rid of the colored woman, and took this time to frighten her, by telling her that an officer from the South was after her and she would be taken off with him." The newspaper learned, however, that the officer had attempted to handcuff Mary, "and this occasioned her fright." A later report indicated that the men were Mary's former owner Whim and a Baltimore constable named Hayes. Mary told an investigating committee that "she is sure that she is not mistaken, either as to Mr. Whim, or Mr. Hayes, as she has unfortunate reasons for remembering them both." Mary told the committee that when Whim entered, he stated that she was "my girl" and said to her, "I am looking for you, do you know me?" When he stated his intention to take her back to Maryland and tried to handcuff her, the committee reported, "she cried out, when several of the girls of the house came in, and interposed, and there was a scuffle" during which Mary was able to escape.[15] Joseph Ricketson, whose domestic help was involved in the affair, wrote a detailed account of the reaction of the community to the rendition attempt.

> The colored women were the first to hear it & they went in a body down there & in a few minutes the alarm was general—The colored men were at work or just returning & they spread it like wild fire from house to house, where colored persons lived—Some one left word at our House. John was about washing the dishes, he remembered us however by putting them all in the sideboard unwashed & locked it, & went on the Hill like a Race Horse—Mary, who is one of the best of women & kind disposition, was raging—she went ditto—& so did every one I presume—Mary when she returned told me would fight to the death because she would be doing God's service—says she, I would hurl down the top or covers of range & stove on their heads like brick bats. I would fight like a Horse—and her eyeballs glistened I assure you & then she exclaimed—they not only [illegible] the body but the brains yes says she & even the soul—Eliza, who lives at Mr. Emersons, when she heard it she cried out—why want I up there to grasp him by the throat, says she I would hold him till I had choked him—And Ralty [?] in the fulness of heart said, I will be the sacrifice, let them take me if they want any body—I guess they would soon get enough of me. . . . The colored people tried hard to find out were the men staid, but could not—if they had been at the Parker House when they inquired, I think they would have mobbed the house if they could not have got them otherwise—In the evening every colored man had a club—John says he never saw so many clubs in his

life—all the colored churches are shut up this evening & they have a public meeting in Sears Hall, where I presume they will vote to take a bold stance at least—It was a bold step on the part of the slave holder, as he did not even have a writ. I would not be surprised in the least to hear of the Death of the Rascal but I hope not—I want them to go away satisfied they can do nothing in New Bedford.[16]

Ricketson noted too an outrage among New Bedford whites, even among "Webster retainers." "There seems to be but one opinion among the white people, the colored people can depend on them fully," he wrote. ". . . One . . . told me he would even shoot Webster himself, if he came to his house for a slave; another told me he would fight to the last if he was a colored man. . . . Others say they would tar & feather the slave holders if they took them, or would like to have them treated so." Even the victimized Mary attended the Sears Hall meeting of citizens, and an investigating committee appointed that night soon reported that fully forty persons in New Bedford knew Hayes and that more than a dozen had seen him in the city within the week. Among those were probably twenty-four-year-old Mary Blair, who lived at Ricketson's house and had been born in Maryland, and Elizabeth Patterson, a thirty-six-year-old woman born in Baltimore who lived in the house of principal John F. Emerson. Neither was listed as a New Bedford resident before 1850, and it seems likely that both were fugitives living in the homes of two of the city's most dedicated abolitionists.

The investigating committee, irritated that both the *Mercury* and the *Republican Standard* had said that Mary's kidnapping charge was "unfounded," also refuted the rumor that the girl had been intoxicated at the time and that the owner of the Franklin House wished to be rid of her. Several of the committee saw her less than half an hour after her escape and reported her sober, and the investigators interviewed one employee who said that the owner in fact found Mary both likable and valuable. The fact that no other hotel employees would speak to the committee indicated, members said, that they were prostitutes, "under the influence of the woman who keeps the house, and makes them available to bring her corrupt gains, and that it is she who commands their silence." The attempt had taken place at a time when the community of color had lost most of its leaders and potential leaders, including Frederick Douglass, Ezra R. Johnson, Nathan Johnson, John Jacobs, and Lloyd Brooks, to California or to the national anti-slavery campaign, but enough men remained for the investigating committee. Fugitive William Henry Johnson, local black leaders J. B. Sanderson and D. W. Ruggles, and Samuel Thomas, who had come to New Bedford from Washington, D.C., the year before and may not have been a free man, were committee members; J. W. Smith may have been the black mariner John Watson Smith, who may also have been a fugitive; Edward Parker was a black shoemaker of unknown origin; member John Kelley was probably white. The committee noted a rash of recent attempts to capture fugitives, including that involving Henry "Box" Brown in Providence just four days after the New Bedford case, and warned about the passage of Clay's compromise in the Senate, "with provisions designed to give them [slaveholders] increased facilities for enslaving us. Slaveholders are already becoming emboldened. . . . Should this bill pass the House of Representatives, and receive the sanction of the President, God have mercy upon the colored people!"[17]

On the same day that the committee's report was published in the newspapers, the House voted exactly as the committee hoped it would not, sanctioning the fugitive slave provisions of the compromise by a vote of 109 to 76. Six days later, on 18 September 1850, Fillmore signed the Fugitive Slave Act into law. Persons who claimed people of color as their slaves had to secure an affidavit attesting their ownership and could seek a warrant from a special federal commissioner for their arrest and rendition. These commissioners were authorized to enlist the aid of anyone to enforce the law; fugitives were denied the right of trial by jury and could not testify in their own behalf. Any law officer who failed to cooperate with federal officials and any citizen who obstructed a fugitive arrest or concealed a fugitive were liable to heavy fines and imprisonment. The conservative *Mercury* conceded that while "the general government of the free States have no right to interfere with the peculiar institution in the several slave holding States," no one had the right to command assistance to slaveholders endeavoring to repossess their slaves once on "free soil." Such southerners, the newspaper vowed, "are greatly mistaken if they think the people of New England will enter upon the laudable business of slave catching with increased alacrity on account of the passage of this bill. . . . It seldom happens that a fugitive slave is claimed in New England, but whenever such a claim shall be made, we shall test the stuff that the new law is made of."[18]

Attempts to implement the new law soon followed, including the arrest of James Hamlet in New York City on 28 September, and concern grew in New Bedford as the *Mercury* reported rumors of slave catchers near at hand in Springfield and Worcester and the wholesale exodus of fugitives from such cities as Pittsburgh. On 1 October a rumor spread that a federal marshal had arrived in town on a slave catching errand. "The rumor spread like wild fire among the colored people," the *Mercury* reported, "who naturally became much excited, and commenced arming themselves, determined to maintain their freedom with their lives." Yet it was a false alarm: the uniformed man was a marshal from Charlestown, near Boston, who had come to the city to get information on a "truant son" supposed to have sailed on a whaling vessel.[19] Abandoning his peace principles in the heat of the moment, Morgan wrote in his diary that day, "Our black population are now in a good deal of alarm—under the new fugitive slave bill—several have already been taken back to slavery from New York & I have no doubt it will be attempted here—and blood shed will ensue—for they are a powerful body and determined to be free or die—and I hope they will carry it out & that no white man can be found to aid & abet the man stealers, when they appear among us."

Two days later New Bedford's community of color met at one of its churches to decide a course of action upon learning the "horrid news" that Hamlet had been returned to slavery from New York. Residents at the meeting resolved to do much as Morgan suspected they would: they vowed to "resist every attempt to take persons into slavery" and appointed what amounted to a vigilance committee "to incite our brethren to prepare for action in the event of any contingency." The new Fugitive Slave Act was in their eyes "a DEAD LETTER, and we will trample its provisions under our feet, and our blood should flow freely from every vein, and mingle with the blood of our revolutionary fathers, who fell on the field of battle defending the liberties of the country, before we should consent to be taken from the pure soil of Massachusetts as fugitive slaves." The act effectively disenfranchised them utterly, the meeting declared, "robbed" them "of our every right," and left them no choice but to defend themselves, "even to death."[20]

New Bedford's white abolitionists staged a meeting soon afterward, on 8 and 9 October, "to give public & loud expressing to the ruling sentiment of this town—which is one of the greatest assylums of the fugitives," Morgan wrote.[21] Morgan was appointed vice president of the meeting, along with John Emerson and two others; Thomas Arnold Greene, the nephew of the Providence abolitionist who was his namesake, was president. The more outspoken of them were outraged that Joseph Grinnell, a New Bedford Whig then serving in the U.S. House of Representatives, "was away from his seat when he knew the bill was under discussion, thereby negatively giving his assent to such a wicked measure." "I am ashamed of him," Edward Mott Robinson declared. "He was at the Treasury Department, was he? He had no business there. We didn't elect him to represent us at the Treasury Department. . . . When the most important bill of the whole session was up for consideration, and he knew it, he was not in his place, but at the Treasury Department!" Robinson asked why Grinnell, who was in New Bedford at the time, had not attended the meeting. "I have made some small speeches and spent money to elect him," he added, "but he will never get my vote again to represent me any where!"[22] The year before, Grinnell had offended city abolitionists by failing to support a resolution that would have abolished slavery in the District of Columbia on the grounds that its wording was such that no southerner would vote for it, and his seeming avoidance of the compromise vote made it impossible for former local Whigs who had thrown support to the Free Soil party to support him.[23]

But the meeting failed to create resolutions that satisfied all of those who attended, and the wording of those pronouncements showed the unraveling of abolitionist consensus, tenuous if it existed at all, over the question of forcible resistance. The meeting stated that it "sympathized with our colored citizens in their danger and distress" but promised only such assistance as "we may rightfully afford them"; whites pledged themselves to protect and defend fugitives to the extent that "a generous construction of the law will allow, and which it does not imperatively forbid." The next resolution was even more contingent: "while we cannot as a community array ourselves in opposition to any law of the land, however odious and unjust," it stated, the meeting refused to acknowledge that Congress could compel "the people of Massachusetts to become the hunters of Slaves."²⁴ A letter to the editor of the *Standard*, signed "Free Soil," promptly castigated the meeting and its resolutions as nothing short of hollow:

> What advantage will it be to the poor slave for us to mount the rostrum and quote the sacred and hallowed language of our Forefathers, and swell with indignation and disgust at the odious slave-catching law, if *our indignation* is only *deep rooted* enough to talk loud when surrounded by a crowded assemblage, and when the chance that we shall have to back up our indignant language by FORCIBLE RESISTANCE to the United States law is small? . . . If our speeches are only made for the occasion to catch the votes of our colored citizens and make them satisfied that we are the true friends of the fugitive and are ready to fight for them, and our resolves are *so bold* and *so mild* that our neighbors in the District and County will admire us for our conservatism and moderation, we had better, *far better* say nothing, than encourage our colored brethren with *false hopes.* We want men here to incur the penalty of the law, *"fine and imprisonment,"* rather than suffer a slave to be dragged from our city. We want a Representative in Congress who will not shrink from rendering assistance to the slave even at the CAPITOL *itself* if need be.²⁵

Another letter in the same issue of the *Standard* suggested deleting the word "rightfully" from the phrase "we freely tender them whatever aid we may rightfully afford them" in one resolution and eliminating the phrase "while we cannot as a community array ourselves in opposition to any law of the land" from the resolution stating that the meeting did not recognize Congress's authority to compel assistance in apprehending fugitives. At the 10 October meeting at Liberty Hall, "crowded to suffocation," white abolitionists followed the lead of the black community by appointing sixty residents, ten from each of the city's wards, to a "Vigilant Committee," but that act was the only consensus the meeting achieved. Rodney French offered nearly identical amendments to the resolutions as had been stated in the *Standard.* The first meeting's resolutions, French stated, "did not go far enough. . . . He wanted Resolutions that would mean something, that would test men," the *Standard* reported, that would compel them to "show their true colors. . . . If they meant to stand by the Fugitive, let them say so." Edward Mott Robinson allowed that "it would be better to have Resolutions passed which would receive the sanction of the whole community, rather than those so strong as to give but a bare majority," even as he agreed with French that "we should not vote for any thing we did not mean."

French's amended resolutions, which essentially removed any language that suggested forcible resistance would not be used, passed the meeting "by a large majority," whereupon meeting president Thomas Arnold Greene stated that he was unable to support any statement advocating "physical force." French allowed that Greene's "conscientious scruples in regard to resisting the slave catcher with physical force" were valid but called upon him to resign his post as a consequence. The *Standard,* sympathetic as its Free Soil editor Edmund Anthony was to him, noted that French "was sometimes quite sarcastic and severe in his remarks"; Morgan, vice president of the meeting, characterized French's amendments as "verbose & violent—and I fear pledging us to oppose it [the law] by force & violence. This drove Thos A Greene from the chair as a quaker & peace man." Greene did resign. In his place the meeting elected Robinson, who "threw himself into the current," Morgan wrote, "& went with them to the extreme." Two secretaries also resigned, and in the *Mercury* Daniel Ricketson, another of the meeting's secretaries, stated that, while he agreed fully with the "general spirit and tenor" of the resolutions, he could not "consistently with my peace principles . . . subscribe to them." For its part the *Standard* voiced its regret about the "division among those who sympathize with our colored population" and stood behind the use of force. "Before we would suffer a natural brother or son of ours to be taken by a slave-catcher, we should use such forcible weapons in defence as we could command," the newspaper stated, and added the hope that "the present state of feeling here" would keep slave agents and owners out of the city altogether and thus avert any need to test "the faith or professions of any of our people in this particular."[26] The ever moderate Morgan left the meeting, he said, "disheartened & discouraged":

> I wanted a firm & universal expression of opinion—no division—no strife—now all is confusion and I do not expect to sign the bill and shall have to appeal to the public with my reasons—I think the coloured people behaved most injudiciously for their own interests—they advocated loudly and noisily the extremest measures— instead of thankfully accepting a sympathy which would have been so universal, as to have been their best protection—now many will desert them—and I should not be surprised if a sentiment in favour of upholding the law—being a law—should arise—and thus defeat their aim altogether—well I must obey God rather than man & if I do not fight against the law I can & will suffer its penalties before I will aid or abet delivering one fugitive up to slavery.[27]

Morgan's account was the only one to mention the presence of people of color—except for fugitive (William) Henry Johnson, who spoke—at these meetings, and that they might support what he termed "the extremest measures" might have been expected from their active and armed response to the attempted kidnapping at the Franklin House the month before. The next day Morgan confirmed, at least for himself, his sense that "the coloured people have lost a great deal of sympathy and support" and expressed his frustration, common among New Bedford Whigs, with Rodney French. "This French has the faculty and talent to outrun and distract every meeting he attends," he wrote, "& he generally is successful."

One abolitionist seemingly lost to the cause after these meetings was Samuel Rodman, then engrossed in supply and labor troubles at his cotton mill in Fall River. He did not mention these meetings in his diary, and his only comment on the Fugitive Slave Act was a record of a discussion he had the next month with Nantucket's Nathaniel Barney, "my kind cousin." Rodman wrote, "I was obliged to differ from him on the duty of acquiescence in act, overt at least, in the supremacy of the late law of Congress for the restoration of fugitive slaves from the Southern states. I think his benevolent feelings disturb the action of his reason, as is unfortunately the case with too many of the good people of our free labor states." It seems clear that Rodman could not support the use of force in the aid of fugitives. He seems in fact to have sided with Webster on the supremacy of the Union; two days before Christmas he noted in his diary that he had finished reading "Professor Stuart's pamphlet on Webster's speech in the Senate at the last session which has drawn so much sensure [*sic*] from Abolitionists and Free Soilers. The pamphlet is a complete vindication," Rodman wrote, "and a severe rebuke upon the slavery agitators of this section."[28] Morgan also ceased to attend many abolitionist meetings, and his tone changed; after a town meeting on the fugitive slave law in early 1851, he wrote in his diary, "the abolitionists & negroes had it all their own way."[29]

Perhaps French's resolutions had become widely enough known that New Bedford began to be perceived, even more than it had previously, as a place for fugitives who wished to remain in the country. In November the *Standard* reprinted the response of a "wealthy Friend (Quaker) of New Bedford" to a Boston correspondent asking whether fugitives would be safe in the former city: "I profess to be a free soiler and hold to the 'high law.' God helping I mean to obey *that*. Therefore send along the 'good likely' fugitive, and if he is hungry we will feed him, if naked clothe him. He will be safe here. We have about 700 fugitives here in this city, and they are good citizens, and here we intend they shall stay. We do not counsel bloodshed, but shall suffer fines and imprisonment to any extent rather than allow that law to be carried out.—So let him come, we will do all we can for him, both for the outer and inner man."[30] The women of New Bedford, always apt to take a less conservative stand on antislavery matters than the city's men, did their part in December 1850 by gathering 1,729 signatures on a petition demanding repeal of the Fugitive Slave Act. The lead signature was that of Elizabeth Rodman, the widow of Samuel Rodman Sr. and daughter of William Rotch Sr. and then ninety-three years old. The women gave the petition to French to transmit to Horace Mann because, French wrote, "they doubted Hon. Joseph Grinnells willingness to serve them, in this respect." French wrote Mann that the petition carried "the names of the principle part of the most respectable ladies in this city. Very few indeed, who were called upon, declined signing it."[31]

In January 1850, about a month before Clay proposed his compromise, Massachusetts abolitionists seemed to feel fugitives quite secure within the state's boundaries. "In this state & in others an attempt at recapture is unheard of, & none has been made here for more than seven years," the board of managers of the Massachusetts Anti-Slavery Society stated in its annual report. "The fact seems to have become an established one that the trouble & expense of reclaiming a slave that has reached one of the New England states, is more than he is worth."[32] The conservative Boston *Traveller* professed itself at a loss to understand the concern of people of color over the possibility of capture even after the law had passed. The newspaper deemed it "hardly probable that any [effort to seize fugitives] will ever be made" and discerned "no sufficient reason" for the "considerable panic among the fugitive slaves who have been, some of them, for a number of years, quiet residents of the city." In an account reprinted in the *Mercury* just days after the October meetings at Liberty Hall, the *Traveller* reported that "quite a number of families in this city, where either the father or mother are fugitives, have been broken up, and the furniture sold off, with a view of leaving for safer quarters, in Nova Scotia or Canada." And the *Traveller's* earlier assessment of the safety of fugitives in Boston proved faulty when, about 22 October 1850, slave catchers arrived in the city to attempt the rendition of William and Ellen Craft. John Thomas, a fugitive from Cecil County, Maryland, who had taken the name James Williams, had come to Boston from Philadelphia immediately after the Fugitive Slave Act passed. But when the attempt was made to return the Crafts to slavery Thomas left Boston for New Bedford, where he stayed about three weeks before returning to Philadelphia. Shortly after the Vigilance Committee in Boston sent the Crafts to England, sometime between the end of October and the end of the year, the city's Vigilance Committee sent the fugitive Andrew Jones to New Bedford; no record of a man of color with this man is known to exist.[33]

Then, on 15 February 1851, the waiter Shadrach Minkins was arrested in Boston by a Norfolk, Virginia, constable with power of attorney from Minkins's professed owner. Word of the event spread rapidly, and as white abolitionists worked to arrange his defense, a group of about fifty men of color entered the courtroom where Minkins was being held and bore him away. They took him to an attic in the home of a black woman on Beacon Hill, and Lewis Hayden had a cab drive them both to Watertown. From there Minkins was relayed north until he reached Montreal on 21 February.[34] His successful rescue infuriated the South, elicited a formal rebuke from President Fillmore, and triggered a new exodus of fugitives from Boston.[35] Within weeks New Bedford was warned that slave agents were on their way to attempt arrests among the city's fugitive population. In mid-March 1851 the Boston Vigilance Committee had heard that William O. Russell, a New Bedford man who had just been appointed U.S. deputy marshal, had planned a foray into his native city aimed at "the seizure of and carrying away of fugitive slaves from New Bedford" because slave agents had been so unsuccessful in Boston. Russell was rumored to have declared "that he would take a fugitive from New Bedford it if cost him his life."[36]

Russell allegedly delegated to one Pat Riley, a deputy of federal marshal Charles Devens, the task of finding a steamer that would carry some one hundred to two hundred "marines" who presumably were to scour New Bedford for fugitives, though no report even hints that the excursion was prompted by specific certificates presented by southern slaveholders; one local history states that the marines were to seize fugitives "supposed to be in hiding awaiting transit to Canada by the Underground Railroad." Riley, the report continued, hired the brig *Acorn*—

the infamous vessel that carried Thomas Sims back to slavery a month later. On attempting to telegraph the report to New Bedford abolitionists, the Boston Vigilance Committee discovered that the "wires were broken, or cut, probably by design," so it sent two men to travel all night over the roads to New Bedford with the news. These men, S. P. Hanscom, a reporter for the Boston *Commonwealth,* and one Potter, were "staunch friends of liberty," the *Standard* reported; they rode in a chaise to Mansfield and then took "the steamboat train" to New Bedford, where they arrived at 4:30 in the morning. The *Standard* noted, "They called on some of our most respectable citizens, made known to them the circumstances, and presented letters from the Boston Committee of Vigilance. The alarm bell was sounded as a summons for assembling. The bell continued tolling about an hour."

That alarm bell was the bell in Liberty Hall, which had been placed in its steeple in the 1790s when the building was a Congregational meeting house; Aaron Childs, the only man of color listed as a New Bedford householder in the first federal census, was one of the largest subscribers to the campaign to finance it. The newspaper stated that ringing the bell was "the signal informally agreed upon by the Committee of Vigilance and their friends, to be used in case of the discovery of danger to fugitive slaves in this city" and reported that it began to toll at 6:00 A.M. One report asserted that Rodney French had seen a "strange vessel" in the harbor and tolled the bell. Yet no such vessel actually entered New Bedford harbor, and no marines appeared on a slave-catching expedition. The *Commonwealth* afterward insisted that the visit had indeed been planned and had failed to materialize only because of "*the non-arrival of the requisite papers from the South* which were expected by the evening mail." This fact the newspaper had learned "from other and better sources" than the "word of Deputy Marshals, some of whom we know have lied under oath." The *Standard* noted that "the old Hunker Boston papers" had derided the notion that such a plan was afoot. One of them printed a cartoon spoofing the anticipated raid, showing the obvious caricature "Sam Jonsing" searching for the "phantom schooner" and poking fun at French and his bell ringing (fig. 54). Theodore Parker saved the cartoon and wrote in its margin, "I put this miserable print here to show the spirit which prevails in Boston. . . . This is all the sympathy we can expect in Boston for a deed which saved the lives of I know not how many men."[37] The *Standard* defended the alarm its community had shown. "People had better be too vigilant than too careless in such cases, and besides danger may yet be impending," the newspaper warned. "We understand that a number of fugitives have this week left the city for a region where color is not a crime punishable by enslavement."[38]

After the scare, New Bedford's people of color held a day and an evening meeting to pray "for those who were supposed to be in peril of capture, and for their wives and children." The newspaper reported that about nine hundred people of color were present at the daytime meeting; if the 1850 census is presumed to be accurate, this number would have comprised almost nine-tenths of the city's

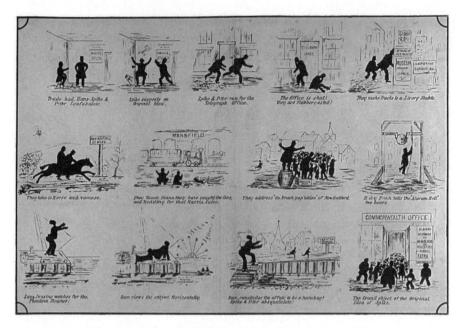

FIGURE 54. "The Geography of a 'Sell!' Or Pot & 'Scum's ride to NEW-BEDFORD,"
lithograph by Atwood, Boston, 1851. Courtesy Trustees of the Boston Public Library.
Found among Theodore Parker's papers, this broadside pokes fun at the rumored
attempt to capture fugitives in New Bedford in March 1851.

entire population of color. In the evening French and Hanscom addressed the
crowd, and an unidentified black minister presented a resolution, "responded to
enthusiastically by his colored brethren . . . to use all peaceable and lawful means
to prevent arrests but in the last resort to fight to the death."[39] Samuel Rodman
had heard that the city's people of color "meditate resistance and are armed. It is
to be hoped on all accounts that no such insane scheme will be attempted either
by the colored people or those who sympathise, as all do here with them in these
alarming circumstances and liabilities under the Law of 1850." Decades later Rodney French's daughter, Melancie French Hitch, recalled how an aged female black
domestic told her after the purported capture attempt "that when the first note
of the bell sounded, she grasped a carving knife off the table—the nearest weapon
at hand—and made haste to the [Liberty] hall."[40]

Instead what happened next was another meeting at the end of the month, this
one called by Mayor Abraham Hathaway Howland to "take such constitutional
measures of precaution to guard our citizens against the undue operation of the
Whig Kidnapping Act of 1850," as the *Standard* put it. The meeting apparently
aimed to take up where the city's women had left off in December by stating the

community's belief that the act should be repealed; failing that, the common-wealth should take declarative steps to enforce its own personal liberty law over the federal law. But the meeting turned into a "Whig dodge," the *Standard* de-clared, as "the supporters of this fugitive-hunting and slave-catching administra-tion" attempted through John Henry Clifford, then attorney general of the state, to declare that there was no sense or need in the city's attempting formally to seek repeal of the Fugitive Slave Act. Clifford claimed impractical a proposed resolu-tion that citizens of New Bedford instruct their representatives to secure passage of an act mandating trial by jury for alleged fugitives and insisted that state law granted such a right already; he thought it foolish to insist that legislators refuse to allow state prisons to be used to hold those accused of violating the act. In sum, Clifford declared, passing resolutions "purporting to express the sense of the city on the state of affairs, while they could do nobody any good, they would be certain to do harm." Any such resolves would be fodder for "South Carolina secessionists," Clifford warned, and he expressed his extreme reluctance "to have it go forth that this, the third commercial city in the Union, was seeking to em-broil herself with the general government in opposition to the laws of the United States."[41]

The *Standard* suggested any "unprejudiced observer" at the meeting would have surmised that Clifford was essentially filibustering in order to make it im-possible for Howland and others who called the meeting to declare and gain sup-port for their objectives. Indeed, the newspaper reported, Clifford moved for ad-journment as soon as he determined that enough like-minded people had assembled to second and approve the attempt. After Rodney French rose to repri-mand Clifford (who, the *Standard* stated, "grinned horribly a ghastly smile" at the rebuke), the motion for adjournment was defeated overwhelmingly, by a vote of 148 to 46. "Then followed some applause, you had better believe," the news-paper reported. In a "spirited, racy, and caustic speech, in which he handled the slave hunters, their *attornies,* apologists and abettors, without gloves," the news-paper reported, French claimed the act had passed the House of Representatives when most of its members were intoxicated and proceeded to gather a committee to form resolutions, among them that the commonwealth's 1843 personal liberty law held sway over the federal act and that fugitives had a right to a jury trial. The meeting approved the committee's report "as the sense of the citizens of New Bedford" by a vote of 148 to 4; 2 of the 4 voting against it were Lindsey of the *Mercury* and "whig attorney" J. H. W. Page, who claimed that the meeting was not representative. Edward Mott Robinson sided with French once again, term-ing the act "cruel" and stating his wish "to have the voice of New Bedford go farther against it." Robinson also voiced his suspicion that "influences had been used to keep people away from the meeting," though he did not specify whose influences and who had been warned off.

The New Bedford meeting apparently caught the attention of at least one New

York paper, the *Express,* which suggested that the influence of the *Mercury* had been responsible for the "agitation." The *Standard* found the idea ridiculous. The *Mercury* "clique," the newspaper charged, "was constituted of the editor of the Mercury alone . . . he was top bottom and sides of the whole concern. 'Influence of the Mercury!' Ha! ha! ha! The idea is a rich one! Why, we have half a pew in church, and we will give a seat for a year to every one who will make oath that he was ever influenced by the Mercury's advocacy of any thing, unless to take up on the opposite side."[42] The Boston *Commonwealth* also reported on the New Bedford meeting, to the *Standard's* obvious delight. "The poor Hunkers, whose lives hang on catching a negro, now give it up that they have been beaten in New Bedford. Gen. Clifford had arranged his campaign to kill off the meeting, but could not rally his forces. The meeting was enthusiastic and very large considering the time of day. Mr. French who took a leading part, was fully prepared to prove that the intention of a 'NAVAL KIDNAPPING EXPEDITION' against New Bedford was a reality, and that Deputy Marshals Riley and Byrnes were at the Navy Yard on Saturday, and arranged to send the new propeller 'John Hancock' to Buzzard's Bay with a large force on Monday, but Clifford and his clique did not deny the fact nor challenge the proof."[43]

The story of New Bedford's refusal to abide by the Fugitive Slave Act and of French's ringing of the bell in Liberty Hall had spread beyond New York and Boston by the fall. Rodney French had plenty of enemies locally: Whigs viewed him as a caustic and opportunistic upstart, and he had rankled the clergy in 1841 when he had called them "a great brotherhood of thieves."[44] To these he added the merchants of New Bern, North Carolina, who in late September 1851 announced a boycott of his lumber vessel and encouraged other southern merchants to do the same.[45] They resolved to offer "no support, no aid, no employment, whereby he may receive one *cent* from us, a portion of the people of the South, of whom he has been so liberal in his abuse." The merchants had heard that French "called on the fugitive slaves and free negroes to arm themselves, and prevent the taking away runaway slaves" after attempts to implement the Fugitive Slave Act with slave extraditions in Massachusetts. Finally New Bernians resolved that they were happy to do business with "that portion of the North who have manifested a disposition to carry out in good faith the fugitive slave law."[46]

In a published response to New Bernians, French relayed his understanding that the vessel's captain, also a part owner, had expressed to them a wish to divest himself of his partnership with French. He promised to sell his share in the sloop as soon as it arrived in New Bedford, "*no matter the sacrifice,* and my business in your State will be closed forthwith." That French occupied "some humble place in the ranks," as he claimed, was disingenuous, but his denial that he had urged people of color to arm themselves in resistance may not have been. "The fugitive slaves and free negroes here, needed no word of mine to excite them to resist 'the taking away runaway slaves,'" French wrote, and added an anecdote his North Carolina readers must have found harrowing:

One of our Judges of the Court of Common Pleas said to a fugitive who asked him for money to enable him to go to Canada, No! Not a dollar, but if you want a 'six-barrel Pistol' to defend your liberty on Massachusetts soil, and will promise to use it if necessary, I will give it to you, and any other arms you may require. The mere mention, in the papers, of the passage of that law was enough to 'excite' them to arm themselves with as fixed a determination as Jackson prepared to resist the British at New Orleans, and in the estimation of many of our citizens in quite as commendable and praiseworthy a cause.[47]

French declared that whether his vessels were boycotted or not, even if New Bernians had burned his lumber boat as it lay in the harbor, "I shall be quite as reluctant to assist in carrying back to bondage those who have escaped from the South, and shall not be withheld in the least in any efforts I may be able to put forth in behalf of the down-trodden and the oppressed." The Fugitive Slave Act, which he denounced in the most unconditional terms, was based on the absurd notion that a person could own another person, French insisted to New Bernians, and he would not obey it, help to carry it out, or cease working for its repeal.

As New Bedford's white population wrangled over resolutions and struggled with outsiders' perceptions of their city, anxiety among the population of color only grew more intense, particularly after fugitive Thomas Sims was arrested in Boston on 4 April 1851. "Our poor colored inhabitants live in a constant state of alarm, many of them thinking that they shall be looked up as soon as warm weather comes on," New Bedford's M. B. Eddy wrote to Anne Weston two days after the event. "Some have left town. Others are going, but of course there are many who cannot go. Is it not horrible?"[48] Sims had made his way to Boston in late February 1851 by stowing away on a vessel in Savannah. He made the mistake of wiring his wife for money, a message that agents intercepted and used to find his lodgings, a boardinghouse for black mariners. There he was arrested. "We shall now see whether a slave can be taken from Massachusetts," Morgan wrote in his diary. "The Abolitionists are leaving nothing undone—to get delay—throw in obstacles & get the people excited, but all will not do I think to prevent the law taking its course."

While Sims remained in custody, Morgan saw little chance that he might be released. "No doubt he must go—Sad though it is nothing but blood & revolution can prevent it—and I for one will not join in that. The antislavery people are moving Heaven & earth to prevent it & get up excitement but the police are determined and public sentiment generally will side with them." On 11 April, the day Judge Woodbury remanded Sims to his owner, Morgan was more certain than ever of the outcome he had predicted and summed up the sentiment about the case. "The excitement does not seem very general," he observed, "but the abolitionists are trying hard to raise it to fever heat." On 12 April Morgan recorded that Sims "has been sent back—and no attempt at rescue made—he goes back by sea. Rumours are now rife that warrants for slaves are out here."[49] On 21 April the *Mercury* announced that "a very large number of fugitive slaves," aided by many of city's most affluent and respected citizens, had left for Canada, and more were preparing for departure.[50] Fully 256 persons of color, comprising 180 individuals and family groups, were listed in the 1850 New Bedford census or in local records from 1851 but not again shown as residents before the Civil War; when compared with the record of the 1850 population of color as a whole, proportionately more of the birthplaces of those 256 persons were "unknown" or left blank and were in one of the slave states (as well as in New York, Rhode Island, and Connecticut). Proportionately fewer persons of this group were born in free states.[51] This accounting of population lost after 1851 may thus hint at the departure of fugitives, but because of the high degree of transience in general and of transience related to whaling and coasting specifically, it is impossible to determine precisely who, and how many, might have left New Bedford because of the fugitive apprehensions of 1851.

Despite the reported exodus from New Bedford, many fugitives continued to view the city as a refuge. The population of color in fact grew between 1850 and 1855, from 1,008 to 1,527 persons. And it continued to grow at a faster rate than the city's white population, as it had since 1840. Among the fugitives who came to New Bedford in the years after the Fugitive Slave Act was William Winters, whose name in slavery was Daniel Fisher. Born in Virginia and sold to South Carolina, Fisher escaped with another slave and made his way back to his native Westmoreland County plantation to ask his former owner to buy him back. The owner was too poor to do so and advised instead that he stow away on a northern-bound vessel. "As the north meant freedom," he wrote, "I decided to act on his advice." For three months Fisher and his compatriot hid in dens they had dug in the woods until a sympathetic captain took them aboard a vessel carrying wood to Washington. Ultimately he was advised to go to Deep River, Connecticut, where he lived in apparent security until the Fugitive Slave Act passed. Fisher, who by then had taken his new name, stated that he was "always afraid of being taken by day or night and carried again to the South." Because he had learned that Massachusetts was "more friendly to escaped slaves than Connecticut," he came to New Bedford, where he lived and worked as a waiter until the signing of the Emancipation Proclamation made him feel safe enough to return to Connecticut.[52]

At a 14 October 1850 meeting in Boston on the Fugitive Slave Act, Frederick Douglass told the story of another fugitive, a woman "now in New Bedford" who had come to Boston on a vessel that had been smoked on the suspicion that a slave had hidden aboard. "The woman lay there in the hold, almost suffocated," Douglass told his audience, "but she resolved to die rather than come forth." Smoking was, as Douglass pointed out, a common strategy, but it may be possible to identify the woman he described. Two years later Wendell Phillips cited in more detail the case of Elizabeth Blakesley, with whom he had shared the stage at a meeting at Fanueil Hall. Blakesley, he said, was "a mulatto girl, of Wilmington, North Carolina" who had hidden on a Boston-bound brig. Her owner came aboard and, when she refused to answer his calls or show herself, he smoked the vessel three times with sulphur and tobacco. "Still she bore it," Phillips noted. "She came North, half frozen, in the most inclement month of the year—this month [January]. She reached Boston just able to crawl."[53]

In 1851 New Bedford seemed a safe haven to Cornelia Grinnell Willis, who sent Harriet Jacobs, a nurse in her family, into hiding in the city after Jacobs read of the arrival in New York of her former master's daughter.[54] In the same year the fugitive grandson of a minister in a black church in Portsmouth, Virginia, came to New Bedford and changed his name to James Pritlow. Pritlow was never enumerated in any city listing, but he was in the city in 1853 when the fugitive George Teamoh came to New Bedford and was there still in September 1855, when the Reverend William Jackson listed him among the members of the Second Baptist Church, one of four black churches in the city at the time.[55] And in August 1851 Joseph Ricketson, under whose roof Henry "Box" Brown had lived in 1849, provided shelter to two more fugitives of unknown identity. "I shall not have time to write about the Slave woman & child consigned to me," he wrote to Debora Weston. "Her story is a long one—She seems very bright & is now very cheerful."[56]

The Fugitive Slave Act seemed even more iniquitous to the city's people of color when Thomas Scott Johnson, a free black mariner from New Bedford, was arrested in late June 1851 after the vessel on which he served, the brig *Commerce* of Nova Scotia, was shipwrecked on Wreck Island near Alexandria, Virginia. Since the 1830s New Bedford's people of color had protested the fact that free blacks were severely circumscribed if they attempted to enter the South, and now, when the North was being asked to assist under penalty of law in the rendition of fugitives, a freeborn mariner was put in jail on the mere suspicion that he was a fugitive. Johnson, about twenty-one years old, was the son of Jacob Johnson, an esteemed man of color who had come to New Bedford from New York in the early 1800s and had died of cholera in 1834. Thomas Johnson's mother Mary had remarried a Cape Verdean man named Domingo Barrows, and the family lived in Jacob Johnson's longtime home at 91 South Water Street. His brothers David, Edmund, and Jacob were mariners as well. New Bedford learned that Thomas Johnson had been taken from the vessel through Elisha Card, a mariner with family ties in the city who was master of the *Commerce*. Card wrote that because Johnson had no free papers with him, officials took him to be a fugitive slave and were preparing to sell him when Card posted a five-hundred-dollar bond until Johnson was able to produce his papers. Johnson told Card his mother's name and address and added that William C. Taber and two other whites in the city could attest to his free status. Card asked New Bedford's Benjamin Sandford to visit Johnson's mother for the requisite documents while he remained in Norfolk getting his damaged brig repaired. "I should feel sorry to see him sold as a slave, as he appears a sober, steady fellow," Card wrote to Sandford. "I have no doubt but that he was born as free as myself, but unless he can show it, and pay the costs, he must inevitably be sold."[57]

Sandford must have done as he was asked, for by the first of July Johnson's papers were drawn up, signed by Mayor Howland and some of the city's "most respectable citizens," and sent to Card. Johnson was still in Portsmouth on 14 July, when he wrote his mother to report that he was free and "very grateful to the New Bedford folks for their kindness toward me in testifying to my freedom." He had an opportunity, he said, to ship out on the *Commerce* again but had not made up his mind to do so. "She is in trouble," he stated, "and I am not."[58]

The success of the Johnson incident may have carried over into the mood of the First of August celebration two weeks after he wrote home to report his release. New Bedford's black community had organized anniversary celebrations of emancipation in the British West Indies since 1844, events that gathered people of color from a wide region, including marching bands of men of color from other towns, and usually featured a procession through the city center and a picnic and speeches at the grove near John Avery Parker's imposing County Street mansion in the northwestern part of town. Both of the city's newspapers customarily reported on the celebrations—invariably noting how "orderly" they were, as though they fully expected otherwise when such a large number of people of color crowded the town—and diarists among the large body of white spectators occasionally described them in more detail. In 1851 William C. Nell, by then a close associate of Douglass and an intimate of J. B. Sanderson, Charles Lenox Remond, and the attorney Robert Morris, the only lawyer of color to serve on Shadrach Minkins's Boston defense team, spoke to the assembled at Parker's Grove. Morris, Nell noted in the *Liberator,* "alluded to the prosperous condition of the colored citizens of New Bedford, promoted, as he was glad to believe, by a favorable public local sentiment, which he hoped would soon extend itself throughout the entire Bay State and New England."[59]

In his report, Nell, then embroiled in a long legal struggle to end segregated schools in Boston, claimed that the fact of integrated public schools in New Bedford by itself accounted for "the respectful attention of the entire citizens of New Bedford relative to the procession and the day's observances—the most sensitive colored person meeting with no chilling pro-slavery look, word or deed." Rodney French invited some of the party and the military companies to his Purchase Street home, and James Arnold asked the visiting black military company from New York to visit his home and grounds, by then an impressive, pastoral garden that residents of the town were free to use on Sundays. Joseph Ricketson reported that Arnold's wife Sarah, who showed the company around her house, told his cousins "almost with <u>tears</u> in her eyes, that she considered it her <u>duty,</u> to contribute to their comfort & happiness, & compared her own situation with the downtrodden and oppressed." "What a striking contrast to the cottonocracy of Boston," Ricketson wrote "—Would that all the wealthy & powerful would do likewise—how soon Slavery would be abolished."[60]

The tendency was strong among white abolitionists in New Bedford and elsewhere to credit the efforts of whites in antislavery reform with more effect than they probably had. Nell did not value integrated schools because of the "improving" access children of color had to white students and teachers but because of the equal access it presumably gave them to resources and because day-to-day interaction between white and black children was bound to have a humanizing effect on both. His colleague Douglass argued that integrated schools were more important in the fight for equal rights than gaining the vote, for voting involved a momentary interaction once a year; school, by contrast, brought black children "into contact on equal terms with white children and youth, three hundred days in the year, and from six to ten hours each day," he wrote in *Douglass' Monthly* in March 1859. "And these children, in a few years, become the people of the State." Jeremiah B. Sanderson stated it somewhat more directly; because black and white children learned together in New Bedford schools, "a sense of equality is cultivated—a spirit of emulation is awakened among all classes." Black abolitionist and minister Samuel Ringgold Ward inverted the conventional argument: people of color needed integrated schools and neighborhoods because whites, he wrote, "need to be taught even the first ideas of civilization, by being near to enlightened and progressive coloured people."[61] Whites seemed to miss the possibility that even lacking access to capital, education, property, and the other measures of status that existed in American society, people of color might yet work by and among themselves toward their own enlightenment. Sarah Arnold told Joseph Ricketson's cousins that "she had never had a more orderly & well behaved set of people in her house" than the visiting black military company, the unspoken and shared premise being that they expected, or feared, the opposite. When he still thought of himself as an abolitionist, Samuel Rodman expressed what was probably a common view in his comments on the 1844 First of August celebration. "Considering the disabilities under which they labor," he wrote in his diary the day after visiting Parker's Grove, "I think our colored citizens deserve great commendation for their good morals and industrious and prudent habits and for their title to this praise they are largely indebted to the zealous efforts of the 'abolitionists' for their elevation in intelligence and morals."[62]

The same tendency to laud white abolitionists reemerged soon after the false alarm of March 1851. In April 1852 a letter from "an abolitionist" attempted to answer a question the *Standard's* Anthony had put the week before—"What progress has been made in the *abolitionist* cause since R----y F----h rang the bell?" His response, if the views of Rodman and Morgan can be taken to represent the view of the city's Whig establishment, was of course that much progress had occurred. Charles Sumner, once denounced as an ultra-abolitionist whose election to the U.S. Senate would sunder the Union, was in his sixth year of public

service in that body with no untoward result; congregations that had not permitted abolitionists to meet in "their splendid cushioned churches" now offered
space to appeals for fugitives. In summing up, however, the abolitionist hinted at
a unity that did not exist:

> Why, sir, before that BELL struck terror into the hearts of the Fillmore and Webster
> slave catchers, and their "southern dirt" eaters, every thing that savored of "Abolition-
> ist" from Garrisonian to Freesoilism, or even Coalitionism here, was cast out as evil.
> Those who were suspected of the least sympathy in that direction were held in very
> low esteem, if, indeed, they escaped open denunciation from "Old Liners" (as they
> claimed to be) who were for sending all the "NIGGERS" back to slavery, to save the
> Union. . . . That "bell" in the tower of Liberty Hall, on that memorable and never
> to be forgotten Sabbath morning, "rang" a peal, that with the aid of electricity and
> steam, was heard in the twinkling of an eye, as it were, over both Continents, and
> which was a prelude to most glorious results.[63]

That French rang the bell of Liberty Hall on that March Sunday in 1851 almost
instantly became a legend, tying in as it did so neatly to the use of the Liberty
Bell in Philadelphia as an antislavery emblem and the use of the term as the title
of Maria Weston Chapman's famed annual gift book. In November 1854, when
the building was destroyed by fire, the *Republican Standard* called Liberty Hall
"the far famed temple of liberty, within whose hallowed walls freedom for all men
has been so frequently proclaimed, and from whose tower the note of warning to
the poor, trembling fugitive from oppression, has so often been sounded." In 1863
William H. Carney Jr. called Liberty Hall "a sacred edifice. Like the Temple of
Diana which covered the virgins from harm in olden time, so old Liberty Hall in
New Bedford protects the oppressed slave of the 19th century."[64]

The 1854 Liberty Hall fire was so intense that the bell melted, and the newspaper noted that many citizens were then "obtaining relics of the venerated lost one
for the purpose of preservation."[65] The abolitionist unity such symbols proffered,
perhaps especially in their own time, concealed the widening rift between Garrison's continued disdain for political antislavery and the appeal of the Free Soil
party. Dissatisfied with the ability of both major parties to address the issue of
slavery in a forthright way, alienated Democrats, "Conscience" Whigs (as opposed to "Cotton Whigs," the old elite with financial interests in Southern cotton), and members of the short-lived Liberty Party formed the Free Soil party in
1848, dedicated to stopping the expansion of slavery in American territories but
not, as Douglass and others pointed out, to eradicating American slavery altogether. Daniel Ricketson and others remained faithfully Garrisonian; before the
1852 election Ricketson argued in the *Liberator* that only by spreading "a healthy
moral tone into the community" would slavery be overcome and that the mind
could only accept as much if it "be left free, and not shackled by any political
machinery." Ricketson added, "I hope no colored voter will be deluded into the
idea, that by casting a vote for either a Whig or Democrat, he will further the

object he has at heart." Still, the Free Soil party garnered the support of many black and white abolitionists, including *Standard* editor Edmund Anthony, and even before its formation the gathering power of the coalition it harbored had helped place Abraham Hathaway Howland (whom Morgan called a "renegade Whig") in the mayor's office in New Bedford in 1847. In 1851 the Free Soil vote is believed to have placed Charles Sumner in the U.S. Congress. Such achievements as these made former Garrisonians question whether political action was as pointless as they had long believed. In a report on Garrison's February 1852 address to the city's Female Anti-Slavery Lyceum, the *Standard* termed it "an abolition lecture of the olden time, in which political action is opposed, and the old abolition organization declared to be the only hope of the slave." Without naming his own political affiliation, Anthony offered that other groups were now "laboring against the giant evil" and that men opposed to slavery need no longer withhold their votes. Before the 1851 election, a man of color rose at a New Bedford anti-slavery lecture by Lucy Stone and the couple Abby Kelly and Stephen Foster to repudiate Foster's contention that voting was inconsistent with antislavery principles. "After Mr. Foster had concluded," the *Standard* reported, "a colored man got up and exhorted his brethren not to be led astray by the remarks which had been made, but rather to attend the polls upon the 10th day of November, and vote the free soil ticket."[66]

New Bedford's people of color grew even more leery of Whigs and Whig coalitions when Horace Mann, Daniel Drayton's defender four years earlier, ran for governor in 1852. At a convention of people of color in Cincinnati, Mann had propounded the theory that people of African descent were "inferior in intellect" to Caucasians but superior "in sentiment and affection"; once antislavery commotion had died down, he stated further, blacks would be restored to their natural part of the world, that "band of territory around the earth, on each side of the Equator." On behalf of the voters of color of New Bedford, Ezra R. Johnson wrote Mann to ask him to elaborate on his ideas, a request Mann immediately honored. He meant only, he wrote Johnson, that Caucasians were adapted to colder climates and Africans to warmer ones and that each race would progress better in the climates God had made for them. When "justice is done," Mann reasoned, blacks would "see reason gradually" and return to these regions to build up "a civilization peculiar of their own."[67]

To Johnson, Ruggles, William Henry Johnson, and other men of color, Mann's ideas were nothing short of an endorsement of colonization, a movement to which the Fugitive Slave Act had given new life. Earlier in 1852 a meeting at the city's Third Christian Church that claimed to represent the thirteen hundred citizens of color in New Bedford protested, as it had twenty years earlier, the American Colonization Society. The meeting resolved, "Here we were born, here will we live by the help of the Almighty, and here we will die and let our bones lie by our fathers."[68] Mann's statements brought the frustrating issue before them again. His views were "untenable, illiberal, unjust, and only sustained by that partial judgment, which measures men by their complexion," a meeting of citizens of color argued in October. And for them to leave behind millions of American slaves to resettle in Liberia, the West Indies, or Canada would be "a strange incongruity," they pointed out, if Mann's theories about the affectional superiority of African peoples were valid. Daniel Ricketson, who attended the meeting, was also dismayed by Mann's views and took them as evidence of the futility of political action. "What, then, are our colored friends to learn from this," he asked, "but that they have little to hope for from political abolitionists—that the overthrow of slavery, and the proper social standing of the free colored people will be but little promoted, for the present, at least, by the use of the ballot-box."[69]

Whether Free Soil or Garrisonian, New Bedford's black antislavery activists appear to have devoted themselves more concertedly to the assistance of escaping slaves in this decade, when a visitor to the city described the city's reputation as a fugitive haven in a letter to the *New York Tribune*.

> The colored population of New Bedford is very large, numbering not less than 1,000. Very many of them are fugitives from 'Southern *service.*' . . . I passed an erect, intelligent looking negro, trimming the street lamps. I asked Canada, the negro who was driving, who he was. 'Oh!' he replied, 'he has been here only a year from Virginia. He is a brother in the same church as I am.' I inquired how he escaped. Canada continued, 'Well, he was in a *box* several days, and once *at sea,* he came pretty fast. His wife had given him up, though she had waited years. Liberty is sweet, and the first time he came into church, I thought he would set it on fire. I tell you he *blowed* there!' The illusion to a whaling phrase is significant. A fugitive could not be taken here, it is believed.[70]

That a fugitive-assisting local network of people of color had developed by the 1850s, if not earlier, is documented in the autobiography of George Teamoh, born a slave in Norfolk in 1818 (fig. 55). Like the coachman Canada, Teamoh also used a maritime metaphor to describe why he held New Bedford in such high esteem. The people of the city, "with a zeal which knew no bounds, had long years ago, laid down as a principle and nailed to the mast-head of their little bark that had crossed so many rugged waters,—the full and untrammeled possession of one's ownership of himself," he wrote, and because of this New Bedford was a "magnet of attraction" for fugitives. Teamoh had worked in his early twenties as a manual laborer on Fort Monroe, a federal installation across Hampton Roads from Norfolk, and as a caulker and ship carpenter at the Gosport Navy Yard in Portsmouth; his owner, Josiah Thomas, was also a carpenter there. Ten years later the owner of Teamoh's wife and children sold them from Portsmouth, and the Thomases made arrangements for Teamoh to become free. In August 1853 they signed him on as a carpenter on the merchant ship *Currituck*, which carried tobacco to Bremen, Germany, and when the vessel returned with German immigrants to New York City Teamoh jumped ship, hired a lawyer to secure his back pay and formally declare him free, and then came to New Bedford about 1 De-

FIGURE 55. George Teamoh,
photograph, about 1865.
Courtesy Library of Congress.

cember.[71] In his autobiography, Teamoh described the sentiment he met in the city, a position he assumed was widely known:

> In New Bedford I passed under the appellation of "fugitive" which at once commanded the sympathy of that patriotic and generous people, and of whom it would seem useless that I should mention a single word after saying what, perhaps most readers know,—that this locality has always been considered the fugitive's Gibraltar—a truth which puts poetry and fiction to blush; as I had been there but a short while when, acting as without the intervention of reason or deliberation its good citizens gathered around me with charitable offerings and a protest of eternal hatred to slavery and all its alliances. . . . And so with that loyal people, they had no argument for slavery but that of instant death to the institution.[72]

But Teamoh found his celebrity as a fugitive short-lived. "Notwithstanding their repeated manifestations of kindness, I was doomed to share a hard lot in that wealthy city," he noted, and added wryly, "Once there you were 'free indeed,' and then thrown upon your own resources after a few weeks of indulgence." Arriving as he had in winter, when work on the wharves had stopped, Teamoh made himself a snow shovel and looked for work. But he found much of the shoveling done by "experts" and contracted for in advance, for the season. In general New Bedford's "laboring classes" did little work of any sort during the winter, Teamoh stated. He spent all his money but refused, he said, to beg. One morning, standing on the corner of Union and South Water Streets in front of the auction house of Nehamiah Waterman, Teamoh saw James Pritlow, who he knew by a different name, riding in a chaise.[73] Pritlow had escaped Portsmouth in 1851 and "possessed a heart truly in sympathetic beat with the fugitive sufferers where ever known." Pritlow sensed Teamoh lacked work and money and took him to the boardinghouse keeper William Bush (see fig. 22). To Bush seems to have fallen the mantle of fugitive assistance; Nathan Johnson, who had earlier played that role for Frederick Douglass and others, had by then left the city for California.

When Teamoh met Bush, the former grocer apparently had returned to manual labor to supplement what he earned from boarding. He had a large family, a wife and eight children, to support (his eldest daughter Julia, by then married to William Castle, had not yet moved to New Bedford from Washington), as well as, Teamoh noted, others:

> Quite a large number of fugitives for a time stayed at his house and received the same hospitalities as did his regular boarders, notwithstanding the former were not able to pay their way. If any reliance may be placed in the statement of many of the older citizens of N.B. Deacon Bush,—now deceased,—has been one of the most zealous, hard working and liberal friends the fugitive ever found. Over such, I have often seen him weep in bitterness of soul while rendering all the aid and comfort within his power. In this respect he did what he believed constituted one of the most essential principles of his profession as a christian, "love thy neighbor as thyself." Mr. Bush has sacrificed much in delivering numbers of our people from the many deep distresses consequent upon human oppressions. . . . Mrs. Bush, indeed the whole family were not less humane in their devotions to mortal sufferers.[74]

"No better Patriot," Teamoh wrote of Bush, "none who could enter more fully in to the feeling and measure the depths of human woes—ever trod the soil of New England."

Teamoh said Bush would take any job "of an honorable character," and through the winter they often worked together much as Frederick Douglass had in his early days in the city—"lading, or unlading coal vessels; with pick-axe and spade digging through the rocky and frosted soil of the city for foundations upon which to erect edifices and other buildings, rolling staves—cording wood &c. &c." Bush would often find a sailor's jacket in his boardinghouse for Teamoh, who had no clothes for such cold weather. Teamoh stayed at Bush's home through the winter, and Bush laid his board charges up against his future wages. When spring arrived Teamoh applied for work at Cannon's shipyard on Commercial Wharf, but Cannon told him he would not hire men of color because a man named Brown who had once worked for him left with his family for Canada when work was unavailable in New Bedford.[75] Teamoh then went to the Stowell Brothers (Daniel and Columbus), caulking contractors who hired him at three dollars a day, a "usual wage" for New Bedford but almost twice what Teamoh had earned at his trade in Virginia. The work with Stowell was not steady but was intermittently heavy: Teamoh worked when needed six days a week. "The old gentleman—father to the Stowells—like his boys, always seems to have been touched with the feelings of human sympathy, as they have steadily given the fugitive something to do for a lively-hood," Teamoh wrote. "Such christian hearted people," he declared, were "the soul of a city."[76]

When the onset of winter stopped caulking work in 1854, Bush helped Teamoh find domestic work in Providence by writing "to a good old fugitive friend" who found him a job as a butler to Thomas Dorr, the governor who had made a name for himself among poor people, including people of color, by fighting against restrictions on male suffrage in Rhode Island. In the spring he returned to New Bedford but could not find work, not even with the Stowell brothers.[77] Teamoh wrote to one of his half-brothers living in Boston—either Thomas, born in 1831, or John William, born in 1827, both of them waiters—and upon word that work was available there, Teamoh left New Bedford for Boston. By then, 1855, a woman of color named Grace Teamar was in New Bedford with her elderly mother, Margaret Wilson, and an eight-year-old daughter Mary; she had come from Norfolk and told the overseers of the poor that she was the widow of William Teamer, who "was never here." Her late husband may have been brother to George, for the latter mentioned that his mother had had "three or four" other children before her death, when he was a boy.[78]

By the time Teamoh arrived in New Bedford, the *Standard,* having openly taken up the fugitive's cause, made frequent note of the travel through or presence in the city of fugitives. The firsthand accounts compiled by William Still in Philadelphia document scores of fugitives sent on to New Bedford from Philadelphia.[79] That fugitives arrived in New Bedford expecting to find friends and family who had previously escaped is patent, suggesting that the city's reputation among people of color in the South was well made, as it had come to be among its own citizens.

Among southern slave owners, the view of the city as a tolerant and liberty-loving haven was of course turned on its head. Southerners had been complaining about northern abolitionists and their presumed accomplices, mariners, for years. The *Wilmington Aurora* in North Carolina stated of black sailors in particular, "They are of course, all of them, from the very nature of their position, abolitionists, and have the best opportunity to inculcate the slaves with their notions." Officials in Norfolk, Virginia, called abolitionists "a desperate and lawless gang of atrocious fanatics" in 1835, and the same year the *People's Press* of Wilmington, North Carolina, used the discovery of a fugitive aboard the Fall River–bound schooner *Butler* to complain about "strangers," meaning the crew who were suspected of helping the slave aboard, "meddling with our municipal laws, even to their infraction—laws that in no way affect them, either in person or property, but which are essential to our self-preservation. They will intermeddle, although they know that to carry away a slave, intentionally, is death on conviction," the newspaper argued. ". . . Our insulted commonwealth can find no salvo in the presumption that those who are guilty are misled by unprincipled fanatics—that Garrison and Tappan, and other diabolical intriguers have perverted the understandings and excited a false sympathy in the breasts of those who come among us for commercial purposes." Ten years later, Maryland slaveholders gathered in Port Tobacco to discuss how to confront "the reckless efforts of fanaticism in the Northern portion of the United states, to subvert the institutions of the State," and "to consider what measures were most likely to put a stop to the elopement of their slaves." Just before Clay presented his compromise in Congress, a special committee of the Virginia legislature had concluded, "The fact is notorious and undeniable that [abolitionists'] emissaries have penetrated into the very hearts of the slaveholding states, and aided the escape of slaves whom they had seduced from the service of their owners." At about the same time one Wilmington newspaper declared that traffic on the Underground Railroad through that city's harbor was "getting to be intolerable." [80]

After the Fugitive Slave Act the generalized bitterness of the South over its loss of slaves took a more personal tone when slave owners in Norfolk and neighboring Portsmouth, Virginia, began to suspect the existence of a direct Underground Railroad route between those cities and New Bedford. The historian Gary Collison has noted that more than one hundred of the four hundred fugitives named in Philadelphia Vigilance Committee records from 1852 forward were from the Norfolk area. Before 1853, when a truly inimical relationship between the ports of Norfolk/Portsmouth and New Bedford emerged, thirty-four people of color from those southern cities who can be identified by name had lived in the northern city—ten heads of household, four spouses, seventeen children, and three transient mariners. Certainly the actual number was larger, as such unrecorded individuals as James Pritlow and George Teamoh suggest. William Jackson, whose father had been a branch pilot in Norfolk, had left that city in 1831 and was living and preaching in New Bedford by 1852 (fig. 56). Louisa Cotton, who lived with her three children in a basement tenement on Mill Street, had come from Norfolk to New Bedford in 1843. Robert Eliot had come to the city at least as early as 1836 and had been almost constantly at sea. James and Keziah Fuller and their seven children had come from Norfolk in August 1846; James and Charity Wilmot left Norfolk with their five children and settled in New Bedford in 1849. Mercy Francis left her birthplace blank when the census taker came to where she lived, the First Street home of Anthony G. Jourdain, in 1850, and she was probably a fugitive; when Ellen Saunders (Elizabeth Francis in slavery) reached New Bedford four years later after escaping from Norfolk, she reported to William Still that she had work and had found her friends and her sister well. "I do not think of going to Canada now," she wrote. [81]

The first hint of trouble was a report in the *Republican Standard* in mid-February 1853 that a "spy," a woman who had once lived in Norfolk but most recently made her home in New Bedford, had returned to Norfolk for a visit and

FIGURE 56. The Reverend William Jackson, by unidentified photographer, 1860–65; private collection; photograph by John Robson.

"gave the owners of slaves information in reference to certain fugitives in New Bedford, telling them they could get their slaves again, by making an effort, &c., &c." The newspaper had learned of the trip from a Norfolk informer.[82] About a month later the same newspaper reported that two fugitives were then "in or near" New Bedford and were perhaps part of a group known to have escaped by vessel from Portsmouth. Then, in mid-January 1854, the *Republican Standard* reported the failed attempt of Portsmouth slaveholders Hodsdon, Binford, Smilley, and others to take the two escapees.[83] "Man-hunting and woman-stealing is considered rather mean business in New Bedford," the newspaper clucked, "and we imagine that all scoundrels who should attempt it here, would meet with a proper reception from the persons pursued." The incident again involved bell ringing, what Hodsdon took to be "a species of telegraph" to fugitives but Elizabeth Buffum Chace claimed only signaled the beginning of the school day.[84]

Clearly incensed by the affair, Hodsdon told the Portsmouth and Norfolk papers that he and his party had had to endure "the taunts and jeers of the press," among them the reference to the group as "scoundrels." "This is one of the many outrages our citizens have to submit to from the lawless abolitionists that make up that sweet, glorious New England," the *Beacon* surmised; "there is it appears

no redress. The Constitution, the laws, the Compromises may all go to the devil"
as far, apparently, as Massachusetts abolitionists were concerned. The *Standard,*
relishing the confrontation, applauded the fugitives for being "more shrewd and
ingenious than the fellow Hodsden . . . and in language quite forcible and emphatic 'stepped out,' illustrating affirmatively the question in some minds,
whether negroes know enough to take care of themselves. They took care of
themselves by taking themselves off."[85] A week later the newspaper documented
the spread of southern outrage by quoting an article in the *Petersburg Express*
about Massachusetts, New Bedford, and the New Bedford *Standard* itself:

> We were actually not aware of the existence of that dirty (and greasy) sheet, until the
> copy containing the assault upon us was kindly left at our office. . . . we question
> whether Virginia girded about by the conservative influences of her social system, is
> not in a better condition with her seventy-seven thousand white adults unable to
> read or right [*sic*], than Massachusetts with her free schools at every cross road, and
> her thousands of fanatics in religion, in politics and in government. The state is a
> seething cauldron of all sorts of abominations, infidelity, communism, woman's
> rights, spiritualism, *et id genus omne.* She has taught all her children the elements of
> knowledge, and how some of them used these elements, her crowded Lunatic Asy-
> lums will testify.[86]

Despite the *Standard's* claim that the two escaped slaves had left New Bedford,
at least one had probably simply been hidden. On 18 February, two days after
New Bedford citizens read the Petersburg newspaper's comments about them and
their Free Soil newspaper, abolitionist Andrew Robeson wrote to Nathaniel B.
Borden apparently about this case. This letter, quoted in a 1930s Fall River newspaper, is the only direct evidence of Robeson's assistance to fugitives despite the
fact that the Weston sisters considered him one of the staunchest abolitionists in
New Bedford, one who had remained active in antislavery meetings when such
men as Samuel Rodman and Charles Morgan had ceased to attend them. Robeson asked Borden to conceal the fugitive for "a short time."[87] And the fugitive
may have been the same one Chace described as having been delivered to her
home in Valley Falls by Robert Adams of Fall River one evening. When she answered the door, she met Adams and a person "apparently in a woman's Quaker
costume, whose face was concealed by a thick veil." This person was, she learned,
a man of color who had escaped with his wife and child from Virginia to New
Bedford and had worked in the city eleven months until his former owner discovered his whereabouts; perhaps he was the man informed upon by the "spy" who
visited Norfolk in March 1853. The fugitive told Chace that his former owner had
gone to Boston to get a constable and had himself spent an entire day searching
for him in New Bedford before returning to Boston. "The colored people of that
town discovering the purpose of the searchers, communicated with some of the
few Abolitionists, and the man was hurried off to Fall River before the man-
stealer had time to find him," Chace recollected, "and my sister Sarah and her

husband Nathaniel Borden, dressed him in Quaker bonnet and shawl, and sent him off in the daylight, not daring to keep him till night, lest his master should follow immediately." The men told Chace he had a revolver because he would never again be a slave. The Chaces kept the man overnight and saw him off on an early morning train the next day bound for an unstated destination. Within a few days, she wrote, they learned he had arrived safely, had found work, and had sent for his wife and child.[88]

In mid-March 1854 Portsmouth citizens met at a town meeting to discuss the attempt of Hodsdon and his fellow slaveholders. The meeting drew up a statement to the effect that the group had "ample evidence" that the fugitives had been in New Bedford and were "secreted within the precincts of the town" when Hodsdon and his party arrived; it was only through the "inefficiency and wilful carelessness" of public officials that the group "failed in securing their property." The meeting resolved to travel to Washington to present this statement to the president, to which the *Standard* responded that a New Bedford party, led by black activist Henry O. Remington, would be only too happy to meet them there.[89]

On the same day that the *Standard* reported the Portsmouth meeting, it also noted that the Underground Railroad, "this glorious railroad of humanity," had brought two fugitives into the area "within the past few days." One of these may have been Daniel Wiggins, who escaped Norfolk after the death of his elderly master in early March 1854. As was so often reportedly the case, Wiggins's owner had promised to free him but had died without making a will stipulating as much. So as not to fall into the hands of the "reckless" son, Wiggins escaped, first to Philadelphia. "While he had always been debarred from book learning," William Still wrote, "he was, nevertheless, a man of some intelligence, and by trade was a practical Corker," or caulker. In his journal Still noted that Wiggins's wife was named Mary Ann and was free, as were his three children, and that Wiggins "belonged to the Methodist Church." The Philadelphia Vigilance Committee boarded Wiggins for a day and a half, paid for a carriage to take him either to a train or boat out of town, and gave him $2.75 in cash. Still stated that the committee sent Wiggins, who had changed his name to David Robinson, to Canada, but on 22 March Robinson wrote Still from New Bedford, where he had arrived that morning. "I am, sir, to you and others under more obligations for your kindly protection of me than I can in any way express at present," Robinson wrote. Robinson was still in New Bedford in 1855, when state census takers listed him as a caulker, and by then his wife Mary Ann and three children had joined him. At his death in New Bedford in 1883 he left money to his church, the Bethel AME, for "support of the Gospel" and a home for the church's needy members, as well as two houses on a small lot, a small cottage on Martha's Vineyard, and four dollars' worth of caulker's tools.[90]

By this time the *American Beacon* of Norfolk claimed that the escape of slaves from this Virginia port was "almost a daily occurrence." During 1854 more than 150 vessels entered New Bedford from southern ports, almost forty from Virginia ports and most of those from Norfolk/Portsmouth or Suffolk/Nansemond River, just south and west of Portsmouth.[91] Slave owners in Virginian port cities had largely ceased to advertise for runaway slaves in the 1850s, despite the Fugitive Slave Act, which suggests the perceived futility of attempting to recover them; it was pointless to advertise locally in any event if, as seemed certain by now, most fugitives escaped by vessel.[92] At the end of March, after noting that a male slave belonging to Richard Doyle had escaped "a few days ago" for the North, the *Beacon* estimated that the slaveholders of Norfolk and its environs had lost more than thirty thousand dollars' worth of slaves "by the aid of abolitionists" in the past year. "We would ask if New Bedford, Boston, or any other community of abolitionists were losers in any kind of property, would they sit so quietly and not call for redress from the 'powers that be,' " the *Beacon* asked. "It is time that the South should take some action. Forbearance has ceased to be a virtue."[93]

Within two weeks of Wiggins's arrival, the *Liberator* noted that fugitives "continue to disappear suddenly and mysteriously" from Portsmouth, including, mostly recently, two men and two women who belonged to Mrs. Berkley and William Broecks. Six or seven weeks later, in late May, the *Standard* reprinted an article from the *Beacon* about the schooner *Ellen Barnes* of Wareham, whose captain, mate, and one of its black crew were arrested in Norfolk for having aided in the escape of two slaves who were "the property of Mrs. Berkley of Portsmouth." The schooner must have carried the fugitives North in April or late March, for in early May it had come into the port of Norfolk in distress, having become somehow disabled while carrying ice from Wareham to Elizabeth City, North Carolina. The *Ellen Barnes* had changed owners, the *Beacon* noted, and sailed in early May under a different captain, which to the newspaper suggested something shady about its earlier voyage. The *Beacon* added that crew member Thomas Murray, who had been among the earlier crew, and "a negro sailor" had admitted the slaves had stowed away on the vessel "and were taken charge of by some men when they arrived at Wareham."

The two slaves were probably the men known in New Bedford as William and Charles Armstead, who had tried to escape Portsmouth with their sister, known in slavery as Clarissa Davis and owned by "Mrs. Brown and Mrs. Burkley of Portsmouth," Still noted. When Davis reached Philadelphia, she told Still that her brothers had succeeded in getting away but she had failed, so she had gone into hiding immediately in what Still described as a "miserable coop" with scarcely any light or air. While she hid, she told him, her brothers had "passed safely on to New Bedford," and seventy-five days later she learned that the steward aboard the steamboat *City of Richmond* had agreed to hide her on board. This was probably the man of color Still identified only as Minkins, and it is at least possible that Davis used as an intermediary Henry Lewey, a slave whom Still labeled "one of the most dexterous managers in the Underground Railroad agency in Norfolk" and known by the name "Blue Beard"; he is said to have helped slaves find spaces on packet boats running between Norfolk and Philadelphia. The *City of Richmond,* which went into packet service in the early 1850s, was commanded by Captain Alfred Fountain, who frequently took fugitives from Norfolk to the North; historian Gary Collison has identified him as the only vessel master working in the clandestine trade from Norfolk who was not caught.[94] Davis dressed herself in men's clothes and made her way to the vessel about three o'clock in the morning, during a heavy rainstorm. There William Bagnal, whose wife was a slave, placed her in "a small box near the Furnace," Still wrote in his journal, "where it was very hot—where she suffered & thought she must die, wanted water very much but was unable to get any—suffered on in that condition until she reached here. A reward of $1000 was offered for Clarissa & her two Bros."[95] Bagnall watched over her on the trip and delivered her to Still in Philadelphia.

Still and other committee members advised Davis to drop her old name and gave her a new one, Mary D. Armstead. She told the committee that she wished to go to New Bedford "to join her brothers and sister" and added that her father had also managed to escape to the city while she was in hiding; an old man, he was either freed or allowed to purchase himself. "Slaveholders would, on some such occasions, show wonderful liberality in letting their old slaves go free, when they could work no more," Still observed, tongue in cheek. Still's journal documents that Davis arrived in Philadelphia on 22 May 1854, and his book reprints one of her frequent letters to him from New Bedford:

> Mr. Still:—I avail my self to write you thes few lines hopeing they may fine you and your family well as they leaves me very well and all the family well except my father he seams to be improveing with his shoulder he has been able to work a little please remember my Dear old farther and sisters and brothers to your family kiss the children for me I hear that the yellow fever is very bad down south now if the underground railroad could have free course the emergrant would cross the river of gordan rapidly I hope it may continue to run and I hope the wheels of the car may be greased with more substantial grease so they may run over swiftly I would have wrote before but circumstances would not permit me Miss Sanders and all the friends desired to be remembered to you and your family I shall be pleased to hear from the underground rail road often.[96]

Davis used the name Mary D. Armstead in her letter to Still in August 1855, but she appears to have taken back her given name by the time the census was taken that year. There she is undoubtedly Clarissa Armstead, born about 1831 or 1832 (Still had noted she was "about twenty-two" in 1854) in Virginia. In the same household were seventy-year-old Samuel Armstead, thirty-year-old William, twenty-eight-year-old Charles, and Ann Scott, aged thirty-five. Ann Scott was the sister Clarissa had alluded to in her conversation with Still; she had married Joseph M. Scott in Norfolk by 1855, but he had apparently not made his way to New Bedford by the time the 1855 census was taken.

While Clarissa Davis hid in Norfolk awaiting safe passage to New Bedford, o 1 19 April the *American Beacon* reported in evident frustration the escape of five slaves belonging to the slave trader William W. Hall, a man named Sigourney, and a Mrs. Shepherd. "How and by what means so many of our slaves procure through tickets by this under ground railway, to convey them to their abolition allies, has not as yet been discovered," the editors noted, but they promised some of the network's principals "a gallows as high as Haman's." One of these fugitives was surely Robert McCoy, who took the name William Doner in Philadelphia. When he reached Still's office in early October 1854, he reported that he had been in hiding for five months "in a place in the city" after his owner, Hall, threatened to sell him. Still reported him to be about twenty-eight years old and suffering from "symptoms of consumption" and rheumatism; he had had to leave his slave wife Eliza behind but hoped she would be able to escape soon. Like Davis, he wished to go to New Bedford, "where, he was led to feel, he would be happy in freedom," Still wrote.

Doner's wife apparently escaped at the same time, for she told Still when she reached Philadelphia about the first of November that she had been owned by Andrew Sigany of Norfolk and had been in hiding herself about seven months. Unlike her husband, who was Hall's personal servant and not one of the slaves in his pens, Eliza McCoy had been treated harshly in slavery and that, coupled with her concealment in "close quarters," kept her in Philadelphia to recuperate before she was sent on to New Bedford. Still somehow let McCoy, now Doner, know of her arrival, and he wrote back immediately. "I rejoice to heare of the arrival of my wife, and hope she is not sick from the roling of the sea," Doner stated, "and if she is not, pleas to send her on here Monday with a six baral warlian and a rifall to gard her up to my residence." Doner reported to Still that he was "getting something to do every day" and that "Mr. R. White . . . says he is very much indebted to you . . . he desires to know wheather his cloths has arived yet or not." In 1855, William Doner and his wife, who had taken the name Mary, were living at 232 Middle Street with Henry and Harriet Kent, who had come to New Bedford from Norfolk in 1847. Henry Kent was a mariner, probably then at sea, and Harriet Kent had two children, Jerome and Napoleon Cross, both born in Norfolk. Napoleon was eighteen and working as a barber at 66 William Street, next door to the dentist's office opened that year by Thomas Bayne, a Norfolk fugitive.[97]

In late April the *Standard* took another swipe at Virginia after it heard that men were again in pursuit of fugitives in the city. The newspaper had learned that the escaped slaves had been passed on "to a place of safety" and asserted again how fruitless the men's efforts were bound to be in the city. "It is probably a great exhibition of 'chivalry' in Virginia eyes, for a Southern slaveholder and kidnapper to come here in disguise, and sneak and skulk around our city, like a thief, in pursuit of *men* who have escaped from bondage," the *Standard* noted, "but tastes *do* differ, and the slave catching *sneaks* find New Bedford very poor hunting ground." Several weeks later Anthony lit into "our *freedom-loving* contemporary, the Boston *Post*, whose mind has been so much exercised because a poor, unfortunate slave obtained his liberty." Gleefully the *Standard* reported that the man,

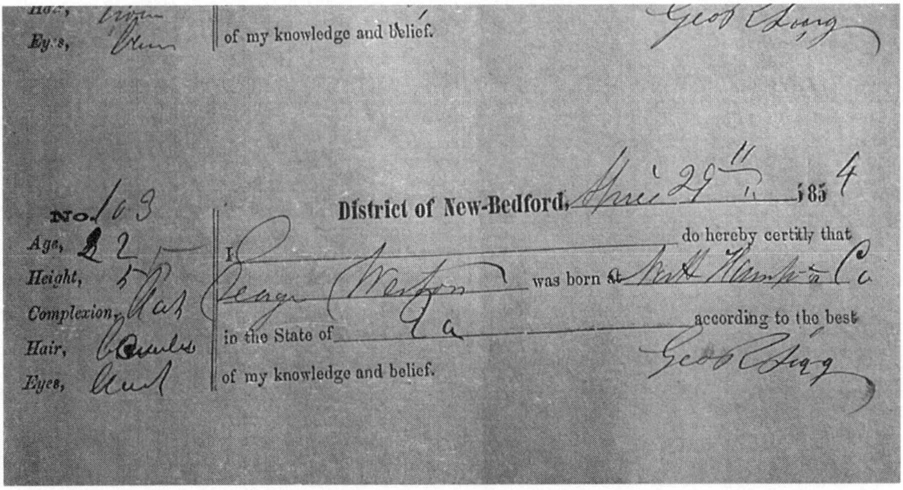

FIGURE 57. Record of seaman's protection paper issued to George Weston, New Bedford, 29 April 1854. Used with permission of the Board of Trustees of the New Bedford Free Public Library.

"Weston," had sailed from New Bedford on a three-year whaling voyage. "The *Post* may put this in its pipe and smoke it," Anthony retorted. "Weston" was the twenty-two-year-old George Weston, who listed his birthplace as Northhampton County, Virginia, on both his protection paper and the crew list of the brig *Ocean*, which left New Bedford on 2 May (fig. 57). Unlike Jacobs and Thompson and many other men of both races, Weston chose to remain in whaling; he was listed among the crew of both the *Hecla* and the *Edward* in 1856 (whether he actually shipped out on either is not known) and shipped out on the bark *Wave* in 1860.[98]

Slaveholders in Norfolk and Portsmouth were puzzled about exactly how these escapes were accomplished. It seemed unlikely that fugitives could get aboard vessels in the harbor, one "slaveholder" noted in a letter to the *Beacon,* although it is clear from numerous statements in the same newspaper that vessels were not routinely searched despite the repeated escapes.[99] To this correspondent it seemed more likely that fugitives "are taken on board after the vessels have left our port, from Lambert's or Sewall's point, or some designated place on Hampton Roads, known only to the parties interested." Probably, the correspondent suggested, the many smaller vessels that plied the rivers and coves around Hampton Roads "day and night, almost without observation," were taking fugitives from designated points on shore to coastwise vessels anchored at one of these points. These smaller boats must be searched: they should "heave to" at Fort Monroe for "a rigid examination." The writer noted that slaves were "almost daily being enticed off and stolen from us" by "abolition thieves," no doubt "in our very midst," and these

regular escapes were demoralizing for the people of color of Norfolk and Portsmouth as well as damaging to the fortunes of widows who depended upon the
wages of slaves for their income.[100] Another letter by "a Citizen" declared, "That
we have abolition agents among us is beyond question, and we have reason to
believe that white men as well as negroes are engaged in this business." Vessels
anchoring constantly at Norfolk and bound for northern ports, he argued, "leave
no money among us and steal away our slaves in the bargain." This correspondent
recommended a more thoroughgoing set of remedies. All vessels should be in-
spected before leaving port; black Sunday Schools, funerals, and "debates in negro
churches" should be stopped at once; no person of color should be on the streets
after 10:00 at night without a pass nor belong to a society other than a church
under penalty of public flogging; no oyster boats operated by black men should
be permitted to leave the harbor after dark, and a watch should be established to
stop all vessels from leaving Norfolk at night; Norfolk ought to create a secret
police force; free men and women of color should not be allowed to gain legal
residence in the city; and any free black not attached to a vessel who came into
Virginia from the free states should be sold.[101]

Even as they seemed unable to fathom how their slaves managed to escape, the
rendition of Anthony Burns the next month probably buoyed such complainants
by making them think the Fugitive Slave Act could be enforced and could obviate
the need for tougher controls on southern ports themselves. Burns had escaped
from his Alexandria owner, Charles F. Suttle, and settled in Boston, and on 24 May
1854 he was arrested as he left the Brattle Street clothing store where he worked
on the false charge of having robbed a jewelry store. While he lay in jail at the
city's federal courthouse, his lawyers, including Robert Morris, prepared his defense, abolitionists held meetings about the arrest all over the state, and Boston's
people of color planned an intense assault on the courthouse. Five days after
Burns's arrest, Morgan was sure that his freedom would be purchased so as to
avert his rendition, but on 2 June U.S. Commissioner Edward Greeley Loring
ordered Burns returned to his owner. Morgan was in Boston that day with his
daughter and described the scene before him:

> It was a solemn & sad day for Boston—the Fugitive slave was remanded to slavery—
> The city was full of soldiers—the court house guarded with artillery—and hundreds
> of troops U States & volunteers—They drove the people from [illegible] to the court
> house & to the route to the wharf—every where bayonets bristled—Thousands of
> people thronged the borders of the proscribed district & waited for hours to see the
> execution as they called it—I left Bessie at Tremont house and went for a while to
> the scene—witnessed the quarrelling of the people with the military—who were
> very patient—but the mob pressing on the order was given to charge on them and
> a dreadful rush took place and I had to run to prevent being crushed—and then
> backed out having no idea of getting killed in a mob—and walked away sorrowful
> to see such a sight in Boston—The people all seem to think alike and the general

feeling is that there shall never again be such a scene be the consequences what they may—Let the slave hunters look out, for all the people are now incensed.[102]

When the news of Loring's decision reached New Bedford, one church tolled its bells, and three days later New Bedford's community of color met to declare that "the names of Cain, Benedict Arnold, and Edward Greeley Loring, form a beautiful trio, the last one being the Boston kidnapper and slaveholders' pimp," and they pledged to use whatever means available to get him removed from office (in addition to being a federal commissioner, Loring was the judge of the Suffolk County Probate Court). Burns's rendition was the last straw for such men of color as Solomon Peneton, Ezra Johnson, Augustus Munroe, and John Freedom, for the meeting ultimately concluded that "the one grand vital issue to be made with the Slave Power is the dissolution of the present existing American Union." The *Republican Standard* said of the Burns rendition, "The deep disgrace of that day's proceedings is the blackest that anywhere attaches to the name of Massachusetts."[103]

On top of the lingering tension Burns's case created and the growing rancor over the Kansas-Nebraska Act came another report that slave agents planned an attempt to seize a fugitive in New Bedford. "The arrangements are already making, and the declaration has gone forth from the slave power, that New Bedford must be humbled as well as the home of the Adamses," the *Standard* noted on 15 June, and it advised fugitives in the city to leave for Canada at once or "be prepared for the worst." "If Massachusetts can afford no protection to those who have achieved their freedom by a heroism unsurpassed in the annals of fame, let them flee from within our borders, shaking off the dust of their feet against us, in testimony of our great moral delinquency, and our oft-repeated defalcations in the great matter of human freedom," Anthony's newspaper intoned, and it asked the citizens of the city if they would allow it to be "everlastingly disgraced by following in the footsteps of so humiliating an example" as Boston's in the Sims and Burns cases:

> Is there a Court-house here, that can be turned into a slave pen? Is there a building here, that can be obtained for the purpose of imprisoning a human being, claimed as a slave? Is there a $10 Commissioner here, who will sit in judgment upon a person claimed as "owing service of labor" to a "Legree," or a "Suttle," and return him or her to a Southern plantation, to be *scourged to death,* as was poor Simms?
>
> Shall it ever be recorded upon the pages of our history, that a slave hunt was successful in New Bedford? God forbid. Will not all people say AMEN?[104]

Appalled by the marvelous inconsistency between the provisions of the Fugitive Slave Act and the protections constitutionally accorded every American citizen, the black activists of New Bedford suggested a more emphatic response:

> This meeting recommends to any fugitive, (if there are such in our midst,) while they remain here, to practice the art of using firearms, as the most efficient means of

defence, and if the kidnappers pounce upon him, to shoot them down; then the State will take him under its protection, and give him a trial by jury, and if the jury do not deem it expedient to bring in a verdict of "justifiable homicide" but manslaughter, he will be further protected in the State Prison until this slave question is settled, (for settled now it has got to be.). There, he will be better fed, clothed and treated, than in the rice swamps and cotton fields of the South, and have some chance to obtain mental and spiritual culture. This is a significant commentary upon the nineteenth century, that in Massachusetts an outcast can elevate himself into citizenship by committing homicide, and that our State Prisons offer better schools for human beings than Southern Institutions.

Several weeks later the city's citizens of color announced their plan to form the Union Cadets, "to hold themselves in readiness at all times for the protection of the civil rights of the community." By October 1855—despite the decision a month earlier by Massachusetts Attorney General John H. Clifford of New Bedford to refuse the request of a Boston black military company to borrow state arms and equipment—this "colored military company" persevered and was shortly renamed the New Bedford Independent Blues.[105]

Whether such measures reached the ears of southern slaves hoping to escape, the fact remains that a fugitive had never been taken from New Bedford to that time, and fugitives continued to come. In September 1854 one Edinbur Randall escaped Jacksonville, Florida, aboard the bark *Franklin,* carrying pine lumber to Bath, Maine. But when the vessel moored at Holmes Hole on Martha's Vineyard, Randall, who suspected the captain had discovered his presence and had gone to arrange his return, escaped into the community of Gay Head Indians and blacks with the aid of the crew. He hid at the home of Beulah Salsbury Vanderhoop, whose husband, like New Bedford's Anthony Jourdain, had descended from the slave population of Suriname and had come north with Jourdain in the early 1830s. "Antislavery friends" on the Vineyard notified the New Bedford Vigilance Committee of Randall's presence and, working with its Boston counterpart, the committee managed to convince Randall's pursuers that he had gone on to Bath. Vanderhoop hired two boatmen to take Randall to the home of a New Bedford abolitionist during the night. Under the alias Edgar Jones, Randall is said to have worked on the New Bedford wharves "for some time" and, at the time the Civil War broke out, moved to San Francisco or Canada.[106]

In September 1855 the community managed to foil another rendition attempt, this from a "former owner" who had traced a woman of color from New London, Connecticut, to New Bedford, to which she had come about 1850 to work as a domestic in a family. The *Standard* reported that her erstwhile owner had come to the city and spent five days searching for her, but she had been moved to "a place of safety"; her pursuer gave up. "The curs of high and low degree who would enforce the odious slave law, may snap and snarl as much as they please," the newspaper almost chortled. "They can effect nothing."[107] Earlier that year the newspaper had reported statistics on Underground Railroad traffic to New

Bedford: one "conductor" had stated that between March 1, 1854, and January 1, 1855, forty-three fugitives had passed over the "route." Another "nine or ten" were reported to have been in the New Bedford area in early February, in May an unstated number were sent to New Bedford from Martha's Vineyard, and in November sixteen more came through the city. "The number of slaves in Virginia is fast melting away," the *Standard* crowed rather disingenuously, for Anthony must have known that the flow of fugitives to the free states, Canada, and England, to say nothing of New Bedford, scarcely put a dent in the three million who remained in slavery; in Virginia alone the number of slaves had climbed from 292,627 in 1790 to 472,494 in 1860.[108]

The flow of fugitives from Norfolk and Portsmouth continued and may have accelerated in mid-1855 when a yellow fever epidemic struck the two ports.[109] "Our Southern contemporary says that one of the termini of the road is at New Bedford," the *Standard* reported after reading the Norfolk newspapers. "If it be so, we would urge our friend to watch the affairs of the route closely, and to see to it that all passengers arriving here are properly provided for."[110] William Still's journal documents that New Bedford was virtually the only place other than Canada to which he regularly sent letters. By the time Sam Nixon arrived in New Bedford in June 1855, he found "many old friends from Norfolk." Nixon, who took the alias Thomas Bayne, had apprenticed to a white dentist in Norfolk and was apparently, according to Still, "quite active and successful as an Underground Rail Road agent" in that city. He told Still he left Norfolk because he suspected slaveholders were aware of his activities; if he remained, he said, he would soon be in "hot water up to his eyes."[111]

Nixon knew the vessel captains who were willing to take fugitives north, but because of the intense suspicion respecting them he felt their activities, as his, would be stopped if he were not extremely secretive in his movements. He did not tell his wife and children, owned by a Norfolk hardware merchant, of his plan to escape. Nixon and perhaps three other Norfolk men of color were taken out of that port by an unnamed schooner and landed on the New Jersey coast; from there the group walked to the Salem, New Jersey, home of the Quaker Abigail Goodwin. Goodwin did not trust Nixon—she called him "a great brag"—and, when he told her that he was a dentist, she wondered whether he was an imposter. Yet she sent him on to Still in Philadelphia and recorded at his request the names "of nine more who expected to get off soon and might come here." When the fugitives reached Philadelphia, Still and others of the Vigilance Committee tried to persuade them to go on to Canada. Nixon, however, had his sights set on New Bedford.

Once in the city, by mid- to late June 1855, Nixon took the name Dr. Thomas Bayne and wrote Still to say he had "received my things" and that he need not say anything to "Bagnul" about them—no doubt William Bagnal, who had helped Clarissa Davis get aboard the *City of Richmond*. Bayne also asked after the nine possible fugitives he had told Goodwin about. Apparently five or six of these nine had tried to escape on 10 June through the agency of a Norfolk drayman named William Sales, who had paid a Captain Goodrich of the Boston schooner *Grace Darling* to take them. Goodrich, a native of Mansfield, Massachusetts, took the money and promptly turned them in, but somehow they managed to escape on a different schooner, commanded by a "Captain B.," probably William B. Baylis of Wilmington, Delaware, master of the *Keziah*. The Norfolk paper identified the fugitives as "a man owned by Mr. Turner, of the firm of Herman & Co., and negro woman and child of T. Bottimore, and Mr. S. March, and a slave of L. Stosser"; they are the same persons, "a woman and child 2 or 3 men belonging to Marsh Baltimore, L. Slosser and Herman & Co—and Turner—all of Norfolk, Va.," about whom Bayne wrote Still that month. "They are all my old friends and we are waiting their arrival," Bayne wrote, and he suggested to Still that they may stop at Goodwin's in Salem en route. Bayne may have expected them to come to New Bedford, but, perhaps because they were being pursued, Still forwarded them to Canada.[112]

Bayne mentioned in his June letter to Still that "John Austin are with us" and "C. Lightfoot is well and remembers you and family." Lightfoot was a fugitive whose name in slavery was Charles Baker, Still recorded in his journal, and by 1860 he was listed under the former name in the New Bedford census. That year too he applied for poor relief, and the record states that he told overseers that he and his wife Elizabeth were both born in Virginia and came to New Bedford in 1855. Lightfoot remained in the city with his wife and two New Bedford–born daughters until his death in 1904.[113] But John Austin and his family were probably free when they left Norfolk.[114] At least some of the twenty-one fugitives Captain Fountain took from Norfolk in November 1855 came to New Bedford aboard a schooner loaded with wheat; Fountain had managed to fool inspectors who boarded his boat by taking an axe to it himself wherever the inspectors bid him to (fig. 58). They reached Philadelphia without further incident, and on 22 August 1855 the man known as Michael Vaughn in slavery wrote Still under the alias William Brown from New Bedford. He reported to Still that he expected his wife Esther and child Louisa soon to escape and told him to direct them to 130 Kempton Street in New Bedford, where he then lived; the fugitives William and Nancy Ferguson had lived at that address when they came to New Bedford in 1848.[115] Vaughn's wife may have been the woman Winnie Patty, who reached the Wilmington, Delaware, home of the Quaker abolitionist Thomas Garrett about 10 May 1856. After her husband escaped in 1855, Patty and her child had hidden under the floor of a house in Norfolk for five months, from October 1855 to March 1856. Garrett wrote to Still that he believed Patty's husband "went some nine months previous to New Bedford"; presumably she wished to go there as well.[116]

A party of fifteen Norfolk fugitives came to New Bedford by way of Philadelphia's vigilance committee in the summer of 1856; they may have been the sixteen unidentified fugitives the *Republican Standard* reported to have come through the area on 23 July that year. Still learned on 4 July 1856 that the schooner carrying them from Norfolk was expected to land late that evening on Philadelphia's League Island (fig. 59). Their escape had been difficult from the start. While they waited at the shore of the James River for the boat that would row them to the waiting schooner, they believed they heard watchmen approaching and so hid in the river behind a boat on the stocks for an hour and a half; then an oyster boat picked them up and took them to the schooner, which had loaded with corn. The schooner had a compartment built especially for fugitive passengers, but two of them, a 260-pound woman named Mrs. Walker and another woman too large to enter it, were hidden behind some corn in back of the cabin. When the captain suspected he was being pursued, the two women were forced to take off nearly all their clothes and squeeze into the hiding place so that the inspection could proceed without discovery. Still stated that Walker "went with the most of her company to Boston, and thence to New Bedford, where she was living when last heard from." Also on this voyage was Rebecca Lewey, the wife of the famed Henry "Blue Beard" Lewey, who ultimately went on to Canada, where her husband later met her, and Sophia Gray and her children Mary and Henry. When they reached New Bedford, Henry Gray was apprenticed to learn a trade—he is listed in the 1860 New Bedford census as a barber—and Mary was sent to live with an aunt, also a fugitive, who worked in the home of George S. Hilliard of Boston. Still visited her at Hilliard's home in 1859, but by 1860 she too was living in New Bedford.[117]

So too was the Norfolk fugitive Stethy Swons, whose slave status apparently was not documented until his widow and daughter sought to receive pension benefits from his service as a colonel's orderly, under the name John L. Wright, in Company C of the Massachusetts Fifty-fourth Regiment. In 1881 one of his daughters, Nancy, a laundress who had married Hezekiah Webb of New Bedford, deposed that she was "the daughter [of] Stethy Swons and Sarah Wiggins Swons. My father and mother were slaves in Virginia where I was born. I am informed that he run away to the north two or three years before the war broke out. He left my mother and three children in Virginia. He came through Philadelphia, Pa on his way north and then to New Bedford Mass where he [illegible] made his home. He changed his name to John L. Wright after he came here. He was married to Fanny Wilkins after he came here and he lived with her until she died. . . . After my father run away from Slavery, my mother remained in Va. at Keep Creek Va until after the close of the war. Then she went to Newark N.J." Webb said she herself had come to New Bedford to look for her father.[118] The presence of other fugitives is far less well documented. One is the arrival of a slave and her son and daughter aboard a coasting vessel whose master may have been New Bedford's Gideon B. Wixon. The three were brought, apparently with the captain's knowledge and assistance, to Clark Point's Light in New Bedford; the vessel had been commissioned to carry supplies to lighthouses along the Atlantic coast. Five times between 1850 and 1858 the Boston Vigilance Committee sent fugitives from

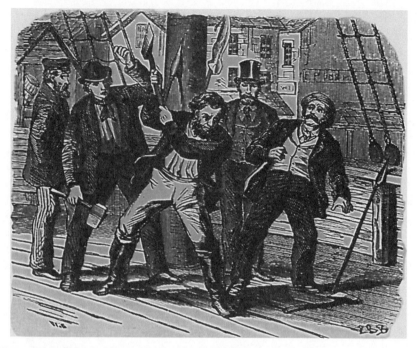

FIGURE 58. "The Mayor and Police of Norfolk Searching Capt. Fountain's Schooner," engraving in William Still, *The Underground Railroad* (1871).

FIGURE 59. "Heavy Weights—Arrival of a Party at League Island," engraving in William Still, *The Underground Railroad* (1871).

Boston to New Bedford, but of the thirteen (three individuals and two families) the committee's records list, only the two families may have left a record of their presence in New Bedford. Of the nine fugitives sent by the Vigilance Committee in New York between June 1855 and July 1856 another record exists definitely for one and possibly for another.[119]

With Thomas Bayne, William H. Carney Sr. and his son William Jr. became the most well-known Norfolk fugitives in New Bedford. Carney was identified as a fugitive in an 1863 article in the *Standard*, which stated that he had lived in New Bedford about five years. Still noted the escape in 1857 of a William Carney, a fifty-one-year-old slave who belonged to the estate of the large slaveholder Sarah Twyne. Carney was hired out, mostly in oystering, and in November 1856 Twyne died. As had other owners of fugitives, Twyne had promised to free Carney and even to send him and her other slaves to Liberia, but she failed to state as much in her will. So Carney left behind his wife Nancy and seven children and escaped to Philadelphia with Andrew Allen, a slave from the same estate. Carney went on to New Bedford, and by 1859 he had saved enough money, or so he thought, to purchase the freedom of his wife. He went to see Loum Snow, the New Bedford merchant and ship outfitter who had arranged for the slave girl Isabella White to be shipped to the city in a barrel marked "sweet potatoes." Snow wrote on Carney's behalf to George M. Bain, a white minister in Norfolk who knew the community's people of color and had arranged for the manumission of five slaves in 1853. Snow enclosed eighty dollars that Carney had raised and asked Bain to offer it to Nancy Carney's owner, Joseph Carter. Apparently Nancy had already contributed some funds toward her purchase, but Bain went to see her and learned Carney had not understood, or had not been given to understand, the true amount of her purchase price. "She thinks there has been some misunderstanding about the amount of money wanted to secure her freedom," Bain wrote to Snow in early September 1859. "In the place of its being $80 wanted the balance is $80 that she has secured, and the balance $220 is the amount wanted, as her Master has agreed to sell her, her time for $300—I have seen her Master also, and that is the sum he agrees to take, and gives her until the end of the present year to make up the amount."

Snow accordingly sent Bain another $140 in addition to the $80 Carney had already arranged to send. "Will you have the goodness to use this money to purchase and set Nancy Carney free," Snow asked. "She will on arrival at New Bedford call at my house 153 County St., or office, 29 Front St." Bain negotiated the purchase, undertook the legal recording of her manumission, and sent Nancy Carney to New Bedford. Their children—probably Simon Henry, Sarah, Mary Ann, and Elizabeth—apparently reached the city about 1863, two years after Union troops seized and occupied Portsmouth. William, the Carneys' eldest son, was not among them (fig. 60); by his own account he had left his job working on coasters in Norfolk in 1856, and the *Standard* said that he "confiscated himself" and came to New Bedford soon after his mother arrived in the fall of 1859. It was

FIGURE 60. William H. Carney Jr., photograph by unidentified photographer, about 1865–70. Courtesy Carl J. Cruz, New Bedford Historical Society.

from William Jr. that Carney learned where his other children were, the newspaper stated. In 1863, after his heroism at Fort Wagner as a member of the Fifty-fourth Massachusetts Regiment of Volunteer Infantry, Carney wrote at the request of his military commander, who wanted information on his life for Massachusetts Governor John Andrew, that his mother had been freed by an owner of a different name before she came to New Bedford; with the outcome of the war highly uncertain, Carney probably lied to conceal his true status, as other fugitives in the regiment also did.[120]

Carney also stated in 1863 that at the age of fourteen, about 1854, he had been sent to a "private and secret school kept in Norfolk by a minister"; one suspects this was George Bain. Bain may also have had some relationship with a slave in Portsmouth named Eliza Baines, whom the Norfolk fugitive Elizabeth Cooley identified as the woman who assisted in her escape and who, according to Cooley's statement, helped other fugitives escaped on Boston- and New Bedford–bound vessels.[121] Bain may also have known the Reverend William Jackson, a Norfolk native and a free man of color who had come to New Bedford as pastor of the city's Second Baptist Church in early December 1851 (see fig. 56). Jackson had been jailed in Philadelphia for having assisted in the release and escape of fugitive slave William Taylor in that city after the passage of the Fugitive Slave

Act, and he is believed to have left Philadelphia shortly after serving his term for Nantucket, Martha's Vineyard, and then New Bedford.[122] He and his parents had moved to Philadelphia from Norfolk after the Nat Turner rebellion of 1831, and by 1842 Jackson had abandoned his life as a mariner for the ministry. He was pastor of West Philadelphia's Oak Street Baptist Church in the 1840s and later served parishes in Wilmington, Delaware, and Newburgh, New York, perhaps on evangelical assignment to foster revivals and increase converts. In February 1852 Jackson offered the prayer at a meeting of New Bedford people of color protesting the American Colonization Society and performed the same role at the West Indian Emancipation celebration in the city that year; he was ordained minister of New Bedford's Second Baptist Church in 1855.

Jackson knew William Still and helped him in at least one instance when Still tried to forward fugitives to Canada. Jackson's journal noted on 14 June 1857, "I have dureing the past week been very successful in helping two men to obtain their freedom one from washington and one from Kentucky." His daughter Mary Alice, born about 1845, recalled later in life that fugitives often came to the family's New Bedford home at 198 Smith Street, and she once stated that "the doorbell would ring, and a man with thick glasses and dark clothes would say, 'I'm sending you a shipment, and they're going to go to Canada.'" She once told her grand-nephew that this bespectacled man was the Quaker Thomas Garrett. It is not known that Garrett was ever in New Bedford, but that Jackson identified the Wilmington abolitionist by name strongly suggests that her father had had some contact with him.[123]

William Jackson was involved in the first documented schism within the city's black community involving fugitive slaves. It may have been in Jackson's church that a collection "for the benefit of persons escaping from slavery" was amassed in December 1855, and by March 1856 he, Solomon Peneton, Thomas Bayne, William Henry Johnson, Lloyd H. Brooks, John Freedom, and other people of color who had formed themselves into a "Vigilant Aid Society" called a meeting to consider "the pro-slavery character of the African M. E. B. Church on Kempton street." The Bethel church had refused to permit the society to hold meetings there "for the purpose of raising money to assist such as are daily making their escape from some portion of the slave States, and whom Divine Providence may direct among us, destitute of the means to make them comfortable." Of the known members of the Vigilant Aid Society, only John Freedom is believed to have been born free; Bayne and Johnson were fugitives, and Peneton and Brooks probably were. Born either in Prince George's County, Maryland, or the District of Columbia, Brooks had worked as a waiter for whaling merchant James Arnold in 1845. Peneton, who never stated the same birthplace in four known listings, was probably from Baltimore and worked for George Howland. Both Howland and Arnold were abolitionists, and many accounts attribute Arnold with having sheltered fugitives. Only one source retrospectively claimed that Arnold had housed fugitives in his County Street mansion, and Howland's house has to this day a legendary Underground Railroad association. If they did not literally shelter fugitives, both gave them work, as Rodney French, the Stowell brothers, Zenas Whittemore, and others were wont to do. By 1856 Peneton and Brooks were in business together, selling groceries and provisioning vessels.

The Vigilant Aid Society claimed that the Bethel church, organized in 1843, "refused their house, for ten or fifteen years, to assist even their own mothers, fathers, sisters, brothers, uncles, and aunts" in their escape from slavery and professed it the duty of the meeting to hold the Bethel "up to the gaze of all Christians, the scorn and contempt of the civilized world" and to warn all fugitives that they should not join the church (though Bayne himself was a member) until it abandoned its "present disgraceful and pro-slavery position." As a test the society asked to use the Bethel for a meeting in mid-December 1855, and the next day its clerk, John Warfield, responded that the structure was engaged every night that week and that the church in any event had a right to govern itself. "While we co-operate with the Vigilant Aid Society in their sympathy toward the oppressed and down-trodden, and are willing to aid them by our means at any time when practicable," Warfield wrote, "yet we cannot admit public meetings to be held in our church or house of worship." The Vigilant Aid Society resolved that the Bethel AME church had "arrayed itself against God, liberty and the bleeding bondman, by shutting its doors against a society, which has for its object the fundamental principles of the Gospel, and aids the poor panting fugitive out of the clutches of wicked human bloodhounds, and gives him a crust of bread and a cup of cold water, and bids him God speed on his way from the prison-house of bondage." After "warm debate" on the resolutions at the March meeting—which may have involved the concern of Bethel members that any affiliation with the society would cast suspicion upon their own status—the group declared the Kempton Street church "anti-Christian, a blind guide, a synagogue of Satan, a cage of unclean birds."[124] By 1859 Bethel's stance seems to have softened, for in August that year Jermain W. Loguen, "general agent of the Underground Railroad" in Syracuse, New York, spoke there to the "friends of freedom" and raised twenty dollars to assist his work.[125]

William Still, the city poor relief records, and Civil War pension depositions recorded the presence of numerous other fugitives who first came to New Bedford in the 1850s and early 1860s. Gertrude Smith told census takers in 1860 that she had been born in Massachusetts in 1788, but her poor relief records identified her as a "Fugative Slave" who "came here, alone, has no family, 3 years ago, from Maryland Va, she is 72 years old, wants coal." Another widowed fugitive, Charity Ellit, sought the same assistance in the same year. Her eleven-year-old daughter Charlotte had escaped with her from Virginia, but she left her teenage sons Moses and William behind. Ann Bird escaped Savannah without her husband and two children, but she was pregnant when she left and "near confinement" when she applied for wood from the overseers in November 1860. Still provided a detailed description of the ordeal of William Jordon (alias William Price), who hid in the forests around Cape Fear, North Carolina, for ten months before escaping in December 1855, and that of five men who came from the same state to him in November 1856; both Jordon and one of those five wanted to go to New Bedford, the latter because he had a brother and cousin there. But records document the presence of neither man. Nor do they indicate that the "Jones & wife & Charles Ames" whom the Boston Vigilance Committee sent to New Bedford in 1861 stayed in the city. And the only record that may relate to the fugitive Caroline Harris, who escaped with her two-year-old child in December 1860 and lived in the rear section of the home of Nathan and Polly Johnson, is a letter Joseph Ricketson wrote to Debora Weston two months after Harris applied for poor relief in February 1861 "I think Quincy (I suppose it was him) was right when he wrote that the Lion of Democracy need lie down with the Lamb of Free Soilism, & a little negro was leading them," Ricketson wrote as New Bedford prepared for civil war. "I told this to Caroline a fugitive slave today & she said it must be the child John Brown kissed."[126]

Among the more obscure fugitives in the city in these post-Fugitive Slave Act years was one Anthony Blow, alias Henry Levison, who left Norfolk for Philadelphia in November 1854. Put in contact with the city's vigilance committee, Blow told Still that he had been shot three times in his life (twice for resisting a whipping and a third time for resisting an attack by three white men) and that the son-in-law of his deceased owner threatened to sell him on 1 January 1855. Facing imminent sale, Blow was hidden by the steward Minkins on the *City of Richmond,* the vessel that had earlier brought Clarissa Davis to Philadelphia. Still did not mention his plans for Blow, but an 1856 letter from a fugitive living in Upstate New York reminded Still that he had met him on 1 November 1854 and added, "You will remember that Mr. Blow, who went to New Bedford was there at the same time."[127] No man of color named Blow or Levison is shown in any official record of New Bedford inhabitants at that time, but given the conditions of his escape, he probably kept as much out of sight as he could.

It could be that Blow somehow found his way to William Bush's boardinghouse, for in 1848 he had been accused of having tried to escape on Daniel Drayton's *Pearl.* By the time Blow came to New Bedford, Drayton had been to New Bedford often. He had stopped at the port on his coastal trading voyages, and he returned for the first time since his incarceration only three weeks after Massachusetts Senator Charles Sumner presented a petition for his release (begun by Drayton's wife and signed by twenty-one of the forty-one owners whose slaves attempted to escape on the *Pearl*) and persuaded President Millard Fillmore, who had just lost the Whig nomination for president, to pardon and release him. On 12 August 1852 Drayton returned to his impoverished wife and children in Philadelphia, and on 9 September he spoke before a large crowd of both races at New Bedford's Sears Hall to "marked effect." There his account was corroborated by Charles Thomas, a man of color who had come to New Bedford from Washington with his wife Hannah about 1851. Thomas, who then worked as a laborer and lived at "Mormon Hall," a boardinghouse in the Marsh area of town on lower Howland street, offered the audience "quite a graphic description of several scenes which came under his immediate observation, connected with the affair," incidents the *Standard* did not report.

The newspaper did, however, state that Drayton stayed in the area as the guest of "that tried friend to the oppressed, Capt. William Anthony, of South Dartmouth" and presented another lecture in that smaller town just west of New Bedford. Both meetings took up a contribution for Drayton, struggling financially and debilitated in body and mind after his imprisonment. At the New Bedford meeting, Ezra Johnson, who later corresponded with Drayton about the progress of black settlements in Canada, presented resolutions honoring "his intrepidity . . . his unspotted integrity and unbounded humanity," expressing sympathy for Drayton's condition and joy at his reunion with his family, and praying a "long life of usefulness" for him, "the Martyr to Liberty." In January 1854, just after the narrative of his ill-fated venture was published, Drayton again toured Massachusetts to sell the volume and seek additional support.[128]

On this trip, however, Drayton may have been seeking funds for more than his family's support. The failure of the *Pearl* attempt and his damaging confinement seem only to have strengthened his resolve to carry out a large-scale fugitive rescue. He had stated in his narrative that the "more dangerous" an attempt to help a fugitive, the "more meritorious" it would be, possibly a hint of his intention. In the summer of 1855, Drayton wrote to Francis Jackson, secretary of the Boston Vigilance Committee and in charge of the effort to raise money for Drayton's support, asking his advice about an idea he had to carry numbers of slaves from a different southern port. Jackson was clearly alarmed, wrote back right away, and mailed a confidential copy of his reply to Wendell Phillips asking for any "suggestions that occur to you—probably I shall hear from him again—his sanguine temperament will not give up a favorite scheme in a hurry":

> Capt. D. Dr Sir I have rec. yours of 21st & given its contents careful consideration. Your project will require time to mature the proper means, & also a trusty agent in Norfolk & Portsmouth, who has a general acquaintance with the colored people, so that he can be safe in making known to them the plan of their deliverance, as traitors among them, is not at all uncommon, & one such would be sufficient to destroy success. It is much more difficult of accomplishment than your voyage in the Pearl, and that failed, by causes much more likely to occur in this attempt, than in that— Then you had the slaves all ready waiting for you, whom you knew, & who knew your object, & yet you were betrayed, by a colored hackman.
>
> Now you & your object, will be all unknown, & without some ally there you will be much more likely to be betrayed than before—Your feeble state of health is strongly against it.
>
> I am therefore not in favor of the attempt, and would, if you will allow me, advise you to abandon it.

Do not despond Captain, but keep up good spirits & courage—Abolitionists must never despair—We will make another appeal to the Anti-Slavery friends in your behalf, whenever your necessities become urgent.[129]

As Jackson made plain, most abolitionists were unwilling to involve themselves in an action that, to use the slaveholders' favorite term, enticed slaves directly from the South; one gets the impression that Jackson would rather not have known of Drayton's plan at all. Even the most reviled Underground Railroad "conductor," Thomas Garrett of Wilmington, Delaware, defended himself staunchly against the charge of enticement. Over thirty-eight years, from about 1825 to 1863, Garrett by his own count helped 2,322 fugitives escape. He knew the vessel captains who were willing to take fugitives and seems very often to have known their schedules. But more than once Garrett insisted that he had never gone into the South to invite slaves to escape nor even encouraged those he knew in Delaware to do so.[130] He admired Harriet Tubman, but he was not Harriet Tubman, and Francis Jackson and Wendell Phillips were not Daniel Drayton.

Jackson's reply to Drayton was another discouragement in the life of a man who knew little good fortune and had not even, he must have thought, been able to make an effective sacrifice. He spent the winter of 1856 living at the sailors' home at Snug Harbor, New York; what had become of his family is unknown. In 1857 the *Standard* noted that Drayton had "frequently visited New Bedford, and usually called upon us; and we rejoiced as much to take him by the hand as we do to greet one of the venerable Revolutionary patriots." In late June that year he checked into the Mansion House in New Bedford and went to see "an old friend," William Bush. The *Standard* speculated that "in consequence of low spirits, probably induced by broken health, Capt. Drayton has probably for sometime meditated self-destruction" and reported that he told Bush "he came here to die, and wished to be properly interred." Bush believed he was joking. But about six o'clock one evening Drayton returned to his hotel room with a vial of laudanum he had bought at a New Bedford apothecary. When hotel employees broke his door down twenty-two hours later, they found Drayton dead on the floor, an empty laudanum vial on his night table and a wash basin full of blood; he had, the newspaper reported, "severed arteries in both legs, with the view, doubtless, of preventing spasms from the effect of the laudanum." There was no baggage in his room and only twelve dollars in his pocket.[131]

The *National Anti-Slavery Standard* concluded that Drayton must have been "partially deranged" from his ordeal, but New Bedford gave him a hero's funeral nevertheless. On 30 June 1857, in a part of the city's rural cemetery where many people of color had been buried, the city selected a plot for his interment. William Jackson and John Weiss spoke about Drayton while J. W. C. Pennington, the black fugitive minister who had married Frederick Douglass in 1838, gave the closing prayer. The city took responsibility for the funeral "in accordance with the sentiments and wishes of our citizens, to whom he has endeared himself by a long and familiar acquaintance." The board of alderman wired Drayton's wife and family about his death and funeral, but none of his kin attended. The newspaper noted that "appreciating friends" planned to erect a monument on the lot in which he had been interred, and in August the Reverend Photius Fisk, a naturalized American born in Greece and a chaplain in the U.S. Navy, visited New Bedford to deposit sixty dollars with Rodney French toward the monument.

Two years later unnamed city residents were raising money to build a fence around Drayton's grave, and before his death in November 1860 Henry O. Remington, a leader in the city's black community, paid for the lot's perpetual care. The Union Club, a group of men of color formed during the Civil War, also helped finance its care. Fifteen years earlier Daniel Ricketson had suggested that "the great amount of feeling and sympathy existing among" the people of color of New Bedford had kept their requests for public relief few in number, and there was also no discernibly greater tendency of southern-born men of color to lend active support to abolition and fugitive slaves than northern ones. Remington was born in Rhode Island and was almost surely born free, but his feeling about Drayton reflected his sense of responsibility for his offended race. He not only remembered "those in bonds," as the Bible put it, but he felt "bound with them."[132]

8

Practical Abolitionism

UNTIL 1860, New Bedford's First of August celebrations of West Indian Emancipation followed a fairly predictable course. Men of color met in May or June to
discuss which orators, marching bands, and military companies they might invite. When the invited visitors came in by train, men of color who had organized
themselves into the New Bedford Blues, later the New Bedford Attucks Frontiers,
met them at the depot, near the waterfront at the bottom of Pearl Street. The
companies would march south together to the town hall, on Pleasant Street at
Market Square, and there assemble with the people from town and from a wide
region who had come to New Bedford to take part in the day's celebration. The
participants formed a procession that snaked its way through downtown streets
to County Street and then north to the grove of John Avery Parker in the Acushnet Heights section, north and west of downtown. At the grove the women of
color served a picnic, and the crowd listened to speakers.

But in 1860 the First of August format seemed unsatisfying to at least some
men of color, perhaps because John Brown's execution only six months before
the planning committee first met had made the processions seem inappropriately
festive, even frivolous. New Bedford's black community met the day after Brown's
2 December 1859 hanging and again the next week to thank the churches in the
city that had tolled their bells that day and to express their sorrow that Brown's
attempt to take the Harper's Ferry federal arsenal had not succeeded. They pronounced Brown "the greatest martyr of the nineteenth century" and promised to
teach their children to revere his name. Ezra Johnson rose to deny the charge
rampant in the nation's press that Brown was a fanatic; the difference between
Brown and other abolitionists, the *Standard* quoted Johnson to state, was that
"his abolitionism is practical, while theirs is theoretical."[1] The divide between
action and words was complete; no longer Garrisonians in that respect, New
Bedford's black activists stood resolutely on the side of action.

When the First of August planning committee met, a resolution offered to
hold the usual "parade, pic-nic, and oration" failed; in its place another resolution suggested holding a "New England States Convention" in New Bedford to

celebrate the event, a "warmly discussed" proposal that ultimately passed.[2] The community divided over the issue despite the vote. Two sorts of celebrations took place on 1 August, one the usual with a procession and picnic and the other the New England States Convention. Strangely, the *Standard,* not customarily shy about reporting events in the city's black community, described only the procession; it noted only that one portion of the meeting met in convention "for the purpose of mutual consultation and encouragement."

The New Bedford Attucks Frontiers, in their first public appearance since the company's formation in June, met the Boston Liberty Guards and the Malden Brass Band at the depot and marched down Purchase Street, up Union Street, and back north to Market Square, where "quite a large crowd had collected . . . the fair sex predominating," the newspaper noted. William Henry Johnson, by then practicing law, gave a speech at Market Square about men of color, particularly Crispus Attucks, who had served their country.[3] William H. W. Gray (see fig. 23), who had been born in Maryland or Virginia and had served as crew on New Bedford whalers since 1842, had married William Bush's daughter Martha in 1858 and had become a barber in the city by 1860. He was named chief marshal for the procession, which included as well a group called the Sons of Liberty, "a company of lads neatly and uniformly dressed." Hacks and open wagons followed the bands and military companies, and throughout the procession there were banners. One of them read, "This Day the Manacles fell from 800,000 human beings, Aug. 1, 1834"; another read "Am I not a Man?" with "Am I not a Brother?" on the reverse; one offered the *Liberator's* longtime slogan, "No Union with Slaveholders"; another, "Equal Rights for All."[4] As it passed the 57 Third Street home of Mayor Isaac C. Taber, whom the "colored abolitionists" had supported in his bid for a seat in the state legislature in 1838, the parade made a salute, and it offered another at the offices of Anthony's *Republican Standard.* New Bedford's activists of color recognized both as friends to their long-held cause.

The Boston *Pilot,* however, was not as favorably disposed to the celebrants; indeed, it regarded the racial mixing that took place during these annual events with evident disgust. "The sidewalks and public streets are monopolized by Africa's descendants, and whites and blacks are promenading arm-in-arm, or side-by-side," the *Pilot* reported. The newspaper called New Bedford "stronghold of Abolitionism—the very Sebastopol of Niggerdom."[5] Few in the city seemed inclined to dispute such epithets. At the annual meeting of the Massachusetts Anti-Slavery Society in Boston that same year, the Reverend William Jackson of New Bedford stood up to show the assembly a small bell Rodney French had given him (fig. 61). It was made, a Boston newspaper reported, "from the fragments of the Liberty Hall bell, in that city, which had often been rung to give the fugitive warning." French not only had rung the bell, as abolitionists loved to recall, but had been mayor when the Liberty Hall fire melted it; he probably gave Jackson the souvenir, one of several he had had made, in recognition of his own role in

FIGURE 61. Miniature replica of bell from Liberty Hall, New Bedford, 1854, owned by Rodney French and given to the New Bedford Free Public Library by Melancie Hitch, French's daughter; the Reverend William Jackson also owned one of the replicas and is said to have used it in his latter days as a town crier on Martha's Vineyard. Used with permission of the Board of Trustees of the New Bedford Free Public Library; photograph by Maria Melo.

fugitive escapes.[6] A fugitive slave named James Williams is said to have rung another one, owned by French himself, from the rebuilt Liberty Hall on the day John Brown was executed.[7]

In 1863 James Bunker Congdon, in a scathing response to a query from the American Freemen's Inquiry Commission,[8] offered a tongue-in-cheek proposal that showed how thoroughly he believed in New Bedford's identity as a "fugitive's Gibraltar." The commission posed two questions to Congdon—"What is the position, morally, mentally, socially of the African in New Bedford? Not of the 'mixed races'—of the 'pure African descent,'" and "Has he taken such a position as would enable one to say of him that he is, *in any sense,* the equal of whites?" Congdon thought both queries ludicrous, the first ignorant and the second patronizing, and in answering he dissected them. "No human being can select from among the 'colored people' of New Bedford, those who are of 'pure African descent,'" he replied, because of the intermixture of New Bedford people of African descent with Native American, Portuguese, Cape Verdean, Polynesian, and Caucasian peoples. In fact, some of the city's people of color, Congdon noted, "claim consanguinity with the Lees, the Pinkneys and the Masons of the South. . . . If the blood of the two races is not the same," he added, "it must be allowed that it mingles easy."

Congdon suspected the intent behind the second query. "If your object is to determine the *position,* that you may judge of the *capacity* of the unmixed African, you are engaged in a difficult undertaking," he wrote. "I can give you but little aid." Instead, because he assumed the commission was composed of "practical men," he proposed an experiment to determine what positions Africans "pure and undefiled" might occupy if placed in different circumstances. Congdon proposed that the commission take "a hundred or two" from an intercepted slaver— "you will not be obliged to wait long," he noted sarcastically—"before they land and soon after being caught" so that "the mixing process can hardly have occurred." The commission should bring that group to New Bedford. Then, in a reply written as though he wished it were an oration, Congdon outlined how the experiment would proceed:

> Bring them to New Bedford. We shall recognize them as men and women. They will be protected and educated. There will be seen in them a God-given humanity, and our laws will protect it from being crushed out by slavery and our social, educational and religious institutions will train it to manhood.
>
> Bring them to New Bedford. We will guard them and train them. They will dwell here in safety and in peace, and the image of God in their souls will find acknowledgment and respect. They will live in the sunshine of civilization. They will be nurtured by the warmth of the sentiment of a common brotherhood. The germs of mental power & of moral and religious truth found in God's children everywhere will meet with fitting aids to development in our schools and churches. . . . We shall extend to them all that social, civil and legal aid and protection which it is evident to us is due to them in that "pursuit of happiness" which is an instinct of our nature as well as a self evident right.
>
> At any rate we think this the fairest method of trying the experiment. We think it more just than that which makes it a penal offence to teach them to read; which takes for its rule of action the maximum of labor with the minimum of tow-cloth and corn; which substitutes brutal fear for the hopes of reward, and the brutal instincts for holy affection; and which makes the blood-hound, the branding-iron and the lash, the exponents of the white man's ideas of a proper discipline and training for human beings.

Congdon suggested further that an equal number of Africans from the slave ship be sent to South Carolina and given "all the advantages of the slave-holding methods." After thirty years the two groups should be brought together, he concluded, "and judgment pronounced." An "inventory of the material wealth of the respective parties," not to the accounted in terms of "pounds of cotton, grown and sold for the white man's profit," would be blank for the South Carolinians but filled with "leases houses and lands, saving-bank deposits and bank stock, homes and the house-hold goods" among the New Bedford people, homes that were not "huts merely" but family sanctuaries. "How much of this belongs to the bondman?" Congdon asked, and then asked and answered his own question. Why had the commission chosen free people of color as "the subject of such an inquisitorial proceeding"? The query, he declared, embraced "a foregone conclusion that it must result in placing these people, comparatively, in a low and degraded condition." Congdon wished to know, "With what class of 'whites' must I compare them that I may determine the question of their inferiority, equality or superiority?" A "just estimate" of their position could be made by no one, he averred, but "the All Knowing."

Among such men as Congdon, Ricketson, French, and Taber, all of them influential in city politics and culture, free people of color and fugitives alike may have felt relatively safe. In the early years of the Civil War, New Bedford's Eunice Congdon, then teaching in schools for people of color near Danville, Virginia, aided in the fugitive Edward Turner's escape to the city, and in 1863 poor records note the presence of a fifty-year-old Maryland fugitive named John Gardner. In March of the next year Gardner was living in the home of New Bedford oil merchant Horatio Leonard but had such crippling "palsy" that he could not work. The overseers of the poor sent the city's physician, Andrew Mackie, to check on Gardner, and because Mackie felt Gardner would probably never be able to work again, the city paid ninety cents to buy him a train ticket to the state almshouse.[9]

Yet New Bedford was not the only place in the United States that regarded itself as a safe harbor for fugitives. In 1855 two abolitionists told Garrison that Salem, Ohio, "has the honor to be a place . . . from which it is useless to attempt the recovery of a fugitive slave"; four years earlier Child wrote the Quaker Joseph Carpenter that the firemen of Medford, Massachusetts, had elected a fugitive to membership in their company and agreed "at a given signal, to rally for his defence in case he was pursued, and to stand by him to the death, one and all." Earlier Joseph Sturge had been told that in Albany "public opinion had become so strong in favour of self-emancipation, that if a runaway were seized in the city, it is probable he could be rescued by the people." Slave pursuers had been hounded out of Worcester as well after the Fugitive Slave Act passed. "Let the Underground Railroad stop here! . . ." one abolitionist minister proclaimed at the time. "Hear O Richmond! and give ear Old Caroline! henceforth Worcester is Canada to the Slave!"[10]

Still, the sheer size of the black population indicates that people of color generally regarded New Bedford as a different sort of place than Worcester. In 1860 Worcester's population of some 24,000 included just 272 persons of color, compared to 1,518 persons of color among New Bedford's officially tallied 22,300 persons.[11] New Bedford's population of color also stood outside the norm of population growth for northern cities, nearly all of which experienced a decline in their populations of color between 1800 and 1860. In Providence people of color occupied less than half the proportion of total population in 1850 that they had in 1800, while in New Bedford nonwhite persons rose from 3.7 percent of the 1800 population to 6.3 percent in 1850 and 7.5 percent in 1855. Other towns known for protecting fugitives tended to lose population in the five years after the passage of the Fugitive Slave Act; 487 of the 943 people of color living in Columbia, Pennsylvania, in 1850 had left by 1855, and two hundred of Boston's fugitives—

whose number Theodore Parker had estimated at four to six hundred when the act passed—are believed to have left in those years as well. In Buffalo the non-white population rose from approximately seven hundred in 1850 to approximately eight hundred in 1860, but the increase may be explained by the fact that Canada was an easy trip from that city; one might leave the United States at virtually a moment's notice.[12]

George Teamoh held that New Bedford people generally believed that once on the city's free soil, a man of color, "striking out for success with his own independent arm, [might] exhibit to the world that nothing but oppression alone degrades an individual or a race when the colored man's misfortunes have been viewed from a complexional stand point." But whether this was so, and whether on measures other than population New Bedford differed greatly from other port cities in the northern United States, are far from clear. Statistics exist that permit an occupational profile of the New Bedford workforce of color in 1836, 1845, 1850, 1855, and 1856, but comparing these figures to those developed for other cities is compromised by the fact that scholars categorize occupations differently. Still, Leonard Curry's comparison between free people of color in fifteen antebellum cities and New Bedford is at least suggestive. Curry's work showed that the proportion of local black workers in unskilled, semiskilled, and service occupations rose as one advanced northward along the Atlantic coast, which reflected the much greater employment of free blacks and slaves in skilled trades in the South. Between 70 and 75 percent of the black workforce in New York, Brooklyn, Albany, and Providence were in unskilled, semiskilled, and service jobs in 1850 and more than 77 percent of Boston's black workforce was so employed in that year. In New Bedford nearly 85 percent of the local black working population was employed in these occupations. At the same time, though, the population of strictly unskilled workers—people listed as laborers, seamen or mariners, and stevedores—tended to decline among New Bedford's workers of color over time. In 1836, 71 percent were unskilled, and in 1856, 54 percent were.[13] And the percentage of artisans among New Bedford residents of color compares favorably with what prevailed in other northern cities. In 1850, 5.8 percent of all free men of color in Boston were artisans, 5.5 percent were in Providence, and 5.4 percent were in New York. But in New Bedford 9.3 percent of the black workforce was in skilled trades in 1850, a higher proportion than in any northern city Curry studied.[14] And this skilled proportion tended to grow, at least in the short term: artisans were 11.5 percent of the black workforce in New Bedford in 1856, during a decade when men of color in most other cities complained that white workers, sometimes Irish immigrants, had crowded them out of not only skilled positions but semiskilled and service jobs as well. When artisans, entrepreneurs, and professionals are combined, New Bedford also compares well to other northern cities. In New York, Boston, and Providence between 1845 and 1855, 10.4, 16.1, and 12.8 percent of the workforce of color were in such jobs respectively; in New Bedford about 21 percent were.[15]

According to another measure—the proportion of men of color working in skilled maritime-related trades, as shown in contemporary counts in Philadelphia in 1849, Boston in 1837 and 1850, and Massachusetts as a whole in 1860—New Bedford also seems to have been slightly more open to the presence of men of color in these lines. In 1837 Boston no men of color were listed as blacksmiths, caulkers, coopers, ropemakers, sailmakers, ship carpenters, or shipwrights; in New Bedford in 1836 twelve men were, or 5.7 percent of the black male workforce. In 1849 Philadelphia 3.5 percent of black males were in skilled maritime work, compared to 1.9 percent in 1850 Boston and 4.6 percent in 1850 New Bedford. In Massachusetts 1.5 percent of all men of color were in such skilled jobs in 1860, compared to 4.6 percent in 1856 New Bedford.[16]

At the same time, however, New Bedford's proportion of men of color working as laborers grew greater over time—from 35.6 percent in 1836 to 48.4 percent in 1899—even as the proportion of men of color in unskilled work declined. A comparison of black and white occupations in the 1836 directory may suggest why so many men of color worked as laborers. In 1836 only 17 percent of New Bedford's white workforce did unskilled work, compared to 71.2 percent of the town's workers of color. While 9.2 percent of the workforce of color had skilled occupations, fully 36.8 percent of the white workforce did. The proportion of white proprietors and managers, both petty and major, was 21.6 percent of the white workforce in New Bedford; 13.8 percent of black workers occupied such positions. This comparison suggests that the need for skilled labor in New Bedford, even before the whaling industry's peak of prosperity, was greater than the need for unskilled labor; it may in fact have been great enough that even a comparably high proportion of the workers of color could find jobs in the skilled trades. White workers seem to have been able to afford to leave much unskilled work to them, and they could continue to occupy those jobs because the city's immigrant population remained minuscule before the Civil War. That may explain why almost no racially motivated labor action—aside from the verbal conflict between white caulkers and Frederick Douglass in 1838, the year after a severe nationwide financial panic—is known to have occurred in New Bedford before the war; although the city certainly had poor and idle people, it was for the most part a full-employment economy in these years.

Yet employment does appear to have been constricted in racial terms in two occupational categories. New Bedford men of color were never well represented in the transportation trades; except in 1836, when 4.6 percent of workers of color were teamers or cart, dray, truck, or coach men, the proportion of the workforce of color in these trades never exceeded 2 percent before the war. This may not have been unusual in New England, for the proportion of transportation tradesmen who were men of color in Boston and Massachusetts as a whole is comparable to that in New Bedford. In Philadelphia 8.2 percent of employed men of color worked in transportation trades in 1849, which was probably a smaller proportion than it had once been; one newspaper in the city that year noted,

"Within a few years they [men of color] have ceased to be hackney coachmen and draymen, and they are now almost displaced as stevedores. They are rapidly losing their places as barbers and servants. Ten families employ white servants now, where one did twenty years ago."[17] Some historians have argued that competition from Irish immigrants for such jobs accounts for the decline, a factor not noticeably influential in New Bedford.

Second, the percentage of mariners in the city's workforce of color dropped steadily between 1836 and 1856, from 35.6 percent in the earlier year to 14.9 percent in the later one. Because total crew numbers have never been compiled in New Bedford, it is not possible to compare the proportion of total New Bedford mariners who were men of color to that in others; but their declining representation amid a constantly growing population is surely significant in itself.[18] Jeffrey Bolster has suggested that the shift in hiring responsibility from captains and vessel owners to "crimps," middlemen who worked with boardinghouse keepers to recruit sailors and who epitomized the rising interest in a racially exclusive workingmen's movement, probably accounted for the diminishing presence of men of color in crews. Crimps tended to hire "whites first," Bolster has noted. In 1863 James Bunker Congdon noted the trend locally. Captain Gideon Randall, his father-in-law, once carried twenty men of color in a crew of thirty on a vessel owned by the Rotch family, and another New Bedford whaling master told him that ten of the sixteen crew members on his first whaling voyage, probably in 1818, were men of color and that he had hired a black officer for three of his voyages. "My impression is clear that then a free negro was considered first rate material for a whaleman," Congdon wrote, but their presence on whaling crews was at that time "not as great now as formerly. . . . The proportion gradually diminished until in a majority of cases the cooks and stewards only were colored. For the most part this is now the case, but it is, without doubt, almost wholly owing to the prejudice of the whites. Colored men have held every position on board of our whale ships; but the reason why they are not oftener there as seamen, and very rarely there as officers, is the same that must be given for their exclusion from any other position of authority or fellowship."[19]

Ezra R. Johnson noted the other racial dimension to New Bedford's occupational profile in a response to a query from the 1855 national convention of people of color about black participation in the "mechanical branches." There does not appear any great desire on the part of parents to secure trades for their children," Johnson wrote. "I think the chances for them to obtain situations as apprentices, very few and difficult. There is little or no disposition to encourage colored men in business, who have means to carry it on. We have several colored men who possess their thousands, accumulated in California, and are anxious to start in some business, but from well-grounded fear of success, either do nothing here or return to California. Our colored mechanics are principally from the south."[20] Indeed, in 1855 65.8 percent of New Bedford's skilled workers of color listed southern birthplaces in the census and only 34.2 percent were northern-born;

these proportions were about the same in 1850. It is at least possible that skilled workers found that they could not advance either in income or through the occupational hierarchy in New Bedford and abandoned the place, as did sailmaker Shadrach Howard and even, for a time, the sailmaker, trader, and botanic physician Ezra Johnson himself. New arrivals from the South, fugitive or free, occupied those vacancies, though certainly not all of the skilled southern-born men of color could find such openings. What Congdon noted of seamen's positions seems also to have applied to the skilled trades. "I found prejudice so great in the North that I was forced to come down from my high position as captain, and take my white-wash brush and wheelbarrow and get my living that way," the former Virginia slave George Henry wrote of his new life in Providence. One observer wrote of skilled men of color in 1859, "Less than two-thirds of those who have trades follow them. A few of the remainder pursue other avocations from choice, but the greater number are compelled to abandon their trades on account of the unrelenting prejudice against their color." In Philadelphia the percentage of skilled black artisans not working at their trades increased from 23 percent in 1838 to about 38 percent in 1856.[21] Men with skills found themselves forced to work in unskilled jobs at various times in New Bedford as well. William Ferguson had been a butcher for fourteen years in Norfolk, but in New Bedford he was a laborer and city crier; the blacksmith John Taseo sold bread on the port city's streets; Frederick Douglass could not get work as a caulker. In statistical terms these evidences of occupational discrimination do not surface. Yet it may be true that on the whole it was hard for a family of color to make ends meet in New Bedford no matter what sorts of jobs its breadwinners occupied. It is hard to understand the notable movement of enterprising African American men from New Bedford to San Francisco in other terms. And when M. B. Eddy noted in 1851 that many New Bedford fugitives "cannot" move to Canada, he surely meant they lacked the financial means to do so.

In residential terms, New Bedford's population of color seems to have reflected the pattern in many other antebellum cities: people of color were not segregated, but they did live in discernible clusters that grew more noticeable toward midcentury (figs. 62 and 63). When their residential distribution can first be plotted, in 1836, a group of dwellings appears on Elm and Middle Streets about a block west of County Street; on Ray Street (later Acushnet Avenue) between Maxfield and Campbell Streets, near the northern section of the working waterfront; on South Water, First, and Second Streets as these proceed south from Union Street; and at the junction of Bedford, Wing, Sixth, and Allen Streets, in the area that came later to be called "Dog Corner." They were noticeably absent from the most affluent neighborhoods, both south of Union Street—the growing one west of County and the older one east of County Street to about Fourth Street. By 1856 the concentration of renters and owners of color at Dog Corner had grown somewhat denser, but the Elm and Middle Streets area, the city's West End, was occupied almost exclusively by people of color and had extended its reach northward

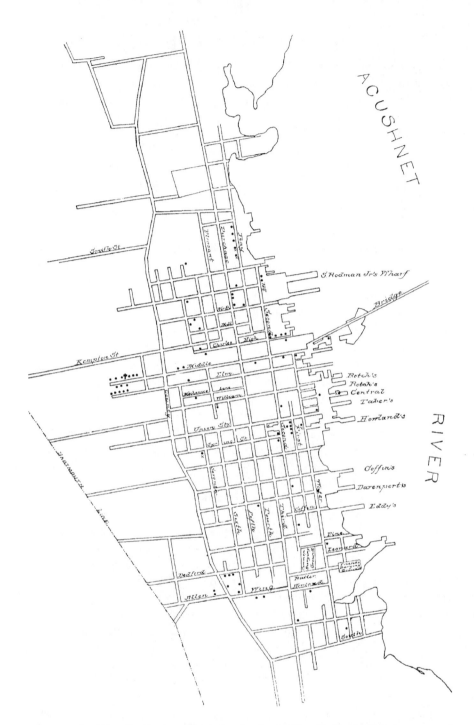

FIGURE 62. The distribution of people of color in New Bedford, 1836; map created by Michael Bachstein. Dots signify known sites of residences; crosses, churches (just one in 1836, on Middle Street); and xs, locations of businesses run by people of color.

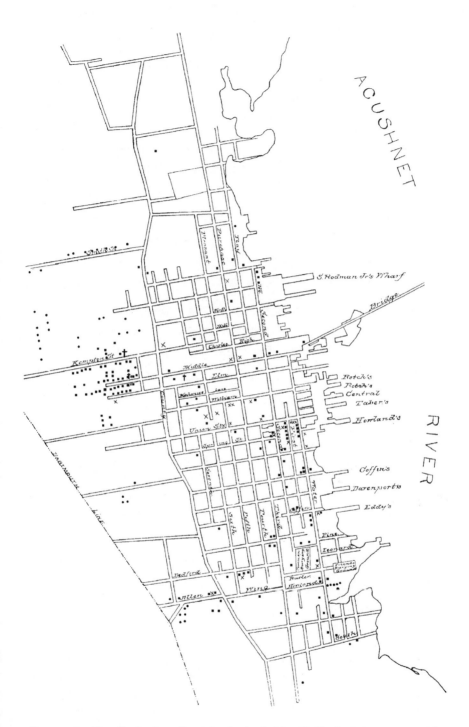

FIGURE 63. The distribution of people of color in New Bedford, 1856; map created by Michael Bachstein. A fourth symbol, blocks, indicates approximate residential locations.

to Hillman Street, west to Chancery Street, and south to the terminus of Cedar Street. Hard-Dig reached into the westernmost part of this neighborhood, which was probably the "negro suburb" Charles Congdon recalled from the late 1830s and 1840s.[22] In addition, Smith Street, a relatively new road, was heavily populated by people of color, including the Reverend William Jackson.

In 1856 people of color inhabited what must have been an integrated neighborhood of poor or lower-working-class people along South Water Street, the area that became the city's gateway neighborhood when immigration began in earnest after the Civil War. And businesses owned or operated by people of color clustered among others in a roughly five-block-square area on both sides of Union Street, from School Street on the south to Middle Street on the north and from the waterfront to North Sixth Street east and west. Here were the hairdressers and barbers W. H. Wood, Napoleon Cross, Henry Vincent, Charles Potter, Samuel Marsh, Anthony and Hepsibeth Jourdain, and John West; the restaurateurs John Kasson, Peter Howard, Abraham Conklin, and William Strother; the grocers Brooks and Peneton and E. R. and R. C. Johnson, who also sold clothing; clothiers J. W. A. Smith and Henry Brown; the confectioner Thornton Smith; the dentist Thomas Bayne; the boot- and shoemaker Willis Lucas, and the boardinghouse of John Warren. Barbers, boardinghouse keepers (including William Bush), grocers, and clothiers lived in other neighborhoods to the south and north; the better-known confectioner Polly Johnson operated from her home just south of the commercial core, at 21 Seventh Street.

By 1856 both the residential distribution and density of New Bedford's population of color had thus increased, and, though by 1860 they lived in all of the city's six wards, they were most prevalent in the third and fourth, the West End wards.[23] Homes and businesses owned and occupied by people of color tended still to be absent from the older and newer affluent neighborhoods and now, notably, from the neighborhood of skilled workers that had grown up in North Bedford, east of County Street between the city's common at Pearl Street on the north and North Street on the south. But by that year, despite the fact that the homes and tenements of people of color were dispersed over the rest of the city, the city's West End, with its markedly heavier concentration of people of color, must clearly have been perceived as a "negro suburb" by people other than Congdon. The density there and at Dog Corner had spawned the creation of court-like streets, short passages laid between smaller structures that had originally been built in the rear of existing residences to house more people within an older, developed neighborhood. In 1838 a survey by the Pennsylvania Society for the Abolition of Slavery found that nearly 22 percent of people of color with known addresses lived in alleys, courts, or at rear of other buildings; by the late 1840s one observer found the city's black population often "crammed into lofts, garrets and cellars, in blind alleys and narrow courts." In 1843 Daniel Ricketson noted in the fourth annual report of the New Bedford Benevolent Aid Society, "Your committee are often called into scenes of suffering, that would rather seem to belong to the crowded cities of the old world, than to one of the most flourishing towns of our flourishing republic. . . . Widowed mothers with little children struggling against the severest want, miserably clad and wanting food collected in some damp unwholesome room half underground . . . these and many others of a kindred character are often to be met with." Two years later Ricketson, who clearly subscribed to a sort of environmental determinism, remained profoundly disturbed at housing conditions among the city's needy.

> Among the most prolific causes of evil among the poor in our town, is the bad state of their tenements. In the spirit of gain, which is ever connected with a thriving place like ours, cheap and hurriedly built tenements are got up for the poor. Many of these are by no means sufficient to protect the occupants from the rigours of our climate, being but half finished and little better than hovels. And others that claim a little better character are often occupied before the dampness has left them, and thus become productive of sickness and suffering. There is one class of tenements, which we cannot fail to make a particular mention of, as detrimental to the comfort of the poor—We mean those called, *basement rooms*—they are usually half underground, and the evils produced by them on the health of the poor are very numerous—not only the great amount of dampness; but the inefficient means of ventilation contribute to this end. These rooms are often under a very respectable house, whose owner may be living in quite a comfortable or even genteel style, little heeding or in many instances being unaware of the sufferers below them.[24]

Living in such places seems to have been no more common among people of color, however, than among whites in the city. The Benevolent Society and its successor municipal agency certainly assisted, proportionately, at least as many white as black persons, and when Congdon encountered the unhealthy and crowded conditions at James Dyer's boardinghouse in 1834, he clearly regarded them as well below the norm. Virtually all persons of color listed in the 1856 directory as living in the rear of structures were living behind black-owned or -occupied residences, a fact which, lacking other evidence, is potentially as indicative of the preference of people of color to live together and support each other as it is of the inability of people of color to secure housing in other neighborhoods. Only two were shown as basement dwellers. These two, and a few others whom poor relief records indicate were living in basements, lived below the floors whites occupied; this fact suggests that they may have been servants there. The condition and appearance of the dwellings of New Bedford's people of color can only be guessed at. During the Ark riot of 1826, the *Mercury* had described the houses occupied by people of color in Hard-Dig as "huts," and in 1863 James Congdon had noted that the home of John Cory, who "had about him every type of the pure African" and for years worked as a steward on New York–New Bedford packets, measured only seven by nine feet. Congdon at the same time stated that the South Water Street home of Henry O. Remington was a neat, tasteful, and "singular looking cottage," a description that raises many more questions than it answers.[25] It seems safe to say that the degree of residential dispersion or clustering in New Bedford does not appear to have been markedly different from what prevailed in other northern port cities with sizeable populations of color, and evidence of racially variable housing conditions is absent or inconclusive.[26]

The incidence of racially motivated crowd action in New Bedford is also difficult to assess. After the Ark riots of the 1820s, the only other notable riot in the city, the so-called Howland Street riot of 1856, does not appear to have been directed even in part at people of color. Still, the repeated coincidence of such events as the black community's meeting on John Brown's raid and "incendiary" fires may indicate the presence of racial tension. Aside from the attack on homes occupied by people of color in Hard-Dig in 1830 and 1835, New Bedford largely escaped the rioting that struck most other northern cities in the 1830s, mob actions that historians tend to lay to the threatening organizing activities and rhetoric of abolitionists and resentment of "foreign" influences such as George Thompson. Local historian Zephaniah Pease likened an 1840 "outbreak" at Dog Corner to the Ark Riots in that the mob singled out "infamous resorts" such as the Gray Eagle and the North Star. Moreover, Pease noted, " 'Hard-Dig' was more flaunting than ever; there were a two-story dance hall and many shambles at Hard-Dig. Again 'Jerry' was invoked," and the west side neighborhood was again torched.[27] In 1847 four men of color were accused of rioting at a "pro-slavery lecture," much as Nathan Johnson and others had been accused of rioting twenty years before in the interests of protecting fugitives. The blacksmith Lewis Temple, the boardinghouse keeper John Adams, the waiter John H. Brown, and "Simmons" (either Amos, Charles, or John G., all laborers) disrupted an unidentified lecturer at Concert Hall in July that year and were later tried in the Court of Common Pleas; the outcome of the case is unknown.[28]

Because the newspapers covered events so erratically, it is hard to judge whether race-related violence increased in the 1850s. The reports that do exist, however, suggest that it may have. In 1850, just days after the *Mercury* reported that Frederick Douglass had been mobbed in Columbus, Ohio, "ruffian and unprovoked attacks of the devotees of intemperance and licentiousness" who gathered nightly in Hard-Dig had seriously injured two people, but the correspondent who described the incident in the *Mercury* did not identify their race. In July 1852 "a gang of young rowdies" assaulted a visiting Providence minister of color at Smith and County Streets. In 1855 and 1856 the barn of Cuffe Lawton near the town line with Dartmouth and the Third Christian Church on Middle Street were set on fire, the latter twice in the same year, and in August 1858 police believed arsonists were responsible for the destruction of a barn off Dartmouth Street in which "Messrs. Potter and Fairweather," both men of color, had stored a tent they meant to use at the First of August picnic that year. Within a week of John Brown's execution in 1859, the *Standard* reported that the fire that destroyed the William Street barber shop and an adjoining one-story wooden building owned by Thomas Bayne, one of the organizers and speakers at the colored community's meeting on the failed raid, had been arson; Bayne was able to get much of the furniture and the instruments he used in his dental practice out before the flames gutted both structures. In April 1860 arsonists were believed responsible for the fire that destroyed the uninsured, wooden AME Bethel church on Kempton Street, and two years later they destroyed the church's vestry.[29] In 1856 the How-land Street riots, which the *Mercury* actually accused the *Standard* of having instigated (by publishing a retrospective account of the Ark riots when the first signs of trouble occurred), struck the Marsh district of the city and seem, like the Ark riots, to have been sparked by a series of deaths of mysterious character. All named participants in this crowd action were white or identified in the newspaper as "Spanish" or Portuguese. A Native American woman living in one of the probably ramshackle boardinghouses in this Marsh district was one of three who died before and during the event, and the Marsh area was, like Dog Corner and Hard-Dig, well populated by people of color living in poverty. But the incident does not seem to have had the racial dimension of the Ark and other lawless actions.

In 1863 the city was threatened with a local version of the New York City draft riots, an action that seemed an effective barometer of the local belief, even among whites, in the ultimate necessity of violence. The New York incident, provoked by Lincoln's institution of a conscription to fill the Union forces, involved four mid-July days of rioting, arson, and lynching in neighborhoods of color; William P. Powell's boardinghouse for black mariners was burned, and he and his family, who had returned to the United States from Liverpool two years earlier, fled to New Bedford. In 1861 Powell had helped his son William set up practice as a physician in New Bedford, and that year his sons Edward and Sylvester took out protection papers in the city and shipped on whaling vessels. According to *Douglass' Monthly*, Powell himself presided over a "very large and enthusiastic meeting of the colored citizens of New Bedford" in early October 1861. In 1863 Powell had spearheaded the formation of the American Seamen's Protection Union Association, the first "quasi-trade union" for American mariners, and had begun to use his boardinghouse as a union hall, to "shape up" gangs of men of color to ship out and thus to circumvent the use of crimps.[30] It is not known exactly when Powell and his family fled to New Bedford after the draft riot, but he may have walked into the teeth of the rumored assault on New Bedford. Joseph Ricketson described it, almost as though nothing of the sort had ever happened in New Bedford before, in a letter to Debora Weston two days afterward:

> Soon as the news of the New York Riot reached here, the low murmurings of discontent were heard and soon it was ascertained that there was to be a combined effort of the lower classes in Fall River, Wareham & Bridgewater & other adjoining towns to burn & pillage New Bedford—The Programme as far as ascertained was to burn the Mansion House first, then Dam's Eating Saloon, & then Ricketson's Block corner of Union & Purchase or rather 4th St, where the Provost Marshalls office is— But I am not in the least apprehensive of any danger; for we are prepared for any emergency, and we are determined—there will be no blank cartridges—We have in

our two Forts, Fort Phoenix at Fairhaven and Fort Taber at the Point 150—Heavy Artillery Men of the U.S. Army—last Wednesday they received 146 muskets with full cartridges from Springfield—we have also two Home Guard Companies amounting to 150 more, also a Dragoon Co who have had their sabres sharpened & are armed with carbines, as well as two pieces of Artillery, and also Capt Hurlburt with his company just returned from Newbern—Capt Hurlburt is in command of the whole. The US Cutter is also at the foot of our st Union st, with her guns shotted—150 extra police here on duty—& we have pickets extending for several miles out of town—Our sea captains are armed with revolvers, & our citizens mostly armed also—Your humble servant nor none of his family are armed—There is but one opinion here as regards the colored man, we are going to stand by him in the name of the Lord Jesus Christ—Thursday the colored chaplain of the 55th Mass Regt [William Jackson], came along by the Bank, where five of us were standing, & said he wanted a Revolver for himself—this was all he said each one of us gave him a dollar, and Major Geo A Bourne told him to wait—in ten minutes or less enough was raised & Bourne bought a $1.16 revolver for him—Our first citizens giving freely—our military sleep on their arms every night in City Hall & other public buildings—One man was heard a few days since to say that he would head a mob & burn the Negro houses in the west part of town—Twenty Negros patrolled, armed with revolvers, around his House intending to shoot him if he came out.[31]

The raid, like the one rumored to round up New Bedford fugitives in 1851, did not materialize, and Jackson probably returned to the Fifty-fifth Regiment's training camp at Readville, Massachusetts, afterward. He served as chaplain to the company of soldiers of color formed after the Fifty-fourth had been filled, and both regiments contained New Bedford men who had enlisted for the most part in February and March of 1863, probably for some of the same reasons William Powell had returned to the United States—because they believed the war would both end slavery and give them a chance to prove to the nation their right to be treated as full citizens. By the time of the alleged New Bedford riot, the Fifty-fourth had already shipped out to South Carolina and its storied, ill-fated assault on Fort Wagner.

James B. Congdon, who had helped organize recruiting for the black regiments in New Bedford early in 1863, told Governor Andrew that 189 men were eligible for military service in the unprecedented regiment. Twenty of them, however, had already enlisted in the navy and in other regiments in 1863; at the end of January 1862, for example, Anthony G. Jourdain Jr. (fig. 64) had left New Bedford to serve as barber for the Eighteenth Massachusetts Regiment, then at Hall's Hill, Virginia.[32] Congdon told the state recruiting committee that another thirty-seven of the city's men of color were "abroad," mostly in California. By then J. B. Sanderson, David W. Ruggles, Shadrach Howard, Ezra R. Johnson, James P. Dyer, Emory Waters, Edward R. Phelps, Lloyd H. Brooks, Charles Gibson, John T. Jenifer, Daniel Seals, and Solomon Peneton had moved to the western state and had become primary supporters of the *Pacific Appeal,* its black newspaper; Nathan Johnson, Thomas Buchanan, George Page, and Samuel and Nancy

HANNAH H. WORTHING,   30 Purchase Street

FIGURE 64. Anthony G. Jourdain Jr. and his wife, the former Anna E. Bush, photograph by Hannah H. Worthing, New Bedford, 1867 or 1868. Courtesy the descendants
of Anthony G. and Anna E. (Bush) Jourdain Jr. Born in December 1837, Jourdain was
the son of Anthony Jourdain Sr., born in Suriname, and Hepsibeth Johnson, a Gay
Head Wampanoag Indian. Jourdain served as one of three secretaries of the 1858 colored
people's convention in New Bedford and was one of the first men of color to enlist in
the Union forces from the city.

Woodland may still have been in California as well. Thomas Bayne, who spoke at the Fifty-fourth's farewell meeting in New Bedford, soon afterward returned to Norfolk (George Teamoh would return to Portsmouth in 1865). Congdon concluded that 132 men of color were recruitable, and by mid-March he reported that thirty had already enlisted. The local effort may have been helped by a letter in the *Mercury* a few weeks earlier by a then-anonymous member of the new Fifty-fourth, later identified as James Henry Gooding, who had enlisted in Company C in New Bedford. In his view, joining the regiment was "probably the only opportunity that will ever be offered them [the men of color of New Bedford] to make themselves a people":

> There are a great many I must confess, who, Micawber-like, 'are waiting for something to turn up'; but they will have to learn sooner or later, that if anything does 'turn up' to their advantage, they will have to be the means of turning it up themselves; they must learn that there is more dignity in carrying a musket in defence of liberty and right than there is in shaving a man's face, or waiting on somebody's table.—Not that it is any degradation to perform those offices, but those who perform them are considered nothing but appendages to society. . . . If the colored man proves to be as good a soldier as it is confidently expected he will, there is a permanent field of employment opened to him, with all the chances of promotion in his favor.[33]

In the end about fifty New Bedford men of color served in the Fifty-fourth (thirty-three of them in Company C alone) and the Fifty-fifth, and more joined the Fifth Cavalry and the U.S. Navy. A private, local committee gave twenty-five dollars to the family of every recruit of color, and on 4 March 1863 fifty-four men each were given a pair of mittens before they boarded a train for Readville's Camp Meigs. The New Bedford Ladies' Soldiers' Relief Society sent sewing kits, shirts, handkerchiefs, and stockings to them in camp; Lindsey sent magazines; "unknown friends" shipped them apples, mirrors, towels, and shoe blacking and brushes; and John Goings, a longtime domestic servant in the city, sent them tobacco.[34] On 18 May at Readville Governor Andrew pronounced the regiment prepared to "vindicate . . . the character, the manly character, the zeal, the manly zeal, of the colored citizens of Massachusetts, and of those of other States which have cast their lot with ours." He then presented the regiment both its American flag and "the State colors of the old Bay State,"

> borne already by fifty-three regiments of Massachusetts soldiers, white men thus far, now to be borne by the Fifty-fourth Regiment of soldiers, not less of Massachusetts than the others. . . . I have the pride and honor to declare before you, your regiment, and these witnesses, that from the beginning till now, the State colors of Massachusetts have never been surrendered to any foe. The Fifty-fourth now holds in possession this sacred charge, in the performance of their duties as soldiers. You will never part with that flag so long as a splinter of the staff or a thread of its web remains within your grasp."[35]

It is almost impossible not to imagine New Bedford's William Carney listening to Andrew's words and taking this passage in particular as his charge. Carney earned the first Congressional Medal of Honor ever awarded to an African American for having taken up the flag of the regiment's injured standard-bearer and, though wounded three times, advancing with it to the parapet of Fort Wagner. M. S. Littlefield, who commanded the regiment after the death of Robert Gould Shaw at Fort Wagner, wrote that Carney had taken the "regimental colors" and moved forward near Shaw as Shaw led the regiment over a ditch toward the fort's wall; Carney's 1889 reminiscence stated that as he saw the color-bearer fall, he threw his gun away, seized the colors, and made for the head of the column. "In less than twenty minutes I found myself alone, struggling upon the ramparts, while all around me were the dead and wounded, lying one upon another," Carney wrote; Confederate fire, Littlefield noted, had "melted away" the men advancing before him. Carney himself was shot in the thigh and knelt with the flag in his hand. "He kept the colors flying till the second conflict was ended," Littlefield wrote. "When our forces retired, he followed, creeping on one knee, *still holding up the flag.*" He was shot twice more as he made his way to the rear. New Bedford's Lewis A. Fleetwood, who served with Carney in Company C, later recalled that Carney refused to surrender the flag to anyone but the men of his own regiment. "Boys I only did my duty," Fleetwood remembered him to have said. "The old flag never touched the ground." This statement, in one version or another, was one of the war stories repeated across the nation; in 1908 one local historian claimed Carney's words "are known by every schoolboy in the land."[36]

To a fugitive from slavery like Carney, to serve in the Union Army as valiantly as he could must have been the ultimate assertion of his willingness to accept all the responsibilities of citizenship even as American society denied him and other people of color—free, fugitive, or enslaved—all of its rights, those "positions of authority and fellowship" to which Congdon had alluded. Unlike other national conflicts where the enlistment of men of color was encouraged by the promise of emancipation, the Civil War held no such overt promise for Carney. Slavery in the territories had been abolished in June 1862, and Lincoln's Emancipation Proclamation of 1 January 1863 declared that slaves in areas still involved in rebellion against the Union would be "forever free," even though those seceded areas were no longer under federal jurisdiction and thus not bound to accede to Lincoln's edict. As a fugitive, Carney remained in limbo, at least technically, until the war ended. For men like James Henry Gooding, serving in the Union Army meant a chance at last to take action to end slavery, rather than simply pass endless resolutions that it must end. He made this argument in the *Mercury* toward the end of April in an effort to persuade more men of color to enlist:

> Let them consider that a chance to obtain what they have 'spouted' for in 'convention assembled' now presents itself by works, not by words! And let them remember

that the Greeks lost their liberties by 'too much talk'; thinking that talking would accomplish more than fighting, but they saw their mistake when it was too late. Let our people beware. Their fate will be worse than that of the Greeks, if they do not put forth an effort now to save themselves. As one of the race, I beseech you not to trust to a fancied security, laying comfort to your minds, that our condition will be bettered, because slavery must die. It depends upon the free black men of the North, whether it will die or not—those who are in bonds must have some one to open the door. . . . Now is the time to act, . . . if our people will only take hold of the matter in earnest it can be done.[37]

Some white abolitionists shared this impatience with talk. In one 1847 letter to the *Liberator*, New Bedford's John Bailey wrote bitterly how "satisfied with small favors" the New England Yearly Meeting of Friends seemed to be with respect to its action on slavery. The meeting had appointed no committee on slavery, but Bailey had no doubt that if it had the result would have been identical to the report made by the committee studying the meeting's proper relation to Native Americans—"that they had *done nothing.*" Bailey added, "I confidently expected the meeting would have felt a *concern* for the slave, inasmuch as this query is always before the meeting—'Do you bear a faithful testimony against slavery?'" But he doubted what underlay the concern Friends ("incorrigible Whigs" to a man, he noted) did seem inclined to express:

I have no hesitation in saying, that should a few of our whale ships be taken by some foreign power, Friends would feel a "concern" to ask and seek for an indemnity, and would be at no loss in finding a way. They say—"We have been concerned that our members may keep ever before them the miseries and sinfulness inseparable from the practice of holding our fellow-men in bondage, and its utter inconsistency with the command of Christ—". . . . If nothing is done for the slave more than has been done, for the last ten or fifteen years by the Friends, I think their concern will be gratified to its utmost extent, in keeping before them the miseries, &c.[38]

British abolitionist Joseph Sturge had observed in 1841 that "a direct and extensive pro-slavery interest" had developed in the North because "the North Eastern States have by far the greater part of the whole commerce of the Union, and are the medium through which the planter exchanges his cotton for provisions and clothing for his slaves, implements for his agriculture, and his own family supplies," to say nothing of the "family-alliances, the interchange of hospitalities, and a fusion of sentiments" created by southern families vacationing in the North each summer. Six years earlier the Reverend Samuel J. May found his efforts to win the Yearly Meeting's pronouncement against slavery stymied by "wealthy cotton manufacturers and merchants, [who] had bestirred themselves to prevent such an 'intrusion,' as they were pleased to term it." These men had tried to persuade the operator of the Newport hotel May intended to stay in to refuse his patronage, but forty Friends staying at the same place—who, "though of less account in the meeting . . . were more weighty in the receipts of the hotel-keeper"—interceded on May's behalf. The landlord instead agreed to serve the meals of those who tried to oust May in a separate dining room, "so that their eyes might not be offended at the sight of the antislavery agent in the common dining-hall."[39]

Friends like these were part of what Daniel Ricketson once termed the "cottonocracy." Others called them the "Cotton Whigs," those "lords of the loom" who existed, Charles Sumner charged, in an unholy alliance with Southern "lords of the lash." In this respect the reluctance of their organized Yearly Meetings to take a decided stand against slavery was no more or less than a reflection of the general American sentiment on abolition.[40] As Frederick Douglass, Samuel Rodman Jr., and Debora Weston noted, antislavery was not popular, despite New Bedford's reputation as a stronghold of positive regard for the fugitive; the "wharves and churches," Weston wrote, were arrayed against the movement. One writer reporting on the 1847 lectures of the abolitionists Stephen Foster and Parker Pillsbury in New Bedford argued in the *National Anti-Slavery Standard* that the effort "Boston cotton-Whigs" made to assure the annexation of Texas as a slave state reflected a more general sensibility. "Why did they act thus?" he asked rhetorically. "Because they hoped by it to make the Union *last their day,* and go on making their millions at Lowell, and who cares what comes afterward? . . . It is the feeling of thousands of business men at the North, who do not want their trafficing interfered with. This is what makes them so patient under the kicks and insults of the South. . . . While Northern commerce flourishes Slavery will not be abolished."[41]

Because of the nature of the city's industry, it would be hard to argue that commercial considerations generally clouded the view or inhibited the actions of New Bedford's abolitionists. Such men as Joseph Grinnell, Andrew Robeson, Samuel Rodman Jr., and Charles W. Morgan had invested in cotton textile manufacturing (though only Grinnell invested in New Bedford's Wamsutta Mill, the city's sole textile factory before 1871), and Morgan was clearly worried about the effect of the Fugitive Slave Act on this sphere of his enterprise. "I dont fear for our nonmanufacture so much as for the Cotton," he wrote on 10 October 1850, and about a year and a half later, having noted the arrival of three whaling ships in port, "all good voyages," he reported, "At present rates of oil everything that arrives makes money—my business however cotton & iron looks rather gloomy."[42] But New Bedford was clearly not, to use the words of Wendell Phillips, "wholly choked with cotton dust," as Boston seemed to be in his eyes.[43] Its commercial interest in slavery was more indirect—it was probably involved in the coastwise traffic in shoes and hats; its oil supplied lighthouses along the coast—but whaling, where the great bulk of the city's capital was committed, never depended in any great measure on southern markets. The South lacked the two things that whale and sperm oil industry thrived on—factories and cities. New Bedford merchants looked abroad and to their own region, not generally southward. The city's interests seem rather to have inclined it to welcome not only fugitives but an end to slavery; Daniel Ricketson once argued that emancipation would create a vast new market of whale oil consumers. And, though no clear evidence of a sustained labor shortage in New Bedford exists, the city seemed to need the labor of men of color on the wharves and whaling ships.

Thus, arguably, New Bedford abolitionists could afford to be abolitionists, yet both whites and blacks noted that antislavery was "far from popular," that the wharves and churches were "mean." This incongruity suggests another impulse behind anti-abolitionism to which New Bedford may have been more susceptible. Few white abolitionists, except perhaps John Bailey and Joseph Ricketson Jr., were to fugitives what Nathan Johnson was to Frederick Douglass or what William Bush was to George Teamoh (fig. 65). Because they possessed most of the political and economic power, they could employ them, shelter them for a night or a week, write letters to cohorts in other cities to assist them in their passage, even invite them to parties. But by doing so publicly they put themselves on the line, for they recognized that being the sort of abolitionist who actively helped fugitives

FIGURE 65. Nathan Johnson's gravestone, Oak Grove Cemetery, New Bedford, photograph by John Robson. After more than twenty years in the West, Johnson returned to New Bedford after his wife's death in 1871. He seems to have returned in precarious financial condition, for he wrote the abolitionist Gerrit Smith in February 1873 for assistance. He had been at various times a prospective Quaker, a Universalist, and a Spiritualist, but he was committed to equal rights throughout his life; the inscription on his headstone reads, "Freedom for all Mankind."

classed one with the radicals, such men as Garrison, the flamboyant foreigner George Thompson, or, locally, Rodney French; identified as such they stood to lose friends, social standing, perhaps even business and political clout.

For most Americans had accepted the polemic advanced in most of their news-papers, including, often, the *Mercury,* that abolitionists were extremists who thought little of the threatening, even revolutionary, consequences of what they advocated. The *Mercury's* Lindsey was frequently upset by the rhetoric abolition-ists used: when the fugitive Henry Bibb wrote in an address to his former master about the "slave holding, rum-sucking, rum-selling, bloated, reeling, staggering, swearing, vomiting, disgraceful bar-room lounger, who talks loudly over the rum-jug, among a lot of loafers, about what they would do, and how they would take a man's liberty or life, whose chief crime has been to run away from slavery," Lindsey professed that Bibb's "intemperate language . . . does him and his cause more harm than good."[44] Though Lindsey never put it in such terms, talk like that contained the seeds of revolt. Abolitionists would force integrated schooling, promiscuously support intermarriage, heedlessly advance the rights of black workers over white, and once again subject the United States to the high-minded thrall of the British. For that reason the great mass of white antislavery activists, even those who declared themselves abolitionists, feared abolitionism in varying degrees.[45] And in New Bedford, the lingering effect of Quaker ideology set pecu-liar limits on abolitionism when it veered toward the use of force or even, for some, intemperate language. Anti-abolitionists were the people who took their insurance business away from Joseph Ricketson and avoided the shop of John Bailey so assiduously that the abolitionist felt compelled to abandon the city for the friendlier climes of Lynn. "N. Bedford seeks to starve & freeze his antislavery fidelity out of him," Samuel J. May wrote in 1848 as Bailey packed to leave.[46] Orville Dewey, minister to New Bedford's new Unitarian congregation in the 1820s and a cleric whom abolitionists came to despise, asserted in 1847, "Almost every respectable and influential man who comes before the public, whether in speech or print, to declare his protest against Slavery, or to reason against the system, takes special pains to say that he is not an abolitionist. Men avoid the name as they would a pestilence."[47]

When Bailey left, the New Bedford Anti-Slavery Society declared that "it is unquestionably true, that his identity with, and consistent advocacy of the un-popular anti-slavery cause, provoked the ill-will and hatred of the sectarian-minded and pro-slavery-hearted, who have exerted an influence injurious to his business. . . . His house was ever open to shelter, as were the hearts of his family to sympathize with, the poor and suffering. Hundreds of fugitives have known his benevolence. Many, in this place, will bless his memory." The meeting passed a resolution to honor Bailey as a "beloved friend and fellow-laborer," but the only members mentioned in the meeting report in the *Liberator* were men of color— Nathaniel A. Borden (then president of the society), J. B. Sanderson (its secre-tary), Lloyd H. Brooks, Solomon Peneton, John Butler, Robert Goldsberry,

Seth B. Toleson, James P. Dyer, David W. Ruggles, and Thomas Buchanan.[48] If white abolitionists attended the meeting and supported the resolution, Borden and Sanderson did not state as much; if they met to pass a similar "testimonial of respect," the *Mercury* did not report it.

Some white antislavery activists, and some abolitionists, were stuck on the bar that separated political and social equality. Antislavery may not have been popular in New Bedford, but Morgan was probably correct when he defined opposition to the Fugitive Slave Act as "the ruling sentiment of this town"; that is to say, many men who possessed social standing and economic power in town were against slavery, and of those a fair share, including the town's most affluent families, were abolitionists. Indeed, just as Quaker ideas constrained the abolitionism of some, it gave a radical cast to the abolitionism of others. In the first decade of the city's existence, it was headed almost exclusively by abolitionists or men from abolitionist families. Abraham Hathaway Howland, the city's first mayor, was the brother of William Penn Howland, who ran a free labor grocery store in the city and attended many antislavery meetings, and the son of Weston Howland, part owner of the vessel on which John Randolph came to New Bedford in the late 1810s. Rodney French, not well liked by the local Whig establishment, became mayor in 1853 in a close contest against incumbent William J. Rotch, who served only one year and was not known for his antislavery views. George Howland Jr., who may have employed more men of color than any other white merchant in the city, succeeded French as mayor. James Bunker Congdon, Isaac C. Taber, and others identified as abolitionists frequently occupied city offices, and in the late 1850s the city's Common Council not only paid for Daniel Drayton's funeral but also wrangled over whether to make an appropriation, like the one it regularly offered the city's Fourth of July committee, to the organizers of the First of August West Indian Emancipation Day ceremonies.[49]

Such actions, and the willingness of men like Joseph Ricketson Jr. and John Emerson to house and employ fugitives, marked the city as willing to stand politically for people of color, but whether abolitionists generally were willing to accept them socially is questionable in New Bedford as elsewhere. Daniel Ricketson, who before his conversion to abolitionism told John Bailey that "no respectable person" would join with the abolitionists, later found mystifying the "colorphobia" that banned two free women of color from a Boston concert. "A colored person, even of the deepest dye, may stand by our chair while at our meals and wait upon us—may cook our food—ay! put their dark hands into our bread— 'tend and nurse our children, and nothing is thought of it—but to sit near us in a concert room, a lecture room, or a church, this is by no means to be thought of," he noted wryly.[50] When the city's newfound antislavery society pledged itself to "elevate the character" of people of color, when Charles Morgan spoke of Henry "Box" Brown having earned his freedom, and when Samuel Rodman claimed that New Bedford's citizens of color were "indebted" to abolitionists "for their elevation in intelligence and morals," they spoke the same language as the

Bostonians Ricketson complained of, a language of improvement that suffused their thought and revealed a lingering and almost unconscious belief in the prevailing racial order of things. It was a different language from the one Thomas Rotch spoke when he hoped that Ohio would admit settlers of color freely, for they would become "useful members of Civil Society" once permitted to "emerge from the state of degradation to which they have been subjected." Thomas Rotch was probably not the sort of abolitionist who, as antebellum black leader Martin Delany once said of antislavery societies generally, "presumed to *think* for, dictate to, and *know* better what suited colored people, than they know for themselves."[51]

That people of color might think and act for themselves was an idea that many whites, North and South, did seem to push away. Southern slaveholders needed to believe that white northern abolitionists, and the seamen of color they had reputedly indoctrinated, induced their slaves to escape because they could not directly confront the possibility that enslaved people of color were capable of escaping on their own, to say nothing of contemplating escape. Northerners needed to believe that white abolitionists led the struggle against slavery and enhanced the lives of free people of color in the bargain (fig. 66). New Bedford has long linked the city's first Friends meetinghouse with Frederick Douglass's first home as a free man, even though the building no longer belonged to the city's Quaker congregation at that time, no evidence exists that Douglass lived in it, and Douglass himself stated repeatedly that he lived with Nathan and Polly Johnson in their home next door. In June 1920 the New Bedford *Sunday Standard* published an extensive article about a "secret chamber," complete with a "signaling device," in the home of one of the city's white merchants on Sixth Street. The report left no question, even as it presented no documentation, that the room was built to conceal fugitive slaves. "Everybody knows the part New Bedford played in pre–Civil War days, how runaway slaves were sheltered here, and how staunch abolitionists made this city the greatest New England terminal, next to Boston, on the underground railway system," the *Standard* noted. "New Bedford was the keystone link in the great chain of underground railways."[52]

Among some abolitionists, like the Westons, there is no doubt that fugitives were critical promotional tools. Yet others showed a more heartfelt commitment to them. There is no reason to question the sincerity of such people as Elizabeth Rodman, who told Debora Weston that "when she sits alone thinking over the horrors of slavery & the sufferings of the slaves it seems as if she could not bear it," or Sarah Arnold, her eyes brimming with tears as she proclaimed it "her duty to contribute to the comfort and happiness" of people of color. Women like these, socially proscribed from overt action despite their Quaker backgrounds and the efforts of such abolitionists as the Grimké sisters and Abby Kelley, did what they could for the cause: Arnold invited First of August celebrants into her home, and Rodman told Weston, "I'll give my money & my labour & my influence to the cause" even if she refused to petition "such a set of men as there are in Congress"

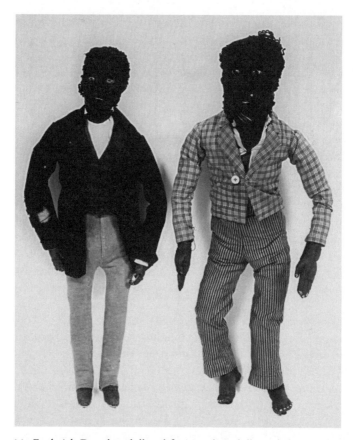

FIGURE 66. Frederick Douglass doll and fugitive slave doll, made by Cynthia Hill, late 1850s. Courtesy Old Dartmouth Historical Society / New Bedford Whaling Museum. According to her great-great-granddaughter Grace Howland Sargeant, who donated the dolls to ODHS, Hill made them to celebrate Douglass's passage from a slave to a free man at a time when the city was enamored of its role in such transformations.

on the subject.[53] For those abolitionists who are known to have helped fugitives, the ability to assist in some way in their dramatic escapes or in their northward flight confirmed—indeed, materialized—their professed antislavery sentiments. Northerners reveled, and arguably still revel, in the idea of their region as a safe haven, an area completely distinct from the slaveholding South, and assisting fugitives was the only action they perceived as available to make their commitment real. New Bedford abolitionists might give a fugitive a job, or shelter, or clothes, or food, and become thereby "practical" abolitionists.

So assured, white abolitionists were not necessarily called upon to address themselves to the larger question of race in their society, to whether New Bedford really was, as May asserted, the best place in the United States for a person of color, whether it was not itself prone, as Susan Paul, a Bostonian of color, complained, to the "spirit which persecutes us on account of our color—that cruel prejudice which deprives us of every privilege whereby we might elevate ourselves—and then condemns us because we are not more refined and intelligent."[54] People of color never talked about New Bedford in quite the same way that white people like May did; to Charles B. Ray the city's people of color were probably "better off than in any other place", to William Wells Brown they were "in advance of the colored people of any other place that I have visited in the State." In other words, in their eyes New Bedford was not the best place, but it was, considering how circumscribed their lives were everywhere, better than most. The city did not seem resistant to the settlement of people of color; it seems to have offered them work; people of color did for at least some of the time have political power; and some people of color were able to prosper. At the same time, the city was not so good that it kept its greatest antebellum achievers, such men as Sanderson, Borden, Nathan and Ezra Johnson, and Thomas Bayne, but it is possible that they took what they had learned in New Bedford to other places that, in their view, needed them more.

All of this is not to say that abolitionists who did not assist fugitive slaves were somehow not good or true abolitionists; it is only to say that for those who did, such assistance somehow proved their abolitionism. For New Bedford people, what fugitives did was a concrete symbol—as the *Standard* put it, "a heroism unsurpassed in the annals of fame"—that for a time drew together an antislavery community otherwise fractured by ideological difference and, most of the time, by race.[55] It may be true, in New Bedford as elsewhere, that white abolitionists were drawn to the principles they represented as much as they were to the practical need to assist them. George Teamoh noted that "after a few weeks of indulgence . . . you were 'free indeed,' and then thrown upon your own resources." It was then that black abolitionists, who saw the situation through a different lens, stepped into the fugitive's life.[56] White abolitionists on the whole came only gradually to the recognition that slavery was not merely a sectional issue; it took the passage of the Fugitive Slave Act for Charles Morgan to recognize, for example, that slavery was a curse upon the entire country. Because whites had not made that cognitive, and surely also emotional, leap, it was easy for them to separate the plight of the slave and the fugitive from the plight of the free northern person of color. But abolitionists of color, at least in New Bedford, never separated themselves from the enslaved millions who lived in the South; from the first days of their organization as antislavery advocates, their declarations suggest their assumption that free blacks were inseparable in every respect from slaves. Thus assisting fugitives in the long term was as much a part of their lives as finding enough work to support themselves and their families. Nathan Johnson took Frederick Douglass in, taught him about the community, lent him his sawhorse and saw, and would have protected him, Douglass trusted, if slave catchers came in his pursuit; Johnson did so much for him that Douglass, having later read "Lady of the Lake" himself, believed that "the noble hospitality and manly character of Nathan Johnson, black man though he was, he, far more than I, illustrated the virtues of the Douglas of Scotland."[57] To George Teamoh, William Bush was the greatest "patriot" in New England. Surely hundreds of men and women of color whose efforts have gone unrecorded, except perhaps in family stories, gave such sustained aid to fugitives. We know so comparatively little about them in large part because they assisted persons escaping slavery on an everyday level, that level of historical detail that generally eludes the public record. These men and women clearly recognized, whether free or fugitive themselves, that the line separating them from people of color in flight had never been well drawn and was often imperceptible. William Bush, Nathan Johnson, and other abolitionists of color were not afraid of abolitionism and what it might mean; their lives were already on the line, everywhere in the United States, no matter how far advanced a community of color was proclaimed to be.

Notes

Introduction

1. Daniel Ricketson, *History of New Bedford* (New Bedford, Mass.: By the author, 1858), 252.

2. See Elmo Paul Hohman, *The American Whaleman: A Study of Life and Labor in the Whaling Industry* (New York: Longmans, Green, 1928), 55; Margaret S. Creighton, *Rites and Passages: The Experience of American Whaling, 1830–1870* (New York: Cambridge University Press, 1995), 50; Zephaniah W. Pease, ed., *The Diary of Samuel Rodman: A New Bedford Chronicle of Thirty-seven Years, 1821–1859* (New Bedford, Mass.: Reynolds Printing, 1927), entry for 10 December 1822.

3. Leonard Curry, *The Free Black in Urban America: The Shadow of the Dream* (Chicago: University of Chicago Press, 1981), 129–32, has noted that only 10 of 3,269 cases of outdoor relief in Cincinnati in the early 1850s were for people of color, and those 10 were for burial costs; in New York City "sober colored widows, with small children, in extreme necessity" were denied poor relief until 1850. Philadelphia and Albany, however, did grant outdoor relief to people of color. I know of no study that has analyzed poor relief extended to fugitives.

4. Curry, in ibid., 60–61, notes that city directories tend to list residences with greater precision than censuses and permit examination of residential concentration over ward lines but that they probably underreport the presence of people of color in wards that were largely white. Directories tended not to list live-in servants or transients and only included heads of household.

5. Jeffrey Bolster, "'To Feel Like a Man': Black Seamen in the Northern States, 1800–1860," *Journal of American History* 76, 4 (March 1990). 1173 n. 2; Virginia M. Adams, ed., *On the Altar of Freedom: A Black Soldier's Civil War Letters from the Front* (Amherst: University of Massachusetts Press, 1991), xxii.

6. Lance E. Davis, Robert E. Gallman, and Karin Gleiter, *In Pursuit of Leviathan: Technology, Institutions, Productivity, and Profits in American Whaling, 1816–1906* (Chicago: University of Chicago Press, 1997), 81; Martha S. Putney, *Black Sailors: Afro-American Merchant Seamen and Whalemen prior to the Civil War* (Westport, Conn.: Greenwood Press, 1987), 2, 11.

7. Alexander Starbuck, *History of the American Whale Fishery* (1878; reprint, Secaucus, N.J.: Castle Books, 1989). Starbuck's research first appeared as vol. 4 of the *Report of the U.S. Commission of Fish and Fisheries for 1875–1876*.

8. M. M. Fisher, Medway, Mass., to Wilbur Siebert, reply to the UGRR Circular, 23 October 1893, in vol. 13, "Massachusetts," Wilbur Henry Siebert Collection (hereafter cited as Siebert Notebooks), Houghton Library, Harvard University, Cambridge, Mass.; Elizabeth Buffum Chace, "My Anti-Slavery Reminiscences" (1891), in *Two Quaker Sisters from the Original Diaries of Elizabeth Buffum Chace and Lucy Buffum Lovell* (New York: Liveright Publishing, 1937), 130.

9. Charles T. Davis and Henry Louis Gates Jr., *The Slave's Narrative* (New York: Oxford University Press, 1985), 319–27, includes a selected bibliography listing 106 autobiographical and slave narratives written by people of African descent between 1760 and 1865. This list does not include the narratives of John S. Jacobs, Edmund Kelley, or George Teamoh. William L. Andrews, *To Tell a Free Story: The First Century of Afro-American Autobiography, 1760–1865* (Urbana: University of Illinois Press, 1986), 335–342, lists 112 works of African American biography but not Teamoh's or John Jacobs's.

10. The year 1790 seemed a reasonable starting point as well because New Bedford was established as a customs district in 1789; the Dartmouth Monthly Meeting of the Society of Friends permitted New Bedford Quakers to establish their own meeting in 1792; and the first federal census was taken in 1790.

11. "Excelsior," "Increase of Cotton Manufactures" (1853), written in pencil "D. R./for the Standard" in New Bedford Benevolent Society Papers, Massachusetts Historical Society (hereafter cited as MHS), Boston; I. C. Ray, New Bedford, to Olive Hinckley, Marstons Mills, Barnstable, Mass., 28 March 1848, Isaiah C. Ray Papers (hereafter cited as Ray Papers), New Bedford Free Public Library (hereafter cited as NBFPL).

12. Davis et al., *In Pursuit of Leviathan,* have found that captains and first and second mates on New Bedford whalers tended to earn more than their counterparts on merchant vessels between 1840 and 1866, while cooks, skilled seamen, and semiskilled seamen tended to earn less in this period. Compared with average monthly wages for artisans ashore between 1840 and 1856, boatsteerers, carpenters, cooks, and stewards—all positions but carpenters most apt to be filled by men of color—uniformly made less, while captains and first mates uniformly made more. In ten of those eighteen years, second mates earned more per month than onshore artisans, and both third mates and coopers earned more in three of those years. Unskilled seamen on whalers always earned less than unskilled workers in the Northeast as a whole, unskilled workers in the region's textile mills, unskilled factory workers, and common laborers. See tables 5.6 and 5.8.

13. Henry Howland Crapo, "Memorandum of Tax Delinquents," 1837–41, NBFPL.

14. An advertisement calling for the retrieval of "a black Sailor, by name JESSE CARPENTER" who had deserted the ship *Eliza* described him as wearing "when he went away, a blue sailor's jacket, the seams covered with white canvass, and a pair of new blue cloth trousers in shape much larger at bottom than usual." New-Bedford *Medley,* 24 June 1796, 3:4. On sailor's clothing generally, see Marcus Rediker, *Between the Devil and the Deep Blue Sea* (New York: Cambridge University Press, 1979), 11, and Jeffrey Bolster, *Black Jacks: African American Seamen in the Age of Sail* (Cambridge: Harvard University Press, 1997), 91–92. The ratio of Quakers to seamen is based on Elmo Hohman's estimate of the number of whaling crew in New Bedford in 1855 (10,000) and the New Bedford Monthly Meeting's tally of membership in 1857 (267). See Hohman, *American Whaleman,* 42, and "Record of the Members Births &c of the Monthly Meeting of New Bedford" (beginning February 1793, and hereafter cited as NB MM Records), New England Yearly Meeting of Friends Records, Rhode Island Historical Society (hereafter cited as RIHS), Providence.

15. Hohman, *American Whaleman,* 51–52; Charles T. Congdon, *Reminiscences of a Journalist* (Boston: James R. Osgood and Company, 1880), 14–15. Congdon was born in New Bedford on 7 April 1821; see *Dictionary of American Biography,* s.v. "Congdon, Charles Taber."

16. Thanks to the New Bedford Election Commission and Michael Bachstein of the city planning department for these figures, which came from the 1990 census and from the Portuguese consul.

17. Milton Meltzer and Patricia G. Holland, *Lydia Maria Child: Selected Letters, 1817–1880* (Amherst: University of Massachusetts Press, 1982), 80; Thomas Wentworth Higginson, Glimpsewood, Dublin, N. H., to Siebert, 24 July 1896, in vol. 14, "Massachusetts," Siebert Notebooks.

18. Wilbur H. Siebert, *The Underground Railroad in Massachusetts* (Worcester, Mass.: American Antiquarian Society, 1936), 5. Siebert's citation of this case, involving Josiah Quincy, appears to have been an article in the *Boston Globe,* 15 September 1900.

19. Wm Rotch Jr., Newport, 8 mo 27 1789, to Moses Brown, Moses Brown Papers, RIHS.

20. Larry Gara, *The Liberty Line: The Legend of the Underground Railroad* (Lexington: University of Kentucky Press, 1961), 18, 130–31, 160; E. Delorus Preston, "The Genesis of the Underground Railroad," *Journal of Negro History* 18, 2 (April 1933): 144.

21. Gara, *Liberty Line,* 18, 90, 92–93.

1. "The True Ring of Freedom"

1. This letter from Robeson was quoted in Edward S. Adams, "Anti-Slavery Activity in Fall River," *Fall River Herald News,* 7 March 1939. The original letter has not been found, and no other correspondence from Robeson on fugitive slaves is known to exist. Gary Collison has noted that 1854 was a "particularly bad year" for slave owners in Norfolk and adjacent Portsmouth; see his *Shadrach Minkins: From Fugitive Slave to Citizen* (Cambridge: Harvard University Press, 1997), 45.

2. The names of some of those in Hodsdon's party appeared in "Virginians Aroused!," *Republican Standard,* 13 March 1854, 2:1.

3. "From the Portsmouth Globe of Friday: Insult and Outrage upon the Rights of the South!" *The American Beacon, and Norfolk and Portsmouth Daily Advertiser,* 17 January 1854, 2:1. The incident was reported in the *Republican Standard* as "Fugitive Slaves," 12 January 1854, 2:3, "Tempest in a Teapot," 9 February 1854, 2:4, and "Virginians Aroused!"

4. Chace, "My Anti-Slavery Reminiscences," 130.

5. "Insult and Outrage upon the Rights of the South!"; "Tempest in a Teapot" quotes an unnamed Virginia newspaper's opinion of Anthony.

6. "Meeting of the Citizens of New-Berne," *Republican and Patriot* (Goldsboro, N.C.), 2 October 1851; thanks to Paul Cyr of the New Bedford Free Public Library for providing me with a photocopy of this article.

7. "Reply to a Portion of the Citizens of Newbern, in Council," *National Anti-Slavery Standard,* 20 November 1851, 101:1–4; substantially the same account appeared in the *Daily Evening Standard* (New Bedford, Mass.), 28 October 1851, 1:1, 4:1.

8. Petersburg *Express,* quoted in *Republican Standard,* 16 February 1854, 2:4.

9. "Tempest in a Teapot"; Daniel Ricketson to the *Standard,* 17 March 1853, clipping in New Bedford Benevolent Society Papers, MHS; William Still, *The Underground Railroad. A Record of Facts, Authentic Narratives, Letters, &c., Narrating the Hardships Hair-breadth Escapes and Death Struggles of the Slaves in Their Effort for Freedom, as Related by Themselves and Others, or Witnessed by the Author . . .* (1871; reprint, Chicago: Johnson Publishing, 1970), 263; F. N. Boney, Richard L. Hume, and Rafia Zafar, *God Made Man, Man Made the Slave: The Autobiography of George Teamoh* (Macon, Ga.: Mercer University Press, 1990), 106–7, 109.

10. Samuel J. May, *Some Recollections of Our Antislavery Conflict* (Boston: Fields, Osgood, 1869), 293; *Republican Standard,* 13 December 1860, 2:3; Frederick Douglass, *Narrative of the Life of Frederick Douglass, an American Slave: Written by Himself* (1845), in *Frederick Douglass: Autobiographies* (New York: Library of America, 1994), 94; *Colored American,* 22 July 1837 2:4, 3:1.

11. "An Abolitionist" to editor of *Republican Standard,* 24 March 1853, 1:3; Congdon, *Reminiscences of a Journalist,* 17; Frederick Douglass, *My Bondage and My Freedom* (1855), in *Frederick Douglass: Autobiographies,* 355–56; Caroline Weston, New Bedford, Mass., to Wendell Phillips, 9 February 1845, Weston Papers, Boston Public Library. The records of the New Bedford Benevolent Society at Massachusetts Historical Society indicate that Daniel Ricketson wrote the letter from "an abolitionist."

12. See especially William McFeely, *Frederick Douglass* (New York: W. W. Norton, 1991), 76–77; Earl Francis Mulderink III, " 'We Want a Country': African American and Irish American Community Life in New Bedford, Massachusetts, during the Civil War Era" (Ph.D. diss., University of Wisconsin, Madison, 1995), 2–4, 26–27; and Robert J. Cottrol, *The Afro-Yankees: Providence's Black Community in the Antebellum Era* (Westport, Conn.: Greenwood Press, 1982), 153–54.

13. Caroline Hazard, *Thomas Hazard son of Robt call'd College Tom: A Study of Life in Narragansett in the XVIIIth Century* (Boston: Houghton, Mifflin, 1893), 49–50.

14. Zephaniah W. Pease, *History of New Bedford* (New York: Lewis Historical Publishing, 1918), 1:11; Edward Byers, *The Nation of Nantucket: Society and Politics in an Early American Commercial Center, 1660 1820* (Boston: Northeastern University Press, 1987), 106, 115. Byers quotes Rev. Samuel Danforth of Taunton.

15. Pease, *History of New Bedford,* 9–10; Byers, *Nation of Nantucket,* 32.

16. Everett S. Allen, *Children of the Light: The Rise and Fall of New Bedford's Whaling and the Death of the Arctic Fleet* (Boston: Little, Brown, 1971), 67.

17. Alice Sue Friday, "The Quaker Origins of New Bedford, 1765–1815" (Ph.D. diss., Boston University, 1991), 252, 315; Henry B. Worth, "Sketches of Old Dartmouth Presented to New Bedford Chapter, D.A.R." (Paper, 28 December 1922), 15, NBFPL.

18. See the numerous entries related to the war, beginning about December 1775, in *The Records of the Discipline of Friends, in the Monthly Meeting of Dartmouth Containing a Register of the Several Transactions, in the Affairs of the Church; from the Tenth Month A. D. 1727, old stile, to the Ninth Month A. D. 1762, new stile, inclusive,* vol. 2 of Record of Men's Friends, Dartmouth Monthly Meeting Minutes, Whaling Museum of Old Dartmouth Historical Society (hereafter cited as ODHS), New Bedford, Mass., and "Memorandum Written by William Rotch in 1814 in the Eightieth Year of His

Age," in John M. Bullard, *The Rotches* (New Bedford, 1947), 176. According to George H. Moore, *Notes on the History of Slavery in Massachusetts* (New York: D. Appleton, 1866), 109, the Nantucket Monthly Meeting also declared in 1716 that "it is not agreeable to truth for Friends to purchase slaves and hold them [for] term of life."

19. Joseph L. McDevitt, *The House of Rotch: Massachusetts Whaling Merchants, 1734–1828* (New York: Garland Publishing, 1986), 197, states that at the beginning of the war, Nantucket and Dartmouth were not only the chief suppliers of whale products to England but their fleets were together 70 percent of all whaling vessels in the American colonies.

20. McDevitt, *House of Rotch,* 247–49.

21. "Memoir of William Logan Fisher (1781–1862) for His Grandchildren," *Pennsylvania Magazine of History and Biography* 99 (1975): 92–103.

22. Ibid., 367–68, 385, 403, 406, 410–11; Hazard, *College Tom,* 30.

23. Jeremiah Winslow, Havre, France, to "Ma Chere Elizabeth," 26 March 1838, Rotch Family Papers, 1824–39, MHS; "Memoir of William Logan Fisher," 97; "Reminiscences of New Bedford by William Logan Fisher," part 1 (manuscript, Wakefield, Pa., December 1856), NBFPL.

24. Friday, "Quaker Origins of New Bedford," 532, states that of the top 2 percent of taxpayers in New Bedford in 1795 (13 individuals), more than two-thirds were Quaker.

25. McDevitt, *House of Rotch,* 193; Davis et al., *In Pursuit of Leviathan,* 43, table 2.5.

26. Allen, *Children of the Light,* 82; Boston *Traveller* quoted in New Bedford *Mercury,* 9 July 1830, 2:5.

27. Pease, *History of New Bedford,* 37; Davis et al., *In Pursuit of Leviathan,* 4, 16–17, 29–30; Hohman, *American Whaleman,* 4–5; Allen, *Children of the Light,* 171.

28. Davis et al., *In Pursuit of Leviathan,* 14–15, 49, 158–60, 179–85; Hohman, *American Whaleman,* 15–16, 222–23; Bolster, *Black Jacks,* 220–29; "Sundry Accounts Dr to Whaling Voyages. . . . For the ship Frances Henrietta's cargo of sperm & whale oil & bone as she arrived from Pacific Ocean 2 mo 19th 1843. Wm N Raynard mas. Absent 3 yrs 6 mo 16 days," Waste Book, 21 Dec 1842–30 Nov 1850, collection 27, vol. 24, Charles W. Morgan Papers, G. W. Blunt Library, Mystic Seaport Museum, Mystic, Conn.

29. J. Ross Browne, *Etchings of a Whaling Cruise* (1846), ed. by John Seelye (Cambridge: Belknap Press of Harvard University Press, 1968), 495–96.

30. Hohman, *American Whaling,* 13; Davis et al., *In Pursuit of Leviathan,* 158.

31. *Whalemen's Shipping List,* 15 August 1854, cited in Davis et al., *In Pursuit of Leviathan,* 4 n. 11; "The Material Wealth of New Bedford," *Republican Standard,* 23 August 1855, 2:4; New York *Evening Post* quoted in *Republican Standard,* 16 August 1860, 2:5. The 1855 *Standard* article featured the wealth of the city broken down by ward, the number of poll tax payers in each ward, and the aggregate value of both personal and real estate in each ward. The total population was derived from the Massachusetts Census, 1855, vol. 6, Bristol County.

32. Pease, ed., *Diary of Samuel Rodman,* 37–38.

33. Debora Weston, New Bedford, to Caroline Weston, 5 October 1836, Weston Papers; "Municipal," *Republican Standard,* 28 April 1852, 1:2; Letter from Young Men's Benevolent Society to *Mercury,* 7 February 1840, 3:1; *Republican Standard,* 15 April 1852; "An Exodus," *Republican Standard,* 12 June 1856, 2:1.

34. Jean R. Soderlund, *Quakers & Slavery: A Divided Spirit* (Princeton, N.J.: Princeton University Press, 1985), 170–71, 186; Frost cited on page 170.

35. Quakers were 2 percent of the population of the United States in 1800, but 19 percent of all woman's rights activists born before 1830; 40 percent of female abolitionists were Friends. Cited in Friday, "Quaker Origins of New Bedford," 27.

36. Soderlund, *Quakers & Slavery,* 3, 185.

37. Frederick Douglass, *My Bondage and My Freedom,* in *Frederick Douglass: Autobiographies,* 355–56; *Life and Adventures of Robert, the Hermit of Massachusetts, Who Has Lived 14 Years in a Cave, Secluded from Human Society. Comprising, an Account of His Birth, Parentage, Sufferings, and Providential Escape from Unjust and Cruel Bondage in Early Life—and His Reasons for Becoming a Recluse. Taken from His Own Mouth, and Published for His Benefit* (Providence, R.I.: H. Trumbull, 1829), 15,

20; Charles L. Blockson, *The Underground Railroad: Dramatic Firsthand Accounts of Daring Escapes to Freedom* (New York: Berkley Books, 1987), 22–23, 43; Leonard Black, *The Life and Sufferings of Leonard Black, a Fugitive from Slavery. Written by Himself* (New Bedford: Benjamin Lindsey, 1847), 22–27; Chace, "My Anti-Slavery Reminiscences," 163; Rev. W. H. Robinson, *From Log Cabin to the Pulpit; or, Fifteen Years in Slavery,* 3d ed. (Eau Claire, Wis.: James H. Tifft, 1913), 12; *Liberator,* 4 July 1851.

38. I. C. Ray, New Bedford, to Olive Hinckley, Marstons Mills, Barnstable, Mass., 15 November 1847, Ray Papers; Pease, ed., *Diary of Samuel Rodman,* entries for 6 April 1843 and 25 January 1844; R., "Anti-Slavery Appeal," New Bedford *Mercury,* pencil date 1845, clipping in Ricketson's notebook, New Bedford Benevolent Society Records, MHS; J. B., "The Society of Friends," *Liberator,* 16 July 1847, 115:2. See also May, *Some Recollections of Our Antislavery Conflict,* 147, in which he stated that early members of the New England Anti-Slavery Society regarded Quakers as " 'birthright' Abolitionists."

39. Thomas D. Hamm, *The Transformation of American Quakerism: Orthodox Friends, 1800–1907* (Bloomington: Indiana University Press, 1988), 10; Soderlund, *Quakers and Slavery,* 18, 185; Ward quoted in Benjamin Quarles, *Black Abolitionists* (New York: DaCapo Press, 1969), 72.

40. Gara, *Liberty Line,* 5–6.

41. Chase, "My Anti-Slavery Reminiscences," 115–17.

42. Ibid., xxiii, 122; Meltzer and Holland, eds., *Lydia Maria Child,* 140; Joseph Sturge, *A Visit to the United States in 1841* (1842; reprint, New York: Augustus M. Kelley, 1969), 6.

43. "Withdrawal from the Society of Friends," *Liberator,* 10 February, 1843, 2:2.

44. Meltzer and Holland, eds., *Lydia Maria Child,* 40.

45. Pease, ed., *Diary of Samuel Rodman,* entries for 6 April 1843, 25 Jan 1844.

46. May, *Some Recollections of Our Antislavery Conflict,* 147, states that among Garrison's "earliest supporters" were "the large-hearted, open handed Andrew Robeson and William Rotch," both of New Bedford.

47. Meltzer and Holland, eds., *Lydia Maria Child,* 83; Herbert S. Aptheker, "The Quakers and Negro Slavery," *Journal of Negro History* 25, 3 (July 1940): 339–40.

48. Hazard, *College Tom,* 187–88, states that William Rotch Sr. was a member of the Providence Abolition Society, but he is not listed among the founders and was living in Dunkirk, France, in 1790; he may have joined at a later date.

49. "An act to incorporate certain Persons by the Name of the Providence Society for promoting the Abolition of Slavery, for the Relief of Persons unlawfully held in Bondage, and for improving the condition of the African race," June 1790, Series B, Folder 1, Austin Collection of Moses Brown Papers, in Archives of New England Yearly Meeting of Society of Friends, Rhode Island Historical Society, Providence, (hereafter cited as Austin Collection); Friday, "Quaker Origins of New Bedford," 1835; Moore, *Notes on the History of Slavery in Massachusetts,* 117.

50. Bullard, *The Rotches,* 218; Byers, *Nation of Nantucket,* 96, 166–67. Byers notes that indentures were a common agreement between whaling captains and islanders who had Indian or black servants; Indians in debt to whites on the island often entered into a form of servitude to work it off. The indentures were equivalent to hiring own's time as a slave in the South. On Rotch's vessels, the non-English members of the crew were, Byers notes, "more than twice as likely as their English counterparts to be working as indentured servants with their earnings going to their master," and he cites the case of Captain Noah Pease, who received from Rotch the "lay," or proportion of the voyage's profit, of his indentured servant Antony, whose contract he had purchased in the West Indies.

51. William Rotch Sr., Nantucket, to Moses Brown, 8 November 1787, Austin Collection.

52. Rotch Sr. to Brown, 8 November 1787.

53. See William Rotch Jr., New Bedford, to Moses Brown, 5 mo 6 1789, Moses Brown Papers, RIHS, and Elizabeth Donnan, *Documents Illustrative of the History of the Slave Trade to America,* vol. 3, *New England and the Middle Colonies* (New York: Octagon Books, 1969), 348–58.

54. William Rotch Jr., Newport, to Moses Brown, 8 mo 27 1789, Brown Papers; William Rotch Jr., New Bedford, to Uncle Francis Rotch, 7 mo 10 1792, quoted in Bullard, *The Rotches,* 263.

2. Origins

1. See Hohman, *American Whaleman,* 27–29, 144.

2. Byers, *Nation of Nantucket,* 156.

3. Richard Ellis, *Men and Whales* (New York: Alfred A. Knopf, 1991), 143, dates the introduction of tryworks on vessels to as early as 1750, though no scholar has been able to pinpoint when they became common. Starbuck, *History of the American Whale Fishery,* 43, states that a 1760 deed from William Wood to Elnathan Eldredge, both of Dartmouth, makes clear that a "Try house and Oyl shed" stood on the Acushnet River at New Bedford in that year.

4. Hohman, *American Whaleman,* 28–29.

5. Ibid., 25–26; Byers, *Nation of Nantucket,* 5–7, 159, 163.

6. On 19 November 1754 the state's General Court and governor ordered "that the Assessors of the several Towns and Districts within this Province, forthwith send into the Secretary's Office the exact Number of the Negro Slaves, both Males and Females, sixteen Years old and upward, that are within their respective towns and Districts." Dartmouth's report was signed 19 January 1755 by Bartholomew Taber and Abraham Sherman. 1754 Census of Slaves, Massachusetts Archives, Boston. J. H. Benton Jr., *Early Census Making in Massachusetts 1643–1765 with a Reproduction of the Lost Census of 1765 (Recently Found) and Documents Relating Thereto* (Boston: Charles E. Goodspeed, 1905), 11–12, 68–71, gives the number of slaves in Salem as 83 in 1755 and 176 in 1765.

7. Byers, *Nation of Nantucket,* 159, 255.

8. Ibid., 159; *A Narrative of the Life and Adventures of Venture, A Native of Africa, But Resident above Sixty Years in the United States of America. Related by Himself* (1798), reprinted in *Five Black Lives: The Autobiographies of Venture Smith, James Mars, William Grimes, The Rev. G. W. Offley, James L. Smith* (Middletown, Conn.: Wesleyan University Press, 1971).

9. Massachusetts Archives, 161:19; Friday, "Quaker Origins of New Bedford," 259, states that 2.3 percent of Dartmouth's population was black in 1776; the total population of Massachusetts was 349,094 in 1774, of whom 5,249 were black. See Lorenzo J. Greene, *The Negro in Colonial New England* (1942; reprint, New York: Atheneum, 1971), 74.

10. Which of the Kempton and Maxfield families these homes belonged to is unclear. On New Guineas elsewhere, see Byers, *Nation of Nantucket,* 167, 255; Horton and Horton, *In Hope of Liberty,* 77; Leon F. Litwack, *North of Slavery: The Negro in the Free States, 1790–1860* (Chicago: University of Chicago Press, 1961), 168 n.; Col. Gardner Morse, "Recollections of the Appearance of New Haven and of Its Business Enterprises and Movements in Real Estate between 1825 and 1837," *Papers of the New Haven Colony Historical Society* 5 (1894): 98–99.

11. "Reminiscences of New Bedford by William Logan Fisher," part 3 (January 1857). Fisher stated that at the turn of 1800 "there were many Indians in the neighborhood of New Bedford" and that "some of the gravest men in New Bedford went out to dine with Pero," whose house was accessible by a path through the woods. Aaron Childs, the only householder of color identified in the 1790 census, was the largest subscriber to the purchase of the bell placed in the village's first Congregational church, later Liberty Hall, in 1796.

12. William D. Piersen, *Black Yankees: The Development of an Afro-American Subculture in Eighteenth-Century New England* (Amherst: University of Massachusetts Press, 1988), 164; Greene, *Negro in Colonial New England,* 74. The 1790 and 1800 figures for people of color are from my own research; the town population totals are from the First Census of the United States (1790), Bristol County. In New Bedford alone, the proportion of total population that was black rose from 1.14 percent in 1790 to 3.66 percent in 1800.

13. On the transactions of the Dartmouth Monthly Meeting with respect to Friends who owned slaves, see DMM, 7 mo 1772; 1, 4, 9, and 11 mo 1774, and 1 and 2 mo 1777, the last of which is a record of a manumission of John Akin's Indian slave Hazzard. For the text and signers of the 1780 petition, see the Paul Cuffe Papers, NBFPL, and the transcript in Herbert Aptheker, ed., *A Documentary History of the Negro People in the United States* (New York: The Citadel Press, 1962), 14–16. For information on Pero Howland, see his obituary in the New Bedford *Mercury,* 11 September 1829. Benton Jr., *Early Census Making,* and Bettye Hobbs Pruitt, ed., *The Massachusetts Tax Valuation List*

of 1771 (Boston: G. K. Hall, 1978), offer population figures predating the first federal census, though the 1771 census for Dartmouth is incomplete; the manuscript page showing population total for the town notes that seventeen pages preceded it, of which only eight have survived. See Pruitt, ed., *Massachusetts Tax Valuation,* 792. On Venter Sampson, see Bullard, *The Rotches,* 16, and Leonard Bolles Ellis, *History of New Bedford and Its Vicinity, 1602–1892* (Syracuse, N.Y.: D. Mason, 1892), 60–61. On Leonard Jarvis's two slaves, see Leonard Jarvis, Newport Accounts, Mss 491, Rhode Island Historical Society.

14. On the numbers of slaves in mid-eighteenth-century New England and on the slave trade, see Bolster, *Black Jacks,* 11; Daniel M. Johnson and Rex R. Campbell, *Black Migration in America: A Social Demographic History* (Durham, N.C.: Duke University Press, 1981), 10; Piersen, *Black Yankees,* 18, 44, 164 table 2, 165 table 4; Jay Coughtry, *The Notorious Triangle: Rhode Island and the African Slave Trade, 1700–1807* (Philadelphia: Temple University Press, 1981), xi, 37, 47, 165, 169, 245–50, 295 n. 28; Greene, *Negro in Colonial New England,* 88, 344 appendix D; for documents on the involvement of Lopez and Rivera in the slave trade, see Donnan, *Documents,* 3:205–6, 211–13, 275.

15. Cottrol, *Afro-Yankees,* 16.

16. According to Edward Channing, such names as Updike, McSparran, Fayerweather, Hazard, and Robinson were among the "leaders" of Narrangansett planter society. See Channing, "The Narragansett Planters: A Study of Causes," *Johns Hopkins University Studies in Historical and Political Science,* 4th ser., 3 (March 1886): 7, 15–16.

17. Rhode Island Monthly Meeting Slave Manumissions, 1708–1827, RIHS.

18. Greene, *Negro in Colonial New England,* 350–59 appendix H.

19. Lamont D. Thomas, *Paul Cuffe: Black Entrepreneur and Pan-Africanist* (Urbana: University of Illinois Press, 1986, 3–4).

20. Piersen, *Black Yankees,* 4, 6–7; "Death of an Aged Woman," *Republican Standard,* 28 April 1853, 2:4. Piersen's statement that probably "more than three-quarters of New England's black immigrants were African by birth" does not attach the estimate to a particular year, but he seems to be making a general statement about the eighteenth century. It does not tally very well with Peter Kolchin, *American Slavery, 1619–1877* (New York: Hill and Wang, 1993), 49, which asserts that by the time the Revolution began "about 80 percent of blacks in America and as many as 90 percent of those in the upper South and in the North were American-born."

21. New Bedford Overseers of the Poor, vol. 3, 19 October 1864 (hereafter cited as NB Poor Records). There were three state almshouses, all created in 1852, at Bridgewater, Tewksbury, and Monson. Presumably Makela was sent to Bridgewater. Others who claimed African nativity were Martin Coryell and Catherine Goings, both listed in the 1860 federal census, Benjamin Ross, Newport Gardner, and Janme Fute (sometimes shown as Jesse Fate); a section of the highlands of Guinea was then called Futa Jallon. A William Thompson, born in Africa about 1801, shipped out on the New Bedford whaler *Montezuma* in 1846. Robert Fogel, *Without Consent or Contract* (New York: W. W. Norton, 1989), 32, has estimated that just more than 20 percent of the black population in the United States in 1790 were born in Africa.

22. J. L. Dillard, *Black Names,* vol. 13 of *Contributions to the Sociology of Language,* ed. Joshua A. Fishman (The Hague: Mouton, 1976), 91; John Thornton, "Central African Names and African-American Naming Patterns," *William and Mary Quarterly,* 3d ser., 50, 4 (October 1993): 727–28.

23. Quaco Bailey married and purchased land in Dartmouth, on the road leading into New Bedford from the west, in 1796, and lived in the city at 29 Allen Street until his death about 1850. His sons, Abraham, George, and Humphrey, and daughter, Martha, who married David Fletcher, were also lifelong New Bedford residents. Cugo Canaday, identified as a "negro" of Dartmouth, married "negro" Rebeckah Shaw of the same town on 12 January 1749.

24. See William Anthony Jr., Dartmouth, to Peter Quanwill, Dartmouth, 3 February 1783, Book 10, Page 379, "Old Deeds," Bristol County Registry of Deeds, New Bedford, Mass (hereafter cited as Bristol County Deeds). Quanwell seems to have married twice; he published a notice in the 23 January 1795 New Bedford *Medley* that his wife "Mather . . . has eloped from my bed and board" and stated that he refused to pay any debts she might incur. He married Hannah White of Westport in 1810 and died six years later.

25. On Peter Quanwell, see page 113 of the ledger book of William R. Rotch and Company, Rotch Papers, MHS; on Joseph, see NB Poor Records, vol. 1 (1845–52), 89, NBFPL. On James Quanwell, see Putney, *Black Sailors*, 113 n. 23.

26. Lorenzo J. Greene, "The New England Negro as Seen in Advertisements for Runaway Slaves," *Journal of Negro History* 29, 2 (April 1944): 130–31; Gary B. Nash, *Forging Freedom: The Formation of Philadelphia's Black Community, 1720–1840* (Cambridge: Harvard University Press, 1988), 81.

27. Pease, ed., *Life in New Bedford*, entry for 11 September 1823. Two persons of color are listed as living in Anthony's household in the 1820 federal census. One of them was probably Henry, or Harry, who in late June 1823 escaped from the house through a window; Anthony suspected he had gone to Haiti in the sloop *William*. Scipio might have been another; Scipio Rome was listed in his own household in 1810 but not in 1820, and from 1836 he appears in his own home in directories.

28. Dillard, *Black Names*, 18; Nash, *Forging Freedom*, 83 table 1. James Oliver Horton, *Free People of Color: Inside the African American Community* (Washington, D.C.: Smithsonian Institution Press, 1993), 154, suggests that "the classical slave names (Cato, Caesar, and Pompey) so fashionable among slaveholders were discarded by many African Americans as they became free." See also James Oliver Horton and Lois E. Horton, *In Hope of Liberty: Culture, Community, and Protest among Northern Free Blacks, 1700–1860* (New York: Oxford University Press, 1997), 78, on the persistence of African names.

29. Thornton, "Central African Names," 737–38. Thornton notes that most slaves in smugglers' inventories were listed by a single name such as Gombe, Pary, and Samba, which implies that they came from "a non-Christian population," while a "large minority" had double names.

30. Pruitt, ed., *Massachusetts Tax Valuation List;* Earle quoted in Carter G. Woodson, "The Relations of Negroes and Indians in Massachusetts," *Journal of Negro History* 5, 1 (January 1920): 47; Daniel R. Mandell, "Shifting Boundaries of Race and Ethnicity: Indian-Black Intermarriage in Southern New England, 1760–1880," *Journal of American History* 85, 2 (September 1998): 466.

31. The painting, titled *Indian Annis and the Thomas Taber House,* is in the collections of Old Dartmouth Historical Society, New Bedford. Born between 1740 and 1775, Anna had married the mariner Hezekiah Sharper, who died in 1810, and she lived alone in the small, old Taber house until 1851. Reuben Sharper, possibly a brother of Hezekiah, lived in New Bedford with his wife, Rebecca Talbot Sharper, from the 1820s to at least 1838; Reuben Sharper worked at least some of the time as a butcher, dressing Samuel Rodman Jr.'s hogs in 1829. See Pease, ed., *Diary of Samuel Rodman,* entry for 15 December 1829. These Sharpers may have some relation to the slave Sharper belonging to Colonel Enoch Brown of Middleboro; in 1775 James Bowdoin wrote Josiah Quincy that Sharper was "on a trading journey to Dartmouth, and the neighboring towns." Bowdoin and Temple Papers, 6th ser., 4, 393–94, MHS.

32. Martha Simon may have been one of the children of William and Nabby Simons, who lived in Fairhaven at the end of Sconticut Neck; Ricketson stated that the Wampanoags maintained a summer camping ground there. The New Bedford *Mercury* of 11 November 1842, 1:6, reported the death at about age 80 of Sally Simons, daughter of William and Nabby Simons and born on Sconticut Neck. A coroner's inquest the day before had determined that she died of "intemperance and exposure." The *Mercury* stated that Sally was "supposed to be the last of the Pawkananket tribe of Indians," Pawkananket or Pokanoket being another term applied to Wampanoags.

33. James Bunker Congdon, answer to the American Freeman's Inquiry Commission, 1863, NBFPL.

34. See Marilyn Halter, *Between Race and Ethnicity: Cape Verdean American Immigrants, 1860–1965* (Urbana: University of Illinois Press, 1993), for an excellent treatment of the early and later Cape Verdean presence in southern New England. It seems possible that such popular names as Antone, Vincent, and Nicholas may indicate the island of birth of some Cape Verdeans; among the twenty-one islands in the archipelago are nine permanently inhabited ones, including Santo Antao, São Vicente, and São Nicolau. Yet I have seen no literature suggesting as much. Cape Verdeans from the islands of Brava and Fogo are far more numerous in New Bedford and surrounding towns, but no surnames that I know of indicate those origins. Halter states that Cape Verdeans emigrated to the United States from all nine islands, and according to her analysis from a later period (1900–1920),

8.6 percent of Cape Verdean immigrants to New Bedford were from São Nicolau, 4.0 from Santo Antao, and 2.6 percent from São Tiago. See 24 n. 1, 42.

35. Allen, *Children of the Light,* 180–83.

36. James Bunker Congdon, "Cholera in New Bedford, August and September 1834," NBFPL.

37. Hohman, *American Whaleman,* 53–55. Hohman listed other names ascribed to Sandwich Islanders and pointed out that Hawaiians had to have a license from an island's governor in order to sign onto a whaling crew, and captains had to put up a bond of $200 guaranteeing the man's return within three years. Hohman suspected that these mandates "were honored more in the breach than in the observance" (53). My compilations of crews of color between 1833 and 1860, based partly on a synopsis of crew lists compiled by Charles Watson of Roger Williams University, Bristol, Rhode Island, and partly on my own analysis, shows the most Sandwich Islanders, 25, aboard whalers in 1853, when total crew of color was 156 persons.

38. Ibid., 42; Davis et al., *In Pursuit of Leviathan,* 42 table 2. 4. It is at least possible that John and Margaret Carmacker, who both married New Bedford people of color on the same July day in 1827, and George and Mrs. T. M. Carnacker, whose deaths are noted in Rev. William Jackson's vital statistics for Salem Baptist Church in 1861, were also Hawaiian.

39. NB Poor Records, vol. 3, entry for 11 February 1861.

40. Ship Outfits, Cargoes, Crew Lists, 1836–43, vol. 26, collection 27, Morgan Papers; Congdon, "Cholera in New Bedford."

41. The statement about William Vanderhoop comes from a notebook of genealogical information compiled by Charles Dudley Onley of New Bedford; many thanks to Carl Cruz for making this book available to me. On Randall, see John W. Blassingame, ed., *Slave Testimony: Two Centuries of Letters, Speeches, Interviews, and Autobiographies* (Baton Rouge: Louisiana State University Press, 1977), 320–25; Netta Vanderhoop, "The True Story of a Fugitive Slave; Or, the Story a Gay Head Grandmother Told," *Vineyard Gazette,* 3 February 1921; and "The Slave Case at Holmes Hole," *Republican Standard,* 30 September 1854, 2:5. Indian census taker John Milton Earle stated that Gay Head Indians were a mix of Indian, white, and black and also had "an infusion of the blood of the chivalry of the South as well as of the Portuguese and Dutch, as might be inferred from the names of Randolph, Madison, Corsa, Sylvia and Vanderhoop being found among them." See Woodson, "Relations of Negroes and Indians in Massachusetts," 48.

42. Horton, *Free People of Color,* 26; Theodore Hershberg and Henry Williams, "Mulattoes and Blacks: Intra-group Color Differences and Social Stratification in Nineteenth-Century Philadelphia," in Theodore Hershberg, ed., *Philadelphia: Work, Space, Family, and Group Experience in the 19ᵗʰ Century* (New York: Oxford University Press, 1981), 400 table 2.

43. Figures on Philadelphia's black population differ markedly from source to source, ranging from 4.8 to 8.8 percent of total population in 1850. See Curry, *Free Black in Urban America,* 246 table A-2, who cites the higher figure, and Hershberg, ed., *Philadelphia,* 465 table 1, 399. Philadelphia's free black population declined between 1840 and 1850 and increased at a much slower rate than it had historically between 1850 and 1860. James Oliver Horton and Lois E. Horton, *Black Bostonians: Family Life and Community Struggle in the Antebellum North* (New York: Holmes & Meier, 1979), 2, state that people of color made up 3.9 percent of Philadelphia's population in 1860.

44. These returns were reported in the *Republican Standard,* 22 December 1853, 28 September 1855, 17 July 1857, and 6 August 1857.

45. These figures come from federal population schedules. My own count puts New Bedford's black population at 1,011 persons in 1850. The black population increased greatly over the course of the decade, reaching 1,657 in 1855, and then appears to have declined slightly to 1,518 by 1860.

46. Samuel Ringgold Ward, *Autobiography of a Fugitive Negro* (1855; reprint, New York: Arno and New York Times, 1968), 3–4.

47. On Ferguson, see NB Poor Records, 1:122, and his obituary in the *Standard Times,* 15 May 1910; many thanks to Raymond Patenaude of New Bedford for making his clipping files available to me. On Handy, see NB Poor Records, 1:5.

48. Putney, *Black Sailors,* 125 table 6, 11.

49. Ibid., 11–12, 15; New Bedford Port Society Crew Lists, 1850, Old Dartmouth Historical Soci-

ety. Rarely are the total crew listed by year in any source on the whaling industry, but in 1850 Port Society records were.

50. Dorothy S. Provine, *District of Columbia Free Negro Registers, 1821–61* (Washington, D.C.: Heritage Books, n.d.), Reg. No. 1630, manumission recorded 25 May 1839; marriage licenses for persons of color in the District of Columbia, 1811–58, are recorded at the back of this volume. See also NB Poor Records, 1:149, and Fleetwood's death notice in *Republican Standard,* 18 October 1855, 1:4.

51. Provine, *District of Columbia Free Negro Registers,* Reg. Nos. 743 and 1250. Provine states that George Bell was a leader in Washington's black community and one of the founders of first school for children of color in the District. In his 1844 will he left one of the houses he owned to his son Lloyd, but Enoch was not mentioned.

52. Ibid., Reg. Nos. 175, 361, 362, 702, 1966, and 2156; see also the marriage licenses in this volume for William and Lucy Bush and Julia Ann Bush and William Cassel.

3. Fugitives, the Sea, and the Coasting Trade

1. Joseph Bates, *The Autobiography of Elder Joseph Bates, Embracing a Long Life on Shipboard, with Sketches of Voyages of the Atlantic and Pacific Oceans, the Baltic and Mediterranean Seas; Also Impressment and Service on board British War Ships, Long Confinement in Dartmoor Prison, Early Experience in Reformatory Movements; Travels in Various Parts of the World, and a Brief Account of the Great Advent Movement of 1840–44* (Battle Creek, Mich: Steam Press of the Seventh-Day Adventist Publishing Association, 1868), 18.

2. Douglass, *Narrative,* 59; Jesse Lemisch, "Jack Tar in the Streets: Merchant Seamen in the Politics of Revolutionary America," *William and Mary Quarterly* 25, 3 (July 1968): 375, 377.

3. McDevitt, *House of Rotch,* 61; Virginia Bever Platt, "Tar, Staves, and New England Rum: The Trade of Aaron Lopez of Newport, Rhode Island, with Colonial North Carolina," *North Carolina Historical Review* 48, 1 (January 1971); William F. Macy, "North Carolina Nantucketers," *Proceedings of the Nantucket Historical Association* (1934): 21; William Rotch Jr. to Zacchariah Hillman, 27 November 1791, in Bullard, *The Rotches,* 259–60; New Bedford *Medley,* 27 November 1792 and 21 July 1794; Letter Book No. 2 Belonging to William Rotch Jr., Commencing 7 month 1792, Subgroup 3, Series A, Box 3, Rotch Collection, MSS 2, ODHS.

4. Collison, *Shadrach Minkins,* 46.

5. Massachusetts Supreme Court Justice William Cushing wrote in the third and final decision about the status of Quock Walker, "The idea of slavery is inconsistent with our own conduct and Constitution; and there can be no such thing as perpetual servitude of a rational creature." See Donald M. Jacobs, "David Walker and William Lloyd Garrison: Racial Cooperation and the Shaping of Boston Abolitionism," in *Courage and Conscience: Black and White Abolitionists in Boston,* ed. Donald M. Jacobs (Bloomington: Indiana University Press for Boston Athenaeum, 1993), 7. For background on the Quock Walker litigation, see also Helen Tunnicliff Catteral, ed., *Judicial Cases concerning American Slavery and the Negro,* vol. 4, *Cases from the Courts of New England, the Middle States, and the District of Columbia* (New York: Octagon Books, 1968), 465–67, and Moore, *Notes on the History of Slavery,* 214–15.

6. Thomas Hazard Jr., New Bedford, 24 June 1792, to Moses Brown; Thomas Rotch, New Bedford, 1 July 1792, to Brown, Brown Papers, RIHS.

7. Bullard, *The Rotches,* 263.

8. New Bedford *Medley,* 26 August 1794, 28 April 1797, 24 June 1796, and 26 April 1799.

9. The vessels that Paul Cuffe built and/or owned were recorded in a memorandum by his brother John, transcribed by Joseph Congdon of New Bedford and now in the Cuffe Papers, NBFPL. On Cuffe's trading sphere, see George Salvador, *Paul Cuffe, The Black Yankee, 1759–1817* (New Bedford: Reynolds-DeWalt Printing, 1969), 15; Horatio Howard, *A Self-Made Man, Capt. Paul Cuffee* (New Bedford: Press of New Bedford Standard, 1913), 8–11; Thomas, *Paul Cuffe,* 18.

10. William Rotch Sr., New Bedford, to Samuel and Miers Fisher, 3 mo 22 1797, Moses Brown Papers, RIHS.

11. Thornton quoted in Nash, *Forging Freedom,* 101.

12. Paul Cuffe, Sierra Leone, to William Allen, 24 April 1811, quoted in Rosalind Cobb Wiggins, ed., *Captain Paul Cuffe's Logs and Letters, 1808–1817: A Black Quaker's "Voice from within the Veil"* (Washington, D.C.: Howard University Press, 1996), 120; Cuffe, Westport, to Simeon Jackson, 25 October 1816, quoted in Wiggins, 466; Cuffe to Allen, probably mid-June 1812, quoted in Wiggins, 226; Cuffe, Westport, to Peter Williams Jr., 20 August 1816, quoted in Wiggins, 450; Cuffe, Westport, to Thomas McTroy, 7 September 1816, quoted in Wiggins, 453.

13. See ibid., 214, 216 n. 6.

14. Sarah Howard, Bridgewater, to Paul Cuffe, 3 July 1816, quoted in ibid., 420. Cuffe noted the books she lent Howard in his letterbook, 3 October 1816, Cuffe Papers, NBFPL. For his loan to Reed see ibid., 186. The multivolume Clarkson work in Cuffe's library was no doubt *The History of the Rise, Progress, and Accomplishment of the Abolition of the African Slave-Trade by the British Parliament* (London, 1808); the Hicks volume was Elias Hicks, *Observations on Slavery* (1811). The other titles seem to have documented the deliberations in the British Parliament in advance of passage of the 1807 English law banning the slave trade.

15. Thomas, *Paul Cuffe*, 75.

16. Paul Cuffe, Westport, to Samuel J. Mills, 30 April 1814, in Wiggins, *Cuffe's Logs and Letters*, 283; see also 286–88.

17. These three were Aaron Richards, George Davis, and Moses Jenkens; Davis returned to Sierra Leone on Cuffe's 1816 voyage. See ibid., 260.

18. Thomas Rotch, Kendal, Stark County, Ohio, to Benjamin Ladd, 6 m 28 1817, transcript in Rotch-Wales Papers, Friends Historical Library, Swarthmore College, Swarthmore, Pa.

19. Rotch to Ladd, 6 m 28 1817; William F. Wickham, Richmond, Virginia, to Thomas Rotch, 14 November 1817, notes that Gist's 400 slaves were manumitted 14 November 1817, and a note in the handwriting of Mrs. Horatio W. Wales, to whom these papers passed and who donated them to the Massillon (Ohio) Public Library, on this letter reads, "Gist negroes settled near Hillboro [*sic*] in the 1830's on 'hundreds of acres of good farmland' after litigation says Grace Goulder." In 1962 a microfilm of these papers was made for the Friends Historical Library at Swarthmore, where the collection is called the Rotch-Wales Papers.

20. See the Cuffe Papers, 16 May 1816, NBFPL, and Wiggins, *Cuffe's Logs and Letters*, 216.

21. Gardner Wainer, London, Ontario, to John Cuffe, 1832, Cuffe Papers.

22. Gerald W. Mullin has noted that owing to the South's "insufficient urbanization and home manufactures," skilled slaves filled a critical gap on plantations large and small, the smaller ones making use of slave artisans trained on the largely self-sufficient larger ones. See his *Flight and Rebellion: Slave Resistance in Eighteenth-Century Virginia* (New York: Oxford University Press, 1972), 3 and 9. Frederick Douglass wrote that the home plantation of Colonel Edward Lloyd near Easton, Maryland, "wore the appearance of a country village. All the mechanical operations for all the farms were performed here. The shoemaking and mending, the blacksmithing, cartwrighting, coopering, weaving, and grain-grinding, were all performed by the slaves on the home plantation. The whole place wore a business-like aspect." See Douglass, *Narrative*, 22.

23. Ira Berlin, "Time, Space, and the Evolution of Afro-American Society on British Mainland North America," *American Historical Review* 85, 1 (February 1980): 62; Philip D. Morgan, "Colonial South Carolina Runaways: Their Significance for Slave Culture," *Slavery and Abolition* 6 (December 1985): 63–65; David S. Cecelski, "The Shores of Freedom: The Maritime Underground Railroad in North Carolina, 1800–1861," *North Carolina Historical Review* 71, 2 (April 1994), 193; Peter P. Hinks, *To Awaken My Afflicted Brethren: David Walker and the Problem of Antebellum Slave Resistance* (University Park: Pennsylvania State University Press, 1997), 3–4; Gara, *Liberty Line*, 23.

24. *The Experience of Thomas H. Jones, Who Was a Slave for Forty-Three Years: Written by a Friend, as Given to Him by Brother Jones* (Worcester, Mass.: Henry J. Howland, 1857). The Singleton episode is cited in Cecelski, "Shores of Freedom," 193 n. 78. On Baltimore, see Christopher Phillips, *Freedom's Port: The African American Community of Baltimore, 1790–1860* (Urbana: University of Illinois Press, 1997), 79.

25. Bolster, *Black Jacks;* Ira Berlin, *Many Thousands Gone: The First Two Centuries of Slavery in North America* (Cambridge: Belknap Press of Harvard University Press, 1998), 58, and Berlin, "Time,

Space and . . . Afro-American Society," 47–49; Rediker, *Between the Devil and the Deep Blue Sea,* 62, 106; Gary B. Nash, *The Urban Crucible: Social Change, Political Consciousness, and the Origins of the American Revolution* (Cambridge: Harvard University Press, 1979), 55–57; Nash, *Forging Freedom,* 11; Nash, "Slaves and Slaveowners in Colonial Philadelphia," *William and Mary Quarterly* 30, 2 (April 1973): 249–51.

26. Higginson to Siebert, 24 July 1896, in vol. 13, Siebert Notebooks.

27. Litwack, *North of Slavery,* 156; "Rights of Northern Colored Seamen," *Liberator* 11, 8 (24 February 1843): 4:1, Gara, *Liberty Line,* 23.

28. Mullin, *Flight and Rebellion,* 34–35; Berlin, "Time, Space and . . . Afro-American Society," 67; Douglass, *Narrative,* 20; *Narrative of the Life of Henry Box Brown, Written by Himself,* first English ed. (Manchester: Lee & Glynn, 1851), 7.

29. Mullin, *Flight and Resistance,* 34–37; Freddie L. Parker, *Stealing a Little Freedom: Advertisements for Slave Runaways in North Carolina, 1791–1840* (New York: Garland Publishing, 1994), 244.

30. John W. Blassingame, ed., *The Frederick Douglass Papers: Series One: Speeches, Debates, and Interviews. Vol. 1: 1841–46* (New Haven: Yale University Press, 1979), 5; *Life and Sufferings of Leonard Black,* 56–57.

31. Mullin, *Flight and Resistance,* 36; Morgan, "Colonial South Carolina Runaways," 58, 62, 69. See also Cecelski, "The Shores of Freedom," 176, who has noted that documents about specific antebellum North Carolina runaways "represent only the tip of an iceberg."

32. Morgan, "Colonial South Carolina Runaways," 63–65; Mullin, *Flight and Resistance,* 38, 94–98. It is worth noting that slaves in shoreside maritime work, such as coopers, shipwrights, and caulkers, were less apt to run away according to their share of the skilled slave population. These maritime artisans were 26.4 percent of this skilled group but constituted only 9.9 percent of all runaways.

33. Marvin L. Michael Kay and Lorin Lee Cary, "Slave Runaways in Colonial North Carolina," *North Carolina Historical Review* 63, 1 (January 1986): 14–21, found that 2.2 percent of slave runaways in North Carolina between 1748 and 1775 were watermen, whereas they were only 0.6 percent of the slaves on the Pollock Plantations between 1770 and 1809. Field hands were 87 percent of runaways and 90.1 percent of Pollock slaves. Their statistical findings are quite different from those presented in Cecelski, "Shores of Freedom," but Cecelski was looking at nineteenth-century data. They also differ markedly from those of Morgan and Mullin but are based on a much smaller sample. Still, Kay and Cary suggest with others that watermen probably ran away more frequently because of their level of acculturation, their "geographical sophistication," and the ease with which they could market their skills. Yet there may have been a relatively high number of African-born men among North Carolina watermen, and unlike Mullin and Morgan, these authors suggest that "the especially wrenching separations and traumas they experienced" may have accounted for their escape "in relatively large numbers"; African-born slaves, they state, were 54.1 percent of slave runaways in North Carolina between 1748 and 1775. These findings are opposite of Mullin's, whose analysis of 1,500 runaway notices placed in Williamsburg, Fredericksburg, and Richmond newspapers between 1736 and 1801 found that 1,000 of 1,138 runaways were American-born. The differences between these two studies may rest on their differing periods. Kay and Cary did not analyze post-Revolutionary runaway advertisements, and Mullin has noted that after 1775 runways changed their usual course. Rather than escape south to visit friends and relatives or to work, they increasingly ran north as slavery was outlawed in various northern states. See Mullin, *Flight and Resistance,* 129 and note to table 4.

34. Parker, *Stealing a Little Freedom,* 5, 621; Cooper's statement, made in the novel *Miles Wallingford,* is cited in Putney, *Black Sailors,* 11; Cecelski, "Shores of Freedom," 174.

35. Harriet A. Jacobs, *Incidents in the Life of a Slave Girl Written by Herself,* edited by Jean Fagan Yellin (Cambridge: Harvard University Press, 1987), 111–15, 128–29, 150–59.

36. Austin Bearse, *Reminiscences of Fugitive-Slave Law Days in Boston* (Boston: Printed by Warren Richardson, 1880), 8–10.

37. Austin Bearse is listed as a laborer living in the basement of 80 Maxfield Street in New Bedford in the 1845 city directory, and he is listed as a New Bedford subscriber to the *Liberator* who had moved to Centerville on Cape Cod by 9 January 1846 in Liberator Mail Book No. 1, Massachusetts

Account Book, 1840–60, Exclusive of Boston, MS.B.3.1, vol. 2, William Lloyd Garrison Papers, Boston Public Library.

38. Bates, *Autobiography of Elder Joseph Bates.*

39. James Brewer Stewart, "Boston, Abolition, and the Atlantic World, 1820–1861," in Jacobs, ed., *Courage and Conscience,* 106–7, has noted that Massachusetts's growing shoe industry "came to depend increasingly on southern markets," and the involvement of the state's textile mills in the production of slave clothing has also been documented. It seems logical to suppose that some of these products were taken south by New Bedford vessels. Historians have estimated that from 20 to 25 percent of New England textile production may have been "Negro cloth," made from very short, low-grade waste fibers, sometimes from lint on the floor. The records of the Hazard family's Peacedale mill in Rhode Island, preserved at Baker Library, Harvard University, refer to this cloth as kersey, Carolina plaid, and osnaburg, though other mills often called it Negro cloth. Before the war, Worcester County, Massachusetts, was a major center for the manufacture of brogan shoes and palm leaf hats for slaves. See Myron O. Stachiw, "'For the Sake of Commerce': Slavery, Antislavery, and Northern Industry," in *The Meaning of Slavery in the North,* edited by Martin H. Blatt and David Roediger (New York: Garland Publishing, 1999), 33–44.

40. W. C. Whitridge, New Orleans, to Benjamin Rotch, Cambridge, 29 January 1838, Rotch Papers, MHS. Samuel Rodman Jr. noted in his diary on 27 November 1837 that New Bedford's Henry Blood had visited him before leaving for New Orleans to attend to the business he had recently established there with William O. Whitridge. See Pease, ed., *Diary of Samuel Rodman.* See also Mary R. Bullard, *Robert Stafford of Cumberland Island Growth of a Planter* (Athens: University of Georgia Press, 1995), which documents the presence of the Rhode Island family of Nathaniel R. Greene on the Georgia Sea Islands before 1813.

41. Martin J. Butler, "A Study of William T. Russell's Role in New Bedford's Coastal Trade, During the 1820's" (typescript, Munson Institute, 1966), Blount Library, Mystic Seaport Museum.

42. See, for example, "Marine News," *American Beacon,* 18 January 1854, 2:6, and 19 January 1854, 2.5.

43. See Cecelski, "Shores of Freedom," 192; R. C. Smedley, *History of the Underground Railroad in Chester and the Neighboring Counties of Pennsylvania* (Lancaster, Pa.: Office of the Journal, 1883), 353–56; Irving H. Bartlett, "Abolitionists, Fugitives, and Imposters in Boston, 1846–1847," *New England Quarterly* 55, 1 (March 1982): 101.

44. William F. Macy, "Migration of Nantucketers to the South and West," *Proceedings of the Nantucket Historical Association, 39th Annual Meeting* (1933): 24–27, and Macy, "North Carolina Nantucketers," 21–25; Stephen B. Weeks, *Southern Quakers and Slavery: A Study in Institutional History* (Baltimore: Johns Hopkins Press, 1896), 107–8, 231–32, 237–38, 242; and Blockson, *Underground Railroad,* 61–63, 78–81, 192–94. Macy has stated that forty-one of fifty certificates of admission to the New Garden Monthly Meeting between 1771 and 1775 were from Nantucketers. Levi Coffin left North Carolina for Newport (now Fountain City), Indiana, in 1826, and his home and store became a lynchpin in fugitive slave traffic through the Midwest; Macy suggests that many who moved to the Midwest from the South, including Coffin, had suffered "great persecution" for their antislavery views and so moved to free states. According to Quarles, *Black Abolitionists,* 144, Coffin helped more than two thousand slaves escape over thirty-five years; one of them, Blockson notes, was Eliza Harris, who escaped first to the home of Quakers Simeon and Rachel Halliday, then to Coffin's at Newport, and then with other fugitives to Sandusky, Ohio, and across Lake Erie to Chatham, Canada West.

45. *Personal Memoir of Daniel Drayton, for Four Years and Four Months a Prisoner (for Charity's Sake) in Washington Jail: Including a Narrative of the Voyage and Capture of the Schooner Pearl* (New York: American and Foreign Anti-Slavery Society, 1853), 10, 20–22.

46. *Life of William Grimes, the Runaway Slave, Brought Down to the Present Time: Written by Himself* (New Haven: Published by the author, 1855), reprinted in *Five Black Lives,* 104–5.

47. See *Mercury,* 14 March 1817, about the possible dissolution of the partnership between Mingo and Allen; *Mercury,* 13 June 1817, 3:4, features an advertisement for "New Goods—for Cash. William Mingo, at the store lately occupied by ALLEN & MINGO, has just received an assortment of DRY GOODS and GROCERIES.... Please to call at Store No. 2, where the small commands will be promptly attended to./Dartmouth, June 12."

48. Letter from an unidentified New Bedford correspondent to John Parrish, Philadelphia, 9 August 1807, Cox, Parrish, and Wharton Papers, vol. 5, page 85, Historical Society of Pennsylvania.

49. In the 1850 census, Johnson's birthplace was listed as either "PA" or "VA"; no other statement about his birthplace is known to exist, and no record of a seaman's protection paper appears to exist. On Cuffe's trading, see Thomas, *Paul Cuffe*, 41–43, 79, 94; on the Howards, see their advertisements, usually on page 3, column 4, in the *Mercury*, 7 July and 24 October 1809, 30 October 1812, 14 January 1814; New Bedford Manifests, 3 October 1811, 4 January 1815, and 22 January 1817; on Johnson's trading, see Manifests, 29 April 1812; *Mercury*, 4 February 1814, 3:4, and 13 January 1815, 3:5; and Howard and Johnson to Paul Cuffe, 19 July 1816, Cuffe Papers.

50. Starbuck, *History of the American Whale Fishery*, 700.

51. William Rotch to Thomas Rotch, 14 November 1812, in Bullard, *The Rotches*, 251.

52. The New Bedford and Fairhaven populations were aggregated in the 1810 census and separated in 1820; Fairhaven was set off from Bedford village in 1812. New Bedford's population was 5,651 persons in 1810 and 3,947 persons in 1820, but adding Fairhaven's 2,733 persons to the last figure brings the total for the two "urban" towns in what had been Dartmouth to 6,680, a 18.2 percent increase in population over 1810. Growth had averaged about 30 percent per decade between 1790 and 1810.

53. These are the households of Michael Wainer, John Master, Alvin Phelps, Paul Wainer, John Cuffe, Thomas Wainer, Gardner Wainer, and Paul Cuffe. Master married Michael Wainer's daughter Mary, and Phelps married Paul Cuffe's daughter Mary.

54. On Benjamin Cook's death, see Paul Cuffe to Thomas Wainer, July 1815, and Cuffe to Gardner Wainer, 17 July 1815, in Wiggins, ed., *Cuffe's Logs and Letters*, 365–66.

55. See *Medley*, 23 January 1795, 3:4, and Peter Quanwell inventory, 6 April 1816, Bristol County Probate Court, New Bedford.

56. William R. Rotch & Company paid Williams three times in August and September 1828, and in April 1829 he advertised his clothes washing and mending service in the *New Bedford Mercury;* by November 1832 Williams advertised that he was cleaning and dressing "gentlemen's coats, pants, vests &c at his residence, No. 11 First Street." See Rotch & Co. Ledger, 37, 40, ODHS; *Mercury*, 3 April 1829 (ad placed at the end of January 1829 and 14 November 1832).

57. Nash, *Forging Freedom*, 136 table 3; Bolster, " 'To Feel Like a Man,' " 1183; Putney, *Black Sailors*, 94–95.

58. Bolster, *Black Jacks*, 191.

59. Hinks, *David Walker*, 50–59; Bolster, *Black Jacks*, 50–59, 193–94; Sidney Kaplan and Emma Nogrady Kaplan, *The Black Presence in the Era of the American Revolution* (Amherst: University of Massachusetts Press, 1989), 6–11; Horton and Horton, *In Hope of Liberty*, 52–53; Lemisch, "Jack Tar in the Streets," 399–400; *Monthly Repository* quoted in Thomas, *Paul Cuffe*, 17.

4. The 1820s

1. Sarah Morgan, account book, household expenses, 1820–35, vol. 43, collection 27; Charles W. Morgan, New Bedford, to William Logan Fisher, Philadelphia, 9 March 1822, box 1, folder 18, Morgan Papers. Sarah Morgan's account book documents that Polly Johnson worked for the couple at least through 1826 and that the couple also hired Rhoda Durfee, a daughter from Polly Johnson's first marriage, in 1820.

2. Griffith's "sworn narrative" of his trip to Nantucket and New Bedford is quoted verbatim in "The Quakers and Slavery: A Fugitive Slave Case in New Bedford Fifty Years Ago," *Republican Standard* (New Bedford), 14 May 1878, 3: 1–3.

3. *Commonwealth of Massachusetts v. Camillus Griffith*, October 1823 term, and *John Randolph v. Camillus Griffith*, April 1824 term, Records of Bristol County Supreme Judicial Court, 1822–28, vol. 4, Massachusetts Archives, Boston.

4. On the Randolph incident, see ibid.; "Quakers and Slavery"; Catterall, ed., *Judicial Cases concerning American Slavery*, 4:500, and New Bedford *Mercury*, 8 November and 6 December 1822, 28 February and 2 May 1823. In his diary entry of 17 March 1823, Joseph R. Anthony wrote, "Mr.

Griffiths came in the stage to attend the trial next week in Taunton for his assault on John Randolph, a slave, whom he attempted to carry off." See Zephaniah W. Pease, ed., *Life in New Bedford a Hundred Years Ago: A Chronicle of the Social, Religious and Commercial History of the Period as recorded in a Diary kept by Joseph R. Anthony* (New Bedford: For the Old Dartmouth Historical Society by George H. Reynolds, 1922).

5. Cooper was chair of the Nantucket colored citizens' meeting that termed the plan to colonize blacks in Africa "wholly gratuitous, not called for by us, and in no way essential to the welfare of our race; and we believe that our condition can be best improved in this our own country and native soil, the United States of America." See "A Voice from Nantucket," *Liberator,* 20 August 1831, 3:2. "Quakers and Slavery" states that Arthur Cooper died about 1852 and Lucy about 1862; she was supposed to be 107 years old.

6. *Mercury,* 8 November 1822, 2:5.

7. For the text of the South Carolina law, see Philip S. Foner and Ronald L. Lewis, *The Black Worker to 1869,* vol. I of *The Black Worker: A Documentary History from Colonial Times to the Present* (Philadelphia: Temple University Press, 1978), 218–20. See also Horton and Horton, *In Hope of Liberty,* 203, and Philip M. Hamer, "Great Britain, the United States, and the Negro Seamen Acts, 1822–1848," *Journal of Southern History* 1 (February–November 1935): 3–28, esp. 7–9.

8. William P. Powell, "Coloured Seamen—Their Character and Condition, No. II," *National Anti-Slavery Standard,* 24 September 1846, 66:1.

9. See Davis et al., *In Pursuit of Leviathan,* 372–77 tables 9A 1–3.

10. Ibid., 379 table 9B.1.

11. By the end of January 1823 Joseph R. Anthony had coupled "the great scarcity of money" and "disputes on Religious matters" as "the great topics of conversation" throughout Bedford village. See Pease, ed., *Life in New Bedford,* entry for 27 January 1823.

12. Charles W. Morgan to William L. Fisher, 18 March 1824, box 1, folder 18, Morgan Papers.

13. In a 19 November 1821 letter to his son Thomas in Kendall, Ohio, William Rotch Jr. documented the home building in New Bedford: "Joseph spent the summer with us finishing his house, and early in 10th month went for his family. . . . After spending a few weeks with us, they are now settled in their new mansion and appear well pleased with it. . . . J. Arnold's house is nearly plastered but they do not change until spring. B. Rodman got into his house last week. A. Robeson's house is nearly plastered. It is of brick in father's meadow, opposite Benjamin's." Rotch Papers, MHS.

14. Job Otis, a local apothecary and Old Light Quaker, made this statement in a now-lost manuscript describing the crisis among New Bedford Friends, cited in Frederick B. Tolles, "The New-Light Quakers of Lynn and New Bedford," *New England Quarterly* 32 (September 1959): 292.

15. See especially February (2 mo) 1772, May 1781, March 1785 in vol. 3 (October 1762–June 1785), Records of Men's Friends, Dartmouth Monthly Meeting Minutes, ODHS.

16. Samuel Rodman Sr., to William Logan Fisher, 15 September 1819, Rodman-Fisher Correspondence, Providence (R.I.) Public Library; Morgan diary, 30 March 1855, MR 121, Morgan Papers; Pease, ed., *Life in New Bedford,* entry for 23 March 1823.

17. New Bedford Monthly Meetings, vol. 401 (6 month 1808–6 month 1828), Records of the New England Yearly Meeting of Friends, RIHS. See especially the records of 8 month 1820 and 1 month 1821 for William Rodman Rotch, 9 and 10 month 1821 for Thomas Rotch, and 7 month 1822 for James Arnold.

18. Morgan to Fisher, 9 March 1822, box 1, folder 18, Morgan Papers.

19. Tolles, "New-Light Quakers," 297; Morgan to Fisher, 14 July 1822, box 1, folder 18, Morgan Papers.

20. NB MM Records. See also part 1 of "Reminiscences of New Bedford by William Logan Fisher," which states that about 1800 New Bedford people were "superior in virtue, to any town of the same number of inhabitants at that time in New England. They were good without ostentation, and wise without pretence." Fisher added, "I do not believe there was a single piano among them." Thanks to Tina Furtado and Paul Cyr, NBFPL, for making a transcript of Fisher's reminiscence available to me.

21. Pease, ed., *Life in New Bedford,* entries for 11 and 19 February and 3 and 24 April 1823. Pease's

edition of the diary of Joseph R. Anthony, disowned in 1820, is an excellent account of the dissension between Old and New Lights in New Bedford.

22. These figures come from Record of the Members, Births &c of the Monthly Meeting of New Bedford, [begun] 2 Month 1793, RIHS.

23. Tolles, "New-Light Quakers," 291–319, has argued that New Lights in New Bedford were "to be found among the wealthiest families in the city, families prominently engaged in whaling and other mercantile and manufacturing pursuits, at least eight of the most conspicuous were later listed among the richest men in the state." Though some historians have argued that the early 1820s schism among New Bedford and Lynn Quakers anticipated the Hicksite separation later in the decade, New Bedford New Lights did not tend to be the "struggling farmers and small merchants" who became Hicksites. See Hamm, *Transformation of American Quakerism,* 184 n. 18. According to Rev. Alfred Rodman Hussey, "Life of Charles W. Morgan" (1921), box 4, folder 22, Morgan Papers, New Bedford never had a Hicksite meeting, though New Lights did for some time meet separately in the old Friends meetinghouse, purchased at auction by New Light Gilbert Russell (father of the disciplined Russell sisters) in 1824; here in 1828 the abolitionist Benjamin Lundy presented what may have been the first public antislavery lecture in the town. New Lights also discussed but quickly discarded the notion of establishing themselves as a separate Quaker congregation in 1832. Many instead joined the city's Unitarian church. On the independent Quakers and Lundy's visit, see Pease, ed., *Life in New Bedford,* entries for 9 August and 2 and 9 November 1823, and 4 April 1824; *New Bedford Courier,* 1 July 1828, 3:3, Pease, ed., *Diary of Samuel Rodman,* entry for 28 October 1832.

24. Otis quoted in Tolles, "New-Light Quakers," 293.

25. Byers has argued that after the Revolution, Quakerism on Nantucket narrowed from a ruling oligarchy into a "sectarian faith," a change that "prevented the emergence of a consensus among the new leaders, who vied fiercely for power." After the War of 1812, private, voluntary organizations emerged to restore "moral order and social discipline" as Quaker hegemony continued to disintegrate and leading Quaker merchants increasingly retreated from the "world." This "tradition of privatism" cast government mostly as an organ through which to accomplish private ends, not an entity dedicated to the public good. "Because Quakerism no longer served to palliate social and economic differences or provide a set of common values and standards of behavior," Byers has argued, the rise by the 1820s in child poverty and vagrancy became a more serious social problem. Byers has concluded that Nantucket's experience coheres with a "new generation of community studies" that demonstrate "a degree of market orientation, individualistic behavior, contentiousness and social disorder, wealth stratification, and economic exploitation that would surprise readers who have relied on earlier historians for their picture of New England village life." See *Nation of Nantucket,* 7–10, 255–56, 261.

26. Byers has noted that Nantucket did not establish a public school system until July 1827; by 1829, when 627 children were attending public school on the island, more than one thousand were being taught in thirty-eight private schools or by private instructors. Ibid., 306.

27. Pease, ed., *Life in New Bedford,* entry for 12 April 1823.

28. Starbuck, *History of the American Whale Fishery,* 228–29, 238–39; the background on the *Camillus* appeared in "Burning of the 'Ark,'" *Evening Standard,* 5 April 1856, 3:2.

29. Pease, ed., *Diary of Samuel Rodman,* 37–38; Ellis, *History of New Bedford,* 245–51; Leonard Bolles Ellis, *History of the Fire Department of the City of New Bedford, Massachusetts, 1772–1890* (New Bedford: Printed for the author by E. Anthony & Sons, 1890), 27–28; *Mercury,* 9 August 1850, 4.1; "Burning of the 'Ark'." Contemporary accounts do not proffer the origin of the term "Hard-Dig," though the aged widow of African American mariner Samuel Cuffe suggested one to a reporter who interviewed her in 1903: "she has a perfect recollection of the old Cannonville hill in Kempton street which was so steep that it was locally known as 'Hard-dig.' It was very difficult for wagons to climb this hill, and even pedestrians found it no easy matter. Mrs. Cuffe recounted the fact that when her mother came over to New Bedford she and her sisters used to come as far as the hill in order to help the old lady up." See *Evening Standard,* 11 July 1903; thanks to Raymond Patenaude of New Bedford for making me aware of this article.

30. Curry, *Free Black in Urban America,* 100, 102, 112; Moore, *Notes on the History of Slavery,*

237–41; Horton, *In Hope of Liberty,* 164; Cottrol, *Afro-Yankees,* 54–57. Curry has suggested that the 14 July 1826 riot in Boston may have been related to rioting among Irish workers in the Broad Street area several days earlier, though Broad Street was on the other side of the peninsula Boston occupied.

31. Pease, ed., *Diary of Samuel Rodman,* entry for 18 July and 4–5 August 1826.

32. Ibid.; Ellis, *History of the Fire Department,* 28–28; Ellis, *History of New Bedford,* 246; "Fire!" *Mercury,* 11 August 1826, 3:2; "Riots," *Mercury,* 18 August 1826, 3:2.

33. Pease, ed., *Diary of Samuel Rodman,* entry for 23 August 1859; "The Ark," *Mercury,* 28 August 1829, 2:5; Ellis, *History of New Bedford,* 249–52.

34. "The Ark," *Mercury,* 28 August 1829, 2:5.

35. *Mercury,* 20 June 1830, 2:3, 2 July 1830, 2:3.

36. Pease, ed., *Diary of Samuel Rodman,* entries for 22 September 1829 and 16 and 23 October 1830.

37. It is possible that Johnson came to New Bedford with Charles W. Morgan from Philadelphia; his death certificate and his seaman's protection paper of 1848 record his place of birth as Philadelphia. Other accounts suggest he was a slave in Virginia and/or that he had purchased his freedom. Since 1821 the wages of his wife, Polly, and her daughter Rhoda Durfee, both also working for the Morgans, were credited to Nathan Johnson's account with Morgan. As Johnson purchased property in New Bedford in 1826, these credits may have gone toward this acquisition, though it is also theoretically possible that Morgan served as the intermediary in Johnson's purchase of himself. No manumission record for Johnson is known to exist, however. See Sarah Morgan Account Book, Household Expenses, 1820–35, vol. 43, collection 27, Morgan Papers; Charles W. Morgan to William Logan Fisher, 9 March 1822, box 1, folder 18, Morgan Papers; Charles W. Morgan, 1822 bills, microfilm 25, Morgan Papers. For an account of Johnson's New Bedford property holdings, see Kathryn Grover, "Nathan and Mary Johnson Properties" (New Bedford Historical Society National Historic Landmark Nomination, New Bedford, Mass., 20 January 1999), New Bedford Historical Society.

38. *Mercury,* 9 July 1830, 1.1; advertisement placed 28 May.

39. *Commonwealth of Massachusetts v. Thomas Williams et al.,* no. 71, April 1827 term, Bristol County Supreme Judicial Court Records, vol. 4; Pease, ed., *Diary of Samuel Rodman,* 26 April 1827.

40. On 25 January 1830 John E. Howard witnessed a seaman's protection paper for James H. Howard, born in Baltimore, a resident of New Bedford, and identified as his brother; Howard's poor relief record from 1848–49 states that the family came from Pennsylvania about 1820.

41. George W. Forbes, "William P. Powell" (mimeographed typescript, n.d.), Ms. AM 282 (19), Department of Rare Books and Manuscripts, Boston Public Library. Forbes cited 19 October 1833 as the exact founding date of the New-Bedford Union Society.

42. On the influence of organized abolitionism on racial rioting, see Leonard L. Richards, *"Gentlemen of Property and Standing": Anti-Abolition Riots in Jacksonian America* (New York: Oxford University Press, 1970), 17–18; Curry, *Free Black in Urban America,* 99–100, 110–11. Curry also suggests the possibility that increased immigration may have had a role in these crowd actions. In 1855, 55 percent of the population of Lawrence was foreign-born and 37.5 percent of Boston's, but New Bedford had 2,875 foreign-born in a total population of 20,389, or only about 15 percent. These statistics are cited in Mulderink, " 'We Want a Country,' " 48–49.

43. Scobey's research, presented in the paper "Transit Strikes and the Contesting of Urban Public Space, 1870–1920" at the American Studies Association annual meeting, Boston, 6 November 1993, seems to fit well such earlier crowd actions as those in New Bedford and Providence.

44. "Riot and Fire," *Mercury,* 22 October 1830, 2:3; Jeremiah Winslow, Havre, to "Ma. Chere Elizabeth" [his daughter], 26 March 1838, Rotch Family Papers, 1824–39, MHS.

45. Paul Boyer, *Urban Masses and Moral Order in America, 1820–1920* (Cambridge: Harvard University Press, 1978), 4, 7.

46. Ibid., 65, 68. Thanks to the Bostonian Society for helping me pin down the date of the first Boston atlas.

47. According to one retrospective account, New Bedford in the 1820s had earned the nickname "Mobtown." See "Burning of the 'Ark,' " 3:2.

48. Curry, *Free Black in Urban America,* 108.

49. According to Greene, *Negro in Colonial New England,* 117, citing the collections of MHS, 2d.

ser., 3:29, on some whalers in the late eighteenth and early nineteenth centuries nearly half the crew was black. As late as 1807 larger whaleships were reported to carry twenty-one men, of whom commonly nine were black; smaller vessels carried sixteen men, of whom seven were black. In 1807 the whaleship *Lion* carried three officers, eight white men, a boy, and nine men of color.

50. David R. Roediger, *The Wages of Whiteness: Race and the Making of the American Working Class* (New York: Verso, 1991), 106–8; the quotation is Roediger's, citing the work of David Dalby.

51. Pease, ed., *Life in New Bedford,* entries for 17, 20, and 27 January 1824.

52. See ibid., 110. Based on his far-reaching analysis of northern and southern cities before the Civil War, Curry has pointed out that no southern city had anything "remotely resembling a black residential area," while in "every real race riot from Cincinnati to Boston, the mob invaded the nineteenth-century equivalent of the black ghetto."

53. There are few statistics on population mobility in the literature that pertain to this period. Stephen Thernstrom, *Poverty and Progress: Social Mobility in a Nineteenth-Century City* (Cambridge, Mass.: Harvard University Press, 1964), 31, compared later data—the 1850 census in Newburyport, Massachusetts, with the 1849 and 1851 city directories—and found that 45 percent of the "laboring families" in the town in 1850 could not be located in either directory. Peter Knights, *The Plain People of Boston, 1830–1880* (New York: Oxford University Press, 1971), 105, found in a sample of city residents in 1830, 1840, and 1850 that between 28 and 36 percent could be presumed to have left Boston, because they could not be accounted for at the end of a given decade.

54. Putney, *Black Sailors,* 33, mentions the runaway aboard the *Abigail.* Starbuck, *History of the American Whale Fishery,* does not list a vessel of that name leaving New Bedford in 1823 or 1824, though does list one leaving New Bedford on 19 December 1825; see pages 254–55. *Mercury,* 2 July 1830, 2:4. Smith's narrative is quoted in Robert C. Hayden, *African-Americans & Cape Verdean-Americans in New Bedford: A History of Community and Achievement* (Boston: Select Publications, 1993), 29. Hayden states in addition that Smith secured work through "the black anti-slavery and Underground Railroad worker, William Bush," but Bush was not in New Bedford until 1849.

5. The 1830s

1. Johnson's brother had also planned to escape, but in the end only Johnson and his mother went aboard. His brother, Johnson later learned, was sold to New Orleans, along with huge numbers of other slaves sent to the Deep South as its new cotton lands boomed, and was freed only by the Emancipation Proclamation. His account of his life and escape appears in "William Henry Johnson Dead," *Evening Standard,* 19 December 1896, and Warren E. Thomson, "William Henry Johnson," in Federal Writers' Project, *The American Slave: A Composite Autobiography,* reprinted in "The Underground Railroad in New Bedford," *Spinner* 4 (1988): 68; Thomson seems to have found the narrative in *Boston Globe,* 19 July 1925, in the Boston Globe Scrapbook, 60–61, NBFPL.

2. Johnson never mentioned in print that he worked on a whaling vessel, though his descendants recall his having stated as much.

3. A William Ransom Johnson (1782–1849) of Chesterfield, Va., father of the architect John Evans Johnson, is credited with having made horse racing popular in that state in the 1830s and was one of the first to race southern against northern mounts; no Andrew Johnson appears in the family genealogy or in the Richmond-area censuses of this time. See Henry W. Lewis, *More Taste than Prudence: A Study of John Evans Johnson* (Chapel Hill, N.C.: Borderer Press, 1983). Thanks to Melissa Morgan Radtke for searching for Andrew Johnson.

4. "Rev. Mr. May's Tour," *Liberator* 5, 2 May 1835, 2:4–5.

5. "A Voice from New-Bedford!" *Liberator,* 10 March 1832; Wiggins, *Cuffe's Logs and Letters,* 277, 298 n. 1. On the African Christian Church, see Charles Cook, *A Brief Account of the African Christian Church in New-Bedford* (New Bedford: Benjamin T. Congdon, 1834), NBFPL; "Legislature," *Mercury,* 5 February 1836, 2:3, which states that Charles K. Cook and other New Bedford residents had petitioned the Massachusetts House to incorporate the society; and "History of the New Bedford Churches: African Christian Church," *Republican Standard,* 14 September 1854, 1:4.

6. *Minutes and Proceedings of the Third Annual Convention for the Improvement of the Free People of Colour in these United States, Held by Adjournments in the City of Philadelphia, from the 3d to the 13th of June inclusive, 1833* (New York: Published by Order of the Convention, 1833), reprinted in Howard Holman Bell, ed., *Minutes of the Proceedings of the National Negro Conventions, 1830–1864* (New York: Arno Press and New York Times, 1969); see also *Liberator,* 10 March 1832, 22 June 1833, 24 May and 1 November 1834. The date of the founding of the New-Bedford Union Society comes from Forbes, "William P. Powell."

7. Henry Mayer has pointed out that the role of people of color in the founding of the New England Anti-Slavery Society has long been obscured because of their preference for retaining their own association. See Henry Mayer, *All on Fire: William Lloyd Garrison and the Abolition of Slavery* (New York: St. Martin's Press, 1998), 130–31.

8. Pease, ed., *Diary of Samuel Rodman,* entry for 23 October 1831: "Benj'n Lundy of Washington, Ed'r of the Gen's of Un'l Em'rs called and attended m'g with me. Afterwards called at J. Arnold's, father's, and Uncle Wm's"; 24 October 1831: "Rode to Tiverton to secure a 2d mate for the Margaret. Called with B. Lundy at Uncle Wm's and again in the ev'g." It was on Lundy's first trip through New England in March that he converted William Lloyd Garrison to abolitionism; his second trip to the region was in July the same year, when he had "large and successful" meetings in New Bedford, New Haven, Lynn, Salem, and Andover. See Mayer, *All on Fire,* 51–55. On Rodman's work with the antislavery petitions, see ibid., entries for 11–16 January 1832.

9. Pease, ed., *Diary of Samuel Rodman,* entries for 7–9 July 1832; Mayer, *All on Fire,* 130–31; Dorothy Porter Wesley, "Integration versus Separation: William Cooper Nell's Role in the Struggle for Equality," in *Courage and Conscience,* 214; *First Annual Report of the Board of Managers of the New-England Anti-Slavery Society, Presented Jan. 9, 1833. With An Appendix* (Boston: Printed by Garrison and Knapp, 1833), 7.

10. *Proceedings of the New-England Anti-Slavery Convention, Held in Boston, on the 27th, 28th, and 29th of May, 1834* (Boston: Garrison & Knapp, 1834), 48–50.

11. Dartmouth Monthly Meeting Minutes, Records of Men's Friends, vol. 4, 18 July 1785–6 June 1803, ODHS; New Bedford Monthly Meeting Minutes, vol. 402 [book 3], 1828–1850, RIHS; on Choules, see also Congdon, *Reminiscences,* 43, who noted that he was a friend of Cornelius Vanderbilt and "was particularly well versed in the history of dissent." Choules was also one of nine counsellors to the Bristol County Anti-Slavery Society in October 1837.

12. *Mercury,* 4 July 1834, 2:1, 3:1.

13. Hinks, *David Walker,* 160–71.

14. Richards, *"Gentlemen of Property and Standing,"* 21–25. Richards notes that there were four local antislavery societies in two states in 1832 but forty-seven in ten states by 1833.

15. Ibid., 11 July 1834, 2:3; 1 August 1834, 2:3.

16. May, *Some Recollections of Our Antislavery Conflict,* 144; Mayer, *All on Fire,* 103–4, 194; Pease, ed., *Diary of Samuel Rodman,* 19 April 1835; "Rev. Mr. May's Tour," *Liberator,* 2 May 1835, 2.4; "Letter from J. Walker," *Liberator,* 26 May 1848, 83:2–3; *Trial and Imprisonment of Jonathan Walker, at Pensacola, Florida, for Aiding Slaves to Escape from Bondage, with an Appendix, Containing a Sketch of His Life* (Boston: Anti Slavery Office, 1845). "Judge Jay's Inquiry," cited by May, was one of the pamphlets written by William Jay (1789–1858), son of the American statesman, who was a jurist, an active abolitionist, and a decided opponent of colonization.

17. "Abolition of Slavery," *Mercury,* 1 May 1835, 2:2.

18. Congdon, "Cholera in New Bedford"; "Black Spirits and White," *Mercury,* 18 July 1834, 2:3; 6 February 1835, 1:2; 12 June 1835, 1:1; "Daring Assault," 12 June 1835, 1:1, 18 December 1835, 2:2; "Court of Common Pleas," 25 December 1835, 1:5. Congdon noted that Dyer could find "no one among the coloured population to help him. So indignant were they at his conduct that they held a public meeting and passed resolutions strongly reprobating his outrageous attack upon me." When Dyer was due to be released in December 1839, Congdon wrote Jared Curtis, chaplain of the Massachusetts State Prison, to see what could be done to prevent his return to New Bedford. "I am afraid to have him come back," Congdon confessed, and he noted that neither his wife nor son, a mariner, wanted him to return. Mary Dyer had since taken up with another man, Congdon noted; he was

probably John Swain, a Hawaiian-born mariner whose name she had taken by 1850; he seems also to have been married when he came to New Bedford.

19. Clare Taylor, *Women of the Anti-Slavery Movement: The Weston Sisters* (New York: St. Martin's Press, 1995) provides biographical background on the Weston family.

20. Anne Warren Weston, New Bedford, to Maria Weston Chapman, 1 August 1835, Weston Papers.

21. Maria Weston Chapman, n. p., to Debora Weston, n.d. (probably late 1830s), Weston Papers.

22. Debra Gold Hansen, *Strained Sisterhood: Gender and Class in the Boston Female Anti-Slavery Society* (Amherst: The University of Massachusetts Press, 1993), 18.

23. Debora Weston, New Bedford, to Anne Warren Weston, 22 January 1836, Weston Papers.

24. "The rashness of enthusiasts" is attributed to Daniel Webster in Mayer, *All on Fire*, 53, see also ibid., 75.

25. Ibid., 241; Hamer, "Negro Seamen Acts," 14, 18; Cecelski, "Shores of Freedom," 202. In 1830 both the city of Savannah and the state of North Carolina forbade black sailors or northern free blacks generally from communicating in any way with southern blacks, although the latter's legislature overturned the state law in the next session because merchants there relied so heavily on black maritime laborers.

26. May, *Some Recollections of Our Antislavery Conflict*, 134–35; "To the Public," *Mercury*, 28 August 1835, 4:5 [reporting May's address of 17 August before the Massachusetts Anti-Slavery Society]; *Mercury*, 28 August 1835, 1:2.

27. May, *Some Recollections of Our Antislavery Conflict*, 134; *Mercury*, 14 August 1835, 1:5.

28. The merchants were David R. Greene, Charles Grinnell, Frederick Parker (the son and business partner of John Avery Parker), Pardon Tillinghast, George Randall, Isaiah Burgess, Samuel G. Stevenson, and Nathaniel Hathaway; the attorneys and officials were Greene, Clifford, Charles H. Warren, and E. N. Chaddock; Rowland Crocker was secretary of the Commercial Insurance Company and James H. Crocker was a cashier at the Commercial Bank; W. H. Crocker and Caleb S. Tobey were dry goods merchants; Jethro Hillman and James Durfee Jr. were artisans (a shipwright and blacksmith, respectively); and the occupations of two, Joseph R. Williams and William C. Whitredge Jr., whose father was a physician, are not stated in the 1836 directory. Whitredge was probably a trader as well. See "Public Meeting," *Mercury*, 28 August 1835, 1:3.

29. Anne Warren Weston, New Bedford, to Maria Weston Chapman, 1 August 1835, Weston Papers.

30. "Legislature," *Mercury*, 14 April 1837, 1:2; H249, 1837, House Unpassed Legislation, SC1, 230, Massachusetts Archives. Of the 122 men of color who signed the petition, at least 88 can be identified as New Bedford residents; of the 107 women, 101 were New Bedford people.

31. Hinks, *David Walker*, 118–19, 123, 135, 137–38, 138 n. 55, 142–45; Foner and Lewis, *The Black Worker*, 1:435–36 n. 30; Philip S. Foner, "William P. Powell: Militant Champion of Black Seamen," in *Essays in Afro-American History* (Philadelphia: Temple University Press, 1978), 88–111; Quarles, *Black Abolitionists*, 17.

32. See Pease, *History of New Bedford*, 37. New York, Boston, and New Orleans exceeded New Bedford in tonnage, and New Bedford's registered tonnage was nearly twice that of Philadelphia in 1845.

33. These figures are derived from my own census research. While the percentage of blacks living in white households steadily decreased in New Bedford between 1810 and 1840, from 50.2 to 10.9 percent, the proportion living in white households in rural Dartmouth and Westport rose over the same years, from 3.7 to 18.4 percent. That increasing percentage suggests the diminishing viability, for people of color, of making an independent living outside the port villages.

34. Martha S. Putney, "Richard Johnson: An Early Effort in Black Enterprise," *Negro History Bulletin* 45 (April–June 1982): 46–47.

35. "Rev. Mr. May's Tour," *Liberator*, 2 May 1835, 2:4–5; Works Projects Administration, "Ship Registers of New Bedford, Massachusetts" (Boston: National Archives Projects, 1940), 1:76, shows Johnson as part-owner of the *Draper* with Asa T. Lawton, John A. Parker and his son Frederick, Oliver Prescott, and William R. Rotch when the 1816 vessel was reregistered on 16 December 1847.

36. The Johnsons' ad appeared in *Colored American*, 9 May 1840. According to Hohman, *Ameri-

can Whaleman, 101, much of the clothing sold to crews was made in port towns through a putting-out system; outfitters bought cloth for local women to fashion into garments in their homes "at rates strangely prophetic of the later sweated trades in the clothing industry."

37. Charles B. Ray, "The Brig Rising States," *Colored American,* 11 March 1837, 4:2–3; Ezra Johnson, New Bedford, letter to the National Negro Convention in Buffalo, 12 August 1843, in *Minutes of the National Convention of Colored Citizens: Held at Buffalo, on the 15ᵗʰ, 16ᵗʰ, 17ᵗʰ, 18ᵗʰ, and 19ᵗʰ of August, 1843 . . .* (New York: Pierce and Reed, 1843).

38. "A Card," *Liberator,* 13 June 1835; "A Card," *Liberator,* 15 August 1835; "An Eastern Brother," *Colored American,* 24 June 1837; "Extracts from the General Agent's Letter," *Colored American,* 1 July 1837, 3:3; Charles B. Ray to "Brother Cornish," *Colored American,* 22 July 1837, 2:4, 3:1. Ray noted in July 1837 that it was difficult to estimate the size of the community of color because it had "never been the custom to discriminate between color, in taking the census," but this was not so; the first local listing of residents, the directory of 1836, did indicate whether a resident was "colored" with a "c." after his or her name. The practice continued through the 1845 directory.

39. Moore, *Notes on the History of Slavery,* 196–200. William C. Nell claimed that the February 1780 petition submitted to the state's General Court by Paul and John Cuffe and other Dartmouth men of color, which protested the fact that they were taxed for real property yet excluded from the franchise, compelled the passage of legislation guaranteeing the vote to men of color. But nineteenth-century historian George Moore found no evidence of legislation and cited historian Jeremy Belknap's 1795 opinion that nothing in the state's constitution, approved by the people four months after the Dartmouth petition, disqualified black men from voting or running for office. John Cuffe noted that Dartmouth blacks received no tax abatement from the 1780 petition and planned to renew the plea in early 1781.

40. "Colored Citizens in Massachusetts," *Emancipator,* 16 November 1837, in microfilm edition of *Black Abolitionist Papers,* Lamont Library, Harvard University.

41. Henry H. Crapo, comp., *The New Bedford Directory, Containing the Names of the Inhabitants, Their Occupations, Places of Business, and Dwelling Houses . . .* (New Bedford, Mass.: J. C. Parmenter, 1845), 42. Crapo also described Hard-Dig as "a small collection of houses on the north side of the Smith's Mills road a little east of Cannonville"; Cannonville was a neighborhood "at the junction of Noel Tabor and Smith's Mills road near the Meeting House." Smith Mill's Road is now Kempton Street; Noel Tabor Road, which ran north from Smith Mill's Road, is now Rockdale Avenue.

42. *Mercury,* 3 December 1830, 2:1.

43. On 19 December 1834, for instance, the *Mercury* (2:2) reported an "Incendiary Attempt" on the Bethel or Seamen's Chapel in New Bedford; and a week later a special town meeting was called to beef up the local fire department's arsenal and to compensate Richard Johnson and a white property owner for the damage to their properties from the November fire. See "Special Town Meeting," *Mercury,* 26 December 1834, 2:4.

44. "Destructive Fire," *Mercury,* 21 November 1834, 2:2; Pease, ed., *Diary of Samuel Rodman,* entries for 18 November 1834 and 25 October 1835; Joseph Ricketson Jr., New Bedford, to Benjamin S. Rotch, 25 October 1835, Rotch Papers, MHS. None of the men involved in these incidents appears in the city's first directory, issued in 1836, and Gibson is not listed in any census or tax listing in greater New Bedford before 1860. In 1918 Pease, in *History of New Bedford,* 146, noted that a one-story house belonging to the blacksmith Jonathan Smith, grandfather of Asa Smith of Ark fame, was "moved up to Nigger Town and is now cut in two and makes the two William Reed houses west of Dudley's. (This was Chepachet)."

45. *Mercury,* 29 July 1836, 3:1.

46. Debora Weston, New Bedford, to Anne Warren Weston, 1 February 1837, Weston Papers.

47. "Anti-Slavery Fair," *Liberator,* 23 August 1839, 135:1; "Free Labor Produce," *Mercury,* 28 December 1838, 3:1. Antislavery fairs had been organized in Boston since 1834 and, according to Hansen, *Strained Sisterhood,* 127–28, emerged from the "vanity fairs" that upper-class women's charities staged at that time. Maria Weston Chapman, Hansen adds, viewed the antislavery fairs as more like the male "Mechanic's Fair in attraction, and productiveness."

48. In August 1837 the General Association of Massachusetts Congregational Churches had issued

a "Pastoral Letter" denouncing women reformers and lecturers as "unnatural" and their activities as "a shame and scandalous offense against propriety and decency"; Garrison called the clergy "nothing better than hirelings, blind leaders of the blind, dumb dogs that cannot bark . . . [that] love the fleece better than the flock"; he wrote, "Abolitionism brings ministers and laymen upon the same dead level of equality and repudiates all clerical assumption, all spiritual supremacy." See Hansen, *Strained Sisterhood,* 22–23.

49. "Public Meeting in New Bedford," *Liberator,* 27 September 1839; "A Voice from the Colored People of New Bedford," *Liberator,* 21 June 1839, 2:2.

50. "Proceedings of the Meeting of Colored Citizens," *Mercury,* 1 November 1839, 4:6. Richard Johnson chaired the meeting, Nathaniel A. Borden served as secretary, and Ezra R. Johnson, Solomon Peneton, and Peter Nelson prepared resolutions.

51. Debora Weston, New Bedford, to Maria Weston Chapman, 8 November 1839, Weston Papers.

52. Debora Weston, New Bedford, to Anne Warren Weston, 25 November 1839, Weston Papers.

53. "The Election," *Mercury,* 15 November 1839, 1:1; *Mercury,* 20 December 1839, 3:1, Debora Weston, New Bedford, to Anne Warren Weston, 25 April 1839, Weston Papers.

54. Hansen has stated that Med was adopted by *Liberator* printer Isaac Knapp. See "Another Slave Case," *Mercury,* 26 August 1836, 1:6, "A Slave Case," *Mercury,* 6 April 1837, 2:1; Collison, *Shadrach Minkins,* 120; Hansen, *Strained Sisterhood,* 17–18. Horton and Horton, *Black Bostonians,* 97, states that the Robinsons claimed to belong to no antislavery society and cite 1827 instead of 1837 for this event.

55. Lydia Child, South Natick, Mass., to Esther Carpenter, 4 September 1836, in Meltzer and Holland, eds., *Lydia Maria Child,* 52–53.

56. "Trial for Kidnapping in Boston," *Mercury,* 29 December 1837, 1:5.

57. Debora Weston, New Bedford, to Anne Weston, 19 November 1837, Weston Papers.

58. "The Kidnapping Case in Boston," *Mercury,* 5 January 1838, 1:1–2.

59. Ibid., 74–76; Douglass, *My Bondage and My Freedom,* 354; Frederick Douglass, *Life and Times of Frederick Douglass Written By Himself* (1893) in *Frederick Douglass: Autobiographies,* 646–50. It is not known whether Joseph Ricketson Sr. or Jr. met Douglass. The elder Ricketson died 9 October 1841; the younger, born in 1815, would have been twenty-three years old at the time. Douglass stated that he carried with him "a line from Mr. Ruggles" for Nathan Johnson in *My Bondage and My Freedom,* 353.

60. The 1830 census shows 26 persons in households headed by persons named Johnson, while the 1840 census shows 29. These figures are probably next to worthless, however, as they could include boarders with different surnames and probably did not take into account all families of color in the village.

61. Douglass, *Narrative,* 94.

62. On Douglass's work in New Bedford, see his *Narrative,* 95; *My Bondage and My Freedom,* 358–59; and *Life and Times,* 655–57. The sailing dates of the *Java* and *Golconda,* as well as their ownership by George Howland, are in Starbuck, *History of the American Whale Fishery,* 354–55. The Ricketson candleworks was probably owned and operated by Joseph Ricketson Sr., not his son and namesake.

63. On Briggs, see *Liberator,* 1 November 1834; *Emancipator,* 16 November 1837; and L. A. Scruggs, *Women of Distinction: Remarkable in Works and Invincible in Character* (Raleigh, N.C.: L. A. Scruggs, 1893), 345–46. On Peneton, see John A. Collins, *Right and Wrong among the Abolitionists of the United States,* 50, in microfilm of *Black Abolitionist Papers; Liberator,* 27 March 1846, 11 August 1848, 16 June 1854, 28 July 1854, 14 March 1856, and 9 July 1858; *Mercury,* 19 April 1847; Ripley, ed., *Black Abolitionist Papers,* 4:391–94; *Pacific Appeal,* 8 November 1862; *Frederick Douglass Monthly,* June 1863.

64. Douglass, *My Bondage and My Freedom,* 357–58. It seems possible that the incident Douglass described here and in the *Narrative,* 94–95, was the John Howard incident of 1827, though Douglass stated that a meeting had been called at the African Christian Church which the would-be informer was somehow lured to attend. At this meeting, the "old man" presiding over it, "one of the numerous family of Johnsons," gave a prayer and then rose and said, "Well, friends, we have got him here, and I would now recommend that you young men should just take him outside and kill him." The

congregation, Douglass was told, "made a rush at the villain," but he escaped through a window and was never again seen in New Bedford. In the *Narrative,* Douglass stated that "some more timid" members of the meeting restrained those who wished to take the man.

65. Pease, ed., *Diary of Samuel Rodman,* entry for 13 April 1839.

66. Debora Weston, New Bedford, to Maria Weston Chapman, 15 April 1839, Weston Papers; Pease, ed., *Diary of Samuel Rodman,* entry for 16 April 1839.

67. Douglass's name is written in on *List of Voters in the Town of New-Bedford* (New Bedford: Benjamin Lindsey, 1839), NBFPL.

68. Documents and accounts of this case are in the Gibson Papers, NBFPL.

69. Patrick Gibson, Creighton Island, Ga., to Nathan Johnson, 17 November 1834; Gibson, New York City, to Johnson, 11 October 183?, Gibson Papers.

70. Gibson to Johnson, 17 November 1834; Gibson, Creighton Island, to Johnson, 15 June 1835; Gibson, Creighton Island, to Johnson, 13 February 1836, Gibson Papers.

71. William Gibson, Creighton Island, to Johnson, 24 March 1837; Edmund Molyneux, Newport, R. I., to Johnson, 15 August 1837; Molyneux, Savannah, Ga., to Johnson, 19 April 1839, Gibson Papers.

72. Molyneux, New York City, to Johnson, 19 August 1839, Gibson Papers.

73. David W. Ruggles, 17 February 1840, Gibson Papers.

74. See Earl F. Mulderink III, " 'The Whole Town Is Ringing with It': Slave Kidnapping Charges against Nathan Johnson of New Bedford, Massachusetts, 1839," *New England Quarterly* 61, 3 (October 1988): 350–53; Benjamin Rodman, New Bedford, to Edmund Molyneux, 6 November 1839; Molyneux, Savannah, to Rodman, 13 November 1839, Gibson Papers. Rodman's statement in the *Mercury* is quoted in Mulderink, " 'The Whole Town is Ringing with It,' " 351.

75. Debora Weston, New Bedford, to "Aunt Mary," 19 January 1840, Weston Papers.

76. Mulderink, " 'The Whole Town Is Ringing with It,' " 354.

77. Jacobs's anonymous narrative was serialized as "A True Tale of Slavery" in the English periodical *The Leisure Hour* 476, 7 February 1861, 85–87; 477, 14 February 1861, 108–10; 478, 21 February 1861, 125–27; and 479, 28 February 1861, 139–41. I am grateful to Jean Fagan Yellin for having identified Jacobs's narrative in the notes to her edition of Harriet Jacobs's *Incidents in the Life of a Slave Girl;* see 260 n. 1.

78. "Murder," *Mercury,* 9 August 1839, 1:4; Lindsey wrote, "Williams, as we learn, sailed from this port in the whaling ship Francis Henrietta, on Sunday morning, and has thus for the present eluded the pursuit of justice."

79. Log of the ship *Rebecca,* September 1791–10 January 1792, Log 50, Mystic Seaport Museum.

80. William P. Powell, "Coloured Seamen—Their Character and Condition, No. X," *National Anti-Slavery Standard,* 29 October 1846, 86:2–3.

81. In 1846 Powell estimated that 2,930 men of color served on whaling vessels, 1,008 of them from New Bedford. However, based on Charles Watson's compilation of crew lists, my own analysis found only 209 men of color on whaling crews sailing from New Bedford that year; 126 of them listed New Bedford, Dartmouth, Fairhaven, or Westport as their places of birth. Martha Putney's analysis showed only 51 men of color on New Bedford crews in the same year. Powell's estimate was based on multiplying 252 whaling vessels sailing from the port by an average of 4 men of color per vessel. See Powell, "Coloured Seamen—Their Character and Condition, No. II," *National Anti-Slavery Standard,* 24 September 1846, 66:1, Putney, *Black Sailors,* 125 table 6.

82. In *Black Jacks,* 211, Bolster has stated that Powell "created a network of antislavery messengers," among them stewards, who were often men of color. In a letter to a friend living in the United States, Powell asks that he send antislavery books "by Mr. Fisher, Steward of the ship Saranak or Mr. Freeman, Steward of the ship Tonawanda, both Philadelphia packets running to L'pool, either gentleman will be glad to serve." For more on Powell, see Foner, "William P. Powell," 88–111; Forbes, "William P. Powell"; Horton, *Free People of Color,* 68–70; *Liberator,* 24 May 1834, 15 August and 13 June 1835, 21 June, 19 July, and 27 September 1839, 9 May 1840, 21 July and 8 September 1843; "Colored Citizens in Massachusetts," *Emancipator* 16 November 1837; William P. Powell, Boston and New Bedford, to Gerrit Smith, 4 September 1861, Gerrit Smith Papers, Arendts Research Library, Syracuse University, Syracuse, N.Y.

83. The total numbers of crew members on New Bedford whalers by year have never been tabulated.

84. The remaining portion of black crew were natives of foreign countries, claimed not to know their birthplaces, or identified a place with a very common or very obscure name whose specific location cannot be determined.

85. Putney, *Black Sailors,* 36.

6. The 1840s

1. Joseph Sturge, *A Visit to the United States in 1841* (1842; reprint, New York: Augustus M. Kelley, 1969), 95. According to Lydia Child, Northampton, Massachusetts, was similar in this respect to Newport. "This town is a great resort for Southerners in the summer season," she wrote to Abby Kelley in October 1838, "and never in my life have I witnessed so much of the lofty slave-holding spirit." See Meltzer and Holland, eds., *Lydia Maria Child,* 90. Background on Sturge is in David Brion Davis, *Slavery and Human Progress* (New York: Oxford University Press, 1984), 185–86. That some Quakers viewed Sturge as an unsavory radical is indicated in Elizabeth Buffum Chace's observation that a "leading minister" of her monthly meeting who had indicated his wish to call on her and her husband changed his mind after she gave him a copy of Sturge's address "to American friends on their inconsistent attitude toward the slavery question." See Chace, "My Anti-Slavery Reminiscences," 121–22.

2. Pease, ed., *Diary of Samuel Rodman,* entry for 20 June 1841; Eliza Rodman Diary, 1 January–31 December 1841, entries for 20 and 21 June, misc. vol. 632, Mystic Seaport Museum.

3. Sturge, *Visit to the United States,* 100. That Sturge's hotel was the Mansion House is revealed in Pease, ed., *Diary of Samuel Rodman,* entry for 20 June 1841.

4. New Bedford Overseers of the Poor Records, vol. 3, 7 January 1861, NBFPL.

5. Debora Weston, New Bedford, to Maria W. Chapman, 4 March 1840, Weston Papers.

6. William C. Coffin, New Bedford, to Maria W. Chapman (care of Henry A. Chapman, Boston), 5 September 1840, Weston Papers.

7. M. W. Chapman, *Pinda: A True Tale* (New York: American Anti-Slavery Society, 1840). Taylor, *Women of the Anti-Slavery Movement,* 91, cites the title as *Pindar, a True Tale* and states that it was Chapman's only novel. Though rarely encountered, Pinda may have been a classically based female slave name, from the Greek lyric poet Pindar. The vessel name *Pindus,* registered in Fairhaven from 1819, may have had a similar root, or may have been named for the mountain range in Greece bearing the same name. According to the novel, "officers" of some sort told Pinda, after her owner brought her to Boston on the ship *Eli Whitney* in 1836, that she was free, but because she wished to return to her husband Abraham, she refused to leave the vessel. When she returned to Savannah, Abraham advised her to escape at her first opportunity, and on a trip to New Hampshire to "wait upon Missis," as Chapman put it, she did. Chapman then told how "Mr. Logan of Savannah" had risen at the sixth annual meeting of the Massachusetts Anti-Slavery Society in Boston to tell the assembly how content his slaves were, but after the meeting someone brought Pinda to Chapman's West Street home. There Pinda confessed that she wished to be free and that Logan was her master. According to Chapman's account, Pinda lived on West Street (perhaps in Chapman's home) for several weeks.

8. On the Faggins case, see "Slave Case," *Mercury,* 9 July 1841, 2:5; *Mercury,* 16 July 1841, 1:1, 1:2, 2:6; New Bedford *Register,* 14 July 1841, 2:1, 3:1; S. T., New Bedford, to Debora Weston, 18 July 1841, Weston Papers; and W. C. N. (William C. Nell) to the *Liberator,* 16 July 1841, reprinted in C. Peter Ripley, ed., *Black Abolitionist Papers,* 3: 362–64.

9. Henry Ludlam, "For the Mercury," *Mercury,* 16 July 1841, 1:2.

10. New Bedford *Register,* 14 July 1841, 2:1.

11. S. T., New Bedford, to Debora Weston, 18 July 1841, Weston Papers.

12. In Ripley, ed., *Black Abolitionist Papers,* 3:364, n. 5, Joseph Eveleth is identified as the sheriff who served the writ in New Bedford, but his name is not mentioned in any other account. In his forthcoming biography of John Murray and Charles Spear, John Buescher identifies Pratt as Jabez Pratt and provides a detailed account of the Faggins case; many thanks to him for sharing part of his manuscript with me. Spear had come to New Bedford in 1835 as pastor of the First Universalist

Society, which he had earlier helped organize. He was a member of the New England Non-Resistance Society and had three times introduced antislavery resolutions to the Old Colony Conference of Universalist ministers; only one, in 1840, was endorsed. His own congregation did pass a resolution on slavery in 1841; Buescher notes, "Among formally constituted Universalist groups, it was almost alone in taking a stand against slavery." Spear and his brother Charles organized the First Universalist Anti-Slavery Convention, held at Lynn about November 1840.

13. James's account appears in his autobiography, *Wonderful Eventful Life of Rev. Thomas James, by Himself* (Rochester, N.Y.: Post-Express Printing Co., 1887), reprinted in *Rochester History* 37, 4 (October 1975): 1–32.

14. Theodore Chase, "A New Bedford Lawyer 140 Years Ago," *Boston Bar Journal,* March 1979, 9. Chase's account, based on Colby's unpublished diary, states that Colby visited the owner of Robeson's wife and children, a physician named Toulson, in Maryland in February 1839 to negotiate the purchase of Celia Robeson and the couple's children. Within three weeks Colby had raised $1,530 for the arranged purchase, and by 1840 Robeson's household contained five persons of the correct age ranges as are shown for his wife and children in the 1850 census. Colby was the son-in-law of attorney John Henry Clifford. Many thanks to Carl Cruz for making a photocopy of the Chase article available to me.

15. Background on the Faggins sisters is derived from the family Bible and the reminiscences of Charles Dudley Onley, the grandson of Henry Onley, and was made available to me by Carl Cruz of New Bedford. Thanks also to Raymond Patenaude for the undated clipping of Lucy Faggins Henson's obituary, before 12 June 1891, which contains an abbreviated version of the 1841 case. For the quote, see "A Slave Set Free," *Boston Morning Post,* 12 July 1841. Many thanks to John Buescher for calling my attention to the *Post* article.

16. J. B. Sanderson, New Bedford, to W. C. Nell, 16 July 1841, Isaac and Amy Post Papers, University of Rochester, Rochester, N.Y.

17. Daniel Ricketson, "Brooklawn, near New Bedford," to Wendell Phillips, 25 July 1856, Wendell Phillips Papers, Houghton Library, Harvard University. See also Daniel Ricketson, New Bedford, to Sydney Howard Gay, 17 March 1845, Sydney Howard Gay Papers, Columbia University Libraries Special Collections, in which he stated, "I used to take the [National Anti-Slavery] Standard because I was a moderate Abolitionist. I now would take it because my strength & convictions are increasing & that I still wish them to increase."

18. "Slave Case," *Mercury,* 16 July 1841, 1:1.

19. I. C. Ray, Nantucket, to H. G. O. Colby, 1 December 1842, Isaiah C. Ray Papers, NBFPL.

20. James stated that he had offered a resolution strikingly similar to the one quoted here after he learned that the Rev. Henry Jackson of New Bedford had been party to a petition before the Maryland legislature to expel free blacks from the state. James's resolution stated "that the great body of the American clergy, with all their pretensions to sanctity, stand convicted by their deadly hostility to the Anti-Slavery movement, and their support of the slave system, as a brotherhood of thieves, and should be branded as such by all honest Christians." James seemed to indicate that the meeting at which he offered this resolution was a local one. He stated that the resolution was published and a meeting called to which all of the village's ministers were invited. Fully thirty attended, and all of them denounced "the obnoxious resolution and its author." The "prejudice" James's resolution inspired against him was compounded, he said, by his role in the Faggins affair. See *Wonderful Eventful Life of Rev. Thomas James,* 8–9.

21. "The Election," *Mercury,* 15 November 1839, 1:1, notes that French, supported by the "colored abolitionists," ran as a "Van Burenite," or Democrat, for the state legislature. See also Morgan Diary, 9 October 1850; Pease, ed., *Diary of Samuel Rodman,* entries for 18 and 20 March and 1 April 1841; "The Church and the Clergy," *Mercury,* 11 June 1841, 1:4; Caroline Weston, New Bedford, to Wendell Phillips, 1 May 1844, Phillips Papers.

22. Mary T. Congdon, the stepdaughter of James Bunker Congdon, noted in a letter to Debora Weston that the "new organization," the Massachusetts Abolition Society, was meeting little success in finding converts in New Bedford, but that among those who had joined them was John Elsimore, a Maryland-born black laborer who had lived in New Bedford since at least 1830. She stated, "Reports says that John Elsinore a coloured man who has recently been licensed to preach has joined

their faction. His having become one of the clericals will sufficiently account for his defection. You know we were very suspicious that the Johnsons (Richard jr. and Ezra) were of the 'pealer' order. I was informed yesterday that Cummings invited them to join the new soc. but they declined; alleging as a reason that they already belonged in one soc. and saw no reason why they should change. What has produced such a change in their sentiments I know not—even their father considered them identified with 'those who went out from us because they were not of us.'" Mary T. Congdon, New Bedford, to Debora Weston, 25 July 1840, Weston Papers. The term "unhappy dissencions" was Congdon's. On the proposed black newspaper, see "The Colored Convention," *National Anti-Slavery Standard*, 7 September 1843, 53:4–5.

23. This report of the 25 May 1840 meeting of people of color in New Bedford is found in the microfilm edition of the *Black Abolitionist Papers* and is attributed to J. A. Collins, *Right and Wrong among the Abolitionists of the United States*, 50.

24. "The Colored Convention," *National Anti-Slavery Standard*, 7 September 1843, 53:4–5. Only two Massachusetts people of color, Charles Lenox Remond and Douglass, who listed his residence then as Boston, attended the Buffalo convention as delegates. New England was represented there by only three other delegates, two from Connecticut and one from Maine. Thirty-six delegates attended from New York, by far the greatest representation from any state; three represented southern states and fourteen the Midwest. See *Minutes of the National Convention of Colored Citizens: Held at Buffalo, on the 15th, 16th, 17th, 18th and 19th of August, 1843 . . .* (New York: Pierce and Reed, 1843).

25. "Meeting of Colored Citizens," *New-Bedford Register*, 7 July 1841, 3:1, indicates that Douglass chaired the meeting opposing the plan of Maryland slaveholders to send free blacks in that state to Africa. In *My Bondage and My Freedom*, 364, and *Life and Times*, 660, Douglass simply stated that he wanted a vacation from his foundry job and went to Nantucket to the antislavery meeting, but Blassingame, ed., *Frederick Douglass Papers*, 1 xlvi, states, "His first brief speech before the Garrisonian Bristol County Anti-Slavery Society in New Bedford on 9 August 1841 so impressed his audience that a group of abolitionists paid his expenses to Nantucket." *Wonderful Eventful Life of Rev. Thomas James*, 8, states that on an undated occasion James invited Douglass to "relate his story" to a white audience after James himself had spoken on antislavery, "and in a year from that time he was in the lecture field with Parker Pillsbury and other leading abolitionist orators."

26. Blassingame, ed., *Frederick Douglass Papers*, 1:xlix, xlix n. 93; Quarles, *Black Abolitionists*, 63; Congdon, *Reminiscences*, 289.

27. "Labors of New-Bedford Boys," *Liberator*, 13 October 1843, 161:6. David W. Ruggles, or D. Wright Ruggles, was a contemporary of David Ruggles of the New York City Vigilance Committee and may have been related to him; Dorothy Porter, "David Ruggles, An Apostle of Human Rights," *Journal of Negro History* 28, 1 (January 1943): 26, suggested that David W. Ruggles was the brother of New York's David Ruggles. Ruggles of New York was born in Connecticut about 1810, while Ruggles of New Bedford was probably born about 1823. He was in New Bedford by 1838 working in the home of Andrew Robeson; he remained there through 1841 and was working for Robeson's son Thomas by 1845. In 1838 he was among the owners, all of them men of color, of the whaleship *Rising States*, which in its three voyages carried an all-black crew. It is not known whether Ruggles was free or a fugitive, though Johnson's letter seems to suggest that both had once been slaves. If Ruggles, like David Ruggles of New York, was born in Connecticut, he could have been a slave until he came to New Bedford. Connecticut's gradual manumission law stipulated that persons of color born as slaves after 1 March 1784 had to serve as indentured servants until they reached the age of twenty-five. See Horton and Horton, *In Hope of Liberty*, 73.

28. Rudolph Lapp, "Jeremiah B. Sanderson: Early California Negro Leader," *Journal of Negro History* 53, 4 (October 1968): 322. Sanderson was the son of Daniel and Sarah Sanderson and may have descended on his mother's side from Jeremiah Burke, a Dartmouth "mustee" who had married Nancy Quash in Dartmouth in October 1784. Sanderson is said to have been of African, Indian, and Scottish descent, according to a typewritten, but undated and unsigned, biography of him, now apparently lost. Sanderson's sister Elizabeth, born in 1823, provided contradictory accounts of their parents' background to the local overseers of the poor; in 1859 she said her parents came from Bristol, Rhode Island, to New Bedford, and that her father had died in 1827 (he is listed, however, in the 1830 New Bedford census), and in 1861 Elizabeth stated that her father had come from Boston, her

mother from Rhode Island, and that her father "went off" about 1828, when she was five years old, and was "never heard from." In a third poor relief record dated 27 February 1865 she stated that her father had died when she was four—that is, in 1827 or 1828. On taking over the *Liberator* agency, see J. B. Sanderson to William C. Nell, 26 June 1841, *Black Abolitionist Papers* microfilm 04:0075. On his participation at antislavery meetings, see record of the New Bedford meeting in John A. Collins, *Right and Wrong among the Abolitionists of the United States,* 50, excerpted in *Black Abolitionist Papers* microfilm frame 4662; Lapp, "Jeremiah B. Sanderson," 321, and Sanderson to Nell, 25 January 1842, *Black Abolitionist Papers* microfilm 04:349.

29. Pease, ed., *Diary of Samuel Rodman,* entry for 6 May 1839. On Cuffe's experience at a local tavern about 1807, see unidentified correspondent, New Bedford, to John Parrish, 9 August 1807, Cox, Parrish, and Wharton Papers, box 2, HSP.

30. William C. Coffin, New Bedford, to Debora Weston, 1 January 1841, Weston Papers.

31. *Register,* 28 June 1841, 1:6; "David Ruggles," *Liberator,* 9 July 1841, 111:3; "Meeting of Colored Citizens," *Register,* 7 July 1841, 3:1; Report of investigating committee, *Register,* 21 July 1841, 1:5. The hearing on the matter was reported in the *Mercury,* 23 and 30 July 1841, 2:1 and 2:6, respectively.

32. See, for example, *Liberator,* 10 February 1843, 3:5–6, and, on Douglass, G. F. [George Foster], "A Shameful Deed," *Colored American,* 30 October 1841.

33. "To the Public: Riot on the New Bedford and Taunton Rail Road," *Liberator,* 18 February 1842, 28:4–5; *Mercury,* 4 February 1842, 2:1, and 11 February 1842, 1:5. The outcome of the trial is not known.

34. Douglass, *My Bondage and My Freedom,* 397; "A Christian Example," *National Anti-Slavery Standard,* 19 May 1842, 198:3; *National Anti-Slavery Standard,* 28 December 1843, 117:6, 118:1. The *Standard* noted that neither the New Bedford *Mercury* nor the *Bulletin,* another short-term rival, would publish Barney's 1842 letter, though the *Register* did. On Barney, see Walter M. Merrill, ed., *No Union with Slave-Holders, 1841–1849,* vol. 3 of *The Letters of William Lloyd Garrison* (Cambridge: Belknap Press of Harvard University Press, 1973), 272 n. 2.

35. Douglass, *My Bondage and My Freedom,* 359–61, 374; "American Prejudice and Southern Religion: An Address Delivered at Hingham, Massachusetts, on 4 November 1841," in Blassingame, ed., *Frederick Douglass Papers,* 1:10–12.

36. Congdon, *Reminiscences,* 37–8; John Cuffe, Westport, Mass., to Freelove Slocum, 8 June 1832, Cuffe Papers.

37. Anne Weston, New Bedford, to Debora Weston, 26 October 1842, Weston Papers; Caroline Weston, New Bedford, to Wendell Phillips, 30 June 1843, Phillips Papers.

38. Debora Weston, New Bedford, to Anne Weston, October 1845, Weston Papers.

39. Pease, ed., *Diary of Samuel Rodman,* entry for 1 November 1845.

40. Caroline Weston, New Bedford, to Wendell Phillips, 2 November 1845, Weston Papers. What Weston meant about Robeson's being unable to speak is unclear, unless she implied that he had nominated Ruggles as a member as well and could not speak in his behalf.

41. M. M. Brooks, Concord, Mass., to Caroline Weston, 24 November 1845; [Daniel Ricketson], New Bedford, to George A. Bourne, Esq., 18 November 1845, Weston Papers.

42. Caroline Weston, New Bedford, to Wendell Phillips, 2 November 1845.

43. Joseph Ricketson, New Bedford, to Wendell Phillips, 17 November 1845, Phillips Papers.

44. Caroline Weston, New Bedford, to Wendell Phillips, 22 November 1845, Phillips Papers.

45. "New Bedford Lyceum," *National Anti-Slavery Standard,* 22 January 1846, 134:1–2, reprinted from the *Mercury.* See also *Liberator,* 16 January 1846.

46. Daniel Ricketson, "Brooklawn, near New Bedford," to Wendell Phillips, 25 July 1856, Phillips Papers; "Annual Meeting of the Massachusetts Anti-Slavery Society," *Liberator,* 6 February 1846, 22:3; the *People's Press* article was a clipping found among the New Bedford Benevolent Society Papers at MHS; Ricketson was its secretary and kept many of his published letters to newspapers in his minute book.

47. Jeremiah B. Sanderson, New Bedford, to Frederick Douglass, *North Star,* 5 January 1849; Joseph Ricketson, New Bedford, to Horace Mann, 23 October 1846, Horace Mann Papers, MHS; Joseph Ricketson, New Bedford, to Deborah Weston, 8 October 1847 (with enclosure from newspaper announcing lecture series); Joseph Ricketson, New Bedford, to Caroline Weston, 17 October 1847, Weston Papers.

48. Debora Weston, New Bedford, to Maria Weston Chapman, 12 April 1837, Weston Papers; Douglass, *My Bondage and My Freedom,* 357; J. B. Sanderson, New Bedford, to Frederick Douglass, 20 December 1848, printed in *North Star,* 5 January 1849; Congdon, *Reminiscences,* 37–38; Josephine Brown, Woolwich, [England], to Samuel J. May, 27 April 1854, reprinted in Dorothy Sterling, ed., *We Are Your Sisters: Black Women in the Nineteenth Century* (New York: W. W. Norton, 1984), 146–47.

49. Morgan Diary, 25 April 1841; "Frederic Douglas in Behalf of George Latimer," *National Anti-Slavery Standard,* 8 December 1842, 105:5–6, reprinting his 8 November 1842 letter to Garrison.

50. *Mercury,* 13 January 1843, 3:5; Pease, ed., *Diary of Samuel Rodman,* entry for 20 January 1843.

51. Anne Weston, New Bedford, to "Aunt Mary" and Debora Weston, 31 October 1842, Weston Papers; "Frederic Douglas in Behalf of George Latimer"; on Latimer, see Quarles, *Black Abolitionists,* 193–95; Horton and Horton, *Black Bostonians,* 99; Collison, *Shadrach Minkins,* 87; and Horton and Horton, "The Affirmation of Manhood: Black Garrisonians in Antebellum Boston," in *Courage and Conscience,* 144–45. On *Prigg v. Pennsylvania,* see Stanley W. Campbell, *The Slave Catchers: Enforcement of the Fugitive Slave Law, 1850–1860* (Chapel Hill: University of North Carolina Press, 1970), 14–15.

52. "A True Tale of Slavery," 21 February 1861, 127; Jacobs, *Incidents in the Life of a Slave Girl,* 136. Jacobs's wages are recorded in Waste Book, 21 December 1842–30 November 1850, under "Sundry Accounts Dr to Whaling Voyages. . . . For the ship Frances Henrietta's cargo of sperm & whale oil & bone . . . ," collection 27, vol. 24, Morgan Papers. These accounts also document that Morgan paid $12.78 on Jacobs's behalf to captain William N. Reyard "for his bills of clothing &c" and that Jacobs seemed to have rights to a share of the oil on board ("Jno S. Jacobs for 2 cask sperm body oil contg 265 2 [sup] Net Gs 1 cask head matter contg 162 net gs + 4072 gs @ 50 203 73"), though it is unclear whether this was part of or a supplement to his stated wage.

53. John S. Jacobs, Chelsea, Mass., to Sydney Howard Gay, 4 June 1846, Gay Papers. Jacobs wrote Gay earlier, on 7 September 1845, from 36 Grove Street in Boston; see Jacobs to Gay of that date, Gay Papers.

54. Alvin F. Oickle, *Jonathan Walker: The Man with the Branded Hand* (Everett, Mass.: Lorelli Slater, 1998), 16–18, states that Walker moved to New Bedford "almost immediately" after his marriage to Jane Gage of Harwich in October 1822. Between 1816 and 1833 he was regularly at sea; from 1831 (?) through 1836 he was working as a shipwright in New Bedford and Fairhaven.

55. *Trial and Imprisonment of Jonathan Walker,* 21, 32–33, 40–41; *Mercury,* 1 November 1844, 2:1; Caroline Weston, New Bedford, to Ann Terry Phillips, n.d., Weston Papers.

56. *Liberator,* 15 October 1847, 167:3–4; Ripley, ed., *Black Abolitionist Papers,* 1:492–93 n. 4; "Incidents in Western New York," *Liberator,* 31 March 1848; "Jonathan Walker and John S. Jacobs," *North Star,* 31 March 1848.

57. On Fairbank and Hayden, see Quarles, *Black Abolitionists,* 149–50, 164–65; Ripley, ed., *Black Abolitionist Papers,* 4:268–69 n. 3; William Lloyd Garrison, Boston, to Sydney Howard Gay, 31 March 1846, in Merrill, ed., *Letters of William Lloyd Garrison,* 3:334; and "Rev. Calvin Fairbank," *National Anti-Slavery Standard,* 13 September 1849, 62:5–6. The Haydens' presence in New Bedford is documented in Lewis Hayden to "My Dear Wife," 22 April 1847, Miscellaneous Collections, American Antiquarian Society, Worcester, Mass. Lewis Hayden wrote the letter from Boston to his wife in New Bedford and referred to his health "since I left New Bedford"; "you may come to Boston next Wednesday if you will or the first opportunity you can get," he wrote. The Haydens probably were staying with "sister Easton," to whom Hayden asked to be remembered. She was most likely Rhoda Cuffe Easton, one of the daughters of Paul Cuffe. Thanks very much to Joel Strangis, author of *Lewis Hayden and the War against Slavery* (North Haven, Conn.: Linnet Books, 1998), for making me aware of this Hayden letter. Quarles, *Black Abolitionists,* 47, has stated that "in the operations of the Underground Railroad the conductors, those who ventured into slave terrain seeking out prospective escapees, were invariably black," but Walker, Fairbank, Torrey, and, later, Daniel Drayton and Alexander M. Ross were white.

58. Bearse, *Reminiscences of Fugitive-Slave Law Days,* 7, dedicated his book to Torrey, among others. For background on Torrey, see F. N. Boney, *Slave Life in Georgia: A Narrative of the Life, Sufferings, and Escape of John Brown, a Fugitive Slave* (Savannah: Beehive Press, 1972), 179, and Meltzer and Holland, eds., *Lydia Maria Child,* 144 n. 3.

59. Little is known about Boyer. At least four protection papers were issued to a man of color with this name, but the ages, heights, and birthplaces listed do not reconcile with one another. Boyer is listed with another in his household, presumably his wife, in the 1840 New Bedford census, where his date of birth was listed between 1804 and 1816. He may have been the son of James Boyer and Jamaica-born Nancy Davis of New Bedford, but his parents are not mentioned in any account, and if the man listed in the 1840 census is the same man listed in protection papers, his birthplace was shown as either New York City or Philadelphia. Protection papers for a man of color born about 1813–15 were issued in 1837 and 1838, and a man of similar physical description received a protection paper in 1830 in New Bedford. His name is sometimes shown as Bowyer or Boyc. His wife may have been Sophia Johnson; a marriage is recorded between people of these names in New Bedford in 1834, though neither is listed as a person of color. One of Boyer's three children may have been the Henry Boyer born in 1842, also a New Bedford steward, who enlisted in the Union Navy as an ordinary seaman on 12 September 1863. Thanks to Lisa King of Howard University for Boyer's enlistment details.

60. Unsigned letter, New Bedford, to William Lloyd Garrison, 29 December 1844, quoted in "Case of Capt. Ricketson," *Liberator*, 3 January 1845, 3:6. For more on Boyer's case, see also *Mercury*, 3 January 1845, 1:1, reprinting an article from the Portsmouth *Index*; William Lloyd Garrison, Boston, to John Bailey, 10 January and 13 February 1845, reprinted in Merrill, ed., *Letters of William Lloyd Garrison*, 3:274–75, 281, "For the Register," *Register*, 21 January 1845, 2:4; "To the Public," *Liberator*, 24 January 1845, 2:6, *National Anti-Slavery Standard*, 30 January 1845, 139:4; Caroline Weston, New Bedford, to Wendell Phillips, 9 February 1845, Weston Papers; "Capt. Ricketson's Defence," *Liberator*, 21 Feb. 1845, 29:6, Joseph Ricketson Jr., New Bedford, to Debora Weston, 29 April 1849, Weston Papers, and Norfolk County Records, 19 December 1844, Library of Virginia, Richmond. Huge thanks to Melissa Morgan Radtke for searching these records for information on the Boyer and other New Bedford cases and for reading Portsmouth and Norfolk newspapers for this project.

61. "Case of Capt. Ricketson."

62. "Capt. Ricketson's Defence."

63. Garrison to Bailey, 13 February 1845.

64. Weston to Phillips, 9 February 1845.

65. Daniel Ricketson, report on Massachusetts Anti-Slavery Society meeting, Boston, 22–24 June 1845, New Bedford Benevolent Society Papers; Joseph Ricketson Jr., New Bedford, to Debora Weston, 29 April 1849, Weston Papers.

66. William Bush, also born in Loudoun County, was the son of William Bush, from Maryland, and Nancy Grimes, from Loudoun County. Leonard Grimes's parents were Andrew Grimes and Molly Goines. Bush was born in 1798; Grimes in 1815. It is possible that Bush and Grimes were cousins, but family history claims Bush as Grimes's uncle.

67. Carl Cruz made me aware of the work of Philip J. Schwarz, professor of history at Virginia Commonwealth University in Richmond, to whom I am indebted for making available the transcripts of Grimes's case, preserved largely in Letters Received, Virginia Executive Papers, Library of Virginia, Richmond. I have included information from Arrest Warrant, Loudoun County, 20 January 1840; *Alexandria Gazette and Advertiser*, 2 March 1840, 2; and *Alexandria Gazette and Virginia Advertiser*, 17 March 1840, 3. Schwarz also made available to me a transcript of the indenture between Grimes and Bush, in Box 2, Folder 46, Washington, D.C., Deeds Folder, Nidiffer Collection, Special Collections Division: Archives, Manuscripts, Rare Books & Fine Prints, Lauinger Library, Georgetown University, Washington, D.C. According to Schwarz, evidence exists to document that Grimes had been involved in assisting fugitives before this incident. Grimes and his son and namesake, who died at the age of five in 1851, are buried in Woodlawn Cemetery in Everett, Mass. For information on Lewis Hayden, see Blassingame, ed., *Frederick Douglass Papers*, ser. 1, 1.441 n. 1; Horton and Horton, *Black Bostonians*, 41, 47–48; and Robert L. Hall, "Massachusetts Abolitionists Document the Slave Experience," in Jacobs, ed., *Courage and Conscience*, 91–92. Hall states that Hayden moved to New Bedford in 1840, but he is not listed in any city directory before 1845; the Hortons state that he moved to New Bedford with his wife, daughter, and son in the "late 1840s." The Washington, D.C., register of free persons includes this certificate of freedom, number 2264, filed 13 August 1845: "Miss Elizabeth P. Massey swears that she has known the children of Leonard and Octavia 'Jane'

Grimes, who are free persons of color, since they were infants and they were born free. Emily Teresa Grimes is about twelve years old, a very light mulatto with black eyes and long, straight, black hair. . . . Mary Frances Grimes, aged nine, is also a bright mulatto with black eyes and long, straight, black hair. John Andrew, aged six, is almost white and has blue eyes and dark auburn hair." Grimes's marriage to Octavia Janet Colson, or Colston, is recorded to have taken place 27 May 1833 in the same register and thus probably took place before Grimes was imprisoned, not after as the Hortons have stated. See Provine, *District of Columbia Free Negro Registers, 1821–61*. Grimes must have sought his certificate of freedom just before he moved to New Bedford and probably brought his wife, son, and two daughters. The birth of Leonard E. Grimes on 17 June 1846 to Octavia E. "Coliston" and Leonard Grimes is recorded in *Vital Records of New Bedford, Massachusetts, to the Year 1850*, vol. 1, *Births* (Boston: New England Historic Genealogical Society, 1932). Grimes's death record of 14 March 1873 lists his mother as Mary (Polly) Goings and his father as Andrew Grimes. A Patrick Goings witnessed, with his mark, Grimes's deed to Bush. A John Goings, born in either Virginia or Maryland, had lived as a domestic in the New Bedford home of Mary Rotch, daughter of William Rotch Sr., since 1841, if not earlier; whether these persons were related is unknown. Thanks to Carl Cruz for locating Grimes's death record and to Prof. Schwarz for passing along information that helped locate Grimes's burial site.

68. Thanks to Carl Cruz and Randall Bush Pollard, the great-great-grandson of William Bush, for providing me with a photocopy of Anna Jourdain Reed's undated memo. Grimes's exact relation to William Bush is not known, but the relation between Bush's wife Lucinda and Archibald Clark is documented by protection papers, probate records, and vital records. Family records indicate that Lucinda and Archibald Clark were two of the sixteen children of a slave named Tamer and her white owner, named McCarthy. Mary Clark, the wife of New Bedford blacksmith Lewis Temple, may have been another child of this union. Eleanor Clark's status is unclear because two records exist related to her in Provine, *District of Columbia Free Negro Registers*. Registration 175 is a record of manumission dated 2 April 1825 and states, "James Warren, in consideration of five dollars, manumits his daughter, Eleanor Clarke, aged about twenty-five, whom he purchased from James Pumphrey." Registration 362, a certificate of freedom dated 12 October 1827, states, "Sarah Kyle, a free white woman, swears that Eleanor Clarke was born free, as were her three children: Archy, aged ten, Cornelius aged eight, and John, aged six years." Pumphrey is also recorded as having manumitted Lucy Bush well before her oldest children were born, beginning about 1822. See Registration 361, a certificate of freedom recorded 12 October 1827: "Sarah Kyle, a free white woman, swears that Lucy Bush, a mulatto woman aged about twenty-three, was manumitted by James Pumphry. Lucy has three children: Julia Ann, aged six, Susan Ann, aged four, and James William, aged two, who were born long after Lucy's manumission." The marriage of William Bush to Lucy Clark on 14 September 1820 in Washington is also recorded in Provine. The first records of Archibald Clark Jr. in New Bedford are a protection paper dated 1827 and a marriage record, under his alias of Archibald C. Lloyd, in 1828; another marriage record exists for Archibald Clark and the same woman in 1832. That Clark had been in New Bedford for some time is indicated in the 1841 city directory, which lists under Archibald Lloyd "alias Archibald C. Clark, trader 167 County, house 207 Middle."

69. On the *Pearl* incident, see *Personal Memoir of Daniel Drayton;* G. Franklin Edwards and Michael R. Winston, "Commentary: The Washington of Paul Jennings—White House Slave, Free Man, and Conspirator for Freedom," *White House History* 1, 1 (1983): 46–52; Stanley C. Harrold Jr., "The Pearl Affair: The Washington Riot of 1848," in *Records of the Columbia Historical Society of Washington, D.C.* 50 (1980): 140–60; John H. Paynter, "The Fugitives of the Pearl," *Journal of Negro History* 1, 3 (July 1916): 243–64; Harriet Beecher Stowe, *A Key to Uncle Tom's Cabin, Presenting the Original Facts and Documents upon Which the Story is Founded* (Boston: John P. Jewett, 1853; reprint, St. Clair Shores, Mich.: Scholarly Press, 1970), 158–73; "Capture of Runaway Slaves," *Washington Daily National Intelligencer*, 19 April 1848, 3:5; "The Slave Case," *Washington Daily National Intelligencer*, 20 April 1848, 3:3; "$50 Reward," *Washington Daily National Intelligencer*, 20 April 1848, 3:2 (for Evelina, supposed to have been among the *Pearl* fugitives but not jailed); *Washington Daily National Intelligencer*, 21 April 1848, 1:4; "The Slave Abduction Case" and "The Quiet of the City Restored," *Washington Daily National Intelligencer*, 22 April 1848, 3:1, 3:2; *Washington Daily Union*, 19 April 1848, 3:6 (which includes a list of sixty-nine of the fugitives on board by their owners);

"Disturbance," *National Era*, 20 April 1848, 6:7; and "Drayton, Sayres & English, Papers Re: Charges of Assisting Slaves," Slaves and Slavery, Box 1, Folders 8–12, Black History Collection, Library of Congress Manuscript Division. For local coverage of the Drayton case up to his release and arrival in New Bedford in 1852, see *Mercury*, 28 April 1848, 2:6; 25 August 1848, 1:7; 1 September 1848, 1:4, 1:6; 30 November 1848, 3:1; 18 May 1849, 2:3; 25 May 1849, 2:2; 19 August 1852, 1:5; and 9 September 1852, 3:3.

70. *Personal Memoir of Daniel Drayton;* Edwards and Winston, "Commentary," 54.

71. It is tempting to speculate that the woman and six children were the slaves Leonard Grimes helped escape from the Loudoun County plantation of Joseph Mead in 1839 and that the connection between Grimes and Drayton accounts for the connection between Drayton and Bush. The date of this escape is not entirely clear from Drayton's memoir, but the text seems to indicate that it occurred in 1847.

72. Harrold, "Pearl Affair," 141–42; *Personal Memoir of Daniel Drayton*, 24–28, 46, 49. Drayton stated that he met with the man at an unspecified place and then again two weeks later; then he went to Washington to see "what could be done." Jennings's story was different, perhaps protectively so; then owned by Massachusetts senator Daniel Webster, Jennings said that Drayton "seemed to take a great fancy to me" when they met in a Baltimore hotel in March 1848 and approached him about assisting in the escape. Drayton told Jennings that he had received a letter from Jennings's brother Frank stating that he and Drayton would arrive in Washington on 13 April and that Paul Jennings should go on board the *Pearl* that evening so that Frank might give Paul a package for their mother. Drayton explained that the letter was a ruse that Drayton himself had sent so as to let Jennings know when he would arrive and that he, as Paul Jennings put it, "will be ready to take as many of us away as want to go."

73. Horace Mann, *Slavery: Letters and Speeches* (Boston: B. B. Mussey, 1851), 116–17.

74. In his memoir Drayton mentioned the suspicion that Gamaliel Bailey of the Washington newspaper *National Era* had financed the trip, which both he and Bailey denied; see Bailey's response in "Disturbance," *National Era*, 20 April 1848, 6:7. In the 1890s J. W. Hutchinson of Lynn, Mass., stated in a letter to Underground Railroad historian Wilbur Siebert that Bailey himself had told him that he was the prime mover in the *Pearl* enterprise despite his claims not to have been involved; see Alfred Garrett Harris, "Slavery and Emancipation in the District of Columbia, 1801–1862" (Ph.D. diss., Ohio State University, 1946), 135 n. 123. Other sources suggest that the upstate New York abolitionist Gerrit Smith and William L. Chaplin, a traveling lecturer for the American Anti-Slavery Society, helped devise the plan. Chaplin wrote Smith in March 1848 to report that he was waiting for a vessel from Philadelphia to take fifty or more passengers. See Horton and Horton, *In Hope of Liberty*, 233, apparently citing an article by Catherine M. Hanchett in the July 1982 issue of *African-Americans in New York Life and History*. According to Harris, "Slavery and Emancipation," 132 n. 1, Smith contributed more than $15,000 to help pay the fines and secure counsel for Drayton, Sayres, and English. During the trial Drayton stated, as he had in his narrative, that Bell had hired him, but it has never been established that Bell financed the *Pearl*'s voyage.

75. Chase, "Reminiscences," 127–28.

76. *Mercury*, 2 July 1841, 1:5, see also *American Beacon, and Norfolk and Portsmouth Daily Advertiser*, 14 June 1841, which notes the departure of the *Relief* that day. The Young to whom Chace referred may have been the Reverend Joshua Young, whose fugitive slave assistance has been documented by Raymond Paul Zirblis, "Friends of Freedom: The Vermont Underground Railroad Survey Report" (Montpelier: Vermont Department of State Buildings and Vermont Division of Historic Preservation, 12 December 1996).

77. *The Life of John Thompson, a Fugitive Slave, Containing His History of 25 Years in Bondage, and His Providential Escape. Written by Himself* (Worcester: John Thompson, 1856), 103, 107–8.

78. "Went to the jail after dinner to ship two men for the Winslow"; see Pease, ed., *Diary of Samuel Rodman*, entry for 22 August 1840. Davis et al., *In Search of Leviathan*, 158, have noted that labor turnover on whaling vessels increased over time; of the six voyages the *George Howland* made between 1840 and 1866, discharge and desertion averaged 63 percent. Jacob A. Hazen in *Five Years before the Mast* (1837) wrote of having been shipped under close watch from Philadelphia to New York with about twenty "drunken, desparate-looking characters" who on arrival were marched through the streets to the shipping office in columns of two so that the recruiting agent would not

lose any fee. See Hohman, *American Whaleman,* 94–96. Stories abound in New Bedford of agents, or "crimps," filling men with liquor and effectively kidnapping them for whaling crews while they were insensibly drunk.

79. Browne, *Etchings of a Whaling Cruise,* 11.

80. Pease, ed., *Diary of Samuel Rodman,* entry for 2 May 1843.

81. "For the Mercury: Death of Rev. Thomas U. Allen, late of New Bedford," *Mercury,* 5 October 1849, 2:7.

82. "Caution to Abolitionists!" *Liberator,* 30 August 1844, 139:1.

83. Daniel Ricketson, Sixth Annual Report of New Bedford Benevolent Society, 30 November 1845, New Bedford Benevolent Society Records, 1829–1893, MHS.

84. "Fugitive Slaves," *Liberator,* 20 March 1846, 45:3.

85. See *Standard Times,* 15 May 1910; thanks to Raymond Patenaude for providing access to this clipping. Ferguson told the newspaper that he had worked in various trades in New Bedford until 1863, when he took a job as a cook on a merchant schooner bound for California. He stayed in San Francisco for thirteen months and then came back to New Bedford, where he was hired as a ship-keeper by the J. T. & W. R. Wing Company. He worked there twenty-five years and was appointed city messenger in 1874. During the New York City draft riots of 1863, when a similar riot was said to be imminent in New Bedford, Ferguson was appointed captain of a company of men of color who patrolled the city with the sanction of then-mayor George Howland Jr.

86. "Runaway Slaves," *Liberator,* 31 December 1847, 2:6; John Bailey, New Bedford, "Information Wanted," *Liberator,* 21 January 1848, 11:6. In December the *Liberator* quoted another paper citing a report in the Springfield, Massachusetts, *Gazette* that nine runaway slaves, "the cause of considerable excitement at Mount Holly, N.J., short time since," were then living in Springfield. Apparently a settlement of fugitives at that New Jersey place had been threatened when Maryland slave owners recognized some of their former slaves there and launched a suit for their recovery. The community of color attempted their rescue, but militia were summoned and a jury ordered their rendition. Upon that outcome many who had been living at Mount Holly escaped farther north.

87. Armstrong's story is recorded in the records of the first Boston Committee of Vigilance, transcribed in Bartlett, "Abolitionists, Fugitives, and Imposters in Boston," 107.

88. On Duval, see Ripley, ed., *Black Abolitionist Papers,* 1:255–57, 257 n. 2; *Republican Standard,* 17 April 1851, 2.6; *National Anti-Slavery Standard,* 1 May 1851; *Liberator,* 13 June, 25 July, and 5 September 1851.

89. The date of the sale of Brown's wife is derived from J. M. McKim, Philadelphia, to "friend," 28 March 1849, James Miller McKim Papers, Rare and Manuscript Collections, Carl A. Kroch Library, Cornell University, Ithaca, N.Y. Brown stated that he had been married fourteen years by that point, which would put their marriage at 1834.

90. Still, *Underground Railroad,* 68–71, states that James A. Smith addressed the box in which Brown was hidden and that Samuel A. Smith delivered it. McKim's letters of 1849 are addressed to S. A. Smith, the man later arrested for trying to accomplish the escape of slaves in the same way. It is unclear whether James A. Smith or Samuel A. Smith was the underground railroad "conductor" to whom Brown referred. Brown traveled in England with J. C. A. Smith, nicknamed "Boxer," who had helped him. Ripley, ed., *Black Abolitionist Papers,* 1, 174 n. 11, 298 n. 2, notes that Samuel Smith was put in prison for seven years for helping Brown escape and that J. C. A. Smith, a free black, was able to avoid prison and paid a $900 fine. McKim actively discouraged Smith from trying to send more fugitives in crates to the North; "you say you know there is no danger," he wrote. "I tell you you know nothing about it. It was a miracle that your friend did not lose his life. You dont know half the dangers that he escaped; and it is absurd to attempt a similar project till you know the particulars of this." See McKim, Philadelphia, to S. A. Smith, 12 and 16 April 1849, McKim Papers.

91. See Gara, *Liberty Line,* 50; "Curious Occurrence," *Liberator,* 10 November 1848, 180:2, and J. M. McKim, Philadelphia, to S. A. Smith, 16 April 1849, McKim Papers. Gara states that Smith was later arrested and convicted for using the method Brown made famous.

92. On Still, see Ripley, ed., *Black Abolitionist Papers,* 2:205 n. 1, and James A. McGowan, *Station Master on the Underground Railroad: The Life and Letters of Thomas Garrett* (Moylan, Pa.: Whimsie Press, 1977), 88.

93. McKim to "friend," 23 March 1849, McKim Papers; Still, *Underground Railroad,* 70–71.

94. Ibid.; Still, *Underground Railroad,* 68; Morgan Diary, 4 April 1849.

95. Ricketson wrote Debora Weston, "The said slave came consigned to me about three weeks since from S. H. Gay who received him from J. McKim Philada." Ricketson, New Bedford, to Weston, 29 April 1849, Weston Papers.

96. Joseph Ricketson, New Bedford, to S. H. Gay, 30 March 1849, Gay Papers.

97. Although Alexander Duval reached New Bedford in October 1848, he was apparently not the man Ricketson described; Duval had a wife and a young daughter only. In the 1850 census Mary Blair, a woman of color who gave her age as twenty-four and her birthplace as Maryland, was living in Ricketson's home at 179 Union Street, and probably by 1853 her children—Lewis, William, Jefferson, Agnes, Sarah, and John, all recorded as born in Virginia between 1825 and 1850—were living in the city as well. To the overseers of the poor Blair claimed that her husband, also named Jefferson, had died before she came to New Bedford and that her actual birthplace was Richmond. She claimed, falsely, to have settled in the city in 1853. Her son William was identified as an "adult" in her first poor relief listing in 1858, and Lewis was not mentioned until she sought aid again in 1860; he was then living in Boston. She never stated the same age in any two listings. Whether she was the wife of the fugitive Ricketson mentioned and claimed that her husband had he died in order to protect him is unknown.

98. Ricketson to Weston, 29 April 1849.

99. Morgan Diary, 4 April 1849.

100. Thanks to Judy Downey, librarian at the Whaling Museum, ODHS, for determining when the Russell and Purrington panorama was first exhibited. I surmised that Brown may have taken the whaling panorama (also titled *A Whaling Voyage Round the World*) as his model when I was working as editor with Nancy Osgood on her article "Josiah Wolcott: Artist and Associationist," *Old-Time New England* 76, 264 (Spring/Summer 1998): 5–34. In his diary entry for 20 December 1848, Charles Morgan mentioned having gone to see the whaling panorama in New Bedford. The panorama is on view at the Whaling Museum.

101. Brown also attempted to secure a $150 loan from Gerrit Smith to finance the panorama, but whether Smith sent him the money is not known. Henry Box Brown, Boston, to Gerrit Smith, 1 February 1850 and 13 September 1850 (from Springfield, Mass.), Smith Papers. James A. "Boxer" Smith, Manchester, Eng., to Gerrit Smith, 6 August 1851, stated that the panorama had not raised the funds it had been expected to for the antislavery cause and expressed his regret the Brown did not seem to want to raise or pay $1,500 to redeem his wife and children from slavery. Broadside, Smith Papers. Brown and Smith had dissolved their partnership twelve days earlier. See Osgood, "Josiah Wolcott," 19. The panorama apparently has not survived.

102. Cynthia Griffin Wolff, "Passing beyond the Middle Passage: Henry 'Box' Brown's Translations of Slavery," *Massachusetts Review* 37, 1 (Spring 1996): 30, 41; Osgood, "Josiah Wolcott," 17–19; Marcus Wood, " 'All Right!'. The Narrative of Henry Box Brown as a Test Case for the Racial Prescription of Rhetoric and Semiotics," *Proceedings of the American Antiquarian Society* 107, part 1 (April 1997): 75–77.

103. "Anti-Slavery Meetings in New Bedford," *Liberator,* 16 February 1849, 27:1.

104. Douglass, *My Bondage and My Freedom,* 339.

7. The 1850s

1. Morgan Diary, 31 December, 28 November, 28 October 1848. Morgan also owned a foundry in Wareham, Massachusetts, a small town about ten miles east of New Bedford with rich bog iron deposits. His attribution of his financial trouble to his "investments in Pennsylvania" is in the diary on 2 October 1849.

2. *Mercury,* 15 July 1842, 1:5; Herman Melville, *Moby-Dick; or, the Whale* (1851; reprint, New York: Library of America, 1983), 828.

3. Morgan Diary, 2 and 12 December 1848.

4. Another migrant of color to California was John Thomas, alias James Williams, whose *Life and Adventures of James Williams, a Fugitive Slave, with a Full Description of the Underground Railroad*

(San Francisco: Women's Union Print, 1873) describes his escape from Elkton, Maryland, at age thirteen in 1838. Williams was active in Underground Railroad work in Lancaster, Reading, and Philadelphia, Pennsylvania, and went to Boston after the passage of the Fugitive Slave Act. When he learned of imminent efforts to take fugitives William and Ellen Craft from Boston, Williams went to New Bedford, where he remained only three weeks before returning to Philadelphia. He left New York for California on 3 March 1851. Thanks to Guy Washington of the National Park Service for making a copy of Williams's narrative available to the New Bedford Historical Society.

5. Rudolph M. Lapp, *Blacks in Gold Rush California* (New Haven: Yale University Press, 1977), 19.

6. Morgan Diary, 14 December 1848, 18 January and 1 and 22 April 1849; Joseph Ricketson, New Bedford, to Debora Weston, 29 April 1849, Weston Papers.

7. Morgan Diary, 5 March 1850.

8. Ibid., 11 and 14 March 1850; *Mercury,* 15 March 1850, 1:7.

9. Ibid., 27 July and 1 August 1850.

10. *Mercury,* 2 August 1850, 2:3; letter from "Law and Order," *Mercury,* 9 August 1850, 4:1, "Abolition Convention," *Mercury,* 30 August 1850, 1:6.

11. See Jacobs, *Incidents in the Life of a Slave Girl,* ed., Yellin, 186, 230 n. 2, 287 n. 2 on Joseph Jacobs. Jacobs's name is not listed on crew lists for 1845 or 1846, but because he was issued a protection paper and is known through his mother's correspondence to have returned by 7 May 1849, it is possible that he shipped under an alias on the *Charles Drew,* John W. Coffin, master, which left New Bedford on 1 September 1846 and returned 5 May 1849; a boy listed as Samuel Humpsen of Boston, with yellow complexion and black hair, is listed among the crew members of that vessel. Joseph Jacobs was light enough to be mistaken for white, he came to New Bedford from Boston, and he was fifteen or sixteen in 1846.

12. *Experience of Thomas H. Jones;* Cecelski, "Shores of Freedom," 174–76; J. Bigelow, Washington, D.C., to I. C. Ray, 29 April 1850, Ray Papers, NBFPL. Araminta may have been Araminta Nevitt, whose poor relief record notes came from Washington to New Bedford in 1850 and whose children are listed as born in Washington in Provine, *District of Columbia Free Negro Registers.* According to his nephew W. B. Williams, Jacob Bigelow also helped numerous fugitives in addition to his effort to help secure the purchase of "colored people" in Washington at the behest of Harriet Beecher Stowe and Henry Ward Beecher; I assume Williams referred to the Edmundsons. Williams also described an elaborate system of signs and messages that he used in helping fugitives escape. See W. B. Williams, Charlotte, Mich., to Wilbur Siebert, 30 March 1896, in Siebert, "The Underground Railroad in the District of Columbia," vol. 24, Siebert Notebooks. Cecelski has argued that "runaway slaves regularly headed to the coast instead of attempting overland paths out of bondage" and that documents attesting "several dozen" specific cases of slaves escaping aboard ships from North Carolina between 1800 and 1861 "represent only the tip of an iceberg."

13. Collison, *Shadrach Minkins,* 1, 54.

14. "A Great Haul," *Mercury,* 14 January 1848, 1:7; *Republican Standard,* 15 April 1852; H. Johnson, J. W. Smith, Edward W. Parker, John Kelley, J. B. Sanderson, D. W. Ruggles, and Samuel Thomas to the *Republican Standard,* 12 September 1850, 1:4. In 1852 a municipal survey found seventy-eight "liquor shops" and fifty-six "houses of ill repute" in the city; see *Republican Standard,* 28 April 1852, 1:2. The 1849 and 1852 city directories list only four hotels in the city, only one of them near the depot. The 1845 directory lists eleven hotels, four of them in that area, at 248, 252, 258, and 258½ Purchase Street—the Pearl Street House, the Exchange Hotel, the Atlantic House, and the Albion House. The Franklin and Railroad Houses are not listed in any of these years.

15. *Republican Standard,* 5 September 1850, 2:1, and H. Johnson et al. to the *Republican Standard.*

16. Joseph Ricketson, New Bedford, to Debora Weston, 1 September 1850, Weston Papers. Ricketson noted later in the same letter, "Mary has just returned from the meeting and says, they have appointed a committee to call on our city officers after twelve oclock for a writ to arrest the slaveholder George W. Wim & the constable a Sheriff Hays by six oclock in the morning, for violating our laws."

17. See "Bold Attempt to Kidnap!" *Liberator,* 20 September 1850, reprinted from the New Bedford *Republican Standard;* "Attempt to Kidnap Henry Box Brown," *Mercury,* 6 September 1850, 2:3.

18. "The Slave Bill," *Mercury,* 20 September 1850, 1:1.

19. See the *Mercury,* 4 October 1850, 2:4, on Hamlet's arrest, and, in the same issue, "Slave Catchers in Worcester," 2.4, "Slave Excitement in Pittsburgh, Pa.," 2.4, and the article on the Charlestown marshal, 2:5.

20. "Meeting of Colored Citizens," *Republican Standard,* 10 October 1850, 1:3. The *Mercury* did not report the meeting of members of the black community.

21. Morgan Diary, 5 October 1850.

22. "The Meeting Last Night," *Daily Evening Standard,* 9 October 1850, 4:3.

23. "Mr. Grinnell's Position on Slavery," *Mercury,* 23 February 1849, 1:1.

24. "The Fugitive Slave Law: Meeting at Liberty Hall," *Daily Evening Standard,* 8 October 1850, 2:2.

25. "For the Standard" by Free Soil, *Daily Evening Standard,* 8 October 1850, 4:4.

26. "For the Standard," *Daily Evening Standard,* 8 October 1850, 4:4; "The Meeting Last Night," *Daily Evening Standard;* Morgan Diary, 8 October 1850. See also the *Mercury,* 11 October 1850, 1:5, 2:5, which reprinted French's amended resolutions in full, and 3:2 for Ricketson's letter.

27. Morgan Diary, 8 October 1850.

28. Pease, ed., *Diary of Samuel Rodman,* entries for 13 November and 23 December 1850.

29. Morgan Diary, 31 March 1851.

30. "A City of Refuge," *Republican Standard,* 1 November 1850, 2:3, reprinting an article from the (Boston) *Chronotype.*

31. Rodney French, New Bedford, to Horace Mann, 19 December 1850, Horace Mann Papers, MHS.

32. "Escaping Slaves" (excerpt from the annual report presented to the Massachusetts Anti-Slavery Society by its Board of Managers, January 23, 1850, 47, in vol. 13, Siebert Notebooks.

33. *Mercury,* 11 October 1850, 2:6; *Life and Adventures of James Williams.* By the beginning of March 1851 Thomas left Philadelphia for New York City, where he took passage on a steamboat bound for California on 3 March. Thanks to Guy Washington of the National Park Service's Golden Gate National Recreation Area for making me aware of Thomas's account and providing a photocopy of it. On Andrew Jones, see "Fugitive Slaves aided by the Vigilance Committee since the Passage of the Fugitive Slave Bill," Massachusetts Anti-Slavery Society Papers, New-York Historical Society. I am indebted to Jim Driscoll of the Queens Historical Society for letting me know about this list and providing a photocopy.

34. Collison, *Shadrach Minkins,* 110–69.

35. Ibid., 149–50.

36. "Fugitive Slave Excitement in New Bedford," *Republican Standard,* 20 March 1851, 2:3.

37. "Fugitive Slave Excitement"; Ellis, *History of New Bedford,* 306, which states incorrectly that this rumored trip occurred at the time of Thomas Sims's rendition from Boston. The cartoon is titled "The Geography of a 'Sell!' Or Pot. And 'Scum's Ride to New-Bedford," Broadside XpbH.90.299, Department of Rare Books and Manuscripts, BPL.

38. "The Fugitive Excitement," *Republican Standard,* 20 March 1851, 2:5 Collison, *Shadrach Minkins,* 190, has accepted that the New Bedford expedition was planned and has stated that "a terrific storm at sea apparently forced the mission to be canceled."

39. "Fugitive Slave Excitement in New Bedford."

40. Pease, ed., *Diary of Samuel Rodman,* entry for 16 March 1851; Stella M. Hay, "A Station on the Road to Liberty," *Sunday Standard,* 20 June 1920, 25:1–4. The resolution to use force among the city's fugitives was attested anecdotally by Congdon, *Reminiscences,* 17, probably writing about the late 1820s and 1830s New Bedford: "We had a cook in our family who was a runaway, and who kept a long and exceedingly sharp knife always at hand. This she showed me in strict confidence, to my great terror, and informed me that it was intended for the reception of her old master if he should ever come after her."

41. "New Bedford Awake! Great Anti-Fugitive Slave Law Meeting at City Hall!!" *Daily Evening Standard,* 1 April 1851, 2:1–3.

42. *Republican Standard,* 10 April 1851, 1:3.

43. "The Meeting in New Bedford," Boston *Commonwealth,* reprinted in *Republican Standard,* 1 April 1851, 3:2.

44. "The Church and the Clergy," *Mercury,* 11 June 1841, 1:4. French had supported this opinion, articulated by Henry C. Wright, as a resolution at the New-England Anti-Slavery Convention anniversary meeting in Boston. Abolitionists Nathaniel P. Rogers and Stephen S. Foster also supported it, with Garrison taking "the middle road." The resolution did not pass.

45. Being vilified, French admitted, "is no new thing. I have received similar treatment before, and bore it cheerfully. In New England—in Massachusetts; yes, in the city of New Bedford, I have been proscribed for opinion sake, and compelled by a sense of duty to others, to dissolve with my partner in business. I am getting accustomed to these things." "Reply to a Portion of the Citizens of New-Berne," *Evening Standard,* 28 October 1851, 1:1, 4:1, reprinted in the *Liberator,* 20 November 1851, 101:1–4.

46. "The True Remedy," *Republican and Patriot* (Goldsboro, N. C.), 25 September 1851, and "Meeting of the Citizens of New-Berne," *Republican and Patriot,* 2 October 1851; thanks to Paul Cyr of the New Bedford Free Public Library for making me aware of these articles. See also "Reply to a Portion of the Citizens of New-Berne."

47. "Reply to a Portion of the Citizens of New-Berne."

48. M. B. Eddy, New Bedford, to Ann W. Weston, 6 April 1851, Weston Papers.

49. Collison, *Shadrach Minkins,* 190–91; Horton and Horton, *Black Bostonians,* 106; Campbell, *Slave Catchers;* 117; Quarles, *Black Abolitionists,* 206–7; Morgan Diary, 7, 8, 11, and 12 April 1850.

50. "Extradition Extraordinary," *Mercury,* 21 April 1851.

51. Of the 256 persons, 9.0 percent had "unknown" birthplaces and 7.8 percent were shown with birthplace left blank, compared with 7.4 and 4.3 percent of the 1850 population of color generally. Of the 256, 45.3 percent showed free-state birthplaces and 35.1 percent listed slave-state birthplaces; among the recorded New Bedford black population these figures were 53.2 for free states and 29.9 percent for slave states.

52. See "Narrative of Daniel Fisher" in Blockson, ed., *Underground Railroad,* 58–60, and Horatio T. Strother, *The Underground Railroad in Connecticut* (Middletown, Conn.: Wesleyan University Press, 1962), 104.

53. Blassingame, ed., *Frederick Douglass Papers,* 2:246; Bearse, *Reminiscences of Fugitive-Slave Law Days,* 31–32.

54. See Jacobs, *Incidents in the Life of a Slave Girl,* ed. Yellin, 194, 290 n. 10, and "True Tale of Slavery," 127, on Jacobs's trip to New Bedford. Cornelia Grinnell Willis, the second wife of journalist Nathaniel Parker Willis, was the adopted daughter of Joseph Grinnell of New Bedford. John Jacobs stated that Harriet fled "a few months after the passing of the Fugitive Slave Law," while Yellin suggests it was spring of 1851. Based on Harriet's statement that Willis sent her "into New England, where I was sheltered by the wife of a senator" who had not voted for the Fugitive Slave Act because he was opposed to it, Yellin has suggested that Jacobs stayed in the County Street home of Joseph Grinnell, who was in fact a member of the House of Representatives between 1843 and 1851. Yellin adds that Grinnell "absented himself" from voting on the act to ensure its passage. Grinnell, Yellin states, worried about Jacobs staying in his home and so sent her "into the country" with the Willises' baby for about a month. She then returned to New York. The Willises owned New Bedford property as well, having purchased the dwelling at 198 Fourth Street in the fall of 1848.

55. Boney et al., *God Made Man,* 109; Record of Second Baptist Church, New Bedford, kept by William Jackson, 1855–62, collection of Julian E. Youngblood, New Bedford. Many thanks to Mr. Youngblood for his gracious assistance with this project and for allowing me to review the papers of William Jackson, his great-grandfather.

56. Joseph Ricketson, New Bedford, to Debora Weston, 11 August 1851, Weston Papers.

57. "Beauties of the Slave System/Attempt to Kidnap a Free Citizen of Massachusetts!" *Republican Standard,* 3 July 1851, 2:3.

58. "Virginia Enslaving a Shipwrecked Massachusetts Freeman!—The Case of Johnson," *Republican Standard,* 31 July 1851, 1:1. The case was also described briefly in Samuel J. May, *The Fugitive Slave Law and Its Victims,* rev. ed. (New York: American Anti-Slavery Society, 1861), 18.

59. W. O. M., "First of August in New Bedford," *Liberator,* 15 August 1851, 113:2.

60. Ibid., "British West India Emancipation," *Republican Standard,* 7 August 1851, 1:1; Joseph Ricketson, New Bedford, to Debora Weston, 11 August 1851, Weston Papers. On the Boston school desegregation case, see Horton and Horton, *Black Bostonians,* 71–75.

61. Ward, *Autobiography of a Fugitive Negro,* 205; Douglass quoted in Litwack, *North of Slavery,* 143; Sanderson to Douglass, 20 December 1848.

62. Pease, ed., *Diary of Samuel Rodman,* entry for 2 August 1844.

63. "An Abolitionist" for the Standard, *Republican Standard,* 21 April 1852, 1:3.

64. "Interesting Correspondence," *Liberator,* 6 November 1863, 180:5–6.

65. *Republican Standard,* 16 November 1854, 1:1, 2:2, and 2 February 1860, 1:3.

66. Richard H. Abbott, *Cotton and Capital: Boston Businessmen and Antislavery Reform, 1854–1868* (Amherst: University of Massachusetts Press, 1991), 22; Horton and Horton, *Black Bostonians,* 87; Quarles, *Black Abolitionists,* 185–88; "To the Colored Citizens of New Bedford," *Liberator,* 29 October 1852, 174:1–2; *Republican Standard,* 12 February 1852, 2:3, and 6 November 1851, 2:6.

67. "Meeting of Colored Citizens in New Bedford" and "Hon. Horace Mann and the Colored Citizens of New Bedford," *Liberator,* 22 October 1852, 170:4–6; "Meeting of Colored Citizens," *Frederick Douglass' Paper,* 22 October 1852, reprinted from New Bedford *Standard;* "To the Colored Citizens of New Bedford," *Liberator,* 29 October 1852, 174:1–2.

68. "A Voice from 1300 Colored Citizens," *Republican Standard,* 19 February 1852, 3:3.

69. "Meeting of Colored Citizens in New Bedford."

70. *Liberator,* 3 February 1854, quoted in Sidney Kaplan, *American Studies in Black and White: Selected Essays, 1949–1989* (Amherst: University of Massachusetts Press, 1991), 157 n. 39. The driver "Canada" might have been George Canada, listed in the 1855 New Bedford census. Henry Foster, a man of color listed as born in Virginia in the same census, was listed as a lamplighter in the 1856 city directory, as was Thompson Hill (who at other times listed birthplaces other than Virginia). John Kasson was a lamplighter in 1855 as well but stated his birthplace as New Jersey.

71. Boney et al., *God Made Man,* 7–9, 84–6, 180–1 n. 40, n. 41. Ten years before his escape, Teamoh was working as a domestic servant for Melzar Gardner, the Massachusetts-born editor of the Portsmouth *Chronicle,* when Gardner was shot to death by a slave-owning lawyer in 1843. Gardner's paper, for white working men, openly opposed slave labor. Teamoh, who lived in the basement of a boardinghouse Gardner owned, joined the protest over the murder and helped prepare Gardner's body for its journey north.

72. Ibid., 106–7.

73. Ibid., 186–87 n. 73.

74. Ibid., 109–11.

75. This Cannon may have been Edward, who was in business as a rigger on Commercial Wharf with Richard Curtis in 1856.

76. Boney et al., *God Made Man,* 108–11. Who the Stowell brothers' father was is not clear. It might have been William H. Stowell, who had once professed his abolitionism during a run for public office in the late 1830s; he was a merchant with a counting room at Coffin's Wharf, lived on South Water Street in 1836, and was a linseed oil manufacturer in 1845. In 1845 two caulkers, George W. Stowell and Joseph Stowell, were listed; either could have been the father of Columbus and Daniel.

77. Ibid., 111–15. In 1838 Douglass had not been able to get a job in New Bedford doing the same work, perhaps at least in part because of the response of white workingmen to the scarcity of work induced by the panic of the previous year. But by 1845, Douglass noted, black caulkers were able to get work in the city. See Douglass, *Narrative,* 95.

78. Ibid., 187–88 n. 78. Grace Teamar was born about 1809, nine years before George Teamer. His half-brothers were born of a different mother. George's half-brother John William married a Florence P. Gault of Norfolk in Leonard A. Grimes's Twelfth Baptist Church in Boston. Grace Teamar's older daughter Margaret, born in 1827, came to New Bedford in August 1864, with the three children of her first marriage to William Galt of Portsmouth, "who went off, when the children were very small," about 1851 or 1853. I have not been able to fathom the relationship that this coincidence of names suggests. See New Bedford Overseers of the Poor Records, vol. 2, 12 January 1859; vol. 3, 12 March 1860, 11 February 1861; vol. 4, 14 October 1864.

79. Unfortunately, the records of the New Bedford Overseers of the Poor covering from 1852 to 1858, the years of Still's documented activity on behalf of fugitives, are missing.

80. Collison, *Shadrach Minkins*, 21; *People's Press* quoted in *Liberator*, 6 June 1835, 2:4–5; "Meeting of Slaveholders," *Liberator*, 1 August 1845, 2:3; Campbell, *Slave Catchers*, 6; Cecelski, "Shores of Freedom," 174, 201–2. *Autobiography of Elder Joseph Bates*, 278, 281, relates being asked in 1843 by a slaveholder on Maryland's Eastern Shore, where he had gone to proselytize adventism, "Mr. Bates, I understand that you are an abolitionist, and have come here to get away our slaves." Always alert to an entry for conversion, Bates replied, "I am an abolitionist, and have come to get your slaves, and *you too*! . . . We teach that Christ is coming, and we want you all saved."

81. Collison, *Shadrach Minkins*, 46–7; Still, *Underground Railroad*, 283; NB Poor Records, vol. 1, 72, 74, 111.

82. "A Spy," *Republican Standard*, 17 February 1853.

83. "Fugitive Slaves," *Republican Standard*, 12 January 1854, 2:3; "Tempest in a Teapot," *Republican Standard*, 9 February 1854, 2:4; "Virginians Aroused!" *Republican Standard*, 13 March 1854, 2:1. "From the Portsmouth Globe of Friday. Insult and Outrage upon the Rights of the South!" *American Beacon, and Norfolk and Portsmouth Daily Advertiser*, 17 January 1854, 2:1.

84. Chace, "My Anti-Slavery Reminiscences," 130.

85. "Tempest in a Teapot."

86. *Republican Standard*, 16 February 1854, 2:4.

87. This letter from Robeson, dated 18 February 1854, was quoted in Edward S. Adams, "Anti-Slavery Activity in Fall River," *Fall River Herald News*, 7 March 1939, 18:3. The original letter has not yet been found.

88. Chace, "My Anti-Slavery Reminiscences," 130.

89. "Virginians Aroused!" *Republican Standard*, 16 March 1854, 2:1; see also *Liberator*, 31 March 1854, 51:4.

90. "The Underground Railroad," *Republican Standard*, 16 March 1854, 2:2; Still, *Underground Railroad*, 228–29; "Journal C of Station No. 2 of the Underground Railroad, 1852–57," Pennsylvania Anti-Slavery Society (hereafter cited as Still Journal), AMS 232, reel 32, HSP.

91. *American Beacon*, 20 April 1854. The figures on ship arrivals from the South were derived from a survey of the "Marine Intelligence" column in New Bedford *Evening Standard* in 1854.

92. On this point, see Kay and Cary, "Slave Runaways in Colonial North Carolina," 7, who have noted that not all of colonial North Carolina runaways were advertised; "owners wherever they lived tended to advertise as a last resort, except when they lived near a newspaper and thought their runaways were lurking about the neighborhood."

93. *American Beacon*, 31 March 1854.

94. Collison, *Shadrach Minkins*, 49–50; Thomas Garrett, Wilmington, Del., to William Still, 10 July 1862, HSP, noted, "I have made inquiry for Alfred Fountain and the Bailey's. The rebels burn'd Fountain's vessel at Norfolk, last year, and he is now a volunteer in McClellan's Army."

95. The Portsmouth and Norfolk papers show no advertisements of rewards in this amount for fugitives at this time.

96. *American Beacon*, reprinted in *Republican Standard*, 25 May 1854, 3:3; *Liberator*, 7 April 1854, 55:4; Still, *Underground Railroad*, 589, 44–46; Still Journal. No reward was advertised for Davis and her brothers in the *American Beacon* through end of June 1854; thanks to Melissa Radtke for this survey.

97. *American Beacon*, 19 April 1854; Still, *Underground Railroad*, 281–84. Doner's letter to Still is dated 3 November 1859, but from other statements Still made in this section it seems clear that 1859 is a typographical error and should be 1854. Jerome Cross was about fifteen years old in 1855 and worked as a laborer; he is probably the Jerome B. Corss who on 1 December 1863 enlisted in the Fifty-Fourth Regiment of the Massachusetts Volunteer Infantry but transferred to the U.S. Navy on 16 May 1864. See Luis F. Emilio, *A Brave Black Regiment: The History of the 54th Massachusetts, 1863–1865* (1894; reprint, New York Da Capo Press, 1995), 389. Wm. W. Hall advertised "Negroes Wanted" of both sexes between the ages of 5 and 45 in the 4 and 26 June 1854 *American Beacon*.

98. "The Slave Hunters on the Rack Again," *Republican Standard*, 27 April 1854, 2:4; "Weston, the Slave," *Republican Standard*, 11 May 1854, 2:4.

99. That vessels were not regularly searched is indicated in the letter to the *Beacon* from "a Citizen" and from this statement in the *American Beacon,* 28 June 1855: "Our commerce with the North is increasing daily, Northern vessels are multiplying in our harbors, and in the wood trade upon the rivers, hundreds of negroes are employed in loading these vessels. Some rigorous system of inspection, then, must be adopted. Every craft leaving our waters for the Northern port must be thoroughly searched, and the law must be enforced to the letter, or the increasing insecurity of slave property in Virginia must materially depreciate its value."

100. "A Slaveholder," *American Beacon,* 22 April 1854.

101. "A Citizen," *American Beacon,* 25 April 1854.

102. Morgan Diary, 27 May and 2 June 1854; Horton and Horton, *Black Bostonians,* 107–11; Quarles, *Black Abolitionists,* 207–9.

103. "The Verdict Rendered," *Liberator,* 16 June 1854; *Republican Standard,* 8 June 1854, 2:3, 3:4.

104. "An Important Matter," *Republican Standard,* 15 June 1854, 2:3. A "$10 Commissioner" refers to the Fugitive Slave Act's stipulation that any authorized federal commissioner who issued a certificate permitting the return of a fugitive to a master was to receive ten dollars; if the commissioner refused to grant such a certificate he received only five dollars.

105. *Republican Standard,* 22 June 1854, 1:2; "The Union Cadets," ibid., 13 July 1854, 2:3; "The Colored Military Company," ibid., 11 October 1855, 2:3. This last article reported that the officers were Henry Johnson, commander; Isaac Guinn, first lieutenant; James Fairweather, second lieutenant; and Robert Gibson, orderly sergeant. Fairweather was from Rhode Island, but Gibson was from Georgia and Guinn and Johnson from Virginia. See "The Opinion of the Attorney General," ibid., 13 September 1855, 1:2 on Clifford's decision. The *Standard* noted, "It is to the Attorney that we may trace the veto of the Personal Liberty Bill, the retention of the slave commissioner Loring, and all those fogie-hunker acts which have so peculiarly characterized the present State administration."

106. *Republican Standard,* 29 and 30 September 1854; Blassingame, ed., *Slave Testimony,* 320–25, reprinted from the *Liberty Bell* (Boston, 1858); Netta Vanderhoop, "The True Story of a Fugitive Slave: Or the Story a Gay Head Grandmother Told," *Vineyard Gazette,* 3 February 1921. Randall by that name or Edgar Jones was never listed in a New Bedford census or directory despite the fact that, according to Vanderhoop's account, he remained in the city for almost a decade.

107. *Republican Standard,* 6 September 1855, 1:2.

108. "The Underground Railroad," ibid., 25 January 1855, 1:2; "Still They Come!" ibid., 8 February 1855, 2:3; ibid., 17 May 1855, 1:4; "The Underground Railroad—*A Good Business,*" ibid., 29 November 1855, 1:2. The quotation is from "The Underground Railroad," ibid., 4 January 1855, 1:2. Statistics on Virginia's slave population have been taken from Jeffrey B. Morris and Richard B. Morris, *Encyclopedia of American History,* 7th ed. (New York: HarperCollins, 1996), 745, 748.

109. Boney et al., *God Made Man,* 3–4, noted that yellow fever first appeared in June 1855 in the ports and was spread by mosquitoes that had been brought into Portsmouth on a cargo ship; the epidemic spread into Norfolk and by the time it ended in October had killed more than two thousand people and struck ten thousand. A columnist for the Portsmouth *Star* noted that the epidemic actually started in Norfolk in a section on the waterfront called Barry's Row; this area was barricaded and burned, but then the fever appeared across the river in Portsmouth's Irish Row. Jeffrey T. Wilson, "Colored Notes," *Portsmouth Star,* n.d., Black History Collection, Portsmouth Public Library, Portsmouth, Va.

110. "The Underground Railroad," *Republican Standard,* 4 January 1855, 1:2.

111. Still, *Underground Railroad,* 260–65.

112. "Break Down on the Underground Railroad," *Southern Argus* (Norfolk), 12 June 1855; *Norfolk Herald and American Beacon,* 28 June 1855, reprinted as "Another Stampede," *Republican Standard,* 28 June 1855, 1:4. "Mr. S. March" or Marsh was probably Seth March, who claimed to own Anthony Hanly, whose letter to Still made it clear he had reached St. Catherine's, Canada West, by late August 1855. Still identified that slave belonging to "Turner" as William Nelson, who had been a packer for the Norfolk firm Turner and White for twenty years before he escaped; his wife Susan was owned by Thomas Baltimore (Bottimore in the Norfolk papers), and the couple had a daughter nearly two years old. Nelson changed his name to Thomas Russell and wrote Still on 28 June 1855 from Elmira, New York, en route to St. Catherine's. Louisa Bell, possibly the sister of Susan Nelson, was owned

by the Norfolk confectioner L. Stasson but married to a free man of color. Another who escaped was Elias Jasper, who had arrived in St. Catherine's with Louisa Bell by early July 1855. See Still, *Underground Railroad,* 264, 267–71. The likelihood that Captain "B" was William Baylis is suggested by Still's numerous references to him and by a report in an 1858 issue of the *National Anti-Slavery Standard* that Baylis and his schooner had been overtaken after leaving Petersburg, Virginia, with five slaves and that Baylis was convicted and sent to jail for forty years. He died in a Virginia penitentiary in the summer of 1859. See May, *Fugitive Slave Law,* 99, from the 12 June 1858 *National Anti-Slavery Standard.* On Goodrich, see "Excitement in Norfolk," *Republican Standard,* 28 June 1855, 2:3.

113. Still Journal, NB Poor Records, vol. 2, 1 February 1860.

114. See Still, *Underground Railroad,* 264; NB Poor Records, vol. 3, 8 February 1861. The 1850 Norfolk census, which recorded only white and free black families by name, listed a man of color named John Austin, born about 1805–10, his wife Ardell, born 1823, and children Mary F. Hurder, born 1841, and Nancy, born 1848 or 1849. The birthdates and children's names do not match, but a Virginia-born John Austin was listed in the 1860 New Bedford census and the 1861 poor relief records with a wife named Ordelia or Delia and children named Mary, born about 1848, and Anna, born 1851.

115. Still, *Underground Railroad,* 161–69; Brown's letter is on 166–67. People of color had lived at 130 Kempton since at least as early as 1838, when the widow Esther Hackett was listed there. Lewis Douglass of Washington lived there at the same time the Fergusons did in 1849, as did Eliza Curtis, a widow born in Washington or Virginia, the laborer William Patterson, about whom almost nothing is known, and the Maryland-born porter Thomas H. Williams, who had come to New Bedford from Rochester, New York. Two women of color—Catherine Hill, born in Virginia or Pennsylvania, and Anna M. Johnson, the widow of Josiah, born in the South—lived at this address in 1864. See NB Poor Records and city directories.

116. Ibid., 402.

117. Ibid., 585–90; *Republican Standard,* 24 July 1856, 1:2.

118. Mulderink, " 'We Want a Country,' " 309 n. 25. Webb deposed that she followed her father and that he had come "two or three years" before 1861, but she was in New Bedford in 1858 and told the overseers of the poor in 1864 that she had come to the city in 1853. Her census and poor records show her first name as Elizabeth; I've assumed her to be the same person as Nancy Webb because she had a son named Hezekiah, the name of her husband as she deposed in 1881.

119. The story of this arrival was apparently first published in Emma C. Gartland, *New Bedford Stories for New Bedford Children,* published about 1936. Gartland there identified the coasting vessel master as her grandfather; Carl Cruz identified Wixon, master of the schooner *William* in 1844–45, as Gartland's only grandfather in maritime work. Gartland stated that the family stayed in New Bedford and that the son, identified only as "Charlie," was a well-known livery hack driver in the city in the 1890s. Efforts to identify the family and the vessel in which they may have come to New Bedford have so far been fruitless. Gartland's story was repeated in Edward Rowe Snow, *The Lighthouses of New England* (New York: Dodd, Mead, 1945, 1973), 305–6. "Letter from Jonathan Walker," *Liberator,* 15 October 1847, 167:3–4, identifies Captain Wixon as the vessel master who carried the sixty-six slaves freed by the will of Carter Edloe of Virginia north to Boston. Walker identified Wixon as one of very few Cape vessel masters who showed a concern for slaves, Wixon was a native of Dennis on Cape Cod. Thanks to Mary Walsh of New Bedford and Jeremy D'Entremont of Boston for making the story and its source in Rowe known to me; Carl Cruz found the source in Gartland. On the fugitives the Boston Vigilance Committee sent to New Bedford, see "Fugitive Slaves Aided by the Vigilance Committee." "Thomas Clark wife & child" sent to New Bedford in 1851 may be the "Thomas and Emily Clark (c) with child Mary Jane b Sept 1850" listed in the first volume of the overseers of the poor records; the family received coal and wood in 1851 and 1852 and claimed to have come to Massachusetts from New Jersey in November 1837. There is no record before this one of a Thomas Clark with a wife by this name, though. A laborer by this name was shown living on Howland Street in the 1856 city directory; a lamplighter by the same name was shown living in the African American neighborhood on Middle Street in the 1859 directory. "Nancy Johnson & 6 chil." sent to New Bedford in 1853 may be the widow of color listed in the 1855 and 1860 censuses and in the 1856 city directory and poor relief record; in the census and the last record five children were listed. She

provided contradictory information about her birthplace and her late husband in all accounts. "The Record of Fugitive Slaves" (1855–58), two notebooks in the Sydney Howard Gay Collection at New-York Historical Society, includes a record of Charles Carter, sent from Richmond to New Bedford in part because he had friends in the city, who may the same listed in the 1860 census. A record also exists of the transfer of Winny Patty from Norfolk, whose husband was in New Bedford; her case was described in detail in Still, *Underground Railroad*, 401–3. Immense thanks to Jim Driscoll for letting me know about both of these sources.

120. Still, *Underground Railroad*, 453–55; Loum Snow II, New Bedford, to George M. Bain, 22 August 1859; Bain, Portsmouth, Va., to Snow, 26 August and 26 and 30 September 1859. These letters were in the possession of "the Misses Snow" of 10 Hawthone Terrace, New Bedford, in April 1939, when they showed them to the WPA Writers Project's G. Leroy Bradford, who transcribed them. The location of the originals, if extant, is unknown. The Snow women, the daughters of Loum Snow II, also told Bradford that their father had paid the way of the Carneys' children to New Bedford in 1861. See *Daily Evening Standard*, 24 March 1863, on William Carney Jr.'s status and the arrival of the couple's children in New Bedford, and see "Interesting Correspondence," *Liberator*, 6 November 1863, 180 5–6, for the younger Carney's letter, dated 15 October 1863 and written at Morris Island, S. C., at the request of M. S. Littlefield of the Fourth South Carolina Volunteers, who in late July 1863 had been assigned temporary command of the Massachusetts Fifty-fourth (Emilio, *Brave Black Regiment*, 107). Carney here said his mother's name was Ann Dean and that she had been freed by the will of one Major Carney, but the will of Major Richard Carney of Portsmouth, who died on 30 August 1842, mentions freeing no slave by the name of Ann or Nancy. Many thanks to Mae Haywood of Portsmouth for sending me a photocopy of Carney's will from Norfolk County Wills, book 6, 152–55, Norfolk County Probate Court, Norfolk, Va.

121. Elizabeth Cooley, 62 Phillips St., Boston, to Wilbur Siebert, April 1897, in Siebert Note-books, vol. 14, "Massachusetts," included under Suffolk County, Houghton Library. Cooley did not say whether Baines was free or a slave, but she is not listed in the 1850 Norfolk or Portsmouth census as a free woman.

122. The statement about Jackson's role in his rescue is recorded in Jackson's journal in October 1850: "more trubl—[illegible] to the late act of Congress alowing the slave holder the privelege of taking his slave where ever he can find him—And in giveing one his freedom I have the honour of being the first [illegible; possibly 'martyr'] by going to Prison." Jackson Journal, collection of Julian E. T. Youngblood, New Bedford, Mass. The fugitive is identified as Taylor in a handwritten manu-script by his great-great-grandson Youngblood, New Bedford, dated 1996. Mr. Youngblood kindly made these documents available to me during a series of interviews I conducted with him on 30 January and 3 and 9 February 1998 in New Bedford. That Jackson aided a fugitive in Philadelphia was also stated in "Rev. William Jackson Dead," *Evening Standard*, 19 May 1909.

123. Jackson's journal entry of 7 May 1860 mentions having had tea with William Still in Philadel-phia, and he apparently received a letter from Still in 1855, the original not extant, about sending fugitives to Canada. His journal mentions helping the two men on 14 June 1857. Julian Youngblood recalled, "Every time we used to go to 198 Smith Street they used to tell them not to go in cellar, in the northeast corner they used they used to hide slaves there; they said the slaves used to go through the window, but there's no window there now. Yet I can remember a window down there." Jackson's ordination at the Second Baptist Church was reported in the *Mercury*, 12 April 1855.

124. "Public Meetings," *Liberator*, 14 March 1856, 43:4; *Republican Standard*, 6 December 1855, 2:4. Bayne's affiliation with Bethel is documented in the *Republican Standard*, 11 October 1855, 2:2, which announced the laying of the cornerstone for an enlarged sanctuary.

125. *Republican Standard*, 14 August 1859, 2:4.

126. Joseph Ricketson, New Bedford, to Debora Weston, 28 April 1861, Weston Papers.

127. Still, *Underground Railroad*, 46–48; John Cannon, Cayuga County, N.Y., to William Still, 19 May 1856, in Still Journal.

128. "Meeting on Sunday Evening," *Republican Standard*, 9 September 1852, 3:3; *Republican Stan-dard*, 5 January 1854, 3:2, reprinting an article from the Boston *Commonwealth*.

129. Francis Jackson, Boston, 24 August 1855, to Wendell Phillips, Phillips Papers.

130. McGowan, *Station Master of the Underground Railroad*, 127.

131. "Death of a Martyr," *Republican Standard*, 2 July 1857, 1:2.

132. *Republican Standard*, 20 August 1857, 2:2; "Daniel Drayton," ibid., 21 April 1859, 2:2; "City Government," ibid., 21 April 1859, 3:1; *National Anti-Slavery Standard*, 9 July 1857, 1:3; J. B. Sanderson, Lowell, Mass., to William C. Nell, 20 July 1842, *Black Abolitionist Papers* microfilm, 4.453. Very little is known about Photius Fisk. Austin Bearse dedicated his book to "my anti-slavery friend, Rev. PHOTIUS FISK" as well as to Drayton, Charles T. Torrey, and Jonathan Walker. The last three had themselves gone into the South to help fugitives escape, and Bearse's inclusion of Fisk among them suggests that he may also have done so. See Bearse, *Reminiscences of Fugitive-Slave Law Days*, 7. Fisk changed his name from Kavasales to Fisk and was commissioned as a chaplain in the U.S. Navy in March 1842. Edward Callahan, ed., *List of Officers of the Navy of the United States and of the Marine Corps from 1775 to 1900* (New York: L. R. Hamersly, 1901), 195, lists Fisk as having retired on 18 July 1864 and having died 7 February 1890. Navy Registers at the National Archives indicate that he served at the Washington, D.C., Navy Yard in 1847–49, when the *Pearl* incident occurred, and in 1855 at the Navy Yard in Pensacola. Many thanks to Bob Huddleston for forwarding this information on Fisk to me. On Fisk's contribution to Drayton's monument, see *Republican Standard*, 20 August 1857, 2:2.

8. Practical Abolitionism

1. "Execution of Brown—Meeting in Liberty Hall—Tolling of Bells, Emblems of Mourning, &c," *Republican Standard*, 8 December 1859, 1:3; "John Brown Meeting at Liberty Hall," ibid., 2:3.

2. Ibid., 14 June 1860, 2:3.

3. Johnson claimed that he had qualified for the bar in 1842, yet he did not begin his practice at that time. He must have been struggling to make ends meet when he applied for poor relief, in the form of heating coal, in January 1851. In May 1848 New Bedford had made him a city crier, a position often reserved for respected men of color, and by the fall of 1859 he was practicing law. The *Republican Standard* reported at that time that Johnson "rather astonished the Rhode Island people" in his defense arguments in a divorce case in the Rhode Island Supreme Court; "here his eloquence has been so long known, that his pleas at the bar excite no particular interest, not more than other distinguished advocates," the newspaper added. See "A Prophet Not Without Honor," *Republican Standard*, 6 October 1859, 1:3. By this time Johnson is called "Wm. Henry Johnson." He may have altered his name because another prominent Henry Johnson, a minister from Queen Anne's County, Maryland, had settled in the city in 1855. Many men by the name of William Johnson, and some fewer of the name Henry Johnson, are listed in directories and among those seeking protection papers throughout the antebellum years.

4. *Republican Standard*, 21 June 1860, 1:3, and 2 August 1860, 2:4.

5. Boston *Pilot*, 11 August 1860, quoted in Mulderink, " 'We Want a Country,' " 3.

6. Reprinted in *Republican Standard*, 2 February 1860, 1:3.

7. Hoy, "Station on the Road to Liberty." Melancie French Hitch claimed that the wooden handle of the bell French owned was made from the piece of "the staunch old frigate Constitution" and still bore the black bow that French or Williams had wrapped around it when it was rung in 1859.

8. J. B. Congdon, response to the American Freemen's Inquiry Commission, Special Commission to Inquire into the Condition of the Colored Population of New Bedford, 1863, NBFPL.

9. NB Poor Records, vol. 4, 23 and 24 March 1864.

10. Gara, *Liberty Line*, 99; Child to Joseph Carpenter, 24 August 1851, in Meltzer and Holland, eds., *Lydia Maria Child*, 260; Sturge, *Visit to the United States*, 52–53; Benjamin Drew, *The Refugee: A North-side View of Slavery* (1855; reprint, Reading, Mass.: Addison-Wesley, 1969), xvi.

11. On Worcester's population, see Nick Salvatore, *We All Got History: The Memory Books of Amos Webber* (New York: Times Books/Random House, 1996), 97–100.

12. Horton, *Free People of Color*, 28, 172; Quarles, *Black Abolitionists*, 200; Jean Fagan Yellin in Jacobs, *Incidents in the Life of a Slave Girl*, 290 n. 6; Curry, *Free Black in Urban America*, 2; Fred Landon, "The Negro Migration to Canada after the Passing of the Fugitive Slave Act," *Journal of Negro History* 5, 1 (January 1920): 25.

13. These statistics are based on an analysis of the 1836, 1845, and 1856 directories, the 1850 federal

census, and the 1855 state census. The percentage of the black workforce that worked in unskilled jobs was 71.2 in 1836, 63.9 in 1845, 68.6 in 1850, 70.2 in 1855 (perhaps reflecting an infusion of fugitive slaves), and 54.4 in 1856. In 1856 eight men of color worked in soap, candle, and oil factories, five of them at George T. Baker and Son at 52 South Water Street, then run by William G. Baker. For roughly comparative data, see Curry, *Free Black in Urban America*, 260–62 tables B-1, B-2, B-9. With some minor modifications, I have used the occupational typology developed by Peter Knights, *Plain People of Boston*, 149–56 appendix E.

14. Curry, *Free Black in Urban America*, 260, calculated that 5.5 percent of employed free black males were artisans in Providence in 1850, but Cottrol, *Afro-Yankees*, 134 tables 4–5, 4–6, claimed that 15.6 percent of employed black males in the city were artisans. African American local studies would benefit tremendously from the development, acceptance, and standard use of occupational classification so that comparative studies have more meaning.

15. The figure for New Bedford here is an average of the proportions for 1845, 1855, and 1856.

16. Figures for other cities were reprinted in Foner and Lewis, *Black Worker*, 1:120–34.

17. Quoted in Litwack, *North of Slavery*, 166.

18. Bolster, " 'To Feel Like a Man,' " 1175, 1178, provides data on mariners of color in terms of the percentage of total berths on vessels held by them. Amassing comparable data on New Bedford was outside the scope of this study.

19. Bolster, *Black Jacks*, 225–29; Congdon to American Freeman's Inquiry Commission.

20. *Proceedings of the Colored National Convention, Held in Franklin Hall, Sixth Street, Below Arch, Philadelphia, October 16th, 17th and 18th, 1855* (Salem, N.J.: National Standard Office, 1856), 16, reprinted in Bell, ed., *Minutes of the Proceedings of the National Negro Conventions.*

21. Henry quoted in Bolster, *Black Jacks*, 176; Curry, *Free Black in Urban America*, 19; Hershberg, ed., *Philadelphia*, 376.

22. See Congdon, *Reminiscences*, 37–38: "Forty years ago this colorphobia was in full and fierce and most uncharitable force. I do not know how many towns had their negro suburb, but I know that we had one."

23. Mulderink, " 'We Want a Country,' " 46, has determined, based on the 1860 federal census, that New Bedford's 3rd ward was 12.8 percent black and its fourth ward 9.5 percent black. People of color were least apt to live in the first ward, the most northern and rural of the wards, and the second, fifth, and sixth wards were between 5.2 and 6.5 percent black.

24. Curry, *Free Black in Urban America*, 48–52; Ricketson, "Fourth Annual Report of the New Bedford Benevolent Society" (n.d., probably November 1843) and "Sixth Annual Report of the New Bedford Benevolent Society" (30 November 1845). For more information on court and basement dwellings in Boston, see Collison, *Shadrach Minkins*, 63–64.

25. *Mercury*, 18 August 1826, 3:2; Congdon to American Freeman's Inquiry Commission.

26. For comparative data, see Hershberg, ed., *Philadelphia*, 372, 374; Curry, *Free Black in Urban America*, 48–58; Phillips, *Freedom's Port*, 102–3. Most historians suggest that residential segregation of people of color seems to have increased after 1830 (in Baltimore) or 1838 (in Philadelphia) to 1860. Curry has noted that the data on this question are "inconclusive" for the fifteen cities in his study, though residential segregation seems to have risen in all of them except Washington, Baltimore, Providence, and possibly New Orleans, Albany, and Cincinnati.

27. Pease, ed., *Diary of Samuel Rodman*, 40.

28. "Police," *Mercury*, 30 July 1847, 2:6.

29. Letter from "Law and Order" to *Mercury*, 9 August 1850, 4:1; "Assault by Rowdies," *Republican Standard*, 29 July 1852, 2:3; *Republican Standard*, 20 September 1855, 1:2; *Republican Standard*, 14 August 1856, 2:3; "Fires on Saturday Night," *Republican Standard*, 5 August 1858, 2:5; *Republican Standard*, 15 December 1859, 2:3; *Republican Standard*, 19 April 1860, 2:3; *Republican Standard*, 3 April 1862, 2:4. The same newspaper reported incendiary fires in 1860 at two vacant houses in Hard-Dig and one occupied by Israel Young, a man of color living in a one-story house on Court Street.

30. See Foner, "William P. Powell," 100–105, and Forbes, "William P. Powell." Powell described the riot and his family's escape in a letter to the *Liberator*, 24 July 1863.

31. Joseph Ricketson, New Bedford, to Debora Weston, 19 July 1863, Weston Papers. Mulderink, " 'We Want a Country,' " 158–59, quoted another letter Ricketson wrote about the incident to George

P. Guerrier, then serving in the Union Army. Here Ricketson stated that the chaplain was William Jackson, that the man who went to raise money for a firearm was Jonathan, not George A., Bourne, and that the amount raised was $16, not $116.

32. *Republican Standard*, 30 January 1862, 1:3.

33. "G—One of the 54th" [James Henry Gooding] to the *Mercury*, 3 March 1863, reprinted in Adams, ed., *On the Altar of Freedom*, 3–4.

34. Ibid., 8, 8 n. 7, 9, 11.

35. Andrew's speech is quoted in full in Emilio, *Brave Black Regiment*, 25–30. On the Fifty-fourth, see Adams, ed., *On the Altar of Freedom*, xvii–xxx, 17, 17 n. 23; Adelaide M. Cromwell, "The Black Presence in the West End of Boston, 1800–1864: A Demographic Map," in *Courage and Conscience*, 163; *Mercury*, 23 March 1863. Adams noted that New Bedford men of color wanted to call themselves the Morgan Guards in honor of S. Griffits Morgan, Charles Morgan's nephew, but he suggested instead the name Toussaint Guards, in honor of the eighteenth-century Haitian hero.

36. M. S. Littlefield, Morris Island, S. C., to Col. A. G. Browne Jr., 15 October 1863, reprinted as "Interesting Correspondence," *Liberator*, 6 November 1863, 180:5–6; Ellis, *History of New Bedford*, 348; "Sergeant Carney Dead," *Evening Standard*, 9 December 1908. Fleetwood, who made this statement in support of Carney's Congressional Medal nomination, is quoted in Mulderink, " 'We Want a Country,' " 177–78, but Mulderink identifies him as Christian A. Fleetwood, who did not serve with Carney. Christian Fleetwood was a sergeant major in the Fourth U.S. Colored Troops and, like Carney, received the Congressional Medal of Honor. Gooding wrote after the Fort Wagner attack, "One man succeeded in getting hold of the State color staff, but the color was completely torn to pieces." See Adams, ed., *On the Altar of Freedom*, 39. Contemporary accounts were not consistent on whether the flag Carney seized was the national or state banner, but the photograph of Carney holding the standard shows it to have been an American flag.

37. J. H. G. [James Henry Gooding] to the *Mercury*, 21 April 1863, in Adams, ed., *On the Altar of Freedom*, 12–14.

38. J. B., "The Society of Friends," *Liberator*, 16 July 1847, 115:2.

39. Sturge, *Visit to the United States*, 182–83; May, *Some Recollections of Our Antislavery Conflict*, 147–48.

40. See Gienapp, "Abolitionism," 32, who has argued that no more than 200,000 of the North's 20 million people could be classed as abolitionists.

41. "From Our New Bedford Correspondent," *National Anti-Slavery Standard*, 15 April 1847, 183:1–4. On Friends and antislavery, see Chace, "Reminiscences," 114–15.

42. Morgan Diary, 10 October 1850, 22 April 1852.

43. Phillips quoted in Abbott, *Cotton and Capital*, 72.

44. *Mercury*, 2 November 1849, 1:6.

45. Foner, *Black Worker*, 1:176, noted the analysis of five white "working men" at Columbia, Pennsylvania, a reputed fugitive stronghold, to riots that had just taken place there in August 1834: "The cause of the late disgraceful riots throughout every part of the country may be traced to the efforts of those who would wish the poor whites to amalgamate with the blacks, for in all their efforts to accomplish this diabolical design, we see no intention in them to marry their own daughters to the blacks, it is therefore intended to break down the distinctive barrier between the colors that the poor whites may gradually sink into the degraded condition of the Negroes." See also Richards, *"Gentlemen of Property and Standing,"* 166. The discussion of British influence relies heavily on Richards, *"Men of Property and Standing."* On attitudes toward abolitionism, see I. C. Ray, Nantucket, to H. G. O. Colby, 1 December 1842, Ray Papers.

46. Samuel J. May, Boston, to "Miss Weston," 17 October 1848, Weston Papers.

47. "Rev. Dr. Dewey's Lecture," *National Anti-Slavery Standard*, 19 August 1847, 45:2–3; see also *Mercury*, 13 August 1847, 2:5–6.

48. "Testimonial of Respect," *Liberator*, 11 August 1848 (letter to William Lloyd Garrison from N. A. Borden and J. B. Sanderson), in microfilm edition of *Black Abolitionist Papers*.

49. See *Republican Standard*, 14 May 1857, 2:7.

50. Daniel Ricketson to the *Republican Standard*, 18 May 1853, in New Bedford Benevolent Society Papers. Harriet E. Wilson, who wrote the autobiographical novel *Our Nig; or, Sketches from the*

Life of a Free Black, in a Two-Story White House, North. Showing that Slavery's Shadows Fall Even There. By 'Our Nig' (1859; reprint, New York: Vintage Books, 1983), 129, expressed the same idea as she recounted her efforts to find work to sustain herself and her child in New Hampshire and Massachusetts: "Strange were some of her adventures. Watched by kidnappers, maltreated by professed abolitionists, who did n't want slaves at the South, nor niggers in their own houses, North. Faugh! To lodge one, to eat with one; to admit one through the front door; to sit next one; awful!"

51. Delany quoted in Gienapp, "Abolitionism," 41.

52. Stella M. Hay, "A Station on the Road to Freedom," *Sunday Standard,* 20 June 1920, 25:1–4.

53. Debora Weston, New Bedford, to Anne Warren Weston, 1 March 1840, Weston Papers.

54. Paul quoted in Hansen, *Strained Sisterhood,* 14.

55. *Republican Standard,* 15 June 1854.

56. My interpretation of New Bedford abolitionism coheres with that advanced by Thomas P. Slaughter, *Bloody Dawn: The Christiana Riot and Racial Violence in the Antebellum North* (New York: Oxford University Press, 1991), 42; he has argued that the efforts of white abolitionists "were aimed at the eradication of slavery and repeal of the Fugitive Slave Law, not the betterment of local conditions for African-Americans; on a day-to-day basis, Lancaster's blacks generally found themselves on their own. . . . It was possible to sympathize with the general plight of African-Americans, to give individual blacks some food, hire their labor to bring in the crops, pass on used clothing, and even harbor and assist fugitives from slavery without believing that blacks really belonged."

57. Douglass, *Narrative,* 94–95; Douglass, *Life and Times,* 651.

INDEX